BLUE GUIDE

PARIS

DELIA GRAY-DURANT

SOMERSET • LONDON

CONTENTS

Twelfth edition 2015

Published by Blue Guides Limited, a Somerset Books Company
Winchester House, Deane Gate Avenue, Taunton, Somerset TA1 2UH
www.blueguides.com
'Blue Guide' is a registered trademark.

ISBN 978–1–905131–67–9

A CIP catalogue record of this book is available from the British Library.

Distributed in the United States of America by
W.W. Norton & Company, Inc.
500 Fifth Avenue, New York, NY 10110.

The author and the publishers have made reasonable efforts to ensure the accuracy of all the
information in *Blue Guide Paris*; however, they can accept no responsibility for any loss,
injury or inconvenience sustained by any traveller as a result of information or advice
contained in the guide.

Statement of editorial independence: Blue Guides, their authors and editors,
are prohibited from accepting any payment from any restaurant, hotel, gallery or other
establishment for its inclusion in this guide, or for a more favourable mention than
would otherwise have been made.

Every effort has been made to contact the copyright owners of material reproduced in this
guide. We would be pleased to hear from any copyright owners we have been unable to reach.

Your views on this book would be much appreciated. We welcome not only specific
comments, suggestions or corrections, but any more general views you may have: how
this book enhanced your visit, how it could have been more helpful. Blue Guides authors
and editorial and production team work hard to bring you what we hope are the best-
researched and best-presented cultural guide books in the English language. Please
write to us by email (editorial@blueguides.com), via the comments page on our website
(www.blueguides.com) or at the address given above. We will be happy to acknowledge
useful contributions in the next edition, and to offer a free copy of one of our titles.

Edited by Annabel Barber

Maps: Dimap Bt.
Floor plans: Imre Bába
Architectural line drawings: Michael Mansell RIBA & Gabriella Juhász
All maps, plans and drawings © Blue Guides.
Cover: Arc de Triomphe, by Michael Mansell RIBA & Gabriella Juhász © Blue Guides.

Photographs: Image research by Hadley Kincade, pre-press by Anikó Kuzmich.
Images by Gábor Fényes (pp. 8, 34, 122, 139, 263, 440), Rosemary Flannery (p. 149),
Phil Robinson (pp. 64, 133, 152, 276, 296, 341), © Florian Monheim/Bildarchiv-Monheim/
Arcaid/Profimedia (p. 86), iStock © rocsprod (p. 170), iStock © Oliver Malms
(p. 280), iStock © Brendan Hunter (p. 294), © Atlantide Phototravel/Corbis/Profimedia
(p. 320), iStock © Jorisvo (p. 347), © Frederic Soltan/Corbis/Profimedia (p. 392),
© Martin Jones/Corbis/Profimedia (p. 447), © Antoine Gyori/Corbis/Profimedia (p. 449),
© Massimo Listri/Corbis/Profimedia (p. 453), © Sung-Il Kim/Corbis/Profimedia (p. 463),
© Arcaid/Corbis/Profimedia (p. 495), Shutterstock © Ivan Bastien (p. 466),
Wikicommons (pp. 114–5), Tom Howells (pp. 97, 187, 229), James Howells (pp. 127, 500).
All other photography by Annabel Barber.

All material prepared for press by Anikó Kuzmich.

The first Blue Guide to Paris was published in 1920, edited by Findlay Muirhead. Since then
it has gone through numerous re-editions, successively revised and rewritten by L. Russell
Muirhead, Stuart Rossiter, Ian Robertson and Delia Gray-Durant.

Acknowledgements:
The author would like to thank her Paris-based friends, Marie Eymard,
Yvonne Laugier-Werth, Geraldine le Clerq and John Welz,
as well as Claire Parker, who provided help and support.
Thanks are due also to Sophie Patrie and Catherine Barnouin of the Paris Region
Tourist Board, Jean-Marie Bruson of the Musée Carnavalet and André Arden
of the Musée Carnavalet, Crypte Archéologique and the Catacombes; and to
Mickaël Blasselle and Boris Bouget of the Musée de l'Armée-Invalides, Claire Séguret and
Audrey Defretin of the Musée du Moyen Âge-Cluny, Peggy Delahalle of the Musée d'Art
Moderne de la Ville de Paris, Maryvonne Deleau of the Musée Cernuschi, Fabien Durand of
the Musée National d'Archéologie, Dominique Gandolfi of the Office de Tourisme, St-Denis,
Véronique Gautherine of the Musée Zadkine, Clémence Goldberger of the Musée Rodin,
Raphaëlle Fauvette of the Musée National des Arts Asiatiques-Guimet, Anne Le Floch of the
Petit Palais, Nelly Girault and Élise Maillard of the Musée du Louvre, Angelina Infanti and
Cécile Venot of the Centre Pompidou, Sylvie Legrand-Rossi of the Musée Nissim de
Camondo, Allison Macgillivray of the Cité de l'Architecture, Marianne Mathieu
of the Musée Marmottan. Sylvie Perrin of the Cité de la Céramique, Pascale de Sèze
of the Musée des Arts Décoratifs, Amélie Simier of the Musée Bourdelle and
Sandrine Adass of the Musée d'Art et d'Histoire de Judaïsme.
With thanks from the editor to Duncan Barclay, Emily Barber, Neil Dodds, Philippe Cothier.

Printed in Hungary by Dürer Nyomda Kft., Gyula.

Introduction

Paris, on the face of it, is reassuringly still the city of one's memory or imagination: the skylines, the monuments and cityscapes; the Eiffel Tower and the Champs-Élysées; the Seine and Notre-Dame are still there to be wondered at, photographed, explored and admired. But the city does not exist in aspic. Over the last decade, gradual but significant changes to the urban landscape have been taking place, including improvements to the transport system, the restoration of monuments, the enhancement of the riverside, the reopening of museums and the inauguration of new arts centres. The cultural life of Paris abounds with music festivals, film festivals and arts festivals and the city in many respects has become more visitor friendly: on public transport, in hotels and restaurants, and especially in the museums and monuments, where the increase in the number of cafés and restaurants is a much-appreciated touch. Nevertheless, almost every art gallery or public monument rigidly maintains the tradition of closing one day a week. Markets selling items ranging from exotic fruit to stamps and bric-à-brac are still popular, and added to these now are a number of Christmas markets.

At the end of 2014 came two long-awaited events in the art world. The first was the reopening of the Picasso Museum, beautifully displayed in the elegantly revamped Hôtel Salé. The second was the inauguration of the Louis Vuitton Foundation in a sensational new building designed by Frank Gehry, with fly-away glass roofs reminiscent of a great sailing ship.

Two of the oldest and most revered monuments of Paris, both on the Île de la Cité, have been enhanced using modern technology. Notre-Dame Cathedral has received sophisticated new LED lighting to enable flexible illumination of the interior. And laser technology has been used to meticulously clean and restore the coloured glass of the Sainte-Chapelle. Also on the Île de la Cité is Archaeological Crypt beneath the forecourt of Notre-Dame, which provides a fascinating insight, enhanced by modern technology, into the evolution of Paris since earliest times..

At the Louvre in 2012 the outstanding Arts of Islam department opened in a specially-created space. More recently, in 2014, the Louvre opened its completed Department of Decorative Arts. Around the same time, the *Winged Victory of Samothrace* and the *Venus de Milo*, following cleaning and restoration, were returned to their rightful places.

Other museums to receive an overhaul include the Hôtel Biron, home to the Musée Rodin, and the Musée Marmottan, which has been rearranged and extended. The

Musée d'Orsay has completed a long-term reorganisation which gives easier access to the Impressionist galleries. Two smaller museums in Montparnasse, dedicated to the sculptors Bourdelle and Zadkine, have also been refreshed; and the best-known work in the Musée de Cluny, the Lady with the Unicorn tapestries, returned in late 2013 after an in-depth restoration and cleaning. The Eiffel Tower now has a glass floor for greater viewing effect; and Les Invalides has brought a new look to its vast collections, including the innovative 'Historial de Gaulle', which is a multimedia presentation— no objects.

A major cultural event of 2015 was the opening of the Paris Philharmonie at La Villette, a vast new concert hall of revolutionary design due mainly to Jean Nouvel. The Bibliothèque Richelieu, the oldest of the five libraries of the Bibliothèque de France, is undergoing a long structural overhaul while still remaining open to the public.

Parts of Paris have become more pedestrian-friendly, including Place de la République, and certain sections of both banks of the Seine are now closed to vehicles on Sundays (between 9am and 5pm). New footbridges (*passerelles*) link left and right banks: one between Musée d'Orsay and the Jardin des Tuileries and another between Quai Branly and Quai de New-York near the Palais de Tokyo. There are now two Paris Plages: the original one between the Louvre and Pont de Sully, and Paris Plage Bassin de la Villette alongside the canal in the 10th arrondissement between Place de Stalingrad and Rue de la Crimée. The Josephine Baker pool and solarium at Bercy is part open-air. A major urban transformation is also happening at Les Halles, where a glass 'Canopée' now floats over the previously rather grim Métro station. The old department store La Samaritaine (1870), an iconic building near the Hôtel de Ville, is due to be repurposed. Less controversial, but lengthy and costly, is the restoration of the Panthéon, which began in 2013.

It is important to remember that objects in permanent exhibitions tend to be rotated, so works described in the text may not necessarily be on view. It is also worth remembering that most of the 14 museums run by the City of Paris are free, including the Musée d'Art Moderne, the Petit Palais, the Carnavalet, the Zadkine and the Cernuschi. Also remember to take advantage of special offers/combined tickets (e.g. Musées Rodin and Orsay), and where to possible to buy tickets online, to avoid queues, which can be lengthy.

Out of town visits are pleasant, especially in summer. Easy to access are the Cité de la Céramique at Sèvres or the former royal châteaux of Vincennes or St-Germain-en-Laye, the latter home to the National Archaeological collection, and each with a Sainte-Chapelle. Or perhaps you might make a visit to the Paris Zoo in the Parc de Vincennes. The Grand Palais usually puts on something special for the winter.

History of Paris

by Matthew Kidd

The Paris of the popular imagination is a sensuous place, as captured by phrases such as '*belle époque*' and '*ville lumière*'. And it is easy to approach the city in this way: the phrases do reflect elements of Parisian history, and Paris has for centuries attracted to it artists and intellectuals, French and foreign. But it is not the full story. For Paris has also known hard times: disease, famine, economic hardship, absentee rulers, political strife. It has undergone repeated siege and occupation. These aspects too have left their traces on the Paris we see now and on the character of its inhabitants, and can help us to understand how it came to be as it is, and what deeper currents underlie the gaiety.

THE BEGINNINGS

The Seine was a navigable river and a commercial highway as far back as historical evidence can take us. At what is now Paris, the river intersected with a main north–south route; and the islands in the river offered natural defensive advantages. The first people to establish a permanent base here, probably in the 4th century BC, were a Celtic tribe later called (by the Romans) *Parisii*. They established themselves on what is now the Île de la Cité, the biggest of what were then a dozen islands, in a river probably twice as wide then as now. They were semi-nomadic, trading up and down the river, leaving no trace of grand buildings or paved streets, and with no bridges to connect their settlement to the banks. They worshipped the water: a fact worth recalling when one sees modern Paris' coat of arms (of a ship afloat) and motto (*fluctuat nec mergitur*: she is tossed on the waves but not engulfed). And Paris remains a working port, France's fifth largest, with a freight canal running directly beneath the Place de la Bastille.

The Romans arrived in 54 BC. Julius Caesar identified the settlement (apparently known to the Celts as *Louk-tier*, place of marshes) as a good base for his campaign to subjugate the tribes of northern Gaul. The Romans Latinised the name as *Lutetia*. The Romans built the first bridges, connecting the Île de la Cité to both banks. The settlement slowly expanded, particularly on the southern side. By the 2nd century AD, they had built a forum (on the hill where the Sorbonne now stands), an arena (remains still visible near the Rue Monge) and baths. The size of the arena suggests a population of 20–30,000. There was a temple to Jupiter on the island where Notre-Dame now stands.

Christianity came to Lutetia probably in the 3rd century. The first bishop, Dionysius (or Denis), was martyred on the hill north of the city which later became known as Montmartre (*Mons Martyrum*). The legend had it that, after his head had been cut off, he picked it up and carried it to where the cathedral of St-Denis was later built in his memory (providing the mausoleum in which a thousand years of French kings were buried).

By the end of the 3rd century, Roman Gaul was under attack from Goths and Huns. The emperor Constantius Chlorus made Lutetia for the first time the provincial capital, closer than Lyon (the previous capital) to the front line at the Rhine. In the mid-4th century, the emperor Julian (nephew of Constantine the Great and known as the Apostate) spent three years in Lutetia, writing affectionately of its charms, and in effect making it the capital of the Western Empire. He was formally acclaimed Augustus there in AD 360, an event not to be repeated until Napoleon's imperial coronation in 1804. Julian changed the city's name from Lutetia to *Civitas Parisiorum*, combining Roman status with Celtic history.

The barbarian pressure on Roman Gaul grew over the following century. In 451 Attila the Hun led a fierce army against Paris but the inhabitants kept their nerve, urged on by a young girl, later St Geneviève, who had had a vision that he would turn away. Indeed he did. In 497, however, Paris was occupied by the equally fierce Franks under Clovis. Geneviève this time advised the Parisians to open their gates to him as long as he converted to Christianity. Clovis did so, defeated the Romans, and made Paris the capital of a Christian Frankish kingdom in 508. His name—the modern Louis—has proved the most popular of all French royal names, reflecting his status as the founding father of France. His dynasty (the Merovingians, after his grandfather Merovius) remained based in Paris for two and a half centuries. The Roman buildings, including the city walls, were plundered for their stone, thus leaving Paris vulnerable. But the first monasteries were founded (including the abbey of St Geneviève, where Clovis was buried, and where the Lycée Henri-IV now stands; *map p. 587, E3–E4*). The first proto-French texts were written.

The later, weaker Merovingian kings allowed power in the city to pass into the hands of indigenous *maires*: already in the 8th century sowing the seeds of conflict between local power brokers and an alien monarchy. The best known *maire*, Charles Martel, succeeded in checking the Muslim advance into France, at Poitiers in 732, and used the authority he had won by so doing to depose the last Merovingian king in 754 and impose his own son instead, establishing the Carolingian dynasty. His grandson Charlemagne (r. 768–814), crowned Holy Roman Emperor in 800, had no use for Paris, and moved his capital to Aachen (Aix-la-Chapelle). By the 9th century Paris had shrunk back to its original dimensions on the Île de la Cité; and, like the rest of what had once been Gaul, was weakened by the squabbling of Frankish nobles. It lay wide open to the attacks of the Norse invaders.

Six times they came between 825 and 925, mostly by ship, the fiercest assault being in 885–6 when Paris, under Eudes (or Odo), eldest son of Robert the Strong, Count of Anjou, withstood a year-long siege. It was the first time that any Frankish settlement had dared to resist the Norsemen so robustly; three years later Eudes was crowned king. By the early 10th century, the Norsemen were established permanently in Normandy (hence the name), and challenged the Franks for territorial supremacy. In 987 the Franks picked Hugues Capet (r. 987–96), Parisian and great-nephew of Eudes, as their leader, replacing the enfeebled Carolingians. He was crowned in Paris, establishing his dynasty, the Capetians.

THE CAPETIANS

Hugues Capet's kingdom was modest—just Paris and the hinterland of the Île de France—and its inhabitants lacked even a common language. But during the three centuries of Capetian rule, Paris started to grow, both physically and intellectually. Hugues Capet's son, Robert le Pieux, was perhaps the first ruler since the Romans to take an interest in the city's fabric. He restored the Palais de la Cité and started rebuilding the monasteries outside the walls. A century later, Suger, Abbot of St-Denis, became the first in a series of ecclesiastical administrators and patrons who over the centuries, in the name of the kings they served, both provided government to France and changed the face of Paris. Suger ordered the rebuilding of St-Denis (1136–47), stimulating the development of the Gothic style in cathedrals across northern France. He encouraged also the building of Notre-Dame, though it was started only after his death. Under the authority of Louis VI (r. 1108–37), he had marshlands on the Left Bank drained, and had the fort (or *châtelet*, hence the name of today's Métro station) which guarded the northern end of the bridge linking the Île de la Cité to the Right Bank rebuilt of stone, creating thereby a new focal point for the expanding city.

In the same generation, Peter Abelard transformed the status of Paris as a seat of learning. Romantics may know him better for his love story with Héloïse but he also transformed Paris' intellectual life, bringing a new questioning spirit to the theological seminaries already present, and starting the process of consolidating them into a single university. Maurice de Sully, who oversaw the construction of Notre-Dame from 1163 onwards, also led the building of Paris' first hospital, the Hôtel-Dieu, next door. It was a period of enlightenment, of intellectual and artistic experiment. The decision to knock down buildings around Notre-Dame, in order to allow straight roads over which the stone for the cathedral could be more easily hauled to the site, must have seemed a radical change of priorities.

Philippe-Auguste (r. 1180–1223), Louis VI's grandson, was one of the kings of France who had most impact on the development of Paris, despite many conflicting calls on his attention: Crusades, tangling with the pope and fighting the English. He ordered the construction of the first complete stone wall around the city, up to six metres high (with traces still visible today; see p. 65). He built aqueducts to bring fresh water, and sought (without much success) to alleviate the problems of refuse and sewage. He gave the University of Paris its first charter and its students ecclesiastical privileges (which led to town-versus-gown frictions over the centuries to come). He promoted trade by establishing the first permanent market at Les Halles. He built the first fortress on the site of the Louvre, then outside his city walls. He strengthened the city's mechanisms for running its own affairs, including allowing it to levy taxes on river traffic. Much of the funding for his projects came from money confiscated from the Jews; Philippe-

Auguste's persecution of them in the 1180s stained his record, and his partial relenting in the following decade was prompted less by conscience than by a realisation that without them his funds were running dry. But Paris as a whole profited from his reign. He promoted the city's sense of itself as capital of France, for example by holding there the triumphal procession following the Battle of Bouvines, the victory over King John of England and his allies which resulted in French gains of English lands in France, and established France as a military power. By the time Philippe died, Paris' population had grown to 200,000.

The 13th century saw a growth in the influence of the Parisian bourgeoisie, supported by the city's growing trading wealth. Philippe-Auguste's grandson, Louis IX (r. 1226–70; later St Louis after being canonised by Pope Boniface VIII for his personal holiness and his contribution to the Crusades), set up administrative structures for France (courts, treasury and a parliament, though without legislative powers) which remained in place until 1789. He turned the old Palais de la Cité into an administrative centre. He also incorporated into it the Sainte-Chapelle, one of the only elements to survive today, to house the Crown of Thorns, which he had acquired from the Frankish emperor of Constantinople (*see p. 35*). The university was further developed, and acquired its name (from Robert de Sorbon, Louis IX's personal confessor). But Louis turned his back on the free thinking of the previous century, even allowing the Inquisition, which St Dominic in his preaching against the Albigensians had introduced to southern France some years before, to establish itself in Paris.

Few of the later Capetians left much trace on the city. The exception was Philippe IV (Philip the Fair; r. 1285–1314), who continued his grandfather Louis' work on France's administration. When he died, France was more populous than at any point over the next four centuries, and Paris had 300,000 inhabitants. But Philippe was a spendthrift, always in need of new sources of revenue. Having harassed the Jews and the Lombards, he turned his attention to the Knights Templar, long and prosperously established in the area still known as the Quartier du Temple (*map p. 588, A1–B1*). With the connivance of Pope Clement V, their headquarters were raided, the knights tortured and burnt by the Inquisition, their property seized by the state. As their Grand Master was burnt at the stake, roughly where the statue of Henri IV at the western end of the Île de la Cité now stands, he cursed both pope and king; within the year, both were dead. Within fifteen more years Philippe's three sons, kings in succession, had died too, all childless.

THE END OF THE MIDDLE AGES AND THE RENAISSANCE
For France and for Paris, the 14th century was marked by the long attrition of the Hundred Years War against England. In addition, the Black Death hit Paris in 1348, following several years of famine. Public disenchantment with the kings' insistence on pursuing the war burst out into rioting, led by the merchant class. Unlike other French cities, Paris had no charter to protect it from the monarch's caprices. In 1355 Étienne Marcel, merchants' provost, sought to establish a new constitution limiting the king's powers over the city. But his revolt was put down, and he lost public support by seeking alliance with the enemy King of Navarre.

By the beginning of the fifteenth century the English had established a military advantage, and pressed it home through the Battle of Agincourt in 1415. They occupied Paris in 1420 with their Burgundian allies; the Duke of Bedford (brother of the English king, Henry V) ran the city from the Palais des Tournelles, on the site of what is now the Place des Vosges (*map p. 588, B2*). In 1429 came an attempt—in which Joan of Arc participated—to storm the Porte St-Honoré. It was unsuccessful, and the English remained in occupation until 1436, having the young Henry VI (Henry V's son) crowned King of France in Notre-Dame in 1431.

After the end of the Hundred Years War, in 1453, when England was expelled from all her holdings in France except Calais, France recovered quickly—though successive French kings involved themselves in fighting for territory on the Italian peninsula, with a series of expeditionary campaigns culminating in humiliating defeat at Novara in 1513. But these campaigns also provided a conduit for the ideas of the Italian Renaissance. Cultivated Frenchmen decorated their speech with Italianisms. This was also the period when Paris acquired its first printing press, in 1470. The kings of the late 15th century spent little time there, however; and the first evidence of new architectural styles reaching France was rather to be seen in the Loire châteaux.

François I (r. 1515–47) had to contend with a new strategic threat: the Holy Roman Empire under the Habsburg Charles V, who ruled both Austria and Spain. The contest culminated in François' defeat and temporary imprisonment after the Battle of Pavia in 1525. He nevertheless gave Paris plenty of his attention. He had the Marais cleared and opened for development by private entrepreneurs. He built the first stone quays along the Seine. He demolished the old fortress of the Louvre and started its reconstruction in the new style as a residential palace. He founded the Collège de Paris, not only to teach the new humanism emanating from Italy, but to do so in French (this was the period when Rabelais was giving the language a new vigour). He brought to Paris the paintings which were to form the nucleus of the Louvre's collections, including the *Mona Lisa*. Indeed, François was Leonardo da Vinci's last and most generous patron, inviting him to France and giving him a country house near Amboise. Leonardo died there in 1519.

François also brought from Italy, as a bride for his second son (later Henri II), Catherine de Médicis, of the Florentine ruling house. Henri II (r. 1547–59) died in a jousting accident in the courtyard of the Palais des Tournelles. Catherine was mother of the next three kings, all of whom inherited the throne young and died young, leaving her influential as regent. This period saw bitter conflict between Catholics and Protestants (the Wars of Religion). In Paris, the populace were mostly Catholic, as were the feudal nobility. But many in the merchant classes had embraced Protestantism, partly out of disenchantment with the monarch's claim of divine right as well as with the corruption and degeneracy of the court.

In 1572, Catherine's second son, the young Charles IX (r. 1560–74), was brought to issue an order for the massacre of Protestants (or Huguenots, from the German *Eidgenossen*, confederates) on St Bartholomew's Eve (23rd August). Six days before, at Catherine's instigation, his sister Marguerite de Valois (later La Reine Margot) had been married to the Protestant Henri of Navarre, an event which brought many

Protestants into the city. Some estimates suggest that up to 15,000 were killed, as the massacre spread from Paris to other cities. Paris' international reputation (and consequently its trade) suffered. Over the following decade it fell further, as the city came under the influence of the vigilantes of the Catholic League, led by the Duc de Guise. The League operated in open rivalry to the king, the unpopular and irresolute Henri III (r. 1574–89), the youngest of Catherine de Médicis' sons. In 1588 Henri nerved himself to order the assassination of the Duc de Guise. In revenge he himself was stabbed to death by a Dominican friar at St-Cloud.

THE BOURBONS TO THE REVOLUTION

There was no direct heir. The Catholic League hoped to manoeuvre their way to the succession. But Henri III proposed on his deathbed that the throne should pass to his brother-in-law and distant cousin, Henri of Navarre, even though he was a Protestant. Henri had to fight for this inheritance. After failing to defeat the League in open battle, and concluding that the walls of Paris, built by Philippe-Auguste nearly four hundred years earlier, were too strong for him to storm the city, he laid siege to it. Famine ensued; 30–40,000 died, and still the Catholic hard-liners urged no surrender. The hard-pressed populace became increasingly impatient for a solution. Eventually, after three years of siege, a deal was reached: Henri submitted to Catholicism in a formal mass at St-Denis in July 1593, and the following spring the city opened its gates to him. He ascended the throne as Henri IV (r. 1589–1610), the first of the Bourbon monarchs of France. His dynasty, destined to occupy the thrones of France, Spain and Naples, was to struggle for the next century and a half for hegemony in Europe.

One of Henri IV's first moves was to announce a general amnesty, and the same year he issued the Edict of Nantes, establishing freedom of religion. He then turned his attention to transforming Paris, which after the siege, and two outbreaks of plague in the 1580s and 1590s, was in a sorry state. He had the Pont Neuf completed and other bridges modernised. He started a programme of replacing medieval wooden buildings with new squares of brick and stone, of which the Place des Vosges is the best completed example (compare with the nearby Rue du Prévôt to understand how novel it must have seemed). The transformation he set in hand led to a 50 percent increase in population over the first half of the following century. It all cost money (Pont Neuf was funded by a tax on wine) but Henri IV preferred to invest in his own capital city rather than follow the fashion of seeking territories in the New World (French colonisation of Canada had begun under François I). Despite all his efforts to rule equitably, the Catholic League remained active. There were frequent assassination attempts on him. In May 1610 a fanatical would-be monk named Ravaillac stabbed him fatally as he sat in his carriage in the Rue de la Ferronnerie (still there, near Les Halles; *map p. 587, E1*), trapped in a traffic jam caused by an overturned cart of straw.

The next three Bourbon rulers, Louis XIII, XIV and XV, reigned for a successive 164 years. Each inherited the throne as a child, the first two under the regency of their mothers. None of the three felt particularly at home in Paris. Louis XIII (r. 1610–43) preferred to be out hunting, and built himself a hunting-box at Versailles. Louis XIV (r. 1643–1715) hugely enlarged it, and it remained the residence of his successors until the Revolution. Louis XIV returned to his capital only 25 times in the last 40 years of his reign.

Paris certainly changed during this long period. But others were primarily responsible. Louis XIII's mother had the Palais du Luxembourg built (later a prison under the Revolution, now the home of the Sénat). Cardinal Richelieu, Louis XIII's chief minister, created the Île St-Louis, joining two existing smaller islands, embellished the Sorbonne and built himself the Palais Cardinal, which later became the Palais Royal (*see p. 309*). This helped to stimulate growth of the city westwards and northwards from the Marais.

Richelieu's tyrannical ways created predictable public resentment, intensified by the cost of the Thirty Years War against Spain and Austria. Richelieu died in 1642, Louis XIII the following year. Louis XIV's mother, Anne of Austria, as regent, called on Richelieu's secretary, Mazarin, to succeed him as First Minister. In 1648, Mazarin sought to re-impose an unpopular tax, and provoked riots which forced the boy king and his mother to flee Paris. The rioters used the catapult, or *fronde*, as their weapon; the rebellions against the crown during these years came to be named after it. Several years of confusion followed, with rebellious nobles joining the urban rioters in seeking to bring the king down. But in 1652 Mazarin prompted the formation of a unified royal party, to support the queen and her young son, which rapidly gained backing. But the experiences of the Fronde had brought the king to the conclusion that to rule effectively, he must rule absolutely. Three years later, still only seventeen, he was told while out hunting that the *parlement* had met without seeking his approval. He appeared at their session and laid down the law: '*l'État, c'est moi*'.

Louis conducted a series of wars, in Spain and the Netherlands, to extend the territory of France, and Paris saw the effects in projects designed to commemorate his victories: the adjacent triumphal arches at the Porte St-Denis and Porte St-Martin, and the Place des Victoires. The Hôtel des Invalides was founded, to accommodate up to 7,000 war veterans. It was an era with a taste for grandeur and spectacle. Parts of the earlier fortifications were demolished to make room for grand boulevards (named after the bulwarks they replaced). Pageants were popular, including the one in 1662 in which Louis XIV wore for the first time the symbol of the sun, which became identified with him. This was also the great age of the Paris theatre, with Corneille and later Racine writing tragedies, Molière comedies and Lully incidental music. Wealthy nobles vied to build elegant châteaux around Paris. But the king did not care to be outshone: when his finance minister Fouquet invited him to a splendid pageant at his new château at Vaux-le-Vicomte, Louis had him arrested for embezzlement.

While Louis was conquering on land, his able new finance minister, Colbert, was seeking to make France mistress of the seas. France now administrated colonies in Africa and the Americas, and exotic commodities were pouring into the capital, along with considerable wealth. During this period Paris saw its first cafés, its first streetlights and fire service, the first carriages for public hire (known as *fiacres*, because they waited to be hired by the church of St-Fiacre, now remembered only in a tiny alley in the Beaubourg, diagonally opposite the church of St-Merry). It had by now a population of half a million, the rich increasingly in the west, where the prevailing winds left the air fresher, the poorer in the east. But taxes to pay for the wars were heavy and the court was not popular. In 1682, Louis XIV decreed that he would rule henceforth from Versailles. Work on his projects in the capital, including completing the Cour Carrée of the Louvre, was suspended (and the scaffolding remained up for the next seventy years). But the withdrawal of the court did little to dent Paris' prosperity. If anything, it had less impact than the Revocation of the Edict of Nantes in 1685, which led to another exodus of Protestants, who took with them their wealth and skills. Persecution of Protestants was followed by action in 1709 to break up the convent at Port-Royal, home of the Jansenists, an austere Catholic sect (though marked by Calvinist ideas) unsympathetic to the luxury of the court but attractive to influential figures such as Pascal and Racine.

The Duc de Saint-Simon's memoirs give a picture of the stultifying life of the Versailles court in Louis XIV's last years. The king's insistence that his nobles remain in attendance on him there made it hard for them to engage in political activity or to administer their own estates effectively. Gloom was heightened by a famine following a failed harvest in 1693; and by the coldest winter ever in Paris, in 1709. The king sought to strengthen his position in Europe by uniting the French and Spanish crowns, in the War of the Spanish Succession. But he suffered a series of military reverses in the first years of the new century, seeing French armies defeated by the Duke of Marlborough at Blenheim, Ramillies, Oudenarde and Malplaquet, and in 1707 Dutch cavalry scouts almost reached the gates of Versailles. In 1715, Louis XIV died, having outlived his son, two out of his three grandsons and his oldest great-grandson.

Louis XV (r. 1715–74), another great-grandson, was five when he came to the throne. Philippe, Duc d'Orléans, son of Louis XIV's younger brother, was appointed regent. In his forties, free-thinking and licentious, he moved the court back to Paris. He was initially popular, especially for negotiating settlements of France's wars. But the public never forgave him for the collapse of his attempt to introduce a paper-based bank, which then speculated heavily in developing Louisiana (New Orleans was named after him).

When Philippe died in 1723, Louis XV moved back to Versailles. Without Louis XIV's early experience of hardship, he had grown up feckless and extravagant, accustomed to flattery. He engaged France once again in dynastic wars: those of the Polish and Austrian successions, and the Seven Years War against Prussia. Under the influence of Madame de Pompadour, his mistress for 20 years, there were some further grand projects in Paris: the École Militaire, and the Place Louis-XV (now Place de la Concorde), which moved the city's centre of gravity a further step westward. The decorative arts flourished, as seen in the works of Boucher, Boulle and Gouthière. But the contrast between the light comedies of Marivaux, popular at Versailles, and the intellectual ferment stimulating Diderot and the *encyclopédistes* in Paris (and Voltaire from his exile near Geneva) is telling. Louis lived for the pleasures of the day and neglected his people; as Madame de Pompadour expressed it, '*après nous le déluge*'. His popularity in Paris declined so far that he preferred to travel from Versailles to Fontainebleau without passing through the city. It took three successive subscriptions to raise the funds for his pet project, the Panthéon. When he died, in 1774, his burial at St-Denis had to be conducted in secret.

His successor, Louis XVI (r. 1774–93), inherited a dire economic situation. But he was not strong-minded enough to endorse, over the resistance of his court, reform proposals which would have abolished some of their tax privileges. Instead, France's public purse remained over-burdened by accumulated debt and continuing military expenditure, even while private wealth funded the building of elegant *hôtels particuliers* in the areas west of the Place Louis-XV. The population continued to grow, now reaching 600,000; and the economic screws continued to tighten. In 1784 an unpopular new wall was built around Paris, to enable customs dues to be collected more efficiently on goods entering and leaving the city (*see p. 405*). The harvest failed across France in 1787 and 1788. In May 1789, the king convoked (for the first time since 1614) a full meeting of the États-Généraux (the closest equivalent to a parliament) to consider further reform proposals prepared by his finance minister, Necker. The États-Généraux had three constituent parts: the First Estate (the clergy), the Second Estate (the nobility) and the Third Estate (the commoners). The Third Estate, always liable to be outvoted by the other two, then proceeded to meet independently and proclaimed itself an assembly in its own right. Louis responded by sacking Necker. But he had misjudged the popular mood, especially in Paris. The mob attacked Les Invalides, capturing 30,000 muskets, and the next day, 14th July, they stormed and occupied the Bastille prison, symbol of royal autocracy, and freed the (in fact, few) prisoners. The French Revolution had begun.

THE FRENCH REVOLUTION

The next decade and a half saw France ruled in a bewildering succession of political formats (*see p. 584*). Paris was at the centre of the turmoil and bloodshed, losing a tenth of its population. The fabric of the city suffered too: royal buildings were damaged and statues toppled, Church property was sequestrated and churches themselves either given new functions or pulled down (with the atmospheric paintings of Hubert Robert recording their decay). But bringing down the monarchy was not the rebels' immediate objective. A new constitution, sworn into operation on the following 14th July, including by the king himself, still provided for a constitutional monarchy, although it severely diminished the powers of the Church.

This new constitution then came under increasing attack from both sides. Radicals, especially those known as the Jacobins (because they met in what had been the Jacobin convent off the Rue St-Honoré), felt that it did not go far enough. Conservative Catholics, swayed by the pope's condemnation of it, felt that it went too far and sought to recover the ground it had ceded. Caught in the middle were the moderate Girondins (so called because many of their leaders came from the Gironde region around Bordeaux). In June 1791 the king and his queen, Marie-Antoinette, tried to flee, and were captured at Varenne in eastern France; but, though the Assembly took this as a reason to suspend Louis from his functions, he was later reinstated. Émigrés, and the wealth they had taken with them, and those priests refusing to accept the constitution, were more urgent targets of popular wrath.

Over the winter of 1791–2 a third focus for resentment developed: the foreign powers thought to be scheming to reverse reforms. In April 1792 the king, reflecting the will of the Assembly, declared war on Austria and Prussia. But the weak French army's disastrous performance encouraged public suspicions that the king and his Girondin government had sought to bring about French defeat. The mob stormed the Tuileries; the Assembly established a Convention to draw up a new, more radical, republican constitution; and the royal family was imprisoned in the Temple Tower. Radical and popular frustration boiled over: prisons were stormed and emptied, and nobles executed. The king himself was guillotined in January 1793, after a show trial. Marie-Antoinette met the same fate in October. The Convention established a Revolutionary Tribunal and a Committee of Public Security which gradually assumed power and pursued anyone suspected of royalist or clerical sympathies, whether presenting any real threat to the regime or just attracting resentment. Twenty thousand died in the Terror, including Madame du Barry, the former mistress of Louis XV, who went to her death pleading with the executioner for '*encore un moment...encore un petit moment...*'.

Conditions in Paris started to approach a sort of vindictive anarchy, against a background of near economic collapse. Only by the second half of 1794, by which time many of the Committee's own original leaders (including Danton and Robespierre) had been executed, did the pendulum swing back. In 1795 a five-member Directoire took power. Though feeble, increasingly corrupt, and dependent on the Army, it was committed to trying to restore stability. The following years saw military success too, especially under the young Corsican general Napoleon Bonaparte; and at home, after the Terror, people began to develop a taste for self-indulgence. The first restaurants were established, mainly run by former chefs to aristocrats: it was thought democratic to eat well in public. Clockmakers and other craftsmen easily incorporated republican motifs into their luxury products.

NAPOLEON AND THE FRENCH EMPIRE

Bonaparte's military successes continued apace. In 1797 he extinguished the Venetian Republic; in 1798 he occupied Rome, declared a Roman republic, and took the pope into custody to France; in 1799 he usurped the Directoire and established a Consulat, with himself as First Consul. Fortified by his crushing of the Austrians at the Battle of Marengo in 1800, he became consul for life. Then he declared himself Emperor, and staged a coronation in Notre-Dame in 1804, in evocation of the papal coronation of Charlemagne (in this case, however, Napoleon placed the crown on his own head rather than allowing the pope the right to do so). In 1805 Napoleon crowned himself with the iron crown of Lombardy in Milan. In 1806 he abolished the Holy Roman Empire and married Marie-Louise, daughter of the last Holy Roman Emperor Francis II, as a way of brokering peace between France and Austria, just as Louis XVI had married Marie-Antoinette. Napoleon had created a new European empire, and Paris was its capital.

Though often absent from Paris, Napoleon nevertheless took a close interest both in France's civil administration and in the amenities of the city. He had four new bridges started. He remodelled the Madeleine, began the Rue de Rivoli, and had medieval houses around Notre-Dame removed to make more space for his coronation parade. He planned his Arc de Triomphe, but in open country to the west of the city rather than in the Place de la Bastille as first intended, because of popular disillusionment with his policies. He inaugurated the Louvre as a museum, in particular to display his spoils from Italy and Germany.

By 1810, Napoleon's luck seemed to change. The long campaign in Spain ended in defeat; so did the disastrous march on Moscow. At home, there was a financial crash in 1811. In March 1814, the combined forces of France's enemies, led by Austria, Prussia and Russia, occupied Paris, the first time it had been occupied by foreign troops for four centuries. Napoleon abdicated, and in May Louis XVI's younger brother returned to reoccupy the royal throne. (He took the title Louis XVIII, remembering Louis XVI's eight-year-old son, the Louis XVII that might have been, thought to have been murdered in the Temple after his father's death.)

The occupying forces behaved magnanimously, though the Cossacks' impatience in restaurants (*bistro* = quickly) gave rise to a new form of eating establishment. But the new king did little to endear himself. When Napoleon, the following year, escaped from Elba and sought to re-establish his empire, Paris received him phlegmatically back. After the Battle of Waterloo finally settled his prospects, the Allies occupied Paris once again, while Napoleon was exiled to St Helena.

THE RESTORATION, JULY MONARCHY AND SECOND REPUBLIC

Louis XVIII (r. 1815–24) returned, this time supported by 300,000 soldiers, equivalent to half the population of the city. He surrounded himself with ministers of reactionary tendencies, tendencies which were only encouraged by the assassination of his nephew, the Duc de Berry, outside the opera in 1820.

Economically, France and Paris recovered well under Louis XVIII and his brother Charles X (r. 1824–30). Albeit later than London, Paris started to see the effects of the Industrial Revolution. But Charles was even more resistant to the pull of democracy than his brother; and his attempt in 1830 to dissolve the Chamber of Deputies and suspend freedom of the press led to riots. The rioters took over the whole city in three days in July, using urban guerrilla tactics which the narrowness of the streets made it hard to counter.

Rather than re-establish the Republic, however, the rebels invited Louis-Philippe (r. 1830–48), Duc d'Orléans, to become 'citizen-king', establishing the 'July Monarchy'. Although he was a direct descendant of Louis XIII, he carefully distinguished his style from that of the Bourbons. He had been a prosperous banker, and he continued to promote bourgeois interests. Most of the changes to Paris during his reign were new residential developments in areas such as the Batignolles. His reign saw the first omnibuses and the first department stores. The railway arrived. The city's population increased by a third in only a generation, to over a million for the first time. Balzac's novels chart this rapidly changing city. But the king's popularity declined, not helped by the authoritarian ways of his police force, nor by the cholera epidemic of 1832 and food shortages in 1847. When a small demonstration in February 1848 was violently suppressed, with several hundred deaths, the National Guard took the insurgents' side and France's last king fled. The rioters sacked the Tuileries and burnt the royal throne in front of the Place de la Bastille monument to those who had died in the 1830 riots.

During 1848, that year of upheaval across Europe, France saw four forms of government. After the monarchy came the Second Republic, unprepared and ineffectual. When, within months, it proved unable to meet public expectations, and unemployment in Paris rose alarmingly, there was more rioting, this time savagely put down by Cavaignac, Minister for War. Several thousand were killed, many more imprisoned or deported; for a while Paris was under effective military dictatorship. Finally, at the end of the year, elections—the first with mass male suffrage—brought Napoleon's nephew-by-marriage, Louis-Napoléon to power as President, his 75 percent of the vote reflecting how strong Bonapartist feeling still was in the provinces compared to radical, republican Paris.

FROM EMPEROR NAPOLÉON III TO THE COMMUNE

Three years later, he mounted a coup against his own presidency and was appointed Emperor in a plebiscite. As Napoléon III (in acknowledgement of the two-week reign of Napoleon Bonaparte's four-year-old son in 1815), the new emperor had ambitious ideas for Paris. He and Baron Haussmann, appointed as Préfet de Paris, wanted wide modern streets and were ruthless in demolishing the crowded and insalubrious old quarters that stood in their way. Planning regulations required housing to follow uniform proportions, emphasised by long horizontal lines of balconies overlooking the new boulevards. The emperor's great pride in his city, and in its railway stations and other public buildings exploiting the developing possibilities of iron and glass, was reflected also in Great Exhibitions in 1855 and 1867.

Napoléon III's foreign policy was less successful. Militarily he was an adventurer, and involved France in a number of wars, including the battle to drive Austria from Italy in return for Savoy and Nice. Disaster struck when he was manoeuvred by Bismarck into declaring war on Prussia in 1870. Within six weeks, the French army had to surrender at Sedan. The emperor was captured, deposed, and a (Third) Republic was declared, under Favre and Gambetta. The Germans occupied Versailles and besieged Paris. The city, unprepared, quickly ran out of food and was reduced to communicating with the outside world by sending out hot air balloons, made of cotton, varnished and filled with coal gas. Finally, it had to capitulate. The Germans imposed harsh terms: France was to cede Alsace and part of Lorraine, pay a hefty indemnity, and recognise Germany as an empire under Kaiser Wilhelm I.

The government saw no alternative to accepting. The poorer classes in Paris, however, were in no mood to sit quiet. Napoléon III's modernisation had created an outwardly grandiose city, but his town planning was socially divisive: the poor could not afford the new rents and had retreated to the eastern districts, where gentrification emphatically did not reach. Now, still bitter at the killings of 1848 and fearing that their interests were once again being sacrificed to those of the bourgeoisie, they seized an armoury of weapons and succeeded in occupying the whole of Paris and declaring a Commune.

The Communards, however, had no strategy for holding on to what they had gained, and a government counter-strike forced them to retreat gradually back across Paris. The traditional barricades were less effective at holding the new broad streets than they had been in the cramped medieval alleys of the pre-Haussmann era. As they retreated eastwards, the Communards set fire to the *quartiers* they were leaving. Within two months it was all over, after a last stand in Père-Lachaise cemetery (in the corner where later French Communist Party leaders liked to be buried). Three to four thousand Communards had died in the fighting; another 20,000 were executed in retribution. The chasm between bourgeois and working class left by Paris' experience of the Commune added a further depth to the tensions visible across France, between Church and State, between conservative provinces and a radical capital. The Dreyfus affair (in which a Jewish officer was accused, falsely as it was eventually proven, of passing military secrets to Germany) polarised society for a decade.

Economic and cultural recovery was nevertheless rapid, and the reparations imposed by the Prussians were quickly paid off. Already by 1878 the city was confident enough to put on another Great Exhibition; and another in 1889, for which Eiffel built his Tower. The Impressionists held their first exhibition in 1874. Ironically, too, the 'scorched earth' policy of the Commune made it all the easier to complete Haussmann's plans. In 1898 the first Métro lines opened, with stations designed in the Art Nouveau style by Guimard (who also designed the little synagogue in the Rue Pavée in the Marais). By 1914 Paris' population stood at 2.5 million: it had quintupled within a century.

PARIS IN THE TWO WORLD WARS

When the First World War came in August 1914, France—although united by resentment of the Germans—was neither politically nor militarily prepared. Within a month, German forces came within 50 miles of Paris and the city faced siege again. The government fled for Bordeaux. But lucky capture of a German campaign map enabled veteran general Gallieni to counter-attack. The city's taxis made an odd but essential logistic contribution by bringing troops to the front line. The Germans retreated to northern France, where fighting descended into trench warfare for the rest of the war, though Paris experienced bombardment again in the spring of 1918 during the Germans' last, unsuccessful offensive.

After the War, the peace treaties were negotiated in Paris. The French Prime Minister, Clemenceau, insisted that they be signed in the Hall of Mirrors (Galerie des Glaces) in Versailles, where Bismarck had had the German Empire proclaimed in 1870. The treaties left France dissatisfied. Exhausted and resentful, having sustained huge loss of life and a ravaged land, she felt angered that Germany was being allowed to survive. On the day of the signing in Versailles, the Paris bus-drivers went on strike.

Recovery was slow. Though the fortifications built around Paris after the Franco-Prussian War (where the Boulevard Périphérique now runs) were dismantled, there were no ambitious ideas—and no funds—for using the space created. Immigration into Paris, from abroad and from the provinces, combined with economic depression, led to social tensions and anti-Semitism. There were serious riots in 1934; and in the seven years up to 1939 no fewer than 19 governments. One of them, in 1936, brought together Socialists and Communists in a pioneering Popular Front under Léon Blum. Mutual suspicions between the two soon undermined it, however, as did a wave of celebratory strikes and factory occupations which put economic revival at risk. But some of its innovations (such as paid holiday entitlements) have kept its memory fresh, and Léon Blum has lent his name to a square in the 11th arrondissement.

Despite this political background, the period between the wars saw Paris attract a distinguished generation of artists and writers, including Pablo Picasso, James Joyce and Ernest Hemingway. The work of all of them was marked by the city; there are accounts from the period of some incongruous meetings between them. This was also the period of Art Deco design and of the flowering of a tradition of *haute couture* set off by the arrival of the Englishman Charles Frederick Worth in the 1890s, and now taken forward by Chanel and others.

On the outbreak of the Second World War, France was in no state to resist the Germans when they sidestepped the defensive Maginot Line in May 1940 and marched once again on Paris. The Germans occupied the northern half of France, including Paris, while a collaborationist government was established at Vichy. French officials connived at the deportation of around half of Paris' Jewish population. But many French began to resist the German occupation, especially once Germany had attacked the Soviet Union. Over the four years to 1944, around 11,000 partisans of various political leanings were killed. In 1944, the Allied forces landed in Normandy, prompting insurgents of both Left and Right to try to take control of Paris. General de Gaulle persuaded the Allied commanders to help his Free French forces take the city, to prevent it falling into Communist control. General Leclerc arranged to enter the city by the Porte d'Orléans, as Napoleon had in 1815. Meanwhile, the departing German Kommandant ignored Hitler's orders to destroy the city behind him. Two days later, to make clear that Paris was once again under French authority, de Gaulle marched from the Arc de Triomphe to the Place de la Concorde, courageously ignoring the danger from Communist snipers still active.

THE FOURTH AND FIFTH REPUBLICS

De Gaulle remained in control of France until the end of the war, and claimed for it a place among the victorious Allied Powers. But the shattered economy needed external support, from the US Marshall Plan. Savage reprisals were taken against alleged collaborators with the Germans: the underlying moral dilemma helped stimulate the development, by Sartre and others, of Existentialism. In 1946 de Gaulle stepped back from power, and the (Fourth) Republic was established. It struggled to achieve economic recovery due to endemic strikes; joined the first efforts to build a new peaceful community between the states of Europe; and grappled with colonial problems, first in Indochina, then in Algeria. It successfully disentangled France from the former but lacked the strength to deal with the latter's demands for independence, especially once the violence spread to France itself.

In 1958 the Republic collapsed and was replaced by a new Constitution (the Fifth Republic), designed by de Gaulle around a powerful President: himself. It came as a shock to many of his supporters when in 1962 he decided to grant Algerian independence. There was fierce resistance within France to this decision (including attempts to assassinate him), led by disaffected generals.

During the 1960s he was able to turn his attention to cleaning up Paris. For the first time, some official support was provided for preserving the city's existing character, starting in the Marais, rather than just imposing new development. This was, nevertheless, also the era of the Tour Montparnasse, still one of only two skyscrapers inside the Périphérique, and of the decision to demolish the old Halles market. In 1968 there were, once again, serious riots in Paris, started this time by students. Though de Gaulle re-established control, he stepped down the following year.

All of de Gaulle's successors as President have sought to leave their mark on Paris, though none have been Parisians by origin. Georges Pompidou (1969–74) commissioned the Pompidou Centre to house a modern art museum and archive. François Mitterrand, the longest serving (1981–95), initiated the most ambitious projects: a new opera house at the Bastille; a new arch at La Défense, to continue westwards the perspective of triumphal arches from the Arc du Carrousel to the Arc de Triomphe; and the glass pyramids at the Louvre. Paris is still a magnet for the country's intellectual and artistic vitality. The Fondation Louis Vuitton in the Bois de Boulogne is perhaps the latest example of how the city can provide a setting for architectural ambition. But it is also still the crucible in which France's social and political tensions—between Right and Left, city and countryside, and now between the established population and new immigrant communities—are managed, and occasionally explode to the surface. The shootings at the offices of the satirical magazine *Charlie Hebdo* in January 2015 showed both how strong those tensions can be, but also how determined Paris' population as a whole is to contain them, and prevent them from undermining the city's liberal spirit.

Every visitor sees his or her own Paris, maybe a different one on each visit. But there can be few cities where the fabric visible today reflects so directly more than fifteen hundred years of growth and reverses, sophistication and struggle, passion and political theory. Whether it be Henri IV's Pont Neuf, the gentle curve of the Boulevard Haussmann, the provocative political statement of the Sacré Coeur on Montmartre, or the series of plaques around the monument in Place de la République recording the stages of France's republican evolution, history lies close to the surface here, ready to be decoded and appreciated.

NOTRE-DAME
St Denis flanked by angels. Detail from the Porte de la Vierge.

The Islands in the Seine

At the heart of Paris, where the River Seine widens to encompass them, are two islands, the Île de la Cité and the Île St-Louis. Closely connected but different in character, their history and position on the Seine makes them attractive and interesting places to visit.

The Île de la Cité was the earliest inhabited part of Paris. It is of major historical and administrative importance and has outstanding monuments, including the Cathedral of Notre-Dame, the Sainte-Chapelle and the Conciergerie. The Crypte Archéologique gives a superb understanding of the spread of the city from ancient times. The island is linked to both left and right banks by numerous bridges, and it has its own Métro stop (Cité; line 4).

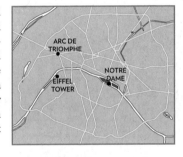

HISTORY OF THE ÎLE DE LA CITÉ

According to Julius Caesar, the Île de la Cité was the site of the *oppidum* of the Celtic tribe known as the *Parisii*. The island was settled c. 52 BC by the Romans and became known as Lutèce or *Lutetia Parisiorum*. There was a temple towards the east, on the site of the present cathedral, and traces of the Roman settlement have been discovered (*see p. 36*). Lutetia gradually spread to the Left Bank and c. 300 the settlement became known as Paris, chosen as the capital of the Franks in 508, under Clovis I (r. 481–511). The island, protected by the river, but also a convenient crossing place, close to ancient overland routes, became a strategic focal point. From the 10th century, the Capetian kings were responsible for the great buildings of the Cité, including the palace (now the Conciergerie).

For many centuries the island continued to be the royal, legal and religious centre, with 14 parishes in the Middle Ages. It remained barely altered from 1300 until the mid-19th century, when the medieval quarters were run through by Baron Haussmann's city improvement projects (*see p. 284*), creating pretty much what can be seen today. The island continues to be an ecclesiastical, judicial and legal centre.

NOTRE-DAME DE PARIS

Map p. 587, E2. Open weekdays 8–6.45, Sat–Sun until 7.15. T: 01 42 34 56 10. Individual tours/audioguides available. www.notredamedeparis.fr. Free. The cathedral is on the itinerary of every visitor to Paris and queues can be long.

NOTRE-DAME DE PARIS: WEST FRONT

The oldest of the great emblems of Paris, Notre-Dame cathedral, attracts some 13 million visitors a year and is almost always busy. It has been described as the ribcage of the city, with all its associations, from pre-Christian times to Quasimodo via royal marriages and presidential funerals. The building of Notre-Dame played an important role in the history of medieval architecture and despite successive alterations, this building represents a textbook example of the evolution of the Gothic style from the 12th–14th centuries. The cathedral has survived many threats to its safety: during the Revolution a festival was held consecrating it as a temple of Reason rather than superstition; over-zealous 19th-century restorers tried to repair the damage and created infelicities of their own; the Communards planned to set fire to it. It survives today as an embodiment in stone of the motto of Paris itself (see p. 311).

The cathedral rises to the east of a vast forecourt, **Parvis Notre-Dame**, which was increased sixfold in the 19th century. In the past, ecclesiastical authorities brought condemned heretics to trial on the Parvis, where they begged for absolution before execution. Road distances are calculated from a symbolic centre in the Parvis (the 'Point zéro'), marked by a bronze plaque in one of the flagstones.

To the left of the cathedral is the **Hôtel-Dieu**, the oldest hospital Paris, rebuilt in 1868–78, north of the first hospital, founded c. 660 by St Landry, Bishop of Paris. The old Hôtel-Dieu, built in the 12th century at the same time as Notre-Dame, was razed by Haussmann. At the time of writing, the hospital was gradually being closed, though a decision about its future use had yet to be taken.

To the right of the cathedral is a tall equestrian **statue of Charlemagne**. The building that closes the Parvis at the far end, dramatically illuminated at night, is the Préfecture de Police.

Bishop Maurice de Sully (d. 1196) was the inspiration behind the move to replace two earlier churches, St-Étienne and Notre-Dame, by a single building on a much larger scale. St-Étienne, founded by Childebert in 528 and dedicated to the first Christian martyr, Stephen, had itself replaced a Roman temple dedicated to Jupiter. Part of the outline of the old church is traced on the paving of the Parvis. Tradition holds that the foundation stone of the new cathedral was laid by Pope Alexander III in 1163. It expanded on the new style initiated at St-Denis (see p. 505), which became known as Gothic and in its turn went on to influence ecclesiastical architecture not just in the Île-de-France but all over Europe.

EXTERIOR OF NOTRE-DAME
NB: Numbers relate to the plan on p. 32.

The west front, composed of three distinct levels, is a model of clarity and harmony. A masterful design of verticals and horizontals divides the elevation into regular and complementary sections. From 1190–1220 it was built up to the rose window, and construction of the remainder continued through the first half of the 13th century. The central **Porte du Jugement (1)** (c. 1220) is medieval only in essence. The figure of Christ on the trumeau dates from 1885, the *Last Judgement* was restored by Viollet-le-Duc, and most of the other sculptures are also 19th century.

The **Porte de la Vierge (2)** on the left is slightly earlier. The Virgin on the central pier has been restored, and the statues of saints remade by Viollet-le-Duc. However, the scenes relating to the life of the Virgin in the tympanum are 13th-century: in the lower register, the *Ancestors of the Virgin*; in the middle, the *Resurrection of the Virgin*; and in the upper register, her *Coronation*. The sculptures of the **Porte de Ste Anne (3)** are mainly of 1165–75, designed for a narrower portal, and added to c. 1240. On the pier is St Marcellus (19th century); above are scenes from the life of St Anne and her daughter the Virgin, and the *Virgin in Majesty*, with *Louis VII* (right) and *Maurice de Sully* (left). The two side doors retain their medieval wrought-iron hinges.

In the buttress niches flanking the doors are modern statues of *St Stephen*, the *Church*, the *Synagogue* and *St Denis*. Above, across the full width of the façade, is the **Gallery of the Kings of Judah**, reconstructed by Viollet-le-Duc. Its 28 statues were destroyed in 1793 because the revolutionaries assumed that they represented the kings of France. Fragments discovered in 1977 are in the Musée du Moyen Âge (*see p. 55*). Above them, on one side of the parapet is a statue of *Adam*, on the other, *Eve*. In the centre is a group of angels in adoration of the Virgin.

The magnificent **rose window** (1220), 9.6m in diameter, is flanked by double windows within arches. Higher still is an open arcade on slender columns. The **flèche** (90m above the ground), a lead-covered oak structure, was rebuilt by Viollet-le-Duc in 1860.

Like the west front, the side façades and apse also consist of three distinct and receding storeys; the bold and elegant flying buttresses of the latter were an innovation by Jean Ravy. The mid-13th-century **north porch (4)**, by Jean de Chelles, has an original statue of the *Virgin* and, in the tympanum, the *Story of Theophilus*. Just to the east of it is the graceful **Porte Rouge (5)**, probably by Pierre de Montreuil (the maple leaf garland carved around it on the left-hand side is thought to be typical of his work). There is a *Coronation of the Virgin* in the tympanum. This was originally the door into the cathedral choir from the cloisters, now demolished but which once occupied much of what is now Rue du Cloître. Just beyond Porte Rouge, below the windows of the choir chapels and continuing around the apse, are seven 14th-century **bas-reliefs of the life of the Virgin** according to the *Golden Legend*. Some of them are badly damaged but the scene of the *Dormition* is well preserved, as is the *Funeral of the Virgin*, showing her bier being attacked by an unbeliever.

The **south porch (6)**, according to a Latin inscription at the base, was begun in 1257 (slightly later than the north porch), again under the direction of Jean de Chelles. It can only be viewed from a distance, from the public park known as Square Jean-XXIII (after Pope John XXIII), laid out on the site of the 17th-century archbishop's palace (demolished in 1831). A statue of St John Paul II now stands directly opposite the south porch. In the tympanum is the *Story of St Stephen* (a reference to the earlier church dedicated to him) and the medallions depicting student life are original. From the garden there are excellent views of the east end of the cathedral with its flying buttresses. These were begun by the master mason Jean Ravy, to take the strain of the high vaults. Their dramatic proportions encourage comparisons with the rigging of a ship.

NOTRE-DAME
Dormition of the Virgin, exterior north side (14th century).

INTERIOR OF NOTRE-DAME

The interior is fairly regular in its layout, with a barely discernible shift in axis between the nave and the choir. The nave is flanked by double aisles and a double ambulatory surrounds the choir (five bays) and 37 chapels surround the whole. The total length of the cathedral is 130m.

Between 1163 and the consecration of the main altar on 19th May 1182, the choir and double ambulatory were finished except for the high vault. The second phase of work, which completed the transepts and most of the nave, extended from c. 1178–1200. Between about 1190 and 1220 the second nave aisle was being erected, by which time modifications were already being made to the earlier sections of the fabric, notably the enlargement of the clerestory windows. In 1235–50 a series of chapels was built between the nave buttresses. Around 1250 the north transept was extended (and the porch built) by Jean de Chelles, who began c. 1257 the extension of the south transept which was completed by Pierre de Montreuil. Pierre de Chelles built the jubé at the beginning of the 14th century and he, followed by Jean Ravy, was responsible for the chapels around the apse (1296–1330). Ravy's successors, Jean le Bouteiller and Raymond du Temple, completed work on the great ensemble by the second half of the 14th century.

For some three centuries the fabric of the cathedral remained relatively untouched and provided the setting for many important events. The School of Music at Notre-Dame was influential during the late 12th and 13th centuries. In 1186 Geoffrey Plantagenet (son of Henry II of England) was buried here after his sudden death in Paris, and in 1431 at the age of ten, Henry VI of England was crowned King of France here. Many royal marriages were celebrated within its walls, including those of James V of Scotland to Madeleine of France (1537), François II to Mary Stuart (1558), Henri of Navarre, the future Henri IV, to Marguerite de Valois (1572), and Charles I of England (by proxy) to Henrietta Maria (1625).

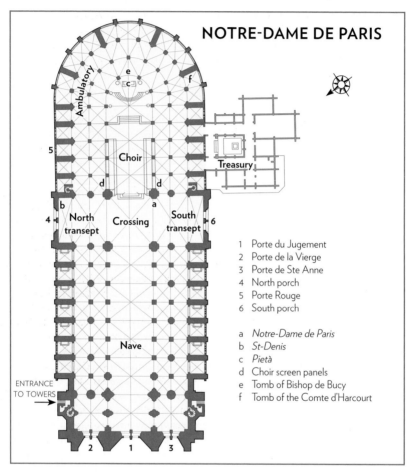

NOTRE-DAME DE PARIS

Ambulatory

Choir

Treasury

North transept

Crossing

South transept

Nave

ENTRANCE TO TOWERS

1 Porte du Jugement
2 Porte de la Vierge
3 Porte de Ste Anne
4 North porch
5 Porte Rouge
6 South porch

a *Notre-Dame de Paris*
b *St-Denis*
c *Pietà*
d Choir screen panels
e Tomb of Bishop de Bucy
f Tomb of the Comte d'Harcourt

Changes in taste and emphasis during the reigns of Louis XIV and Louis XV brought about major alterations. Tombs and stained glass were destroyed, the jubé and the stalls were condemned, and in 1771 Soufflot desecrated the trumeau and part of the tympanum of the central portal to allow a processional dais to pass through. Much of what survived this destruction was lost during the Revolution. But the cathedral was still used for great ceremonies: in 1804, Napoleon was crowned Emperor here by Pius VII and in 1853 Napoléon III and Eugénie de Montijo were married here. By 1844, due in great part to Victor Hugo's novel *Notre-Dame de Paris* (1831), which helped to engender an interest in Gothic architecture, the cathedral was considered worth a thorough restoration. This was begun under the direction of Lassus and Viollet-le-Duc. A century later, on 26th August 1944, the thanksgiving service following General de Gaulle's entry into liberated Paris took place at Notre-Dame. The cathedral has continued to be the scene of occasional ceremonial functions, including the state funeral of François Mitterrand in January 1996. The first stage of a long renovation was completed to coincide with the start of the 21st century. On Easter Sunday 2013, eight new bells and a *bourdon* (great bell) were rung for the first time as part of the 850th jubilee celebrations. One bell was named Maurice, after the first bishop, Maurice de Sully, and another Jean-Marie after Cardinal Jean-Marie Lustiger, 139th Archbishop of Paris, who died in 2007. And new light has been shed—literally—on the once-sombre cathedral interior. Using LED technology, a sophisticated system of illumination was inaugurated in 2014, which can be adjusted to suit the situation—religious, musical, touristic—with spotlights which can subtly enhance specific features such as the rose windows or the statue of the Virgin and Child.

The nave and west end: The height of the ten-bay nave, 33m, very daring for the time, confirmed the prestige of the principal ecclesiastical building in Paris. The sheer elevations of the nave and shallow mouldings of the upper storey emphasise the slenderness of the walls relative to their height. In contrast, short cylindrical piers, a throwback to St-Denis, surround the nave and the apse. Triple shafts of equal size rise uninterrupted from the capitals to the springing of the sexpartite vaults. A vaulted triforium overlooks the nave whereas the gallery around the choir has double openings. The change in the master of works c. 1178 resulted in the contrast between the piers with shafts to the east and the piers with pilasters to the west.

The **rose window** in the west wall contains scenes of the Labours of the Months, the Signs of the Zodiac, Vices, Virtues and prophets with the Virgin, though almost entirely remade in the 19th century and obscured from many angles by the great **organ**, built in 1868 by the Cavaillé-Coll workshops. The Cavaillé-Coll dynasty originated in the south of France; the best known of them, Aristide (d. 1899), was one of the originators of the symphonic organ.

In the side-chapels of the nave hang seven **17th-century paintings** (all that remain from an original total of 76) by Charles Le Brun, Sébastien Bourdon and others, presented to Notre-Dame by the Goldsmiths' Guild of Paris between 1630 and 1707.

LOUIS VIERNE, ORGANIST OF NOTRE-DAME

Louis Vierne (1870–1937) was organist at Notre-Dame for 37 years from 1901. He found inspiration in the magnificent Cavaillé-Coll instrument here and was one of the first organists to give recitals. Born almost completely blind but with a clear talent for music, he became a pupil first of César Franck and then of Franck's successor, Charles-Marie Widor, whose assistant he became at St-Sulpice. Between 1899 and 1930 he wrote six organ symphonies, the first of which, Symphony No. 2, was highly regarded by Claude Debussy. His *Pièces de fantaisie* (1926–7) include the 'Carillon de Westminster', its finale inspired by the chimes of Big Ben. In 1937, on 2nd June, during his one thousand, seven hundred and fiftieth concert, Vierne suffered a heart attack and died here, at his beloved keyboard.

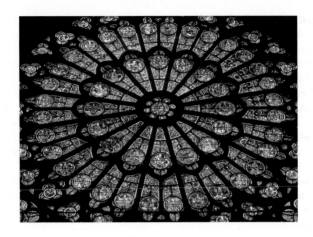

NOTRE-DAME
The north rose window, which retains some of its 13th-century glass.

The transepts and crossing: The shallow transepts each contain **rose windows** that have retained some original 13th-century glass. The north, the finest and best preserved, represents kings, judges, priests and prophets around the Virgin. The south was much restored in 1737 and, with Christ at the centre, it depicts saints, apostles and angels, with the *Wise and Foolish Virgins*. The upper part of the transept bays and west bay of the choir were remodelled in the 19th century to approximately their original 12th-century disposition.

Against the southeast pillar at the crossing stands a 14th-century sculpture of the Virgin, as *Notre-Dame de Paris* **(a)**. In the north transept is *St Denis* **(b)** by Nicolas Coustou (18th century) and the 19th-century reliquary casket of St Geneviève.

The choir: The choir was completely altered in 1708–25 by Louis XIV, in fulfilment of his father's vow of 1638 to place France under the protection of the Virgin should he father a son; this vow was realised after 23 years of marriage, when the future Louis XIV was born. The work was carried out under the direction of Robert de Cotte, though much of what you see today is due to the hand of Viollet-le-Duc. (*NB: The choir can usually only be viewed from the bottom of the chancel steps, but it is nevertheless possible to identify the works of art described below.*)

Above Viollet-le-Duc's altar rises a sculpted *Pietà* **(c)** (1723) by Nicolas Coustou, the base by Girardon, part of the *Voeu de Louis XIII*. The altar is flanked by statues: *Louis XIII* (south), also by Coustou, and *Louis XIV* (north) by Coysevox (both 1715). Of the original 114 **stalls**, 78 remain, adorned with bas-reliefs from the designs of Jules Degoullons, with canopied archiepiscopal stalls at either end. The **bronze angels** (1713) against the apse-pillars are rare survivors of the Revolutionary melting-pot.

The ambulatory: Around the exterior of the choir, in the first four bays, are the remains of the mid-14th-century wooden **choir screen (d)**, which until the 18th century extended round the whole apse. The expressive carved reliefs were restored and repainted by Viollet-le-Duc. In the blind arches below the carved scenes are listed some of the eminent people buried in the church. The ambulatory contains the tombs of 18th–19th-century prelates. Behind the high altar is the **tomb-effigy of Bishop Matiffas de Bucy (e)** (d. 1304). In the second chapel south of the central chapel is Jean-Baptiste Pigalle's theatrical **tomb of the Comte d'Harcourt (f)** (d. 1769). At the other end of the same chapel are the restored tomb-statues of Jean Jouvenel des Ursins (d. 1431), with his wife (d. 1451) kneeling behind him.

On the south side of the ambulatory is the entrance to the **Treasury** (*open Mon–Fri 9.30–6, Sat 9.30–6.30, Sun 1.30–6.30; entry fee; opening hours may vary at certain times of the ecclesiastical year, check www.notredamedeparis.fr*), which has a collection of ecclesiastical plate, cult objects, reliquaries and, most importantly, the Holy Relics of the Passion, the Crown of Thorns and pieces of the True Cross.

THE CROWN OF THORNS

The three most revered objects among the Holy Relics of the Passion (though none can be conclusively authenticated) are a nail of the Crucifixion, a fragment of the True Cross discovered by St Helen, mother of the emperor Constantine and, most sacred of all, the Holy Crown of Thorns with which, according to St John's Gospel, Jesus was crowned at the Crucifixion by the soldiers who mocked him. The veneration of these relics was widespread from the 4th century. From the 7th–10th centuries they were gradually translated by the Byzantine emperors to Constantinople for safekeeping.

In 1238 Emperor Baldwin II, in need of funds, offered them for sale to King Louis IX of France (the future St Louis) although they were pledged as surety by the emperor to Venetian bankers; Louis had to refund this pledge. On the 10th August 1239, he received the 29 relics at Villeneuve-l'Archevêque (Burgundy) and, simply dressed and barefoot, accompanied the Crown of Thorns to Paris. The importance that he attached to them is reflected in the grandeur of the Sainte-Chapelle, which he built to house them, in the form of a reliquary casket (*see p. 38*).

The Crown of Thorns is a chaplet of reed canes, 21cm in diameter, bound with gold thread. The thorns within it, of the species *Zizyphus spina-christi*, were dispersed over the years, by emperors, kings and prelates who gave them as gifts. The Crown is kept in a circular tube of crystal covered with a gold filigree mount with a spina-christi design. The relics are shown in Notre-Dame on the first Friday of each month, every Friday during Lent (3pm), and on Good Friday (10–5).

THE TOWERS OF NOTRE-DAME

Open daily April–Sept 10–6.30, July–Aug Fri–Sat to 11pm; Oct–March 10–5.30; last entry 45mins before closing; free for under 18s (family visit), for 18–25-year-old EU citizens and for non-EU residents of France under 26. Entrance on Rue du Cloître Nôtre-Dame. T: 01 53 10 07 00, www.monuments-nationaux.fr.

The massive towers (1225–50), which never received the spires that were originally intended for them, contain 387 steps. The climb is worthwhile for the view of Viollet-le-Duc's flèche and the rooftops of Paris. The visit includes an exhibition about the building and a close-up from the gallery between the towers of the suitably chimerical creatures redesigned by Viollet-le-Duc. The great bell, *Emmanuel*, recast in 1686 and weighing 13 tonnes, was made famous by Victor Hugo's novel *Notre-Dame de Paris* and his hunch-backed bell-ringer Quasimodo, who was found on the cathedral steps by Archdeacon Frollo on the first Sunday after Easter and was named from the introit for that day: *Quasi modo geniti infantes*, 'As new born babes'. The story of Quasimodo and his devotion to the gypsy girl Esmeralda has been the subject of at least five film adaptations—although the central character of the novel remains the cathedral itself.

CRYPTE ARCHÉOLOGIQUE

Open 10–6, closed Mon and holidays. Audioguides. No disabled access (though this is scheduled to change). T: 01 55 42 50 10.

This small museum provides a fascinating insight into the ancient history of Paris. Enter at the west end of the Place du Parvis Nôtre-Dame, where steps lead down to a modern display of the archaeological underworld of the Cité. Revealed in 1965 during excavation work for the underground car park, the crypt museum was created in 1980, and the presentation was updated and greatly enhanced in 2012–14.

The 2000-year history of Paris is evoked chronologically by combining the superimposed layers of archaeological fragments of buildings and streets, from Roman times to the 19th century, with state-of-the-art museology. Every effort is made to bring the different periods to life by means of spot-lights, reproductions of ancient maps and pictures, a hypothetical bird's eye view of Lutetia-Paris in the 4th century, touch screens, electronic displays and background sound effects.

It is divided into four main sections: the Metamorphosis of Lutetia-Paris; Classical Antiquity, when ancient Lutetia was threatened by Germanic invasions; the Middle Ages and the building of the Cathedral of Notre-Dame; the Emergence of Modern Paris in the 18th and 19th centuries. Scant remains of the Roman river port can be seen and there is also a reconstruction of a Roman thermal baths. The museum display is based on archaeological evidence of the site itself and of archaeological sites in or near Paris of the same period and with similar functions, such as Bercy, where pirogues (dugout canoes) were found in 1991–2 (now in the Musée Carnavalet). These, alongside the writings of Caesar and the emperor Julian, together with documentary evidence, paintings, drawings and plans of medieval Paris, as well as records kept during Haussmann's time, contribute to understanding the history of the Île de la Cité.

THE EMPEROR JULIAN ON WINTER IN PARIS

I happened to be in winter quarters at my beloved Lutetia, for that is how the Celts call the capital of the Parisians. It is a small island lying in the river; a wall entirely surrounds it, and wooden bridges lead to it on both sides. The river seldom rises and falls, but usually is the same depth in the winter as in the summer season, and it provides water which is very clear to the eye and very pleasant for one who wishes to drink. For since the inhabitants live on an island they have to draw their water chiefly from the river. The winter too is rather mild there, perhaps from the warmth of the ocean, which is not more than nine hundred stades distant, and it may be that a slight breeze from the water is wafted so far; for sea water seems to be warmer than fresh. Whether from this or from some other cause obscure to me, the fact is as I say, that those who live in that place have a warmer winter. And a good kind of vine grows thereabouts, and some persons have even managed to make fig-trees grow by covering them in winter with a sort of garment of wheat straw and with things of that sort, such as are used to protect trees from the harm that is done them by the cold wind.

Tr. W.C. Wright, 1913

PALAIS DE JUSTICE, SAINTE-CHAPELLE & CONCIERGERIE

The Palais de Justice (*map p. 587, E2*), standing on Boulevard du Palais, is a huge block occupying practically the width of the island, the great but inglorious result of 19th-century rebuilding under Louis Duc and P.-J.-H. Daumet. The main courtyard, **La Cour du Mai** (named after the maypole once set up here annually by the society of law clerks), is dominated by the domed **Galerie Marchande**, a colonnaded façade (1783–6). The Conciergerie and the Sainte-Chapelle are part of the huge complex.

The site was occupied in the Roman period by the palace where Julian the Apostate was proclaimed emperor in 360; the Merovingian and Carolingian kings, when in town, divided their time between the *thermae* (*see p. 57*) and their palace within the city walls. Louis VI died here in 1137 and Louis VII in 1180. Louis IX (St Louis) altered the building and built the Sainte-Chapelle. From 1431 it was occupied entirely by the *Parlement de Paris*, the first supreme court of justice in the kingdom, which had previously shared it with the king, but at the Revolution it acquired its present function. Here, in the 16th *Chambre Correctionelle*, the trials of Flaubert's *Madame Bovary* and Baudelaire's *Les Fleurs du Mal* took place (29th January and 20th August 1857). The 18th-century buildings were greatly enlarged in 1857–68 and again in 1911–14. The clock tower, **Tour de l'Horloge**, at the northeastern corner of the building, dates to the 14th century and with Vincennes was the first public clock in Paris. The clock face was largely rebuilt c. 1585 by Germain Pilon, when the sculptures representing *Justice* and *Law* were added, reinforcing the judicial role of the former royal palace. Damaged at the Revolution, there were more repairs in the 19th and 20th centuries. In 2012 the clock had a total clean and overhaul and was returned to its original splendour.

VISITING THE PALAIS DE JUSTICE

The Palais de Justice (Law Courts) may be visited (*identification needed*), accessed up steps from the Cour du Mai. The main point of interest is the **Salle des Pas-Perdus**, a magnificent hall which replaced the great chamber of the medieval palace where in 1431 the coronation banquet of Henry VI of England was celebrated after his crowning in Notre-Dame. Rebuilt in 1622 by Salomon de Brosse, it was restored in 1878 after being burned by the Communards. The room is divided in two by a row of arches and at the far end is the entrance to the Première Chambre Civile, a vestige of the old palace and perhaps originally the bedroom of Louis IX. It was later used by the *Parlement*, in contempt of which Louis XIV here coined his famous epigram *L'État, c'est moi*.

THE SAINTE-CHAPELLE

Combined ticket for La Sainte-Chapelle and Conciergerie. Open daily March–Oct 9.30–6, 15 May–15 Sept until 9, Nov–Feb 9–5; closed 1 Jan, 1 May, 25 Dec. Entrance on Blvd du Palais. Binoculars are useful to study the stained glass. Narrow stairs link the lower and upper chapels. Sharp or pointed metal objects are forbidden. T: 01 53 40 60 97, sainte-chapelle.monuments-nationaux.fr.

The Sainte-Chapelle was built by the pious Louis IX (*see p. 14*) and dedicated in 1248. It is best known for its remarkable concentration of medieval stained glass in a building of exceptional lightness and delicacy.

It was planned both as the royal chapel of the palace and as a resting place for the precious and costly relics acquired from Baldwin II, the new Emperor of Constantinople, among them the Crown of Thorns and fragments of the True Cross, in 1239. The Crown of Thorns cost more than building the chapel itself, which takes the shape of a medieval reliquary. An acquisition of both religious and political significance at the time, the importance attributed to these relics is reflected in the sumptuousness of the building, whose design has been attributed on stylistic grounds to the architect Pierre de Montreuil, who also worked at St-Denis, Notre-Dame and St-Germain-des-Prés. The west window was replaced in 1485 by a Flamboyant rose. Damaged by fire in 1630, the chapel was slowly rebuilt only to be put under risk of demolition at the end of the 18th century as the Revolution left it in a perilous state. Thankfully the chapel, including many of the statues, was saved by the archaeologist Alexandre Lenoir (*see p. 93*). Restoration was undertaken between 1837 and 1857 by Duban, Lassus (who reconstructed the leaden flèche in 15th-century style, the fifth on this site), Viollet-le-Duc and his successor Boeswillwald. A subsequent long and complicated restoration of the chapel and its glass has been underway since the 1970s. The year 2015 was the 800th anniversary of the birth of St Louis.

From the outside, the impression of great height, actually 42.5m, in proportion to its length (36m) and breadth (17m) is accentuated by the buildings that crowd in around it. The balustrade is decorated with a motif of *fleurs de lys* and carved on the pinnacle above the south tower is a Crown of Thorns. The exterior of the chapel has been cleaned and returned to its original colour, and the statues were also restored; in 2013 the statue of the Archangel Michael was replaced after eight years of absence.

The chapel consists of two superimposed levels: the lower one, the Chapelle Basse, and the upper Chapelle Haute, where the sacred relics were kept.

CHAPELLE BASSE

The lower chapel is dedicated to the Virgin Mary, whose image is above the entrance, and was for the use of royal servants and retainers during solemn Mass. The interior, devoid of windows, with carved oak bosses and 40 columns supporting the upper chapel, has a 19th-century reproduction of its medieval decoration, painted with the *fleurs de lys* of France and the towers of Castile (emblem of Blanche of Castile, mother of Louis IX). The glass is also 19th-century. The mural of the *Annunciation* is the oldest in Paris (13th century). The low vaults are supported by blind arches and there are several 14th/15th-century tombstones in the floor.

CHAPELLE HAUTE

The upper chapel (20.5m high), richly endowed with lofty windows and medieval stained glass, was originally connected directly with the palace and was reserved for the royal family and court. The narrow staircase by which visitors enter today was not the route taken by royalty, who entered directly from the west at the upper level from buildings now demolished. In contrast to the gloominess of the lower chapel, the upper chapel is a revelation, appropriate to the shrine of the holy relics. In one of the greatest virtuoso achievements of medieval architecture, the structure is reduced to an essential skeleton of tracery, likened to the filigree work of a goldsmith, supporting walls of richly coloured glass totalling almost 600 square metres. It was designed to house the supremely important relic of the Crown of Thorns, which Louis IX had acquired from Constantinople in the aftermath of the Fourth Crusade of 1204, when the Byzantine emperors were ousted by Frankish and Venetian 'Crusaders' and the short-lived Latin Empire was set up. The Crown of Thorns is now kept in the Treasury of Notre-Dame (*see p. 35*). The decorative scheme, originally inlaid with gilt and glass to give the effect of enamels, emphasised the relationship of the chapel to a shrine or reliquary. The effect, with the stained glass, was a powerful and splendid setting designed to echo the physical reality and the mystical significance of the relics. Linking the blind tracery of the arcades in the lower part to the soaring windows are statues of Apostles under baldachins—the fourth and fifth on the left and the fourth and fifth to the right are 13th-century. The two deep recesses under the windows of the third bay were the seats reserved for the royal family. On the south side is a small chapel built at the time of Louis XI to enable the monarch to participate in Mass without being seen. In the centre of the restored arcade across the apse is a wooden canopy beneath which the relics used to be exhibited on Good Friday.

The **stained glass** was restored in 1845, and although much has been lost, some two-thirds date from the 13th century. Over time, however, due to accumulation of dirt, dubious conservation, and condensation, the clarity had dulled. Begun in 2008 was a campaign to clean and restore the glass, lead fittings and tracery. Each of the 15 windows has been dismantled and cleaned using laser lighting. New glass, which is placed on top of the old to protect it, has been specially moulded to match the irregularities of the ancient coloured glass. The effect is breathtaking.

There are 15 windows containing a total of 1,113 scenes. The lateral windows have four lancets each, those in the apse only two. The sequence reads from left (northwest) to right (southwest) and individually from bottom to top.

1: Genesis
2: Exodus
3: Numbers
4: The Book of Joshua
5: The Book of Judges
6: The Book of Isaiah and the Rod of Jesse
7: The life of St John the Evangelist and the Childhood of Christ
8: The Passion (central window). This is considered the most outstanding of all the windows
9: Stories of John the Baptist and the Book of Daniel
10: The Book of Ezekiel (92 of the 121 scenes are original)
11: The books of Jeremiah and Tobit
12: The books of Judith and Job
13: The Book of Esther
14: The books of Kings
15: The legend of the True Cross with illustrations of the translation of the Relics to Paris by St Louis. However, this contains only 26 of the original 67 scenes (which read in a serpentine sequence)
16: Rose window (west end). The 86 panels from the Apocalypse, which are the easiest to read of all the windows, were a gift from Charles VIII (15th century).

THE CONCIERGERIE

Combined ticket for the Conciergerie and La Sainte-Chapelle; opening times and details as for the Sainte-Chapelle. Enter from Blvd. du Palais. No wheelchair access. conciergerie.monuments-nationaux.fr.

The Conciergerie occupies part of the lower floor of the Palais de Justice and was a stately royal palace before becoming one of the world's most infamous prisons during the Revolution. The medieval rooms constitute a very fine and rare example of medieval architecture in Paris.

HISTORY OF THE CONCIERGERIE

Roman governors and the French kings had palaces on this site until the second half of the 14th century. This was the first seat of power of the Capetians, c. 1000, and Clovis V's ancient palace. By the end of the 14th century, it was abandoned as a residence in favour of the Louvre and Vincennes (*see p. 512*) but remained the seat of royal justice and administration, and a prison. The three distinctive round towers facing the river are vestiges of the royal residence built by Philippe IV le Bel (1285–1314). After the old palace was abandoned in the 14th century, it was used only for major receptions and celebrations.

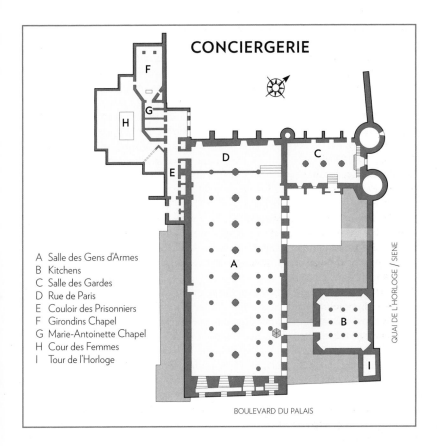

CONCIERGERIE

A   Salle des Gens d'Armes
B   Kitchens
C   Salle des Gardes
D   Rue de Paris
E   Couloir des Prisonniers
F   Girondins Chapel
G   Marie-Antoinette Chapel
H   Cour des Femmes
I   Tour de l'Horloge

QUAI DE L'HORLOGE / SIENE

BOULEVARD DU PALAIS

It became the seat of power for the *Parlement*, a judicial body, and residence of the *Concierge*, a high-ranking officer of the Crown with powers of justice. Over time it became associated solely with the place of imprisonment of those judged and its infamy grew during the Revolution when some 2,780 people, both Royalist and Jacobin, passed their last hours here. Among them were Queen Marie-Antoinette, Mme du Barry, Camille Desmoulins, Charlotte Corday, Danton, the poet André Chénier, and Robespierre. From 1793 the Revolutionary Tribunal was installed in the Salle des Gardes, marking the reign of the Terror.

VISITING THE CONCIERGERIE
The visit includes what remains of the medieval palace and the Revolutionary jail. The present entrance is 19th-century (the original palace entrance was from the eastern side of the Cour du Mai). It opens into the impressive vaulted **Salle des Gens-d'Armes (A)**, a rare and magnificent example of secular Gothic architecture and the oldest surviving medieval hall in Europe. It was constructed for Philippe IV le Bel,

begun in 1302 and completed c. 1313 under the supervision of Enguerrand de Marigny, with the royal apartments above. Measuring 63.3m in length and divided into four aisles by more than 60 large columns, it functioned as a refectory, with space to feed some 2,000 members of the royal household and was originally heated by four fireplaces. It was here that Philip IV le Bel sponsored eight days of celebration, when the whole island was illuminated, to welcome his son-in-law Edward II of England; Charles V held a reception for the Emperor Charles IV in 1378; wedding celebrations included François I's marriage to Eleanor of Habsburg in 1530, and Mary, Queen of Scots to François II (1558). Against the south wall is a portion of the black marble table once used for important receptions. Massive medieval **kitchens (B)** built at the time of Jean II le Bon (1350–64) were in a separate annexe to the east, to minimise fire risk: the lower, vaulted part of these has survived. The king's residence had its own kitchen directly connected to the upper floor.

The smaller **Salle des Gardes (C)** (c. 1310), with central columns, was the dining hall for the garrison below the Grand'Salle of the king and had access to the king's courtyard. The capital of the central column is carved with two figures with their heads together, thought to represent Héloïse and Abélard. The Revolutionary tribunal sat here in 1793–5.

The four bays at the western end of the great hall are known as the **Rue de Paris (D)**, after the executioner during the Revolution who was known as Monsieur de Paris. The overflow prisoners, or *pailleux* (prisoners who slept on straw, being too poor to pay for their term in jail), slept here. Beyond is the Revolutionary Prison of 1780, rebuilt following a fire and altered again in the 19th century so that visitors now see only a small portion of the original. The **Couloir des Prisonniers (E)** is lined with small spaces reserved for the Clerk, who took the prisoners' names, the Concierge's office, and the Salle de la Toilette, where prisoners were prepared for execution. In an upper room is a list of the prisoners who were guillotined. The chapel where the Girondins were incarcerated **(F)** is on the site of a small royal oratory modified in 1776. The **Marie-Antoinette Commemorative Chapel (G)** was built at the Restoration on the exact site of the queen's cell, and a poignant reminder of the tragic past of the Conciergerie is the re-creation of her cell in the last room on this level. Outside, the **Cour des Femmes (H)**, where the female prisoners took exercise, has a fountain and stone tables. Above are prison memorabilia, the blade of a guillotine, lists of names, keys and locks and reconstructions of cells. But the modern rendition of the situation here during the Reign of Terror comes nowhere near the pitiless horror of that period.

THE WESTERN PART OF ÎLE DE LA CITÉ

Opposite the Palais de Justice, Rue de Lutèce between (left) the Domed Tribunal de Commerce (Bailly, 1860–5) and (right) the Préfecture de Police on Quai de la Corse, is the **Marché aux Fleurs Reine Elisabeth II**, renamed since a British royal visit in 2014. It provides a colourful and sweetly-scented contrast to the sombre judicial buildings. It is supplied with drinking water from a Wallace Fountain (*see p. 319*) and a bird market is held here on Sundays.

The **Quai des Orfèvres** on the south side of the island owes its name to the goldsmiths established here between 1580 and 1643. Much later, as the site of the headquarters of the detective branch of the French police, the *quartier* became famous through Georges Simenon's fictional detective, Chief Inspector Jules Maigret of the *Brigade spéciale* (Homicide Squad), hero of 103 novels and short stories written between 1930 and 1972. Maigret entered his office in the Palais de Justice from the Quai des Orfèvres.

Behind the Palais de Justice is the newly-planted **Place Dauphine**, a quiet and lovely oasis, named in honour of the future Louis XIII—as was the road on the Left Bank—and flanked by some attractive old houses, their ground floors occupied by cafés, restaurants and galleries. You will get a good meal at Le Caveau du Palais, overlooking the *terrain de boules* at nos. 17–19 (*see p. 49*).

From Quai des Orfèvres there are ramps and a stairway leading down to the walkway beside the Seine, which takes you underneath Pont Neuf.

THE BRIDGES OF ÎLE DE LA CITÉ

Rue de la Cité, which crosses the island roughly in the middle, is an ancient route which crossed Roman bridges. These are replaced to the south by the **Petit Pont** (1853) and to the north by **Pont Notre-Dame** (rebuilt 1913).

Pont d'Arcole (1855) is named after a youth killed in 1830 leading insurgents against the Hôtel de Ville. Rue d'Arcole was the site of the now-demolished church of St-Pierre-aux-Boeufs (*see p. 70*), where Diderot was married in 1743. The **Pont au Double** (1882), leading from Notre-Dame to the left bank, replaces a mid-17th-century bridge where the toll was a diminutive coin known as a *double*. **Pont de l'Archevêché**, also leading to the left bank from the gardens of the old archbishop's palace, is one of the bridges from which lovers like to hang padlocks (*see p. 97*).

From the Palais de Justice, the Boulevard du Palais leads north to Place du Châtelet, over the **Pont au Change** (1860), thus named in the 12th century when goldsmiths and moneylenders set up shop on the bridge. The present bridge replaces a 17th-century stone causeway lined with buildings; its counterpart to the south, **Pont St-Michel**, rebuilt several times since the late 14th century, most recently in 1857, leads to Boulevard St-Michel and the Latin Quarter.

The newest bridge is **Pont St-Louis** (1969). The oldest surviving, and the finest, linking Île de la Cité with both left and right banks, is **Pont Neuf**.

PONT NEUF

The picturesque Pont Neuf (*map p. 587, D2*) is in fact two bridges which meet on the western point of the island between the Quai du Louvre and (south) the Quai des Augustins. The two parts are unified by the same cornice supported by corbels decorated with expressive and varied heads. Despite its name (New Bridge), this is the oldest surviving bridge in Paris, begun by Jean-Baptiste du Cerceau. It was conceived so that the king could travel between the Louvre and the Abbey of St-Germain-des-Prés and was the first bridge to be lined with sidewalks instead of houses. Henri III laid

PONT NEUF
Equestrian statue of Henri IV, *le Vert Galant* (1818).

the foundation stone in 1578; it was completed in 1607 and since then required little maintenance until major renovations in 2006. Much admired from the start, it was a favourite subject with artists, and paintings of it in former times can be seen in the Musée Carnavalet. Christo and Jeanne-Claude wrapped it in 2007.

The **Pointe de la Cité**, a shaded area with fine panoramas of the banks of the Seine (*access from the river pathway or down steps from Pont Neuf*), is known as the Square du Vert-Galant, alluding to the legendary womaniser who inherited the crown of France in 1589 as King Henri IV. Before and during his two marriages—the first to Marguerite de Valois, which was annulled, and the second in 1572 to Marie de Médicis—he had many mistresses, including Gabrielle d'Estrées (portrait in the Louvre) and Henriette d'Entragues, and sired many illegitimate children. Above the gardens, on an elevated piazza opening off Pont Neuf, is an **equestrian statue of the king** by Lemot, unveiled in 1818 to replace an original, destroyed at the Revolution, commissioned from Giambologna and given to Paris in 1604 by Marie de Médicis. It was the first royal statue to be erected in a public place. The four *Slaves* of the pedestal, begun c. 1614 by Pierre de Francheville and completed by Bordoni, are now in the Louvre (Richelieu Ground Floor Sculpture Gallery, Room 16). A few surviving fragments of horse and rider are in the Musée Carnavalet. On the balustrades around the statue, 'love locks' (*see p. 97*) have begun to crop up.

From the Pont Neuf is a view (right bank) of **La Samaritaine**, the 19th-century department store whose future has long been under debate. Created by Ernest Cognacq (*see p. 366*), using a then-pioneering iron frame, it developed into a vast enterprise from 1900–30 to become the largest department store in Paris. However, after a lengthy decline it finally closed. LVMH, owned by France's richest man, Bernard Arnault, won the battle in April 2014 to transform it into a glass-fronted structure masking a luxury hotel, duty-free shop, designer stores, offices and local-authority spaces. At the time of writing it was due to reopen in 2016.

River cruises (Vedettes du Pont Neuf; *see p. 529*) leave from the Square du Vert-Galant.

ÎLE SAINT-LOUIS

On the eastern tip of the Île de la Cité, in Square de l'Île-de-France, is the stark and deeply moving **Mémorial des Martyrs et de la Déportation** (1962), designed by G.-H. Pingusson and opened by General de Gaulle (*open daily except Mon April–Sept 10–12 & 2–7, Oct–March 10–12 & 2–5; T: 01 46 33 87 56*). The names of some 200,000 French men, women and children deported to German concentration camps during the Second World War are recorded here.

From here it is a short walk to the other island in the Seine, Île Saint-Louis, across the Pont St-Louis (1969).

Île St-Louis (*map p. 588, A2–A3*) is a tranquil and elegant residential area. The island boasts no major monuments, nor a Métro station, but it does shelter some pleasant hotels, shops and restaurants. The island was formerly two small islets, Notre-Dame and Île des Vaches. The former belonged to the cathedral canons and was a favourite place for Louis IX to find peace and pray (he is said to have prayed here before leaving on the Eighth Crusade). The two islets became one and now bear the name of the saintly king. They were linked together in the 17th century when, as an annexe to the Marais, this became the site of a number of imposing mansions, several of which were designed by Louis Le Vau (*see below*), the leading French Baroque architect. They jostle for place in the few narrow streets, the best presenting a dignified and subtly-hued cordon facing out to the river. Four bridges link the island to the 'mainland': Pont Marie (1635), in the middle, was named after the original developer of the island, Christophe Marie.

LOUIS LE VAU

The leading Baroque architect at the time of Louis XIV, Le Vau (1612–70) was a highly successful master of the grand manner and overall effect, if not of fine detail. His works combine ingenuity and drama and he knew how to adapt to his clients' tastes. He also had a talent for designing showy interiors, on which he worked with a dedicated team of decorative craftsmen. Born in Paris, he learned his trade from his father, a master mason, and in the late 1630s built himself a house on the Île St-Louis. There followed several private commissions for mansions on the island, which at that time was in full expansion. The most outstanding of these is the Hôtel de Lambert (1641–4; *see below*). In 1643 Le Vau was engaged by the king's *surintendent*, Nicolas Fouquet, for the Château de Vaux-le-Vicomte, and after Fouquet's fall managed to keep in good grace with Colbert, subsequently succeeding Lemercier as *Premier Architecte du Roi*. From 1661 he worked at the Louvre, on the rebuilding of the Galerie d'Apollon and with Perrault on the great east façade. He produced the first designs for the Institut de France, begun in 1662, and at Versailles in 1669 he remodelled the garden façade, altered later by Hardouin-Mansart.

RUE ST-LOUIS-EN-L'ÎLE

This is the main street of the island. It has no river frontage, is filled with shops, crêperies and restaurants, and has retained an aura of times past. It is also endowed with one or two good buildings, including, at no. 51, the **Hôtel Chenizot**, with a fine decorated doorway and balcony of 1726. The ground floor is now home to a butcher and a delicatessen.

Further on, across Rue des Deux Ponts, past a baker (good mini quiches) and a cheese shop, is the **church of St-Louis-en-l'Île** (*open 9.30–1 & 2–7*). Its grimy façade could be passed by unnoticed—but look up to see the curious openwork spire and the clock of 1741. Begun in 1664 to replace the then-outgrown original chapel, it was based on designs by the great architect Louis Le Vau (*see above*) and completed in 1726 by Jacques Doucet. The bright Baroque interior has ornamental stone-carving executed under the direction of Jean-Baptiste de Champaigne, who is buried here (d. 1681). A statue of St Louis stands at the head of the nave. As well as several 18th-century paintings and furnishings of some interest, the church contains a 16th-century Flemish polychrome wood relief of the *Dormition of the Virgin* (in the Chapel of the Sacré Coeur; south side) and some fine Nottingham alabaster reliefs: two in the Chapel of the Magdalene (south side); another, of the *Crucifixion*, also in a chapel on the south side; and directly opposite in the Chapel of Compassion (next to the organ), a 14th-century relief of the *Assumption*.

Opposite the church is the wonderful **Librairie Ulysse** (no. 26), an antiquarian travel bookshop (*open Tues–Fri 2–8*), founded in 1971 and proudly claiming to be the first bookshop in the world dedicated exclusively to travel.

QUAI D'ANJOU

Typical of the grander *hôtels particuliers* built on the eastern part of the island is the **Hôtel Lambert** (*privately owned*), at the corner of Rue St-Louis en l'Île and Quai

ÎLE SAINT-LOUIS
Fish-head drainpipe on Hôtel de Lauzun.

d'Anjou. It was begun in 1641 by Le Vau. The interior was decorated by Eustache Le Sueur and Charles Le Brun, among others.

Over three centuries, Quai d'Anjou has seen a variety of illustrious residents (almost all the buildings along the waterfront have plaques). Le Vau himself lived at no. 3 and no. 9 was the home from 1846 of the artist Honoré Daumier, whose paintings, inspired by the quays, include *La Blanchisseuse* (c. 1863, Musée d'Orsay). Born in Marseilles, Daumier was apprenticed to a bookseller but soon discovered that his passion lay in drawing and politics. He studied the former under Alexandre Lenoir, and his interest in the latter contributed to his incisive caricatures of contemporary political figures. In 1832, his caricature of King Louis-Philippe as Gargantua earned him six months in prison. Baudelaire considered Daumier one of the greatest artists of his day.

No. 17, the **Hôtel de Lauzun** (1657; *occasional visits with the CMN, see p. 540 or www.monuments-nationaux.fr*), was the residence from 1682–4 of the Duc de Lauzun, commander of the French forces at the Battle of the Boyne in Ireland in 1690, where he was defeated by William of Orange. From 1842, as the Hôtel de Pimodan, this grand old address hosted the Club des Hachichins, a popular meeting place for artists and writers to experiment with cannabis, an exotic import that had arrived in the wake of Napoleon's North African campaigns. Charles Baudelaire (1821–67) rented three rooms on the top floor and squandered his inheritance here from 1843–5, although according to Théophile Gautier, who became a regular visitor, the great Romantic poet did not indulge. The artists responsible for the splendid decoration of the *hôtel* were Le Brun, Le Sueur, Patel and Sébastien Bourdon.

The English writer Ford Madox Ford published the literary periodical *Transatlantic Review* (*see p. 72*) from no. 29 around 1919; Hemingway was its deputy editor.

QUAI DE BOURBON AND QUAI D'ORLÉANS

The painter Émile Bernard, 'father of Symbolism', lived at no. 15 **Quai de Bourbon** for the last years of his life, until his death in 1941. The sculptor Camille Claudel (*see below*) lived at no. 19 from 1899–1913, the date when, according to the plaque, her 'brief career as an artist came to an end and the long night of her internment began'.

To the south, at no. 6 Quai d'Orléans is the **Polish Library and Museum** (*see p. 518*). After the Polish uprising against Russian occupation in 1831, the island became a refuge for a number of Polish immigrants, including the Romantic poet Adam Mickiewicz, who was a friend of Chopin and Victor Hugo.

CAMILLE CLAUDEL

An exceptionally gifted artist and Rodin's pupil and lover, Camille Claudel (1864–1943) lived and worked for a productive but difficult period of her life at no. 19 Quai de Bourbon on the Île St-Louis. She first met Rodin in 1883 when at the Académie Colarossi studying under Alfred Bouchier. Strong, passionate, beautiful, independent and serious about her artistic future, she had rebelled against her parents and by the age of 20 was established in her own studio on the Left Bank. Rodin was bowled over by Claudel. She joined his studio in 1884, as model and assistant, which resulted in an intense love affair and a deeply rewarding artistic partnership. During their association Rodin derived the inspiration for a more profound expression in his works. Their tempestuous affair lasted for eleven years in the shadow of Rose Beuret, Rodin's lifelong companion. This situation provoked Claudel to make vicious drawings aimed at the couple, as she came to realise that Rodin would never marry her. The relationship had become intermittent between 1889 and 1894, and by 1898 they no longer had any contact. As the affair waned, however, Claudel's strength as a sculptor emerged: despite similar characteristics, her work tends to be more lyrical and imaginative than Rodin's. Claudel made her first maquette of *L'Âge Mûr* in 1894, an allegory of the breakup: one figure, *The Implorer*, was produced as a separate edition. Her work was well received at the 1903 Salon d'Automne and *The Wave* (1897) shows a conscious advance on the Rodin years. From 1905 her mental health deteriorated and she destroyed many works. After her brother, the poet and diplomat Paul Claudel, married and moved abroad, she took refuge from the world in her studio, accusing Rodin of plagiarism. She was not informed of her father's death in 1913, and was committed to a psychiatric hospital by her mother. Despite pleas from medical staff that her daughter should return to her family, her mother refused. Camille Claudel died on 19th October 1943, after 30 years in an asylum. About 90 of her sculptures, sketches and drawings survive. The biographical film *Camille Claudel* (1988) stars Isabelle Adjani and Gérard Depardieu. In the 2013 film *Camille Claudel 1915*, Juliette Binoche portrays Claudel during her tragic confinement in the hospital. The Musée Rodin (*see p. 130*) has good examples of her work.

EATING AND DRINKING ON THE ISLANDS IN THE SEINE

ÎLE DE LA CITÉ

There are numerous cafés, brasseries and sandwich bars here. For a more elegant experience, seek out €€ **Le Caveau du Palais**, in an attractive, secluded setting behind the law courts, with good reliable fare and tables outside in summer (*17–19 Place Dauphine, T: 01 43 26 04 28, map p. 587, D2*). **Au Rendez-Vous des Camionneurs** (*72 Quai des Orfèvres, T: 01 43 29 78 81, www.aurvdescami-onneurs.com, closed Sun and Mon*) has also won plaudits.

ÎLE SAINT-LOUIS

€€ **Brasserie de l'Île Saint-Louis**. The first place you see as you cross Pont St-Louis. Good for an al fresco beer and unpretentious cooking. Closed Wed. *55 Quai de Bourbon. T: 01 43 54 02 59, www.labrasserie-isl.fr. Map p. 587, F2.*

Along Rue St-Louis-en-l'Île, are a great variety of places, both simple and sophisticated. At no. 92, on the corner of Rue Jean du Bellay, is the popular **St Regis** (*6 Rue Jean du Bellay, T: 01 43 54 59 41, www.cafe-saintregisparis.com, map p. 587, F2*), a modern recreation of a traditional bistrot serving plates of *charcuterie*, *confit de canard*, snails and other classics, as well as burgers and salads. €€ **Mon Vieil Ami** (*90 Rue St-Louis-en-l'Île, T: 01 40 46 01 35, www.mon-vieil-ami.com, map p. 587, F2*) is a simple bistrot offering a modern slant on Alsatian cooking based on seasonal

availability, including vegetable-only 'Cabbage Patch Classics' as well as meatier dishes and fixed-price menus (open daily). €€€€ **Le Sergent Recruteur** (*41 Rue St-Louis-en-l'Île, T: 01 43 54 75 42, www.lesergentrecru-teur.fr, map p. 587, F2*) has a Michelin rosette and extremely fine cooking using the best available produce in an historic venue. €€ **Le Caveau de l'Îsle** (*36 Rue St-Louis-en-l'Île, T: 01 43 25 10 26, www.lecaveaudelisle.com*) is small and charming with a vaulted cellar and 17th-century fireplace. It serves traditional dishes including *escargots* and *soupe à l'oignon*.

Beyond the busy Rue des Deux Ponts crossroads is €€ **Le Tastevin** (*46 Rue St-Louis-en-l'Île, T: 01 43 54 17 31, www.letastevin-paris.com*), with wood panelling, white tablecloths and a traditional zinc bar. It offers dishes such as *foie gras*, *rôti de boeuf* and profiteroles).

Numerous cafés in Paris sell Berthillon products (and use the name) but the original **Berthillon ice-cream parlour** is at no. 29–31 (*T: 01 43 54 31 61*), usually identified by the line of people waiting to taste the frozen nectar.

Refined Japanese cuisine is served at €€ **Isami** (*4 Quai d'Orléans, T: 01 40 46 06 97, map p. 587, F2*). The modern bistrot € **Les Fous de l'Île** is at 33 Rue des Deux Ponts (Pont Marie end; *T: 01 43 25 76 67, www.lesfousdelile. com, map p. 587, F2*).

THE LEFT BANK

The Seine arrives from the south and describes a large arc dividing Paris in two, then leaves the centre by the southwest. The smaller section of the capital within the arc, relative to the flow of the river, is the Left Bank or Rive Gauche. Gallo-Roman Lutetia spread onto the mainland here opposite the islands, the area which later became the academic, or Latin Quarter, around the medieval university reaching as far as the Montagne Ste-Geneviève. The abbey of St-Germain was established in the fields (prés) west of the medieval fortified walls.
By the 17th century this area was expanding, with the construction of major buildings such as the Luxembourg Palace, the Institut de France, Les Invalides, the Jardin des Plantes and the Salpêtrière hospital. Each introduced a certain distinction and character, particularly around St-Germain, which became an increasingly fashionable residential area. By the 18th century the École Militaire and the Champs de Mars were created. These districts correspond today to the 5th, 6th and 7th arrondissements. It was not until the 19th century, when the faubourgs and outlying villages became part of Paris, that new districts such as Montparnasse, Vaugirard, Grenelle and Tolbiac, the 13th, 14th and 15th arrondissements, came into existence. The National Assembly and the Senate are both on this side of the Seine, as are the Eiffel Tower and the Musée du Quai Branly.

The Latin Quarter

*The Latin Quarter is one of the oldest parts of Paris. It contains the
majority of the educational and scientific institutions of the University and
there are still many signs of student life—though probably little Latin spoken.
During the student revolution of 1968, the old pavés (paving stones)
were used as missiles, to be replaced by dull slabs. Cafés and bookshops abound,
and the two major Gallo-Roman remains of Paris—the Arènes de Lutèce and
the Thermes de Cluny—are here, along with interesting lesser-known
medieval churches and the great necropolis on the hill, the Panthéon.*

The Latin Quarter holds a vague yet irresistible attraction for many visitors, and although the crass commercialism, fast-food restaurants and constant frenetic bustle of the main artery, the *Boul Mich* (Boulevard St-Michel, part of Haussmann's scheme), can be a disincentive to linger, there is a more picturesque character to be discovered in the clustering side streets, which despite being bisected by Boulevard St-Germain in the mid-19th century still harbour many reminders of the past.

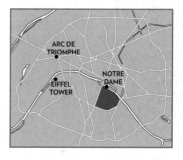

WHY THE 'LATIN' QUARTER?

By the 1st century AD, Roman *Lutetia* began to spread from the Île de la Cité to the left bank of the Seine. A military camp was established on Montagne Ste-Geneviève, and the forum, amphitheatre, theatre and three thermae were constructed, while an aqueduct carried water from the Bièvre valley in the south. The main Roman roads south from the Île de la Cité were the *Via Inferior*, roughly the route of Boulevard St-Michel (*map p. 587, D3–E3*) and the parallel *Via Superior*, the present Rue St-Jacques (*map p. 587, E3*).

Overrun by the Huns in the 5th century, Paris' salvation c. 451 is traditionally attributed to the courageous example and prayers of a young Christian woman, Geneviève (Genovefa), born c. 420 at Nanterre, who came under the protection of St Germanus (Germain) of Auxerre. Although romantically described as a shepherdess, she was in fact from a prosperous Gallo-Roman background. Her faith and generosity of spirit raised her to sainthood and she became patron saint of Paris.

Latin was the language spoken by the students who gathered around the brilliant and outspoken theology scholar, Pierre Abélard (d. 1142) on the Montagne Ste-Geneviève. He settled on the Left Bank following his removal, c. 1100, from the school attached to Notre-Dame where he had confounded his master, Guillaume of Campeaux, in disputation. Abélard continued to challenge the Church and later proved to be a writer of genius, but his place in history was established by the scandal of his seduction and marriage of his pupil Héloïse, niece of Canon Fulbert of Notre-Dame. After the couple failed to keep their vow of celibacy, Fulbert ordered Abélard's castration. They are commemorated at Père-Lachaise Cemetery (*see p. 392*).

MUSÉE DU CLUNY: MUSÉE NATIONAL DU MOYEN ÂGE

Map p. 587, E3. 6 Place Paul-Painlevé. Métro 10 to Cluny-La Sorbonne. Open Wed–Mon 9–5.45. Closed Tues, 1 May. Free on the 1st Sun of the month and for under-18s. Audio guides available in English, for children and adults; sound and touch equipment available for the non- or partially sighted (T: 01 53 73 78 16). Frequent guided tours, cultural activities and concerts. Garden accessible to wheelchair users but no lifts in the museum, though a new entrance and improved access for the disabled are planned. T: 01 53 73 78 22, www.musee-moyenage.fr.

With gardens on both sides, the popular Cluny Museum, with collections of European medieval art and architecture, stands in a small oasis in the Latin quarter. The entrance opens into the courtyard of the 15th-century Hôtel de Cluny, which is not only one of the finest surviving examples of medieval French domestic architecture in Paris but also incorporates the best-preserved vestige of the antique city, a section of the Gallo-Roman *thermae*. Gathered here in the Musée National du Moyen Âge (National Museum of the Middle Ages) are precious collections of religious and domestic art and artefacts dating from Gallo-Roman times to the 15th century, exhibited in 23 smallish rooms on two levels. The greatest single attraction is the series of late 15th-century tapestries, *The Lady with the Unicorn*.

HISTORY OF THE HÔTEL DE CLUNY

From around 1280, young monks from the great Benedictine monastery of Cluny in Burgundy lived in the Collège de Cluny while attending the University of Paris. In 1340, Pierre de Chalus, Abbot of Cluny and chancellor to Philippe VI, purchased land in the area to establish a residence in the capital. His 14th-century building was replaced by the present U-shaped *hôtel particulier* built by Jacques d'Amboise, Abbot of Cluny, in 1485–98. His emblems are on the stair-tower in the courtyard. The building is an early example of a house standing between courtyard and garden, an arrangement developed further in later centuries. Although rarely used by the abbots, it was important enough to be mentioned by Rabelais in *Pantagruel*; Louis XII's widow, Mary Tudor (1496–1533), younger sister of Henry VIII of England, lived here for a time, as

MUSÉE DU MOYEN ÂGE
Heads of the Kings of Judah from Notre-Dame, defaced during the Revolution when it was believed that they depicted kings of France.

did James V of Scotland before his marriage to Madeleine, daughter of François I. By the 17th century the building was neglected. In the 19th century, isolated by the new Boulevard St-Michel, it became national property. Alexandre du Sommerard moved in with his family and the treasures that he had spent his life collecting. After his death, the collection was purchased by the state and supplemented during the long curatorship of his son, Edmond du Sommerard (d. 1889). Objects from the Renaissance period, part of the collections of this museum, are at Écouen (*see p. 509*).

Ground floor

Rooms 2–3: These rooms are used for special exhibitions from the collections.

Room 5 (corridor): Exhibited here are 15th-century alabasters, mainly from Nottingham and Burton-on-Trent (England).

Room 6: The small panels of stained glass (12th–14th centuries) displayed at eye level include a section of a panel from St-Denis (before 1144) of two monks watching St Benedict's ascension, and several panels from the Sainte-Chapelle of the history of Samson; one scene depicts Samson tearing the jaw of the lion.

Room 7: This corridor linking the medieval and antique buildings contains 13th–14th-century tombstones and the doorway for the Lady Chapel of St-Germain-des-Prés by Pierre de Montreuil (*see p. 503*).

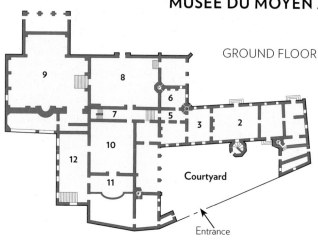

MUSÉE DU MOYEN ÂGE

GROUND FLOOR

GROUND-FLOOR HIGHLIGHTS

6   Glass from St-Denis and the Sainte-Chapelle
7   Door by Pierre de Montreuil

8   Sculpture from Notre-Dame
9   Roman *thermae*
10–12   Romanesque and Gothic

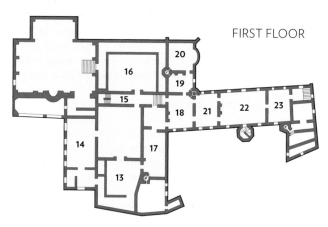

FIRST FLOOR

FIRST-FLOOR HIGHLIGHTS

13   *La Dame à la Licorne*
14   Late medieval painting and sculpture
16   Gold and enamelwork

18   Beauvais choir stalls
19   Basel altar frontal
20   Chapel

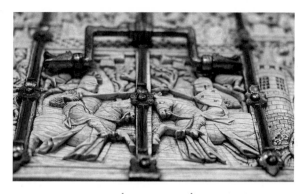

MUSÉE DU MOYEN ÂGE
Detail of the lid of an ivory casket known as the *Assaut du Château d'Amour*,
showing jousting knights outside a castle.

Room 8: This larger space (where concerts are held) contains fragments of sculpture from Notre-Dame that was defaced and removed during the Revolution, including the original 13th-century heads from the Gallery of the Kings of Judah, and the nude *Adam* (c. 1260), attributed to Pierre de Montreuil, originally forming part of a statue group with *Eve* on the south transept façade.

Room 9 (*thermae*): Here we take a leap back in time to the frigidarium of the Gallo-Roman thermal baths, unique in France in that its 1st-century vaulting is still intact. This large space (14m high), plus the piscina on the northern side, are the best preserved remains of the baths, probably built during the 1st century and modified c. AD 212–17. Partial ruins remain of the tepidarium, the caldarium and palaestra (gymnasium), and underground chambers still exist. The rest were demolished in the 16th and 19th centuries. Exhibited here is the *Pilier des Nautes* (c. AD 14–37), an offering to the emperor Tiberius from Parisian boatmen who were hedging their bets: the dedication is to a syncretism of a Celtic and a Roman god. The votive *Pilier de St-Landry* (2nd century) is dedicated to Roman divinities. Both pillars were discovered on the Île de la Cité. (There are twice-yearly temporary exhibitions in the frigidarium.)

Rooms 10–12: These rooms are devoted to objects from the Romanesque and Gothic periods, including the original medieval capitals from St-Germain-des-Prés. Finely-carved ivories (4th–12th centuries) include a 12th-century English crozier and a casket with scenes of courtly love, *L'Assaut du Château d'Amour*. There are also two wooden *Crucifixions* from the Auvergne and an ivory Virgin with a 'Gothic sway' following the curve of the elephant tusk. Keystones demonstrate the Gothic inspiration from vegetation.

First floor

Stairs lead up to Room 13, which contains the series of six exquisite *millefleurs* tapestries known as ***La Dame à la Licorne*** (*The Lady with the Unicorn*), now seen to even greater effect following their restoration in 2013.

LA DAME À LA LICORNE

These beautiful and intriguing tapestries were woven, in silk and wool, somewhere in northern Europe between 1484 and 1510. They were probably designed by a Parisian artist and were commissioned by Jean V le Viste or Antine le Viste, from a family of Lyonnais lawyers whose coat of arms—gules, a bend azure with three crescents argent—is frequently repeated in the designs. The tapestries hung for a long time in the Château of Boussac in the Creuse until brought to public notice by Prosper Mérimée, Inspector of Historic Monuments, and the writer George Sand. They were acquired by the museum in 1882 and have undergone a number of restorations. The latest, completed in December 2013, included 'washing', bringing them closer to their original colours (the bottom section of each panel was rewoven in 1882 using synthetic colours which have faded more than the natural dyes). Although in remarkably good condition, every modern precaution has been used to minimise their deterioration. Of the six tapestries, five of them (which hang in a semicircle) represent the five 'material' senses: *Taste*, where the lady feeds a monkey and a parakeet from a bowl of sweetmeats; *Hearing*, where she plays a portable organ; *Sight*, where the Unicorn gazes into the mirror held before him by the lady; *Smell*, where the monkey sniffs a flower while the lady weaves a garland; and *Touch*, where the lady gently grasps the Unicorn's horn. The sixth tapestry, known by the enigmatic motto *À mon seul désir*, which appears embroidered on the pavilion before which the lady stands, shows her returning jewels to a casket held by her maid.

In the medieval tradition of *millefleurs*, the six panels are scattered with thousands of delicate flower, animal and bird motifs, but here—unusually—they are on a rich background of red rather than blue or green. In each panel the lady stands on a blue island of colour, each with a different type of tree. Her attire varies: she is sometimes accompanied by her maid, and always flanked by the mythical Unicorn, symbol of purity (among many other references), as well as a lion. In several of the panels a monkey and a pet dog are also included. The iconography has given rise to many interpretations, the current proposal being that the last tapestry '*Mon seul désir*', where the lady relinquishes her jewellery, illustrates a sixth sense, love, the closest to the soul or spiritual world.

Room 14: Late medieval religious works include altarpieces as well as representations of the Virgin and female saints. Jan de Molder's altarpiece of the Blessed Sacrament, from Averbode in Brabant (1513), has carved images of the *Mass of St Gregory* and *Last Supper*. An early 16th-century *Virgin reading to the Child* comes from the Lower Rhine and there is an elegantly carved funeral effigy of Jeanne of Toulouse (c. 1280). A rare example of a medieval English painting in a French museum depicts scenes from the life of the Virgin (c. 1325).

Rooms 15–16: In the corridor (15) are furnishings from the Picardy Chapel (c. 1500) and small domestic articles such as aquamanilia, seals, cooking pots and a metal plate from a liturgical book binding.

Room 16 contains a glittering array of the goldsmiths' and enamellers' arts. The centrepieces—part of the magnificent Treasure of Gurrázar, near Toledo, capital of the Visigoth kings—are three Visigothic votive crowns with their pendant crosses (late 7th century) which demonstrate the complexity of the craftsmanship of this civilisation. The fragile Golden Rose (1330), made in Siena in gold and coloured glass, was given by Pope John XXII to a count of Neuchâtel in recognition of his support in a struggle against Emperor Louis of Bavaria. It was a tradition on the fourth Sunday in Lent for pontiffs to give Golden Roses to towns or rulers who had gained their favour. The rose is without thorns, as are those which flower in Paradise, a symbol both of the Passion of Christ and of his Resurrection. This is the oldest Golden Rose in existence. Its creator has been identified by the Vatican as the Sienese goldsmith Minucchio, active in Avignon, which was the papal seat at that time.

Examples of medieval reliquaries and high-quality 12th–14th-century Limoges enamels are two reliquaries of St Thomas Becket (1190–1200), illustrating his murder, and a 13th-century reliquary from La Sainte-Chapelle, commissioned by Louis IX and resembling a miniature chapel. The central plaque of the finely-engraved portable triptych of the *Dormition of the Virgin* (Nuremberg, 15th century) was found in London in 1994.

Rooms 17–18: Room 17 has French and German stained glass (14th and 15th centuries) and a delightful *millefleurs* tapestry with rabbits. The choir stalls in Room 18, from the abbey of St-Lucien in Beauvais (1492–1500), have irreverently carved misericords.

Room 19: Contains a remarkable gold antependium (1002–24) showing a marked Byzantine influence, typical of the early 11th century. It was possibly intended as a donation for Monte Cassino from Emperor Henry II and Empress Cunégonde (who are portrayed as tiny figures at the feet of Christ) but ended up in Basel Cathedral. Here also is the 12th-century Stavelot retable, with a Pentecostal scene. Among late-antique Byzantine and Islamic pieces (in a well-lit showcase) are celebrated ivories such as the sensual *Ariane* (Ariadne; Constantinople, 6th century) sculpted in high relief, found in a grave in the Rhine Valley with the two rock-crystal lion heads; an 8th-century English diptych, re-used in the 9th century during the Carolingian Renaissance, and a *Crucifixion and Saints* from Northern Italy (end 11th/early 12th century). A magnificent 11th-century olifant in elephant ivory (made in Italy) from Metz is engraved with scenes of the Ascension.

Room 20 (chapel): The original late-Gothic chapel is a masterpiece of Flamboyant vaulting which springs from a central pillar. It consists of a fretwork of delicate mouldings between the main ribs and sophisticated undercutting of the architectural canopies. The niches originally contained figures representing the powerful Amboise family (who built the *hôtel*), destroyed in 1793.

A sequence of choir hangings depicting the life and martyrdom of St Stephen and the legend of his relics begins in this room and continues back into rooms 19 and 18. Woven c. 1500 for Jean Baillet, Bishop of Auxerre, for the cathedral of St-Étienne, they were acquired in 1880. They have never been restored although the colours are still strong and every painstaking detail is clearly revealed. Resembling a strip cartoon with captions, the scenes are arranged in alternate interior and exterior settings.

Rooms 21–23: Here are displayed objects of public and private devotion from the late Middle Ages, including reliquaries, pilgrim badges, etc. A charming wooden *Christ astride a Donkey* (late 15th century), on a platform with wheels, is typical of religious processional objects from southwestern Germany until the Reformation. The mid-15th-century painting of the Jouvenel des Ursins family kneeling in line was commissioned for their chapel in Notre-Dame (*see p. 35*). There is also a triptych of *St Gregory's Mass with the Virgin* that opens to reveal images of *God the Father* and *Christ on the Cross*.

Room 22 has domestic artefacts dating from the 11th and 12th centuries until 1500, including games pieces in ivory and bone, wooden combs with intricate decoration, and panels of courtly scenes, rich in detail and carefully executed using *jaune d'argent* on white glass, and dating from the 15th century.

Room 23 contains objects used by medieval knights in the arts of combat as well as for hunting and tournaments, and include shields, helms and items of body armour.

SQUARE PAUL-PAINLEVÉ AND THE JARDIN MÉDIÉVAL

The small **Square Paul-Painlevé**, opposite the entrance to the Musée du Cluny, contains statues of Michel de Montaigne by Landowski and of the painter Puvis de Chavannes by Desbois. The replica of the Roman She-Wolf was given by Rome to Paris in 1962 when the two capital cities were twinned.

On the north side of the museum, the **Jardin Médiéval** was created in 2000 as a contemporary interpretation of themes and symbolism found in the Cluny museum's famous tapestries. Composed of enclosed beds and areas, it includes a vegetable garden, medicinal garden, a lovers' garden and a celestial garden with roses, lilies, iris and other flowers symbolising the Virgin. There is also a play area.

THE PANTHÉON & ITS DISTRICT

Map p. 587, E3. Métro 10 to Maubert-Mutualité. Open April–Sept 10–6.30, Oct–March 10–6; closed 1 Jan, 1 May, 25 Dec; last admission 45mins before closing. At the time of writing the monument was undergoing restoration but was open to the public. Entry fee. Guided tours. T: 01 44 32 18 00, pantheon.monuments-nationaux.fr.

The unmistakable, grandiose bulk of the Panthéon stands on the summit of Montagne Ste-Geneviève, the highest point on the Left Bank (60m), honoured as the burial place in the 6th century of the patron saint of Paris (*see p. 12*).

HISTORY OF THE PANTHÉON

In 1744, lying ill at Metz, Louis XV vowed that if he recovered he would replace the abbey church of Ste-Geneviève, then ruinous, with a new church to house the saint's shrine. Work began in 1755, in the old abbey gardens, but the foundations disappeared into the labyrinth of Roman clay pits dug 16 centuries earlier. Louis finally laid the first stone above ground in 1764. The building was only completed in 1790 and its architect, Jacques-Germain Soufflot, is said to have died of anxiety. By the Revolution there were three churches on the hill: the old abbey church, the new church, and St-Étienne-du-Mont (*see below*). In 1791, the National Assembly decided that the building should be used as a *panthéon* or burial place for distinguished citizens, 72 of whom are buried here. The pediment was inscribed with the words *Aux Grands Hommes la Patrie Reconnaissante*. It was reconsecrated at the Restoration and remained so until 1831, and was consecrated again in 1851, but on the occasion of Victor Hugo's interment in 1885 it was definitively secularised.

At the time of writing the Panthéon resembled an outsize rocket. Following problems of infiltration and deterioration which have beset it over several years, a ten-year campaign of restoration began in 2013. Preparing the site was a huge project considering the size and weight of the scaffolding (315 tons rising to 37m), which could not use the building as a support and is carried on stakes driven 17m into the ground. A 96-m crane capable of raising four tons also needs strong support. Work began on the upper parts and will move down to the porch, the interior, the exterior walls, and the base. The first phase has been to consolidate the cupola. There is an installation of artwork on the exterior until the renovations are complete.

THE BUILDING

Inspired by the Pantheon in Rome, the Paris Panthéon has a dome and columned portico. It is not circular, however, but takes the form of a Greek cross. It is 110m long, 82m wide and 83m high to the top of its majestic dome. It was radically altered after 1791, when the twin belfries were demolished and the pediment above the Corinthian portico was re-carved by David d'Angers. The result is a masterful relief, France between Liberty and History, showing the nation distributing laurels to famous men.

Inside, the effect is coldly Classical, using the giant Corinthian Order but enlivened with a series of huge **murals** (everything is on a colossal scale here), made possible when 42 windows were walled up during the Revolution. The most notable is the series of the life of St Geneviève by the Symbolist painter Puvis de Chavannes, recognisable by their calm dignity and quiet colours. The only true exponent of the technique of fresco painting to work in the Panthéon, and an admirer of the Italian Quattrocento painters, Puvis (who had studied under Delacroix and Couture) began the series in 1874 in this ideal setting and it brought him general acclaim. Note in particular the panel showing the saint watching over Paris and bringing supplies to the city after the siege by the Huns.

At the **east end** is a work representing the Convention, by Sicard, and against the central pillars are monuments (right) to Jean-Jacques Rousseau by Bartholomé and (left) to Diderot and the *encyclopédistes* by Terroir. The **dome**, supported by four piers united by arches, is made up of three distinct shells, of which the first is open in the centre to reveal the second. It carries a fresco by Antoine Gros. Within the dome, in 1852, the physicist Léon Foucault gave the first public demonstration of his pendulum experiment proving the rotation of the Earth, which is dramatically reconstructed in audio-visual displays in the aisles. It is possible to climb up to the colonnade encircling the dome for an unusual and thrilling view of historic Paris. The space below the cupola was intended for St Geneviève's tomb, but it was never moved here.

The **crypt** contains the tombs of Rousseau (d. 1778) and Voltaire (d. 1778) and of the architect, Soufflot. Many famous men have been re-interred in the vaults, including Victor Hugo (d. 1885) and Émile Zola (d. 1902); the chemist Marcellin Berthelot (d. 1907); the socialist politician Jean Jaurès (assassinated 1914); Louis Braille (d. 1852); the explorer Bougainville (d. 1811) and the Resistance hero Jean Moulin (d. 1943). The heart of Léon Gambetta (d. 1882), a proclaimer of the Republic in 1870, is enshrined here. Jean Monnet (d. 1979), the 'Father of Europe', was reburied here in 1988 on the centenary of his birth. More recently, the remains of Pierre and Marie Curie (in 1995; Marie Curie is the first woman thus honoured), former Minister of Culture André Malraux (in 1996) and novelist Alexandre Dumas (in 2002) were re-interred here.

BIBLIOTHÈQUE SAINTE-GENEVIÈVE

Ten-minute accompanied visits possible daily except Sun, Sept–June 10–6; July–Aug 1–6. Open to readers on request in writing or with one-day pass; T: 01 44 41 97 97, www. bsg.univ-paris1.fr or go to the visitor desk.

In the northwest corner of the Place du Panthéon, on Rue Soufflot, is the **Law Faculty building**, begun by Soufflot in 1771 and subsequently enlarged. On the north at no. 10, on the site of the Collège de Montaigu, a theological school founded in 1314, where the Dutch humanist Erasmus, Catholic founder of the Jesuit Order Ignatius Loyola, and the Protestant reformer John Calvin all studied, is the **Bibliothèque Ste-Geneviève**. Formerly housed in the abbey of the same name (where Lycée Henri-IV is now), the library moved in the mid-19th century to the present building, which was designed for it in 1844–50 by Henri Labrouste. It is an important early example of a metal-framed structure, using both wrought and cast iron, the exterior resembling a cross between a 16th-century Florentine palace and a 19th-century railway station. Students work under the splendid iron and glass roof of the reading room. The library contains a large collection of manuscripts and incunabula from the Abbaye Ste-Geneviève and other neighbouring religious houses (St-Victor, St-Germain-des-Prés), some 120,000 volumes from the 16th–19th centuries, as well as MSS of Rimbaud, Verlaine, Baudelaire, Gide and Valéry.

SAINT-ÉTIENNE-DU-MONT

Map p. 587, E3. Open Tues–Fri 8.45–7.45, Sat–Sun 8.45–12 & 2–7.45 (school holidays Tues–Sun 10–12 & 4–7.45). Closed Mon. There are regular guided visits. T: 01 43 54 11 79, www.saintetiennedumont.fr.

Approaching St-Étienne-du-Mont up the pretty, cobbled Rue de la Montagne, you have a sense of approaching the heights of ancient Paris. St-Étienne-du-Mont is an unusually pretty church facing a broad open square and retaining some original features. Essentially a late Gothic structure with Renaissance decoration, it was almost continuously under construction from 1492 to 1586. It has sheltered the shrine of St Geneviève, patron saint of Paris (*see p. 12*), since the destruction of the old abbey church nearby (*see Lycée Henri-IV below*), to which it was originally joined. This may account for the choir, nave and façade being on slightly different axes. In 1610, Marguerite de Valois, first wife of Henri IV, known as *La Reine Margot*, laid the foundation stone of the façade. This has three pedimented tiers with a small rose window in each of the upper levels, in a curious decorative combination characteristic of the transitional style of architecture from late Gothic to Renaissance. The tower, begun in 1492, was completed in 1628. On the north flank is a picturesque porch of 1632.

INTERIOR OF ST-ÉTIENNE

The luminous interior gives an impression of height because of the tall aisles. Several of the large windows contain Renaissance stained glass. The originality of the building lies in the elegant gallery that links the supporting pillars of the nave and choir. The ambulatory is wide with ribbed vaulting and heavy pendant bosses, the longest of which is above the crossing.

The most unusual feature of St-Étienne-du-Mont, however, is its **Renaissance jubé**, or rood screen, a structure rarely found intact in French churches. This celebrated fretted piece of stonework, built in 1525–35, is a *tour de force* of carving, with magnificent sweeping spiral stairways at either side of the central pierced balustrade, more a triumphal arch than a barrier. The design is attributed to the great French Renaissance humanist architect Philibert de l'Orme and the work was probably carried out by Antoine Beaucorps. The date 1605 on the side refers only to the door to the spiral.

The organ, over the west door, has a richly carved case by Jean Buron dating from 1631–2, with *Christ of the Resurrection* at the summit. The organ itself dates from the 17th century, renovated in the 19th. The pulpit is the work of Germain Pilon (16th century), with later, 17th-century sculptures designed by Laurent de la Hyre. At the crossing is a pendant boss with the *Lamb of God*.

There is stained glass dating from c. 1550–c. 1600; the high nave windows by N. Pinaigrier date from 1587–8 and include scenes of the *Resurrection*, *Ascension* and *Coronation of the Virgin*. The transept glass (1585–7), also by Pinaigrier with J. Bernard, includes various saints and *The Crucifixion*. The high windows in the choir contain glass of the 1540s onwards and in the ambulatory are fragments of 16th-century glass mixed with 19th-century work.

SAINT-ÉTIENNE-DU-MONT
Early 16th-century stone jubé or rood screen.

In the chapel south of the choir is the copper-gilt **shrine of St Geneviève** (1853), containing a fragment of her tomb; her remains were burned by the mob in the Place de Grève (now the Place de l'Hôtel de Ville; *map p. 587, F2*) in 1801. Various important monuments include an ex-voto to St Geneviève, with the provost and merchants of Paris, by François de Troy (1726) and higher, to the right, a similar subject painted by Largillière in 1696. In the adjacent chapel are the epitaphs of the philosopher Pascal (d. 1662) and the tragedian playwright Racine (d. 1699), whose graves are at the entrance to the Lady Chapel. In the southwest chapel is a 16th-century *Pietà*.

On the site of the *charnier*, or charnel house, are twelve superb **windows of 1605–9**; the joy of these is that the glass panels are at eye level. The most notable are no. 1, *The Miracle of Rue des Billettes*, depicting a legend concerning a piece of the Host which promptly bled when a Jew, not believing it to be the body of Christ, took it to his kitchen for use as ordinary bread; *see p. 372*); no. 2, *Noah's Ark*; no. 9, *Manna from Heaven* and no. 10, *The Mystic Wine-press*.

LYCÉE HENRI-IV

South of St-Étienne-du-Mont, at 23 Rue Clovis, is the Lycée Henri-IV (*map p. 587, E3–E4; no visits*), one of Paris' great schools, which was built on the site of the old Abbaye Ste-Geneviève in 1796. It was here in 510 that Clovis, ruler of the Franks from 481/2 and who converted to Christianity c. 498, built the first church, dedicated to the Holy

Apostles. It later became the burial place of the king and his wife Clothilde, who had inaugurated the cult of Geneviève and to whom the church was re-dedicated in the 9th century. It became the church of an important royal abbey during the Middle Ages and was also used by the local population. Over time, however, the populace outgrew it, resulting in the construction of a second church in the 13th century, dedicated to St Étienne. In 1744 Louis XV decided to replace the old abbey church, now in bad repair, by a grander building. The result was the Panthéon (*see p. 60*), though it was not completed until after the Revolution. Meanwhile the abbey church was desecrated and the relics of St Geneviève were burned. The abbey buildings became the Lycée Henri-IV and what remained of the abbey church disappeared in 1804 to make way for Rue Clovis. Only the tower with a Romanesque base and Gothic upper storeys and the cloister (1746) remain of the old abbey. The Lycée has many famous alumni, among them Haussmann, Viollet-le-Duc, Jean-Paul Sartre, the film director Éric Rohmer and the engineer Isambard Kingdom Brunel.

Part of Philippe-Auguste's **13th-century city wall** is visible in Rue Clovis.

JARDIN CARRÉ AND SQUARE LANGEVIN

The **Jardin Carré** (*map p. 587, E3*) is a modern public garden with a bronze, *La Spirale* (1986), by Meret Oppenheim. It was created in the courtyard of the former École Polytechnique (*5 Rue Descartes*), which was founded in 1794 for the training of artillery and engineer officers. This was the most prestigious of the *Grandes Écoles*, institutions created by the Convention to provide the technical experts needed by the reorganised nation. From 1805 it occupied old college buildings, and relocated to the outskirts of Paris in 1977. It is now a University.

Steps lead down to **Square Paul-Langevin** (on Rue Monge), with an 18th-century fountain and headless statues from the old Hôtel de Ville, as well as a statue of the poet François Villon.

The private dwellings in the courtyard at no. 34 Rue Montagne-Ste-Geneviève once belonged to the Collège des Trente-Trois, so called after its 33 scholarships, one for each year of Christ's life, established here in 1657. The Musée de la Préfecture de Police occupies the first floor of no. 5 (*see p. 522*).

THE UNIVERSITY OF PARIS & ITS INSTITUTIONS

Map p. 587, D3–E3 and D4–E4. Métro 10 to Cluny-La Sorbonne.

The University of Paris, which disputes with Bologna the title of oldest university in Europe, arose in the first decade of the 12th century out of the schools of dialectic attached to Notre-Dame. It later transferred to the Montagne Ste-Geneviève and in 1215 received its first statutes, which served as the model for those of Oxford and Cambridge and other universities of northern Europe. By the 16th century it comprised no fewer than 40 separate colleges.

THE SORBONNE

Map p. 587, D3–E3. Occasional visits with Centre des Monuments Nationaux (CMN). T: 01 44 54 19 30, www.monuments-nationaux.fr.

The Sorbonne was founded as a theological college in 1253 by Robert de Sorbon, chaplain to Louis IX. Before the end of the 13th century it had become synonymous with the faculty of theology, overshadowing the rest of the university and possessing the power of conferring degrees. It was noted for its religious rancour, supporting the condemnation of Joan of Arc, justifying the St Bartholomew's Day massacre of Protestants and refusing to recognise Henri IV, a former Protestant, as king. In 1470 it was responsible for the introduction of printing into France. Other colleges (from *colligere*, to assemble) followed, with charters defining their principles, which were mainly to provide secure shelter for poor students; study was in the schools, the ancestors of faculties. From the 15th century the university experienced a period of crisis and criticism, and by the end of the next century, the buildings were in poor condition.

Cardinal Richelieu undertook the rebuilding of the Sorbonne in 1629, employing the architect Jacques Lemercier. The huge project continued until Richelieu's death in 1642. In the 18th century the university was still traditional in its teaching and had not accommodated the new thinking in philosophy and the sciences. At the Revolution, in 1792, the Sorbonne was suppressed, to become a Musée des Arts in 1801.

Napoleon refounded the university in 1806–10 and the Sorbonne became the seat of the University of Paris in 1821. During the last third of the 19th century the institutions were reorganised. The college buildings, apart from the chapel, which had fallen into disrepair, were replaced by the present sombre collection (1885–1901). Around a large courtyard with galleries are the great staircase and Grand Amphithéâtre, or main lecture hall, decorated with a mural by Puvis de Chavannes.

THE MODERN UNIVERSITY

Student unrest was simmering in 1968, provoked by poor academic standards and overcrowding. In early May unrest turned to riot at the University of Nanterre on the outskirts of Paris, and spread to the Sorbonne, which was occupied. The leader who emerged was Daniel Cohn-Bendit. The university buildings were closed for only the third time in their history (the first had been during riots in 1229, the second during the invasion in 1940). The student revolt escalated to a nationwide general strike lasting until 30th May, when President de Gaulle's appeal finally restored calm. The action brought about overdue reforms in the university system and in 1970 the University of Paris was replaced by 13 autonomous bodies, the Universités de Paris I–XIII. The 5th arrondissement (the Latin Quarter) is still the historical campus.

Four of the new universities share the premises of the historic Sorbonne building and three have kept the Sorbonne name as part of their official title: Université Panthéon-Sorbonne (Paris I), Université de la Sorbonne Nouvelle (Paris III) and Université Paris-Sorbonne (Paris IV). The universities come under a common chancellor, who is Rector of the Académie Française.

CHAPELLE DE LA SORBONNE

Open during temporary exhibitions or concerts.

The Chapelle de la Sorbonne, facing Place de la Sorbonne, was founded in the 13th century as the private chapel of the college. When Richelieu commissioned Jacques Lemercier to redesign the Sorbonne, the plans included the chapel. The college buildings were begun in 1627, but the chapel, paid for by Richelieu, was begun only in 1635. It was completed in 1642, the year of Richelieu's death. The west elevation makes a direct reference to the Italian Baroque with superimposed orders linked by volutes, innovative in Paris at the time. The unusual plan places the dome centrally, between a nave and choir of equal length, and shallow transepts. Richelieu's dramatic tomb (1694), sculpted by Girardon, is designed to give maximum effect either from the west or from the alternative north entrance.

RUE SAINT-JACQUES & THE COLLÈGES

Behind the Sorbonne runs Rue St-Jacques, an ancient thoroughfare which existed even before it became the *Via Superior* or cardo, the north–south artery linking Gallo-Roman *Lutetia* to northern France and to *Cenabum* (Orléans). It crossed the Seine via the Petit Pont, which until 1782 was defended at the southern end by the Petit Châtelet, the successor of the Tour de Bois that in 885–6 held Viking or Norman marauders at bay. It was adopted in the Middle Ages as the pilgrimage route to Santiago de Compostela, taking its name from a pilgrim hospice dedicated to St James (St Jacques), which was occupied in 1218 by the future St Dominic and Dominican friars from Toulouse. Rue St-Jacques links the Latin Quarter with Montparnasse to the south, and continues northwards on the Right Bank as Rue St-Martin.

COLLÈGE DE FRANCE

The entrance to the Collège de France (*map p. 587, E3*) is in Place Marcellin-Berthelot, Rue des Écoles, a graceful porticoed courtyard with a statue of the scholar Guillaume Budé (Budaeus, 1468–1540), who influenced the founding of the college by François I in 1530 with the intention of spreading Renaissance humanism to counteract the narrow scholasticism of the Sorbonne. Independent of the University, its teaching was free and public. The present building was begun in 1610, completed c. 1778 by Jean-François Chalgrin.

Square A.-Mariette-Pacha, next to the Collège de France, contains statues of Dante (1882), the Renaissance poet Ronsard (1928) and C. Bernard (1946), Professor of Medicine in 1947–78. In Impasse Chartière nearby is a monument to the Pléiade, a group of Renaissance poets that originated in the vanished Collège Coqueret, which occupied this site from 1418–1643.

On Rue St-Jaques is the **Lycée Louis-le-Grand** (*map p. 587, E3*), formerly the Jesuit Collège de Clermont, founded in 1560 and rebuilt in 1887–96. Among those who studied here were Molière, Voltaire, Robespierre, supporter of the Reign of Terror at the Revolution, and another revolutionary, Camille Desmoulins, as well as the painter Delacroix and the writer Victor Hugo.

ON AND AROUND RUE D'ULM

On Rue d'Ulm is the Maronite Catholic Cathedral of **Notre-Dame du Liban** (Our Lady of the Lebanon; *map p. 587, E4*). It was elevated to an eparchy in 2012 by Pope Benedict XVI. The **Collège des Irlandais**, founded in 1578 by John Lee, was re-founded in 1687 as a seminary by English Catholics, at 5 Rue des Irlandais. Now the Centre Culturel Irlandais, it has a wide programme of cultural events, offers residencies for Irish artists and is home to the Irish Chamber Choir of Paris. Events are open to the public (*closed Mon and public holidays, T: 01 58 52 10 30*).

Pasteur from 1864–88, and Pierre and Marie Curie in 1883–1905, worked in the laboratories of the **École de Physique et de Chimie Industrielles** in Rue Pierre-Brossolette. The **École Normale Supérieure**, established in 1793, was, like the École Polytechnique, a *Grande École*, or higher education institution originally created, in this case, to train élite teachers. It has been at no. 45 Rue d'Ulm since 1843 and is one of the highest ranking universities of Paris.

The unadorned Classical church of **St-Jacques-du-Haut-Pas** (1630–88) began as a simple chapel established by Tuscan hospitallers in the 12th century for pilgrims on the road to Santiago de Compostela. Many times altered, its present unadorned 17th-century aspect reflects later Jansenist connections. It was completed in 1712 with the help of the Duchesse de Longueville (d. 1679), who is buried here together with Jean Duvergier de Hauranne (d. 1643), a prominent Jansenist (*see p. 158*), and the astronomer Jean-Dominique Cassini (d. 1712). It has a fine organ, with a case dating mainly from 1609, transferred here from the church of St-Benoît-le-Bétourné (destroyed; the Sorbonne now occupies the site) and entirely rebuilt in 1971.

To the west on Blvd St-Michel, the **Mines ParisTech University** occupies the Hôtel de Vendôme, an 18th–century building enlarged after 1840, its principal façade facing the Luxembourg Gardens. It contains a Museum of Mineralogy (*see p. 522*).

At the corner of Rue de l'Abbé-de-l'Épée, is the **Institut National des Sourds-Muets**, a hospital for the deaf and dumb, founded by the Abbé de l'Épée about 1760. It was taken over by the state in 1790 and reconstructed in 1823. In the courtyard is a statue of the Abbé by Félix Martin, a deaf and dumb sculptor (1789). (*For the Schola Cantorum and votive church of Val-de-Grâce, see p. 158.*)

RUE DE L'ÉCOLE-DE-MÉDECINE

West of Blvd St-Michel, on the corner of Rue de l'École de Médecine and Rue de Hautefeuille (*map p. 587, D3; no. 32*), Gustave Courbet had his studio in the former chapel of the Collège des Prémontrés. Most of the block on Rue de l'École de Médecine is occupied by the Faculty of Medicine, Université René Descartes Paris V, known as Paris Descartes. Jacques Gondouin was responsible in 1769–76 for the courtyard, colonnaded façade and pedimented entrance, a grandiose Classical structure; the building was enlarged in 1878–1900. It contains a library of around 600,000 volumes, the Medical Faculty archives since 1395, and the Musée d'Histoire de la Médecine (*see p. 520*). In the courtyard is a statue by David d'Angers of the anatomist Xavier Bichat (d. 1802), 'father of histology' (the study of tissues).

Opposite Paris V is the entrance to the beautiful Gothic refectory of the **Couvent**

des Cordeliers (*open 10.30–6.30, 10–7 during exhibitions; closed Mon; T: 01 40 46 05 47*), used as a municipal exhibition gallery. The 15th-century Franciscan house was rebuilt c. 1500 around a 13th-century church, on land lent by the Abbey of St-Germain-des-Prés for theology lessons. Space was later rented out, and the urbanist Edmé Verniquet worked here from 1785 on the masterly plan requested by Louis XVI for the restructuring of Paris. In 1790 the chapel became the meeting place of the Cordeliers Club, the most vocal and violent of the pre-Revolutionary groups. Led by Georges-Jacques Danton (d. 1794) and Jean-Paul Marat (d. 1793), who lived nearby, as did Danton's friend, the rabble-rousing journalist Camille Desmoulins (d. 1794), it was even more left-wing than the Jacobins Club. All three men perished during the Terror, when rival factions turned on each other after the execution of the king and formation of the First Republic. Marat was buried in the convent garden after his assassination by the Girondist Charlotte Corday. The club was closed in 1795. After the Revolution, Citizen Verniquet's designs became the basis for the proposal to subdivide nationalised land.

At the western end of Rue de l'École-de-Médecine a flight of steps ascends to Rue Monsieur-le-Prince (de Condé). Futher south, on the corner where it meets Rue de Vaugirard, is the **Lycée St-Louis**, built by Bailly, on the site of the Collège d'Harcourt (1280), where the writers Racine and Boileau studied. Its entrance faces Place de la Sorbonne, which was the site of the Café d'Harcourt (*47 Blvd St-Michel*), where the Nicaraguan poet Rubén Darío famously met Verlaine in 1893 and described the encounter in his memoirs (*see below*). The café closed during the Nazi occupation in 1940. Verlaine died three years after the meeting described below and is buried in the cemetery of Batignolles (*see p. 293*).

A YOUNG POET MEETS VERLAINE

One of my greatest ambitions was to speak to Verlaine. One night, in the Café d'Harcourt, we found the Faun, surrounded by dubious acolytes.

He was precisely as his likeness by the marvellous Carrière. He had clearly been drinking. He responded, from time to time, to the questions put by his companions, intermittently thumping the marble tabletop. Sawa [modernist Spanish writer] and I went up to him and I introduced myself: 'American poet, humble admirer, etc., etc.' In bad French I stammered out all the admiration I could muster and ended with the word glory, '*gloire*'...

Who knows what had happened that evening to the unfortunate maestro? The fact is, that, turning to me and never for a moment leaving off thumping the tabletop, he said, in a low and guttural voice: '*La gloire!... La gloire!... Merde, merde encore!*'

I deemed it prudent to withdraw, hoping to renew his acquaintance under more propitious circumstances.

In this I was never successful, because on those occasions when I did see him again I found him in more or less the same condition; and this was a circumstance both melancholy and unfortunate, tragic and grotesque. Poor 'Pauvre Lélian'! *Priez pour le pauvre Gaspard*!

From the Autobiografía *of Rubén Darío. Tr. A.B.*

SAINT-SÉVERIN

Map p. 587, E2–E3. Métro 10 to Cluny-La Sorbonne or 4 to St-Michel. Open Mon–Sat 11–7.30, Sun 9–8.

The oldest parish church on the Left Bank, St-Séverin, between Rue St-Jacques and Rue de la Harpe, dates from the 13th–16th centuries and combines early and late Gothic styles overlaid by various later modifications. The first church to be built here was a simple building, on the site of an oratory of the time of Childebert I in which Foulque of Neuilly-sur-Marne had preached the Fourth Crusade (c. 1199). It was enlarged at the end of the 13th and beginning of the 14th centuries, but only the first three bays of the nave escaped a fire in 1448. Rebuilding began in 1452 and went on until 1498. In the 17th century the church was drastically altered, like many other churches at the time. The jubé was demolished and the choir partially classicised at the request of Mlle de Montpensier, La Grande Mademoiselle, niece of Louis XIII.

EXTERIOR OF SAINT-SÉVERIN

The early 13th-century **west door**, with foliate carvings between the colonnettes, was brought piecemeal from St-Pierre-aux-Boeufs in the Cité (the *Virgin and Child* is 19th century). St-Pierre-aux-Boeufs stood on Rue d'Arcole until its demolition in 1837. Its name came from the heads of two bulls carved on its façade in honour of two beasts on their way to market who had supposedly knelt in veneration when passing the church.

The upper sections Saint-Séverin date from the 15th century. On the left is a **13th-century tower** completed in 1487, with a door (round the corner) that was once the main entrance; the tympanum of *St Martin and the Beggar* dates from 1853, but at the base of the frame is a 15th-century inscription: *Bonnes gens qui par cy passés, Priez Dieu pour les trespassés* ('Good people who pass through here, pray to God for your sins').

On the south side of the church are the galleries of the 15th-century **charnel house**, the only one to survive in Paris.

INTERIOR OF SAINT-SÉVERIN

The church is impressively broad compared to its length, with a double ambulatory but no transept. The difference in style between the first three bays, built in the 13th century, and the remainder, which are of the 15th century, is quite obvious. The earlier bays contain late 14th-century **stained glass** from St-Germain-des-Prés, but much restored; from the fourth bay on, the glass is mid-15th-century. One of the subjects on the south side of the nave is the murder of Thomas Becket. The west rose window contains a *Tree of Jesse* (c. 1500), masked by the organ of 1745 that was once played by the composers Gabriel Fauré and Camille Saint-Saëns.

The **double ambulatory** is a *tour de force* of Flamboyant architecture, with a dynamic central column around which shafts spiral to burst into leaf in the vaults like a palm tree. The stained glass of the apse chapels is by Jean Bazaine (1966). Off the southeast chapel is the **Chapel of the Sacrament**, designed by Jules Hardouin-

Mansart in 1673. The liturgical furnishings (1985–9) are by Georges Schneider and the chapel contains a series of framed lithographs, *Miserere* (1922–7) by Georges Rouault, displayed here since 1993.

In the **north aisle**, above a small door next to the sacristy entrance, is the funerary monument of Nicolas de Bomont (1547), who kneels before a scene of the *Crucifixion* in the company of his wife and 15 children, ten girls and five boys.

The **area around St-Séverin**, going west towards Place St-Michel, is a corner of old Paris penetrated by narrow, ancient streets or alleys such as Rue de la Huchette, Rue Xavier-Privas and Rue du Chat-qui-Pêche (named after an old shop-sign of a cat fishing). The warren would be picturesque if it were not so completely given over to tourism. Touts stand at every doorway, attempting to lure passers-by inside. On Place St-Michel, the **Fontaine St-Michel** (1860) incorporates a later memorial to the Resistance of 1944.

SAINT-JULIEN & RUE DE LA BÛCHERIE

The church of **St-Julien-le-Pauvre** (*map p. 587, E2–E3; often closed*), rebuilt c. 1170–1230 by monks of Longpont, an abbey attached to Cluny in Burgundy, stands on the site of a succession of chapels dedicated to St Julian the Hospitaller. The present west front was built in 1651. Despite many restorations, the interior retains the air of a solid late-Romanesque country church. There are two original carved capitals in the chancel. St-Julien was used from the 13th–16th centuries as a university church and from 1655–1877 for various secular purposes. Since 1889 it has been occupied by Melkites (the Greek Catholic Church of Antioch) and an iconostasis stretches across the chancel, obscuring the east end. Fixed to the wall in the south aisle is a funerary slab with a vivid resurrection scene.

Rue Galande, left of the church of St-Julien as you come out of it, is one of the oldest streets in Paris (14th century). At no. 42 is a carved relief, mentioned in 1380, of St Julian and his wife ferrying Christ across a river.

The small garden adjacent to the church, **Square René-Viviani**, contains some architectural elements possibly from Notre-Dame and claims the oldest tree in Paris, a Robinia (Locust tree or False acacia) planted in 1601. From here is a classic view of Notre-Dame.

The square bisects **Rue de la Bûcherie**, which runs parallel to the river. In its eastern section (across Rue Lagrange), at no. 13, is the building that was occupied by the École de Médecine for more than two centuries, from 1483–1775. It has a rotunda of 1745. On the western section of Rue de la Bûcherie, at no. 37, is the shabby little second-hand bookshop **Shakespeare & Company**. The first bookshop of this name, founded by Sylvia Beach, was in Rue de l'Odéon, where it was the rendezvous of interwar expatriate writers (*see below*). The bookseller George Whitman took over the name when

Beach died in 1964: his shop here on Rue de la Bûcherie, founded in 1951, had previously been called Le Mistral. For years Whitman (d. 2011, buried in Père-Lachaise Cemetery) ran the shop as a 'socialist utopia' for penniless writers—as it was described by one such, Canadian journalist Jeremy Mercer, in two books: *Time was Soft There* and *Books, Baguettes and Bedbugs.*

THE 'LOST GENERATION'

After the First World War, young American and foreign writers, such as F. Scott Fitzgerald, James Joyce and Ernest Hemingway, came to Paris in search of political freedom and intellectual stimulation. They settled in the Latin Quarter, particularly around Rue St-Jacques (*map p. 587, E3*), to live, work and drink. Gertrude Stein (1874–1946), the writer and friend of Matisse and Picasso, dubbed these disillusioned expatriates the 'Lost Generation'. Stein's apartment at 27 Rue de Fleurus (*map p. 586, C3*) became a place of pilgrimage, although in Hemingway's case their friendship did not last. The expatriate community's base shifted from the Latin Quarter to the cafés of Montparnasse, though the economic Depression following the stock market crash of 1929 forced many Americans to return home. George Orwell meanwhile arrived in 1928, as did Samuel Beckett, and Evelyn Waugh a year later. The second wave descended on Paris in the aftermath of the Second World War, Hemingway notably entering the city with the American troops to 'liberate the cellars of the Ritz'. Many expatriates were attracted to the French capital by nostalgia for the achievements of the 'Lost Generation'. Café culture at this time favoured the watering holes of the St-Germain-des-Prés and Luxembourg districts—Café de Flore, Les Deux Magots, the Mabillon and the Pergola.

During both periods the visitors brought a new energy to the cultural life of Paris and also supported and relied upon English-language presses, periodicals and bookstores. Small presses included the Contact Press (American poet Robert McAlmon), the Three Mountains Press (William Bird), the Hours Press (Nancy Cunard), the Black Sun Press (Harry and Caresse Crosby), the Obelisk Press (Jack Kahane) and the Olympia Press (Maurice Girodias, son of Kahane). They published the works of many writers in Paris, often before they were well known elsewhere, as in the case of Ernest Hemingway and Henry Miller. Most of these early presses disappeared with the Depression, as did many expatriate periodicals, among the more important of which were *The Transatlantic Review*, edited by Ford Madox Ford (and one issue by Ernest Hemingway), and *This Quarter*, featuring poetry, short stories and prose. Possibly the best-known contribution, which Joyce usually called *A Work in Progress*, was later incorporated into *Finnegans Wake* in 1939. The only periodical to survive the onset of the Depression was *transition*, which lasted until 1938. Of the English-language bookstores, the most important was undoubtedly Sylvia Beach's famous Shakespeare & Co., which opened in 1919 on Rue Dupuytren and then removed to Rue de l'Odéon. As well as running the bookstore and library, Beach published Joyce's *Ulysses* in 1922, in an edition of a thousand numbered copies, but business declined during the war and she finally closed her shop in late 1941, after the Nazi occupation of Paris.

SAINT-NICOLAS-DU-CHARDONNET
Tomb of the mother of Charles Le Brun, designed by Le Brun himself.

SAINT-NICOLAS-DU-CHARDONNET
& LES BERNARDINS

On Rue Monge stands the church of St-Nicolas-du-Chardonnet (*map p. 587, E3*), a reminder that an earlier church was built here in a field of thistles (*chardons*). The major part of the present church was built 1656–1709; only the tower (1625) remains from the previous building. In the 19th century, Boulevard St-Germain shaved off the east of the church, necessitating a rearrangement of the apsidal chapel. The main façade on Rue Monge was not completed until the last century.

Le Brun designed the finely-carved door on Rue des Bernardins and in fact this is a good place to see examples of his work. The interior contains many good paintings and sculptures, while the crystal chandeliers in the choir add a secular, ballroom touch. At the west end, on the right as you enter the church, is Le Brun's painting of the *Martyrdom of St John the Evangelist*, and in the first chapel on the right is Corot's study for the *Baptism of Christ* (left wall). In the south transept is the Communion Chapel (*ask the sacristan to unlock it*), with two paintings by Nicolas Coypel on either side of the altar (poorly lit): on the right, *The Fall of Manna* and on the left, the *Sacrifice of Melchisedech*. Also outstanding are a monument by Girardon of Bignon, the jurist (d. 1656; second south ambulatory chapel) and, in the third north ambulatory chapel after the east end, the splendidly theatrical monument to Le Brun's mother, designed by Le Brun and showing the deceased being raised from the tomb. In the same chapel is a

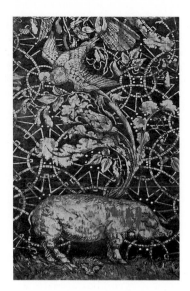

RUE MOUFFETARD
Detail of the sgraffito fresco of a former butcher's shop (1929–31).

monument to Le Brun (d. 1690) and his widow, by the sculptor Antoine Coysevox. Le Brun painted the ceiling fresco of *St Michael*.

COLLÈGE DES BERNARDINS

The medieval Collège des Bernardins (*20 Rue de Poissy; map p. 587, F3; open Mon–Sat 10–6, Sun and holidays 2–6; closed most of Aug and over Christmas*) was a Cistercian monastery founded in 1244 by the English Abbot of Clairvaux, Stephen of Lexington. It became state property at the Revolution. Subjected to many roles since but never totally destroyed, it was re-purchased from the city by the Diocese of Paris in 2001. A lengthy restoration and adaptation of this beautiful building was completed in 2008 and it is now a Christian institution under the auspices of the Cathedral School as a centre for teaching, research and debate; it also holds cultural events. Entrance is free to the main hall and former sacristy. Other parts of the college, including the cellar and upper floor, can be seen on a guided tour (*T: 01 53 10 74 44, www.collegedesbernardins.fr*). The main hall, known as the Large Nave, is a beautiful vaulted room, 70m long, its vaults springing from 32 slender columns. It is overlooked, at one end, by a 14th-century statue of Christ. The space contains a bookshop and café.

At the Seine end of Rue de Poissy, at no. 57 Quai de la Tournelle, stands the restored 17th-century **Hôtel de Nesmond**, now occupied by La Demeure Historique, an organisation founded in 1924 by Dr Joachim Carvallo, owner of the Château de Villandry, to support and preserve historically important private properties across France.

The **Musée de l'Assistance Publique**, with exhibits on the history of Paris hospitals, is at 47 Quai de la Tournelle (*see p. 518*). Rue de Bièvre marks the line of the canal built by the Abbaye St-Victor in the 12th century to re-route the Bièvre river into the Seine.

QUARTIER DE LA MOUFFE

Map p. 587, E4. Métro 10 to Cardinal Lemoine (top of the street) or 7 to Censier Daubenton (bottom of the street and church).

Behind the Panthéon and the Lycée Henri-IV (*see p. 64*) is Rue Descartes and the house where Paul Verlaine died (*see p. 85*). From here, across Place de la Contrescarpe, begins Rue Mouffetard, or Quartier de la Mouffe, an ancient cobbled thoroughfare on a gentle hill slope, described by Hemingway as a 'wonderful narrow crowded market street'. It retains all these characteristics as well as a cheerful, bustling, relaxed atmosphere. Extremely popular and packed with cafés, it also has some interesting old houses. In the lower part of La Mouffe there is a lively street market every morning.

HISTORY OF LA MOUFFE

Rue Mouffetard follows a section of the old Roman road leading from the Île de la Cité out of Paris towards Italy, following the course of the Bièvre river. In the Middle Ages it linked the University quarter and the outskirts of Paris as far as the present Place d'Italie, crossing the semi-rural *bourgs* of St-Médard and St-Marcel. Once a desirable rural area outside Charles V's ramparts, it evolved over the centuries into a thoroughly urban working-class quarter with cabarets and dance halls, its inhabitants employed mainly in leather-related industries, especially tanning, which polluted the river water and filled the air with putrid odours. These smells, described as *moffettes*, may be the origin of its present name (although there are other theories).

The Bourg St-Médard gradually spread as far as the walls of Paris and was annexed to the city in 1724. By then the district was considered dangerous, dirty and generally to be avoided, and its inhabitants participated in Revolutionary uprisings and insurrections. A section of La Mouffe disappeared with Haussmann's urban reorganisation in the 19th century and around 1910 the unhealthy Bièvre was channelled underground. Before the Second World War the area was still insalubrious and many buildings were not linked to main drains. Yet it attracted writers such as Georges Duhamel, Ernest Hemingway and George Orwell, who could live inexpensively here, and its colourful market became famous. In the 1960s it was popular, like Montmartre, for its *chansonniers*. Being close to the University of Paris, it also felt the effects, for better or for worse, of the 1968 student riots. Today it is perhaps a little tamer than it was, but much of the old atmosphere remains.

SAINT-MÉDARD

Open Mon 5–7.30, Tues–Fri 8–12.30 & 2.30–7.30, Sat 9–12.30 & 2.30–7.30, Sun 8.30–12.30 & 4–8.

The church of Saint-Médard is the major monument of the quarter, dedicated to St Medardus, a 6th-century French bishop and the continental equivalent of St Swithin. If it rains, so the legend goes, on his feast day (8th June), it will continue to rain for 40 days thereafter.

The original church on this site was under the protection of the Abbey of St-Germain-des-Prés until the Revolution. The nave and west front are late 15th-century. The choir was constructed in 1560–86 and the aisles from 1665. A classical touch was the fluting of the Doric columns in 1784, at which date the Lady Chapel was also added. Inside there is a fine organ case of 1650 by Germain Pillon. The pulpit dates from 1718. The church was sacked by the Huguenots in 1561. Then, in the early 18th century, it became the centre of a scandal when devotees began to gather round the grave of the Jansenist deacon François Pâris (d. 1727, aged 37). Reports of miracles occurring at the site began to circulate and soon a cult of cures and visions grew up, leading to collective hysteria and violence; female *convulsionnaires*, so it was said, rent their clothes. The cemetery was closed in 1732 and an anonymous message was pinned to the gate that read: *De par le Roi, défense à Dieu de faire miracle en ce lieu* ('By order of the King, God is forbidden to carry out miracles in this place').

INSTITUT DU MONDE ARABE & ENVIRONS

Map p. 587, F3. Métro 7 and 10 to Jussieu. 1 Rue des Fossés-Saint-Bernard. Open daily except Mon 10–6. T: 01 40 51 38 38, www.imarabe.org.

Located beside the Seine, the Institut du Monde Arabe (IMA) is sometimes overlooked by visitors but well known to Parisians for its excellent programme of temporary exhibitions. Inaugurated in 1987, it was founded to further cultural and scientific relations between France and some 21 Arab countries. The sleek and complex building, designed by Jean Nouvel, has nine levels above ground and two below. The design echoes certain aspects of Arab architecture such as the geometric *mashrabiya* window lattices of the south façade, which are designed to function like a camera lens, expanding and contracting either mechanically or in reaction to the sun's intensity, through the medium of a photo-electric cell. The building is arranged around an interior court or *ryad* (with glass lifts) and a book tower or *ziggourat*.

The Institute contains a museum, temporary exhibition spaces, a cinema, book and gift shop, library and documentation centre. It offers a wide variety of cultural activites based on the Arab world and its culture: exhibitions, conferences, cinema, concerts. On level 0 is the Café Littéraire (*open 10–7.30*). On the roof terrace (level 9) are the Zyriab restaurant and the cafeteria 'Self' (*for details, see p. 85*). A bonus is the bird's eye view onto the Seine and Notre-Dame.

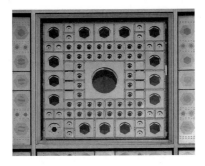

INSTITUT DU MONDE ARABE
Detail of the mechanical *mashrabiya* windows of the south façade.

THE MUSEUM

The permanent collection is exhibited on three levels (starting on level 7 and working down) and is dedicated to the art and civilisation of the Arab world from pre-Islamic times to the present day. Small and elegantly laid out, the museum is mainly concerned with the development of the religion of Islam and the part played by the Arab world in the history of science. Examples of the arts and crafts of Islam include ceramics, manuscripts, metalwork, ivories, fabrics and glass objects; also textiles, rugs, costumes and jewellery from throughout the Arab world.

ENVIRONS OF THE INSTITUT

Behind the Institute, on Place Jussieu, are the Science Faculties of Université Marie Curie, Paris VI and Paris VII, where the **Collection of Minerals** can be visited (*see p. 521*). Here, until their transfer to Bercy in the 19th century, stood the huge bonded warehouses of the Halle aux Vins, itself on the site of the Abbaye de St-Victor. The abbey was dissolved in 1790. Thomas Becket and Abélard had once resided there and Rabelais studied in its library.

The corner site of 15–17 Quai de la Tournelle is occupied by one of Paris's most celebrated restaurants, **La Tour d'Argent** (*see p. 84*). Long-established (although no-one can agree on the date), it is a beautiful place with stunning views of the Seine and Notre-Dame—and is very, very expensive.

The Collège des Bons-Enfants, one of the first colleges of the university to be established (1208), once stood at 32 **Rue du Cardinal Lemoine**. Vincent de Paul founded his congregation of mission-priests here in 1625. No. 49 is the Hôtel le Brun, built by Germain Boffrand and variously occupied at times by the painter Watteau and by the naturalist the Comte de Buffon. At no. 65 is the Collège des Écossais (Scots), where the skull of James II of England is preserved. King James died in exile in St-Germain-en-Laye in 1701.

ARÈNES DE LUTÈCE

Between Rue Monge and Rue Linné is Rue des Arènes, leading to the remains of the 1st-century amphitheatre of Lutetia, the Arènes de Lutèce (*map p. 587, F4*). The second most important Gallo-Roman site in Paris after the *thermae* (*see p. 57*), and one of the largest arenas in France, it now gives little idea of its former glory, when around 17,000 spectators would have watched fights as well as theatre performances. The structure fell into ruin in the 3rd century, was used as a necropolis in the 4th, and the stone was removed. It was mentioned in the 12th century, but was filled in during the building of Philippe-Auguste's city wall and disappeared from view. In 1869, during the Haussmann era, construction works uncovered underlying remains, but despite opposition, it was turned into an omnibus depot. As a result of a public outcry instigated by Victor Hugo, funds were raised that led to more excavations in 1883–5 and to the arena's consequent conservation. Dr Joseph-Louis Capitan restored the ruins to their present state in 1917–18. Square Capitan on two sides of the arena is a green space on the site of an old reservoir. Instead of bloodthirsty spectacles, the Arènes is now a popular place for *le foot, les boules* or eating *les sandwiches*.

MOSQUÉE DE PARIS

To the west of Rue Geoffroy-St-Hilaire is the green-tiled Grande Mosquée de Paris (*map p. 587, F4; guided visits Sat–Thur 9–12 & 2–6 at 2bis Place du Puits-de-l'Ermite; T: 01 45 35 97 33*). Identified by its minaret, the mosque was inaugurated in 1926. It commemorates the 100,000 Muslims who died for France in 1914–18. The religious buildings are grouped around a courtyard and in the prayer room are some magnificent carpets. The decorative materials were made in North Africa and much of the décor is Mudéjar style. The entrance to the souk (shop) is on the corner of Rue Daubenton and Rue G. St-Hilaire; there is also a restaurant and tea shop for mint tea, and a women-only hammam.

The 1960s' utilitarian architecture nearby on Rue Censier belongs to the **University of Paris III**, Faculty of Letters, Languages and Sociology.

MUSÉUM NATIONAL D'HISTOIRE NATURELLE & JARDIN DES PLANTES

Map p. 588, A4–B4. Entrances on Place Valhubert, Rue Geoffroy-St-Hilaire and also Rue Cuvier and Rue Buffon. Métro 7 and 10 to Jussieu or 5 and 10 and RER C to Gare d'Austerlitz. Gardens open daily summer 7.30–7.45, winter 8–5.15. Greenhouses open daily except Tues, summer 10–6 (Sun to 6.30), winter 10–5. The main garden is free. For opening times of the Ménagerie and other museums, see individual entries below. T: 01 40 79 56 01, www.jardindesplantes.net.

The Jardin des Plantes, officially part of the Muséum National d'Histoire Naturelle, exists not only as a public space, but as a centre of ongoing research. It is an oasis of 23.5 hectares, encompassing botanic gardens, a group of museums, a zoo (the Ménagerie) and a small maze, as well as unrivalled collections of wild and herbaceous plants. There are around eleven small gardens, and the displays of peonies and iris in May and June are famous.

HISTORY OF THE JARDIN DES PLANTES

The origin of the Jardin des Plantes is in the medicinal garden created in 1635 by Louis XIII for the cultivation of herbs by the royal physician Guy de la Brosse and first opened to the public in 1640. Its present reputation is mainly due to the eminent naturalist, biologist and mathematician the Comte de Buffon (1707–88), who was superintendent here from 1739, and greatly enlarged the grounds. Known until 1793 as the Jardin du Roi, it was reorganised under its present official title by the Convention and provided at that time with twelve professorships. The National Museum of Natural History is a public institute with the triple goal of research, conservation and the dissemination of knowledge. The library owns a remarkable collection of botanical manuscripts, including the *Vélins du Roi*, illustrated by Nicolas Robert and others; also works by the watercolourist and botanical painter P.-J. Redouté.

Several of the distinguished French naturalists who taught and studied here are commemorated by monuments in or near the garden. An early 20th-century statue by Léon Fagel of the naturalist associated with early theories of evolution, J.-B. Lamarck (d. 1829), faces the Place Valhubert entrance, and another by the same artist of the chemist Eugène Chevreul (d. 1889) stands in the northern part of the gardens. Chevreul's research into the principles of harmony and colour contrasts had an important influence on the colour theories of the Impressionist and Post-Impressionist painters. For a time he was director of the dyeing department at the Gobelins tapestry factory (*see p. 163*). The Administrative Department is housed in the Hôtel de Magny, built in 1690, and behind it is the Grand Amphithéatre, begun by Verniquet, and where Chevreul worked. The Maison de Cuvier was the home of Georges Cuvier (d. 1832), zoologist, palaeontologist and educator, founder of the study of comparative anatomy and Secretary of the Academy of Science from 1803. The house was later occupied by Henri Becquerel (d. 1908), who discovered radioactivity here in 1896.

EXPLORING THE GARDENS

From the west, by the Grande Galerie (*Rue Geoffroy-St-Hilaire*), there is a vista bordered by curtains of plane trees planted in 1882, which creates the structural backbone of the garden. To the north of it is the Ménagerie; to the south, the Minerals Gallery and the galleries of Palaeontology and Comparative Anatomy. Within this framework is a host of smaller gardens including small plots with four types of soil, and a variety of plantings.

The sunken **Alpine Garden**, viewed from Allée Cuvier, protects some 2,000 species of mountain plants. There is a **rose garden** (near the Mineralogy gallery), and the **Peony Collection** is set among magnolias and rocks at the Seine end. Other collections are vegetable, iris and perennial; birds and bees; and the **Stegosaurus Garden** of ancient plants. The **Butte** is a fanciful hillock encased in a small maze. At its foot is the first Cedar of Lebanon to be planted in France (it came from Kew Gardens in 1734) and at its summit an *Acer orientale* (Turkish maple), planted in 1702 close to the **Gloriette**, the oldest metal structure in Paris, dating from 1786 and designed by Edmé Verniquet. A sundial bears the inscription *Horas non numero nisi serenas*: 'I only count the hours of happiness'.

The **Large Greenhouses** (Grandes Serres; *open Wed–Mon 10–6, Sun to 6.30; closed Tues, 1 May and public holidays*) recreate zones as diverse as the deserts of Mexico and the rain forests of New Caledonia.

The Ménagerie

In 1792, animals from the royal collection at Versailles and belonging to street show-men formed the nucleus of the Ménagerie (*open April–mid-Oct Mon–Sat 9–6, Sun and holidays in summer to 6.30; winter 9–5*). Large animals have today been replaced by around 2,000 smaller species of mammal, reptiles and birds. Examples range from red pandas (*Ailurus fulgens*) and binturongs to tarantulas. Divided into five geographic zones or 'biozones', the presentation is sympathetic to the delicate balance of ecosys-tems and the well-being of the animals. The setting is also visitor-friendly and the old buildings (which are listed) have been sensitively modernised.

Grande Galerie de l'Évolution

Part of the Museum of Natural History, the Grande Galerie de l'Évolution (*open Wed–Mon 10–6, last admission 5.15; closed Tues, 1 May; T: 01 40 79 54 79*) combines an excit-ing visual experience with rich natural history content. The exhibition space uses the central nave, balconies and side galleries of the old building of the Zoological Gallery of 1889. The theme of the museum revolves around the history of evolution, whose drama unfolds across the different levels of the building. The innovations of modern museology manage to convey a powerful scientific message in a quite magical way. The permanent exhibition combines carefully selected and restored specimens—the smaller ones suspended in transparent display cases to great effect—with audio visual presentations, models and etched glass. Level 0, excavated to reveal stone arcades, evokes various marine zones, from the deep to the shallows and on to the coast and dry land. Arctic regions have to be crossed on the way to Level 1 and a change in climate. Here, among other displays aimed at demonstrating the wide diversity of animal life above and under water, is a cavalcade of animals across the African savannah and the tropical forests of South America.

Lifts fly you past exotic birds to Level 3 where the balconies, devoted to the evolu-tion of living organisms, provide a spectacular view down onto the nave of Level 1. The exhibition continues on Level 2 with the science of selectivity and mankind's role in evolution, including some of our most disturbing effects on the environment. Behind the balcony on the east side is a gallery devoted to extinct and endangered species. This chapel-like room, with its original wooden display cabinets, is classified as an his-toric monument and contains a clock made for Marie-Antoinette.

Other departments of the Muséum

All open Wed–Mon 10–5; Sat–Sun in summer to 6; closed Tues and 1 May.

The Cabinet d'Histoire du Jardin des Plantes, in the Hôtel de Magny, built by Pierre Bullet in the late 17th century, describes the evolution of the Jardin des Plantes from the oldest object, the chapel bell of the Royal Garden of 1631, to ancient documents shown in rotation.

The Mineralogy and Geology Gallery (*36 Rue Geoffroy-St-Hilaire*) contains a spectacular collection of rocks and minerals, as well as precious stones. Among them is a group of giant crystals from Brazil, originally destined for industrial use, which amount to three-quarters of the world's known stock.

The Palaeontology and Comparative Anatomy Galleries (*2 Rue Buffon*) reopened its doors in 2014 following renovation. The long, iron-framed building dating from 1898 has a glass ceiling and finely-wrought balustrades. It consists of one single span, which is impressively filled with glass vitrines displaying the multitude of skeletons of fish, birds, reptiles and mammals, including dinosaurs and mammoths. The object of the collection is to demonstrate how vertebrates adapted, and to provide comparisons between them. The visit is on two levels. A fine decorative metal ramp sweeps you up, allowing you to appreciate how the ornate iron framework harmonises with the objects on display. On the upper level are some faintly creepy fossilised skeletons, the oldest specimen being the skeleton of the rhinoceros that belonged to Louis XV.

AROUND GARE D'AUSTERLITZ

Map p. 588, B4. Métro 5 and 10 and RER C to Gare d'Austerlitz.

Gare d'Austerlitz is the railway terminus for southwest France. Between 1870 and 1871 (during the Siege of Paris), the station, then known as the Gare d'Orléans, was turned into a hot-air balloon factory. On the riverbank are the Square Tino-Rossi gardens, extending all the way to Pont de Sully and which contain the **Musée de la Sculpture en Plein-Air**. Created in 1980 with examples of large 20th-century sculpture, there are works by some 29 artists, including Ipoustéguy, Augustin Cardenas, Bernard Pagès, Liuba and Nicolas Schöffer.

LES DOCKS, CITÉ DE LA MODE ET DU DESIGN

Map p. 588, C4. 34 Quai d'Austerlitz. Open Tues–Sun 10–8, shops open 12–8. T: 01 76 77 25 30, www.citemodedesign.fr.

Between Gare d'Austerlitz and Bibliothèque François Mitterrand, at the end of Pont Charles-de-Gaulle, the green screen-printed addition to the long, faceted façade makes it impossible to miss Les Docks. The former industrial space, built in 1907 on the Quai d'Austerlitz, was totally revamped (2012) to become the Centre for Fashion and Design. Home to the French Fashion Institute, its objective is to bring the public in contact with all types of fashion, beauty and design and the annual fashion Salons are held here. There are also exhibition spaces. The Musée d'Art Ludique (Fun Art) has frequent exhibitions and there are also temporary exhibitions in conjunction with the Palais Galliera (*see p. 430*). There are boutiques selling up-to-the-minute designer items on the ground floor. The vast roof terrace has a superb view over the city's quays, a garden, and the Moon Roof bar and restaurant (*see p. 84*).

HÔPITAL DE LA PITIÉ-SALPÊTRIÈRE

Map p. 591, D1–E1. Entrance on Square Marie-Curie, 47 Blvd de l'Hôpital. The chapel is usually open to visitors.

The 17th-century buildings of the old hospital are surrounded by the modern wings that make this one of the largest hospital complexes in Paris. As a whole, it is a notable example of the austere magnificence of the architecture of the reign of Louis XIV.

HISTORY OF LA SALPÊTRIÈRE

In the 17th century the state took over from the Church the responsibility for the sick and needy. By an edict of 1656 it created the Hôpital Général to contain all undesirables: the destitute, the poor, the old, women of ill repute and so on. At the same time the huge Hôpital de la Salpêtrière was founded to shelter destitute women. It was built, by Le Vau (*see p. 46*) and Pierre Le Muet, on the site of the old Arsenal (saltpetre being a component of gunpowder, hence the name), at that time on the outskirts of Paris. The domed chapel of St-Louis, built in 1670–8 by Libéral Bruant, who worked on Les Invalides, can hold 4,000 people. The criminal wing, La Maison de la Force, was added in 1680. Mental patients were admitted from 1796. Dr Jean-Martin Charcot (d. 1893), who used hypnosis as a diagnostic tool to study hysteria and was an influence on Freud, is commemorated by a monument to the left of the gateway. In 1964 the hospital was combined with the Hôpital de la Pitié, founded by Marie de Médicis in 1612. Diana, Princess of Wales died in the hospital on 31st August, 1997.

CHAPELLE DE ST-LOUIS DE LA SALPÊTRIÈRE

The Chapelle de St-Louis de la Salpêtrière returned to the Church in 1802 but was then abandoned. Following restoration work it reopened in 1974 as a religious and cultural centre. It is grandiose yet simple and, with Les Invalides and the Val-de-Grâce, is among the most important examples of the Baroque in Paris. In designing the chapel Bruant, *Premier Architecte du Roi*, needed to be ingenious in creating separate areas to accommodate the large numbers drawn from different sectors of the hospital, and yet segregate those who had to be kept apart. His solution was a central domed octagon with four identical rectangular naves separated by small octagonal chapels. Each compartment is linked to the central space by a small arched bay. The articulation of the vast, empty space is unusual in French architecture of the period, and the decoration is minimal. Statues by Antoine Etex were added after 1832. Outside are formal gardens and a sundial on the south wall.

BIBLIOTHÈQUE NATIONALE FRANÇOIS MITTERRAND

The Bibliothèque Nationale de France François Mitterrand (*map p. 591, F2*) stands beside the Seine between the Pont de Bercy and the Pont de Tolbiac. The Tolbiac district has undergone major urban renewal in the last 20 years. It is linked to Bercy on the other side of the river by the **Passerelle Simone-de-Beauvoir**, a footbridge by Feichtinger Architects (2006), the newest of the 37 bridges in Paris.

THE LIBRARY

Upper garden level (haut-de-jardin) open Mon–Fri 10–6, Sat 10–9, Sun 10–7. Closed Mon and holidays and mid-Sept. Guided visits in French Tues–Fri 2.30, Sat–Sun 3pm; also thematic visits. Book in advance, T: 01 53 79 49 49, visites@bnf.fr, www.bnf.fr. The reference library is open to anyone of 16 years and over with a daily or annual reader's ticket (on sale in the entrance halls).

The library is only one part of the Bibliothèque Nationale de France (along with the Bibliothèques Richelieu, de l'Arsenal and Bibliothèque-Musée de l'Opéra in Paris and another site in Avignon) but it has become a veritable fortress for books since the major part of the national collection was transferred here 1996–8 from the Richelieu branch (the Richelieu site has retained certain collections; *see p. 310*). This was the last of Mitterrand's *grands projets*, a controversial mammoth construction designed by Dominique Perrault and begun in 1990. It consists of four L-shaped 80m-high towers, each of 20 storeys, simulating books open at right angles, which stand at the corners of a hollow rectangular podium. The eleven upper floors are lined with wooden shutters for protection. The huge site has 400 linear kilometres of stacks.

The esplanade (60,000 square metres) is approached by wide steps of silvery-grey hardwood and decorated with evergreen bushes. It is arranged around an interior sunken garden of 12,000 square metres.

Escalators (east and west) from the esplanade serve the two main entrances and entrance halls at each end of the *haut-de-jardin* (upper garden level). This level looks down on the glassed-in garden, reminiscent of a cloister. The upper garden level is open to visitors and the upper reading rooms have free open access (*see above*) to some 300,000 specifically-acquired volumes. On the eastern side of the upper garden level is the reception desk for tickets. There is a bookshop and a café as well as a free permanent exhibition (on the west side) of Louis XIV's Coronelli globes and paintings related to them. There are also regular temporary exhibitions.

The reading rooms on the *rez-de-jardin* (garden level) have 2,000 places reserved for accredited readers with access to the closed stack collections.

EATING AND DRINKING IN THE LATIN QUARTIER

The Quartier Latin is excellently provided with places to eat, ranging from snack bars, *boulangeries* and casual bistrots to the finest of the fine. Around Boulevard St-Michel the narrow streets are filled with inexpensive takeaways and cafés, many with an Indonesian or North African flavour. At the other end of the market is one the most famed restaurants in the world, the Tour d'Argent.

€€€ **Atelier Maître Albert**. ■ Across the Seine from Notre Dame, part of Guy Savoy's portfolio, this combines a modern, understated décor with good seasonal cooking. Dishes are a blend of tradition and modern chic. There are also vegetarian options and superb desserts. Daily specials from the slate. Good-value set menus, pricier '*menu dégustation*'. Closed Sat and Sun lunch. *1 Rue Maître-Albert. T: 01 56 81 30 01. www.ateliermaitrealbert.com. Map p. 587, E3.*

€€€ **Les Itinéraires**. Small corner restaurant just off Boulevard St-Germain offering acclaimed modern French cooking. Best to book. Closed Mon. *5 Rue de Pontoise. T: 01 46 33 60 11, www. restaurant-itineraires.com. Map p. 587, F3.*

€€€ **La Tour d'Argent**. On the upper floor of a corner site near the Seine, this restaurant offers wonderful old-fashioned luxury and service, a view of Notre-Dame and a small museum. The dishes are rich and generous and the wines outstanding. A three-course lunch costs under €100; the sky's the limit for dinner. *15–17 Quai de la Tournelle. T: 01 43 54 23 31, www. latourdargent.com. Map p. 587, F3.*

Cité de la Mode. The €–€€ **Moon Roof** bar and restaurant (*open Mon–Sat 12–4, until 5pm on Sun, T: 01 44 24 39 34 or 06 23 04 08 81*) is a place to relax in the lounge bar with a drink or snack and to admire the view. Other places to eat and drink in the Cité include the popular **Wanderlust** restaurant, bar and night club, and the more casual **Café Nüba**. *Quai d'Austerlitz. www.citemodedesign.fr. Map p. 591, E1.*

€€ **Le Moissonnier**. Close to the Institut du Monde Arabe, in the style of a traditional '*bouchon lyonnais*', serving moderately-priced hearty meals in relaxed surroundings. *28 Rue des Fossés-St-Bernard. T: 01 43 29 87 65. Map p. 587, F3.*

€€ **Le Pré Verre**. Very popular, therefore essential to book. An unpretentious setting, excellent modern cooking, good-value midday *formule*. Roast suckling pig is recommended; also an impressive range of coffees. Closed Sun and Mon. *Rue Thénard. T: 01 43 54 59 47, www.lepreverre.com. Map p. 587, E3.*

€€ **Le Refuge du Passé**. Not far from the Jardin des Plantes, near Rue Mouffetard, a friendly, slightly old-fashioned bistrot-restaurant specialising in recipes from southwest France, such as *cassoulet au confit de canard*. Fixed-price menus and music. *32 Rue du Fer à Moulin. T: 01 47 07 29 91. Map p. 587, F4.*

€€ **Terroir Parisien**. ■ Modern bistrot and bar, part of chef Yannick Alléno's portfolio. The emphasis is on seasonal ingredients from the Île de France. Popular, lively and very good. *20 Rue St-Victor. T: 01 44 31 54 54.*

Institut du Monde Arabe. There are transparent lifts to Level 9, where the roof-terrace restaurant €–€€ **Le Zyriab** specialises in Lebanese cuisine and offers set lunch menus (*open Tues–Sun 12–3 & 7.30–midnight, T: 01 55 42 55 42*). There is also a cafeteria or 'Self' (*open Tues–Sun 11–3.30*). On Level 0 is the € **Café Littéraire**. *Map p. 587, F3.*

€ **Brasserie Balzar**. At the heart of the Quartier Latin, this reliable brasserie serves classic French dishes. Family-friendly, with a *plat du jour* Mon–Fri. Closed Sun. *49 Rue des Écoles. T: 01 43 54 13 67, www. brasseriebalzar.com. Map p. 587, E3.*

€ **Le Grenier de Notre-Dame**. Vegetarian, macrobiotic and vegan, this was the first restaurant of its kind to open in Paris, in 1978. *18 Rue de la Bûcherie. T: 01 43 29 98 29, www. legrenierdenotredame.fr. Map p. 587, E3.*

€ **La Maison de Verlaine**. A large plaque records that Verlaine died here on 8th January, 1896. A couple of decades later (1921–5), Hemingway rented a room in the same building in which to work uninterrupted. The smallish restaurant has stone walls, tightly-packed tables, photographs and memorabilia, and tables outside in fine weather. Closed Wed, and Thur midday. *39 Rue Descartes (near Pl. de la Contrescarpe). T: 01 43 26 39 15, www.lamaisondeverlaine.com. Map p. 587, E3.*

€ **Au Moulin à Vent**. Stalwart old bistrot with a loyal following, serving classic dishes (*côte de boeuf, cuisses de grenouille*) in a friendly, lively setting. *20 Rue des Fossés-St-Bernard. T: 01 43 54 99 37, www.au-moulinavent.com. Map p. 587, F3.*

€ **La Mosquée de Paris**. The café attached to the Paris Mosque is relaxed and informal, popular for a simple meal or a cup of mint tea and a sticky sweetmeat. Open daily. *Rue Geoffroy-St-Hilaire. T: 01 43 31 38 20, www.la-mosquee.com. Map p. 587, F4.*

For a feather-light treat, try **Patisserie Ciel** (*5 Rue Monge; map p. 587, F3*). There is a good bakery, butcher and delicatessen in **Place Maubert** (*map p. 587, E3*), where there is also an open-air market.

SAINT-GERMAIN-DES-PRÉS
View down the nave, with its Romanesque arches, to the Gothic choir.

Faubourg Saint-Germain

*As emblematic of Paris as the Quartier Latin or Montparnasse, but
timelessly elegant and fashionable, Faubourg St-Germain fascinates
every visitor to the city. The quartier has famous literary cafés, smart but
discreet hotels and restaurants, antiquarians selling books and bibelots
alongside modern galleries, the best in fashion boutiques as well as
colourful street markets and meandering urban lanes.*

The *faubourg* (suburb) of Saint-Germain (*map pp. 586–7*), named after the oldest of the major churches of Paris, stretches south from the Seine between the Institut de France to the east and the Pont de la Concorde to the west. In the eastern part, between Boulevard St-Michel, Rue des Saints-Pères and Boulevard Raspail (6th and 7th arrondissements), are the churches of St-Germain-des-Prés and St-Sulpice and the Musée Delacroix.

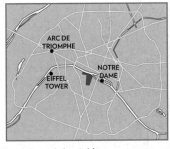

Here too are the Institut de France, Musée de la Monnaie and the Odéon.

In the Middle Ages much of this area, the property of the Abbaye St-Germain-des-Prés, was open country with a *bourg* which developed outside Philippe-Auguste's walls (*see p. 13*), bounded in the 13th century by rues du Vieux-Colombier and des Saints-Pères. Early in the 14th century more houses were built, and in the 17th century the abbey enclosure was gradually dismantled. With the 16th–17th century religious revival, several convents were established and, in 1670, the Hôtel des Invalides was constructed on the western outskirts. By 1685 the new Pont Royal provided easy access to the Palais des Tuileries, the home of the court during the Regency (1715–23). This, together with the creation of the École Militaire, was the main reason for building the new 18th-century aristocratic quarter which gradually supplanted the Marais.

About half of the houses were built in 1690–1725, a quarter between 1725 and 1750, and most of the remainder between 1750 and 1790. In style they are nonetheless very similar; often the more handsome façades face the interior garden, and the gateway or *porte-cochère* from the street leads to the Cour d'Honneur. Baron Haussmann (*see p. 284*) created the new main axes of Boulevard St-Germain, Rue de Rennes and Boulevard Raspail in the mid-19th century, cutting across many small streets and destroying a number of grand houses. Boulevard Raspail is the link between Boulevard St-Germain and Montparnasse.

RUE BONAPARTE

Map p. 587, D2. Métro 4 to St-Germain-des-Prés.

Rue Bonaparte runs south from the Seine towards the Jardin du Luxembourg. It is mainly a commercial street, although along its length are the two main churches of the district, St-Germain-des-Prés and St-Sulpice. The narrower and more interesting stretch, north of Boulevard St-Germain, is a great place to linger among the numerous antique shops and art galleries. The Hôtel du Marquis de Persan (nos 7–9) was the birthplace of the painter Édouard Manet in 1832.

THE CHURCH OF SAINT-GERMAIN-DES-PRÉS

Map p. 587, D2. Open 8–7. Visits to the Chapelle St-Symphorien (guided tour in French) Tues, Thur and third Sun of month at 3pm; T: 01 55 42 81 18.

The revered and reassuring tower of the church of St-Germain-des-Prés dominates its surroundings. Although heavily rebuilt and restored, this is the oldest church in Paris and the only one retaining any considerable remains of Romanesque work.

The church was a part of the great Benedictine abbey founded in 558 by Childebert I, who was buried here and who endowed the abbey with relics of St Vincent of Saragossa. St Germanus, Bishop of Paris (d. 576), was also interred on this site. The church became the burial place of the Merovingians. At the beginning of the 11th century it was rebuilt and the nave was completed up to the vaults in 1050. The massive flying buttresses of the choir are among the earliest in France. The base of the west tower also dates from this time (the bell-chamber itself is of c. 1644). Pope Alexander III consecrated the enlargement of the chancel in 1163 and in the 13th century the master mason, possibly Pierre de Montreuil (*see p. 503*), came up with a solution to the long-standing problem of how to vault the curved section of an ambulatory. The ensemble was embellished at this time with a Gothic Lady Chapel and cloisters. A small section of the cloisters stands in the gardens. Badly desecrated at the Revolution, the church suffered drastic alterations in the 19th century, which included the rebuilding of Pierre de Montreuil's Lady Chapel in 1819, the truncation in 1822 of the two towers flanking the choir and the restoration of the upper part of the west belfry. The church is entered from under the west tower. While the porch dates from 1607, it retains the jambs of a 12th-century door and a battered lintel depicting the *Last Supper*. A fragment of the 11th-century tympanum was found during excavations in 1971–3.

INTERIOR OF ST-GERMAIN-DES-PRÉS

The interior of St-Germain-des-Prés (65m by 21m, and 19m high) provides an important architectural document of the transition from Romanesque in the nave to the earliest Gothic in the choir. It was entirely painted with murals from 1842–64, by Hippolyte Flandrin and friends. By the 21st century, the interior of the church was

SAINT-GERMAIN-DES-PRÉS | 89

in urgent need of restoration and cleaning. A major campaign in five stages, starting in the east, began in 2011. The choir area has received a new stone floor, a new unadorned altar was consecrated in 2012, and modern-style wooden furnishings have been installed. The organ has also been overhauled and work on the church is ongoing.

(A) Chapelle St-Symphorien: The beautiful Chapelle St-Symphorien, begun in the 6th century and once the Merovingian necropolis, is on the south (right) of the entrance. Its high, simple interior is lit by windows high in the lateral walls. At the east end is the former triumphal arch that led to the apse (no longer extant). The soffit of the arch is decorated with fragments of 11th–12th century frescoes. The chapel is reserved for prayer but may be visited at the times given above.

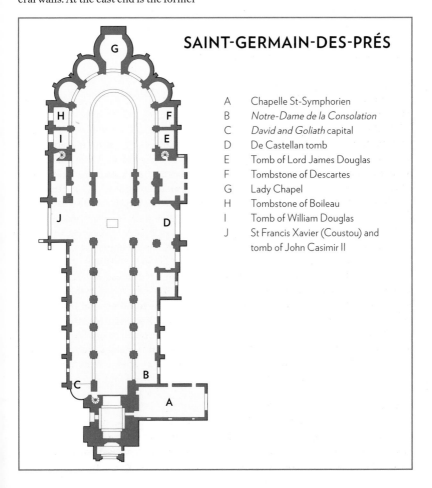

SAINT-GERMAIN-DES-PRÉS

A   Chapelle St-Symphorien
B   *Notre-Dame de la Consolation*
C   *David and Goliath* capital
D   De Castellan tomb
E   Tomb of Lord James Douglas
F   Tombstone of Descartes
G   Lady Chapel
H   Tombstone of Boileau
I   Tomb of William Douglas
J   St Francis Xavier (Coustou) and tomb of John Casimir II

ST-GERMAIN-DES-PRÉS CHURCHYARD
Detail of Picasso's *Head of a Woman* (1959), with the features of his lover Dora Maar, whom he had met in the Café des Deux Magots opposite the church in 1936.

West end: To the right of the entrance is the much-venerated marble image of ***Notre-Dame de Consolation* (B)**, presented to the Abbey of St-Denis by Queen Jeanne d'Evreux, consort of Charles IV, in 1340.

Nave and choir: In the 17th century, when the church was the chief house of the reformed Congregation of St-Maur, the wooden roof of the nave was replaced by a neo-Gothic vault and the transepts were remodelled. The **sculpted capitals** of the nave pillars are copies (1848–53) of the originals now in Musée du Cluny-Moyen Âge, with the exception of one in the northwest corner, which represents David and Goliath **(C)**.

The small marble columns in the triforium of the choir are re-used material from the 6th-century abbey of St-Vincent, and their bases and capitals are 12th century.

South side: In the south transept is the tomb, by Girardon, of Olivier and Louis de Castellan **(D)**, killed in royal service in 1644 and 1669 respectively. Renovations in the ambulatory in the 1950s revealed the 12th-century structure and capitals of some of the eastern chapels. In the first south ambulatory chapel is the tomb of Lord James Douglas **(E)** (d. 1645), commander of Louis XIII's Scots regiment, killed near Arras. In the second chapel is the **tombstone of Descartes (F)** (d. 1650), moved from Ste-Geneviève in 1819. The fourth chapel has fragments of 13th-century stained glass. The Lady Chapel **(G)**, which Pierre de Montreuil had designed and where he was buried, was rebuilt in the 19th century (its doorway is in the Musée du Moyen Âge).

North side: In the north ambulatory is the **tombstone of the poet Boileau (H)** (d. 1711), transferred from the Sainte-

Chapelle; and the tomb of William Douglas, 10th Earl of Angus **(I)**, who died in 1611 in the service of Henri IV. In the north transept **(J)** are a statue of the Jesuit missionary St Francis Xavier, by G. Coustou, and the theatrical tomb, by G. and B. Marsy, of John Casimir II, King of Poland, Abbot of St-Germain in 1669.

ENVIRONS OF THE CHURCH: THREE FAMOUS BRASSERIES

In the little gardens of Square Laurent-Prache, to the left of the church as you face it, are fragments of sculptures from the Lady Chapel (1212–55) and **Picasso's *Head of a Woman***, given in 1959 in homage to Guillaume Apollinaire. In Square F.-Desruelles, on the Blvd St-Germain side of the church, is a statue of the ceramicist Bernard Palissy and a monumental portico in ceramic and stone made at the Sèvres works by Risler for the Great Exhibition of 1900.

Opposite the entrance to the church is a sculpture by Zadkine. Here too, around the lively intersection Place Jean-Paul Sartre et Simone de Beauvoir, is a trio of brasseries made famous by denizens of the artistic and literary world—Romantics, Surrealists and Existentialists—until the 1950s. No longer the haunts of impoverished cutting-edge intellectuals, they are nevertheless still packed with visitors (and the odd local) seeking something of the old atmosphere or a good rendezvous. Each retains a certain individuality: **Café des Deux Magots** is named after the two *magots*, wooden Chinese statues (still preserved inside) and has a corner terrace; next door on Blvd. St-Germain, **Café de Flore** has an Art Deco interior and is marginally less hectic. Across the boulevard is the once ultra-fashionable **Brasserie Lipp**, specialising in the cuisine of Alsace. (*For contact details of the brasseries, see p. 102.*)

MUSÉE DELACROIX

Map p. 587, D2. 6 Rue du Furstemberg. Open Wed–Mon 9.30–5; closed Tues and 1 Jan, 1 May, 25 Dec. T: 01 44 41 86 50. Tickets for the Louvre also valid for Musée Delacroix on the same day.

In 1857, six years before he died, Eugène Delacroix moved from Rue Notre-Dame de la Lorette (*map p. 582, B3*) to the first-floor apartment at 6 Rue de Furstemberg (or Furstenberg). Seriously ill, he needed to be close to St-Sulpice, for which he was preparing three large paintings, and was delighted to discover this abode with its little square of garden (now returned to its 1850s layout). The studio was later shared by Monet and Bazille. The Musée Delacroix is an intimate space that gives a fascinating insight into the artist's life through memorabilia such as his palette and paint table, objects which he brought back from Morocco in 1832, as well as letters written by, and photos of, the painter. There is also a collection of small paintings by Delacroix, including *The Education of the Virgin* (1842; inspired by a scene he observed of a farmer teaching her daughter to read), *Mary Magdalene in the Desert* (1845), other portraits, and works on paper; there are also works by other artists.

Place de Furstemberg is grandly named for something that is no more than a bulge in the street. Picturesquely shaded by four Paulownias and lit by a five-globed street

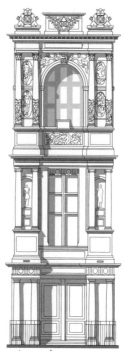

CHÂTEAU D'ANET

lamp, it has been the subject of many paintings. It was opened in 1699 by Cardinal Egon of Fürstenberg, Abbot of St-Germain-des-Prés, to serve the abbey palace and was in fact built as an outer courtyard surrounded by stabling and accommodation, including the house that is now the Musée Delacroix.

ÉCOLE DES BEAUX-ARTS

Map p. 587, D2. Main entrance at 14 Rue Bonaparte. Open Tues–Sun 1–7, closed Mon. Certain buildings can be visited; T: 01 47 03 50 14. Occasional visits with CMN (see p. 540). Entrance for temporary exhibitions at 13 Quai Malaquais.

The origins of the École des Beaux-Arts (School of Fine Arts) go back to L'Académie Royale de Peinture et de Sculpture, which Mazarin created in 1648 and which was partly closed in 1793. The parts of it that continued to function became the École Nationale Supérieure des Beaux-Arts. Its first home was the Louvre, then it moved to Rue Mazarine (*map p. 587, D2*), and since 1829 it has occupied the site of the former convent of the Petits-Augustins, founded in 1608 across the river from the Louvre. The school inherited part of the varied collections of the Royal Academies.

THE BUILDINGS

The large group of buildings making up the School occupies a vast space between Rue Bonaparte and Quai Malaquais. The transformation was begun in 1820 by Debret and finished in 1862 by his pupil Félix Duban. Some parts of the old convent were incorporated into it, notably the 17th-century chapel. It was here that Alexandre Lenoir, archaeologist and fervent protector of French monuments, collected together numerous pieces of sculpture, including the tombs of the kings from St-Denis, saving them from destruction during the Revolutionary period. At the Restoration many, but not all, were returned to their place of origin or dispersed among museums (*see below*). The building was further enlarged in 1883 by the acquisition of the Hôtel de Chimay, built by François Mansart c. 1640 and altered in the 18th century. This was the first great architectural school. Most great names in art studied here at some point during the 19th and 20th centuries.

From the street it is possible to glimpse on the right, against the former convent church, the re-erected central part of the façade of the **Château d'Anet** (c. 1540), a rare extant work of Philibert de l'Orme, celebrated architect to François I. This façade is cited as the earliest example in France of the correct use of the three orders of architecture according to Vitruvius: Doric on the lowest storey, followed by Ionic and then Corinthian. The Château d'Anet, which stood to the west of Paris, had been built for Diane de Poitiers, favourite of Henri II. The hexagonal **Chapelle des Louanges**, on the Rue Bonaparte side, was built by Marguerite de Valois, first wife of Henri IV. Its dome is the earliest built in the city (1608).

ALEXANDRE LENOIR

When in 1793 the Convention ordered the destruction of the 'tombs of kings' and other undesirable monuments of the *Ancien Régime*, a young artist by the name of Alexandre Lenoir (1762–1839) stepped forward to save what he could. Lenoir was not a particularly gifted artist but he did have a keen sense of the value of art and its importance to a nation's sense of itself. Perturbed by the sight of statues of saints with their noses hacked off, the graves of monarchs pillaged and their bones cast into ditches, he gathered together a collection of works from churches, convents, monasteries and other institutions all over France and housed them for safekeeping in the old Couvent des Petits-Augustins. Lenoir was a keen supporter of Napoleon's policy of garnering spoils of war, and while grand works pillaged from Italy and Germany were placed in the Louvre, Lenoir opened the Petits-Augustins as the Musée des Monuments Français. It was an enormous popular success. Later art historians have tended to criticise Lenoir, objecting that his methods were haphazard, his system of dating lamentable, his restorations clumsy and his attributions suspect. He was not, it is true, a trained curator. Instead he was an amateur enthusiast, and it is as such that his achievement should be judged. There can be no doubt that he did France a great service in saving so much from oblivion. After the fall of Napoleon in 1815, many plundered artworks were returned. Likewise Louis XVIII ordered Lenoir to give back what works he could to the institutions they had come from. That there was anything at all to give back is entirely thanks to his dedication and zeal.   A.B.

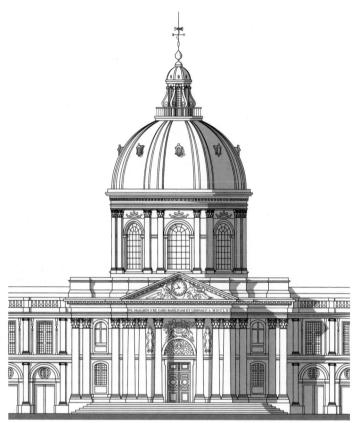

INSTITUT DE FRANCE: CENTRAL NORTH FRONT

INSTITUT DE FRANCE

Map p. 587, D2. Occasional visits with CMN (see p. 540).

Place de l'Institut, on the south bank of the Seine facing the Louvre, is flanked by the curved wings of the Institut de France. These prestigious premises, with their gilded dome, are the most beautiful on this reach of the river.

This is an outstanding structure, without parallel in 17th-century France, the oval cupola and semicircular façade embodying characteristics typical of the Roman Baroque. Louis Le Vau (*see p. 46*) was responsible for the initial design, which was built between 1662 and 1691 on the axis of the Cour Carrée of the Louvre. The architects Lambert and d'Orbay continued where Le Vau left off.

The building was erected in accordance with the bequest of Cardinal Mazarin, powerful statesman and first Minister of France while Anne of Austria acted as regent (1643–61) during the minority of Louis XIV. He gave two million *livres* in silver and 45,000 *livres* a year for the establishment of a college for 60 gentlemen of the four provinces acquired by the Treaty of the Pyrenees: Artois, Alsace, Roussillon and Piedmont (Pinerolo), and the college was always known as the Collège des Quatre-Nations rather than by its official title, Collège Mazarin.

The Institute, founded in 1795, acquired the building in 1806 and moved from the Louvre. The east wing of the complex and the adjacent Hôtel de la Monnaie (*see below*) cover the site of the Hôtel de Nesle (13th century), in which was incorporated the Tour Nesle or Hamelin, the river bastion of Philippe-Auguste's wall (which ran southeast, parallel to Rue Mazarine). The western part, known as the Petit-Nesle (the workshop in 1540–5 of the goldsmith Benvenuto Cellini, who was invited to France by François I), was demolished in 1663. The eastern part, or Grand-Nesle, rebuilt in 1648 by François Mansart, became the Hôtel de Conti, and in 1770, the Hôtel de la Monnaie.

THE ACADEMIES

The Institut de France comprises five academies: the Académie Française, founded by Cardinal Richelieu in 1635 and restricted to 40 members, with the particular task of editing the dictionary of the French language; the Académie des Beaux-Arts (1816), founded by Mazarin in 1648 as the Académie Royale de Peinture et de Sculpture; the Académie des Inscriptions et Belles-Lettres, founded by Colbert in 1663; the Académie des Sciences, also founded by Colbert, in 1666; and the Académie des Sciences Morales et Politiques, founded in 1795 and reorganised in 1832. The Institut is also responsible for several collections, among them the Musée Marmottan Monet (*see p. 431*). An annual general meeting of all five academies is held on 25th October. The Académie Française holds special receptions for newly-elected members who are known as *Les Immortels* (because their ranks are always refilled). In 1980 the first woman member was elected: the writer Marguerite Yourcenar (1903–87), author of the *Memoirs of Hadrian* (1951).

INSIDE THE INSTITUT DE FRANCE

From the first octagonal courtyard (beyond which are two others, one of them the Kitchen Courtyard of the old college), an elegant staircase (1824) by Vaudoyer leads to the Bibliothèque Mazarine, where little has changed since the 17th century. It contains some 450,000 volumes, 4,600 manuscripts and 2,100 incunabula. Originally the cardinal's personal library, it opened to scholars in 1643, became the first public library in France and was considerably augmented by other collections during the Revolutionary period. The Institut library is also in this wing, together with several rooms decorated with academic statues and busts of eminent academicians. In the former chapel in the west wing is the Salle des Séances Solennelles. Restoration has removed many of Vaudoyer's other interventions and Mazarin's tomb, by Coysevox, has been returned from the Louvre. The room contains some 400 seats (green for members of the Académie Française, red for the others) and is used for receptions and general meetings.

MUSÉE DE LA MONNAIE

Map p. 587, D2. 11 Quai de Conti. Open Tues–Sun 11–7, Thur to 10pm; closed Mon and holidays. T: 01 40 46 55 35.

The Monnaie de Paris (or Mint), the oldest of the French institutions, celebrated its 1150th anniversary in 2014. There are regular temporary exhibitions but the permanent museum is undergoing a major project of renovation styled the *Metalmorphosis*. At the time of writing the reopening of the Manufacture and Mansart wing had been scheduled.

The Monnaie de Paris (EPIC) is, since 1st Jan 2007, simultaneously an institution responsible for a sovereign function of the state—the production of official French currency—and an industrial enterprise, a corporate brand, a museum and a home of artistic creation. Its home, the Hôtel de la Monnaie (1768–77), is a vast and handsome building designed by the architect Jacques-Denis Antoine, with a Neoclassical façade 117m long. The pillared entrance, ornamented with Louis XV's monogram and elegant bronze door knockers, gives access to the magnificent Cour d'Honneur, flanked by two smaller courtyards. From the 18th-century vestibule, a double staircase ascends to Salle Guillaume Dupré, a superb Louis XVI-style room named after the chief engraver of medals in the 17th century. This was the first École des Mines. It then became the coin museum until 1983 and the workshops were housed in an adjoining mansion built by Jules Hardouin-Mansart, also in the process of restoration, which will be part of the visit. A long series of rooms overlooking the Seine is dedicated to temporary exhibitions.

Although in 1973 the minting of French coins was transferred to Pessac, near Bordeaux, some pieces, in gold, silver and bronze, are still minted here, continuing a centuries-long tradition. These include medals, trophies, commemorative tokens, tourist and event tokens, customised pieces, as well as collectables and jewellery.

The permanent display plans to show the workshops and previously hidden treasures of the Monnaie de Paris collection, with workshop tours on offer. High-quality metalwork pieces will be on sale in a new shop, with further outlets for luxury goods in the courtyards. Two new places to eat, under the auspices of Guy Savoy, were due to open at the time of writing: a gourmet restaurant on the riverside and the MetaLmorphoses cafe-brasserie in an interior courtyard.

THE QUAYS

The **Quai des Grands-Augustins** (*map p. 587, D2–E2*), between Pont St-Michel and the Pont Neuf, built in 1313, is the oldest in Paris. It took its name from a 13th-century convent which was demolished in 1797, but some fine 14th–16th-century mansions, several now restaurants, have survived. A segment of Philippe-Auguste's wall, built in

1200–10 and which ended where the Institut de France now stands, is visible at the end of the Rue de Nevers (entered below an arch). The embankment or *quai* here, as elsewhere on this reach of the Seine, is lined with the bookstalls of the *bouquinistes*, who sell new and not-so-new publications.

No. 13 Quai de Conti, **Hôtel Guénégaud** by François Mansart (1659), was owned by a Mme Permon who had Corsican connections, and the young Napoleon Bonaparte stayed there briefly. From 1805–32 Napoleon's surgeon, Baron Dominique Larrey, inventor of the ambulance (*see p. 161*), occupied the first floor.

LOVE LOCKS

A growing trend in Paris, 'city of love', in the last few years is for amorous couples to attach padlocks to bridges, an addiction which has become a threat to the bridges and a problem to the authorities. The tradition began in Rome, on the Milvian Bridge, inspired by a scene from *Ho Voglia di Te*, the 2007 film adaptation of a novel by Francesco Moccia, which shows a girl persuading her boyfriend to attach a padlock (a red one, with a long shackle) to the bridge and cast the key into the Tiber, vowing to remain true to her forever after. The thicket of lovers' padlocks that followed this screen declaration was removed from the Milvian Bridge in 2012.

Meanwhile, the craze had spread to Paris, where 54 tons of love locks were recently excised from the **Pont des Arts** (*map p. 587, D2*), which was collapsing under their weight. Glass and fibreboard panels (albeit susceptible to graffiti) have now replaced the mesh to which the padlocks were attached.

Love padlocks are quite a business and are sold in a variety of colours with heart-shaped keys. Pont de l'Archevêché is also badly afflicted, and padlocks are beginning to appear in other places as well, including Pont Neuf and the Eiffel Tower. A.B. & D.G-D.

Quai Malaquais has a number of 17th–18th-century mansions. No. 9, at the corner of Rue Bonaparte, the Hôtel de Transylvanie, is a good example of Louis XIII architecture (1622–8). Henrietta Maria, daughter of Henri IV and widow of Charles I of England, lived at no. 17, part of the Hôtel de Chimay.

Quai Voltaire (*map 586, C2–C1*), between Pont du Carrousel and Pont Royal, was a sought-after address for writers and artists in the 18th and 19th centuries. The controversial writer and philosopher François Voltaire, author of *Lettres philosophiques* (1734), died at no. 27. Dominique Ingres died at no. 11 in 1867, and Delacroix lived at no. 13 in 1829–36, as later did Corot. Baudelaire lived at no. 19 in 1856–8 while writing *Les Fleurs du Mal*, and Wagner completed the libretto of *Die Meistersinger* at the same address in 1861–2; later tenants included the Finnish composer Sibelius as well as Oscar Wilde.

RUE ST-ANDRÉ-DES-ARTS & THE ODÉON

The area around Rue St-André-des-Arts (*map p. 587, D2*), which runs east to Place St-Michel, is a veritable labyrinth of ancient alleys which are fun to explore. In **Rue Hautefeuille** leading south, is the Hôtel des Abbés de Fécamp, at no. 5, with a pretty turret. Rue St-André-des-Arts itself has interesting 17th–18th-century buildings (nos. 27, 28 and 52) and meets Rue Dauphine (1607) at the **Carrefour de Buci**, where there is an enticing street market.

Rue de l'Éperon meets Rue du Jardinet, at the end of which an alley forms the entrance to the **Cour de Rohan** (16th–17th centuries), originally part of the palace of the Archbishop of Rouen, with an old mounting block still in place. Through the arch on the left, behind the window of the boutique at 4 Cour de Commerce-St-André, is the base of one of Philippe-Auguste's towers. Popular myth has it that at no. 9 opposite, Dr Joseph-Ignace Guillotin, professor of anatomy, perfected his 'philanthropic beheading machine', although in fact he merely proposed to the National Assembly that beheading should be the only method of capital punishment, preferably by machine. A mechanic built a model to the specifications of the secretary of the College of Surgeons, Dr Louis, which was put into operation on 25th April 1792, and was first known as the Louisette.

Rue de l'Ancienne Comédie takes its name from the Comédie Française of 1689–1770, which occupied no. 14. Opposite at no. 13 is **La Procope**, claimant to being the oldest café in Paris, with a picturesque interior on three floors and adequate-enough food. Opened in 1686, it was the favourite haunt of many generations of writers—Voltaire, Balzac, George Sand and Oscar Wilde among them.

The extension of Rue de l'Ancienne Comédie, **Rue Mazarine**, runs north to the Institut de France (*see above*). No. 42 was the site of a real tennis court, the Jeu de Paume de la Bouteille, where the Abbé Perrin established the Opéra in 1669–72; it was occupied by Molière's company in 1673–80, followed by the Comédie Française in 1680–9. No. 12 is the site of another *jeu de paume*, where the Illustre Théâtre was opened in December 1643 by Molière's company, and no. 30, known as the Hôtel des Pompes, was until 1760 the headquarters of the *pompiers* or fire brigade of Paris, founded in 1722.

L'ODÉON

South of Boulevard Saint-Germain, isolated and surrounded by arcades, stands the Odéon-Théâtre de l'Europe (*map p. 587, D3; www.theatre-odeon.eu*), a focus of attention during the student protests in 1968. It was built in 1779–82 as the Théâtre Français, in the form of a Classical temple on the site of the former Hôtel de Condé and its gardens, which Marie de Médicis had sold to Henri II, Comte de Condé, heir presumptive to the throne, in 1612. Several generations of Condé lived there, and it was finally acquired by Louis XV who pulled it down to build the theatre. This was the most important work of architects Charles de Wailly and Marie-Joseph Peyre. The name was changed to Théâtre de l'Odéon in 1797 and it had to be rebuilt by Chalgrin following a fire in 1799, to re-open in 1808. The ceiling of the auditorium was decorated by André Masson in 1965 and the theatre has hosted many controversial and memorable plays. In the Grand Foyer is the Café de l'Odéon (*open midday–1am*).

Rue de l'Odéon, bordered by 18th-century houses, slopes downhill towards the Carrefour de l'Odéon. At no. 12 was Sylvia Beach's bookshop, Shakespeare and Co. At the Café Voltaire (closed in 1956), near the Carrefour, a banquet was held in honour of Gauguin before he left for Tahiti in 1891.

ÉGLISE DE SAINT-SULPICE

Map p. 587, D3. Place St-Sulpice. Open 7.30–7.30. Guided visits Sat 2.30–5.30 (meet at the sacristy), Sun 3pm (meet under the organ loft). Visits to the crypt (no large groups) on second Sun of the month at 3.30; contact visites@pssparis.net or T: 01 42 34 59 98.

The wealthiest church on the Left Bank, Saint-Sulpice is a fine Italianate building whose size imposes on the surrounding area. The sober west front, like a Roman theatre, features a two-storey colonnade of superimposed Doric and Ionic orders. The north tower, topped by a balustrade, is 73m high; the unfinished south tower is 5m lower. The scale of the project and the change in style of the elevations, notably the Jesuit or Baroque characteristics of the transept arm, are obvious from Rue Palatine on the south flank.

A succession of masons and a succession of designs mark the character of this church. Begun in 1646 to replace an older structure, it was continued on a larger scale in 1670. After an interval from 1678 to 1719, work was resumed by Gilles-Marie Oppenordt, following Gittard's design, but the tower that was added above the crossing had to be demolished after 1731. The building of the west front was entrusted to Giovanni Servandoni, a Florentine, who was replaced in 1766 by Oudot de Maclaurin. His successor, Chalgrin, built the north tower in 1778–80, but the south tower was left incomplete.

THE INTERIOR

In the form of a Latin cross, the interior is spacious and regular in Counter-Reformation style, measuring 115m long by 57m wide and 33m high, with tall arcades to the aisles. The church is noted for its music and organ recitals. In fact the **organ** is one of the largest in existence (6,588 pipes). It was built in 1781 and remodelled in 1860–2; the case was designed by Chalgrin, with statues by Clodion and decoration by Duret.

Among the other church furnishings are two **holy-water stoups** in the form of huge *Tridacna gigas* (giant clam) shells, presented to François I by the Venetian Republic and supported on 'rocks' carved from marble by Pigalle. Plenty of Paris churches have clam-shell stoups, but not Pigalle's rocks, richly carved with seaweed, squid and other forms of marine life.

SAINT-SULPICE
Jacob Wrestling with the Angel, by Delacroix (1855–61).

The late 18th-century **pulpit**, designed by Wailly, bears gilded figures of *Faith* (with chalice) and *Hope* (with anchor) by Guesdon, and *Charity* (above, with numerous children) by Dumont.

The lateral chapels are decorated with frescoes. The most important are the **late works by Delacroix** in the first chapel on the right (1855–61). These vigorous images of spiritual conflict represent, in the vault, *St Michael Vanquishing the Devil*; on the left, *Jacob Wrestling with the Angel*; and on the right, *Heliodorus Driven from the Temple*. In the fifth right-hand chapel is the **tomb of the *curé* Jean-Baptiste-Joseph Languet de Gergy** (d. 1750) by the Neoclassical Academic sculptor Michel-Ange Slodtz, who trained in Rome for 17 years. The sculpture represents the power of the Christian soul over death, with an angel thrusting back the curtain of mortality, beneath with crouches a skeleton. The influence of Bernini is marked. Languet founded l'Orphelinat-Hôpital de l'Enfant-Jésus in 1724 on Rue de Vaugirard, and in

1802 on the same site the Enfants-Malades, the first paediatric hospital in the world (since 1926 called the Necker-Enfants Malades). The *curé* was also responsible for the completion of the church.

In the paving of the south transept is a marble plaque connected by a bronze **meridian line** to a marble obelisk in the north transept. At noon the sun's rays, passing through an aperture in a blind window in the south transept, strike the meridian at specific points according to the time of year: during the winter solstice the sun strikes the obelisk, and during the spring and autumn equinox, the ray strikes the marble plaque.

The **south sacristy** has some good 18th-century woodwork. The statues against the pillars of the **choir** are by Bouchardon and his workshop (1740). The high windows in the choir are 17th-century except the *Sacré Coeur*, which is of 1885. The sizeable domed **Lady Chapel** at the east end was designed by Servandoni but damaged by fire in 1762; its trappings were restored by Wailly in 1774. The original painting (1731–2) by F. Lemoyne in the cupola (*difficult to see*) has undergone several alterations. The subtly-lit marble *Virgin* (placed here in 1774), in the niche behind the altar, is by Pigalle, with angels by another hand. The bronze altar relief (1730) is another work by Michel-Ange Slodtz.

PLACE SAINT-SULPICE

The large forecourt of the church, Place St-Sulpice, has since 1844 been embellished with the ***Fontaine des Quatre-Évêques*** by Visconti, featuring statues of four famous preaching bishops: Bossuet, Fénelon, Massillon and Fléchier. Hemingway noted that pigeons often settled on their heads: they still do. The square is a charming and elegant part of the Left Bank, with a number of cafés and restaurants. In June it hosts an antiques fair and in December a Christmas Fair. At no. 6 is a dignified mansion by Servandoni (1754), the first of a range which never fully materialised.

Once filled with shops selling ecclesiastical artefacts, the neighbourhood's retail focus for the last few decades has become rather more '*designer*'. North of Place St-Sulpice is a small garden, **l'Allée du Séminaire**, with shady chestnut trees and the *Fontaine de La Paix*. To the south of St-Sulpice, in Rue Servandoni, is Mundolingua (*see p. 518*). **Rue de Cassette** nearby (*map p. 586, C3*) is one of the oldest streets in this district, with 18th–century houses.

EATING AND DRINKING AROUND SAINT-GERMAIN

There is a huge choice of cafés, restaurants and bars of all types in the Saint-Germain area. There is a famous street market and food shops on **Rue de Buci** (*map p. 587, D2*). **La Procope** on Rue de l'Ancienne Comédie (*see p. 98*) claims to be the oldest café in Paris (*open Sun–Wed 11.30–midnight; Thur–Sat 11.30–1am, T: 01 40 46 79 00, www.procope.com, map p. 587, D2*). €€ **Café de l'Odéon**, inside the famous theatre (*map p. 587, D3*), makes full use of the building and its position, with tables under the arcades facing Place de l'Odéon in less clement weather, and spreading out onto the Place in fair weather. The attractively-presented choice of dishes is fairly limited, and tends toward the light and healthy.

Two famous literary cafés/brasseries maintain an aura of times gone by (and all-day service). One is €–€€ **Les Deux Magots** (*6 Pl. St-Germain-des-Près, T: 01 45 48 55 25, www.lesdeuxmagots.fr, open 7.30am–1am; map p. 587, D2*). Founded in 1884, it adopted the name of the shop it replaced and remains fairly traditional. The food is good and on the east side it has a view of the church of St-Germain. Great for a '*pause café*' or '*apéro*' at any time of day. Next to Les Deux Magots is the equally famous €–€€ **Café de Flore** (*26 Rue St-Benoit, T: 01 45 48 55 26, www.cafedeflore.fr, open 7am–2am*), with an Art Deco interior. A brasserie, therefore it serves all meals, it is renowned for its *chocolat chaud* and crunchy baguettes. Opposite is €–€€ **Brasserie Lipp** (*151 Blvd. St-Germain, T: 01 45 48 53 91, open 8.30am–2am*), which preserves much of its 130-year-old charm, with serried rows of tables draped in white tablecloths. The food also retains its Alsace ancestry to a degree, with traditional dishes including *pied de porc farci grillé* (grilled stuffed pig's trotter). It is difficult to get seated in the downstairs area, but much better if you can manage it.

Below are a few other suggestions:

€€€ **L'Atelier de Joël Robuchon**. This was the first bistrot to introduce the idea of customers sitting at a bar around an open kitchen (there are also tables). This is French cuisine with an original twist, both beautiful and delicious, but not inexpensive. The *menu découvert* is a particular treat. *5 Rue de Montalembert. T: 01 42 22 56 56, www.atelier-robuchon-saint-germain.com. Map p. 586, C2.*

€€–€€€ **Le Restaurant**. ■ In the hotel called L'Hôtel (*see p. 530*), this is an elegant choice for a special occasion, offering an intimate dining experience (40 covers) in a room which opens onto a small patio. Service is friendly and the dishes, prepared by Julien Montbabut and which follow the seasons, are a culinary delight. Closed Mon. *13 Rue des Beaux-Arts. T: 01 44 41 99 01, www.l-hotel.com. Map p. 587, D2.*

€–€€ **Le Chardenoux des Prés**. A 1970s' Left-Bank bistrot recreated by chef Cyril Lignac, with a slightly political stance and featuring leather banquettes, busy wallpaper and photos of former Presidents of the Republic, plus excellent food and an affordable lunch menu. (Lignac's other establishments are Le Cardenoux in the 11è and *pâtisseries* in the 11è and 16è.) *27 Rue du Dragon. T: 01 45 48 29 68, www.restaurantlechardenouxdespres. com. Map p. 586, C2.*

€–€€ Le Comptoir du Relais. A small updated brasserie/bistrot (essential to book). *9 Carrefour de l'Odéon (the northern section of Rue de l'Odéon, leading into Blvd St-Germain). T: 01 44 27 07 97. Map p. 587, D3.*

€–€€ Semilla. Modern bistrot with an open kitchen and friendly service. Good food and wine, excellent lunch menus. In the same family as Così. *54 Rue de Seine. T: 01 43 54 34 50. Map p. 587, D2.*

€ Le Bar du Marché. Crowded and buzzing, this is the place to watch the world go by. Known familiarly as BDM. *75 Rue de Seine. T: 01 43 26 55 15. Map p. 587, D2.*

€ Casa Bini. Close to l'Odéon, for a touch of the Mediterranean in Paris. The weekday menus are reasonably priced and choices change regularly. *36 Rue Grégoire de Tours. T: 01 46 34 05 60, www.casabini.fr. Map p. 587, D2.*

€ Così. A place that satisfies any craving you may have for a good, generously-filled fresh focaccia sandwich. *54 Rue de Seine. T: 01 46 33 35 37. Map p. 587, D2.*

€ Da Rosa. Grocery store and bistrot, perfect for a bowl of soup or a light snack. *62 Rue de Seine. T: 01 40 52 00 09. Map p. 587, D2.*

€ Emporio Armani Caffè. Above the shop of the same name on the corner of St-Germain and Rue de Rennes. It offers an opportunity for a glass of wine and an Italian taster during the arduous task of trying on all those designer jeans; prices a bit hefty, matching those of the merchandise, but they have wifi. *149 Blvd. St-Germain. T: 01 45 48 62 15. Map p. 586, C2.*

€ Mariage Frères. One of several Mariage Frères outlets. Head upstairs for brunch (12–6.30) or afternoon tea and *pâtisserie* Parisian style, or a light lunch. *13 Rue des Grands-Augustins. T: 01 40 51 82 50, www.mariagefreres. com. Map p. 587, D2.*

€ Pâtisserie Viennoise. Very small and simple, doing good food, hot chocolate and especially cakes and desserts. *Rue de l'École de Médecine. T: 01 43 26 60 48. Map p. 587, D3.*

Musée d'Orsay

*The grander, western part of Faubourg St-Germain accommodates
the Musée d'Orsay, with its unparalleled collection, and several
embassies and ambassadorial residences in elegant 17th–18th-century
hôtels particuliers. Here too is the Musée de la Légion d'Honneur.
Palais Bourbon is home of the Assemblée Nationale.*

Quai Anatole-France (*map p. 586, B1–
C1*) runs between Pont Royal and Pont
de la Concorde, in front of the Musée
d'Orsay. The improvement of a vast section of the southern banks of the Seine was
begun in 1708 and completed at the beginning of
the 19th century. Quai Anatole-France received
its present name in 1947. The Passerelle de
Solférino (1997–9), a single-span footbridge,
links the southern embankment to the Tuileries

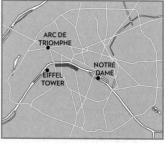

Gardens. It is named after a bloody battle fought in Lombardy in 1859, at which the
combined forces of Piedmont and France, under Vittorio Emanuele and Napoléon III,
were victorious over Austria. It was on visiting the battlefield that Henry Dunant was
moved to found the Red Cross.

Wide steps below the Musée d'Orsay descend to a floating garden, restaurants and
sports and play areas.

MUSÉE D'ORSAY

*Map p. 586, C1. Métro 12 to Solférino or RER C to Musée d'Orsay. Open Tues–Sun 9.30–
6, Thur until 9.45pm; closed Mon; T: 01 40 49 48 00 or 01 40 49 49 78. There are frequent
temporary exhibitions (Level 5), concerts, films and symposia.*

*Like most major museums, the Musée d'Orsay cannot display all its works at any one
time and the presentation is constantly changing. The key works will, for the most part,
remain on display, and overall themes and categories will be maintained, although there
may be changes in emphasis. The location of artworks is updated every morning before
the museum opens: for the latest information consult the museum website (www.musee-
orsay.fr) under the heading 'The Museum in Motion', and 'Calendar' for daily events.*

MUSÉE D'ORSAY

There are three places to eat in the museum: the self-service Café de l'Ours (Level 0); the original restaurant of the railway station, with 1900s décor (Level 2); Café Campana, brasserie-style (Level 5). There is an outlet for takeaway snacks on the forecourt.

The huge and ornate bulk of the former Gare d'Orsay, still bearing the names of destinations it once served—Orléans, Bordeaux, Toulouse—dominates the southern embankment on Quai Anatole-France. It has two great clocks above the massive glazed arcades and large allegorical figures look out from the façade across the river. A favourite museum, mainly for its important Impressionist and Post-Impressionist collections, it attracts large numbers of visitors. Recent reorganisation of the layout has improved circulation, especially in the Impressionist galleries.

HISTORY OF THE BUILDING

The building was originally the Gare and Hôtel d'Orsay, erected in 1898–1900 by Victor Laloux on the site of the ancient Cour des Comptes, set ablaze in 1871 during the Commune (*see p. 22*). The metal frame of the elevation towards the Seine, both functional and decorative, was faced with stone to complement the Louvre on the opposite bank. The old hôtel façade faces west on Rue de la Légion d'Honneur. The artist Édouard Detaille remarked ironically at the time that the railway station looked exactly like a Palais des Beaux-Arts—but 86 years elapsed before the transformation took place. By 1939 the station had virtually outlived its usefulness because of its short platforms and, after a succession of roles, the condemned building was saved in the 1970s thanks to a revival of interest in the conservation of 19th-century industrial architecture. In 1973, during the government of Georges Pompidou, a museum was envisaged but the project only began seriously to take shape in 1978 at the time of Giscard d'Estaing. It was finally opened by François Mitterrand in December 1986.

A team from ACT Architecture undertook the task; Gae Aulenti designed the interior. The intention was to create a museum on a human scale without sacrificing the original perspectives of the building. The central hall alone is 138m long spanned by a glazed and coffered vault with 1,600 rosettes. The installations use a quantity of pale, polished Buxy stone, designed neither to emulate nor to vie with the original building. Certain rooms retain their original Belle-Époque decoration.

THE COLLECTIONS

The Musée d'Orsay continues chronologically where the Louvre leaves off. National collections from the 1840s to the early 20th century were assembled here from the Musée de Luxembourg, the Louvre, the Jeu de Paume, the Palais de Tokyo and provincial museums, as well as through donations and acquisition. The collections include all aspects of the visual arts: painting, sculpture, graphic and decorative arts, and photography. On the museum forecourt are bronzes commissioned for the first Trocadéro Palace built for the Paris Universal Exhibition of 1878, and on Rue de Lille are works of 1925 by Bourdelle.

Some 4,000 works are permanently on display, arranged chronologically and thematically, illustrating the rapid changes and wide range in styles from the mid-19th century to the First World War. The permanent exhibition space is divided into around 80 separate sections or rooms over three main floors. The recommended sequence begins on the ground floor, Level 0 (19th-century works) followed by Level 5 (Impressionism). On Level 2 are Salon paintings, Post-Impressionism and Decorative Arts, as well as large sculptures. Highlights of the collections are given below. Because of rearrangement and the possibility of works being out on loan, the description should not be taken as a catalogue of which works you will see, but as an overview of the styles, mannerisms and preoccupations of French art during the period covered by the museum.

LEVEL 0: BEFORE IMPRESSIONISM

CENTRAL AISLE: SCULPTURE 1850–80

Below the great station clock steps descend into the large, lucid central concourse (Allée Centrale), populated mainly by large sculptures of the period 1850–70, contrasting Classical and Romantic tendencies. Works in the collection include Pradier's composed version of *Sappho* (marble, 1852), challenged by a vigorous plaster model of the same subject by Carpeaux (c. 1855). Also in the collection by Carpeaux, the principal French sculptor of his day, are a passionate *Ugolino* (1862) and maquettes for major public commissions: *La Danse* for the Opéra Garnier and the *Four Quarters of the Globe* fountain for Avenue de l'Observatoire (*see p. 156*), one of his last works. A marble nude, *Woman Bitten by a Snake* (1847) by Auguste Clésinger, caused a double scandal: because of its subject and because the sculptor had made an initial mould directly from life. Barye, best known for animal subjects, is represented here by a plaster model (1860–5) for an equestrian statue of *Napoleon I as a Roman Emperor*. There are also striking works in bronze and onyx by the ethnographic sculptor Charles Cordier.

Halfway up the central aisle, facing it on the right, is Thomas Couture's huge canvas *Romans of the Decadence* (1847). In the guise of a history painting, in which the artist combines Classicism with subtle 18th-century colouring, it was intended as a metaphor for the vices of contemporary society. The work was equally appreciated for its dimensions, technical skill and orgiastic content. Manet studied under this gifted teacher for several years before rebelling against his rigid academicism.

LILLE SIDE, ROOMS 1–3 & 11–13

During the period 1850–80 there was a shift from the Classicism of David towards Romanticism. Ingres' *La Source* (completed in 1856) tends towards Neoclassicism in its refined style, but not so in subject matter. The leading Romantic painter, Eugène Delacroix, drew inspiration from colourists such as Rubens and Veronese and his sketch for *Lion Hunt* is full of energy and turmoil. Préault's bronze relief *Ophélie* (1876) also fits the tenets of Romanticism, whereas the two poles combine in *The Tepidarium* (1853) by Théodore Chassériau, a student of Ingres, admirer of Delacroix and, later, teacher of Moreau. The subject was based on one of the *thermae* discovered at Pompeii. *The Birth of Venus*, a pretext for a luscious nude by Alexandre Cabanel, successful in the Salon of 1863, was purchased by Napoléon III. William Bouguereau tackled the same theme in 1879. Leading French artists who studied at the French Academy in Rome include Ernest Hébert, whose *La Mal'aria* shows Italian peasants escaping a malaria epidemic. He was twice director of the Academy.

Charming records of an affluent society include *The Circle of the Rue Royale* (1868) and *Evening* (1878) by Tissot; Claude Monet's *Women in the Garden* (1861) and Frédéric Bazille's *The Pink Dress* (1864). Paintings of suffering or parting include Alfred Stevens' *We call it Vagrancy* (1854) and *The Break-up Letter*. Degas' pre-1870s experimental work is represented by *Semiramis Watching the Construction of Babylon* (1861), which is influenced by medieval Italian art. The finely-tuned *The Bellelli Family* (1858–69), owes a debt to 16th–17th-century northern painters.

LILLE SIDE, ROOMS 8–10

Late 19th-century artists who paved the way to Symbolism, fired by French writers and poets such as Baudelaire, Rimbaud and Huysmans, include Lévy-Dhurmer, whose pastel *Le Silence* (1895) is a profoundly mysterious and timeless piece; although he had abandoned Symbolism by 1901, his work influenced future symbolists. Odilon Renon was a fine Symbolist artist, represented here in a number of works. Toulouse-Lautrec, a member of the oldest aristocratic family in France, did not fit into any group but admired Degas and absorbed many influences, including Japanese prints. *Rousse* (1889) is a study of a young woman at her toilet, shown with deliberate foreshortening.

SEINE SIDE

Developing social awareness is behind many of the works here. Honoré Daumier, cartoonist and social and political satirist, pokes fun at the ruling classes with his series of 36 painted clay busts of Parliamentarians (from 1831). *The Washerwoman* (*La Blanchisseuse*, c. 1863), a small painting handled in a monumental manner, shows the figures silhouetted against the quays of Paris (Daumier's studio was on the Quai d'Anjou on Île St-Louis). His works contrast with the quiet dignity of everyday toil expressed in Jean-François Millet's celebrated *The Winnower* (1848), *The Gleaners* (1857), *The Angelus* (1859) and *Spring*. In the same vein is C.-F. Daubigny's *Vendanges en Bourgogne* (1863) and Hébert's *Haymakers of San Germano*. Ernest Meissonier, master of Napoleonic subjects and important in his day, was the first artist to receive the Grand Cross of the Légion d'Honneur. Nostalgic works by Jules Breton and Constant Troyon follow in the footsteps of Millet, whereas the gentle silvery landscapes of Camille Corot, together with the Barbizon painters Théodore Rousseau and Diaz de la Peña, who worked in the Forest of Fontainebleau, paved the way for *plein-air* painting.

Large academic paintings of 1850–70 include Paul Chenavard's hugely complex *Divina Tragedia*, purchased by the state for the Luxembourg Museum. Puvis de Chavannes, already successful by 1861, produced large fresco-like murals such as *Summer* (1873). He became a leading Symbolist and had a profound influence on Seurat and Moreau.

Pre-1870s paintings by Cézanne and Manet show their evolution from sombre academicism towards their own individual styles. Cézanne's dark and agonised *Christ in Limbo* (1867) and *La Madeleine* (c. 1869) are thought to be two parts of a mural made

MUSÉE D'ORSAY

LEVEL 0: BEFORE IMPRESSIONISM

1–3 & 11–13	Neoclassicism and Romanticism	14 & 18	Early Manet, Cézanne and Monet
4–7	Realism, Historicism	22–23	Decorative arts
8–10	Symbolism		

LEVEL 2: SCULPTURE AND POST-IMPRESSIONISM

LEVEL 5: IMPRESSIONISM

| 29 *Déjeuner sur l'herbe* | 33 Degas |
| 32 Monet, Renoir | 36 Cézanne |

for the family home in Aix-en-Provence. The *Portrait of Achille Empéraire* (1867–8) was refused by the Salon in 1870 and as a consequence Cézanne abandoned figure painting until 1880. Found later at Julien Tanguy's gallery, it was a revelation to Émile Bernard and Vincent van Gogh.

The five canvases by Édouard Manet demonstrate his increasing versatility and brilliance. Among them are *Monsieur et Madame Auguste Manet* (1860), *Angelina* (1865; she does not look angelic), the lovely *Lola de Valence* (1862) and *The Fife Player* (1866). But undoubtedly the most glorious of all is *Olympia* (1863). Derived from Titian's *Venus of Urbino*, it presents a defiant woman who holds the viewer in her gaze. The black velvet bow, the slippers, the jewellery and the flower in her hair contrast with her pale nudity and intensify the provocation; the little black cat is equally challenging, while the bouquet is a mini-masterpiece of still-life painting.

As a result of Napoleon's Egyptian campaign in 1798, the Near and Middle East opened up to travellers. A 24-volume tome describing Egypt, published in 1809, had a marked effect on French architecture and furnishings. Painters visited the exotic 'Orient' for inspiration; others, like Ingres, were inspired by hearsay. For many, the Orient meant Algeria, colonised by the French in 1830. Representative are Fromentin's *Falconry in Algeria* (1863), Guillaumet's *Evening Prayer in the Sahara* (1863) and *Arab Woman* (1901) by Jules Blanchard.

Gustave Courbet's large and sometimes sombre works were both controversial and influential. A flamboyant, outspoken, anti-clerical republican, Courbet was criticised at the Salon of 1850 for the blatant realism of *A Burial at Ornans*, at a time when Couture's *The Romans of the Decadence* (in the Central Aisle; *see p. 115*) was the received style. Courbet's treatment of a group of humble peasants in the monumental manner was considered shocking. *The Wounded Man* (1844, reworked in 1854) is a self-portrait, of which he painted many. The two nude studies, the voluptuous *La Source* (1868) and the erotic *Origin of the World* (1866), demonstrate Courbet's skill and pleasure in painting luminous flesh.

SEINE SIDE, ROOMS 22–23
These rooms include examples of the decorative arts, including ceramics made at Sèvres, tableware, jewellery and portraits, works by Baccarat and Christofle and examples of furniture by leading Wiener Werkstätte figures such as Josef Hoffmann. There is also a bentwood chair by Adolf Loos.

OPÉRA
At the far end of the building is the Opéra room devoted to the architect Charles Garnier and the construction of the Paris Opéra, begun in 1862 (*see p. 299*).

LEVEL 5: IMPRESSIONISM

The origins of Impressionism are traced through paintings of the 1860s–70s. *The Studio in the Batignolles* (1870) expresses Henri Fantin-Latour's support for the painters who were to become known as Impressionists: at the easel is his friend and colleague Manet. Grouped around Manet are Renoir, Bazille, Monet and Émile Zola. Examples of works by the precursors of Impressionism might include Jongkind or Courbet's *Cliffs at Étretat after the Storm*, a motif painted by Monet in 1868-9 and then some 50 more times. James Abbott MacNeill Whistler was susceptible to influences from Japanese art and developed a way of simplifying shapes and spaces, which led to the austere harmony of *Arrangement in Grey and Black, Whistler's Mother* (1871).

Manet's *Le Déjeuner sur l'Herbe* dates from 1863 (*see below*). Monet painted a similar scene, intended both as a tribute and a challenge to Manet, in 1865-6. A very large work, it was badly damaged by poor storage and only segments survived. Other canvases by Manet here include *The Balcony* (c. 1868-9), a tribute to Spanish painting and Goya in particular, with Berthe Morisot in the foreground; and *Portrait of Zola* (1868) with *Olympia* (*see above*) in the background. Zola spoke out in defence of Manet's work.

Works of the 1870s include Fantin-Latour's *Hommage à Delacroix* and Manet's painting of his sister-in-law, *Berthe Morisot with a Fan* (she was also a painter). Monet's delicate *Coquelicots* (1873), one of his most emblematic works, is a halcyon moment recording his wife and child in a cascade of poppies, while *The Railway Bridge at Argenteuil* (c. 1875) expresses his admiration for 19th-century engineering. There are still lifes by both Monet and Manet, and Sisley's *Snow at Marly-le-Roi* (1875), where he had gone to live the previous year.

One of the three canvases that Cézanne exhibited at the First Impressionist Exhibition in 1874, *The Hanged Man's House* (1873), shows the influence of Pissarro in the lighter palette and looser brushstrokes. Compare it with his *Self-portrait* (1875), which is altogether darker. Manet's captivating *Sur la Plage* (1873) was painted on the beach—grains of sand have been identified in the pigment—but it does not strictly adhere to all the canons of Impressionism: he uses black, the strokes are more fluid, and the shallow perspective is a link to the influence of *Japonisme*. By Sisley is *La Barque pendant l'Inondation, Port-Marly* (1876), one of six versions of the floods.

Works which portray Parisian life in the 1870s include Renoir's *Bal du Moulin de la Galette* (1876), where he uses dappled light to great effect and shows Parisians at play on a sunny Sunday afternoon in Montmartre. Compare it with the more restrained *Danse à la ville*. Degas' moving portrayal of café life, *The Absinthe Drinkers* (1876), is a theme of addiction addressed by Zola in his book *L'Assommoir* (1877) and is an exercise in spatial harmony and colour (Musée d'Orsay also has Picasso's *Absinthe Drinker* of 1901).

Paintings of people at work include Gustave Caillebotte's vigorous *Floor Planers* (1875) and Manet's *La Serveuse de bocks* (1878-9), showing a waitress with mugs of beer in a crowded café, as well as the fatigued and bored *Women Ironing* (1884-6) by Degas. Another side of Parisian life is Manet's *Lady with the Fans* (1873-4), a likeness of Nina de Villard, who held brilliant literary and artistic salons.

Monet, who at this point was leaving the countryside for Paris, was inspired by other painters, as well as by the critics Duranty and Zola, to paint contemporary scenes. He painted seven versions of the *Gare St-Lazare* (1877), where he succeeded in capturing the changing atmosphere, luminosity and geometry.

MANET AND THE *DÉJEUNER SUR L'HERBE*

Courbet's *The Artist's Studio* (1855) is a work where a group of men, all clothed, painted as portraits of real individuals and including (on the right) Baudelaire, are shown surrounding a nude female model. Because the subject was an artist's studio, the painting did not cause undue comment. Two pivotal works painted by Manet eight years later (in 1863), however, caused outrage: *Olympia* (*see p. 110*) and *Le Déjeuner sur l'Herbe*. Both portray naked women and both were considered scandalous and condemned as ugly at the time. They were Manet's last nudes.

Déjeuner follows in the tradition of the '*Fête Champêtre*', such as Titian's *Concert Champêtre* (c. 1510) and Watteau's *Pilgrimage to Cythera* (1717; both in the Louvre). Manet's version became one of the most notorious picnics of all time, heavily criticised not only for its subject matter but also for the non-conformist technique: freely applied paint, 'blocks' of colour, ambiguous perspective, lack of tonal modelling, and a sketchy background. Manet was a bourgeois revolutionary rebelling against the idealism and impersonality of Couture's studio. He was also a true Parisian, loved art, and was seeking a formula to reconcile style and modern life: he was an ardent believer in spontaneously capturing real scenes. Daumier, Courbet and the Barbizon painters had gone some way towards this via landscape, but landscape did not interest Manet in the way that figures did. In 1838 Louis-Philippe's Spanish Collection opened to the public and there Manet discovered works by Velázquez and Goya, which influenced his *Absinthe Drinker* (1858–9), modelled by a rag-picker.

Velázquez's abrupt handling of colour and dramatic contrasts were another influence. *Concert in the Tuileries* (c. 1860–2), using numerous sketches of modern people at leisure, was Manet's first 'instant' record of modern life, but he still kept a foot in the past, a tension that emerges in *Le Déjeuner sur l'herbe*. The idea was based on sketches of bathers in the Seine, but the composition was borrowed from a small group of naked divinities in an engraving of a lost *Judgement of Paris* by Raphael. The huge canvas was painted in his studio using models. The result is a disconnected painting, implausible but fascinating. Predictably it was turned down at the official Salon; and at the alternative Salon des Refusés, crowds came along for a good laugh. Manet's painting proved a *succès de scandale*. Few who derided *Déjeuner* were unaware of its Classical influences. The furore was caused above all by the depiction of an insolent-looking floozy sitting stark naked in the company of men wearing clothes that placed the scene fairly and squarely in the contemporary period. The nude has the face of the artist's favourite model, Victorine Meurent, and the body of his wife Suzanne. But the modernity of it all was incomprehensible to the public: the loose paint handling in the naturalistic background; the almost cut-out figures; the ambiguous perspective and the contrasts of tone; Manet's hallmark strong greens and blacks; the abandoned clothes in the foreground; the man's tasselled hat, of a kind not usually worn out of doors. Everything combined to disturb the accustomed norms. Today, while still provocative and inscrutable, the work is considered a masterpiece.

Degas' statuette of a standing horse, *Cheval à l'arrêt* (1865–81) is modelled in wax on a wire framework (the horse's head is modelled around a wine bottle cork).

Paintings from the 1880s include Renoir's *Maternity* (1885), where the paint handling contrasts with the carefully drawn, smooth finish and soft colours of his future wife, Aline, nursing their son Pierre. Later is the *Girl in a Straw Hat* (1908). Two preparatory drawings made outdoors for *Young Woman with a Sunshade* (1886) show her facing in opposite directions. *Les Glaçons (Ice)* is supremely delicate and looks forward to *Waterlilies*; the *Avenue of Poplars near Moret-sur-Loing* by Sisley shows nature at the height of summer.

Cézanne made many paintings of his wife Hortense, including a head-and-shoulders version of 1885–90; she is also the model for his *Woman with a Coffeepot* (1890–5). In his still lifes he often uses familiar possessions—a chair, a ginger jar, cloths and fabrics, a small armless statuette—as well as a tipped perspective.

The collection has several landscapes by Pissarro and Sisley. Two women painters who exhibited with the Impressionists are Berthe Morisot (*In the Wheat Fields* of 1875 and *The Cradle* of 1872, a tender and delicate painting of her sister and niece) and the American Mary Cassatt, friend of Degas, who studied in Paris (*Woman Sewing in the Garden*, c. 1880–2).

From the last decade of the 19th century come some of the most famous Impressionist paintings. Monet made 'series' paintings on the themes of *Poplars*, *Haystacks* and *Rouen Cathedral* (1892–3), of which the Orsay has five versions, at different times of day, catching the light in a variety of ways and in different weather conditions. He painted the lily ponds at Giverny a multitude of times in the 1890s, and in many different ways, and continued to paint them until the end of his life.

Renoir was fascinated by the subject of girls at the piano and was constantly striving for the perfectly-accomplished result. Degas began painting young dancers, often from an unusual angle, and from then on they became one of his principal subjects; his *Blue Dancers* (c. 1890) are shown in repose behind the scenes. Henri Rousseau is represented by the *Portrait of Madame M.* His flat colours and naïve style were an important influence on the movement which became known as Post-Impressionism.

LEVEL 2

SALLE DES FÊTES
The painted decoration of the Salle des Fêtes, the former ballroom of the station hotel, has been restored to its original Belle-Époque glitter, including gilded mirrors and chandeliers.

ROOM 54: THE MEYER DONATION
Displayed here are works by Cézanne, Seurat, Bonnard, Mondrian and Vuillard, including Vuillard's 'Intimiste'-style *Interior with Three Lamps* (1899).

SEINE SIDE: APPLIED ARTS
Displayed here, together with some paintings, are ornate decorative arts of the 1860s to the turn of the century, from the Second Empire to 'La Belle Époque'. The museum possesses chairs in various historic styles including Georg Hulbe's sturdy carved oak

MUSÉE D'ORSAY

Manet's *Déjeuner sur l'herbe* (1863), which provoked stiff reaction in its day for its loose approach, so different from the academic style exemplified by Couture's *Romans of the Decadence* (1847; right).

and leather chair for Tiffany (c. 1891). Contrasting examples of ceramics and glass include an elegant Baccarat vase (c. 1867) in semi-translucent white and blue glass. Ceramic pieces testify to the fascination with Eastern Asia as does a delicate circular screen of rosewood, gilded bronze and etched glass (c. 1885–90), probably from the exclusive Parisian shop L'Escalier de Cristal. The hand-painted plates of the Lambert-Rousseau Service (after 1884) are inspired by the landscapes of the Japanese artists Hokusai and Hiroshige; outrageously ornate is the idealised medieval style *Toilette* (dressing table) of the Duchess of Parma (1845–51) by F.-D. Froment-Meurice, incorporating gilded silver and copper, enamel, glass, emeralds and garnets.

Art Nouveau and Art Deco pieces from several European countries are also displayed, including jewellery by Lalique and ceramics and enamel work from the School of Nancy (Émile Gallé and Albert Dammouse). Perfectly crafted and sometimes exquisitely over-elaborate furnishings include a chimney piece by Hector Guimard and a dining room of 1901 by Alexandre Charpentier. Other extreme examples are a writing table called *Orchidées* by Louis Majorelle, and the *Nénuphars* bedroom suite (c. 1905) designed by Eugène Vallin. There are also objects by Bugatti and Charles Rennie Mackintosh.

Among French and foreign-school paintings (second half of the 19th century) are Naturalist works on a variety of topical subjects. They include Bastien-Lepage's *Les Foins* (1877), highlighting the plight of agricultural workers, as do works by Léon Lhermitte and Alfred Roll; advances in medical research are treated in Henri Gervex's beautifully composed *Before the Operation* (1887). Marie Bashkirtseff was only 25 when she gained a place at the 1884 Salon with *A Meeting*, a closely observed study of six working-class schoolboys. She died of tuberculosis the same year.

A variety of small sculptures includes the singer *Yvette Guilbert* (1899), captured by Cappiello (1902). By Prince Troubetzkoy are small bronzes of *Léon Tolstoy on Horseback*. Claude Debussy (1884) is portrayed by his friend Marcel Baschet and Clara Rilke-Westhoff captures Maria Czaykowska (c. 1902) in marble.

Bouguereau's *Compassion* (1905) shows off his painterly skills and talent for drama and Georges Rochegrosse, who designed scenery, was inspired by Wagner (as were many artists of the period, particularly the Symbolists) and takes a scene from *Parsifal* in *The Knight of the Flowers* (1894). The mural *La Famille* (1901) is the work of decorator and illustrator Luc-Olivier Merson. Among seascapes by Corot are *Trouville, Fishing Boats Aground* (between 1848 and 1875). By Courbet is the vigorous *Apple Branch in Blossom* (1872).

SCULPTURE TERRACES

Sculpture between 1880 and 1900, allegorical, symbolic and celebratory, large and small, is exhibited on the three sculpture terraces overlooking the Central Aisle. Emmanuel Frémiet's *Archangel Michael Slaying the Dragon* (1897) was a commission for Mont St-Michel after he had exhibited a small bronze version at the Salon of 1879. Eugène Delaplanche's *Virgin with Lily* (1878) is quiet and graceful, with delicate folds of drapery. Ernest Barrias's second version of *Nature Unveiling Herself to Science* (1899) was originally commissioned in marble for the new medical school at Bordeaux, whereas here the sculptor has used coloured onyx and marble to great effect. Among the Rodin plaster casts is an enlarged version of *Ugolin* (1906) from his *Gates of Hell*. Camille Claudel's moving bronze group entitled *L'Âge Mûr* (*Maturity*; c. 1902) symbolises the pain of Rodin's rejection as she reaches out to prevent him leaving. Joseph Bernard's seemingly simple female nude *The Water Carrier* (1912) is an exercise in equilibrium. There are some good examples of work by Maillol and Bourdelle, including a cast of Maillol's *Méditerranée* and his original *Monument to Cézanne*, in Canigou marble, which was rejected by the city of Aix-en-Provence (the Tuileries garden has a cast of the same work). Look out too for the animal sculptures by François Pompon (*see p. 121*).

ROOMS 67–72: NEO- AND POST-IMPRESSIONISM

'Nabis' painters include Félix Vallotton, represented by a portrait of the publisher and collector Alexandre Natanson (1899). It was hanging above Natanson's desk until 1929, when financial problems forced him to sell his collection, and was kept by the family before entering the Orsay in 2005. The Natanson brothers, Alexandre, Thadée and Alfred, published *La Revue blanche* in 1889–1903, to which the Nabis artists were closely linked: Vallotton was a regular contributor. Other Nabis paintings include Pierre Bonnard's *La Crépuscule* (*Twilight*, 1888), one of his earliest works, exhibited in 1892. *Femme assoupie sur un lit* (1899) is one of the first nudes he painted, and *La Table de toilette* (1908) includes one of his favourite conceits, a mirror. Maurice Denis painted *Hommage à Cézanne* (1900), showing artists in Ambroise Vollard's shop grouped around a Cézanne still-life that had belonged to Gauguin: left to right are Redon, Vuillard, Mellerio, Vollard, Denis, Paul Sérusier, Ranson, Roussel, Bonnard and Madame Denis.

Édouard Vuillard's *Le Déjeuner* (1903), a scene of his mother at breakfast, shows him moving away from the stylisation of the Nabis to intimate and autobiographical works. The Orsay has studies by Seurat for *La Grande Jatte* and *Une Baignade à Asnières*, which were among paintings which prompted the English art critic Roger Fry to group styles of this period loosely under the heading Post-Impressionism, encompassing Neo-Impressionism and Divisionism (optical mixing of colours and strict formal composition).

Paul Signac was the most articulate artist to adopt the concept of simultaneous contrasts of colours and minimum modelling of shapes. Matisse and Signac were together in St-Tropez in 1904, when Matisse painted *Luxe, calme et volupté*, based on a poem by Baudelaire: the result is an experimental amalgam of shimmering horizontal dashes captured within an outline. Purchased by Signac in 1905, it did not re-emerge until 1950.

Gauguin lived mainly in Brittany in 1886–90. He and others who worked with him at Pont-Aven, including Émile Bernard and Paul Sérusier, developed a strong and symbolic use of flat planes of colour. In 1888 he spent two months in Arles with Van Gogh where they both painted the Roman necropolis (*Les Alyscamps*), which represents the combined search by the two painters to produce non-naturalistic landscapes.

In *La belle Angèle* (1889), a likeness of Marie-Angélique Satre, a hotel-keeper at Pont-Aven, Gauguin abandoned traditional perspective and followed the Japanese custom of framing the portrait on a decorative background. *Women of Tahiti* (1891) is a confident, elegant and decorative portrayal of two women. In *Arearea* (1892), dream and reality appear to coexist, rendered in a succession of coloured planes. *Breton Village under Snow* (c. 1894) was found unfinished after Gauguin's death, and completed by his friend Daniel de Monfreid. Gauguin died in the South Seas in 1903.

Paul Sérusier met Gauguin in Pont-Aven in 1888 and was taken up by the theories of 'Synthetism'. *La Grammaire* (1892) shows a girl in a Breton headdress reading from a large book framed in a semicircle, like a stained-glass window. Émile Bernard also painted in Brittany around this time: *Harvest by the Sea*, in simplified colours and shapes, is an example.

The Orsay has a representative collection of works by Van Gogh, including *Les Roulettes, Vagabonds' Camp near Arles* (1888), *Starry Night* (1888), his famous self-portrait in a pale blue suit on a pale blue background (1889), *Two Little Girls* (1890; dressed in blue looking rather quizzical) and *In the Garden of Dr Paul Gachet* (1890), the doctor who treated him and befriended painters. *La Méridienne* (1889–90) is a blue and gold siesta under a haystack. Also here is the well-known *Van Gogh's Bedroom in Arles* (1889).

PHOTOGRAPHY, GRAPHIC ARTS AND ARCHITECTURE COLLECTIONS

The Musée d'Orsay has rich **photographic** reserves built up since 1979, which span the period 1848–1914. The aim is to record the development of photography starting from the first daguerreotype cameras and is dedicated to collecting early original prints. The focus is not solely on France; early links between France and England are explored, as is the later spread of photography to other countries.

Graphic arts have always been part of the collection, particularly drawings, but also pastels, architectural drawings, sketches, sculpture models and drawings from foreign schools. The collection now amounts to over 80,000 examples and mainly covers artists born after 1820 and before 1870, though there are some exceptions.

The nature of the building lends itself to the presentation of **Architecture**, which is part of the permanent exhibition, with an emphasis on the construction and decoration of the Opéra Garnier. The museum has some 18,000 architectural drawings, including the remarkable Eiffel Collection.

MUSÉE NATIONAL DE LA LÉGION D'HONNEUR

Map p. 586, B1. 2 Rue de la Légion d'Honneur. Open Wed–Sun and Tues 1–6, closed Mon. Groups only on Tues. Audioguides available. T: 01 40 62 84 25, www.legiondhonneur.fr.

West of the Musée d'Orsay is the colonnaded Palais de la Légion d'Honneur, home to the Musée National de la Légion d'Honneur et des Ordres de Chevalerie. It occupies the Hôtel de Salm, one of the last mansions to be built in Paris, which is distinguished by a triumphal arch, a vast courtyard and an elegant rotunda with Corinthian columns facing the river. Built in 1782–6 for a German count who was put to death in 1794, the house became the Swedish Embassy in 1797. It was here that the writer Mme de Staël, wife of the ambassador, invited to her famous salons members of opposing political persuasions. An early supporter of the Revolution, she switched allegiance to the constitutional monarchy and was forced to flee France after the September massacres of 1792.

In 1804 the palace was bought by the government for the Grand Chancery of the Legion of Honour, which administers the Order. Following a severe fire during the Commune of 1871, it was restored to its original form in 1878 and is now the Grand Chancellor's residence. Since 1925 it has also been home to the National Museum of the Legion of Honour and the Orders of Knighthood, its motto *Honneur et Patrie*. It contains a unique collection of religious, military and secular Orders, including many insignia from other countries. This is a bright and bejewelled collection containing memorabilia, paintings, costumes and fine portraits of illustrious gentlemen with their chests covered in medals.

Four rooms are dedicated to different orders. The ancient religious and chivalrous Order of St John of Jerusalem, now the Order of Malta, began with the Crusades; the insignia is a white cross with eight points. The Order of St Michael (1469) and the Saint-Ésprit (1578) were the first French royal orders of chivalry, reserved for the aristocracy. In 1693, Louis XIV founded the first democratic order of merit, the military Order of St Louis. The badge of the Légion d'Honneur, created in 1802 by Consul Bonaparte, is a white star on a red ribbon.

The oldest world orders still awarded are the Order of the Garter (Great Britain) and the Order of the Elephant (Denmark). Other rooms include the Contemporary History Room, with French decorations since 1789; and a room dedicated to the Legion of Honour schools, two boarding establishments for girls who are descendants of holders of the Légion d'Honneur, in Écouen and in St-Denis.

The Multimedia Resource Centre has profiles of over 300 men and women who exemplify the diverse character of holders of the French National Orders.

HÔTELS DE SEIGNELAY AND DE BEAUHARNAIS

At 80 Rue de Lille, occupying land stretching down to the Seine embankment, is the **Hôtel de Seignelay** (*map p. 586, B1*), built in 1714 by Gabriel Boffrand, France's finest Rococo architect. On the Seine side is a **plaque commemorating Coco**, the spaniel of Marie-Antoinette and her children. The animal is said to have been their faithful companion during imprisonment in the Temple and to have accompanied Princess Marie-Thérèse, the sole survivor, into exile. Boffrand also built the adjacent **Hôtel de Beauharnais** (1713), at 78 Rue de Lille, one of the best *hôtels particuliers* in this area. Sold first to Jean-Baptiste Colbert, nephew of the great statesman, it was acquired in 1803 by the son-in-law of Napoleon and Viceroy of Italy, Eugène de Beauharnais, and was the occasional home of his sister Hortense, whom Napoleon had married to his brother, the King of Holland. In 1814 it became the Prussian legation, in 1871 the German Embassy, and it is now the German ambassador's residence. The curious neo-Egyptian porch characterises a fashion that was introduced after Napoleon's Egyptian expedition of 1798.

AROUND RUE DU BAC

Map p. 586, B2–C2. Métro 12 to Rue du Bac.

A large section of the western end of Boulevard St-Germain, including Hôtel de Roquelaure (no. 246; 1722), is occupied by government offices. Guillaume Apollinaire (1880–1918), poet, writer and champion of avant-garde artists, lived (and died of Spanish flu) at no. 202, near the boulevard's junction with **Rue du Bac**, which weaves south from the river and took its name from the ferry that operated in 1550–64, before the construction of the Pont Royal, carrying stone from the Vaugirard quarries across to the Louvre. The former Dominican **church of St-Thomas-d'Aquin**, begun in 1682 by Pierre Bullet in the Jesuit style, was completed in 1722 with the construction of the monks' choir at the east end behind the altar; the façade dates from 1765–9. The light interior, with pale stained glass, is very effective. The *Transfiguration* on the vaults of the choir was painted by François Lemoyne shortly before his departure for Italy.

Further east off Blvd St-Germain, at no. 27 **Rue St-Guillaume**, is the 16th-century Hôtel de Mesmes. Enlarged in 1933, it is now the prestigious Institut National des Études Politiques or 'Sciences Po'. No. 16, the Hôtel de Créqui, built in 1660–4 and extended in 1772, was for a time the home of poet, statesman and historian Alphonse Lamartine (1790–1866). An early French Romantic, Lamartine was unusual in combining his literary endeavours with a career in politics (though without much success in the latter). Nevertheless, he was involved in the birth of the Second Republic in 1848, advocating the abolition both of slavery and of the death penalty.

ON & AROUND QUAI D'ORSAY

The Quai d'Orsay extends from Pont de la Concorde (*map p. 586, B1*) to Pont de l'Alma (*map p. 585, E1*). Along this stretch of 2.3km the lower quay has been transformed from a fast freeway to a pedestrian walk.

PALAIS BOURBON: ASSEMBLÉE NATIONALE

Map p. 596, B1. 33 Quai d'Orsay. Métro 12 to Assemblée Nationale. Four guided visits every Sat in French: book online (www.assemblee-nationale.fr). When the Assembly is not in session, individual visits can be made four times a day on Mon–Fri; T: 01 40 63 56 00. Audioguides available in English. ID required. To attend a session on a week-day afternoon, reserve at least two months in advance through a Député (member of Parliament).

In 1722–8 a mansion was erected on this site for the Dowager Duchess of Bourbon, daughter of Louis XIV, of which only the inner courtyard and main entrance (at 128 Rue de l'Université) have survived. The Prince de Condé enlarged the palace between 1764 and 1789, incorporating the Hôtel de Lassay. The palace became national property at the Revolution, was transformed into the meeting-place of the Council of Five Hundred, and was later occupied by the Archives (1799–1808). Since 1815 it has been used by the Chambre des Députés, the French equivalent of the British House of Commons. Its name was changed to the Assemblée Nationale in 1946. In 1940–4 the Palais Bourbon was the headquarters of the German military administration of the Paris region. At the time of the Liberation, considerable fighting in the neighbourhood caused some damage to the building and the destruction of over 30,000 volumes in its library.

The **north façade** (1804–7), a neo-Hellenic piece of imperial bombast designed principally to balance the church of the Madeleine (*map p. 581, E4*) when seen from Place de la Concorde, is entirely decorative and consists of a portico of twelve Corinthian columns. The low reliefs on the wings are by Rude and Pradier. Inside, the semicircular **Salle des Séances** (1828–32) has statues by Pradier, Desprez and others, and a Gobelins tapestry after Raphael's *School of Athens*. Other rooms contain historical paintings by Horace Vernet and Delacroix. The Galerie des Fêtes (1848) connects the building to the Hôtel de Lassay (1724), the official residence of the President of the Assembly.

Behind the Assemblée Nationale is **Place du Palais Bourbon**, an elegant ensemble of Louis XVI houses built to the same pattern after 1776. On the northeast corner, on Rue de l'Université is the former Hôtel Turgot (18th century; *entrance at 121 Rue de Lille*), home to the Frits Lught Collection. Lught established the Fondation Custodia in 1947, a collection and study institute whose mission is to serve the history of art. It holds regular exhibitions (*T: 01 45 05 75 19, www.fondationcustodia.fr*).

QUAI D'ORSAY

Next to the Palais de Bourbon on Quai d'Orsay is the **Ministère des Affaires Etrangères** (Foreign Office), built in 1845 (*occasional visits with the CMN; see p. 540*). The embankment then leads west, past the Invalides (*see p. 123*) and at no. 65 on the quay, the neo-Gothic **American Church in Paris** (1927–31; *map p. 585, F1*) to Pont de l'Alma and the entrance to the Paris sewers.

LES ÉGOUTS DE PARIS

Map p. 585, E1. Métro 9 to Alma-Marceau (and walk across the bridge) or RER C to Pont de l'Alma. Open May–Sept 11–5, Oct–April 11–4; restricted entry after heavy rain; closed Thur, Fri and 2 weeks in mid-Jan. T: 01 53 68 27 81.

Famously romanticised in Victor Hugo's *Les Misérables*, the Égouts de Paris (sewers), adjacent to Pont de l'Alma, opposite 93 Quai d'Orsay, make an interesting underground visit. Paris' water system began very modestly during the 14th century with a vaulted drain (as opposed to open drains and sewers) which carried waste into the Seine via the Ménilmontant stream. By 1740 the Grand Égout de Ceinture had been built (the route for Jean Valjean carrying Marius in *Les Misérables*). Progress on further construction was slow until Haussmann's project (*see p. 284*), carried out in 1857–61, which included the cleaning up of the city streets and providing a wider network of drains and fresh water. The engineer Eugène Belgrand was in charge, and by his death 600km had been completed. Now the network stretches for over 2000 km. The first public visits from the Châtelet area were introduced during the Universal Exhibition of 1867, first by small cart, then by boat. Today about 200m can be covered on foot, enlivened by an audiovisual display, numerous maquettes, information panels and machinery.

EATING AND DRINKING AROUND MUSÉE D'ORSAY

At the Musée d'Orsay itself there is the sumptuous and popular €– €€ **Restaurant** on Level 2, decorated in 1900 as part of the old Hôtel d'Orsay and preserving its Belle-Époque ceiling painting, gilding and chandeliers. The tables and chairs are modern, creating an interesting contrast. The cuisine is traditional French, with museum-themed specials. Behind the Impressionist galleries on Level 5 is the € **Café Campana**, an Art-Nouveau-inspired brasserie designed by the Campana brothers, where you can have a simple meal or just coffee and cake. At the left-hand end of the Central Aisle on Level 0 is the self-service € **Café de l'Ours**, named after the bright white sculpture of a polar bear that stands outside it. The sculpture (1923–33) is the work of François Pompon, who began as a marble-cutter for Rodin and Claudel before turning to sculpture in his own right, inspired by the animals of the Jardin des Plantes zoo. The Musée d'Orsay has a number of other works by his hand, including a lovely owl (Level 2 sculpture terrace).

Not far from the Musée d'Orsay is the reasonably-priced € **Le Cinq Mars** (*51 Rue Verneuil, T: 01 45 44 69 13, cinq-mars-restaurant.com, map p. 586, C2*), open daily with seasonally changing modern French cuisine.

LES INVALIDES
View of the gilded dome and Seurre's statue of Napoleon.

Les Invalides

The spacious avenues west of Faubourg St-Germain are dominated
by the magnificent building of Les Invalides, unmistakable for its gilded dome,
under which is the burial place of Napoleon.

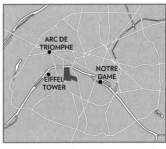

The grandest approach to the sweeping panorama of Les Invalides (*map p. 586, A2*) is from the north, across the ornate Pont Alexandre III. The complex contains the tomb of Napoleon, the Musée de l'Armée and other museums. Esplanade des Invalides, between Place des Invalides and the Seine, is a vast open space which was laid out in 1704–20 by Robert de Cotte, who became *Premier Architecte* to the Crown in 1709. Originally planted with elms, the esplanade was replanted in 1978 with lawns and scented lime trees.

HISTORY OF THE HOTEL DES INVALIDES

The Hôtel des Invalides, covering 13 hectares, was founded by Louis XIV as a home for elderly and/or disabled veterans. It was the first enduring institution of its kind and encouraged recruitment to the king's army. By 1714 the buildings housed about 4,000 pensioners or *invalides*. The majestic ensemble, based on designs by Libéral Bruant, included the Chapel of St Louis. Work began in 1671, and in 1697 Bruant was replaced by the great-nephew of François Mansart, and master of the Parisian Baroque, Jules Hardouin-Mansart, who designed the Église du Dôme. So revolutionary was the idea of the *hôtel* that foreign monarchs came to visit, including Peter the Great of Russia in 1717. Between the Esplanade and Les Invalides are fortifications built at the time of the king's engineer and military designer, Maréchal de France Vauban, with a ditch and bossed walls. Restoration work was carried out under Napoleon, who was later buried beneath its dome (Vauban lies entombed here too). Today Les Invalides is primarily the headquarters of the Military Governor of Paris and it is still a home to retired soldiers: some 80 war veterans are currently accommodated here. The setting and the range and quality of the collections contribute to making this one of the top armaments museums in the world.

The dignified **north façade** is 200m long and four storeys high, with a pavilion at each end surmounted by stone trophies and flags. The decoration is concentrated in the attic storey around the dormer windows. Flanking the main entrance are copies of the original statues of *Mars* and *Minerva* by Guillaume Coustou (1735). In 1815 the equestrian bas-relief of Louis XIV above the central door, accompanied by *Justice* and *Prudence*, replaced the original, designed by Coustou, that was destroyed during the Revolution. Facing the Esplanade des Invalides is an artillery battery composed of foreign bronze cannons captured by the French army, the most remarkable being those made in 1708 to celebrate the creation of the Kingdom of Prussia.

On the south side is the **Jardin de l'Intendant** (*open to all*), a fine formal garden based on plans by Robert de Cotte but carried out only in 1980. It is organised around a large pool and the borders are punctuated by cone-shaped yews. The architect Jules Hardouin-Mansart is commemorated in a 19th-century statue.

MUSÉE DE L'ARMÉE

Map p. 586, A2. Historial de Gaulle closed Mon. Other museums open daily April–Sept 10–6, Oct–March 10–5. Late-night opening April–Sept Tues to 9pm, in winter holidays to 5.30. Closed first Mon of each month Oct–June, and 1 Jan, 1 May, 1 Nov, 25 Dec. One ticket gives access to all museums: Musée de l'Armée, Le Dôme, De Gaulle Historial, Musée de l'Ordre de la Libération and the Plans-Reliefs. Two main exhibitions are held every year and there are frequent concerts. T: 08 10 11 33 99 or 01 44 42 38 77, www. musee-armee.fr. The Hôtel des Invalides site itself is open daily 7.30–7. Enter either from the Esplanade des Invalides on the north side, or from Place Vauban on the south.

The buildings of Les Invalides, with their 60 sculpted dormer windows, surround the vast **Cour d'Honneur** (102m by 64m), with three sundials and 70 bronze cannons which trace the history of French artillery between the 17th and 19th centuries. The Musée de l'Armée was created in 1905, when the Artillery Museum and the Army History Museum merged. It is now divided into seven exhibition spaces around the Cour d'Honneur: the Artillery Collections (the cannons mentioned above); the Cathédral St-Louis; the Dôme des Invalides and Napoleon's tomb; the three departments of the Historic Collections: old, modern and contemporary; and the Historial Charles de Gaulle.

ST-LOUIS DES INVALIDES

The Cathédral St-Louis (the Chapel of Les Invalides or Soldiers' Church), based on designs by Libéral Bruant, was built by Hardouin-Mansart c. 1679–1708. Above it stands Seurre's original bronze statue of Napoleon (restored in 2014–15), which formerly topped the Vendôme Column (*see p. 297*), and an astronomical clock (1781). The bare interior, with a gallery built at the same level as the dormitories of the disabled, is hung with captured regimental colours. In 1837 it resounded to the first performance of Berlioz's *Grande Messe des Morts*. The organ (1679–87) is by Alexandre Thierry,

LES INVALIDES
Detail of the cannon *l'Éclatant*, cast by Bérenguer in Strasbourg in 1757.

the case by Germain Pillon. A sheet of plain glass behind the high altar separates the cathedral from the very different Dôme des Invalides.

DÔME DES INVALIDES

The Dôme des Invalides, in contrast to the cathedral, is all pomp and ceremony. Built in 1677–1706 by Hardouin-Mansart, it was added to the church of St-Louis as a chapel royal to the glory of Louis XIV and the French armies. In the niches on either side of the entrance are statues of Charlemagne and St Louis by Coysevox and Nicolas Coustou. The ribbed dome, the most splendid in France, is roofed with lead and stands on a balustraded base and attic storey. It is crowned with a lantern and short spire rising to a height of 107m. In each bay are trophies, re-gilded in 1989 with 12kg of gold. The entire decorative programme celebrates the military glory of the French monarchy. The interior of the dome is decorated with allegorical paintings (1705) on the theme of *St Louis Presenting his Arms to Christ* by one of Le Brun's most talented disciples, Charles de la Fosse, who also worked at Versailles. The artist was recalled to Paris by Hardouin-Mansart from London, where King William III had been hoping that he would decorate Hampton Court Palace.

The Dôme was converted into a national military pantheon by Napoleon in 1800, with the translation of Turenne's tomb from St-Denis. The 56 metre-square interior, in the form of a Greek cross, has an ornate Baroque decoration of paintings, sculpture and mosaic paving; behind the main altar is a mid-19th-century baldachin and there are paintings by Coypel in the vault. The upper-level chapels (going anticlockwise from the high altar) contain the tombs (some enshrining only hearts) of the following:

Hubert Lyautey (d. 1934): Colonial administrator, Resident-General in Morocco and Marshal of France. Tomb by Albert Laprade.

Vicomte de Turenne (d. 1675): Henri de la Tour d'Auvergne, Marshal of France, was killed by a cannon ball during the Franco-Dutch war. Originally buried at St-Denis, his remains were saved from destruction and brought here. Tomb by Le Brun, Tuby and Marsy.
   In the same chapel, an urn encloses the heart of **Théophile de la Tour d'Auvergne** (d. 1800), created First Grenadier of the Republic by Napoleon, and who died on campaign in Bavaria. A Breton, a linguist and a scholar, we owe to him the words dolmen and menhir.

Jérôme Bonaparte (d. 1860). Napoleon's youngest brother, nominated King of Westphalia (1807–14). He was later Governor of Les Invalides (1848–52).

Joseph Bonaparte (d. 1844): Elder brother of Napoleon, created King of Naples and later of Spain.

Marquis de Vauban (d. 1707): Marshal of France and military engineer under Louis XIV. Tomb of 1847 by Etex.

Ferdinand Foch (d. 1929): Marshal of France and, during WWI, supreme commander of the Allies: France, Great Britain and Poland. Striking tomb, a coffin with pall-bearers, by Landowski.

In front of the high altar is a model of the Hôtel des Invalides before 1757. In the Turenne chapel is a model with a segment cut away revealing the brilliant construction of the cupola and its windows, designed to throw light upwards into the dome.

THE TOMB OF NAPOLEON

From the circular gallery is a view down to the crypt, filled by the imposing Tomb of Napoleon I, designed by Visconti. The Emperor's remains were placed in it in April 1861, 40 years after his death on St Helena. Brought to Les Invalides in December 1840, his remains lay in the Chapelle St-Jérôme while the sarcophagus was being prepared.

Steps descend behind the high altar to the crypt. The inscription above the entranceway is taken from Napoleon's will: *Je désire que mes cendres reposent sur les bords de la Seine, au milieu de ce peuple français que j'ai tant aimé* ('I desire that my mortal remains should rest on the banks of the Seine, in the midst of the French people whom I have loved so dearly'). The vast proportions of the tomb (4m by 2m and

LES INVALIDES
'The principles of disorder fade away, factions bow their heads, parties unite,
wounds heal and Creation seems once again to leave chaos behind.'
The pacific benefits conferred on France by Napoleon.

4.5m high) and its colours (dark red Finnish porphyry for the sarcophagus and green Vosges granite for the plinth) make their full impact down here. The sarcophagus is surrounded by a gallery with ten bas-reliefs after Pierre-Charles Simart representing the benefits conferred on France by the Emperor, making deliberate allusion to the parallels between ancient Rome (*Droit Romain, institutes de Justinien*) and the new statues (*Code Napoléon, justice égale et intelligible pour tous*). The statue of Napoleon in his coronation robes, in a niche, is by Simart himself. On the inner face of the gallery, facing the sarcophagus, are twelve figures by Pradier symbolising Napoleon's victorious campaigns, which are picked out in lettering in the pavement—Rivoli, Pyramides, Marengo, Austerlitz etc. Around them is an inlaid polychrome wreath of green laurel.

THE HISTORIC COLLECTIONS

ANCIENT ARMS AND ARMOUR

The **Royal Room** begins with the Crown Collections, from St Louis (1226–70) to Louis XIII (1610–43), and is decorated with a mural of battle scenes of the Franco-Dutch war (1672–8). Here are French royal weapons, armour and objects from the East. The most famous armour of the collection was made in Austria (1539–40) for François I. A skilfully damascened suit (c. 1536) was made for the future Henri II.

The **Medieval Room**, illustrating the shift from a feudal to a royal army, has some remarkable pieces of ordnance and a collection of medieval swords. The **Louis XIII Room** addresses the Italian Campaigns against the Habsburg Empire. Among the firearms (c. 1520) is one of the first arquebuses with a French-type wheel-lock mechanism. Objects relating to the **Wars of Religion** in the 16th century include a suit of armour weighing 30kg which belonged to Henri I, Duc de Guise ('*le Balafré*').

The Arsenal Gallery recreates the atmosphere of former arsenals, with some 2,500 pieces. Weapons used in **Courtly Leisure Activities** (hunting and tournaments) from the late Middle Ages to the mid-17th century include full plate mail. The collection of **Eastern Armour and Arms** (15th–early 20th century) from Turkey, Persia, Mongolia, Mughal India, China and Japan, and includes the helmet of the Ottoman Sultan Beyazit II.

The **Large Firearms** collection includes around 70 large early portable guns (17th century) produced in great European workshops and used by civilians. The **European Room** (16th–17th centuries) contains superb examples of Italian, German and French armoury made by the greatest European masters. The former Pauilhac Collection, acquired in 1964, has the only remaining example of a 17th-century French painted harness.

LOUIS XIV TO NAPOLÉON III (1643–1870)

This section covers the military as well as the political history of France in five themed stages. During the **Old Monarchy**, in the reign of Louis XIV, a professional army was formed to further the king's policy of conquest. The display includes the cannon ball that killed Turenne in 1675 and the back-plate of his cuirass. Also here is a magnificent ornamental *partisan*, presented to the Gardes de la Manche, King Louis' closest guards, on the occasion of the proxy marriage celebrations of his niece to Charles II of Spain.

Revolution to the Restoration of the Monarchy, reflecting a time of great turbulence, includes a model of the Bastille prison, symbol of royal authority. The era of Napoleon's imperial campaigns is illustrated by examples of arms used and regiments involved (infantry, cavalry, cuirassiers, carabineers and so on). Objects on display include a model of a Foot Grenadier, the toughest elite Imperial Guard. Memorabilia of Napoleon himself includes one of his grey coats, his hats, tent, furniture, the saddle of a dromedary from his Egyptian campaign, the stuffed skin of his white Arab horse, Vizir, and his 'Versailles pistols'. Also shown here is Ingres' celebrated painting, *Napoleon Enthroned* (1806), in which he wears the Order of the Légion d'Honneur (*see p. 118*).

The **Hundred Days** covers the period when, after nearly a year of Louis XVIII's reign, Napoleon returned from Elba in 1815. On 18th June he lost the battle of Waterloo. He abdicated on 22nd June and was imprisoned on St Helena and died on 5th May 1821. Attempts by France to establish her place in Europe resulted in the Franco-Prussian War of 1870–1. The effect of the siege of Paris and, above all, the annexation of Alsace-Lorraine by Germany had a lasting effect, leading to the First World War.

The **Vauban Room**, dedicated to the great military engineer of the 17th century, occupies one of the four former dining halls, with murals, *The Wars of Devolution* (1667–8). The history of French cavalry is presented through a collection of models of horses, some of which were donated from their studios by the artists Édouard Detaille and Ernest Meissonier, who were major supporters of the Musée de l'Armée.

THE TWO WORLD WARS (1871–1945)

The military history of France and the country's part in the world conflicts of the 20th century are evoked through some 4,000 objects, including personal belongings of military leaders, objects from former colonies, historical models, knives, pistols, rifles, machine guns, everyday objects, emblems, personal archives and documentary films, photographs, maps and architectural models.

Following the loss of **Alsace-Lorraine** to Germany, weapons were modernised and military service was gradually introduced. **The First World War: The Joffre Room** covers colonial expansion and the assassination of Archduke Franz Ferdinand in 1914. On show is one of the famous Renault cars, or 'Marne taxis', which carried troops to the Marne Front in September 1914, helping to save Paris from the advancing Germans. The **'Poilus' Room** addresses trench warfare (1915–17) and the suffering of the *poilus* ('hairy ones'), French ordinary soldiers who had no means of shaving. The increasing involvement of the Allies and the new weapons or equipment of this industrialised conflict, including machine guns, shells and protective masks against poison gas, are also explored. Products of the cultural war include propaganda posters. The section ends with the **Foch Room**, dealing with the conclusion of the First World War and the armistice. Over-confident in the strength of the Empire and the Maginot Line, however, France was not properly prepared for the next outbreak of war.

The Second World War: The Leclerc Room covers the campaign of France between 1939 and 1942; its occupation by Nazi Germany; the emergence of General de Gaulle and the Free French forces; the Battle of Britain; the German invasion of the USSR (June 1941); and the Japanese attack against the US Navy at Pearl Harbor (December 1941). The **Juin Room**, 1942–4, celebrates the first Allied victories and the struggle of the French Resistance. Objects include a North African *képi* worn by General Leclerc de Hauteclocque (*see p. 173*) and the uniform of a GI, including a first-generation assault jacket. The standard of the 2nd Regiment of Dragoons was the only flag to receive the *Médaille des Évadés* (the 'escapees'). The **De Lattre Room** evokes Allied landings and the liberation of French territory; and Allied offensives on Berlin and the discovery of the concentration camps. It contains a life-size model of the atomic bomb which destroyed Hiroshima and ended the war in Asia. The section ends with **Berlin and the Cold War**, and the fall of the Berlin Wall in 1989.

L'HISTORIAL CHARLES DE GAULLE

Both monument and memorial, this audiovisual tribute to Charles de Gaulle (1890–1970) was launched by President Chirac and opened by President Sarkozy in February 2008. It is the result of a close collaboration between the Musée de l'Armée and the Charles de Gaulle Foundation. This is not a conventional museum: it takes a multimedia approach and has no 'objects'. Each visitor is equipped with an infrared device to plot their own course through the some 400 audiovisual documents and nearly 20 hours of commentary. It combines audio books, newsreel, film, filmed interviews, photographs, maps and so on. Arranged around three concentric areas, it begins with a 25-minute biographical film, and is followed by 'a wall of images' which provides the background of the century throughout which de Gaulle was so dominant in France. Three rooms propose different ways of interpreting his legacy.

The great French wartime leader became President of the Fifth Republic in 1958, holding the post until 1969. The student revolt of 1968, followed by a general strike, destabilised his government, and though he won the next election, he nevertheless resigned in 1969. The events that symbolise de Gaulle's political career are his 1940 radio address from London, the Liberation of Paris in August 1944, the rebuilding of France in 1944–5, and the foundation of France's Fifth Republic in 1958.

OTHER MUSEUMS IN LES INVALIDES

MUSÉE DES PLANS-RELIEFS

The autonomous Musée des Plans-Reliefs (*open as Musée de l'Armée*), on the attic floor of the building, is a fascinating collection of some 100 relief maps of fortified sites, built to a scale of 1:600, which were created for practical military purposes. Begun from 1668, at the time of Vauban, the practice ended after the Franco-Prussian War (1870–1). The original idea is attributed to Louvois, Louis XIV's minister of war. Secreted until 1776 in the Louvre, the maps were then moved to Les Invalides. The display is divided between fortifications along the Channel, the Atlantic and Mediterranean coasts and the Pyrenees. Today these are a precious record of the history of fortification from the Middle Ages to 1870 (especially of those which have since disappeared) and of siege techniques, as well as of the evolution in the range of the fire of artillery.

MUSÉE DE L'ORDRE DE LA LIBÉRATION

The Musée de l'Ordre de la Libération is in the Robert de Cotte wing, headquarters of the Chancellerie de l'Ordre (*entrance at 15bis Blvd Latour-Maubourg*). It is a repository of memorabilia connected with the fighters for France Libre and the Resistance, between 18th June 1940 and 8th May 1945. It is also a memorial to the 1,036 companions who received the Cross of the Liberation created by de Gaulle in 1940 and to those deported. In six rooms are 3,700 objects and documents.

MUSÉE RODIN

Map p. 586, B2. 79 Rue de Varenne. Métro 13 to Varenne. Open Tues–Sun 10–5.45, Wed to 8.45, closed Mon and 1 Jan, 1 May and 25 Dec. Free first Sun of the month. Reduced admission for garden only. Audioguides, disabled access. Garden café open Tues–Sun 10–5.30, Wed until 8.30pm. T: 01 44 18 61 10, www.musee-rodin.fr.

The Musée Rodin, the 'home of sculpture', has exceptional charm and remains one of the most popular museums in Paris dedicated to a single artist. The fame of the sculptor as well as the setting contribute to the museum's popularity. Towards the end of his life, Auguste Rodin worked for nine years in this building, the Hôtel Biron, an 18th-century mansion with its garden. It now contains a permanent collection of works which were donated to the state by Rodin in 1916.

HISTORY OF THE HÔTEL DE BIRON-MUSÉE RODIN

Built in 1728–30 by Jean Aubert to designs by Jacques-Ange Gabriel, the mansion was purchased by Gontaut, Duc de Biron, Governor of Languedoc in 1753. He held sumptuous receptions here. In 1820 the Duchess of Charost, widow of the last owner, sold it to a religious community, les Dames du Sacré-Coeur de Jésus, which was expelled in 1904. Their chapel of 1876 was built using the proceeds of the sale of painted and gilt panelling from the Hôtel Biron, some of which has now been recovered or replaced. From 1908 Rodin rented a studio in the *hôtel*, alongside other artists and writers including the Austrian poet Rainer Maria Rilke, who was his secretary at that time. The sculptor gradually occupied more rooms and worked here until his death. The chapel, which reopened after restoration in 2005, is used for temporary exhibitions and contains the museum shop and ticket office. Rodin's former home and workshop at Meudon is also open to visitors (*see p. 462*).

AUGUSTE RODIN

Auguste Rodin (1840–1917) opened new vistas in a medium that had stagnated in the 19th century, doing for sculpture what the Impressionists did for painting—although he was not as vigorously criticised. In fact by 1900 he was widely acclaimed. Having trained as a sculptor-decorator for façades, he was, to his great regret, rejected three times by the École des Beaux-Arts. Rodin's technique was to model in clay—he was not a carver. Numerous assistants or trainees copied the clays in plaster, from which bronzes were cast; others carved the marbles under the master's supervision. Throughout his career major commissions were not always arrived at with any degree of ease and were secured on the basis of the plaster casts he presented to his patrons.

His first work accepted at the Salon was *The Man with the Broken Nose*, in 1878. *The Age of Bronze* (1876–7) was Rodin's first free-standing figure and caused controversy as it was erroneously reputed to have been cast from life. In the late 1870s Rodin systematically removed anything superfluous or distracting from his figures—the lance from the *Age of Bronze* or the cross from *St John the Baptist Preaching*—anything that added too precise an explanation. He would often reassemble anatomical elements from one work to create another: St John's vigorous legs became *The Walking Man* (1877–8); or reinterpret fragments of figures: *The Hand of God* is an amplification of a hand from *The Burghers of Calais*. Many of his masterpieces were triggered by parts of previous works, which he enlarged or reduced. He greatly admired Michelangelo and created a technique based on Michelangelo's unfinished works, although in this case the works were brought to a state of perfection, such as a highly polished figure emerging from rough-hewn marble or stone.

Rodin sculpted many men, but he adored women and they were attracted to him likewise. He made many female portraits some of which, like *Eve*, are symbolic. His affairs were legion yet he married Rose Beuret, his life-long companion and the mother of his son, just before her death.

THE COLLECTIONS

The collection includes around 500 sculptures, from early seminal works to the best-known marbles and bronzes, plaster casts, maquettes and 7,000 works on paper. It also includes Rodin's personal collection of art, antiquities and furniture, together with some 8,000 photographs. Masterpieces are displayed here alongside pieces from Rodin's own collection, as well as portrait busts of Rodin by Bourdelle and others, and examples of the pretty potboilers Rodin produced to make a living. Also scattered through the museum are the antiques that he collected from dealers who special-ised in job-lots for sculptors, and from which he drew inspiration. They range from Egyptian, Chinese and Indian to medieval European pieces.

The aim of the display is to present the different stages of the work of a sculptor, with specific examples of Rodin's creative methods. It explores the lengthy and com-plex genesis of a sculpture, including all the stages of preparation from the initial con-cept through sketches, maquettes, clay models, trials and plaster casts, until at last the final work is completed.

Sculptures of couples include *Paolo and Francesca*, the basis for *The Kiss* (1888). Rodin's compositions modelled on Camille Claudel (*see p. 48*) include *La France* and *l'Aurore*. Works by Claudel herself, which express her sensitivity and skill, are the bronze *L'Age Mûr* (1898), the onyx *Gossips* (1897) and *The Wave* (1897–1902) in onyx and bronze. Both Rodin and Claudel were skilled draughtsmen and made many pre-paratory drawings for sculptures. Among Rodin's personal art collection are three glo-rious works by Van Gogh, a female nude by Renoir and a Monet landscape.

THE FORECOURT AND GARDEN

In the forecourt of the museum, along with other bronzes, are the **Gates of Hell**, the result of a commission of 1880 for the entrance to a new Musée des Arts Décoratifs (which never materialised). It is based on Lorenzo Ghiberti's 'Gates of Paradise' (1403–24), the doors for the Baptistery in Florence, and on the iconography of Dante's *Divine Comedy* (1308–21) as well as Michelangelo's *Last Judgement* (1535–41) in the Sistine Chapel. Rodin modelled each figure separately in clay, experimenting with the composition on a wooden door frame. In the swirling cascade of the final version, many figures are illegible and even faceless; some that stand out include the *Three Shades* at the entrance to Hell, the *Thinker* (who is Dante), two *Falling Men*, *Ugolino*, *Paolo and Francesca* and *The Prodigal Son* (slightly amended in *Fugit Amor*). Rodin described this project as his 'Noah's Ark' of inventions, as it provided him with an end-less source of motifs which he re-used, in part or whole, in different positions, alone or in groups, amplified or reduced. The collection in this museum contains many examples. The gates were cast only in 1926 and have stood in the forecourt of the Hôtel Biron since 1939. The figure of the tragic Ugolino (pictured opposite, on all fours) was to inspire a number of French sculptors besides Rodin. Ugolino della Gherardesca, lord of Pisa, was embroiled in the Guelph-Ghibelline squabbles that beset medieval Italy in Dante's day. Captured and arrested during a riot, he was thrown into a dungeon with his two sons and two grandsons and left to starve to death. Rodin's sculpture (and a version by Carpeaux, in the Petit Palais) show him maddened by hunger, reduced

to gnawing his own fingers (Carpeaux) or contemplating devouring the bodies of his children (Rodin).

The elegant three-hectare **garden**, behind the museum, can be visited independently. Its formal layout is divided between lawns and hedges, a pond and rose gardens, framing to advantage the elegant south façade of the *hôtel*. It contains numerous examples of Rodin's bronzes as well as marble sculptures, and scattered around are more of the master's works, including ***The Thinker***, ***The Burghers of Calais***, *Whistler's Muse*, *Cybele*, and statues of the painters Bastien-Lepage and Claude Lorrain; in the pool is *Ugolino and his Children*. A recent trend has been to enliven the garden with modern sculptures.

THE BURGHERS OF CALAIS

This work was designed to commemorate an act of civic heroism in 1347 following a long siege of Calais by the English during the Hundred Years War. It represents the group of six notables who chose to sacrifice themselves to Edward III in return for the cessation of hostilities. In the event, so impressed was the English king by their bravery that they, and the city, were spared. To commemorate this heroic act in the 19th century, the town of Calais commissioned a monument. The committee had visualised something rather staid and allegorical, in the prevailing style of the time. Rodin's conception, however, was based on the description of the event by the 14th-century chronicler Froissart. His ideas evolved as he worked on maquettes from 1884–9; the first maquette is here in the museum. Its uncompromising realism was met with outrage, infuriating Rodin. Funding was slow and installation delayed until 1895. More disagreement followed on Rodin's outlandish suggestions for the plinth, designed either to display the group at ground level or on a 4m-high scaffold. Rodin's work today is considered a masterpiece, a deeply moving portrait of six brave men preparing to meet their deaths, huddled, heavy and agonised, expressing emotions of resignation, fear or despair. Two men, linked by their torment and by the ropes around their necks, carry the keys of the gates of Calais. Some ten versions of the Burghers exist, in Calais, Paris and in cities as far apart as Washington and Seoul.

RUE DE VARENNE & RUE DE GRENELLE

Map p. 586, B2–C2. Métro 13 to Varenne.

Streets such as Rue St-Dominique, Rue de Grenelle and Rue de Varenne—the two latter both deriving their names from *garenne*, or uncultivated land—have examples of the fashionable and handsome 17th–19th-century *hôtels particuliers* which have maintained the elegance typical of the old Faubourg St-Germain.

RUE DE VARENNE AND RUE DU CHERCHE-MIDI

East of the Musée Rodin, on Rue de Varenne, which opened c. 1605, is one of the most beautiful *hôtels* in the *faubourg*, the **Hôtel de Matignon** (no. 57), with an unusually large garden. Built in 1721 by Jean Courtonne and altered later, it has been the residence of the *Président du Conseil* (Prime Minister) since 1935. The novelist Edith Wharton spent 'rich years, crowded and happy...' at no. 53 from 1910–20. The **Hôtel de Gallifet** (no. 50; 1775–96) is the Italian Institute and their embassy is at no. 47. The section of Rue du Bac between Rue de Varenne and Rue de Sèvres is equally endowed; at no. 140 is the **Chapel of the Miraculous Medal**, a destination for many pilgrims because it is here that the Virgin Mary appeared to Ste Cathérine Laboure in 1830 and requested the creation of the medal; and where it meets Rue de Sèvres is the only department store on the Left Bank, the elegant **Bon Marché and La Grande Épicerie de Paris**, one of the best food halls in the city (with very sophisticated takeaway).

Further southwest, on Rue du Cherche-Midi, at no. 85, is the Hôtel de Montmorency-Bours (1743), an aristocratic mansion typical of the second half of the 19th century, former home of Ernest Hébert and now home to the **Musée Hébert** (*see p. 520*). Also on this street, at no. 8, is **Boulangerie Poilâne**, which opened here in 1932, and where the successful brown loaves were first baked. The local bar Au Sauvignon serves Poilâne toast for breakfast.

RUE DE GRENELLE

This was once a street of embassies and ministries, but many have now moved away. The ***Fontaine des Quatre-Saisons*** (*57–59 Rue de Grenelle*), the work of Bouchardon (1739), occupies an exedral façade on a grand scale, designed to maximise the limited space in this narrow street (Voltaire criticised the choice of site). Its purpose was to bring water to the district, but the supply turned out to be limited. The sculptures on the main section represent the City of Paris with the Seine and Marne at her feet, with bas-reliefs of the Seasons on the wings. The land once belonged to the Couvent des Récollets. The poet and dramatist Alfred de Musset lived at no. 59 from 1824 to 1840. In the 20th century, jazz enthusiasts frequented the Cabaret de la Fontaine des Quatre-Saisons. The building is now home to the Musée Maillol (*see below*).

No. 127, the **Hôtel du Châtelet**, is one of the finest examples of the Louis XV style, and was used as the Archbishop's Palace in 1849–1906.

MUSÉE MAILLOL

Map p. 586, C2. 59 Rue de Grenelle. Métro 12 to Rue du Bac. Open daily 10.30–7, Fri to 9.30 including public holidays. Frequent temporary exhibitions. Café on the lower level. T: 01 42 22 59 58, www.museemaillol.com.

The Musée Maillol, which opened in 1995, is an endowment of the Fondation Dina Vierny. Vierny (1919–2009) met Aristide Maillol in 1934: she was 15 and he 73. In her, Maillol recognised the ideal figure he had been modelling all his life. Their association lasted for ten years, during which Vierny began collecting. She opened a gallery in the St-Germain-des-Prés *quartier* after the war and, as a native of Russia, launched avant-garde Russian artists such as Poliakoff. In 1964 she created her foundation and the concept of the museum developed over 15 years. Dina Vierny gave 18 of Maillol's bronzes to the Louvre in 1964–5 (now in the Tuileries) and two more to the Éspace Tuileries in 2001. A major emphasis of the museum is on temporary exhibitions.

ARISTIDE MAILLOL

Maillol (1861–1944) was from a winegrowing family in Banyuls in French Catalonia. The family vineyards were lost to phylloxera in 1880 and the young Aristide pursued his studies on very slender means. Heavily influenced by the Nabis (*see p. 494*) though never strictly part of the group, he studied at the Beaux-Arts from 1887 but left in 1890, impatient with the outmoded teaching of Cabanel and Gérôme. After seeing some works by Gauguin, he began to produce Symbolist portraits of women, using bright, pale colours. He also experimented with pottery and wood-carving and for a time produced tapestry designs, but suffered eye strain from the weaving and elected to focus on sculpture, returning again and again to studies of the female nude, which became his chief mode of artistic expression ever after. His wife and model was Clotilde Narcis, of whom there is a portrait at the Fondation Vierny. After years of toiling in obscurity, he suddenly found himself the centre of attention following a solo exhibition at the Galerie Vollard in 1902. Rodin approved. Maillol began to be talked about and to receive commissions. Three years later, in 1905, *La Méditerranée* (a sculpture of a nude woman with her head bowed, rapt in thought) received an outstandingly good reception at the Salon d'Automne. In contrast to Rodin's more expressionistic work, Maillol's nudes are more condensations of form, placing him in an important position between the 19th century and Modernism. The Hungarian sculptor Béni Ferenczy, a great admirer of Maillol, described his sculptures thus: 'They do not express something, do not point to meanings beyond themselves; they are finished, complete aesthetic entities.'   A.B.

THE COLLECTIONS

Maillol's sculptures, particularly the monumental bronzes, among them *La Méditerranée* (1902–5), pensive and serene, established him among the great modern sculptors. Nine bronzes of between 1900 and 1931 include *Pomone* (1910), *La Rivière* (1938–43) and versions of those now exhibited in the Tuileries. Also here are examples of his work in crayon, pastel, chalk and charcoal and paintings in oils include *Portrait of Dina* (1940) and *Dina with a Scarf* (1941), as well as an Impressionistic earlier painting, *Seated Woman with Sunshade* (1895).

Holdings of sculpture and textiles (not necessarily on display) include examples of ceramics, woodwork and stone carving as well as tapestry designs. Dina Vierny's collection of modern and contemporary art has works by artists from whom Maillol drew inspiration, such as Renoir and Maurice Denis, as well as Gauguin. There are also Matisse drawings, watercolours by Dufy, drawings by Odilon Redon, and prints by Degas, Picasso, Bonnard, Ingres, Cézanne, Suzanne Valadon, Foujita and others. Vierny was an early supporter of naïve artists and the collections include Rousseau, Louis Vivin and Camille Bombois as well as works by each of the Duchamp brothers: Marcel, Raymond Duchamp-Villon and Jacques Villon. Russian non-figurative art includes works by Poliakoff, Kandinsky, Charchoune, Boulatov, Yankilevski and Oscar Rabin, and the Constructivist Jean Pougny.

EATING AND DRINKING AROUND LES INVALIDES

At Les Invalides is there is a café/self-service restaurant, € **Le Carré des Invalides** (*T: 01 44 42 50 71*), near the ticket office. € **Musée Rodin** has a charming garden café for meals and drinks (*T: 01 45 55 84 39; open Tues–Sun 10am–5pm, Wed until 8.30pm*). The **Bon Marché department store** at Sèvres-Babylone (*map p. 586, C3, www.lebonmarche.com*) has a vast and wonderful food store on the ground floor, with a choice of takeway food as well as high-quality groceries. It is the ultimate food market, well organised, beautifully presented and perfect for a gourmet picnic selection. A choice of restaurants in the area is given below:

€–€€ **L'Affable**. Fairly smart modern bistrot with a good-value lunch *formule* (open only on weekdays). Pleasant and relaxed with red upholstery and a zinc bar. The food is good quality and reliable and may include such traditional choices as *cuisses de grenouilles meunières* (frogs' legs), *ris de veau croustillant* (veal sweetbreads) or fillet of beef from the Aubrac, as well as fish choices and freshly cooked vegetables. *10 Rue de St-Simon. T: 01 42 22 01 60, www.laffable.fr. Map p. 586, B2.*

€–€€ **L'Ami Jean**. Off Rue Dominique, close to Les Invalides. Offers a modern slant on Basque cooking. *27 Rue Malar. T: 01 47 05 86 89, www.lamijean.fr. Map p. 585, F1.*

€ **Au Sauvignon**. This modest café on Place de la Croix Rouge has barely altered since the '60s when it was the first café to offer sandwiches made from *pain Poilâne*—and still does, as well as toast for breakfast. The original **Poilâne bakery** is close by at 8 Rue du Cherche-Midi (*www.poilane. com*). *88 Rue des Saints-Pères. T: 01 45 48 49 02. Map p. 586, C2.*

€ **Le Basile**. Popular with politics students from the nearby Sciences Po: informal, part-contemporary, part-traditional décor, with music and inexpensive salads and snacks. Open daily 7–midnight. *34 Rue de Grenelle. T: 01 42 22 59 46, www.lebasile.fr. Map p. 586, C2.*

€ **Bistrot Belhara**. The Basque chef produces traditional dishes with a modern slant. *23 Rue Duvivier. T: 01 45 51 41 77, www.bistrotbelhara.com. Map p. 585, F2.*

€ **Le Petit Lutetia**. Epitomises a traditional, subdued brasserie, with banquettes, mirrors, white tablecloths, and a board with the day's specials, such as *poireaux vinaigrette* (leeks) and *boeuf bourguignon*. *107 Rue de Sèvres. T: 01 45 48 33 53. Map p. 585, C3.*

Quai Branly
& the Eiffel Tower

The Eiffel Tower is the most recognised symbol of Paris, both visible from
all over the city and the best vantage point from which to view it.
In front of it stretches the wide parade ground of the Champ de Mars.
On Quai Branly is the well-known museum dedicated to pre-industrialised cultures.

Quai Branly is named after the scientist Édouard Branly, who in 1890 invented a device for detecting radio waves. The embankment leads between Pont de l'Alma (*map p. 585, E1*) and Pont de Bir-Hakeim (*map p. 584, C2*) and in turn gives its name to the museum of the ethnography and ethnology of parts of Asia, Oceania, Africa and the Americas that occupies a part of its length. A footbridge, Passerelle Debilly, links Quai Branly to the Right Bank.

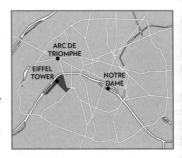

MUSÉE DU QUAI BRANLY

Map p. 585, E1. RER C to Pont de l'Alma. Enter from Quai Branly or from Rue de l'Université. Open Tues, Wed, Sun 11–7, Thur–Sat 11–9; closed Mon. T: 01 56 61 70 00; for reservations, T: 01 56 61 71 72, www.quaibranly.fr. Gardens open Tues, Wed, Sun 9.30–7.30, Thur–Sat 9.30–9.15; closed 25 Dec, 1 May. The ticket office is beneath the building, and the bookshop and Café Branly are in the garden; on the museum terrace is the restaurant, Les Ombres. Audioguides available. Disabled facilities. Ticket includes access to the permanent collections and temporary exhibitions on the mezzanines.

The Musée du Quai Branly opened in 2006, the culmination of a project announced by President Chirac in 1995. It is devoted to the arts and civilisations of pre-industrial societies in Oceania, Africa, Asia and the Americas, dating from the Neolithic era to the 20th century. The objective is to illustrate the lifestyle of cultural and ethnic groups through the objects associated with them. The core of the original collection came from

THE EIFFEL TOWER.

the Musée de l'Homme and the Musée National des Arts d'Afrique et d'Océanie. Of the 300,000 objects in the collection (plus photographs and documents), some 3,500 are on display, of which the majority date from the 19th or 20th centuries, though the cultural traditions that they reflect are much older. A particular emphasis is placed on recent Australian aboriginal art but the collections are rotated at intervals. The museum is also a research and education centre, with a media library open to the public.

THE BUILDING

The eye-catching building is by Jean Nouvel. The horizontal, curved edifice on stilts uses earth colours for the small exhibition spaces suspended from the main Seine façade; the south façade, of glass and stone, is decorated with the work of Aborigine artists. A tall transparent screen protects the site from the noise of the traffic on the quays, and the museum emerges from sloping gardens, planted with trees and varied grasses and has a *mur végétal* or 'plant wall' camouflaging part of the administrative section. The garden is lit at night by 'L'Ô', a 'lake' of phosphorescent tubes installed by Yann Kersalé.

From the vast entrance hall a ramp winds upwards around a glass tower which stretches the full height of the building and contains reserves of the collection of musical instruments. The main floor is wreathed in dramatic obscurity (partly for conservation purposes) and the four main exhibition spaces flow freely into each other around a central 'river', bordered by leather-covered, organically-shaped seating. The geographical regions are colour coded: Oceania red, Asia umber, Africa yellow and the Americas blue, and the floor colour indicates which region you are in. Each section is introduced by a representative group of objects. In the Asian and Africa sectors, some 30 'boxes' contain special exhibits. Although the individual captions for each object are not always easy to read, information is widely diffused through video programmes, multi-media installations and interactive alcoves as well as maps, texts and pictures.

Oceania

Melanesia: The objects from several islands in the Southern Pacific demonstrate the differences and similarities in cultures divided by great distances. Important to all these cultures is ancestor worship. From Papua New Guinea and West Guinea come ceremonial house posts, roof sculptures and masks associated with the ancestor house; ancestor skulls are preserved and embellished with seeds and feathers while carved headrests establish a personal link between owner and ancestors. Objects which are used in male initiation rites range from secret musical instruments to a Bisj pole carved from new wood following a ritual murder. The canoe and canoe sheds held a special role in the Solomon Islands in the head-hunting that was practised there until the end of the 19th century. Reliquaries, such as a dug-out canoe, were beautifully carved for the remains of chiefs. The many and varied symbols of hierarchy include finely-carved wooden dishes or a Rambaramp funerary effigy, with the features remodelled on the deceased's skull.

Masks cover a great diversity of forms and materials. They played a role in key points in public, spiritual and political life. Hemlaur masks of the Sulka people of New Britain are rare, as they are normally burned at the end of a ceremony. Decorated Tapa cloth, made from beaten bark, is found throughout Oceania, in particular in Melanesia and Polynesia.

Polynesia: The relationship between man and his gods is the focus here. Figurative or abstract, divine receptacles were used as containers for the breath of gods and ancestors. To enhance the sanctity of cult objects, sacred materials were used, such as red feathers in Tahiti or bark cloth and feathers in the Cook Islands; in the Fiji Islands coconut fibres cover miniatures of houses to attract spirits, the most important of whom is Tiki, the god-creator. Some images of divinities are made to last so that they can be handed down. Body art, permanent or ephemeral, continues this relationship with the divine: girls from the ages of 8 to 10, and boys at 15, underwent tattooing. Elegant insignia of rank include dishes for kava, the ceremonial drink. There are many and varied emblems of prestige: from the Marquesas, a decorated club in blackened hardwood; from Fiji, a finely inlaid headrest. Artefacts from the Maoris of New Zealand, such as the Korere feeding funnel used during painful facial tattooing, and a Hei Tiki jade pendant, demonstrate their superb skill in carving.

Australia: This section concentrates on contemporary Aboriginal art from Northern and Western Australia, based on an adaptation of ancient forms which is the plastic expression of 'Dreaming'. This refers to all that is known and all that is understood according to the Aboriginal explanation of life. Sacred or body decoration has evolved in modern times into acrylic paintings consisting of brilliant dots, straight or curved lines and circles. A series of shields and spear-throwers carry motifs connected with the modern works. The Bark Chamber contains eucalyptus-bark paintings, using natural pigments from Arnhem Land, that develop and elaborate on motifs of rock painting, both abstract and representational.

Insulindia: Exhibits from Insulindia, an archipelago of around 20,000 islands, including Indonesia, Malaysia and the Philippines, highlight the wide cultural and ethnic diversity of this region, which forms a crossroads between continental Southeast Asia and Oceania. The prehistory and protohistory of Insulindia is presented through recurring forms of metal artefacts and decorative items fashioned from gold, silver, brass and other alloys, as well as megalithism in Sumba, Sumatra and Nias, where ceremonial seats of honour were carved in the form of mythical animals. The spread of the Dong Son civilisation from China to Insulindia is represented by bronze drums traditionally buried with their owner, including a 4th–1st-century BC Dongsonian drum from Java. The largest example of a bronze funeral drum is from Vietnam (18th–19th centuries).

Asia

The collections from the Asian continent cover an area from Siberia to the Middle East, but the greatest number and variety of objects are from Southeast Asia, the former territories of French Indochina. The objects focus on specific themes, such as village and minority cultures, popular religion, and communities living by oral tradition, in recent and even contemporary times. The survival of Shamanism in Siberia is an example.

Costumes and textiles: The backbone of the section is a colourful array of costumes and textiles illustrating the vast range of lifestyles, cultures and climates on the Asian continent, along with the cross-fertilisation of cultures. The collection shows the ways in which raw materials, techniques of weaving and sewing, dyes and decorative elements, are applied in different communities. In Russia and far eastern Siberia, for example, birch-tree bark is a basic raw material, as is reindeer hide; a bride's coat from Nivkh is made from fish skin and embroidered with a bear-head design for protection against evil spirits. Costumes play a major role in art and symbolism, and in exchange and movement, and textiles, dress and adornment tell us much about the role of women and girls. Some 300 examples of textiles and jewellery represent the Miao groups who migrated to the Southeast Asian peninsula. The largest ethnic group, who speak the Tai languages, is represented by many different weaving techniques including ikat, where the thread goes through a tie-and-dye process. There are elaborate jackets from Laos, their designs embroidered from memory and taking nearly a year to complete. The beautifully decorated Akha bonnets worn by the Yao and Tibeto-Burmese indicate age group, from birth to old age.

The identifying dress of Western Asian civilisations includes face veils which go back to c. 1000. The Assyrians were the first to insist that married women cover their heads outside the home, and this custom spread to Greece and Rome. It was adopted successively by Judaism, by Christianity for women at prayer, and by Islam as a sacred duty. An elaborate Burqa face veil from Gaza displays the wearer's wealth in the form of coins, silver, cornelian and agate.

Southeast Asia: Early 20th-century artefacts provide information on the agricultural communities of Southeast Asia: a decorative mask from Myanmar for the lead bull in a caravan; the machete essential for survival in the central highlands of Indochina; and an elaborate *naga* snake sickle from Cambodia. Buddhism was the religion of the plains but did not reach the mountain people, who worshipped a multiplicity of spirits in rituals in which tomb sculptures, such as the wooden image of a seated *bram* (from Vietnam) were carved. Beliefs among ethnic groups of the Himalayas are represented by an 11th-century Shâkyaumini Buddha or a Nepalese anthropomorphic mask in wood with goat's hair, thought to represent a forest spirit.

Central Asia: The two nomadic populations of Central Asia were Indo-Iranians, who lived in goatskin tents and travelled on foot, and Turko-Mongolian yurt dwellers, who followed their stock on horseback. In these societies, jewellery and harnesses, such as the horse's saddle from Uzbekistan, acquired more value than coins. Felt, an ancient fabric made from layer upon layer of compacted fleece, is widely used for waterproof or protective clothing.

Africa

The Africa collection has some 70,000 objects from North African countries, sub-Saharan Africa and Madagascar, dating from the 3rd century BC to 1895. The displays are by region and by theme and include textiles, musical instruments and sculpted representations of the body. The 'boxes' on the north wall have a particular thematic or cultural focus. Nomadic life and a concern with the metaphysical are two themes; objects include dancing masks and examples of body ornament.

North Africa: Examples of the spread of the written word include a 10th-century parchment extract from the Koran and a silver Torah Shield (18th century). Caravan routes across the Sahara from the 3rd century BC facilitated trade in salt and other produce: slaves from the Tuareg Berber north, and gold, ivory and indigo from the Negro south.

West Africa: In the Mandé region on the borders of Mali and Guinea, remarkable masks were produced for male initiation societies, such as the N'tomo mask in wood, brass and aluminium from Malinke. Statues associated with ancestors include a wood carving of a mother suckling a child from Cameroon. Trade with Europe developed in coastal West Africa in the 15th century. Commodities included slaves, but also objects such as ivory horns, salt cellars and spoons.

Gold was invested with considerable powers, and goldsmiths created fine objects such as the appliqué jewel in the image of two facing crocodiles. The lost-wax technique passed from Ife (Nigeria) to Benin and objects made in this way are on display. The first known figurative sculpture in West Africa, modelled by hand with extreme skill, was produced by the ancient Nok culture (1st millennium BC) in Nigeria. The 12th–15th-century Classical period of the Ife and Benin kingdoms includes objects associated with court traditions. A typical head of a royal ancestor marks an artistic high spot during the Benin kingdom's expansion.

Ethnic groups from southwest Nigeria are represented by numerous carved wooden objects, as well as a colourful Egungun cloth mask. Masks in the shape of fish or crocodiles for paying homage to water spirits come from the Niger delta.

Equatorial Africa: Equatorial Africa includes many ethnic groups who created an outstanding range and variety of sculptures, many of which inspired Western artists early in the 20th century. Metal objects carried the ultimate symbolic value, shown for example in a Ngulu reliquary guardian incorporating brass and copper. The *Nkisi nkondi* is a magical male image from Angola, made of wood with iron nails embedded in it. There are also fertility or fecundity images of women, often featuring children.

The Kuba from central Congo participate in lengthy rites of passage to adulthood. Related objects include the *Ndeemba* and *Bwoom* masks.

South and East Africa: In South and East Africa similar rites and rituals to Central Africa determine many of the arts. The staff signifying adulthood in Zulu art traditionally features a male image on the handle. Headrests from Zimbabwe and Mozambique often have a stylised zoomorphic design. Women have long been involved in bead work, first using natural materials, but glass beads became important after they were introduced in the 19th century. Madagascar absorbed traditions from the peoples of the Indian Ocean and Insulindia. The Malgache protect themselves against spirits and supernatural beings with an amulet or *ody*, while the talisman case, or *sampy*, attracts success of

The Americas

This collection is the richest, and is divided into three sections: Pre-Columbian America; Pan America, highlighting through objects the trans-continental unity of native American people; and America from the 17th century to the present.

Pre-Columbian America (or Pre-Hispanic America) refers to the era before the New World was 'discovered' by Columbus in 1492. The archaeological collections give an overview of the many cultures that succeeded one another in the three major cultural areas: Mesoamerica (between the North Mexican deserts and Central America), Central America and the Andes.

Pre-Hispanic Mesoamerica was dominated by the Olmecs between 1200 and 300 BC. They were replaced by the Maya, who created even more impressively monumental sites and developed a calendar, a complex writing system, and made superb ceramics, such as the spherical bowl in the shape of a death's head from Guatemala (300–600). The El Tajín, from the Gulf of Mexico, are represented by hollow ceramic statues, while the Huastecs sculpted unusual figures in limestone such as the old man leaning on a stick. A fragment of paving stone (800–1200) is an example of Zapotec culture. The sophisticated Teotihuacán culture (150–650) on the central Mexican plateau made terracotta objects such as the butterfly vase with a lid. The Aztecs (1350–1521) dominated central Mexico and much of the Pacific

coast for 150 years before the arrival of the '*conquistadores*'. Aztec divinities such as Tlaloc, god of rain and personification of the earth, or Huitzilopochtli, god of war and guiding deity, were carved in stone or green rock.

The Pre-Hispanic Andes benefited from deposits of gold and silver, but also produced terracotta objects, such as the Cauca culture statuette of a seated warrior. The small elegant metal pectoral from Boyacá was an emblem of power for the Muisca culture (1200–1500) in the central high plateau. During the 4th century BC, on the central coast of Ecuador, the Valdivia culture was the first to carve human figurines out of soft stone. By 500–300 BC different styles had developed, such as the Jama Coaque culture in Manabi province, who produced the seated statuette of a chief or priest, with elaborate headdress and piercings.

The great early civilisations of the Central Andes, notably Peru, are represented by ceramics from c. 1800 BC. Regional developments followed a succession of powerful societies which dominated the area, including the Moche (c. 100 BC–c. AD 700) on the north Peruvian coast, who worked gold and silver and decorated terracotta vases with scenes of humans in their environment and performing rituals. The Paracas produced funerary fabrics of great quality; the Nasca are representing by polychrome ceramics; the Recuay by a novel piece representing a warrior and a cat, the cat definitely overpowering the warrior. The Chimú kingdom (c. 11th century AD) dominated the north coast of Peru, its capital Chan Chan covering over 20km square. Each king had his own palace, many fortresses were built and the desert was irrigated. An exhibit from this culture is a ceremonial gauntlet in silver decorated with stylised human and animal motifs. From 1438 the Incas (1200–1500) became the largest Pre-Columbian empire, ruling from their capital at Cuzco. They encouraged the worship of their foremost god Inti, the sun god.

The remarkable textiles from the Pre-Hispanic Andes (2000 BC–AD 1532) are mainly from burial sites in the coastal deserts of Peru and Chile, including knotted cords used by the Incas for counting. There are examples of embroidery and a tapestry with a figure carried on a litter (1100–1450). Textiles and clothing of hide and bark, as well as feather-based artefacts, demonstrate the importance of colour for the American Indians of the Pre-Columbian period.

Pan-American Transformations: The comparison of artefacts relating to common themes and myths from all over the American continent and from all eras suggests the influence of the collective unconscious. This is seen in anthropomorphic objects, utensils in the form of animals, weapons from places as far apart as Guyana and Canada, and bead work and basket work from North and South America.

Colonial and Contemporary America: The period between the 16th and 19th centuries saw an unprecedented mingling of peoples, especially through European colonisation, which introduced Europeans into the New World, and also through the slave trade, which brought millions of Africans to America. Christian traditions were fused with African magic practices. Slaves who managed to free themselves established communities in the Guyanese forests. Many modern musical genres were the result of this cultural blending. Collections of clothing (19th–20th centuries) cover all of America from Canada to Patagonia. Among them are a series of feather-based artefacts from Amazonia and cotton from Brazil. There is a collection of 18th-century painted hides from the northern regions, including a bison-dance coat that once belonged to the French royal collections. There is also a series of paintings by George Catlin, commissioned by Louis-Philippe.

The Inuits of the northwest Canadian coast, who lived by seal farming, made implements from walrus ivory, such as a harpoon support and an *ulu* (woman's knife). The people of the northwest coast participated in potlatch, the exchange of food and gifts to confer power and status, as well as long winter rituals involving masks, such as the remarkable articulated mask made by the Haida people. Totem poles represent clan kinships and stood in front of houses. The figures on a pole erected c. 1880 in Angidah village, British Columbia, tell of the myth of the Peesunt people, descended from twins, half-man half-bear. The art of the Plains Indians—Sioux, Cheyenne and Blackfoot—divides into figurative for men and abstract for women.

THE EIFFEL TOWER

Map p. 585, D2. RER C to Champ de Mars-Tour Eiffel.

The Tour Eiffel, the most emblematic monument of Paris, can be glimpsed from most parts of the city. Standing close to the Seine, its giant presence is the main focus of one of the great city vistas which stretches from the École Militaire down the kilometre-long gardens of the Champ de Mars and across the Seine, spanned by Pont d'Iéna, to the Palais de Chaillot. The view is equally spectacular in the other direction—perhaps better, when the fountains of the Trocadéro gardens are playing in the foreground. The Eiffel Tower attracts huge numbers of visitors. On a clear day, particularly about one hour before sunset, it is the ultimate place from which to view (and photograph) Paris.

The tower is a masterpiece of 19th-century engineering and still, in the 21st century, its audacious proportions (324m high including the television antennae) are breathtaking. At night it shimmers like a golden beacon, thanks to the sodium lamps which illuminate it, the work of lighting engineer Pierre Bideau. Every hour on the hour a shower of sparkles dances up and down the tower, lasting for five minutes. Long an inseparable part of the Parisian landscape, La Tour Eiffel continues to inspire painters, poets and film-makers.

HISTORY OF THE EIFFEL TOWER

Opened in 1889 for the Universal Exhibition held to mark the centenary of the Revolution, the Eiffel Tower aroused as much controversy then as the Pompidou Centre or the Louvre Pyramid did in the 20th century. Originally granted only 20 years of life, its role in radio-telegraphy in 1909 saved it from demolition.

The design was mainly the work of the engineers Maurice Koechlin and Émile Nouguier and the architect Stephen Sauvestre but it was erected by a contracting company owned by the engineer Gustave Eiffel, whose name the tower has borne ever since. The tapering lattice-work structure is composed of 18,000 pieces of metal and weighs over 10,000 tonnes. Its four feet are supported by masonry piers sunk 9–14m into the ground. It is repainted about every seven years in Eiffel-Tower bronze, a colour that is exclusive to the monument and which almost imperceptibly changes from a lighter tone at the summit to a darker one at the base, to give the impression that it is the same colour all the way up.

Today the Iron Lady has met her capacity in the number of visitors she can accommodate, and the new approach is to admit fewer people but to provide improved surroundings. To this end the tower has been undergoing extensive renovations for the first time since the 1980s, while remaining open. Refurbishment of the West Lift has been going on for several years at a cost of some €36 million (causing some delays), and there are major changes on Level 1. The increase in places to eat has been part of the campaign. There are many more costly plans afoot to improve the experience, but decisions still have to be taken.

Visitor information

Open mid-June–early Sept 9–midnight; rest of the year 9.30–11. Easter weekend and spring holidays open to midnight. Guided visits and iPhone app available. T: 08 92 70 12 39, www.tour-eiffel.fr. Ticket sales in the south, north and east pillars.
Access by lift: *Lifts leave from the north and east pillars for Levels 1 (57m) and 2 (115m). On Level 2 you change to a separate lift for Level 3 (276m). Mid-June–early Sept last lift midnight (3rd floor last lift 11pm); rest of the year last lift 11pm (3rd floor 10.30). There can be a long wait for the lift to Level 3 at peak times.*
Ascent on foot: *Mid-June–early Sept last admission midnight; rest of the year last admission 6pm. You can climb the tower to Level 2 (704 steps) and after that purchase a ticket for the lift to the top. Queues for the ascent on foot are considerably shorter.*
Cafés/restaurants: *Snacks are available on all three floors. For details, see p. 151. There is a hole-in-the-wall hatch on Level 3 (grandly called a 'Champagne Bar'), where you can get a flute of fizz.*

Ground Level has a temporary exhibition about the improvements to the Tower. In the South Pillar there are also an ATM, a shop, buffet and post office (for an Eiffel Tower postmark). The 1899 lift machinery is in the basement (*open occasionally*).

Level 1, at 57m above ground, is enclosed, relaxed and was revamped in 2014 to adapt to the increasing number of visitors and to improve disabled access, energy efficiency, visitor services, cafés and shops. Four transparent pavilions with sloping sides following the angle of the pillars have been created, leaving the central area open. The floor surrounding the central space and the protective barriers are now also (non-slip) glass, intensifying the experience of being at such a height. There is an entertaining and educational discovery path, the Eiffel Tower Epic, with information about the monument and its history. The presentations in the Ferrié wing and Cineiffel combine unusual pictures and virtual images. The 58 Tour Eiffel restaurant is here.

Level 2 (115m), open-air and with a promenade deck, is a good place from which to photograph Paris. The 'Story Windows' provide information on the construction of the tower, the lifts and the old hydraulic lift which went to the top until 1983. There are glazed portholes for vertiginous views directly to ground level. It was from this level, in 1912, that the tailor Franz Reichelt tragically jumped to his death. He had invented a wearable parachute and his aim had been to demonstrate its efficacy. In the extremely gusty conditions of that February day, however, it failed to inflate and wrapped itself around his body. There are also shops on this level, a buffet and the Jules Verne restaurant.

Level 3: Glass lifts carry you the final 160m to the top level (276m). There are two tiers, one open-air and the other enclosed, equipped with telescopes and maps to help you make the most of the spectacular panorama, and a scale model of the top floor in 1889. There is also a champagne 'bar' and a reconstruction of Gustave Eiffel's office.

THE CHAMP DE MARS

Map p. 585, E2. Métro 8 to École Militaire.

Positioned between the École Militaire and the Seine, the Champ de Mars was laid out in 1765–7 as a parade ground on the market gardens of the old Plaine de Grenelle. Several early aeronautical experiments were carried out from here by, among others, J.-P. Blanchard in 1783–4. It became the theatre of the celebration to mark the first anniversary of the storming of the Bastille, the *Fête de la Fédération* (14th July 1790), and of Napoleon's *Champ de Mai* on his return from Elba. In 1791 an anti-royalist petition resulted in many deaths when the National Guard opened fire on a crowd led by Danton and Camille Desmoulins. Used as a racecourse after the Restoration, the parade ground was transformed and reduced in 1860 and became the site of five universal exhibitions. In 1908, a 20-year project was initiated to create the park that exists today, with central lawns, avenues of trees and less formal areas on either side.

Among the sculptures is the **Monument to the Rights of Man**, near the Rue de Belgrade (southeast), commemorating the bicentenary of the Revolution. Captain Alfred Dreyfus, a promising young Jewish artillery officer from Alsace, was publicly degraded here in December 1894, the start of the Dreyfus affair, in which he was falsely accused of delivering documents concerned with the national defence to a foreign government.

Champ de Mars is still a rallying ground for demonstrations and major events. The **Mur de la Paix** or Wall of Peace (Clara Halter and Jean-Michel Wilmotte) was erected here in 2000. Inspired by the Wailing Wall in Jerusalem, it has chinks into which visitors can insert messages of peace. But the pugnacious spirit of Mars cannot be so easily appeased on this field: vandals find the broad glass panels of the Peace Wall all too tempting.

ÉCOLE MILITAIRE

The École Militaire on Place Joffre (*map p. 585, E2–E3*), a handsome structure covering part of the former farm and château of Grenelle, was built by J.-A. Gabriel and enlarged in 1856. Eighteenth-century railings separate the Place de Fontenoy from the elegant Cour d'Honneur, profusely embellished with Corinthian columns and pilasters. The figure of *Victory* on the entablature is modelled on Louis XV, but this apparently went unnoticed by Revolutionary iconoclasts, who left it unscathed.

The school was founded in 1751 by Louis XV for the training of noblemen as army officers. Opened in 1756, it was completed in 1773. In 1777 its rigid rules for entry were modified to accept the élite of provincial military academies. Thus it was that in 1784 Napoleon Bonaparte was chosen from the Collège de Brienne. Officer cadet Bonaparte was confirmed in the chapel, which is decorated with nine paintings of the life of St Louis.

The vast complex of buildings is now a staff college, part of the Ministry of Defence, for training the upper echelons of the armed services.

UNESCO
The *Nagasaki Angel.*

UNESCO

Map p. 585, E3–F3. *Group visits only, Tues–Fri, by reservation (visits@unesco.org).*

UNESCO, the UN's Organisation for Education, Science and Culture, has its headquarters on Place de Fontenoy. The building was designed by an international team of French and American architects, Bernard Zehrfuss and Marcel Breuer, and the Italian engineer Pier Luigi Nervi. Construction began in 1954 and the complex was inaugurated four years later. The number of member states of UNESCO has increased from the original 37 to 195, and the multinational character of the organisation is reflected in all aspects of the building design.

The large complex consists of three major buildings and some outstanding artworks. The main part is the Y-shaped concrete and glass **Secretariat** on seven floors, where the Ségur façade is enlivened by a spiral fire escape. The square building to the west has a mosaic by Jean-René Bazaine on one exterior wall, next to which is the Japanese **Garden of Peace**, designed by Isamu Noguchi. It contains the *Nagasaki Angel*, a sculpture fragment from the cathedral of Nagasaki destroyed by the second atomic bomb, and a cylindrical Meditation Space designed by Tadao Ando, with a pond in and near which are stones which were exposed to the bombing of Hiroshima. The **Conference Building** has fluted concrete walls and an accordion-pleated concrete roof covered in copper.

On the vast **piazza**, in the angle formed by avenues Lowendal and Suffren, are works by Alexander Calder, Henry Moore and Giacometti, as well as *Symbolic Globe* (1995) by the Danish engineer Erik Reitzel (who worked on the Grande Arche de La Défense), and *Birth of a New Man* by Zurab Tsereteli (1992), marking the 500th anniversary of the discovery of America.

PLACE DES MARTYRS JUIFS
Detail of the memorial to the victims of the Vél d'Hiv roundup.

ALONG THE SEINE

At 101bis Quai Branly, between the Eiffel Tower and Pont de Bir-Hakeim, is the **Maison de la Culture du Japon à Paris** (*map p. 585, D2; open Tues–Sat 12–7, Thur until 8; closed Sun and Mon; T: 01 44 37 95 01*). Designed by Masayuki Yamanaka and inaugurated in 1997, this provides a permanent centre where Japanese culture can be presented in all its aspects through exhibitions, concerts and other events.

Pont de Bir-Hakeim, on two levels, métro and road, was built in 1903–6 and modified 1930–40. Originally known as Pont de Passy, from the name of the district to which it leads, it was given its present name in 1948, to commemorate the resistance of the Free French against Rommel in Libya in 1942. From it, Boulevard de Grenelle leads southeast. At **no. 8 Blvd de Grenelle** a plaque records the notorious Rafle du Vél d'Hiv, the roundup in July 1942 of thousands of Parisian Jews in the Vélodrome d'Hiver, a covered cycle track that once stood here and where Hemingway used to enjoy watching races. The Jews were kept here for some days before being deported to Auschwitz. Today, on the waterfront, part of the railway line has been covered over (west of the bridge) and named **Place des Martyrs Juifs**. It is home to a moving monument to the deported by Walter Spitzer, himself a Holocaust survivor.

Quai de Grenelle continues southwest past **Square Bela Bartok** (*map p. 584, C3*), a little valley planted with shrubs and bamboos, created in 1981 among the high-rise buildings flanking the Seine. On the opposite bank is the **Maison de la Radio** (Henry Bernard, 1963). Stretching between Pont de Bir-Hakeim and Pont de Grenelle is an artificial island, the **Allée des Cygnes**, with a pleasant, tree-lined walk (accessible from either end). At its western extremity is a scale replica in bronze of Bartholdi's

Statue of Liberty, a gift from the Parisian community in the United States in 1885 in return for the original presented by France to New York.

Further on still is **Pont Mirabeau** (1895–7; *map p. 584, B3*), leading to Auteuil and the Fondation Le Corbusier (*see p. 436*). The bridge was made famous by Guillaume Apollinaire in his poem of 1912:

Sous le pont Mirabeau coule la Seine
  Et nos amours
  Faut-il qu'il m'en souvienne
La joie venait toujours après la peine...

EATING AND DRINKING AROUND THE EIFFEL TOWER

On Level 1 of the Eiffel Tower is the **58 Tour Eiffel**, for 'picnic' lunches or dinner (*see www.restaurants-toureiffel.com to reserve online; the price of the lift ticket will be included*). On Level 2 is the romantic and exclusive €€€ **Jules Verne Restaurant**. Under the direction of Alain Ducasse, it is a wonderful experience altogether, and there is even a separate lift to take you there: much in demand, book well in advance (*T: 01 45 55 61 44, www.lejulesverne-paris.com*).

The **Musée du Quai Branly** has a roof-terrace restaurant (completely glassed over), €€ **Les Ombres**, in the shadow (*ombre*) of the Tour Eiffel. It serves modern international food and is open daily (*T: 01 47 53 68 00, www.lesombres-restaurant.com*). On the garden level is **Café Branly**, for drinks and snacks. Other possibilities nearby include the following:

€€ **L'Epopée**. This is an attractive and pleasant setting to enjoy a good-value seasonal menu. The cooking is inspired by the great gastronomic regions of eastern France: Burgundy and the Lyonnais. Good lunch *formule* and weekday menus where you choose from the slate. *89 Av. Émile-Zola, T: 01 45 77 71 37, www.lepopee.fr. Map p. 585, D3.*

€–€€ **La Cantine du Troquet Dupleix**. A *troquet* is a bar, and the verb *troquer* means to barter. South of the Champ de Mars, near Place Dupleix, is chef Christian Etchebest's good, unpretentious interpretation of the theme, serving specialities from southwest France, notably the Basque country. *53 Blvd de Grenelle. T: 01 45 40 04 98. Map p. 585, D3.*

€ **Le Troquet**. Another '*troquet*' where chef Marc Mouton serves up flavours of the southwest. A friendly and popular place. *21 Rue François-Bonvin. T: 01 45 66 89 00. Map p. 585, F4.*

Luxembourg & Gobelins

The extensive gardens of the Palais du Luxembourg occupy a vast area between Boulevard St-Germain and Boulevard de Montparnasse. South of them are the Paris Observatory and the hospitals of Boulevard Port-Royal. The 13th arrondissement, further east, is home to the Gobelins tapestry manufactory.

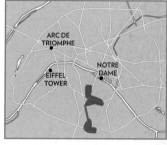

Rue de Vaugirard is the longest street in Paris, stretching from Boulevard St-Michel to the Porte de Versailles. On its south side is the historic **Palais du Luxembourg** and its extensive garden. Further west, on the opposite side from the Luxembourg, is the domed church of **St-Joseph-des-Carmes** (*map p. 586, C3*), once the chapel of a Carmelite convent, dating from 1613–20, containing several 17th-century canvases. In the crypt are the bones of some 120 priests massacred in the convent garden in September 1792. Josephine de Beauharnais (1763–1814), later Madame Bonaparte, was one of many imprisoned here during the Terror. Adjacent are the buildings of the Institut Catholique, founded in 1875, one of the most prestigious Catholic teaching establishments in France. It was there, in 1890, that Édouard Branly invented his coherer, a device for detecting radio waves. South of Rue de Vaugirard is **Rue de Fleurus**, where Gertrude Stein lived, at no. 27 (plaque).

PALAIS DU LUXEMBOURG

Map p. 587, D3. 15 Rue de Vaugirard. RER B to Luxembourg. Occasional visits with CMN (see p. 540) or T: 01 44 54 19 30. Visits can be made to the Senate in session: individuals should check the schedule on T: 01 42 34 20 01, then request a ticket at the Accueil du Sénat (ID required); groups by appointment minimum one month in advance, T: 01 42 34 20 60. Details on www.senat.fr. To visit the palace building, T: 01 42 34 20 60 or email visites@senat.fr. Visits take place on Saturdays at set times.

The Palais du Luxembourg, home to the Sénat, the upper chamber of the French government, was once a royal residence. The northern façade, where the main entrance is surmounted by an octagonal dome, is the 17th-century original; the south façade, facing the gardens, is a 19th-century copy. The two wings, terminating in double steep-roofed pavilions with three orders of columns superimposed, are connected by a single-storey gallery. Architecturally the palace provides an early example of a building visualised in terms of mass as opposed to an emphasis on surface decoration, thus preparing the way for Classicism.

HISTORY OF THE PALAIS DU LUXEMBOURG

Marie de Médicis, mother of Louis XIII and widow of Henri IV, commissioned the most distinguished architect of the time, Salomon de Brosse, to design the Luxembourg. Following the assassination of her husband, the queen supposedly wished to quit the gloomy Louvre for a more rural setting reminiscent of Tuscany; somewhere that recalled the Pitti Palace, her birthplace in Florence. The Luxembourg, built in 1615–27, stands on the site of the Petit-Luxembourg (1570–1612), the mansion she acquired from the Duc de Tingry-Luxembourg. After Louis XIII's death in 1643, the palace passed to Marie's second son Gaston, Duc d'Orléans, and the Palais Médicis became known as the Palais d'Orléans. Subsequently it belonged in succession to Mlle de Montpensier, daughter of Gaston d'Orléans; the Duchesse de Guise (1672); Louis XIV (1694) and the Orléans family. The building was altered in 1808 and enlarged in 1831–44, gaining a new façade facing the gardens. It was used as a prison during the Revolution and in 1794 the Directory transferred the seat of government here from the Tuileries. In 1800 it became the Palais du Consulat; under the Empire it was the Palais du Sénat and later the Chambre des Pairs (House of Lords). Several important people were tried here, including Louis-Napoléon Bonaparte (the future Napoléon III) after his second attempted coup in 1840. From 1852 to 1940, except for a short time, the Palais became the meeting place of the Senate, the upper chamber of the French Republic. Used as the Luftwaffe's headquarters in 1940–5, it reverted to the Senate in 1958.

INTERIOR OF THE PALACE

The interior (*to arrange a visit, see above*), drastically remodelled by Jean Chalgrin under Napoleon, is decorated in the sumptuous 19th-century manner. The series of paintings by Rubens devoted to the life of Marie de Médicis, painted for the palace, is now in the Louvre (*see p. 194*). Of the rooms that can be visited, Marie de Médicis' audience chamber, the **Cabinet Doré**, is outstanding. Other rooms occasionally open to the public are the Salles des Conférences, the hemicycle of the Salle des Séances and the library with paintings by Delacroix.

The adjoining **Petit-Luxembourg**, now the residence of the President of the Senate, was presented to Richelieu by Marie de Médicis in 1626. It includes the cloisters and chapel of the Filles du Calvaire, for whom the queen built a convent; the chapel is a charming example of the Renaissance style; the cloister forms a winter-garden.

MUSÉE DU LUXEMBOURG

Next door to the Petit-Luxembourg, at 19 Rue de Vaugirard, is the charming Musée du Luxembourg. This was the first French museum to be opened to the public, in 1750 and from 1818 became the first museum to show contemporary art. It now holds frequent temporary exhibitions (*open daily 10–7.30, Fri and Mon until 10pm; T: 01 40 13 62 00, www.museeduluxembourg*).

JARDIN DU LUXEMBOURG

Map p. 587, D3. RER B to Luxembourg. Open daily 7, 8 or 8.15–dusk.

The Jardin du Luxembourg was first created for Marie de Médicis against the handsome backdrop of the Luxembourg Palace. Although radically altered in 1782 and 1867, its basic layout still follows to some extent the 17th-century original, which was inspired by the Boboli Gardens, attached to Marie de Médicis' birthplace of Palazzo Pitti in Florence. Altogether less formal and more varied than the Champ de Mars or Tuileries, the 25 hectares are embellished by some 106 statues, two fountains and a pond. There is also an orchard and an apiary. In a quarter with few green spaces, it is pleasantly refreshing and its cafés, bandstand with regular concerts, carousel, marionette theatre and children's play area are very popular on sunny weekends. On clement weekdays, office workers and students come here to eat lunch. Chess-players are frequently to be seen locked in combat and there are photographic exhibitions on the railings. In 2011 a ten-year campaign began to replace the old trees and to include species not previously planted in an overall scheme of diversifying the flora of the gardens. To encourage owls, nesting boxes have been installed.

In the centre of the gardens is an area of lawns surrounding an **octagonal pond** with a fountain. Beyond the formal west terrace (to your right if you stand with the palace behind you) is the **Jardin Anglais**, enclosing a small-scale replica of the *Statue of Liberty* by Bartholdi that was given to the United States in 1886, as well as a stele commemorating Édouard Branly (*see p. 153*). To the southwest is a fruit garden with old apple varieties and there is a collection of orchids. Due south, an impressive perspective stretches between avenues of pollarded trees.

North of the central octagonal pond, opposite the east flank of the palace, is an oblong pool, at the end of which is the **_Fontaine Médicis_**, attributed to Salomon de Brosse (c. 1627), in the style of an Italianate grotto. It was moved here in 1861. In the central niche is *Polyphemus about to crush Acis and Galatea*; on either side are *Pan* and *Diana*, by Augustin Ottin (1866). At the back is a low relief, the *Fontaine de Léda*, brought from the Rue du Regard in 1855.

The many **sculptures** placed around the gardens include a statue of Stendhal by Rodin, a monument to Watteau by Henri Gauquié, a monument to Paul Éluard by Zadkine, a bust of Beethoven by Bourdelle and a monument to Delacroix by Jules Dalou, pupil of Carpeaux. Also here, on the west terrace behind the tennis courts, is Dalou's *Triumph of Silenus* (1884), showing one of the most celebrated companions of Dionysus in a typically inebriated state, just about maintaining his seat on a donkey thanks to supporting satyrs and nymphs. A tremendous piece of neo-Baroque,

JARDIN DU LUXEMBOURG
Detail of the memorial to Éluard by Zadkine (1954).

the sculpture provided inspiration for the *Bacchus* paintings of the 1970s by Elaine de Kooning.

AVENUE DE L'OBSERVATOIRE

Leave the gardens by the south gates. The Esplanade Gaston Monnerville, between the two branches of Avenue de l'Observatoire (*map p. 587, D4*), was achieved at the cost of a Carthusian monastery demolished at the Revolution. You pass, on the right, the neo-Mudéjar brick bulk of the Institut d'Art et d'Archéologie, adorned with terracotta reliefs of famous antique works. The esplanade gives way to another garden, Jardin des Grands Explorateurs with, at the end, the extravagant ***Fontaine de l'Observatoire*** (1875) by Gabriel Davioud, with Carpeaux's group of figures representing the four quarters of the earth, holding aloft a terrestrial globe bounded by a celestial sphere. The concept—and indeed the attributes and physiognomy of the figures—are similar to Bernini's *Fountain of the Four Rivers* in Rome, but this being Paris, the four figures are nude females. The bronze horses and turtles are the work of Frémiet.

CLOSERIE DES LILAS

On Carrefour de l'Observatoire stands François Rude's **statue of Marshal Ney**, who was shot nearby in 1815 for supporting Napoleon on his return from Elba. Just behind it is **Closerie des Lilas** (*see p. 165*), now a smart restaurant, whereas the original

Closerie, a simple *guinguette*, was the first watering place on the road to Fontainebleau. By the end of the 19th century it was a favourite destination on the edge of Paris for the poet Charles Baudelaire and the painter Dominique Ingres (with his models). Writers and poets such as Verlaine, Théophile Gautier, the Goncourt brothers and Émile Zola all frequented the café. In 1901, the American poet Stuart Merrill became an *habitué* as did Strindberg, along with exiles from Café Guerbois such as Manet, Jongkind, Gauguin, Impressionist painters and James McNeill Whistler, the American painter-dandy. The café was rebuilt in 1903 and every Tuesday evening was dedicated to *Vers et Prose*, where the likes of André Salmon, Guillaume Apollinaire or Max Jacob might declaim. In 1925, the Closerie was modernised (according to Hemingway, the waiters were forced to shave their bushy moustaches off) and a banquet in honour of the poet Saint-Pol-Roux turned into a rumpus provoked by leading Surrealist André Breton. Hemingway came here often to write and was particularly fond of the Marshal Ney statue. Seeing him standing there, he writes, and knowing 'what a balls-up he'd made of Waterloo, I thought that all generations were lost by something and always had been and always would be and I stopped at the Lilas to keep the statue company and drank a cold beer.' Today the terrace is populated at midday by business people but remains a wonderfully nostalgic place to sip a *coup de champagne* of an evening.

MUSÉE ZADKINE

Map p. 587, D4. 100bis Rue d'Assas. Open 10–6, closed Mon and holidays. Free. Disabled access. T: 01 55 42 77 20, www.zadkine.paris.fr.

The museum dedicated to the Russian-born Ossip Zadkine (1890–1967) celebrated its 30th anniversary in 2012 with a total overhaul. This intimate space has been deployed to great effect. Zadkine, a member of the Montparnasse-based group of international artists, settled in Paris in 1909. A collector helped him to buy the house in 1928 and the sculptor continued to live and work here until his death. He became a member of the École de Paris, which included Modigliani, and around 1920 his work began to receive public acclaim. According to his wishes, his widow, the painter Valentine Prax (d. 1981), bequeathed the building and his collection, as well as her own paintings, to the City of Paris on condition that it became a museum. The Entrance Hall contains a samovar symbolising Russian hospitality.

Arranged around a garden, the museum derives much of its charm from the juxtaposition of former domestic and work spaces and the preservation of the character of the house. The works on display in seven successive rooms are arranged to demonstrate their synergy with the setting and Zadkine's truth to his materials and tools. His work shows the influence of Modigliani or Brancusi, and qualities of Cubism, Expressionism and Abstraction. His affinity with wood is represented in 24 works. The works in stone include the marble *Tête d'homme* (1919), which was shown in his first monograph exhibition. Towards the end of his life his work became more decorative and abstract. Among the pieces is a model for *La Ville détruite* for Rotterdam and tributes to Van Gogh. Examples of Zadkine's major production cast in bronze, such as *Rebecca (Grande Porteuse d'eau)*, are displayed in the garden, placed there by the sculptor to echo the trees.

PORT-ROYAL, THE OBSERVATOIRE & VAL-DE-GRÂCE

Map p. 590, A1–B1. RER B to Port-Royal or Métro 4 and 6 to Denfert-Rochereau.

To the south of the Jardin du Luxembourg is the district of Port-Royal, an area which developed in the 17th century and is now mainly residential. It takes its name from the Cistercian convent of Port-Royal, founded here by the Abbess of Port-Royal des Champs (southwest of Versailles), Angélique Arnault, in 1625 in the abandoned Hotel de Clagny (built by Pierre Lescot), on the edge of Faubourg St-Jacques. Marie de Médicis and Louis XIV contributed to the restoration and expansion of the convent buildings, but the abbey became an increasingly influential centre of Jansenist philosophy (which developed from Augustinian piety) to the extent that Louis XIV closed it in 1664. At the Revolution the convent became a prison and later a hospital.

On Boulevard de Port-Royal there are now two hospitals. The **Hôpital Cochin** lists George Orwell and Samuel Beckett among its more famous patients. Orwell describes his experience in *How the Poor Die*, concluding, 'The dread of hospitals probably still survives among the very poor, and in all of us it has only recently disappeared. It is a dark patch not far beneath the surface of our minds.'

The maternity hospital, **Port-Royal Baudelocque**, has, since 1818, occupied the buildings of the old Port-Royal convent. The chapel, completed by Lepautre in 1647, still stands, and has kept furnishings such as the woodwork in the chapter house.

JANSENISM AND PORT-ROYAL

Jansenism was a re-interpretation of the doctrine of St Augustine of Hippo by a Flemish theologian, Cornelius Jansenius (1585–1638), who became Bishop of Ypres in 1635. Among other things, it placed an emphasis on original sin and the redemption of a predestined few. Jansenius's book on the subject, *Augustinus*, was published posthumously in 1640, and drew an increasing number of followers to practise a very strict moral code and level of piety.

The Convent of Port-Royal followed the Jansenist creed and taught it in the schools which it ran. Among its adherents were Racine, who received a Jansenist education, and the scientist-philosopher Blaise Pascal, author of *Pensées*. A succession of popes issued bulls condemning the Jansenist propositions and the Jesuits, who did not accept the Jansenist line on predestination, put pressure on Louis XIV to end Jansenism altogether. Jacqueline Pascal, sister of the philosopher, had taken the veil at Port-Royal in 1652, much against the wishes of her brother, who had hoped that she would remain at home to look after him. When required to sign, by decree of Louis XIV, a statement repudiating certain aspects of Jansenist doctrine, Jacqueline suffered a breakdown which led to her early death at only 36.

Eventually the nuns were forcibly removed from Port-Royal and by 1710 the convent was largely destroyed. Philippe de Champaigne's painting of two nuns of the convent is at the Louvre (*see p. 190*).

OBSERVATOIRE DE PARIS

Map p. 590, A1–A2. Apply to attend a guided tour on the first Wed of the month (except Aug), in writing, enclosing s.a.e, to Secrétariat, 61 Av. de l'Observatoire, 75014 Paris. T: 01 40 51 22 21, www.obspm.fr. The Observatory is open during the Journées Européennes du Patrimoine and La Fête de la Science (Oct).

The Observatoire, which comes under the auspices of the Academy of Sciences, is the oldest working observatory in the world. It was founded by Louis XIV at the instigation of J.-B. Colbert. On 21st June 1667, the Meridian of Paris (*see overleaf*) was established and determined the orientation of the building, which was designed by Claude Perrault using no iron, so as not to interfere with the magnetic compass; nor any wood, for fear of fire. Completed in 1672, it has been enlarged many times, most recently in 1951. The four sides of the building face the cardinal points of the compass, and the latitude of the southern side is the recognised latitude of Paris (48° 50' 11" north), which, until 1912, formed the basis for the calculation of longitude on French maps. Famous scientists associated with the observatory include the Danish astronomer Olaf Rømer, who calculated the speed of light here in 1676; Le Verrier, who discovered the planet Neptune in 1846; Esclangon, inventor of the speaking clock (1932); and Lallemand, to whom we owe the electronic camera. Legal French time is still calculated from here. In the entrance is the original speaking clock and on the first floor of the main building is a museum of astronomical instruments. In the east cupola is an equatorial telescope of 38cm aperture. In 1926 the solar observatory at Meudon, on the outskirts of Paris, was taken over by the Paris Observatory and a radio astronomy station is maintained at Nançay, about 160km south of Paris.

Rue Cassini runs in front of the Observatoire. It is named after the family who gave the observatory its first four directors. The last of these, Jean-Dominique Cassini, resigned in 1793 (he was a royalist). The street is lined with early 20th-century buildings in variations on the Modern style, many of which were built as artists' studios. The English engraver Stanley William Hayter, founder of the influential graphics workshop Atelier 17, lived at no. 12, a Bauhaus pebbledash building adorned with a bas-relief of a stylised painter, sculptor and writer. A later resident, in 1943, was Jean Moulin, head of the French Resistance (*see p. 173*). No. 2, one of the oldest houses (1900), is where Alain-Fournier wrote *Le Grand Meaulnes* in 1913. He was killed fighting a year later, in the second month of the First World War.

On the corner of Rue Faubourg St-Jacques, at no.38 opposite Hôpital Cochin, is the **Hôtel de Massa** (1784), transferred here from the Champs-Élysées in 1927 and occupied by the Société des Gens de Lettres, a writers' society founded by Balzac in 1843 to defend the rights of authors. The *hôtel* became a meeting place of the intellectual elite.

Continue down Rue Faubourg St-Jacques until you reach **Boulevard Arago**, on the far side of which is an empty plinth bearing the name Arago. The statue of the scientist, politician and director of the Observatoire was destroyed at the time of the Vichy government and never replaced. Instead, a more unusual memorial was devised:

THE ARAGO MEDALLIONS

The physicist François Arago (1786–1853), known for his work in the fields of wave theory, rotatory magnetism and light polarisation, became director of the Paris Observatoire in 1830. His political sympathies were republican and this, combined with his military streak and his scientific brilliance, have made him a national hero. His statue, on the boulevard which bears his name, was destroyed in 1942 and has never been replaced. In 1994, however, the Dutch artist Jean Dibbets devised a novel way to preserve the great man's memory. Small bronze plaques, the *médaillons Arago*, were fixed to the Paris pavements along a route tracing the path of the Paris meridian, which passes through the former statue's plinth. Small and difficult to spot (and some have come loose and disappeared), they are nevertheless fun to seek out. The Paris meridian line, first calculated by Abbé Jean Picard in the mid-17th century, was thenceforward used by French map makers as the basis for their cartography. Louis XIV ordered the construction of an observatory across the meridian line. Calculated to greater exactitude by Arago, to 2° 20' 14.03" east of 0, the Paris axis long rivalled Greenwich as the prime meridian of the world (Greenwich was adopted as such in 1884). An April Fool's hoax in 2014 attempted to convince people that the Paris meridian was to be re-adopted as prime zero.   A.B.

At no. 65 Blvd Arago is the **Cité Fleurie**, where artists created studios constructed from scraps salvaged from the Universal Exhibition of 1878. The 29 studios and old buildings provided a home for J.-P. Laurens, for the foundry of the bronze caster who worked for Rodin and Maillol and, briefly, ateliers for Picasso and Modigliani. The buildings were saved by the efforts of a sculptor, Armand Lacroix, and his wife, who lived here from the 1950s to the 1980s.

VAL-DE-GRÂCE

On Rue St-Jacques rises the magnificent porticoed and pedimented façade of the church of Val-de-Grâce (*map p. 590, B1; open daily 1–5; Latin Mass Sun at 11am*), one of the best-preserved examples in Paris of the 17th-century Counter-Reformation architecture introduced by the Jesuits. Its dome, one of the finest in France, shows the influence of Roman Baroque. The little clock at the top of the façade is an anachronistic touch.

In 1621 Queen Anne of Austria, wife of Louis XIII, founded the Benedictine convent of Val-de-Grâce, one of many religious houses which, until the Revolution, were established in this district. In 1638, after 23 years of childless marriage, the queen gave birth to the future Louis XIV. In fulfilment of a vow, she planned the building of a church and commissioned François Mansart to carry out the work. The first stone was laid by the young king in 1645 and under Mansart's direction the church was built up to the entablatures of the nave and lower storey of the façade. But a year later Mansart was dismissed and the project was continued by Jacques Lemercier, Le Muet and Gabriel Le Duc, who was responsible for the lead and gilt dome completed by 1667. The king's initial 'L' and the 'A' of Anne are everywhere to be seen in the decoration. In 1624 a Benedictine convent under the patronage of Notre-Dame du Val-de-Grâce was founded, which became a military hospital in 1790 and the Army Medical School was added in 1850. A new hospital was built at the end of the 20th century.

In front of the church is a wide cobbled courtyard with the entrance to the Musée du Service de Santé des Armées, a museum of military medical history within the hospital complex (*see p. 522*), and a bronze statue by David d'Angers of Napoleon's surgeon, Baron Larrey.

LARREY: 'THE MOST VIRTUOUS MAN'

Dominique-Jean Larrey (1766–1842), born in a village in the Pyrenees and orphaned at the age of 13, was brought up by his uncle, chief surgeon at Toulouse. The boy also adopted a medical career, and as Napoleon's chief military surgeon, he followed the commander on all his campaigns. An excellent teacher, Larrey was everywhere recognised by the medical fraternity, in countries that were allies of France as well as in those that were not. In Prussia, the Berlin Anatomical Museum was placed at his disposal. After the Battle of Waterloo, when he was about to be shot by a Prussian firing squad, a Prussian doctor intervened; Larrey was reprieved by Blücher, whose son's life he had once saved.

Larrey is best known today for introducing the field ambulance (*ambulance volante*) so that wounded (and dead) soldiers could be collected immediately from the battlefield. The ambulances were carriages with sprung mattresses. During the advance on Moscow, he is reputed to have personally carried out 200 operations. Larrey's surgical memoirs record his extraordinary career, but his reputation declined alongside Napoleon's and he was stripped of his honours. However, after a visit to Britain in 1826, where his pioneering medical research was widely acknowledged (the Duke of Wellington was an admirer), his title of Medical Inspector General was reinstated. Napoleon, in his will, described Larrey as 'the most virtuous man I have known'. His statue at Val-de-Grâce shows him holding a parchment with those words engraved upon it.

The highly Classical interior of the church was decorated (1662–7) by François and Michel Anguier, Jacques Sarazin and others, and the dome painting, *La Gloire des Bienheureux* (1663) was commissioned by the king from Pierre Mignard, a successful but not hugely inspired painter of church decoration. This was one of his most accomplished works. The high altar, with its six huge twisted marble columns, is inspired by Bernini's baldachin in St Peter's, Rome; the sculpted *Nativity* is a copy of Michel Anguier's original (now at St-Roch; *see p. 299*). In the chapel on the right of the choir is a portrait of Anne of Austria borne by an angel; and in the Chapel of the Sacrament is the *Communion of the Angels* by Jean-Baptiste de Champaigne. The Chapel of St Anne once contained the hearts of royal princes and princesses, the first one said to have been that of Louis XIV's first child, who was stillborn (1662). The remains of other royal family members interred here—there were 45 in all, including Anne of Austria herself and Marie-Thérèse, wife of Louis XIV—were dispersed at the Revolution.

THE SCHOLA CANTORUM

North of Val-de-Grâce at 269 Rue Saint-Jacques (*map p. 590, B1*) is the Schola Cantorum, a private conservatoire of music, established in 1894 by three pupils of César Franck, including Vincent d'Indy (d. 1931). The buildings (1674), by Charles d'Avilère, are those of the English Benedictine monastery of St Edmund, founded in France in 1615, which occupied this site from 1640 until the Revolution and is still English property. The salon and staircase are good examples of 17th-century decoration, and the chapel, where the exiled James II's body lay in state in 1701 (*see p. 489*), is now a concert hall.

LES CATACOMBES: DENFERT-ROCHEREAU

Map p. 590, A2. Métro 4 and 6 to Denfert-Rochereau.

Place Denfert-Rochereau was known as the Place d'Enfer until 1879, when it was named after the defender of Belfort during the Franco-Prussian War in 1870. In the square is a reduced version of the most famous lion in France, the ***Lion of Belfort*** (the original is in Belfort, Franche-Comté) by Bartholdi (designer of the *Statue of Liberty*). In Square Ledoux on the west are the heavily rusticated remains of the twin pavilions of the **Barrière d'Enfer** for collecting tolls, designed by Claude-Nicolas Ledoux, in the old Wall of the Farmers General (*see p. 405*).

LES CATACOMBES

Open Tues–Sun 10–8 (last entry 7), closed Mon and 1 May. Audiogudies. T: 01 43 22 47 63, catacombes.paris.fr. NB: It can be chilly in the catacombs (14°C). There are 130 steps down and 83 up.

Popular with visitors of all ages, the catacombs are entered via the eastern pavilion of the old Barrière. The visit starts with the historic background, followed by a long series of galleries lined with bones and skulls, anonymous and timeless, leading to a huge ossuary containing the debris of over six million skeletons. The labyrinthine series of underground quarries, covering about 850 hectares and 20m down, first provided stone in Roman times, with 160km of tunnels extending from the Jardin des Plantes to the Porte de Versailles and as far as Montrouge and Montsouris. In the 1780s they became a charnel house for bones removed from four overfull graveyards in the city, particularly the Cimetière des Innocents (*see p. 331*), and the remains of most of the victims of the Terror were transferred here; it took 15 months to transport them. In 1944 the Catacombes served as a headquarters of the Resistance Movement.

PARC DE MONTSOURIS AND CITÉ UNIVERSITAIRE

Some way south of Place Denfert-Rochereau is the 16-hectare **Parc de Montsouris** (*map p. 590, A3–A4*), laid out in 1875–8 as part of Haussmann's scheme to provide green spaces around the capital: one at each of the cardinal points (the others are Bois de Boulogne, Parc des Buttes-Chaumont and Bois de Vincennes). The area was a continuation of the Catacombes (*see above*). Built by J.-C. Alphand, Haussmann's engineer, and landscaped by J.-P. Barillet-Deschamps, the gardens imitate the informal English style, with vast lawns, around 1,400 trees in groups, and a lake. As well as sculptures in stone and bronze, such as Etex's *Shipwrecked* (1882) and *Drama in the Desert* (1891), there is also a bandstand, a puppet theatre and playgrounds.

Facing the south side of the park, spread over about a kilometre along Boulevard Jourdan, is the **Cité Internationale Universitaire** (*map p. 590, A4–B4*), founded in 1922 on the site of the 19th-century Thiers fortifications, to provide accommodation for about 6,000 students in a park-like setting. There is an interesting diversity in the buildings and it is worth seeking out the various examples of 20th-century architecture among the 40 national halls of residence (1922–2005), modelled on English colleges and designed to evoke national characteristics in a wide spectrum of styles. Among them are five which are listed historic monuments. The Maison Internationale (1936) was financed by John D. Rockefeller. The most innovative building of the time was Le Corbusier's sleek Swiss Hall (1930–2), which introduces revolutionary new elements including his signature *pilotis*, or piers which support it off the ground. A later example of Le Corbusier's work, in conjunction with Lúcio Costa, is the partly painted, exposed-concrete, brutalist Brazilian Hall (1952). Other important buildings are the Japanese pavilion (P. Sardou); the Netherlands Hall (W.M. Dudok, 1927); and the Fondation Avicenne (1966–8), typical of French architecture of the late 1960s.

MANUFACTURE DES GOBELINS

*Map p. 590, C2. Métro 7 to Les Gobelins. 42 Av. des Gobelins. The **workshops** are open for guided visits only on Tues, Wed, Thur at 1pm (except 25 Dec, 1 Jan, 1 May). Visits last 90mins, in French only (short text in English available). Tickets can be purchased on site* *from 11am; numbers are limited. Advance purchase available only at FNAC; www.fnac. com. Visit includes the gallery (see below) during temporary exhibitions. T: 01 44 08 53 49.*

*The **Galerie des Gobelins** is open during temporary exhibitions, Tues–Sun 11–6 (except 25 Dec, 1 Jan, 1 May); free on the last Sun of the month. Guided visits on Sat at 2.30 and 4. Tickets as above.*

The Manufacture Nationale des Gobelins, famous for the production of tapestries, has been a state institution for over 300 years. It encompasses three great weaving workshops: Gobelins and Beauvais for tapestries, and Savonnerie for carpets.

HISTORY OF LES GOBELINS

The manufactory was named after Jehan de Gobelin (or Gobeelen; d. 1476), from Flanders, who had special knowledge of the use of cochineal as a red dye. He settled in 1443 on the banks of the Bièvre, whose clear, clean, non-calcareous water was ideal for dyeing and bleaching the silk and woollen thread used in weaving tapestries. Such was Gobelin's skill and so numerous were his descendants that the dynasty went from strength to strength, fortune accrued, and the attention of kings was secured. When Berbier du Mets (1626–1709) was director of Les Gobelins, Jean-Baptiste Colbert suggested to Louis XIV that he purchase the workshops, which he did, founding the Royal Manufacture of Tapestries and Furnishings. The *premier peintre* to the king, Charles Le Brun, was made director and, by 1667, the manufactory included the royal furniture factory, with silversmiths and cabinet-makers as well as the best Flemish weavers. The production was destined exclusively for the embellishment of royal palaces and as diplomatic gifts. In 1789 it was closed, to be declared Manufacture Nationale in 1791. Here the chemist Eugène Chevreul researched colours for tapestry dyes which could exactly replicate paintings. The royal carpet factory, established at the Louvre by Henri IV in 1604 and later installed in a *savonnerie* (soap-factory) at Chaillot, was transferred here in 1826. The Beauvais tapestry workshops, founded in 1664, moved to Les Gobelins in 1940 after the destruction of their workshop (although part returned to Beauvais in 1989). A new depot was designed by Auguste Perret for the furniture store in 1934–6. All came under the administration of the Mobilier National in 1937.

VISITING THE MANUFACTORY

The tapestry is woven by hand on both high-warp (Gobelins) and low-warp (Beauvais) looms. The highly skilled weaver works on the reverse side of the tapestry; the painting that he is copying is placed behind him and reflected in a mirror. The average amount of tapestry produced per person per day is 15 square centimetres. Both traditional designs, which feature a border, and modern designs, since 1945 without a border, are used. In the former chapel, designed by Jacques V. Gabriel in 1723, hang two tapestries after cartoons by Raphael's famous series for the Vatican, copied at Gobelins in the early 18th century.

The visit crosses Rue Berbier-du-Mets, which follows the curve of the Bièvre, the river that once flowed between the dye-works and the workshops. Le Brun lived in this street and returned here from his residence in Montmorency shortly before his death, having left 300 *livres* to 300 poor of the parish. The river, polluted by the dye- and leather-works on its banks, was buried in 1912 for health reasons. Square René le Gall was created in 1938 on the former vegetable plots of the Gobelins weavers on the banks of the Bièvre.

CHÂTEAU DE LA REINE BLANCHE

Guided visits April–Sept, Wed and Sun pm; meet at the gate.

Behind the manufactory, in the angle between Rue Gustave-Geffroy and Rue Berbier-de-Mets, in Rue de la Reine Blanche, is the 'Château' of the same name. Built by the Gobelin family it was transformed in 2000–2 into elegant housing conserving the medieval characteristics of the three-storey building on three sides of a courtyard. The oldest wing (1500–35), on the right side of the courtyard, was altered and added to in the 17th century. Overlooking the Bièvre, it would originally have been divided between accommodation and workshops, but by the mid-18th century it was entirely made over to dye shops. The Gobelin family disposed of the property and the buildings later had several uses.

EATING AND DRINKING AROUND LUXEMBOURG

€€ **La Closerie des Lilas**. At the southern end of the Jardin du Luxembourg, this classic has existed since 1847 and the food and service is reliable. Fairly upmarket and patronised by locals, it has a brasserie (no reservations) and a restaurant (which takes reservations) and is also a pleasant rendezvous for an aperitif or late-night drink. There is a piano bar (open to 1am) and a large outdoor terrace. In the winter months *coquillages* (shellfish) and *fruits de mer* are served, while traditional meat dishes include such favourites as *coq au vin*. *171 Blvd du Montparnasse. T: 01 40 51 34 50, www. closeriedeslilas.fr. Map p. 587, D4.*

€ **Au Bon Coin**. Near Les Gobelins Métro, this is a small busy side-street bistro, proud to be 'authentic'. The menu is limited but good. Busy, with very few tourists. A pleasant dining experience. *21 Rue de la Collégiale. T: 01 43 31 55 57, www.auboncoin-bistrot. com. Map p. 590, C1.*

€ **Le Cornichon**. Highly rated for its traditional French dishes made with good fresh produce, such as *salade d'oreilles de cochon croquantes* (crispy pig's ear salad). Closed Sat–Sun. *34 Rue Gassendi. T: 01 43 20 40 19, www. lecornichon.fr. Map p. 578, C4.*

€ **Le Jeu de Quilles**. Tiny wine bar, reasonably priced and very popular: book in advance. The meat is of the highest quality (Le Jeu rubs shoulders with one of the top Parisian butchers, Hugo Desnoyer). Closed Sun, Mon and midday Tues. *45 Rue Boulard (Métro: Mouton-Duvernet). T: 01 53 90 75 22, www.jdequilles.fr. Just beyond map p. 590, A2.*

WALK ONE: LA BUTTE AUX CAILLES

La Butte aux Cailles, between Place d'Italie and Rue de Tolbiac in the 13th arrondisse-ment, preserves a village charm against a background of towering buildings. The nar-row, criss-crossing streets cling to rising ground (62m), lined with low houses, their tiny gardens overflowing with greenery and flowers in summer. Once the Bièvre river, now covered by Rue Vergniaud, flowed at its feet, marking the limit of La Butte. In the 17th century the small hill would have been dotted with vines and mills, and by the 18th century it had been further cut off from the centre of Paris by the Farmers-General Wall (*see p. 318*). The character of La Butte changed in the 19th century with the spread of tanneries, dyeing works, quarries and workshops. Though a working-class district within living memory, today it is a sought-after residential area with many restaurants and shops. The name is not an allusion to any quail (*cailles*) which might have nested here, but to a certain Pierre Caille, a 16th-century vineyard owner.

To begin the walk, take Métro 6 to Corvisart.

TURN LEFT OUT OF THE MÉTRO STATION onto **Boulevard Auguste Blanqui**, notable for its six rows of trees and elevated railway. It runs along the line of a section of the former Wall of the Farmers-General, at a point where it had particularly wide boulevards either side. A street market lines the boul-evard on Tues, Wed and Sun mornings. Auguste Blanqui (1805–81), described as an anarchist and socialist, was one of the chiefs of the Revolution of 1848 and who spent more than 36 years in prison. When he wasn't behind bars he lived in a house on this street, which we shall see at the end of the walk.

The passageway through no. 51, **Rue Eugène-Atget**, is named after the Doisneau of his day, one of the first photographers of Paris, who moved his cumbersome equipment around on a small cart. His images were intended as aids for painters (one user was Maurice Utrillo). A flight of steps leads up to a green area named after another celebrated photographer, Brassaï, a Hungarian called Gyula Halász. He took his working name from his home town of Brassó in Transylvania (now Braşov, Romania). Turn left and walk through the gardens to **Rue des Cinq Diamants**, which has a number of restaurants, including, on the corner, Chez Gladines (*T: 01 45 80 70 10*), where customers are seated cheek-by-jowl wherever there is a space, at tables with check cloths; good helpings are inexpensive with a mainly Basque slant. No. 27 opposite, Au Passage des Artistes, serves couscous in the evenings and mint tea all day, and at no. 25 is a tapas bar/brasserie, Papagallo. The Café du Commerce (*T: 01 53 62 91 04*) at no. 39 has paintings on the walls and jazz on Sundays, and hearty, reasonably-priced dishes.

The pretty **Passage Barrault** descends through overhanging roses and honeysuckle (even an apricot tree) to **Rue Barrault**, known as Little Russia in acknowledgement of the mainly Russian employees of a 1920s' taxi company once established here. Turn left, past a med-

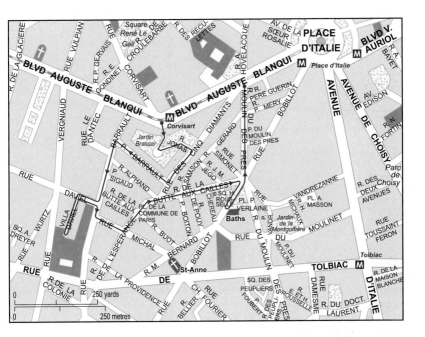

ley of surviving older buildings, 1930s' social housing and modern infill. Many of the walls are adorned with urban street art, some of it by Jef Aérosol.

At the junction of Rue Daviel, go downhill to the right and then left into **Villa Daviel**, a quiet cul-de-sac with immaculately-kept houses of 1912, reminiscent of English brick terraces. There is a variety of designs in the wrought iron, including thistles, acorns and arabesques, and the tiny front yards are packed with scented shrubs. Beyond the end buildings is a glimpse of the Little Russia chalets. Turning back, you face, in Rue Daviel, a chalet-like building (no. 10), 'Petite Alsace', with blue painted timbers, where the archway leads to a garden courtyard. This communal housing was designed by Jean Walter in 1912, for some 300 people.

Return to Rue Barrault and turn left into Rue Michal. On the climb up towards Rue de l'Espérance, the dome of the neo-Byzantine church of **Sainte-Anne de la Butte-aux-Cailles** (1819–1912) is in full view. Although a small community has existed here for centuries, this was the first church to be built on the Butte. There is a small pedimented house on the corner of Rue Michal and Rue de l'Espérance, and old-fashioned street lamps all around. **Rue de l'Espérance** was created in 1845, linking the Rue de la Butte-aux-Cailles to the Bièvre Valley. Turn left into it.

Three roads meet at the tree-shaded **Place de la Commune-de-Paris** (with a Wallace Fountain), the name a reminder of events following the siege of Paris during the Franco-Prussian War (1870–1). The city had capitulated

in January, and the provisional government under Adolphe Thiers was in Versailles. On 25th May 1871, the Butte was the theatre of a bloody battle between the Communards or *Fédérés*, led by Wroblewski, and the *Versaillais* (National Guard). The Communards held Place d'Italie (where this walk ends) long enough to allow many of the insurgents to cross to the Right Bank for the final battle near Père-Lachaise. Go straight on into **Rue de la Butte-aux-Cailles**, the centre of activity on the hill, with galleries, shops, restaurants, bars and a crêperie. Le Temps des Cerises at nos. 18–20 has been a workers' cooperative since 1976. A number of cafés and bars in this part of town have names taken from the famous Commune-era song: Le Merle Moqueur and Folie en Tête are two examples. (*For the song and its origins, see p. 319.*) L'Oisive Thé, on the corner of Rue Jean-Marie Jégo

(*closed Mon*), is a tea room offering light fresh food, good desserts and cakes...and crochet classes.

At the top of the Butte, Square Henri Rousselle and **Place Paul Verlaine** are small parks cut in two by Rue Bobillot, with a playground on one side and on the other a stele commemorating the landing of the first flight by air-balloon (*montgolfière*), by François d'Arlandes and Pilâtre de Rozier, who took off from La Muette, 9km away on the other side of the Seine, in 1783, during the reign of Louis XVI. Also in the Place is a drinking-water fountain, related to the nearby **swimming baths**. Both fountain and baths are supplied by natural spring water. The search for a deep well was authorised by Haussmann in 1863 to supplement the supply of river water to the Butte. Drilling went to a depth of 532m but was abandoned in 1872, to be revived 20 years later with the discovery in 1903 of abundant springs—nearly 6,000 cubic metres per day 582m down—slightly sulphurous and warm (28°C). The exercise lost its utility because the Bièvre was gradually covered and homes were soon supplied with running water. In 1924, however, the hot water came into its own with the creation of a swimming pool and public baths, housed in the small pink- and red-brick building whose architecture is reminiscent of the British Arts and Crafts style, with a wavy roofline. There is an outdoor and an indoor pool (*check opening times, T: 01 45 89 60 05, www. guide-piscine.fr*). It was used by Dr Pierre Macleuf in 1943–6 for research into swimming therapy. When the original borehole was exhausted, a new one was drilled to a depth of 620m, to the benefit of locals who still fill their water bottles with the pure water which flows from the fountain. Across from the swimming pool is a shabby-chic wine bar/restaurant, La Bouche à Oreilles (*T: 01 45 89 74 42*).

A reminder of the mills which once stood in the fields of the Butte is **Rue des Moulins des Prés**, on the corner of which is a charming little restaurant, Chez Nathalie (*T: 01 45 80 20 42*). Go up Rue des Moulins to reach Boulevard Blanqui again, where, on the right-hand corner as you reach it, is the Mercure hotel, occupying the site of Blanqui's former house (on the left is a pleasant café). Turn right and you reach the busy **Place d'Italie**, where there is a Métro station (lines 5, 6 and 7). Its Guimard entrance is a good example of its type, with many of the original features in place, including the two red lamps or *phares*.

The 13th arrondissement is famous for its **Asian restaurants**. Close to the Tolbiac Métro station (line 7) are three excellent ones (*all map p. 579, D4–E4*): **Le Lotus** (Vietnamese; *121 Av. d'Ivry, T: 01 53 61 00 61, www.lelotus13.com*), **Lao Lane Xang 2** (Laotian and Vietnamese; *102 Av. d'Ivry, T: 01 58 89 00 00*) and **Basilic & Spice** (Thai; *88 Av. de Choisy, T: 01 45 85 19 30, www.basilicspice.com*).

MONTPARNASSE
View down the Champ de Mars to the famous (or infamous) Tour.

Montparnasse

*Montparnasse, famous for its literary and bohemian associations
of the 1920s, is a busy shopping and residential district with a slightly seedy charm,
watched over by the dark silhouette of the Tour Montparnasse, yet retaining faded
associations with the artists and intellectuals who once lived here.
Boulevard du Montparnasse is imbued with a modern vitality
in the evenings, when the large brasseries are all crammed to bursting.*

'Mount Parnassus' was named, so it is said, by students from the Latin Quarter, who gathered here on the rising ground outside Paris. In the 18th century, it became a centre of popular entertainment where *cabarets* and *guinguettes* could serve tax-free alcohol, and even when incorporated into Paris in the 19th century the tradition continued. With the construction of Boulevard Montparnasse and the railway station (1852), the ground was levelled. At the turn of the 19th 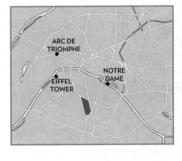 and 20th centuries, Montmartre, suffering from its bohemian fame and rising subculture, was supplanted by the Left Bank as the centre of artistic and literary activity. Montparnasse had abundant new housing and inexpensive studios readily available. Prior to the First World War, artists, musicians and poets began to move in. The social life of the intellectual community was centred on the café-brasseries at the junction of Boulevard Montparnasse and Rue Vavin (*map p. 586, C4*)—Le Select, La Rotonde and Le Dôme—and later La Coupole. During the *Années Folles*, after the First World War, the café society reached its zenith. Everyone and anyone gathered in Montparnasse. Blaise Cendrars, Jean Cocteau, Aragon and André Breton were among the literary newcomers, and musicians included Denis Milaud and Francis Poulenc. Jazz was in the air thanks to the likes of Sidney Bechet; anti-art movements such as Dada and Surrealism were taking off; Paul Poiret liberated women from the corset; and Maurice Chevalier, Mistinguett and Josephine Baker provided entertainment. Young, energetic writers and artists from the United States, escaping prohibition (1919), also gathered in the *quartier*, and many Eastern European and Russian émigrés arrived to swell the crowd. A loose-knit group of immigrant and French artists became known as the School of Paris (*see p. 427*). Although most of the American colony abandoned France during the Wall Street Crash of 1929, the popularity of Montparnasse barely waned during the early '30s. After the Second World War, Americans returned and a new wave of enthusiasm swept over the area, lasting until the '50s. Both Henry Miller and Ernest Hemingway described the café life, disreputable and otherwise, of the district in its heyday.

THE CAFÉS OF MONTPARNASSE

At no. 108 Blvd Montparnasse, **Le Dôme** was, from the 1870s, the original café and meeting place for Germans and East Europeans, including the Bulgarian painter Pascin. In 1907 Matisse, already well regarded, met other painters here as well as Gertrude Stein, and it is suggested that Russian political refugees, including Lenin and Trotsky, were seen at Le Dôme.

La Rotonde at no. 105 started as a modest bistrot, but in 1911 its expansive owner, Victor Libion, extended into the butcher's shop next door. All were welcome and Libion instructed his waiters not to wake the down-and-outs who came to sleep there. Picasso and the Cubist painters, apart from Braque, moved to Montparnasse and frequented La Rotonde. So did Amedeo Modigliani, a most striking character, ceaselessly sketching, who met other émigrés and members of the School of Paris such as Soutine and Kisling. La Rotonde was so famous that it was the first place Charlie Chaplin, accompanied by Douglas Fairbanks and Mary Pickford, visited on his arrival in Paris in 1921—to a tumultuous reception.

In 1924, **Le Select**, at no. 99 Blvd Montparnasse, was the first café to open all night (now only until 2am) and among its specialities was welsh rarebit, which attracted an American clientèle. The café brought together Ernest Hemingway (also fond of Le Cluny and La Closerie des Lilas; *see p. 156*), Henry Miller, Scott Fitzgerald, Ezra Pound, William Faulkner and Alexander Calder, along with James Joyce and T.S. Eliot.

La Coupole at no. 102, which opened in 1927, is the largest and most splendid of them all, with top-quality food and wine. The genuine Art Deco brasserie is supported by 33 pilasters and pillars, with murals which were renovated in the 1990s. Its famous clients were legion, from Cocteau to Man Ray, and from Braque to Simone de Beauvoir and Jean-Paul Sartre. It still has an American bar.

TOUR MONTPARNASSE

Map p. 586, B4. Métro 4, 12 and 13 to Montparnasse-Bienvenüe. Entrance on Rue de l'Arrivée, in front of Gare Montparnasse. Open April–Sept 9.30–11.30; Oct–March Sun–Thur 9.30–10.30, Fri, Sat and days preceding a public holiday, 9.30–11. Last lifts 30mins before closing. T: 01 45 38 52 56, www.tourmontparnasse56.com.

The insolent Tour Montparnasse (210m high), an office skyscraper built in 1973, was the first of its kind and now dominates the area. The only way to beat it is to go to the 56th floor (196m) and revel in one of the most impressive views that the city can offer. The ride in the lift takes 38 seconds and brings you to the Panoramic Floor, totally enclosed by plate-glass windows, for a 360° view. Higher up, accessed by stairs, is the roof terrace, an outdoor platform 200m high. The 360° Café serving snacks and Le Ciel de Paris Restaurant (*reservations only, open 8.30–11; Bar Américain to 1am, T: 01 40 64 77 64*) are the highest eating-places in Europe.

GARE DE MONTPARNASSE

Adjacent to the tower is the mainline station, Gare de Montparnasse, serving Brittany and the Atlantic coast. An 18-storey glass and concrete structure surrounds the station platforms on three sides and above it is **Le Jardin Atlantique**, which can be entered from Place des Cinq-Martyrs-du-Lycée-Buffon or from the mainline station. It combines French formality and English informality, using metal, wood, marble and granite structures to create an urban breathing space. An intermittent fountain (*The Isle of the Hesperides*) evokes the sound of waves on a seashore and coastal plants are used to harmonise with the theme. A raised walkway meanders through small gardens. There are play areas for children of all ages.

MUSÉE GÉNÉRAL LECLERC–MUSÉE JEAN MOULIN

Open Tues–Sun 10–6. Free. Access via the mainline station Platform 1, staircase (only) to Jardin Atlantique. T: 01 40 64 39 44, www.museesleclercmoulin.paris.fr.
At the tower end of the Jardin Atlantique is the entrance to a museum inaugurated in 1994 at the instigation of Jacques Chirac and dedicated to the roles of two heroes of the Second World War: General Leclerc de Hauteclocque of the Free French movement and Jean Moulin, head of the Resistance. General Leclerc was involved with the Free French, the Allies and the aggressors (Rome, Berlin and Tokyo). Jean Moulin was concerned with internal questions within France: the Resistance, Paris, Vichy and the occupying forces. The action of both men is the museum's central theme. Personal memorabilia relative to General Leclerc's role in Africa and Indochina include his colonial helmet and cane; for Jean Moulin there are etchings he made of the poems of Tristan Cobière and drafts of coded messages. The room dedicated to the Liberation of Paris uses the elliptical walls and 14 screens to plunge the visitor into the action. Montparnasse was chosen because of its many symbolic connections, including the site where General von Choltitz signed the ceasefire. The museum also holds temporary themed exhibitions.

THE MUSEUMS OF MONTPARNASSE

L'ADRESSE: MUSÉE DE LA POSTE DE PARIS

Map p. 586, B4. 21 Av. du Maine, Chemin du Montparnasse. Open Mon–Sat 1–6, T: 01 42 79 24 24, www.ladressemuseedelaposte.fr.

This comprehensive and engaging museum tells the story of the transfer of the written message from the time of Louis XI (end of the 15th century) to the present, through the people involved and the variety and development of the means and techniques that they put in place. The germ of a postal museum based on philately goes back to the mid-19th century but it did not take off until 1946. Along the way a variety of related objects and information on evolving technology was gathered, making it much more than a postage-stamp museum, and early on the intention was both to present and instruct. One of its oldest documents is a 12th-century parchment scroll with replies attached, sent between religious houses to announce the death of an abbot. It ended up some nine metres long. The history of the postal service is told through objects such as four postcard albums which belonged to the poet Paul Éluard. The museum has vast archives on the history of the letter and there are examples of contemporary art on postal themes as well a vast photo library.

Among the varied and fascinating objects on display are a postilion's boots weighing three kilos, into which he could put his shod feet, thus protecting him from the harnesses of other travellers. The *Boule de Moulins* was an inventive means of sending letters during the Siege of Paris (1870–1). Watertight balls of zinc, with little fins, which could contain up to 500 letters, were thrown in the Seine upstream of Paris, and eventually trapped in a net. The last one found was in 1982, with 306 letters. The history of airmail began in 1918 with the pioneering efforts of the aviator P.-G. Latécoère, who envisaged carrying mail between France and South America. The ambition was realised in 1929, when Jean Mermoz landed in Chile.

THE AIRMAIL PIONEER

When the young Jean Mermoz flunked his *baccalauréat* in 1919, no one would have guessed that the shy, poetic teenager was destined to become an aviator hero, a flying ace with a physique that turned heads, a man whom Antoine de Saint-Exupéry (author of *Le Petit Prince*) would dub 'Mermoz the Great'. Mermoz took naturally to flying and enjoyed performing stunts. He joined the Latécoère aerial postal service (later Aéropostale), whose first route had been Toulouse–Spain but which soon spread further afield into French colonial Africa. Mermoz delivered the previous day's papers to Marshal Lyautey in Morocco. Casablanca and Dakar were also served by the air routes. It was a dangerous job. Many pilots crashed. In 1926, after engine failure, Mermoz was captured by bandits in the African desert. Flights to South America began in the late '20s. In the 1930s Mermoz was involved in developing the Argentine national airline. His last flight was in 1936, in a four-engine seaplane that should probably never have taken off. It was known to be faulty and had been hastily repaired. It crashed in the south Atlantic and Mermoz and his four crew members perished. His last words had been, 'Let's not waste any more time.'   A.B.

MUSÉE BOURDELLE

Map p. 586, B4. 16 Rue Antoine-Bourdelle. Open Tues–Sun 10–6, closed Mon and public holidays. Free. T : 01 49 54 73 73, www.bourdelle.paris.fr.
Behind an unassuming exterior is the renovated (2012) museum dedicated to the

sculptor Antoine Bourdelle (1861–1929), who left his native Montauban and the south-west of France for Paris in 1884 and worked at this address from 1885 until his death in 1929. His family lived here, as did the artist for a time. Bourdelle's entire collection, including all the memorabilia preserved by his second wife, Cléopâtre, and his daughter Rhodia, passed to the Ville de Paris in 1949.

Not only does this museum provide an insight into the range of Bourdelle's work, it is also a unique opportunity to experience a traditional artist's *atelier* of 19th-century Montparnasse. A pupil of Rodin, Bourdelle's earlier works, such as *Beethoven aux Grands Cheveux* (1891), show his master's influence. He made several studies of Beethoven to whom, as a young man, he felt he had a physical resemblance, and he likened the composer's artistic journey to his own artistic development. A bust of Beethoven by Bourdelle is in the Jardin du Luxembourg. In complete contrast, one of his best-known works, *Pénélope* (1912), which harmonises robustness and simplicity, was in fact a synthesis of his two wives, Stéphanie and Cléopâtre. An example can be seen in the Petit Palais. Bourdelle's Classical style finds expression in the reliefs for the Théâtre des Champs-Élysées (1912–13; *see p. 274*), strongly influenced by the dances of Isadora Duncan. He was also influenced by the Symbolist movement.

Multi-talented, Bourdelle worked in all media: examples include plaster, bronze and marble; he also painted, drew in pastels and made engravings. While he was working for Rodin, others worked for him. The studio was always busy with artists, students, patrons and visitors, and among those who studied under him were Giacometti and Germaine Richier.

A feature of the museum is its contrasting display areas. The courtyard and gardens contain large bronzes; a gallery was added in 1961 to contain major large plaster models such as *Héraklès Archer* (1906–9) and *La France* (1923–5); the workshop has faithfully preserved its original fittings, structure and furnishings and there are smaller galleries which present Bourdelle's work chronologically, as well as photographs. The impressive two-level extension designed by Christian de Portzamparc in 1989–92, creates a setting for works on a monumental scale, such as the monument to General Alvear, for Buenos Aires (1913–23) and the *Monument aux Morts* for the Tarn-et-Garonne. The museum is planning the restoration of part of the old house as exhibition space for Bourdelle's works on canvas and paper. The museum also holds frequent temporary exhibitions.

CARTIER FOUNDATION FOR CONTEMPORARY ART
Map p. 578, C3. 261 Blvd Raspail. Open Tues–Sun 11–8. T: 01 42 18 56 72, fondation. cartier.com.

It is 30 years since the Fondation Cartier was inaugurated at Jouy-en-Josas near Versailles. It moved into its present building, designed by Jean Nouvel, in May 1994. Its patronage has encouraged young, unknown artists as well as promoting less-known aspects of the work of established ones and it holds regular exhibitions of contemporary art by international names. Not limited to the visual arts, the foundation has a policy of bringing together all the performing arts, as well as science and philosophy. The 30th anniversary exhibition in 2014, *Vivid Memories*, brought together works the foundation has collected since 1984 (the collection now comprises some 1,000 pieces). The artworks spread into the surrounding garden, which is a semi-wild urban oasis with some mature trees.

Just north of the junction of Boulevard du Montparnasse and Boulevard Raspail stands the **statue of Balzac** by Rodin.

> ## THE MEMORIAL TO BALZAC
>
> In 1891 Rodin was commissioned by a committee presided over by Émile Zola to undertake the memorial to the eminent novelist Honoré de Balzac (1799–1850). Balzac was an Olympian figure but did not have a Herculean physique. Rodin made multiple studies, seeking a way to depict the man within, but his 1893 version, naked and ugly, was rejected. In 1898 the final draped figure was derided at the Salon as a travesty of the literary giant. Rodin had his supporters, though, among them the sculptors Maillol and Bourdelle. The statue was finally purchased for the city of Paris by public subscription. It stands today as a monument to creative genius and is considered one of Rodin's major achievements, for its psychological insight and relative simplification. Preparatory works for the monument can be seen in the Musée Rodin (*see p. 130*) and include both clothed and unclothed versions.

CIMETIÈRE MONTPARNASSE

Map p. 586, C4. Métro 4 to Edgar-Quintet, 4 and 6 to Raspail, or 13 to Gaîté. Main entrance on Blvd Edgar-Quinet; additional entrances on Rue Froidevaux. A plan is available at the office just inside the main gate.

The land now occupied by this famous cemetery originally belonged to the Hôtel-Dieu hospital beside Notre-Dame and was used by the monks as a burial ground for those who died in the hospital. In the southwest, near Porte Froidevaux, is the tower of a mill that stood here in the 15th century. It became a *guinguette* after the Revolution and, in 1824, when the City of Paris decided to open a new cemetery, it became the custodian's home.

Although this cemetery is not quite as spectacular as Père-Lachaise, its forest of monuments and gravestones is a tribute to all the marble cutters and engravers who found work here in the 19th century, and the list of those buried here is impressive. The writers Maupassant, Baudelaire, Huysmans, Sartre, Ionesco and Beckett lie here. Composers and musicians include César Franck, Saint-Saëns and Serge Gainsbourg. Many artists are also here, such as Fantin-Latour, Gérard, Houdon, Rude, Soutine, Zadkine, Bourdelle, Bartholdi and Brancusi—whose *Le Baiser* (*The Kiss*) is tucked away in the northeast corner. Pierre-Joseph Proudhon, the social reformer, is here too as are Alfred Dreyfus; the scientist and politician Arago (*see p. 160*); the architect Charles Garnier (*see p. 301*); and the car manufacturer André Citroën.

EATING AND DRINKING IN MONTPARNASSE

The brasseries of Boulevard du Montparnasse still carry some historic glamour and all stay open conveniently late. **La Coupole** (*no. 102, T: 01 43 20 14 20, www. lacoupole-paris.com*), **Le Dôme** (*no. 108, T: 01 43 35 25 81*) and **Le Select** (*no. 98, T: 01 45 48 38 24*) are probably more famous now for their history (*see p. 172*) than for their cuisine, but history is a potent reason to pay a visit. Other options include:

€€ **Le Montparnasse 1900**. Built as a brasserie in 1901, the décor dates from 1914—mirrors, mirrors everywhere, on walls, ceiling, and 'twixt the windows—with sinuous Art Nouveau frames. The décor is probably more impressive than the food, which remains very traditional, but it is open every day 12–3 & 7–12. It specialises in *fruits de mer* in winter, and in roasts. The Belle-Époque set menu includes an aperitif, three courses, half-bottle of wine and coffee; portions are generous. *59 Blvd de Montparnasse. T: 01 45 49 19 00, www.montparnasse-1900. com. Map p. 586, B4.*

€–€€ **Le Ciel de Paris**. Whatever you think of the building, a visit to the top of Tour Montparnasse to admire the view is not to be missed and can be combined with a drink at the elegant Bar Américain, or a meal at the restaurant (breakfast, lunch, tea and dinner are served between 7.30am and 11pm). *33 Av. du Maine. T: 01 40 64 77 64, www.cieldeparis.com. Map p. 586, B4.*

€–€€ **La Rotonde**. With its '30s décor in tones of red, this is a reliable place and serves meals until late (2am). The menu combines traditional choices with some surprises, and the ingredients are reliably sourced. *Coquillages* and *crustacés* (shellfish, shrimps, langoustines) are available in season. *105 Blvd du Montparnasse. T: 01 43 26 48 26, www.rotondemontparnasse. com. Map p. 586, C4.*

€–€€ **Toyo**. A Japanese restaurant of repute. *17 Rue Jules Chaplain. T: 01 43 54 28 03. Map p. 586, C4.*

€ **La Cantine du Troquet**. Friendly bistrot, reasonably priced. The cuisine is Basque, under the direction of Christian Etchebest. The dishes of the day are written on a large wall slate. *101 Rue de l'Ouest. T: 01 45 40 04 98* (no reservations). *Métro: Pernety. Map p. 578, C4.*

€ **Le Cornichon**. Between Montparnasse and the Catacombes (*see p. 165*).

€ **Invictus**. Chef Christophe Cabanel's cooking is inspired. *5 Rue Ste-Beuve. T: 01 45 48 07 22, restaurantinvictus.fr. Map p. 586, C4.*

€ **Le Timbre**. The name is no deception: this place really is postge-stamp sized. It is under the direction of an English chef, Chris Wright. The *millefeuille* is particularly good. *3 Rue Ste-Beuve, T: 01 45 49 10 40, www.restaurantletimbre.com. Map p. 586, C4.*

€ **Wadja**. Fun and inexpensive, epitomises the small, old-fashioned bistrot, with a traditional menu (organic produce). *10 Rue de la Grande-Chaumière. T: 01 46 33 02 02. Map p. 586, C4.*

THE RIGHT BANK

The greater part of Paris, encompassing 14 of its 20 arrondissements, lies north of the River Seine. The Rive Droite has no single unifying characteristic, but the quartiers closest to the river are areas redolent of luxury and wealth. In the Middle Ages, the protective fortifications encompassed a far greater area here than on the Left Bank, and the Right Bank was early on associated with royalty, whose palace was in the Marais, the oldest inhabited part. Later the Louvre (today's 1st arrondissement) was remodelled as a kingly residence. The municipal authorities have been based on Place de l'Hôtel de Ville since the 13th century and the square is still a focus of rallies and events. Since 2002 Paris Plage has occupied the area below the Hôtel de Ville, stretching between the Louvre and Pont de Sully, and in winter the square is transformed into a skating rink.

The Champs-Élysées and Place Vendôme, laid out in the 17th century, and Place de la Concorde which was created in the 18th, bear witness to the grandeur of those times, and they remain affluent districts, while finance is centred around the Bourse.

As Paris expanded in the 19th century, many of its famous landmarks were created: Garnier's opera house epitomises mid-century opulence; wide boulevards were built by Haussmann and a multitude of theatres, hotels and mansions accommodated a fun-loving population. The Élysée Palace has been the official residence of the President of the Republic since 1873, and various embassies cluster around it. The great circle of the Étoile, with the Arc de Triomphe at its centre, has twelve radial avenues leading off it.

The Right Bank also claims the famous hill of Montmartre as well as the districts around Place de la Bastille, Place de la République, the atmospheric Canal St-Martin, Parc de la Villette with its new concert hall, Père-Lachaise cemetery, and the residential, multi-ethnic enclaves of Belleville and Ménilmontant.

The Louvre

The Musée du Louvre is the largest and most visited museum and art gallery in the world, its collection spanning many centuries and civilisations.

The huge courtyard known as the Cour Napoléon, with the Pyramid at its centre, is the heart of the Louvre. The museum's twelve departments are housed in three wings around the courtyard: Pavillon Denon to the south, Pavillon Richelieu to the north and Pavillon Sully to the east, occupying all four sides of the smaller Cour Carrée. Outside the Pyramide, lines of visitors wait patiently to get through the security check and down to the ticket hall on the lower level. This is one of the greatest museums in the world, attracting nearly ten million visitors a year. Many of the rooms of the former royal palace still have their original décor, of great interest in itself; the remains of the medieval Louvre fortress and Napoléon III's apartments in Pavillon Richelieu are also part of the museum.

Access and opening times
Map p. 587, D1. Métro 1 and 7 to Palais Royal-Musée du Louvre. Open daily except Tues 9–5.45, evening openings on Wed and Fri until 9.45pm (except public holidays). Closed Tues, 1 Jan, 1 May, 15 Aug, 25 Dec. The main entrance is on the west side of the Pyramide. Other entrances are from the underground Carrousel du Louvre (ticket sales), Porte des Lions-Denon Pavilion (except Fri; ticket sales by machine and card only), Passage Richelieu-Richelieu Pavilion (ticket holders only). A weekly chart in the Hall Napoléon (under the Pyramide) gives up-to-date gallery closures; or check at reception or online in advance. T: 40 20 53 17, www.louvre.fr.

Tickets
Free for under-18s; free for everyone on the first Sun of the month and for under 26s on Fri after 6pm. Reduced admission after 6pm on Wed and Fri. Combined evening ticket for permanent and temporary exhibitions; same-day ticket for Louvre and Delacroix museums. At peak times there can be a long wait to enter the Pyramide. The Louvre has no online ticket sales from its own website. Online tickets can be purchased from TicketWeb (US & Canada), FNAC and Ticketnet; tickets must be collected at the stores listed on those websites. The Paris Pass also includes entry to the Louvre.

Information
There are regular introductory tours (available in English) and guided tours (French only), listed on louvre.fr/visites-guidees. Audioguides on Nintendo 3DS available

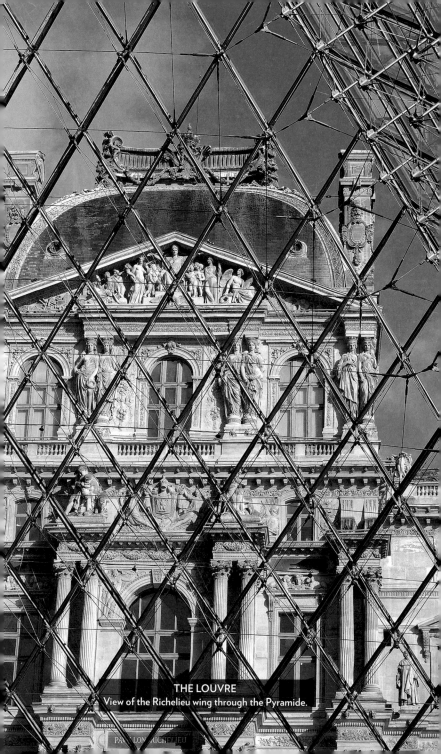

THE LOUVRE
View of the Richelieu wing through the Pyramide.

(ID necessary) under the Pyramide and at top of escalators to the Denon, Sully and Richelieu wings; also audioguide for iPhone and Android (download at home or at the museum). Most galleries have handbills in several languages giving detailed information on exhibits. In certain historic rooms there are wall panels with information on the history and decoration. Visitor Trails (www.louvre.fr) are thematic and can be printed out. The website also has online tours of several departments.

There is a vast range of guidebooks to the masterpieces of the Louvre in several languages. The main bookshop is under the Pyramide, and there are subsidiary book sales and information outlets in the museum. Films of the Louvre are shown in the audio-visual room, open from 10am. Security staff are very helpful.

Photography
Photography is prohibited in the Apollo Gallery and in the galleries of Italian, Spanish and French paintings on the first floor of the Denon wing. Flash photography is strongly discouraged throughout the museum.

Cafés and restaurants
Inside the Louvre are various eating places. Waiter service: Le Café du Grand Louvre (T: 01 40 20 53 41) and Café Mollien, first-floor landing of Mollien staircase (not far from Italian paintings). Under the Pyramide: Le Comptoir du Louvre and Les Cafés de la Pyramide, three food outlets for hot meals and snacks. There are a number of eating places, cafés and takeaways in the Carrousel du Louvre shopping mall (under the Louvre). Close by, in Cour Napoléon, is Café Marly (see p. 241), and in the Tuileries is the Saut du Loup (see p. 261).

Disabled visitors
A map and guide are available online for disabled visitors. There is an entrance with lift on the west side of the Pyramide. Manual wheelchairs are on loan free of charge. Disabled visitors' information, T: 01 40 20 59 90, handicap@louvre.fr. There is an area for visually handicapped visitors in the Italian Sculpture section of the Denon wing, with works that may be touched.

Orientation
It is impossible to see the whole of the Louvre Museum in one day. Orientation leaflets are available free at the information desk (in English and eight other languages). All information in English is signalled in red. The Louvre's collections are divided between eight departments, plus the Medieval Louvre and Primitive Arts. Each department constitutes a museum in itself, and the building is large and complicated to get around. It may help to set out with a preconceived plan tailored to individual preferences and time available. Departments are colour-coded to assist orientation: History of the Louvre—brown; Paintings—red; Prints and Drawings—pink; Greek, Etruscan and Roman Antiquities—blue; Egyptian Antiquities—light green; Near Eastern Antiquities—gold; Arts of Islam–green; Decorative Arts—purple; Sculptures—buff.

THE LOUVRE BUILDING

NB: To read about the history and architecture of the Louvre, see below. To plunge straight into the museum collections, turn to p. 186.

Despite its apparent homogeneity, the palace is the result of many phases of building, modifications and restoration. It is made up of two main parts, the Old Louvre, comprising the buildings surrounding the Cour Carrée to the east and along the bank of the Seine; and the New Louvre, the 19th-century buildings north and south of the Cour Napoléon (which has the Pyramide in its centre). The long extensions to the west were originally part of the now-demolished Tuileries Palace.

HISTORY OF THE PALAIS DU LOUVRE

The derivation of the name Louvre is unclear, but it was already used in relation to the fortress built here by Philippe-Auguste (1190–1215, *see p. 185*), of which it was a part. Extended and improved by Charles V (1364–80), it became an official royal residence, endowed with a library, sheltered within new walls completed in the 1390s. Subsequent monarchs preferred other palaces until François I (1515–47) planned the total demolition and reconstruction of all the west and south sides of the fortress. The west side of the Cour Carrée, south of Pavillon Sully, part of the early 16th-century palace, is the oldest elevation above ground. The work, begun by Pierre Lescot shortly before the king's death, was continued under Henri II. Jean Goujon was responsible for the elegant Classical sculptural decorations which set the tone for all later additions. Charles IX (d. 1574) began the Petite Galerie (or Apollo Gallery) in 1566, the first part of a plan to build a long gallery to connect the Louvre with the Tuileries Palace, his mother Catherine de Médicis' new residence. At the time of Henri IV (d. 1610), the Grande Galerie (1595–1610), or Galerie du Bord de l'Eau, built along the Seine by Louis Métezeau and Jacques II Androuet du Cerceau as far as the Pavillon de Flore, was part of the *Grand Dessein* (royal design) to enlarge the Louvre. The monumental Pavillon de l'Horloge (1639–42; later Pavillon Sully) and the north half of the west façade were the work of Lemercier.

From 1654, during the minority of Louis XIV, Lemercier supervised work on the court apartment of the queen mother, Anne of Austria. Fire destroyed the second floor of the Petite Galerie in 1661, and the royal decision to renew Henri IV's *Grand Dessein* resulted in the Apollo Gallery and further buildings to the west. The Pavillon de Marsan, opposite the Pavillon de Flore, was built in 1660–5 by Louis Le Vau and François d'Orbay (rebuilt 1873). The quadrangle (now the Cour Carrée) was extended and several architects, including Bernini and Le Vau, submitted projects for the main façade to the east. However, the resultant great colonnade of 52 Corinthian columns and pilasters was the work of Claude Perrault and Le Vau. (The decorations of the Cour Carrée were not completed until the 19th century.) Louis XIV, preoccupied with his new palace at Versailles, soon lost interest and these buildings were abandoned in a state of disrepair, to be occupied by the academies. It was not until 1754 that Louis XV commissioned J.-A. Gabriel to renovate and restore the palace.

Under Napoleon part of the North Gallery along Rue de Rivoli was begun and in 1810, the wedding feast of Napoleon and Marie-Louise of Austria was celebrated in the Salon Carré (now part of the Italian Paintings gallery). The building was attacked during the revolutions of 1830 and 1848.

At the time of Napoléon III, Visconti and then Hector-Martin Lefuel completed Henri IV's Grande Galerie linking the Louvre and the Tuileries, as well as new buildings on Rue de Rivoli extending the existing wings. Cour Napoléon was completed in 1857 and the interior decoration in 1861. After 1871, when the Tuileries palace was fired by the Communards, the damaged Pavillon de Marsan (now the Musée des Arts Décoratifs) was rebuilt by Lefuel.

On 10th August, 1793, the Musée de la République was opened in the Louvre, and has remained France's national art gallery and museum ever since. By 1981 the museum lacked sufficient space for both visitors and workshops, so the north wing, occupied by the Ministry of Finance since 1871, was handed back in 1989 and became the Richelieu wing. The Ministry transferred to Bercy.

THE *GRAND PROJET DU LOUVRE* AND THE PYRAMIDE

The ambitious *Grand Projet du Louvre* began in 1983, when President Mitterrand approved the plan proposed by the Chinese-born American architect I.M. Pei to construct a glass pyramid as the new museum entrance. The Cour Carrée was excavated and the foundations of the medieval fortress were exposed.

The Pyramide, elegant and innovative, in the centre of Cour Napoléon, is now almost as well known as the Eiffel Tower. The 30m square by 20m high structure, with transparent walls supported by a trussed steel frame, takes up less space than conventional building shapes. The glass reflects and refracts light as well as permitting uninterrupted views of the palace façades. It shelters the hub of the Louvre Museum, the Hall Napoléon, and is flanked by three subsidiary pyramids and seven fountains with triangular basins of Brittany granite. Between the Pyramide and the Arc du Carrousel is an equestrian statue of Louis XIV, a lead copy of 1988 after Bernini's original at Versailles. The statue—but not the Pyramide—is on the same axis as the Tuileries, the Champs-Élysées and the Arc de Triomphe

In 1993, President Mitterrand dedicated the whole Palais du Louvre to the museum, almost doubling the exhibition space from 31,000 to 60,000 square metres, allowing for improved presentation of the works and more use of natural light. However the Napoleon Hall below the Pyramide is increasingly busy. Originally designed to accommodate 4.5 million visitors, the museum, by the time of writing, had almost ten million passing through. To ease congestion a project is underway to reorganise the space beneath the Pyramide and to improve facilities.

THE CARROUSEL DU LOUVRE

The Carrousel du Louvre is a popular underground shopping mall with a smaller inverted glass pyramid providing daylight. It is accessed directly from the Métro station Palais Royal-Musée du Louvre; via escalators from 99 Rue de Rivoli; and from the Hall Napoléon under the Pyramide. The mall has specialist shops and a large food hall

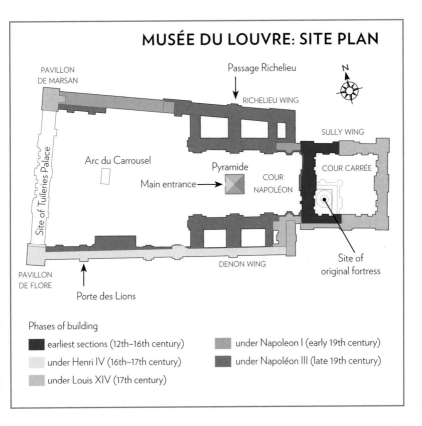

MUSÉE DU LOUVRE: SITE PLAN

PAVILLON DE MARSAN

Passage Richelieu

RICHELIEU WING

N

SULLY WING

Arc du Carrousel

Pyramide

COUR NAPOLÉON

COUR CARRÉE

Site of Tuileries Palace

Main entrance →

Site of original fortress

PAVILLON DE FLORE

Porte des Lions

DENON WING

Phases of building

■ earliest sections (12th–16th century)

□ under Henri IV (16th–17th century)

□ under Louis XIV (17th century)

■ under Napoleon I (early 19th century)

■ under Napoléon III (late 19th century)

with a variety of cafés as well as a post office, cafés and a museum a ticket desk (*open daily except Tues 9.30–7, Wed and Fri to 9.45*).

THE MEDIEVAL LOUVRE

The oldest part of the Louvre (*marked on the plan above*), on the lower ground floor of the Sully wing, is a section of the foundations of **Philippe-Auguste's fortress** of 1190, which was integral to his defensive wall around Paris. An introduction to the history of the early castle is illustrated by maquettes, paintings and fragments of masonry. The re-sited base of a rusticated wall by Le Vau (17th century) creates an impressive entrance to vaulted galleries with information on the excavations of the outer moat in 1983–4. Outlined on the floor is the position of the 12th-century Tour de la Fauconnerie, which became Charles V's library in 1367, when the fortress had lost its defensive role. The massive masonry formed a quadrilateral 72m by 78m, surrounded by moats and punctuated by ten towers and drawbridges. The Grosse Tour (keep), symbol of royal authority, formerly 15m in diameter and 31m high (now 7m), was used as a food store and valuables safe. It was demolished in 1528.

Beyond the moat and keep is the last remaining fragment of the main residence, the **Salle St-Louis**, with Gothic rib vaults (1230–40), where some of the 900 objects and fragments discovered beneath the keep are exhibited.

THE COLLECTIONS

The nucleus of the royal art collection was formed by François I, at whose request Leonardo da Vinci spent the last few years of his life working in France (d. 1519, Amboise). Henri II and Catherine de Médicis carried on the tradition of royal patronage and Henri IV created a room for antiquities. Louis XIV added to the Cabinet des Tableaux du Roi and the Cabinet des Desseins, which became the basis of the present collection. Louis XVI acquired some important paintings of the Spanish and Dutch Schools and planned the opening of a museum in the Louvre. During the 18th century the Académie de Peinture et de Sculpture (founded 1648) had a permanent exhibition and also held biennial exhibitions of the works of its members here which, during the years 1759–81, were the subject of Denis Diderot's invigorating art criticism in *Salons*. In 1793 the Musée de la République was opened to the public and during the next few years a large number of the most famous paintings of Europe—spoils of conquest by the Republican and Napoleonic armies—were exhibited here; after 1815 the French government was obliged to restore some works to their former owners. Under Louis XVIII, the *Venus de Milo* and over a hundred pictures were acquired. Champollion, the Egyptologist, persuaded Charles X to acquire prestigious Egyptian collections. The Louvre's latest project (2012) was the opening of a specially-designed gallery in which to display the extensive collection of the Arts of Islam.

PAINTINGS

The Louvre's Department of Paintings contains works from every European School from the Middle Ages to the mid-19th century.

FRENCH SCHOOL

The collection of French paintings is, as to be expected, second to none, encompassing works by all the greatest French painters from the 13th–19th centuries. There are over 1,000 works on display in 77 rooms, arranged chronologically. The overview of highlights below begins with the earliest, on the second floor of the Richelieu wing.

Medieval works: The department is introduced by the **portrait of Jean Le Bon** (Jean II; before 1350), a rare easel painting on wood and the only existing French portrait of this period. The first rooms are devoted to the International Gothic, which was a style developed by Franco-Flemish artists working in Paris, Dijon and Bourges. It is characterised by elegance, decorative refinement and a celebration of courtly life, as well as a wealth of naturalistic detail. These are

THE LOUVRE
Escalier Daru.

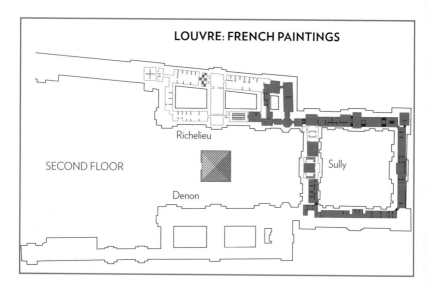

LOUVRE: FRENCH PAINTINGS

Richelieu

SECOND FLOOR

Sully

Denon

combined in *Carrying of the Cross* by Jacquemart de Hesdin. Two paintings commissioned by Philippe le Hardi, Duke of Burgundy, for Champmol, Burgundy, were the *Retable of St-Denis* (1415–16) by Henri Bellechose, showing scenes of the saint's martyrdom, and a large round *Pietà* (c. 1400) attributed to Malouel.

For much of the 14th century, **Avignon** was the seat of the papal court and brilliant works were produced there under the influence of Sienese painters. The greatest of all French paintings to have absorbed this influence is the *Pietà of Villeneuve-les-Avignon* (c. 1455), by Enguerrand Quarton. It is a typically French interpretation, with the body of Christ dramatically outstretched, the Virgin accompanied by Mary Magdalene and St John the Evangelist, and a donor figure on the left.

A bold and monumental form of **portraiture** was practised both in miniatures and full-scale portraits such as that of Charles VII, by Jean Fouquet, who had studied in Rome.

The 16th century: Portraiture was dominated by **Jean Clouet**. The portrait of François I (c. 1530) borrows stylistically from Fouquet's Charles VII as well as on a drawing of the king by Jean Clouet, and also shows a strong Italian influence. The attribution of the painting was long disputed and it is possible that Clouet's son François contributed to it. François succeeded his father as court painter and gave a more marked individual characterisation to his sitters.

The style of the **School of Fontainebleau** goes back to the presence in France of the Italian artists Rosso Fiorentino, Primaticcio and Nicolò dell'Abbate who, invited by François I, participated in the decoration of the Château of Fontainebleau from 1530. They introduced a Mannerist, Renaissance elegance, where mythological and allegorical subjects replaced religious iconography, bringing the freedom to introduce sensual female nudes. Typical is *Eva Prima Pandora*, the work of Jean Cousin the Elder and one of the first nudes painted in France. *Diana the Huntress* (c. 1550; artist unknown) is thought to be an idealised portrait of Diane de Poitiers, favourite of King Henri II. The delicately painted portrait of Gabrielle d'Estrées and one of her sisters (c. 1594), showing the sister pinching Gabrielle's right nipple, may allude to the latter's pregnancy. A mistress of Henri IV, Gabrielle gave birth to his illegitimate son in 1594.

A French painter who reacted against Mannerism and leaned towards the naturalism of the Italian painter Caravaggio was **Valentin de Boulogne**, who as a young man found success in Rome painting genre works such as the *Concert with Antique Bas-relief* and *The Innocence of Suzanne*. **Claude Vignon**, by contrast, remained Mannerist in style.

The court of Louis XIII: Outstanding among the large works by the court painters of Louis XIII are those of **Simon Vouet**, who had a successful career in Italy before returning to France where he painted many altarpieces. Portraits by **Philippe de Champaigne** include *Cardinal Richelieu* and *Louis XIII Crowned by Victory*, commemorating the Siege of La Rochelle (1628), a victory for cardinal and king over the Protestants.

Poussin and Claude: The Louvre owns 38 works by Nicolas Poussin, a quarter of the total in existence. Originally from Normandy, Poussin spent most of his life in Rome, where he concentrated on Classical themes. The evolution of his rigorous, intellectualised style can be followed through these galleries. After the large-scale *Apparition of the Virgin to St James the Greater* (1629), he turned to a smaller format and recreated antiquity for the *cognoscenti*. Among paintings of his first Roman period (1624–40) are *Echo and Narcissus* and *Inspiration of the Poet*, demonstrating his short-lived interest in Venetian art. Works such as *Arcadian Shepherds* or the *Rape of the Sabine Women*, which characterise his mature years, are filled with dramatically posed figures. In order to plan compositions he used miniature scenery and wax models. The grave *Self-portrait* has in the background the *Allegories of Art* and *The Arm of Friendship*.

Poussin's artistic counterpoint, Claude Gellée, from Nancy, known as Le Lorrain or Claude, also spent most of his working life in Rome. Claude created his own brand of Classical landscapes, often based on atmospheric scenes of the Roman countryside or of seaports, idealising nature. He favoured U-shaped compositions that recede into a misty distance, such as *Seaport in the Setting Sun*, *View of a Port with the Capitol* and *Arrival of Cleopatra at Tarsa*.

17th-century masters: The founder-members of the Académie Royale de Peinture et Sculpture (founded in 1648) include Philippe de Champaigne, Charles Le Brun, Sébastien Bourdon, Noël Coypel, Eustache le Sueur and Laurent de la Hyre.

Georges de la Tour is famed for his night-time scenes dramatically lit by candlelight such as *Penitent Magdalene*; but the richly-painted, anecdotal *Cardsharp with the Ace of Diamonds*, one of only two works of his in the Louvre

THE LOUVRE
Mother Catherine-Agnès Arnauld of the Port-Royal nunnery,
by Philippe de Champaigne (1662).

painted in direct light (the other is *St Thomas*), is the masterpiece here. A favourite theme of artists from Caravaggio to Cézanne, the card game provided an ideal opportunity to create a mood, study relationships and moralise on the temptations of gambling, wine and lust. The elegantly-dressed young man on the right is being set up by the other three players, whose body-language indicates what is about to happen, directing the viewer's focus to the hand of the card-sharp on the left.

Philippe de Champaigne abandoned his earlier Baroque style after 1643 as he became more involved in the ascetic Jansenist sect (*see p. 158*). An austere and rigorous masterpiece of 1662, *The Artist's Daughter with Mère Catherine-Agnès Arnauld*, was painted in thanksgiving for the miraculous cure of his daughter, nursed by Jansenist nuns at Port-Royal. The simple, kindly face of the elderly nun and the tired eyes of the palsied girl are brilliantly rendered.

Charles Le Brun, the foremost painter at the time of Louis XIV, remained faithful to the Baroque style in the sumptuous equestrian portrait of Chancellor Séguier (c. 1661). His great *L'Histoire d'Alexandre* (1660) painted at Fontainebleau, depicts Darius' mother prostrate at feet of Alexander the Great, pleading with him to release her son. Jean Jouvenet, a pupil of Le Brun, following paralysis in his right hand, taught himself to paint with his left for the last three years of his life (1715–17).

Other painters at the Court of Louis XIV included **Hyacinthe Rigaud**, who produced the quintessential Baroque portrait of absolute monarchy, the celebrated full-length *Louis XIV*, in 1701 (*see p. 230*).

The 18th century: The Louvre has around a dozen paintings by Jean-Antoine **Watteau**, who died young of tuberculosis in 1721 (he was 37). He began as a decorative painter and his works have a certain wistfulness, including the monumental but enigmatic *Pierrot* (also known as *Gilles*), and *Pilgrimage to Cythera* (1717), his vision of a lazy, melancholic day of late summer, for which the term *fête galante* was coined.

Among genre paintings are those of pure pleasure by **François Boucher**, such as the erotic *L'Odalisque* (c. 1745) and *Rape of Europa*.

Well-known works by Jean-Baptiste-Siméon **Chardin** include *Le Buffet*, in which fruit perilously perched in a stand forms a pyramid of reds and greys. In the last ten years of his life Chardin abandoned oils because of poor health, and worked in pastels (shown in rotation). Outstanding is his *Self-portrait* (1775), made when he was 66. Another pastel masterpiece not to be missed is the portrait of Madame de Pompadour by Maurice-Quentin Delatour (1748–55).

The encyclopaedist Denis Diderot objected to his portrait by Louis-Michel van Loo, complaining that it was too flattering.

The work that made Jean-Honoré **Fragonard**'s name in Paris was *The High Priest Croesus Sacrificing Himself to Save Callirhoë* (1765), but he soon turned to lighter themes, dashed off with rapid, vibrant brushstrokes. *Adoration of the Shepherds* (c. 1775) and *Le Verrou* (*The Bolt*; c. 1777) are pendant pieces which symbolise sacred and profane love; the latter is a masterpiece of Fragonard's ambivalent eroticism: is this free love or is it ravishment?

Hubert Robert's paintings of picturesque ruins in Italy and France are valuable topographical records, as in the *Demolition of the Houses on Pont Notre-Dame in 1786*. Gabriel de Saint-Aubin captures a work by Robert in *Vue du Salon de 1779*, in the Salon Carrée at the Louvre.

Jean-Baptiste **Greuze**, a painter admired by Diderot, was one of the most important of French 18th-century painters. Enormously popular in his day, but long dismissed as sentimental and moralising, he is now being re-evaluated.

One of the most successful portraitists of her time was **Élisabeth Vigée-Lebrun**. Her career was encouraged by Vernet, whom she painted in 1778. At the Revolution she fled France, travelling through Europe as far as Russia, surviving by painting portraits. She is best known for her likenesses of women and children (among her sitters was Marie-Antoinette).

Neoclassical, Romantic and Orientalist works: A number of fine portraits by the Neoclassical painter **Jacques-Louis David** demonstrate his skill in this field.

One room is devoted entirely to **Ingres**, a consummate draughtsman who painted great portraits, including that of the composer Cherubini (Ingres himself was a violinist). He was Director of the French Academy in Rome in 1834. Throughout his long career his style barely altered, but he was especially famous for voluptuous scenes inspired by stories of North Africa (which he never visited), such as *Le Bain turc* and *La Baigneuse de Valpinçon*.

The Romantic painter **Théodore Géricault**'s passion for animals is represented here, notably by paintings of horses; he took an interest also in inmates of Paris asylums, of which *La Folle Monomane du jeu* (c. 1820) is an example. Here too is the first sketch for the *Raft of the Medusa* (*see p. 196*).

The greatest of the Romantic painters was **Eugène Delacroix**. His varied subjects include battles, Greek soldiers dancing, and a portrait of Chopin (a fragment of the painting *George Sand et Chopin* of 1838). *Horatio at the Graveyard* was painted during the artist's visit to England in 1825, and *Self-portrait* in 1837. His visit to Tangiers in 1832 left a deep impression and indeed North Africa was a fashionable source of ideas for a group of painters known as 'Orientalists', among them **Théodore Chassériau**, pupil of Ingres and admirer of Delacroix, who painted mythological, religious and Shakespearian subjects, and the wistful *Portrait de l'artiste tenant une palette.*

19th-century collections: Théodore Rousseau and the **Barbizon School**, notably Paul Huet, pioneers of painting '*en plein air*', provide examples of bucolic landscapes. The Moreau-Nélaton collection contains many works by **Corot**, such as beautiful landscapes and *La Femme à la perle*, as well as works by Barbizon artists who worked in the forest of Fontainebleau. The *Jeune Orpheline au cimetière* is familiar as Delacroix used the image, transformed into a young man, in *Massacres de Chios.*

The **Thomy-Thiery Collection**, donated in 1902, has works by Corot and others. Millet brought dignity to peasant famers at their labours in studies such as *La Bruleuse d'herbes* and *La Lessiveuse,*

the background and colours simplified, the emphasis on the figure.

The works in the **Beistegui Collection**, mainly 18th–19th-century, were donated in 1953 on condition they be kept together. They range from a Flemish 14th-century *Virgin and Child* and a late 15th-century *Portrait of the Dauphin Charles Orlando* (son of Charles VIII and Anne of Brittany) by the Maître de Moulins, to numerous portraits by Fragonard, Largillière, Thomas Lawrence and others. The most eye-catching work is Goya's powerful *Marquesa de la Solana* (c. 1795). It depicts Maria Rita Barranchea, a cultured aristocrat and playwright, who married a friend of one of Goya's patrons, Jovellanos. She was 38 when this portrait was made but gravely unwell, and knew she had little time to live.

The **Croÿ and Lyon collections** were donated in 1930–2 and 1971 respectively. Princess Louise de Croÿ's bequest of 3,800 drawings and paintings consists mainly of Northern School works and landscapes by Pierre-Henri de Valenciennes, responsible for reinvigorating the *paysage historique* with his oil sketches done *en plein-air*. The Hélène and Victor Lyon donation of 17th–18th-century Northern and Venetian paintings includes landscapes by Bernardo Strozzi, a Genoese Capuchin friar, also known as 'il Cappuccino', who moved to Venice in 1631 and whose style has been compared to Rubens and Van Dyck. There are also works by Canaletto and Giandomenico Tiepolo, as well as a cross-section of late 19th-century French works by painters including Cézanne, Degas, Jongkind, Monet, Pissarro, Renoir and Toulouse-Lautrec.

NORTHERN SCHOOLS

The Northern Paintings Department (Richelieu second floor), one of the richest in the world, has on display some 1,200 works by Flemish, Dutch and German artists from the 14th–19th centuries.

International Gothic works from Bohemia, Germany and Austria set the scene for early 15th-century Dutch and Flemish paintings showing the result of a deliberate break by artists from its brilliant but superficial qualities. Exceptional is **Jan van Eyck**'s *Virgin with Chancellor Nicolas Rolin*. Rolin, the donor, who kneels in prayer before the Madonna, was the rich and powerful chancellor of Philip the Good of Burgundy. By **Rogier van der Weyden** is the *Braque Family Triptych* (c. 1450), a work of intense colour and feeling, and the *Annunciation*, with sparkling details. Bruges artists who followed Van Eyck's lead were **Hans Memling**, represented by several works including *The Virgin between St James and St Dominic*. A fragment of an allegorical work depicting avarice, greed and drunkenness, *The*

Ship of Fools (1490–1510), is the Louvre's only work by **Bosch**.

A series of 28 portraits of illustrious or wise men (Room 4) was commissioned from **Joos van Gent** and Pedro Berruguete by Federico da Montefeltro for the Ducal Palace at Urbino. The Louvre now has 14 of them.

Renaissance works between c. 1495 and 1550 are a fusion of German, Netherlandish and Italian art. **Albrecht Dürer**'s finely-drawn *Self-portrait with a Thistle* (1493) was one of the first individual self-portraits in Western painting, although artists had previously included themselves in groups. Dürer painted it at the end of a guild tour through southern Germany. He holds a thistle, possibly a symbol of fidelity to his betrothed, Agnes Frey. The Louvre also

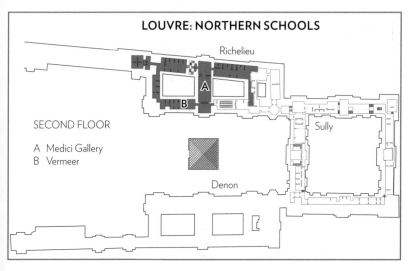

LOUVRE: NORTHERN SCHOOLS

Richelieu

SECOND FLOOR

A Medici Gallery
B Vermeer

Sully

Denon

owns five portraits by **Hans Holbein the Younger**, which belonged to Louis XIV. These include the Dutch scholar Erasmus (painted for Sir Thomas More), Thomas More himself, and the friend of both men, the Archbishop of Canterbury, William of Warham, which was the first work made in England (1526–8) and is considered to be the original version of a copy in London. A popular work is **Quentin Metsys'** *Moneylender and his Wife*, which shows the couple at a table surrounded by a variety of objects including a small round mirror. It can be read as a record of an honest couple at work or as an allegorical piece with references to vanity and avarice, with the scales as symbols of the Last Judgement. **Jan Gossaert** (Mabuse) fuses Italian Renaissance ideas with those of Van Eyck and Dürer to create a beautiful object of private devotion, the *Diptych of Jean Carondelet*, representing the Chancellor of Flanders and the Virgin and Child.

The Louvre has just one painting by **Brueghel the Elder**, *Beggars* (1568), a curious group of five cripples. His younger son Jan, **'Velvet' Brueghel**, visited Rome in 1591 and met Paul Bril there. He returned to Antwerp in 1596 and was a successful portrait and landscape painter. Rubens collaborated with him.

Rubens and Van Dyck: Seventeenth-century Flemish painting was dominated by these two artists. Against the light-green walls of the specially-created Medici Gallery **(A)** are Rubens' 24 huge, resplendent allegorical series depicting the **life of Marie de Médicis**. Designed in 1622–5 to decorate the Palais du Luxembourg, this is the painter's greatest single work and glorifies the life and achievements of the queen in an appropriately exuberant and eulogistic manner. Running in chronological sequence from left to right, each canvas represents a major event of Marie's life, starting with her birth in April 1575. Other scenes include her arrival at Marseilles on 3rd November 1600 to become Henri IV's second wife; the birth of her son, Louis; the *Apotheosis of Henri IV*; and the *Proclamation of the Regency of the Queen*, the key moment in the cycle. The sequence ends with the reconciliation with her son, Louis XIII, in 1619. Above the door, between portraits of her parents, is Marie de Médicis as *Reine Triomphante*. This great series influenced later French artists as disparate as Watteau and David.

Other works by Rubens include a portrait of Baron Henri de Vicq (c. 1625), the ambassador who obtained for the artist the commission to paint the Medici canvases. Among the landscapes is the unforgettable *Kermesse*—the village wedding—a rustic scene superbly observed and peopled.

Several of the works by Van Dyck here came from Louis XIV's collection. They include mythological scenes, such as *Venus and Vulcan* (1626–32), painted just before the painter's departure for England, and two beautifully composed and elegant portraits executed in Antwerp, *A Lady of Quality and her Child* and its counterpart *A Gentleman and his Child*. The full-length portrait of Marchesa Spinola-Doria was made during Van Dyck's stay in Italy (before 1632). From his English period is *Portrait of James Stewart* (1612–55), a private work which introduces an element of mythology with the apple in his hand, possibly an allusion to the Judgement of Paris. *Charles I at the*

Hunt (c. 1637) was paid for by the king in 1635 although not kept by him. It presents him as an aristocratic gentleman rather than as a monarch. The work was already in France by 1738 and was purchased by Louis XVI from Madame du Barry in 1785.

There is a representative selection of Flemish genre scenes and landscapes. Jan Davidsz de Heem's *The Dessert* is an opulent still life, of which Matisse made a version in 1893.

Early 17th-century Dutch paintings

are arranged by genre rather than by artist (with the exception of Rembrandt) and are displayed more or less chronologically. Works by **Frans Hals** include the majestic portrait of Paulus van Berestyn and the later *Old Woman,* which demonstrates his growing preference for restrained colours. Landscapes, often with a brilliantly observed sky, include Van Goyen's *Two large Sailing Boats* and Solomon van Ruysdael's *The Landing-stage.* One of several architecture specialists was **Saenredam**, represented here by *Interior of a Church Haarlem.* Dutch genre scenes are typified by Adam van Breen's *Skaters.* Fine examples of large history or genre painting typical of the **Dutch Caravaggists** are Gerard van Honthorst's *The Concert* and *The Lute Player.* More sober is the work of Ter Brugghen from predominantly Catholic Utrecht.

Rembrandt: Rembrandt van Rijn painted himself through every stage of his life. Of the four self-portraits in the collection, two date from 1633: the introspective *Self-portrait Bareheaded,* and *Self-portrait Wearing a Toque and Chain,* which uses a rich palette and play

of light. From 1660 is the even more self-reflective *Artist in his Old Age at his Easel* (1660). Saskia van Uylenborch, whom Rembrandt married in 1634, brought a considerable dowry. In the period up to her death in 1642 he lived in grand style and beyond his means. During those years he painted the *Philosopher in Meditation* and the *Holy Family.* From his more mature and mystical period is *Christ at Emmaus* (1648). The portrait of *Hendrickje Stoffels with a Velvet Beret* (c. 1654) is a loving painting of the nursemaid to Rembrandt's son, who became his mistress after Saskia died. Hendrickje posed for one of the best known of Rembrandt's works in the Louvre, the monumental, copper-toned *Bathsheba Bathing.* Rembrandt records Bathsheba's dilemma when she receives the note from King David, who had fallen in love with her. To meet his ends, the king banishes Uriah, her husband, to certain death on the battlefield. There are also many works by pupils, imitators and followers of Rembrandt.

Later 17th-century Dutch paintings

include quantities of scenes of everyday life, portraits, landscapes, seascapes and still lifes, a production which reflects the strength of the domestic market for small secular paintings. There are several works by **Gerrit Dou**, including *Old Woman Praying* and a self-portrait.

Among the painters of bucolic landscapes are **Van Ruisdael** (*Le Buisson*), **Cuyp** (*Landscape near Rhenen*) and more works by Dou, such as the atmospheric *Le Gué* (*The Ford*). **Metsu** painted charming compositions of women engaged in domestic tasks, such as *La Peleuse de pommes* (*The Apple Peeler*) and Abraham Mignon's *Flowers in a*

Crystal Jug is representative of Dutch paintings of abundant blooms. **Jan Steen**'s populous *Fête dans une auberge* is typical of his output.

Vermeer: A single room **(B)** is dedicated to this artist (by whom only 35 paintings are known) and his circle. The first of the two Vermeers owned by the Louvre is *The Lacemaker* (c. 1679), the smallest he ever painted (24cm by 21cm), which combines an intensely concentrated domestic scene and a masterful use of colour and light. The book in the fore-ground, which appears to be the Bible, adds a moral dimension. The second Vermeer is *The Astronomer* (1668), from his late period. Here we see a figure in deep contemplation, a conceit much appreciated in Holland at the time, bathed in a cool light which falls on the globe and accentuates the deep folds of the luxuriant fabrics.

Pieter de Hooch painted *The Drinker* (1658) during his stay in Delft. Also here are *Courtyard of a Dutch House* and *Card Players in an Opulent Interior in Amsterdam* (c. 1663–5). In both works the artist makes great play of indirect light and the careful orchestration of fig-ures in perspective. The latter painting apparently set in a brothel.

LARGE-SCALE FRENCH WORKS

An enfilade of rooms **(1)** on Denon first floor contain the most famous large-scale French paintings of the Empire period. Theatrical canvases by David, inspired by antiquity, include *The Sabine Women* (1799) and *The Oath of the Horatii* (1784), widely seen as extolling Republican virtues although commissioned for the Crown. There is also the brilliant historical record of the *Coronation of Napoleon I by Pope Pius VII in Notre-Dame*, on 2nd December 1804 (when Napoleon's impatience with the reluctant old pope led to his seizing the crown and placing it on his own head). David's genius as a portrait painter is amply demonstrated by the famous *Madame Récamier*. Also here is Prud'hon's rather wistful *Empress Josephine at Malmaison* (1805). Ingres' three main themes or genres are also found here: portraits (*The Rivière Family*, 1805); odalisques (*La Grande Odalisque*, 1814); and antiquity (*The Apotheosis of Homer*). By Delacroix are *Death of Sardanapalus*, from the poem by Baudelaire, and the battle-cry of the Republic, *Liberty Leading the People* (1831). Géricault offers high drama in *Raft of the Medusa* (1818–19), based on a true event, the catastrophic shipwreck of the French frigate *Méduse* off Senegal in 1816.

ITALIAN SCHOOLS

The richly-endowed Department of Italian Paintings (600 works) dates back to the reign of François I and constitutes the oldest collection in the Louvre. It also contains the most famous painting in the museum, the *Mona Lisa*. The collection covers works of the 14th–18th centuries, Renaissance works being displayed in the Grande Galerie, part of the old Louvre Palace. This room was used in the 18th century as a repository for military relief plans and in Louis XVI's time the intention was to make it the Musée Royal. In fact the museum was only to open during the Revolutionary period, on 10th August 1793.

The first two rooms, Salle Percier et Fontaine and Salle Duchâtel, contain **frescoes by Florentine masters** of the 13th–16th centuries. Two frescoes of c. 1483–5 by Botticelli were discovered in 1873 near Florence. Also here are a *Crucifixion* by Fra' Angelico (c. 1440–5), and three by Bernardino Luini, a follower of Leonardo.

Cimabue's *Madonna and Child in Majesty with Six Angels* (c. 1240–1302) is an early attempt to bring naturalism and depth to a fundamentally Byzantine composition. In the painted frame are 26 medallions of Christ, angels, prophets and saints. Freer and more lifelike figures are achieved by **Giotto** in *St Francis Receiving the Stigmata*.

The Quattrocento: The Salon Carré **(2)** contains works typical of the Quattrocento (the 15th century). **Fra' Angelico**'s two *Angels in Adoration*, one turned to the right and one to the left, were originally the two wings of a ciborium. **Botticelli**'s *Virgin and Child with the Young St John the Baptist* (c. 1470–5) is considered one of the most moving of the painter's works. The colourful (and charmingly wooden) *Battle of San Romano* (c. 1438), by **Paolo Uccello**, is one of three panels on the same theme (the others being in Florence and London), painted to depict a Florentine victory over the Sienese in 1432.

Siena and Northern Italy: In the collection are 13th–15th-century works by various artists, including Pisanello (active in Bergamo and Verona) and Jacopo Bellini, also active during the heyday of the Venetian republic. The *Portrait of Sigismondo Malatesta* by Piero della Francesca is a fine example of the artist's intellectually rigorous style and predilection for sharp profiles. Smaller works include *Christ Bearing the Cross* (c. 1342), a small, vivid section of a polyptych of the *Passion* by Simone Martini, an artist from Siena who

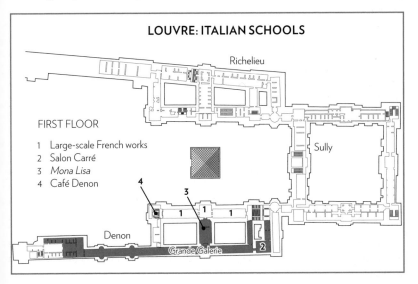

LOUVRE: ITALIAN SCHOOLS

Richelieu

FIRST FLOOR

1   Large-scale French works
2   Salon Carré
3   *Mona Lisa*
4   Café Denon

Sully

Denon

Grande Galerie

worked for a time in Avignon (France), and *The Dead Christ Supported by Two Angels* (c. 1485) by Carlo Crivelli.

Along the great length of the **Grande Galerie** the paintings are arranged to set up dialogues facing each other across the room. The first section has 15th–16th-century paintings from Tuscany and northern Italy. The precise draughtsmanship of **Andrea Mantegna** can be appreciated in the *Crucifixion*, and his fully developed interest in antiquity in *St Sebastian*, painted for the Church of Aigueperse in the Auvergne for the wedding of Chiara Gonzaga to the Count of Montpensier. The exaggerated perspective of the *Virgin of Victory* (1496), made for Francis II Gonzaga, suggests it was intended to be viewed from below.

Domenico Ghirlandaio, from Florence (he taught Michelangelo painting and drawing), painted the tender *Old Man and Young Boy*, of a bottle-nosed old man suffering from rhinophyma and his grandson (the old man is excellently rendered; the boy is perhaps by another hand).

Giovanni Bellini, the greatest artist of his family, raised Venetian art to the level of that of Florence. The development of his personal vision is represented in several works, including *Crucifixion* (c. 1465–70) and *Virgin and Child with Saints* (c. 1487).

Pietro di Cristoforo Vannucci, from Perugia, called **Perugino**, who strongly influenced his pupil Raphael, frequently painted *St Sebastian*, the plague saint, and here the saint is placed in an architectural setting with a delicately-painted landscape in the distance.

The High Renaissance: The end of the Quattrocento and first quarter of the Cinquecento produced some of the greatest Italian painters. One of them was **Leonardo da Vinci** and the Louvre owns five of his works. *The Virgin of the Rocks* (1482), which shows the Virgin Mary and Jesus with the orphaned St John sheltering in a grotto under the protection of the Archangel Uriel, was considered unfinished when Leonardo left Milan in 1499 and replaced by the later version, now in London. *The Madonna and Child with St Anne* is a vital, closely-knit group of three generations expressing tenderness and compassion. The painting was undoubtedly brought to France by Leonardo, but did not enter the royal collections until the time of Louis XIII. Also by Leonardo is a late painting, *St John the Baptist* (1513–16), depicting an eloquent, androgynous figure whose smile is almost as enigmatic as that of *Mona Lisa* **(3)**.

Opposite the *Mona Lisa* is **Veronese**'s magnificent, huge *Wedding at Cana*, painted for Palladio's refectory at San Giorgio Maggiore, Venice, but stolen by Napoleon. A religious subject packed with secular detail, the intensity of its colours were rediscovered when it was restored in 1989–92. It includes Veronese's self-portrait.

Around the walls are works by other Venetian artists, including **Titian**. His *Concert Champêtre* (c. 1509), the first in the tradition of *fêtes champêtres*, was a major influence on Manet, an hypothesis being that the female nudes are allegories, existing only in the imagination of the two seated figures. *The Entombment* (c. 1530) is one of Titian's greatest pictures—dramatic, moving,

MONA LISA

Leonardo's *Mona Lisa*, in the very centre of its gallery, is always surrounded by eager crowds taking photographs. Smiling insouciantly, she is housed in a protected, free-standing display which makes it impossible to get anywhere near close enough to admire her and to understand what makes her so artistically innovative.

The work is traditionally assumed to be a portrait of *Mona Lisa Gherardini* (correctly 'Monna', a variant of *mia donna* the Italian for 'my lady'), third wife of Francesco di Zanobi del Giocondo, the Florentine merchant who commissioned the work. The famous half-smile of the sitter could be a visual pun on this name and the reason why she is also known as *La Gioconda* or *La Joconde*. Leonardo seems to have begun work on the painting in Florence in 1503, taking it to Milan in 1506 and then to France, where he came at the behest of François I in 1517. It was one of his favourite pieces and Leonardo kept it with him when he returned to Italy; it is likely that the French king purchased it for a considerable sum in 1518 from one of Leonardo's two heirs. It was to become the most valued piece in the royal collection. In 1800 it was purloined by Napoleon for his apartments in the Tuileries Palace. It returned permanently to the Louvre in 1804 and has been here ever since, except for a couple of gaps: in August 1911 the painting was stolen, but recovered in Florence in December 1913; during the Second World War it was moved around provincial France for safety.

At some point, probably in the 17th century, the painting was trimmed in size, apparently in order to fit a required frame or hanging space: between two and three centimetres were taken off each of the sides and probably a small amount from top and bottom. In the process the pillared window-frame in which Mona Lisa was originally sitting was lost: the bases of the two columns can still just be seen at the edges. This loss explains the apparently abrupt passage from foreground to background, which would have been more logically solved in the original design. Nevertheless this small portrait still has tremendous and arresting power and magnetism. It brings together all of Leonardo's highly experimental skills.

Mona Lisa's gaze is benign but elusive. She slightly averts her eyes, as if something has caught her attention to her left. The smile, which appears to be the clue to her mood, is gentle but difficult to interpret: is it contentment or irony, nostalgia or self-satisfaction that she expresses? Her hands rest demurely on the arm of the chair in which she is seated and she is dressed in the Florentine fashion of the day. The glow of her skin is offset by the dark blue of her dress with yellow sleeves, and complemented by the light sky. Crucial to the effect of the portrait is the use of *sfumato*, the soft-edged technique which Leonardo perfected, managing the natural transition between light and dark in almost imperceptible degrees. The fluidity of the composition and delicacy of the image was achieved by building up layer upon layer of glazes heightened with tiny amounts of pigment on a medium ground. This proportion of an exceedingly small amount of pigment to a substantial thickness of medium (walnut-oil) accounts for the darkening of the picture—the reds and highlights in her face which Vasari repeatedly mentions have been overwhelmed by oxidation, giving the portrait its predominantly greenish hue. Arguably the most reproduced image in the world, it has inspired endless copies and alternative versions.　　　N.McG.

and ground-breaking in its time, both in tone and technique. Commissioned for the Gonzaga Dukes of Mantua, and bought by Charles I of England in 1627 when their collection was broken up, it was then purchased (for £120) just over 20 years later for Louis XIV by Cardinal Mazarin's agents following the execution of the English king, passing thereby into the French national collection. Much of the core of the Louvre's Italian collection followed this same route from Mantua via London to Paris.

Tintoretto combined the 'colour of Titian and the drawing of Michelangelo' to produce the highly personal style found in *Paradise*, a preparatory work for his masterpiece in the Doge's Palace.

Raphael and Mannerism: The greatest of the Roman School artists in the continuation of the Grande Galerie after the *Mona Lisa* room is Raphael, 30 years younger than Leonardo and the most eclectic of the great masters of the High Renaissance. The type of Madonna for which he became so famous is *La Belle Jardinière* (1507), a work heavy with religious symbolism and one of several versions of the Holy Family to use the pyramidal composition pioneered by Leonardo. The *Portrait of Baldassare Castiglione*, a straightforward but remarkably effective likeness of the poet and diplomat, was purchased by Louis XIV from the heirs of Cardinal Mazarin in 1661. Works commissioned by Pope Leo X for François I include the large *St Michael*, a diplomatic gift painted when the countries were allied in conflict against the Turks.

Giulio Romano, who trained with Raphael and also practised architecture, has been described as a pioneer of the Mannerist style. Typical of **Correggio**, who is associated with an extreme use of *sfumato* and a tender yet voluptuous quality, is the *Mystic Marriage of St Catherine of Alexandria*. Among other Mannerist works are those by the exceptionally accomplished Florentine eccentric Jacopo **Pontormo**.

Caravaggio and the Bologna School: Caravaggio threw himself passionately into both life and work and his artistic influence spread throughout Europe. The *Dormition of the Virgin* (1605–6) was considered scandalous at the time because of the earthy realism of the figures and the dramatic contrasts of light and shade. The **Carracci family** from Bologna is also represented here, notably Annibale; and also **Guido Reni**, who was influenced by the Carracci and was greatly admired in the later 19th century. He is known as a colourist.

A series of rooms at the end of the Grande Galerie contains a miscellany of 17th-century works by artists as various as Salvator Rosa, Pietro da Cortona and Luca Giordano.

The final rooms are devoted to works by 17th- and 18th-century Venetian artists, including **Canaletto**, who is represented with typical scenes such as *The Molo* (c. 1730), of which there are about ten versions. **Francesco Guardi** painted in a freer and more expressive style than Canaletto, as shown by eight scenes depicting festivities for the coronation of the *Doge Alvise IV Mocenigo*. There are also charming and intimate genre scenes by **Pietro Longhi**, and *Susannah and the Elders* by **Sebastiano Ricci**. The great fresco artist **Tiepolo** and his son Giandomenico are also represented.

SPANISH SCHOOL

Limited in number, the **Spanish collection** nevertheless has some masterpieces, ranging from Spanish primitives to Goya. Louis-Philippe amassed a magnificent collection, exhibited in the Louvre in 1838–48; but those works followed the king in exile to London and were dispersed in 1853. Among what remains here are seven large works by **Murillo**, including *Young Beggar* (1650), one of several works by this artist depicting street urchins which began the contemporary taste for sentimental subjects. The *Birth of the Virgin* (1661) is a good example of the use of beautiful soft tints that became characteristic of Murillo's peculiar brand of tender realism.

Francisco de Zurbarán produced rather gloomy paintings of saints for export to South America, but his *St Apollonia*, who carries her attributes—pincers and a martyr's palm—is a charming representation of the saint whose teeth were pulled out before her martyrdom at the stake; she became the patron saint of toothache sufferers.

A characteristic work of heavy pathos by **El Greco**, *Crucifixion with two Donors* (c. 1579, signed in Greek), uses menacing colour and exaggeratedly long limbs. **Goya** is represented by *Woman with a Fan*, and *Still Life with a Sheep's Head*.

Portraits by **Velázquez** include *Queen Mariana of Austria* and *Portrait of the Infanta Margarita*, aged three years.

There is also a room of **Greek and Russian icons**, mainly dating from the 16th–17th centuries.

ENGLISH SCHOOL

The English collection is modest, and contains works by Gainsborough, Constable, Turner, Richard Parkes Bonington, Richard Dadd and Henry Fuseli.

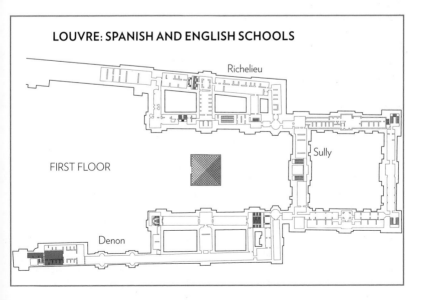

LOUVRE: SPANISH AND ENGLISH SCHOOLS

DEPARTMENT OF PRINTS AND DRAWINGS

Prints and Drawings (Arts Graphiques) have been a department in their own right since 1986, with some 130,000 works on paper (cartoons, drawings, pastels and miniatures). Because they are fragile and susceptible to light, they are not on permanent public display but are exhibited in rotation. Selected pastels and cartoons are on Sully second floor, incorporated into the displays in the plan on p. 188. Temporary displays are shown on Denon first floor, off the Grande Galerie.

Although drawings had already existed in the Bibliothèque du Roi, it was not until 1671, when Louis XIV acquired the 5,542 drawings collected by Everard Jabach (d. 1695), that the nucleus of the royal collection was formed. To this were added drawings by Le Brun, Mignard and Coypel. By 1730 there were some 8,593 works, plus some 1,300 drawings collected by the great connoisseur Pierre-Jean Mariette, purchased in 1776. By 1792 some 11,000 drawings were listed and in the following decades the figure almost doubled. The Codex Vallardi (including a number of drawings by Pisanello) was acquired in 1856 and Jacopo Bellini's sketchbook in 1884. There are approximately 200 pastel portraits including works by Leonardo da Vinci and Rosalba Carriera (d. 1757), who did much to popularise the technique in France. The Edmond de Rothschild collection comprises 3,000 drawings and 40,000 engravings.

GREEK, ETRUSCAN AND ROMAN ANTIQUITIES

This department covers art from ancient Greece, Italy and the whole of the Mediterranean basin, from the Neolithic and Helladic (4th millennium BC) periods to the last days of the Roman Empire (6th century AD). The royal collection formed the nucleus, to which were added objects seized during the Revolution.

LOWER GROUND FLOOR
The chronological circuit illustrates the evolution of pre-Classical Greek civilisations from the 3rd millennium to the start of the 5th century BC. **Cycladic art** (3000–2000 BC) includes the remarkable large marble head of a female statue with schematised features. The function of the statues, which typically take the form of a naked female standing on tip-toe, remains a mystery. The **Dame d'Auxerre** (c. 630 BC), of Cretan origin, is a small, neat figure with her hand on her chest and an Egyptian-style wig. The finely modelled head of a horseman (*Rampin Horseman*, c. 550 BC), originally part of a full statue, was found at the Acropolis in Athens 1877.

SALLE DU MANÈGE AND GALERIE DARU
The magnificent **Salle du Manège (A)** was designed by Lefuel in 1861 for equestrian displays in Napoléon III's new Louvre, and still has part of its original décor. A public space from 1928 to 1969, it is now the gallery where the departments of Greek, Etruscan and Roman antiquities cross over into modern sculpture. Here are great French and Italian collections of antique originals or copies assembled in the 17th and 18th centuries. In the central bay are pieces from the Albani and Borghese col-

lections, and in the side bays are the French royal collections and those of Richelieu and Mazarin. Cardinal Borghese's fine collections of Roman antiquities came to the Louvre in 1807 as a result of negotiations that Napoleon carried out through his brother-in-law, Prince Camillo Borghese. A much-restored sarcophagus panel depicting the death of Meleager (AD 160–170) was in the Villa Borghese in 1615, and from 1784 in the Louvre. Also from this collection are a statue of Eros, a Roman copy of a 4th-century BC Greek original and the *Borghese Dancers*, a 3rd-century BC marble relief.

In the **Galerie Daru (B)** are major pieces including the *Borghese Krater* (c. 50 BC), manufactured in Greece for the Roman market. It was found in 1569 and was in the Borghese collection by 1645. The heavily restored *Borghese Gladiator* is a late Hellenistic piece, discovered at Anzio, Italy, in the 17th century. Signed on the tree-trunk by Agasias (c. 100 BC), it represents a warrior.

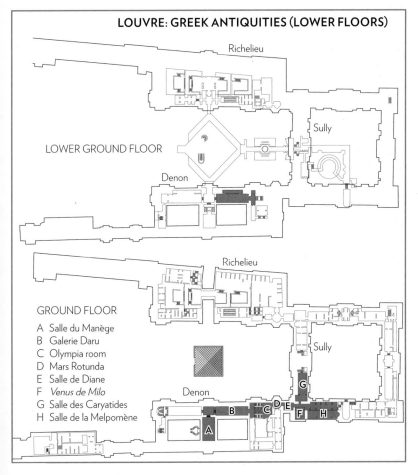

LOUVRE: GREEK ANTIQUITIES (LOWER FLOORS)

Richelieu

Sully

LOWER GROUND FLOOR

Denon

Richelieu

GROUND FLOOR

A   Salle du Manège
B   Galerie Daru
C   Olympia room
D   Mars Rotunda
E   Salle de Diane
F   *Venus de Milo*
G   Salle des Caryatides
H   Salle de la Melpomène

Sully

Denon

ARCHAIC, CLASSICAL AND HELLENISTIC GREEK COLLECTIONS
Ancient Athens, Olympia, the colonies of southern Italy and the Hellenistic world are all covered in the displays following on from Galerie Daru.

The **Olympia Room (C)** contains a model of the Temple of Olympia and fragments of metopes from the Doric frieze (c. 460 BC) and a marble head of Athena with a helmet and metal eyelashes; there is evidence that it was originally enhanced by other metal elements.

The **Mars Rotunda (D)**, created by Louis Le Vau in 1655–8, was the original entrance to the museum in 1809. The hugely ornate ceiling, depicting *Prometheus and Minerva*, was painted by Berthélemy in 1802 and restored and repainted by Mauzaisse in 1826.

The **Salle de Diane (E**; with references to Diana the Huntress in the decor), originally a corridor built 1566, was enlarged 1655 and in 1672 became the first seat of the Académie Française. It contains **sculptures from the Parthenon** (447–440 BC), including fragments of the east frieze which represents the Panathenaic Festival (the greater part of the frieze is in the British Museum) and includes the *Laborde Head*, possibly the head of a goddess from the west pediment, once owned by the Comte de Laborde; *Centaur Carrying away a Lapith Woman*, from the south side, and the beautiful *Plaque of the Ergestines*, showing six draped figures (two priests and four young women). It was originally painted in blue and the heads gilded.

Funerary arts of the period include objects such as urns, jars, stelae, carved reliefs and statues. In the votive relief of Theseus welcoming an Athenian citizen and his son, the names are engraved on the relief and the god is represented larger than the humans. The political and artistic dominance of Classical Athens between 378 and 317 BC is witnessed by the quality of funerary monuments represented, including a head of Hygeia, Goddess of Health, from Piraeus and beautiful stelae, several showing individuals with their dogs. A variety of funerary urns and vessels includes a red-figure wine vase and a black-figure amphora for oil from sacred olive trees.

Magna Graecia: From the 750s BC the Greeks founded coastal colonies in southern Italy and Sicily. These developed their own original artistic production, with ceramics in a variety of types and forms, exemplified by a red-figure volute krater and a rhyton in the form of a donkey, as well as elegant two-handled cups and vases.

Alexander the Great and his successors: Macedonia, in northern Greece, dominated the Greek world during the reign of Philip II (359–336 BC) and his son, Alexander the Great (336–323 BC), who conquered the Persians and extended Greek influence into India. A brilliant and luxurious court art developed among the elite, whose tombs are of a remarkable richness. On display are a bronze head of Demetrios Poliorcetes, who became king of Macedonia, a collection of coins from the reigns of Philip II and Alexander, fragments of architecture, terracotta bowls with relief patterns and small decorative objects including jewellery.

At the death of Alexander, his general Seleucus inherited a huge territory from Syria to Afghanistan, and in 306 BC took the title of king, founding the dynasty of the Seleucids, but over time the boundaries retracted and power was concentrated in northern Syria. In Asia Minor, during the 3rd century BC, the powerful kingdom of Pergamon developed, celebrated for its library and remarkable sculptures. Miletus, Smyrna and Ephesus were also important artistic centres while Myrina, to the north, produced quality terracottas.

In Egypt, Alexander the Gerat founded Alexandria in 331 BC. At his death Ptolemy established his own dynasty, which was to rule until extinguished by Rome. A heroic statue of Alexander, in bronze (end 4th century BC) and the head of a man wearing a bandeau (marble, Roman, late 1st century BC/early 1st century AD) are both outstanding.

Greek sculpture: Most surviving Greek statues were produced in Athens, and extant written descriptions often reveal the circumstances of their creation. Gods, heroes and athletes (who competed nude) afforded excellent opportunities for artists to show an idealised human body. Outstanding is the male nude statuette in bronze, possibly the god Mercury (1st half of the 1st century AD), inlaid with gold and silver, maybe from southern Gaul.

Goddesses, as well as mortal Greek women, were traditionally depicted modestly draped in simple gowns held together by pins or *fibulae* (no stitches). Variety in dress consisted mainly in the way that the fabric was draped and sculptors were adept at varying the effects. It was the Athenian sculptor

Praxiteles (active c. 370–330 BC) who introduced the female nude. Lysippus was a prolific sculptor who worked in bronze. Statues here include *Apollo Sauroctonos*, showing the adolescent god about to kill a lizard, after Praxiteles; *Athena with a Necklace*, a copy of the *Athena Parthenos* of Phidias; the famous nude *Aphrodite of Cnidos* and the *Venus of Arles*. The large *Ingres Minerva*, inspired by Phidias, stood in the gardens of the Villa Medici in Rome when Ingres was director of the French Academy there.

The **Venus de Milo** (c. 120 BC; *see overleaf*) is displayed in the large room **(F)** in which she was originally shown from 1824 to 1848. Also here are fragments which were discovered at the same time, although not connected.

The **Salle des Caryatides (G)** is the oldest surviving room in the palace. Built by Pierre Lescot for Henri II, it is named after the four caryatids designed to support the musicians' gallery sculpted by Jean Goujon. The southern part of this large room contained the royal dais. This was the heart of the old palace. In 1610 the wax effigy of Henri IV was displayed here. Later decoration and the chimneypiece are by Percier and Fontaine (c. 1806). The room contains antique Roman replicas (1st–2nd centuries AD) of Greek works of between the 4th century BC and the Hellenistic period (3rd–1st centuries BC). The *Wounded Gaul* in alabaster, is a vigorous figure with untidy hair, a type which appeared in Greek art following the Galatian invasion in 280 BC. Among portrait heads are Mithridates VI Eupator, crowned with the head of the Nemean lion, and a portrait of Seleucus I, King of Syria.

THE *VENUS DE MILO*

For well over a century this has been the most famous piece in the Louvre's collection of antiquities, and deeply formative of the public's idea of the nature of ancient Greek art. It is a relatively late work from the 2nd century BC and has been the subject of poems, of much admiration and of countless copies. It was found accidentally in April 1820 by a farmer on the Cycladic island of Milos, where it appears the sculpture had narrowly escaped being consigned to a furnace to make mortar. Miraculously it still possessed its original head. A fragment of a statue-base found nearby—almost certainly belonging to the sculpture—carried the signature of the artist, a certain '[Alex]andros of Antioch on the Meander': this base was later conveniently 'lost', perhaps to allow full scope to those experts who wished to believe the Venus might be a work of the golden age of Phidias or Praxiteles. Although consciously 'Classical' in style (especially in the face, distant gaze, hairstyle and proportions of the torso), both the method of carving and the complex spiral of the design, which is made to seem effortlessly natural, date the piece to the late 2nd century BC. She originally may have stood in a niche, gathering her falling drapery with her right hand, and holding an apple in her left. Others have wished to see her admiring her own reflection in a polished shield.

N.McG.

ETRUSCAN ANTIQUITIES

From (c. 530 BC) Cerveteri in western Italy was famous for its clay sculpture, such as the terracotta **Sarcophagus of the Spouses**, discovered in 1845 and purchased by Napoléon III in 1861. Lifelike figures of a man and his wife recline on a funeral couch, as if conversing. The woman wears a cap (*tutulus*) and slippers with neatly turned-up toes; the man, bare-footed, is draped. Further examples of Etruscan antiquities include cinerary urns from Chiusi, several with lids modelled in the form of a female reclining (2nd century BC), others with a frieze; also numerous bronze vessels and figurines, mirrors, jewellery and ceramics.

ROMAN ANTIQUITIES

The ground-floor galleries (plan below) display sculptures, mosaics and funerary arte-facts from the 1st century BC to the early Christian period.

The splendid rooms exhibiting Roman antiquities have occupied the former apartments of Anne of Austria, mother of Louis XIV, since the early 19th century. The display begins with the Republican era (1st century BC), with a bronze *Child Holding a Dove* (mid-2nd century BC) and fragments of fresco.

The next rooms are dedicated to the Imperial period, with portrait heads after Greek models, a sculpture of the Greek heroes Orestes and Pylades, and of the emperors Augustus, Caligula, Claudius and Nero, as well as other portrait heads and a 2nd-century mosaic of the *Judgement of Paris* from Antioch.

There is a likeness of Antinous, the abundant-haired favourite of Hadrian who drowned himself in the Nile at 21 years old, was deified and is here represented as Dionysus; also a fine but subdued Emperor Hadrian in bronze (c. AD 140) and a superb Greek-made bust of Marcus Aurelius (c. AD 161) in marble.

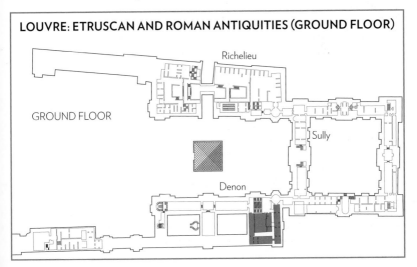

LOUVRE: ETRUSCAN AND ROMAN ANTIQUITIES (GROUND FLOOR)

Richelieu

GROUND FLOOR

Sully

Denon

A statue of the goddess Nemesis shows her with a wheel in her hand and a small figure squashed under her right foot.

Later works of the 3rd–5th centuries include several busts and heads and a statue of Julia Domna, wife of Septimius Severus, partly restored in the 19th century, as a priestess of Isis. There are also elegant decorated pillars from the agora, Thessalonica (early 3rd century AD) and a superbly-carved marble sarcophagus from St-Médard, France (3rd century AD) with the myth of Dionysus and Ariadne on one face and of Selene and Endymion on the other.

Art from Roman Gaul and Christian North Africa includes an antique porphyry urn which was used by Count Caylus for his tomb in Auxerre. The display ends with funerary mosaics and relief sculptures as well as 'school books' of wooden tablets.

ESCALIER DARU

The ***Winged Victory of Samothrace* (1)** was restored to its natural shade of white in 2014. The monument, which weighs 29 tons, is made of different kinds of marble (the breast and left wing are of plaster). In a case nearby is the mutilated right hand found during further excavations in 1950; it may have been held aloft to announce a naval victory. It puts the probable date of the statue at 220–185 BC. Below the *Winged Victory* are restored reliefs from the Temple of Zeus at Olympia (c. 460 BC).

THE *WINGED VICTORY OF SAMOTHRACE*

The *Winged Victory* came to light in excavations in 1863 at the Sanctuary of the Great Gods on the remote Aegean island of Samothrace. The exquisite figure of the flying divinity, Nike, who alights on the prow of a vessel with her drapery pressed against her by the wind, was almost certainly part of an extravagant monument of Rhodian workmanship, erected in the sanctuary to celebrate and give thanks for a great Greek naval victory. This was not an uncommon practice of the period. Much of the piece's significance depended on the original setting: the whole ensemble stood, between mountain and sea, in a pool filled with water and rocks carved to appear like billows. The sanctuary was most frequented by night, and lighting with flickering lamps may have added to the sculpture's powerful effect. Great antiquities often lose their 'presence' when committed to a museum gallery: but the *Winged Victory*'s dramatic setting on the landing of the Escalier Daru gives it a new and different power, ensuring its survival as one of the iconic images of antique art.

N.McG.

GREEK AND ROMAN GLASS, BRONZE AND TERRACOTTA

The collections of Greek and Roman antiquities on the first floor contain many precious *objets d'art* as well as glassware, pottery and smaller sculptures.

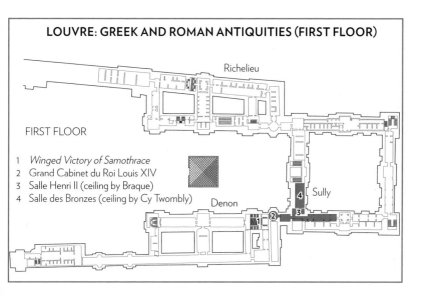

LOUVRE: GREEK AND ROMAN ANTIQUITIES (FIRST FLOOR)

Richelieu

FIRST FLOOR

1 *Winged Victory of Samothrace*
2 Grand Cabinet du Roi Louis XIV
3 Salle Henri II (ceiling by Braque)
4 Salle des Bronzes (ceiling by Cy Twombly)

Sully

Denon

The **Grand Cabinet du Roi Louis XIV (2)**, built by Le Vau c. 1660, is dedicated to some 100 pieces of Greek and Roman glass. The **Salle Henri II (3)**, with a ceiling decorated by Braque in 1953, and the **Salle des Bronzes (4)**, its ceiling painted by Cy Twombly in 2007–9, contain Greek and Roman bronzes and precious objects. The **Treasure of Boscoreale** is a collection of superbly decorated silver objects, buried when Vesuvius erupted in AD 79, and discovered in 1895 in a fine state of preservation. There are also mirrors, jewellery and utensils. Among outstanding pieces of Archaic Greek art are a Minotaur, a statuette of Athena and *Silenus Dancing* (all 6th century BC). Classical Greek statuettes (5th century BC) include a 1st-century BC athlete's head, said to have been found at Benevento, Italy, and probably from Herculaneum. From Roman Gaul is the statuette of a local divinity in silver-plated bronze known as *Fortuna* (1st quarter

3rd century BC), from the Lyon area. Other Roman objects include the *Apollo of Piombino*, a 1st-century BC bronze figure with copper encrustations—lips and nipples—which was retrieved from the sea near Piombino, Italy; *Aphrodite Untying her Sandal* (?1st century AD), with inlaid gold jewellery, from Syria; and the helmet of a Thracian gladiator (3rd quarter 1st century AD).

The Salles Charles X (in the old Musée Charles X) are devoted to **Greek terracotta figurines**, arranged chronologically, geographically and thematically and including objects from Tanagra. The Campana Gallery is named after Marquis Giampietro Campana's superlative collection of **Greek vases**, purchased in 1861, which the Louvre considers to be one of the most complete in the world. Some 2,000 vessels (800–400 BC) can be studied chronologically or thematically according to the various decorative motifs.

EGYPTIAN ANTIQUITIES

This rich department is divided between Pharaonic, Roman and Christian (Coptic) Egypt with collections which date from the late prehistoric civilisations in the Nile Valley (c. 4000 BC) to the Christian era (4th century AD). The spoils of Napoleon's Egyptian campaign of 1798–1801 did not come to the Louvre because they were confiscated by the British, although books published at that time on Egypt, including one by Vivat Denon, fired the public imagination. Small contributions came later from private individuals. Jean-François Champollion (d. 1832), who deciphered the Rosetta Stone in 1922, persuaded the king to buy three major collections (Salt, Durand and Drovetti). Champollion was appointed curator of Egyptian antiquities in 1826.

The collections range over three floors, thematic on the ground floor and chronological on the first floor. On the lower ground floor is the Great Sphinx.

CRYPT OF THE SPHINX (LOWER GROUND FLOOR)

The Great Sphinx is a statue of rare beauty carved from polished red granite, found in 1825 in Tanis. It is inscribed with a palimpsest of pharaohs' names, making it difficult to date. The names of Merenptah (13th century BC) and Shoshenq (10th century BC) are legible, but the sphinx is likely to be much older than this. (*To continue the Egyptian circuit, take the lift or stairs to the ground floor.*)

THEMATIC COLLECTIONS (GROUND FLOOR)

A large statue of *Nakhthorheb at Prayer*, an important figure of the 26th Dynasty, marks the entrance to the department. These are popular rooms which introduce Egypt through vivid presentations of daily life.

The first theme is the **Nile** itself, source of life and fertility, evoked by a long display cabinet containing models of boats of the Middle Kingdom, and figurines of fish, crocodiles, hippopotami and frogs from all periods. A fascinating exhibit is the limestone *Akhethetep mastaba*, a sculpture in the form of a table found at Sakkara decorated with vivid scenes in bas-relief, to ensure that the dignitary *Akhethetep* would be nourished eternally. It includes a depiction of the master's meal enlivened with music and dancing. These scenes of earthly life in the Old Kingdom (2400 BC) are echoed in paintings from the Shrine of Wensu, which lead on to exhibits on the theme of **agriculture**, with tools, papyrus accounts, legal documents and scale models.

The theme of **food** takes as its starting point the ideal menu for the dead sculpted on the walls of a tomb of the Old Kingdom, complete with the names of the delicacies. There are further displays on **writing and scribes**, **weights and measures** and **arts and crafts**, approached through the materials and techniques that were used, along with the stele of the master craftsman, sculptor and scribe Irtysen, on which is inscribed that he excels at his art, a rare record of the subject.

Many objects on the theme of **dwellings and furnishings** come from the sepulchres surrounding the village of the workers who built the royal tomb at

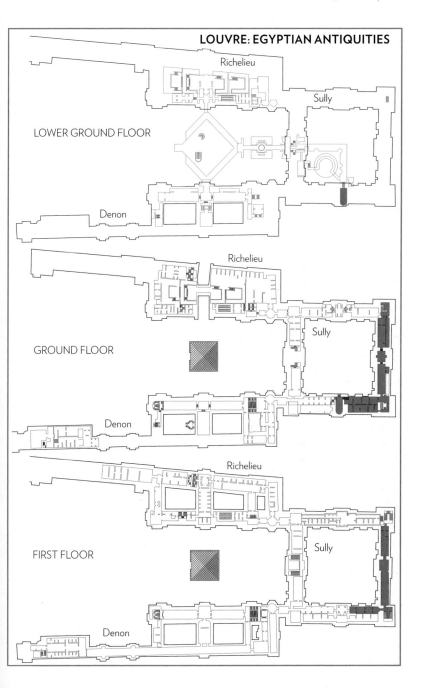

Deir el-Medina opposite Luxor. There are also models of houses, and amphorae are used to evoke a wine cellar.

Adornment is another theme. The *Necklace of Pinedjem I*, of gold and lapis lazuli with lotus-shaped bells, dates from 1044–1026 BC; the heavy gold ring of the Pharaoh Horemheb is also a seal, and contrasts with the delicate *Ring with Lotus Flowers*, encrusted with turquoise and lapis lazuli. There are cosmetics containers too, and spoons for applying creams carved in wood, ivory and faïence.

Among the **musical instruments** are harps, curved and triangular, and a bronze sistrum, as well as images of musicians.

The **Alley of the Sphinxes** represents a long processional walk or dromos marked by an enfilade of six limestone sphinxes from the Serapeum at Sakkara (4th or 3rd centuries BC). The four red granite baboons adoring the rising sun are from the base of the obelisk at the entrance of the **Temple of Luxor** (the pendant to the one on Place de la Concorde). Large sculptures and pieces of architecture evoke the temple and its courtyards. Statues of deities include Sekhmet, the lion-headed goddess (19th Dynasty) from Karnak, and the head and base of a colossal statue of Amenhotep III, 18th-dynasty king of Upper Egypt, in a mitre-shaped crown. The great deeds of the pharaohs are listed on the **Wall of the Annals of King Thutmose III**. At the heart of the temple is the naos, sheltering a statue of Osiris. Objects from the chapels include a large circular sandstone zodiac from the Temple of Hathor at Dendera, showing the sky, planets and constellations in 50 BC.

The Crypt of Osiris: Steps leading down to the Royal Tomb give the impression of the descent to the hypogeum of the Valley of the Kings, the site of most royal tombs. After death, all deceased kings were revered as gods and the decoration of their tombs illustrates this destiny. In the centre is the magnificent pink granite sarcophagus case that once contained the nest of coffins of Ramesses III (its cover is in the Fitzwilliam Museum in Cambridge, England), presided over by the winged goddesses Isis and Nephthys at each end. Egyptians believed that Osiris had reigned in the world before becoming sovereign of the dead.

Sarcophagi and mummies: The oldest sarcophagus in the collections is from Abu Roash (c. 2300 BC), carved from a single block of limestone. The coffin has a number of functions: it is the protective covering of the body; the new home of the deceased; it reproduces the universe in miniature; and it stands in for the life beyond. The collection includes a standing display of wooden mummy cases and a mummy of the Ptolemaic period, with an intricately-painted mummy case (of moulded linen and plaster).

Objects from burial chambers of four different periods show the evolution in funerary customs over more than 1,000 years. There are displays on embalming and the 1st-century BC *Book of the Dead* of the Priest Hornedjitef, preserved almost in its full length (the full scroll would have measured 24m).

Gods and magic: The final rooms bring together animals, sacred and mummified, and the contents of the Serapeum of Memphis. There is also a magnificent statue of the bull Apis.

CHRONOLOGICAL COLLECTIONS (FIRST FLOOR)

Stairs, a lift or escalator lead you up to the first floor. An illustrated chronology consisting of panels, each representing 1,000 years, introduces the circuit which covers some 3,000 years of Egyptian history and art.

Predynastic and Early Dynastic Egypt:

The highlight of the Nagada (or Predynastic) period (c. 4000–3100 BC) is a **dagger from Gebel el-Arak** with a hippopotamus-tooth handle carved with a battle scene, a very early example of relief sculpture. Huge cemeteries have revealed decorated pottery, stone vases and palettes for grinding eye-shadow.

From the Thinite period (c. 3100–2700 BC), the time of the 1st and 2nd Dynasties, is the **stele of King Djet** (or Wadji), the Serpent King, which epitomises the two great phenomena of this period: the unification of Egypt under a single crown and the birth of writing. The name of the king is written with the hieroglyph of the serpent.

Old Kingdom:

The Old Kingdom (c. 2700–2200 BC) was the time of the great pyramids. The individuality of the king and his funerary monument reached its peak in the 3rd Dynasty and the majority of the objects surviving from this period, which reflect the power of the kings, are funerary. A remarkable find from the pyramid of Djedefre, son of Khufu (Cheops), is one of the most popular works in the Egyptian department, a small highly-coloured limestone figure called the **Seated Scribe** (c. 2620–2500 BC), sitting cross-legged, with eyes of white quartz and rock crystal. The stone **stele of Nefertiabet**, a relative of King Khufu, reflects the degree of refinement reached during this period, showing her seated before a funerary banquet guaranteeing her sustenance in the afterlife.

Middle Kingdom:

This period (c. 2033–1710 BC) marks the classical era of Egyptian civilisation, when the kings re-united a realm previously carved up by invaders. Among the outstanding statues is the elegant female **Libation Carrier**, carrying food and water to a departed soul, and remarkable **portrait statues** of Senwosret III and of his son, Amenemhat III. A small corridor contains beautiful **stelae** of this period.

New Kingdom:

The period c. 1550 to 1069 BC was a glorious age, when gigantic temples such as those at Karnak and Luxor were built. Exhibits include the dual portraits of Amenhotep III and his principal wife Tiye, the parents of Akhenaten.

The time of Akhenaten and Nefertiti (c. 1353–1337 BC) left an outstanding artistic legacy. The famous heretic Akhenaten (Amenhotep IV) built the huge open courtyard near Karnak, with massive sculptures in a revolutionary style. The monumental **statue of Akhenaten** from the colossus bears the elongated head that was the trademark of his family. This was the king who introduced the cult of the sun god, Aten. Some of the most beautiful smaller Egyptian pieces in the Louvre include a **torso of Queen Nefertiti**, in red quartzite and a statuette of Akhenaten and Nefertiti holding each other by the hand. Their son was the boy-king **Tutankhamun** (d. c. 1327 BC), who is represented as a small figure with the god Amun.

The upper landing of the south staircase is dedicated to the civilisation of **ancient Nubia**. To the west is the first room of the old Egyptian Museum created at the time of Champollion, in 1827.

The reigns of Ramesses I and other New Kingdom pharaohs (c. 1295–1069 BC) are represented by ceramic decorations from the palaces of the Delta. The great gods are represented by a very fine statuette of Amun and his wife Mut, and the lesser gods by the small stele of the goddess Qetesh and a display devoted to **Ramesses the Great**.

Late Period: The Saite Dynasty was marked by Persian domination (c. 1069–404 BC). It produced the finest Egyptian bronze in the Louvre, the statue of *Karomama, Chantress of Amun*, which is sumptuously decorated with inlays of gold and silver. The art of the last pharaohs of Egypt up to the time of Cleopatra (404–30 BC) bears witness to Hellenistic influences after 322 BC, when Alexander the Great entered Egypt. Here is the abundantly decorated, gilded mummy covering of Tacheretpaankh.

NEAR-EASTERN ANTIQUITIES

This department, established in 1881, has objects which date back 10,000 years and end with the advent of Islam in the 7th century. Exhibits come from a wide array of countries extending from the Indus Valley (Pakistan) to the Mediterranean. Crucial to the collections are early examples of written language, c. 3300 BC, which spread across the whole of the East, including Egypt. The great empires and dynasties of the 3rd–1st millennia included the Akkadian, Babylonian, Hittite, Assyrian and Elamite.

The collections are divided into three sections: Mesopotamia, Ancient Iran and the Ancient Near East.

MESOPOTAMIA

A Greek name for the broad basin of the Tigris and Euphrates, 'between two rivers', Mesopotamia refers mainly to the ancient civilisations of Sumeria, Assyria and Babylon that prospered in the region relating roughly to modern Iraq, eastern Syria, southeastern Turkey and southwestern Iran.

Origins: The development of civilisation in Mesopotamia from its Neolithic village origins to Sumerian primitive urban culture and the city of Mari is illustrated through a plethora of mainly small objects remarkable for their great age as well as beauty. They include a female **fertility figurine** (c. 6000–5100 BC), one of the oldest known. The first known documents, inscribed on clay tablets, are the **pre-Cuneiform writing tablets** from Uruk IV (c. 3300 BC),

accounts or inventories where a notch indicates a number and names are represented by pictograms.

The **relief of King Ur-Nanshe** (2600–2330 BC) is a perforated stone slab carrying relief carvings to commemorate the religious activities of the founder of the First Lagash Dynasty. Fragments of the oldest known historical document in the Sumerian language, carved in text and images, the *Stele of the Vultures* (2600–2330 BC), records

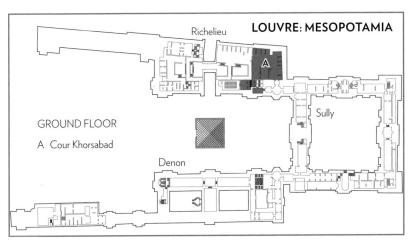

the triumphs of King Eannatum, grandson of Ur-Nanshe.

Beautifully-made **statuettes from the Temple of Ishtar** in Mari (Middle Euphrates, Syria), commissioned by worshippers to depict themselves in perpetual prayer, include Ebhi II, superintendent of Mari (c. 2400 BC), dressed in a *kaunake*, or short sheepskin skirt.

Akkad and Ur: The period c. 2350–2000 BC covers the Akkadian Empire and the last Sumerian dynasties of Ur. Many Akkadian objects were retrieved from Susa, Iran, where they had been taken in the 12th century BC; others are from Tello, and several record important events. Cuneiform script, using wedge-shaped characters, was adapted by the Akkadians and used in the **obelisk of Manishtusu** (c. 2270), King of Akkad, a significant legal document of exceptional quality. The **victory stele of Nahram Sin** (2254–2218 BC) celebrates the triumph of the king in a victory parade which symbolises the sovereign's ascent towards equal status with the gods. **Cylinder seals**, used to endorse documents, appeared in the second half of the 4th millennium BC; several are exhibited with their impression strips.

The brilliant Second Dynasty of Lagash (2150–2100 BC) is represented by **statues in diorite**, the kings' preferred material, imported from Magan (Oman). Prince Gudea, known for his piety and for building temples, is represented by nine diorite statues designed to stand before those temples. The **cylinders of Gudea** (c. 2100 BC) record the construction of the temple of Ningirsu and the enthronement of the divine king and queen of Lagash during the New Year ceremony.

The ***Lament for the Destruction of Ur*** tablets (c. 2000), written at the fall of Ur to the Amorites, represents a poetic genre and includes eleven songs or dirges.

The Amorite Kingdom and First Babylonian Dynasty: The period 2000–1000 BC is illustrated with objects from the sites of Mari, Babylon and Eshnunna. The near life-size, headless **seated statue of a prince of**

Eshnunna (late 2nd–early 3rd millennia BC; diorite) was carried away as a spoil of war in the 12th century BC by the Elamite king of Susa, who had the inscription carved over the original Akkadian one. The ruins of the **Amorite palace of King Zimri-Lim** in Mari revealed the exceptional mural painting of the king's investiture. The bronze lion, with fearsome eyes of limestone and shale, is one of a pair from the Temple of the King of the Land at Mari, as are the **model livers for divination** (19th–18th centuries BC), thought to be the earliest direct evidence of hepatoscopy, the examination by augurs of the liver of a sacrificial sheep.

The First Babylonian Empire, which developed under King Hammurabi (1792–1750 BC), launched a brilliant period. The emblem of Mesopotamian civilisation is the tall black basalt **Codex of Hammurabi** (c. 1800 BC), a complete legal and literary document covered with closely-written text in Akkadian cuneiform script. It constitutes the most complete legal compendium of antiquity, the 282 laws embracing practically every aspect of Babylonian life. It also gives a historical account of the investiture of Hammurabi, and a lyrical epilogue sums up his legal contributions. The superbly sculpted **Royal Head** stylistically dates to c. 2000 BC, but is optimistically described as King Hammurabi, after whose death Babylon declined.

The *kudurru*, a small engraved stele recording a royal gift of land, such as the **Kudurru of King Melishipak II** (1186–1172), first appeared during the revival of the Babylonian Empire under the Kassite Dynasty, whose greatest king was Nebuchadnezzar II (605–562 BC).

Khorsabad: Celebrated sculptures from the great Assyrian palace are displayed in the Cour Khorsabad **(A)**. The Assyrian Empire reached its peak between the 9th and 7th centuries BC and the Cour Khorsabad is designed to evoke the original massive scale of the palace of Dur-Sharrukin, Sargon II's fortress. The five *lamassu*, huge winged bulls with human heads, which protected the palace from evil spirits, have five feet, so that viewed from the front they are in repose and from the side they appear in motion. Three of them are original, one is a 19th-century copy, and the last, a plaster cast from the original in Chicago, has its head turned towards images associated with heroes taming lions, which evoke the divine strength protecting the palace, while the winged Genius wards off evil spirits. Carved reliefs both protected the base of the mud-brick walls and served as forms of decorative official propaganda. Five plaques make up the frieze showing the transportation of cedar wood (partly reconstructed), which explains in cuneiform that timber was carried from Lebanon by land and by sea to timber-poor Assyria on heavily-laden boats with horse-head prows and fish-tail sterns.

Anatolia, Cappadocia and the Hittites: Anatolia, the area of present-day Turkey east of the Bosphorus, was on a major route between Asia and the West and its mineral wealth attracted traders, who in turn introduced cultural influences. There is a Bronze Age rhyton in the form of a lion (c. 1950–c. 1750 BC) and the sophisticated *Stele of Tarhunpiyas* (neo-Hittite, late 8th century BC), showing a child standing on his mother's knee.

Syria, Assyria, Arslan Tash, Nimrud and Nineveh: Artefacts from northern provincial palaces of the neo-Assyrian period (9th–7th centuries BC) include rare **mural paintings from Til Barsip** (northern Syria) and a stele representing Ishtar as a warrior goddess (8th century BC). A bronze **statuette of the demon Pazuzu** (early 1st millennium BC) is one of the finest representations of this type. On the back of his wings his powers are described. It was designed to hang around the neck or above a sick person's bed as protection from Pazuzu's wife, the female demon Lamashtu, who infected humans with disease. A relief lion passant in glazed brick is from the **Processional Way at Babylon**, which passed through the Ishtar Gate during the reign of Nebuchadnezzar II (604–562 BC). An exceptional collection of carved **ivories from Arslan Tash** (Syria) includes a cow licking its young, and part of a piece of furniture, once decorated with gold, depicting the birth of Horus (late 8th century BC).

ANCIENT IRAN

The collection covers Iran and the Iranian plateau (5th, 4th and early 3rd millennia BC) during the ancient civilisations of the Elamites, Persians, Parthians and Sassanids in a region roughly equivalent to modern Iran and parts of Afghanistan. Iran is dominated by two large mountain ranges, the Zagros from the northwest to the southeast, and the Elburz, which follows the curve of the Caspian Sea.

Early Elamite period: The single most important city in ancient Iran was **Susa**, situated in the plain of Susiana (Elam), which extends east from Mesopotamia and was continuously inhabited for 6,000 years, from 4200 BC to the Islamic era. From the early Elamite period (4200–3800 BC) a terracotta of a wild sheep typifies the painted ceramics which are the main artefacts to have survived from the 5th–4th millennia BC, shaped by hand using coils of clay as the

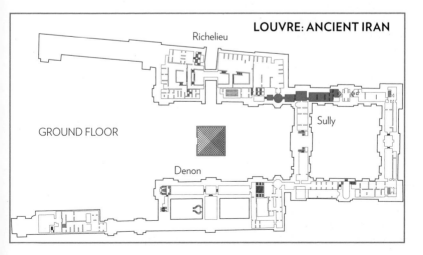

potter's wheel had not been invented. Iran and Susa during the period of Uruk (3800–3100 BC) saw the first attempts at metallurgy: a multitude of copper pins and a small gold dog pendant (3300–3100; the dog provides a clue to the type of domestic dog which existed). There are also small carvings in alabaster, diorite and other types of stone, including a fly-shaped amulet from Luristan. Among objects from the Temple at Susa (2700–2340 BC) is the *Royal Praying Figure* and among exotic imports the statuette of a monkey in red limestone.

Bactria, present-day Uzbekistan and northern Afghanistan, is an area rich in gold, silver and lapis lazuli (the latter used for the woman in childbirth amulet). The ***Bactriana Princess*** (c. 1800 BC) is one of a number of statuettes with detachable parts in serpentine and calcite. Typical of the metalwork are two exceptional little silver dogs.

Middle Elamite period: The display contains numerous moulded terracotta figurines (14th–12th century BC), funerary portraits and statuettes of gods. Royal monuments include the lower part of a statue of King Untash-Napirisha (1340–1300 BC), 'King of Anzan and Susa', as well as a headless bronze statue of his wife, Queen Napir Asu. Small votive offerings include copper figurines, many objects found on the acropolis at Susa. Among superb examples of moulded terracottas are panels with man-bulls protecting a palm tree.

Iron Age Iran: Illiterate nomadic peoples of Indo-European origin, known to us primarily through their tomb artefacts, mark the beginnings of Iron-Age culture in Iran. Artisans from the Marlik culture (14th–12th centuries BC), who settled on the banks of the Caspian Sea, produced zoömorphic vessels such as the hump-backed bull in red terracotta, metal objects such as the moulded silver dish with a roaring lion's head (7th–6th century BC) and a beautiful gold bracelet with lion's-head decoration. From Susa or Susiana are gold earrings in the form of a cluster of grapes and from Luristan are bronze harness decorations.

The Achaemenids: The Persian Achaemenid dynasty was founded by Darius I the Great (522–486 BC), who recognised the strategic importance of Susa. Impressive and beautiful large elements from his palace include the huge capitals shaped in the form of the heads and shoulders of a bull, one of 36 used to support the ceiling of the audience chamber (*apadana*). There are also friezes, including *Persian Archers—the Immortals*, in what appears to be slow procession. Alexander the Great conquered Babylon in 331 BC, extinguishing the Persian Empire.

The Seleucid, Parthian and Sassanian empires: These empires were created following the death of Alexander the Great in 323 BC. Examples of Sassanian arts are stone foundry moulds for making jewellery (3rd century BC–3rd century AD), the bronze bust of a Sassanid king, and a low-relief in stone of a king holding a horn of plenty (2nd-3rd century AD), from the temple of Heracles. Graeco-Roman influences begin to be evident, as seen in the harp-player mosaic from the palace of Shapur I at his capital Bishapur (3rd century AD).

ANCIENT NEAR EAST

The collection is arranged in rooms covering Phoenicia and Carthage, Arabia, Cyprus and the Levant.

The Phoenician Kingdoms and Carthage:

The Phoenicians, maritime traders who dominated the Mediterranean during the 8th–2nd centuries BC, acquired their name from the Greek word *phoinikes* meaning red, referring to the purple-red dye used for textiles. Important producers of luxury objects (glass, ivory and metalwork), the Phoenicians' major cities in the east Mediterranean (modern-day Lebanon) were Tyre, Sidon and Byblos. From **Byblos** comes the lion couchant in basalt (400–350 BC); from **Sidon** are an obelisk dedicated to the god Shalman (300–250 BC). Many of the artefacts show Egyptian influence, for example the Egyptian-style sarcophagus of King Eshmunazor II in black amphibolite (5th century BC).

Carthage, founded in 814 BC, according to tradition by Dido, sister of the King of Tyre, became the main Phoenician trading base on the north African coast until the victories of Alexander the Great (333–332 BC) and the Punic Wars with Rome (264–146 BC). A rich collection of objects includes the varied earthenware amulets and gold amulet cases, Wadjet eyes (Eyes of Horus) and an impressive array of votive stelae (4th–2nd centuries BC). The Phoenicians' progress in glass-making from the 8th century BC enabled the production of many small, multicoloured objects such as a the glass pendant of the bearded head of a man (4th–3rd century BC).

Arabia: The southern part of the Arabian peninsula, ancient **Arabia Felix** (present-day Yemen), was inhabited by several kingdoms which enjoyed a prosperous trade in the export of incense and myrrh to Mesopotamia, Persia and the Mediterranean. Objects include temple furniture and offerings

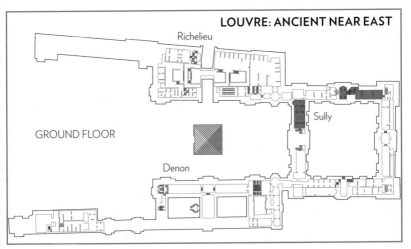

LOUVRE: ANCIENT NEAR EAST

Richelieu

GROUND FLOOR

Sully

Denon

such as the head of a woman carved from reused stone (3rd–1st century BC); the eye sockets, now empty, would have held stones.

The rest of the peninsula, **Arabia Deserta**, was crossed by caravan routes, who broke their journeys at the cities of Dura-Europos and Palmyra. From AD 106 Arabia became a Roman province. From **Dura-Europos** comes the bust of a woman (?Artemis) in polychrome plaster (2nd–3rd century AD) and a graceful marble sculpture (headless) of Aphrodite with a tortoise. **Palmyra**, the site of a large oasis, enjoyed great prosperity during the first three centuries of the Christian era. Its tombs have yielded numerous limestone slabs which closed off burial niches, sculpted with a bust of the deceased. The Graeco-Roman influence is clear, and each bust is inscribed in local script (a dialect of Aramaic) with the name and genealogy of the deceased. Examples include women holding children and priests holding a libation vase and incense box. There are also funerary reliefs of standing figures, and sometimes the same names appear, such as in the bust of '*Tibnan, daughter of Hagegu, son of Maliku*', shown carrying a baby, and the funerary relief of a reclining man in Parthian breeches with a smaller image of his mother, inscribed '*Taime, son of Maliku, son of Hagegu, alas! And of Hadira, his mother, alas!*'

Cyprus: After the Bronze Age, Cyprus was divided into small kingdoms that paid tribute to the King of Assyria (8th–7th centuries BC) and to the king of Persia (6th–4th centuries BC). The collection includes female terracottas engaged in a variety of activities ranging from making music to bearing children.

Other figurines include horses and riders, models of chariots and warriors, models of boats and of fish. There are several male heads in limestone, bearded, wearing a hat and a beatific expression. A fine bust of Heracles shows him wearing the head of the Nemean lion (late 4th century BC).

The Levant: Four rooms in the west of the Sully building cover the Copper, Bronze and Iron ages in Cyprus, coastal and inland Syria, Palestine and Transjordan. **Cyprus**, the most easterly of the Mediterranean islands, was a crossing point of influences. Terracottas from here include a seated female pressing her breasts and a female psi figurine (its form resembles the Greek letter Ψ). There are many Bronze-Age artefacts.

Coastal Syria is represented by furnishings from royal tombs and luxury items from Byblos, ceramics from Ras Shamra (ancient Ugarit), where excavations continue, and objects from the tombs of Minet el-Beida.

Aretfacts from **Inland Syria**, from the earliest times to the Iron Age, include a fine silver pendant in the form of a crescent moon; a Sumerian-style model chariot in bronze (c. 2500–2250 BC) and numerous figurines and fragments of human figures and animals in hand-worked terracotta. Among architectural models is that of a storeyed house (c. 13th–12th century BC). The stele of Zakkur from the Aleppo region has an Aramaic inscription (c. 800 BC).

Objects from **Palestine and Transjordan**, from earliest times to the Iron Age, include miniature pitchers in terracotta, some painted, and scarabs of baked steatite engraved with hieroglyphs.

THE EASTERN MEDITERRANEAN IN THE ROMAN EMPIRE

The display here aims to bring together the collections covering late antiquity in the eastern Mediterranean (previously dispersed between the three archaeological departments). This period is characterised by the emergence of a civilisation founded on the double heritage of Greece and Rome and is explored here in nine thematic presentations. The sequence begins with Egyptian funerary arts, continuing with the funerary arts of the Near East, by way of contrast and comparison. Cult statues, mosaics, fabrics, ceramics, bronze and glass are all part of the display. A small room dedicated to pre-Christian and Christian Nubia leads to the Coptic Egypt rooms.

COPTIC EGYPT

The word Copt originates from the Greek *Aegyptios*, via Arabic. When the Muslims arrived in Egypt it was an entirely Christian country and the word came to refer to the inhabitants, including Nubians, Ethiopians and Armenians. Coptic art is now taken to refer to Egyptian art from the 3rd–14th centuries.

The emergence of a distinctively Coptic style, combining Roman and Pharaonic elements, is seen in the **Horus Horseman** (4th century) and the slightly later **Shawl of Sabina** (4th–5th century), which still clings to themes from pagan mythology and Nilotic motifs. Recognisably and explicitly Christian are the limestone relief with a fish and the Cross (4th–5th century), a wooden panel of the *Virgin Annunciate* and interlocking wooden panels with the design of the Cross (12th century). The extent of conserved **fabrics**, mainly of linen and wool, is impressive and includes several decorative bands, a depiction of Aphrodite and Adonis and of the goddess Gaia.

Among **domestic and decorative objects** are a tankard engraved 'Adrianos' and a

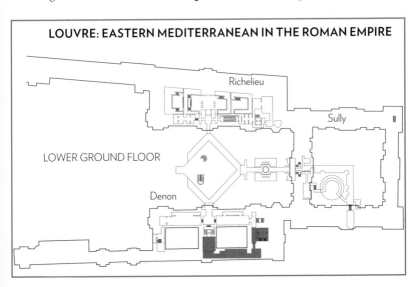

LOUVRE: EASTERN MEDITERRANEAN IN THE ROMAN EMPIRE

Richelieu

Sully

LOWER GROUND FLOOR

Denon

large Byzantine-era fired clay water jar decorated with Coptic designs. A silver incense burner of Graeco-Roman inspiration is pierced with a design of theatrical masks. After the Arab conquest in the mid-7th century, Coptic art begins to display typically Islamic motifs, such as the very fine bronze censer surmounted by an eagle clasping a serpent and the four woven squares displaying the name of Allah (9th–10th century).

The culmination of the Coptic section is the Bawit Room, which contains the reconstruction of part of the 4th-century **monastery church of Bawit**, abandoned in the 12th century and excavated by French archaeologists from 1900. In 1903 Egypt made France a gift of part of the finds. There is an icon of Christ with Abbot Menas and mural paintings from Bawit and from the Hermitage of the Kellia (6th–7th century). Various stone and wooden objects are displayed in the way that they were found in 1902.

The section covering **Roman Egypt** is devoted to funerary objects from the Roman period (1st–4th centuries AD).

THE ARTS OF ISLAM

The first Islamic objects to arrive at the Louvre came from the Royal Collections and these have been supplemented over the years by gifts and acquisition. The inspiring array of some 3,000 objects from the 14,000-strong collection covers a wide geographical area and a rich diversity of the arts from the 7th–19th centuries. Gaps in previously less well represented areas of the collection, such as the Maghreb and Mughal India, have been filled, and modern museology embraces multi-media displays to aid an understanding the history and other aspects of this presentation. The innovative gallery opened in 2012, the Louvre's largest building project since the Grand Louvre of 1993. The upper gallery is enclosed in transparent screens covered by an undulating woven metallic roof.

The display is divided into four time zones: 1. Beginnings to the Foundation of Empire, 632–1000; 2. Break-up and Recovery, 1000–1250; 3. The Second Wind of Islam, 1250–1500; 4. Three Modern Empires of Islam, 1500–1800. Section 5 is dedicated to the Arts of the Book. A dateline and an electronic display illustrating the expansion and recession of the Islamic world introduce each main section; within the four chronological zones are geographic sub-sections. The sequence, which is free flowing, begins on the lower ground floor (Space A) and continues on the level further down (Space B). Many items are displayed in horizontal vitrines which are labelled with sequence numbers and brief titles low on the narrow end.

Beginnings to the Foundation of Empire, 623–1000: Islam was born of the revelation to the Prophet Mohammed of a new monotheistic religion. The Islamic calendar dates from the Prophet's exile or Hegira, in 622, and, at his death in 632, the first Arab State was founded. The first four caliphs conquered the Persian (Sassanid) and Byzantine Empires between 632 and 660 and by c. 750 the Islamic Empire had spread from Spain to Pakistan. The Umayyad capital was at Damascus by 661; the Abassids were in Baghdad by

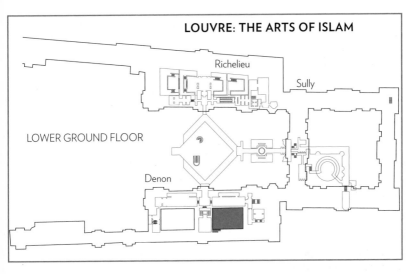

LOUVRE: THE ARTS OF ISLAM

Richelieu

Sully

LOWER GROUND FLOOR

Denon

762; the Fatimids in Egypt by 750 and the Emirs in Cordoba by 756. By the 8th century, not only was there unification of religion and language, but also of the administration, weights and measures and a postal service

The first Islamic art was a synthesis of Christian, Hellenic and Persian art, recognisable in domestic items. Typical of the influence of Classical antiquity is the chequerboard pattern on the small jug with a green squared design (7th–9th century). From the beginning, Abbasid potters attempted to imitate Chinese porcelain, resulting in a version of faïence. Elements of decoration hint at the splendour of the Abbasid caliphs' palace of Jawsaq, north of Baghdad. There are examples of glass from Syria, including a lamp with multiple handles and an elegant copper peacock-shaped ewer made by a Christian artisan and engraved in Latin, 'Work of Salomon Year 1010', and in Arabic, 'Made by Abd al-Malik the Christian'. A rock-crystal ewer (from Egypt or southern Italy) was

presented to the Abbey of St-Denis in Paris c. 1150.

In 638 the Muslims took the ancient city of Susa, which became the capital of southwest Iran for 300 years. It exported expensive goods from the port of Basra and was famed for its opulent palaces. Production from western Iran became increasingly sophisticated during the 11th–13th centuries. One of the most famous pieces is the **candlestick with ducks**, made from a single circular sheet of thin copper. The remarkably skilled technique involves hammering the metal sheet from the interior with an embossing tool. The ducks in high relief and the felines in low relief around the base were created entirely in this way; neither the artist's nor the patron's name is known. High-quality luxury objects from Khorasan (Central Asia) include filigree bronze falcon and feline perfume burners with inlaid blue glass eyes, both animals poised for the chase. From Bamiyan, a former Buddhist centre, is a copper tray inlaid with silver.

Calligraphy: In the area between Space A and Space B are calligraphy displays and exhibits. Sacred texts are widely used in architectural decoration and religious objects. There are examples of the two styles of script: Kufic, the earlier angular style, used in a mainly ornamental way, and Cursive, which is more supple and easier to read. Cursive was originally used only for everyday affairs, but was adopted from the end of the 11th century for Qur'anic texts and is found in decorative applications, such as the ceramic frieze with the *bismillah*: 'In the Name of God, the Merciful, the Compassionate'.

Breakup and Recovery, 1000–1250: During the 11th and 12th centuries there were power shifts in the Islamic world, affecting production but also introducing new artistic stimuli. The Turks, recently converted, occupied Baghdad, established a Sultanate and took Delhi in 1193. Berber dynasties in North Africa embraced Islam and reinforced cultural links with the Iberian peninsula after the fall of the Caliphate of Cordoba (1031). The Islamic territories of Sicily and Jerusalem were lost, although the latter was retaken by Saladin, who also invaded Egypt and Syria.

The **spout of a fountain in the form of a lion**, its flanks and rump inscribed with vows, is typical of fountains with animal features found in palaces in Al-Andalus. A pierced mosque lamp is reputed to have come from the Dome of the Rock. From Iran or Syria are small figurative objects either for functional use, such as a feline pumice-stone holder, or for decoration (man milking a buffalo).

In Iran, the image of the sphinx, symbol of power and protection, often accompanied the image of the sovereign, as in the goblet with sphinx and musicians. Literature, such as courtly verses from the *Book of Kings* (*Shâh Nâmeh*), an epic poem (940–1025), increased in popularity, inspiring the decoration of objects. A virtuoso example of ceramic fretwork is the **ewer with a rooster's-head spout** (13th century) with a slender neck and terrifying eyes and beak. Decorated with a turquoise slip, it has a lively decoration of figures and animals hiding among foliage based on fantasy literary sources, plus inscriptions in Persian and Arabic of poetic verses and vows. It originally had a water-tight skin.

Ceramics, lustreware and metal objects are an important part of the collection. Metalwork flourished in Syria c. 1150–1250 and powerful Ayyubid sultans commissioned richly inlaid vessels. Some 20 examples carry the name of the dedicatee and are occasionally signed by a master brass-worker. A symbol of power, they include all types of abundantly decorated objects. The **candlestick** (1248–9), signed Dawud ibn Salama al-Mawsili, is a glorious piece engraved with saints in arcades around the base, and priests in the convex section, while the large medallions on the side contain scenes from the life of Christ: *Baptism, Circumcision, ?Presentation in the Temple* and *Wedding at Cana*. On the shoulder are the signs of the Zodiac. It is likely that the same artist created the ***Barberini Vase*** (1239–60), commissioned by the Ayyubid sultan of Aleppo and Damascus and one of the most famous pieces in the collection. A uniquely elegant shape with extremely refined decoration, it shows a new dynamic in inlaid metals. The inscriptions alternate between a series of vows and the titles of the last Ayyubid Sultan, al-Nasir Salah al-din Yusuf. The medallions of the lower part frame animated scenes of hunting, entertainment and the training of the military elite. It is named after Pope Urban VIII (Maffeo Barberini), who owned it in the 17th century.

Glassmaking in the Levant, famed since antiquity, used a technique of inlaid gold, and was revived in the 12th–13th centuries. By the 13th century gilded and enamelled glass from Syria and Egypt was being exported to Europe.

The **celestial globe from Isfahan**, Iran, is the third-oldest surviving astrolabe in the world. Signed Yunus b. al-Husayn al-Asturlabi, it is made of bronze, engraved and inlaid with silver, and represents a three-dimensional model of the heavens with the 48 constellations identified by the Greek astronomer Ptolemy in Alexandria in the 2nd century. The 1,025 stars are represented by silver dots varying in size according to the brilliance of the star.

The Second Wind of Islam, 1250–1500: This was a period of great upheaval. The Mongols under Genghis Khan invaded China, the Islamic world and Eastern Europe. Devastation was immense in Iraq, Iran and Central Asia. Baghdad fell in 1258. The Mamluks (1250–1517) dominated Egypt and Syria; Cairo became the largest city in the world. The Mongolian momentum was broken by the Mamluks in 1260, leading to a separation between the Persian-speaking world to the east and the Arabic-speaking world to the west. Sufism spread across the whole community. The Sultans of Delhi dominated two-thirds of India in the mid-14th century, while the Ottomans took Constantinople in 1453. In 1492 Granada was lost and the Arabs left Spain for good.

The cross-fertilisation of Arabic design and Christian iconography produced the Mudéjar style in Spain. Architectural fragments include ceramic lustreware tiles which adorned floors and walls in the Nasrid palaces of Granada and Castile.

The **Baptistery of St Louis**, made in Syria in 1320–40, is a truly outstanding example of Islamic hammered metalwork inlaid with silver and gold. Uniquely it is signed six times by the artist, Muhammad ibn al-Zayn. On the exterior a series of figures moves towards the Hunter Ruler. In the interior, scenes of hunting and battle alternate with an enthroned monarch. In the upper and lower friezes of the exterior two original coats of arms have been hastily covered by a third; the identity of the person for whom it was originally intended therefore remains unclear. The object came from the Sainte-Chapelle at the Château of Vincennes and was used in 1601 for the baptism of Louis XIII at Fontainebleau. In 1783, during the Revolution, it entered the Louvre. An inlaid brass bowl also signed Muhammad ibn al-Zayn features members of the Mamluk elite on the exterior: men of the sword and men of letters or administration (with a writing case). Seated between them is the monarch, carrying a bow, representing power.

In Iran inlaid copper or enamelled glass was highly prized by the Mamluks. The long-necked **bottle of Tuguz Timur** (1345–6) is the largest and most beautiful among the 15 known to exist. Door panels from grand residences, made in wood from India, Madagascar or Central Africa, are decorated with complex geometric patterns. Mamluk ceramic vessels with all-over blue and black designs, rendered watertight by glazing, were often used for transporting pharmaceuticals: some were found at the papal palace in Avignon.

During the mid-13th century the Mongol conquerors of Iran converted to Islam and began renovating religious buildings. The Palace of Takht-e Sulayman was adorned with a sophisticated ceramic decoration honouring the mythical history of Iran through the verses of Shahnameh. Artistic continuity at this time was maintained but Chinese motifs, such as lotus flowers or petals, phoenix and fish, were added.

The mid-14th to the 15th century was a period of intense artistic activity stimulated by Timur (Tamerlane) and his descendants. Architects, highly-skilled artists and manuscript writers arrived in Samarkand from all over the empire. Ceramic decoration was increasingly used on brick buildings, glazed cobalt decoration imitated porcelain and Chinese motifs were freely interpreted and employed (peonies, cranes, dragons and the like).

The Three Modern Empires of Islam, 1500–1800: The Islamic world reached a high point in the 16th century, embracing some 30 percent of the world's population and comprising three major empires. The Ottoman Empire encompassed the Balkans, Turkey, the Arab world (except Morocco) and part of eastern and central Europe. To the east, the Mughals united the Indian Islamic states and had spread into most of the Indian subcontinent by the 17th century. Between these two powers was Iran, under the Safavids (1501–1722), who imposed Shi'ism as the state religion. The Ottoman Empire began to weaken in the face of European expansion and trade in the late 18th century. This was also the time of Bonaparte's expeditions to Egypt, and the beginning of European 'Egyptology', while the British established a new order over India from 1799.

Outstanding pieces of arms and armour from Mughal India are extravagantly embellished with precious metals and gemstones. A supreme example is the dagger handle representing a neighing horse, carved from jade inlaid with gold and gems (jade was introduced into India in the early 17th century). Mughal Indian armour, designed for ease of movement, was much lighter than its European equivalents. Cavalry body armour was made of a supple, damascened steel alloy and velvet. Arms from northern and southern India vary in design: there is, for example, a helmet designed to accommodate the long hair of a Sikh.

A striking variety of metalwork produced in India and exclusive to it was the **Bidriwar technique**, using blackened zinc alloy. Examples include an elegant ewer from the Deccan and a lamp in the shape of a duck.

Iranian carpet manufacture underwent changes in the 15th century, due perhaps to the adoption of designs which facilitated the industry. The Safavid rulers controlled production in centres at Isfahan and elsewhere. The Indian emperor Akbar brought carpet weavers from Iran to Fatehpur Sikri between 1571 and 1584, and further imperial carpet manufactories were set up in Kashmir. The export of carpets to

Europe expanded in the 17th and 18th centuries.

Also during the Safavid period, 'Speaking Works' appear: metal and ceramic pieces which have poetic inscriptions both referring to the function of the object and carrying mystical references. The tall candlestick, *'Moth and Candle'*, is an example and the ceramic tile with a young man smelling a narcissus symbolises love. Safavid rulers collected Chinese porcelain and kept it in a purpose-built room, the *'Chinikhaneh'*, with shaped niches. In the entrance pavilion of the royal palace at Isfahan was a similar arrangement.

There is a plentiful collection of Ottoman ceramics. The earlier Iznik designs (c. 1480–1510) had regular patterns of demi-palmettes (*rumi*) and vegetal friezes. Deep cobalt is found on the oldest pieces, and later turquoise. Iznik and Kütahya artists produced glazed ceramics of great technical perfection. The palette was later enriched with pink and green tones and floral designs. From the 1560s an iron oxide-based glaze obtained a bright red as well as a subtle coral and lavender blue. Fashion later favoured abstract patterns. The three-point shape, Ottoman symbol of strength, became popular, and Iznik animals and boats were added.

Architectural traditions that were maintained in the Arab provinces include *mashrabiyas* (18th century, openwork screens).

The Arts of the Book: This section demonstrates the changes in illuminations and illustrations, and the production of books from the 12th/13th centuries to the 19th century. In Iran, paintings were gradually detached from the text and made into albums. This fashion spread to India and Turkey and included stylised portraits as well as paintings based on nature. By the 13th century, in Iraq, paintings illustrating scientific and literary works were based on figurative scenes of contemporary objects. Towards 1400 a style developed which spread in the 16th century to Turkey and India, characterised by contrasts of bright colours, non-individualised figures and idealised transcriptions of nature. There are examples of the transformation of the Qur'an from manuscripts to printed and bound books.

DECORATIVE ARTS

The department of Decorative Arts is without equal and contains a vast and dazzling array of artefacts, ecclesiastical and secular, predominantly from France. They span the period from the end of antiquity to the 19th century. The collection is displayed in rooms on the first floor, including the great Apollo Gallery.

MEDIEVAL TO RENAISSANCE

A period of about ten centuries is covered in these galleries, from the fall of the Roman Empire (AD 476) to the Renaissance, organised chronologically and geographically. Two porphyry columns from the 4th-century basilica of old St Peter's in Rome flank the door.

The Middle Ages: Under the Merovingians (481–751) the quality of the goldsmiths' art is demonstrated by the **adornments of Queen Aregond** from St-Denis. Several fine pieces from the period of the Carolingian Renaissance include the bronze horseman known as the **statuette of Charlemagne** (9th century) from Metz Cathedral.

The **Treasure of St-Denis** is a collection of superb ecclesiastical ornaments acquired in the 12th century by Suger, Abbot of St-Denis (1122–51). Among them are **Suger's Eagle**, an eagle-shaped antique porphyry vase mounted in silver gilt; the rock-crystal **Vase of Eleanor of Aquitaine**, presented to her by Louis VII and which she gave to Suger; and a ewer in rock crystal, carved in Egypt around the end of the 10th century. The **Coronation sword and scabbard of the Kings of France** is one of the oldest pieces of French regalia, kept in the St-Denis treasury until the Revolution.

From the Gothic period are the **treasures of the Sainte-Chapelle workshop**, founded by St Louis in 1239. Among those acquired by the Louvre in the late 18th century are an ivory sculpture, *Virgin and Child* (c. 1260–70), which is considered a perfect example of the Gothic ideal of beauty and a tribute to the skill of Parisian ivory carvers. An ingenious chess set (15th, 17th and 19th centuries) consists of a German-made board in squares of rock crystal and smoked quartz cased in silver; through each of which a flower design is visible. The crystal and quartz pieces are French.

Impressive collections of 15th–16th-century Hispano-Moorish lustreware have examples of the development of storiated faïence at Faenza, Italy. Metalwork includes an outstanding **medallion with the self-portrait of Jean Fouquet** (c. 1450) and an advance on the technique of painted **enamels from Limoges**.

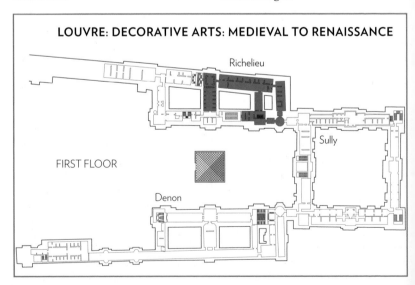

LOUVRE: DECORATIVE ARTS: MEDIEVAL TO RENAISSANCE

Richelieu

Sully

FIRST FLOOR

Denon

THE LOUVRE
Detail of the gilded silver filigree mount and gemstone settings of the so-called
Vase of Eleanor of Aquitaine, from the Treasury of St-Denis.

The later Middle Ages, an important period for woven tapestries, is well represented. The Salle des Millefleurs is named after the delightful medieval tapestry scattered with flowers.

Renaissance: The 16th century is marked by the shift from religious to domestic items: Italian bronzes from Florence and Padua introduced Italian Renaissance ideas to France. Important groups of tapestries include the magnificent *Hunts of Maximilian* series (1531–3), which since the time of Louis XIV has been considered a great masterpiece. The twelve **tapestries of the *Months***, after cartoons by the painter Bernard van Orley, are a unique document of court life and rural landscapes.

The workshops of Léonard Limosin

dominated French painted enamels and include a portrait plaque of the dauphin, the future François II. Doors (c. 1557) from Clermont-Ferrand carved with grotesques and the monograms of Henri II and Catherine de Médicis show the speed with which innovatory decorative influences introduced at Fontainebleau spread to the French provinces.

Among small decorative bronzes from Italy is Giambologna's dynamic *Nessus Carrying off Deianeira*, a gift from André Le Nôtre to Louis XIV in 1693.

Examples of the singular art of the ceramicist **Bernard Palissy** should not be missed. His glazed earthenware dishes are decorated in coloured high relief with animals—snakes, frogs, fish—set in foliage and flowers. He also produced enamelled grottoes for prestigious customers, and possibly had a workshop in the Tuileries.

The early 17th century was of fundamental importance to French furniture, with the appearance of the new technique of *ébénisterie* (cabinet-making).

Representative pieces are a Parisian ebony cabinet, a fine ensemble of a bed (with hangings) and six armchairs with original embroidered velvet from the Château of Effiat.

LOUIS XIV TO THE REVOLUTION

The extraordinary sumptuousness—as well as the constraints—of French royal and aristocratic life are illustrated here in a series of rooms recreating living spaces of the 17th and 18th centuries.

The Grande Siècle: Exemplary pieces are presented in the historic **Council of State chambers (1)**, which have 19th-century ceiling paintings. The sumptuous royal collections are built largely around those assembled by Louis XIV and works formerly belonging to Richelieu or Mazarin. The portrait of Louis XIV (1704) by Hyacinthe Rigaud has been moved here from the French Paintings department. Grouped here are many masterpieces from the great royal factories and Crown workshops, which came under the control of Le Brun from 1667. Le Brun designed the *History of the King* tapestries (Gobelins, 1672), and the Savonnerie carpet for the Grande Galerie du Louvre (1668). Remarkable pieces of furniture include the chest with the arms of Colbert (c. 1690–1700) by Oppenordt, designed by Bérain. There was a marked predilection for **Boulle marquetry** at the time, and on display are several examples which typically use exotic woods, brass and tortoiseshell, among them tall two-door cupboards (1680–1700). There are also examples of work by the cabinet-maker Charles Cressent, who was crucial in the development of the *rocaille* style. From these rooms is a sweeping view beyond the Tuileries to La Défense.

The Rococo period: A major feature of the north wing of the Cour Carrée are the period rooms, saved as far as possible from Parisian mansions and aristocratic country houses and furnished with objects that evoke the grandest interiors of their day.

The **Salle Chagoury** opens the period 1700–80 with a reconstruction of a room from the Hôtel le Bar de Montargis on Place Vendôme, including several original panels and objects by artists who worked at Versailles, including a table by Boulle, bronzes and an elaborate pedestal clock attributed to Oppenordt. Highly elaborate hangings, *Les Attributs de la Marine* (Paris, 1689–92), were commissioned by Jean-Baptiste Colbert de Seignelay, Secretary of State of the Navy, and designed by Jean I Bérain and Jean Lemoine.

The panelled decoration from the **Château de Voré**, which belonged Louis Fagon, *Intendant des Finances* at the time of Louis XIV, is a rare survival from the early 18th century. Nine delicately-painted canvases, *Country Diversions* (c. 1720–3) by Jean-Baptiste Oudry, are reminiscent of a Watteau painting.

The **Salle Rocaille** (1730–52) contains richly ornate original blue and

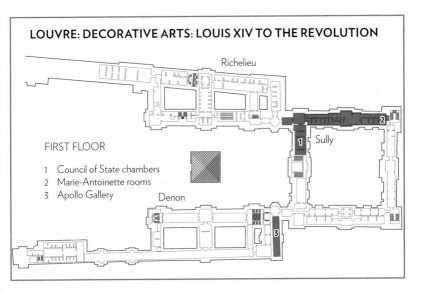

LOUVRE: DECORATIVE ARTS: LOUIS XIV TO THE REVOLUTION

Richelieu

FIRST FLOOR

1 Council of State chambers
2 Marie-Antoinette rooms
3 Apollo Gallery

Sully

Denon

white panels from the Hôtel Villemarie-Dangé, decorated with painted scenes in sculpted and gilded frames, of childrens' games. The green and red damask is a copy of the 18th-century original and the Cabinet Chinois typifies the fashion for *chinoiserie* in the mid-18th century.

The royal possessions in the **Louis XV Room** contains include ornate watches, snuff boxes, a liqueur set and coffee grinder; an elegant pink and green Sèvres porcelain pot-pourri (1760) is a complicated piece of porcelain. The '*nécessaire*' (travelling case) was a gift to Madame de Pompadour from the King and there is a portrait of her and Louis XV (1748) by Quentin Delatour.

The drawing room of the **Château d'Abondant** (c. 1750) is one of the rare examples of the survival of an almost complete interior decoration. The panelling and furniture are perfectly representative of the evolution of the *rocaille* style at this time towards more sober ornamentation. Furnishings include settees and straight-backed armchairs, a harpsichord, an original chandelier and a small round table on two levels by Martin Carlin.

The Neoclassical period: The **Edward de Rothschild Room** contains superb examples of Neoclassical furniture. The **Rotunda**, painted by Antoine-François Callet and Pierre-Hyacinthe Deleuze, came from a mansion close to Les Invalides built for Louis-Joseph de Bourbon, Prince de Condé. This is a rare piece from one of the most famous Parisian follies of the end of the 18th century.

The magnificent **Schlichting Donation** includes a drop-front desk with ebony veneer and inlaid marble and a silver soup tureen and tray from the Orloff Service ordered from Jacques-Nicolas Roettiers de la Tour by Catherine the Great and given to Count Orloff.

Salle Louis XVI has mirrors, painted panels and tapestries, with furniture dating from 1775–90. The *Medici Vase* (c. 1787) was designed by P.-P. Thomire and made at Sèvres for Mme Adélaïde, an aunt of Louis XVI (1780). Among furniture is a pedestal table by Carlin, chairs in gilded walnut by Georges Jacob for the Salon de Jeux at St-Cloud and a rolltop desk attributed to D. Roentgen.

The **David Weill donation** of furnishings from the Château de Bellevue, Meudon, which belonged to Louis XVI's aunts, includes decoration designed to accommodate two sets of over-door panels painted by M.-A. Challe (originally for Mme de Pompadour, who previously occupied the château). Mme Victoire's Commode and two corner cupboards were made by Martin Carlin using lacquered panels from Japan.

Marie-Antoinette rooms: These two rooms **(2)** contain small personal objects which belonged to the queen, including timepieces, hardstones, crystal, lacquer and snuff boxes. The '*nécessaire de voyage*', combines picnic box, make-up box and sewing box. The adjacent room has recreated panelling and silk hanging copied from the original fabric in Louis XVI's bedroom at St-Cloud, and a fireplace from Fontainebleau. These create a setting for some of the queen's furniture, including a cylinder desk (J.-H. Riesener, 1784) from her apartment at the Tuileries Palace, with veneer and gilded bronze decoration, a cabriolet armchair (1787) upholstered in blue from her *grand cabinet* at St-Cloud, made by J.-B.-C. Séné, and a footstool attributed to Georges Jacob.

Apollo Gallery: This room **(3)** is sumptuously decorated with stuccoes and paintings carried out under the direction of Charles Le Brun from 1661–80, on the theme of the Sun, symbol of Louis XIV. The room was restored from 1849 by Félix Duban and Delacroix was commissioned in 1851 to decorate the central part with *Apollo Overpowering the Serpent Python*. The wrought iron came from Château Laffitte. This is the home of items originally in the French royal collection, including vessels made of lapis lazuli, jade and other semi-precious stones. Individual objects include the **crown of Louis XV** (1722; after his coronation the gems were replaced by coloured stones, according to custom). The Crown jewels retained when the remainder were sold in 1887 include the **Regent diamond** (140.64 carats), discovered in India and bought by the Regent, Philippe, Duc d'Orléans, from the Governor of India, Thomas Pitt, in 1717. It was used in royal regalia, including the crowns of Louis XV and of Louis XVI, Napoleon's sword (1812) and Empress Eugénie's crown. The **Côte de Bretagne ruby** has had an illustrious list of owners and was later cut into the shape of a dragon as a decoration of the Order of the Golden Fleece.

NAPOLEON I TO NAPOLÉON III

The galleries on the top west of the Richelieu wing cover the period from the Consulate and the Napoleonic Empire (1799–1814), and the Bourbon Restoration (1814–30) to the July Monarchy (1830–48). They are characterised by Neoclassicism, of which the architects Percier and Fontaine, informed by the study of antiquity, are representa-

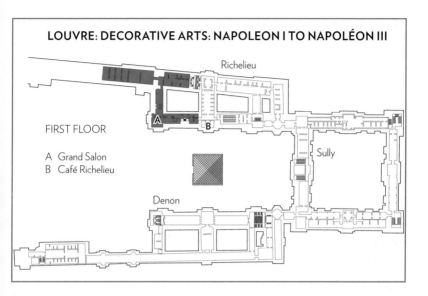

LOUVRE: DECORATIVE ARTS: NAPOLEON I TO NAPOLÉON III

Richelieu

FIRST FLOOR

A Grand Salon
B Café Richelieu

Sully

Denon

tive. They include the models of furniture made by Jacob-Desmalter, metalwork by Biennais, or ceramics from the Sèvres manufactory, directed by Brongniart from 1800–47. Apart from the furnishing of the Hotel Récamier, practically everything at the Louvre comes from imperial, then royal, residences, in particular the Tuileries (jewel-boxes of Empress Josephine, bedroom of Charles X). However, from 1819 the layout is gradually interspersed with pieces presented at the Exhibitions of National Industry, thus reflecting the gradual break with Neoclassicism and the triumph of historicism under the July Monarchy.

Furniture-making during the early 19th century, was dominated by the Jacob dynasty. Georges Jacob usually signed his work 'G. Jacob' and his two sons as 'Jacob Frères' until 1804, after which F.-H.-Georges Jacob-Desmalter worked independently for another decade. His son, Alphonse Jacob (signed 'Jacob') flourished in the 1840s.

The wealthy banker Jacques Récamier purchased the Hôtel Necker in 1798 and appointed the architect Louis Berthault to refurbish it and design the furniture, which was made by Jacob Frères. The painting by F.-L. Dejuinne

shows Madame Récamier, the celebrated *'femme de lettres'*, in the apartment to which she withdrew in 1819 in Rue de Sèvres, and where she held her famous salons: Chateaubriand was a frequent participant. **Julie Récamier's famous day-bed**, on which she posed for her portrait by David (*see p. 196*), and other pieces by Jacob Frères, are gathered here. Her taste was the prototype for Empire-style interiors.

Examples of **Sèvres porcelain** date from the time that Alexandre Brongniart directed the manufacture. Martin-Guillaume Biennais, personal goldsmith to the Emperor, designed a prestigious silver-gilt tea service of 28 pieces, ordered by Napoleon for his marriage to Marie-Louise in 1810 (part of which is here), as well as a superb Sèvres porcelain coffee service, the *Cabaret egyptien* featuring views of Egypt, which the Emperor took with him to St Helena.

Early Empire: Magnificent pieces on display here include the throne (by Jacob-Desmalter) for Napoleon's coronation. There is also Gérard's portrait of Napoleon (1805) wearing his coronation robes.

The *Vase Médicis* (1804), originally commemorated two victories of the First Consul Napoleon (Marengo and Rivoli) but the illustrations were changed to a bacchanal and a boar-hunt during the Restoration. The laurel-wreath design of the handles were also changed and other Napoleonic symbols expunged.

Outstanding among Empire memorabilia from the Élysée Palace is the *surtout de table* in porcelain celebrating Napoleon's victories in Europe.

The Restoration and July Monarchy: Representative pieces which belonged to Louis XVIII include a reconstruction of his blue and gold bedchamber at the Tuileries, later occupied by Charles X. The bed was made by Pierre-Gaston Brion; other pieces are by Jacob-Desmalter and the beautiful blue velvet drapes came from Lyon. The Savonnerie carpet was in Napoleon's bedchamber at the Tuileries.

Exhibitions of industry were encouraged by the Directoire (1795–9) to stimulate national production and limit imports—especially from England.

Among the items made is a spectacular carved crystal dressing table and chair bought by the Duchesse de Berry. There is a set of sacred vessels from the Chapelle Expiatoire; and a pair of vases described as 'seditious' conceal the profiles of Louis XVI and Marie-Antoinette.

As the 19th century progresses, objects become increasingly ornate, such as the bronze-gilt candlesticks (by Picard) and a pair of bronze ewers by Triqueti (1838).

Apartments of Napoléon III: The suite has retained its original furnishings, constituting a unique ensemble of the period. The wing was built during the Second Empire to house the Ministry of State, as part of the project to link the Tuileries Palace to the Louvre. The work was carried out by Hector Lefuel from 1857–61. The apartments miraculously survived the fire of 1871, when they were made over to the Ministry of Finance, who remained here until the Grand Projet du Louvre began.

The **Salle Thiers**, or family salon, links both the small rooms and the large reception rooms. The first is the **Salon Théâtre**, which has a charming floral and musical decoration, and off it opens the **Petit Salon de la Terrasse**.

On the corner, the **Grand Salon (A)**, is the largest and most sumptuous, glittering with gold, adorned with putti, and draped in crimson velvet. The ceiling painting by Charles-Raphaël Maréchal depicts the *Linking of the Louvre and the Tuileries by Napoléon III*.

The rather more sedate tones of sea-green marble and darkened wood in the small **Dining Room** are enlivened by gilding and *trompe l'oeil* painted wallpaper.

SCULPTURE

The Louvre's collection of sculpture from the Middle Ages to the mid-19th century is dominated by French work but also includes significant works from Italy as well as a small number from Spain and Northern Europe.

FRENCH SCULPTURE

French sculpture on Richelieu lower ground and ground floors is arranged around the Cour Marly and Cour Puget. They rise over two levels and larger pieces of sculpture originally designed for royal gardens or public places are displayed to advantage in these light spaces. Crypte Girardon is between the two courtyards and just before it the staircase to the left leads to the chronological beginning of the display.

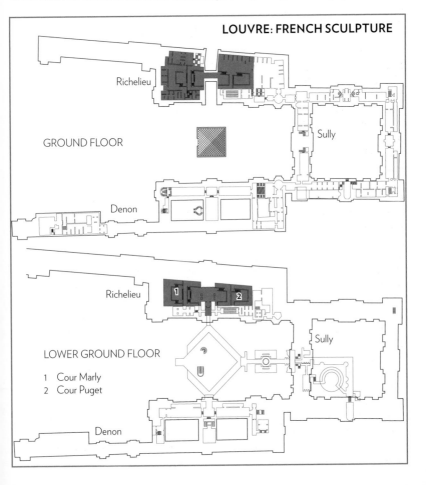

LOUVRE: FRENCH SCULPTURE

Richelieu

GROUND FLOOR

Sully

Denon

Richelieu

Sully

LOWER GROUND FLOOR

1 Cour Marly
2 Cour Puget

Denon

Medieval sacred sculpture: A deeply incised 6th-century capital from Aquitaine, re-carved in the 12th century, comes from the church of St-Geneviève in Paris (demolished). It shows *Daniel in the Lions' Den*, with a pensive Daniel seated between two lions which form the angles, under Ionic scrolls. A late Romanesque relief of the *Annunciation, Virgin in Majesty* and *Baptism of Christ* was found in the church of St John the Baptist, in Carrières-sur-Seine, a dependency of St-Denis. It is considered to be the oldest retable in northern France. Above the arched setting is an architectural design usually thought to represent the celestial Jerusalem.

By the late 12th or early 13th century, in the Île de France and eastern France, the Gothic style was developing. Based on a more naturalistic representation of the world, due to Classical and Byzantine influences, sculpture responded to the new innovations in architecture and free-standing statues were introduced. An example is the elegant 13th-century statue of King Childebert (d. 558), founder of the Abbey of St-Germain-des-Prés, which stood in the abbey cloister at the entrance to the refectory. Fourteenth-century works include several altarpieces, in black and white marble, from the Sainte-Chapelle. A refined and smiling angel (c. 1340) in marble, carrying cruets for wine and water during Mass, is from the altarpiece of the Abbey of Maubuison. It was given by Queen Jeanne d'Evreux, key patron of the arts in the 14th century. Small statues for the tomb of the entrails of Queen Jeanne, and her consort, the last of the Capetians, Charles IV (d. 1328), are by Jean de Liège.

Fifteenth to seventeenth centuries: By the 15th century two important artistic centres, Burgundy and the Loire, developed sculpture along different lines. It was only in this later medieval period that artists were more commonly identified by name. The celebrated tomb of Philippe Pot (d. 1493), Grand Seneschal of Burgundy, from the Abbey of Cîteaux, is supported by eight supple and eloquent mourners. Two more Burgundian-style hooded mourners come from the tomb of the Duc de Berry (d. 1416), brother of Charles V and of Philippe the Bold of Burgundy. The duke planned his tomb for the chapel of his palace in Bourges, and it was begun during his lifetime.

The later Middle Ages and early Renaissance are represented by the superb marble high relief *St George and the Dragon* (1504–9), commissioned from the leading sculptor in the Loire area, Michel Colombe, by Georges d'Amboise for the Château of Gallon. Colombe's influence can be found in other works of the period and later.

The birth of Humanism and the influence of Italy resulted in the more lifelike sculptures in the Renaissance period, among which is an outstanding funerary monument to Philippe Chabot (d. 1543), Admiral of France, who is shown dressed in armour, reclining on one elbow. Attributed to Jean Cousin, the work is only one part of a larger decorative ensemble. The macabre funerary statue of Jeanne de Bourbon, Comtesse d'Auvergne (1521), shows her being devoured by worms.

The monument for the heart of Henri II by Germain Pilon was originally in the church of the Célestins. Also by Pilon is the monumental bronze of Cardinal

René de Birague in perpetual prayer, a moving and deeply expressive portrait and also a crowning achievement of bronze sculpture. A remarkable survival from a commission by Queen Catherine de Médicis for the projected Valois chapel at St-Denis is a terracotta model by Pilon for the *Vierge de la Douleur* (*see p. 353*). Barthélemy Prieur, who succeeded Pilon, continued in a more sober style. He designed the monument for the heart of High Constable Anne de Montmorency (d. 1567; *see p. 509*) and his wife to stand beside that of Henri II.

The oldest surviving garden sculpture in France (restored) is the *Fontaine de Diane*, which undoubtedly refers to Diane de Poitiers, favourite of Henri II and François I. From the Château d'Anet (*see p. 92*), the sculpture is in the Mannerist style of Fontainebleau, but its sculptor remains unknown.

Seventeenth-century sculptures include Simon Guillain's masterpiece, the *Monument du Pont-au-Change*, which once dominated the busy cross-roads opposite the Cité at the time of Louis XIII.

Small-format works: High in drama though small in scale are qualifying works from 1704–91 for acceptance at the Académie Royale de Peinture et de Sculpture, by a variety of artists. The rival portraitists Jean-Jacques Caffieri and Augustin Pajou were eclipsed by Jean-Antoine Houdon, who made like-nesses of his contemporaries such as Voltaire, Rousseau, Diderot, Benjamin Franklin and George Washington. The Galerie de Grands-Hommes has statues of illustrious men commissioned in 1776 during the reign of Louis XVI, including the playwrights Molière and Corneille by

Caffieri, Jean de La Fontaine and Nicolas Poussin in a toga, by Pierre Julien.

Sculpture of the Revolution, Empire and Restoration: This is a period char-acterised by ostentatious allegory. The silver and bronze *Peace* conceived by Vivant Denon, Director of the Louvre, was modelled by Chaudet. *Napoléon I in Coronation Robes* (1813) was carved in marble by Ramey. A mosaic by Belloni, *The Genius of the Emperor, Controlling Victory, brings back Peace and Abundance* (1810), was designed for the floor of the Salle de la Melpomène (*see plan on p. 203*).

The Romantic era: The collection contains many virtuoso and sentimen-tal pieces by James Pradier and others. Some individuality shines through in David d'Angers' *Child with a Bunch of Grapes* (1845) and in the large portrait heads in marble at which he excelled. Works by the famous animal sculp-tor Antoine-Louis Barye include his *Jaguar Devouring a Hare*, and *Roger and Angélique Riding the Hippogriffe*. By the great François Rude are *Mercury, Young Neapolitan Playing with a Turtle* and *Joan of Arc Hearing Voices* (1845), one of a series made for the Jardin du Luxembourg.

Cour Marly: Cour Marly **(1)**, on the lower ground floor, is named after the sculptures from the Parc de Marly (*see p. 496*), acquired by Louis XIV in 1676 as a private retreat from Versailles (*see p. 496*). The architect Jules Hardouin-Mansart embellished the gardens with complicated water features and exuber-ant examples of Rococo sculptures by leading artists. Antoine Coysevox was responsible for part of the cascade featuring the Seine and Marne, Neptune and Amphitrite, and the equestrian groups on the upper level, *Mercury* and *Fame*, each riding Pegasus, which were moved to the Tuileries in 1719. These were superseded at Marly by the magnificent **Horses of Marly** (1743–5) by Guillaume I Coustou, which were subsequently moved to the end of the Champs-Élysées. Now replaced by reproductions, the originals came to the Louvre in 1984.

Crypte Girardon and Cour Puget: Between the two courtyards Crypte Girardon contains 17th–18th-century sculptures by Girardon, Puget and Coysevox. These include a small model for the equestrian statue of Louis XIV by François Girardon, and a marble relief by Pierre Puget, *The Meeting of Alexander and Diogenes* (1671–89), made for Louis XIV. Grandiose busts of bewigged men include Coysevox's marble bust of Jean-Baptiste Colbert and a bronze (posthumous) bust of Louis II de Bourbon, *le grand Condé*.

Scattered across Cour Puget is a disparate collection of 17th–19th-century works which includes monuments for public places and parks, although Pierre Puget's Baroque *Milo of Croton* (1671–82) and *Perseus and Andromeda* (1687–94) were destined for Louis XIV's Versailles and transferred to the Louvre in 1819. Beneath the trees are 17th-century pieces by Sébastien Slodtz and Nicolas Coustou, also made for Versailles but transferred to the Tuileries in 1722. Coysevox's light-hearted *Marie-Adélaïde de Savoie, Duchesse de Bourgogne* (1710), portrays the mother of Louis XV as Diana, while Jean-Baptiste Pigalle's marble *Madame de Pompadour en Amitié* (1753) depicts Louis XV's favourite with flowers of all seasons.

EARLY ITALIAN, SPANISH AND NORTHERN EUROPEAN SCULPTURE

Italian sculpture of the 6th–15th centuries is on Denon lower ground floor, together with pieces from Spain and northern Europe.

Galerie Donatello: Converted from the stables built in 1857–9 by Lefuel, this space on the lower ground floor contains Italian sculpture from the 6th–15th centuries and several images of the *Madonna and Child*, in a variety of materials, such as the lifesize version in painted wood by Jacopo della Quercia. Dominating Italian sculpture in the 15th century are the elegant and sensual works of the Florentine sculptor Donatello. Inspired by antiquity, his *Madonna and Child* in coloured and gilded terracotta is a figure of great delicacy and pathos and was probably one of the last works that he produced before his departure for Padua (1443). The *Virgin Surrounded by Four Angels* by Agostino di Duccio, made for Piero de' Medici, is a virtuoso example of marble bas-relief, and masterly are the three reliefs by Mino da Fiesole of the *Madonna and Child*, which give the effect of transparent fabric.

Bottega della Robbia: This is devoted to a collection of enamelled earthenware, in characteristic blue and white, and yellow and green, from the Florentine workshops of the Della

LOUVRE: ITALIAN, SPANISH AND NORTHERN EUROPEAN SCULPTURE

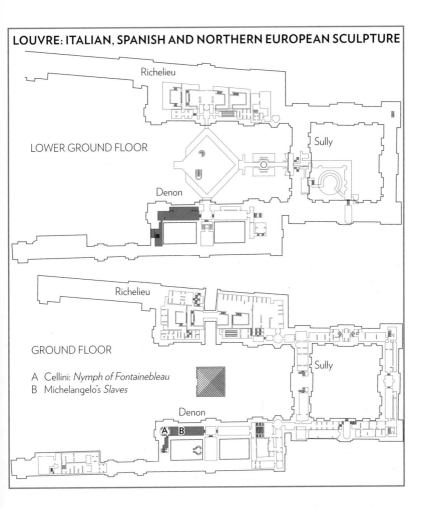

LOWER GROUND FLOOR

Richelieu

Sully

Denon

GROUND FLOOR

A Cellini: *Nymph of Fontainebleau*
B Michelangelo's *Slaves*

Richelieu

Sully

Denon

Robbia (Andrea, 1435–1525), Giovanni (1469–c. 1530), Luca (1475–c. 1548) and Benedetto Buglioni (1459–1521). Terracottas include *St Sebastian*, *Madonna and Child with Three Cherubim* and *Christ on the Mount of Olives*.

Spanish sculpture: Essentially religious, the small collection of 12th–18th-century Spanish sculpture contains several polychrome pieces, some in wood. Capitals date from the Visigothic and Mozarabic periods, and pieces in alabaster are from royal tombs from the Catalan monastery of Poblet. There is a monumental Gothic doorway, richly decorated with vegetal motifs and an *Annunciation* group.

Northern European sculpture: This is a small collection of works from the

12th–16th centuries. From England are 15th-century alabasters typical of Nottingham production. There is a beautiful International Gothic-style *Virgin and Child* (c. 1510) from Isenheim, near Colmar (Lorraine), originally the central part of an altarpiece carved in lime wood, a material that lends itself well to complicated drapery. Among German and Dutch later Gothic reliefs and sculptures is a kneeling *Virgin Annunciate* in painted alabaster, by Riemenschneider; and a naked *St Mary Magdalene* (1510) in painted limewood, made by Gregor Erhart of Augsburg. Her nakedness refers to the legend that she lived as a mystic ascetic in a cave in Sainte-Baume (Provence), clothed only in her hair.

Renaissance sculpture is represented by the tombstone of Jean de Coronmeuse, Abbot of St-Jacques-de-Liège (c. 1525–30). There is a bronze *Mercury and Psyche* (1593) by Adriaan de Vries from Prague, and a spirited model of a sculpture by the Swedish artist Johan Tobias Sergel, *Othryades the Spartan, Dying* (1779), in preparation for the plaster maquette to gain admission to the Paris Academy.

LATER ITALIAN SCULPTURE

Denon ground floor displays works from the 16th–19th centuries, including two famous masterpieces by Michelangelo.

Mollien Staircase: On the stairs up to 16th–19th-century Italian sculpture is the ***Nymph of Fontainebleau***, a bronze bas-relief by Benvenuto Cellini. Cellini trained as a goldsmith, but this was his decisive move into monumental sculpture for which he used the lost-wax technique, casting it in five sections. François I commissioned the work for the Porte d'Orée at Fontainebleau during Cellini's second visit to France in 1540–5, but it was never installed. After the king's death (1547) it was re-erected at the Château d'Anet until the Revolution.

The Michelangelo Gallery: With its low vaults and polychrome marble floor, entered via a monumental portal from the Palazzo Stanga in Cremona, this room makes a grand setting for **Michelangelo's** *Slaves*. The most celebrated works in the department, these two sculptures (1513–15) were famously never completed and the symbolic significance of the powerful and expressive figures remains a mystery. The more rugged of the two, described as the *Captive Slave*, appears to be struggling for release, while the younger, more sensuous version, known as the *Dying Slave*, seems at peace. Both were intended for the tomb of Pope Julius II, alongside other works including the four *Slaves* in Florence and the *Moses* in Rome, but Michelangelo, for financial reasons, gave these two works to the Florentine exile Roberto Strozzi, who presented them to Henri II in 1550. They were kept for some time at the Château of Écouen (*seep. 509*) before being transferred to Cardinal Richelieu's collection.

The outstanding pieces of the high Baroque period are by **Bernini**. They include *Angel Carrying the Crown of Thorns* (c. 1667), a terracotta study for his statue on Ponte Sant'Angelo in Rome, and the bust of Cardinal

Richelieu (1641), Louis XIII's powerful chief minister, dressed in his prelate's robes and wearing the Ordre du St-Esprit. The work was modelled on the triple portrait of Richelieu by Philippe de Champaigne in London.

Canova's *Cupid and Psyche* (1787–93) is an idealised representation of young love and a technically perfect and harmonious composition of interlocking forms.

ARTS OF AFRICA, ASIA, OCEANIA & THE AMERICAS

PAVILLON DES SESSIONS
From 1827 the Louvre had a maritime and ethnographic collection which inspired Fauve, Cubist and Expressionist artists. It was transferred to the museum of ethnography at the Trocadéro in 1878 and then in 2006 to Quai Branly. Today this quiet outpost, in the southwest corner of the Louvre, at the far end of the ground floor of the Denon wing, has some fine examples of artworks from the four main cultural regions: Africa, Asia, Oceania and the Americas.

EATING AND DRINKING AT THE LOUVRE

The Louvre has several cafés and restaurants. Under the Pyramide are € **Le Café du Grand Louvre** (waiter service, classic modern French; *T: 01 40 20 53 41*) and the € **Comptoir du Louvre** for snacks and drinks. On the mezzanine level are three centrally-organised fast-food outlets which provide hot meals and snacks.

The € **Café Richelieu** tea room (Richelieu first floor) overlooks Cour Napoléon and is near the apartments of Napoléon III (*see plan on p. 233*). € **Café Denon**, on the first-floor landing of the Mollien staircase (Denon wing), overlooks French paintings, not far from the *Mona Lisa* (*see plan on p. 197*). There are also cafés and takeaways in the Carrousel du Louvre shopping mall under the Louvre.

€–€€ **Café Marly**, in the Richelieu wing, is accessed from outside (*93 Rue de Rivoli, T: 01 49 26 06 60, cafe-marly.com/fr; map p. 587, D1*). Very trendy and with very chic staff, it has a brilliant location with a view from inside over the French sculpture gallery, Cour Marly, while the restaurant terrace faces Cour Napoléon and the Pyramide. The situation contributes to its popularity and the (fairly limited) choice of food is well cooked and nicely presented.

Musée des Arts Décoratifs & The Tuileries

The Jardin des Tuileries, with its Orangerie housing Monet's
'Water Lilies', is entered from the east through Napoleon's triumphal
Arc du Carrousel. The Musée des Arts Décoratifs is here.
Rue de Rivoli, to the north, has smart hotels and shops.
St-Germain-l'Auxerrois is the former royal chapel of the Louvre.

The former Château des Tuileries has completely disappeared, leaving only fragments at the western extremities of the Palais du Louvre (*see plan on p. 185*): to the south is the Pavillon de Flore and to the north, the Pavillon de Marsan. Both have been restored or rebuilt and the latter houses the Musée des Arts Décoratifs.

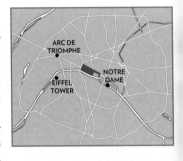

The Tuileries Palace was begun in 1564 by Philibert de l'Orme for Catherine de Médicis as a more comfortable alternative to the Louvre, but she left it in 1570 for the Hôtel de Soissons in the Marais. The two palaces, Tuileries and Louvre, only half a kilometre apart, were eventually linked and the Tuileries became the residence of the ruling monarch. After being brought from Versailles, Louis XVI was confined here until 10th August 1792, and it became the headquarters of the Convention. The Tuileries later became the main residence of Napoleon (when the Arc du Carrousel was erected as the main entrance to the courtyard), as well as of Louis XVIII (who died here), Charles X, Louis-Philippe and Napoléon III. In May 1871 the Communards set fire to the building which, like the Hôtel de Ville, was completely gutted. Its charred remains stood until 1884, when the main wing was demolished, and the site was converted into a garden in 1889. The two pavilions, however, were partly rebuilt and restored in 1875–8 by Lefuel.

ARC DE TRIOMPHE DU CARROUSEL
The Place du Carrousel, which derives its name from an equestrian fête held in 1662 by Louis XIV, lies between the Louvre and the Tuileries gardens. The Arc de Triomphe du Carrousel is a copy on a reduced scale of the Arch of Septimius Severus at Rome

TUILERIES
Sculpture by Aristide Maillol in the lower gardens.

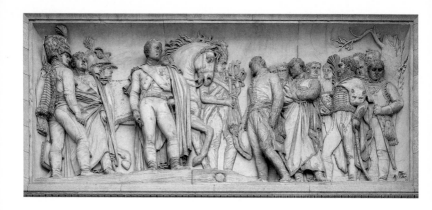

ARC DU CARROUSEL
The Surrender of Ulm, showing the defeated Austrian general Karl Mack
capitulating to a victorious Napoleon in 1805.

(14.6m high instead of 23m), enhanced by pink and white Corinthian columns. It was begun in 1806 from designs by Fontaine and Percier to commemorate the victories of Napoleon in 1805; these are depicted in the marble bas-reliefs on the four sides: facing the gardens, on the right *The Treaty of Tilsit* (concluded between Napoleon and Tsar Alexander I) by Ramey and *Napoleon entering Munich* (left) by Clodion; facing Rue de Rivoli, *Napoleon entering Vienna* by Deseine; facing the Louvre, *The Battle of Austerlitz* by Espercieux (right) and *The Surrender of Ulm* by Cartellier (left); facing the Seine, *The Peace of Pressburg* (concluded with Austria following the above two battles) by Le Sueur. The columns are surmounted by figures of soldiers of the Empire and the arch itself is crowned by a bronze chariot group by Bosio (1828) representing the Restoration of the Bourbons. The original group incorporated the antique horses looted by Napoleon from St Mark's, Venice, in 1797 but returned in 1815. Beyond the arch is a distant view towards the Arc de Triomphe and La Défense.

MUSÉE DES ARTS DÉCORATIFS

Map p. 586, C1. 107 Rue de Rivoli. Métro 1 and 7 to Palais Royal-Musée du Louvre or 1 to Tuileries. Open Tues–Sun 11–6, Thur to 9pm during temporary exhibitions; closed Mon and holidays. Disabled access, audioguides. The Documentation Centre has free access. Excellent shop. Restaurant (see p. 261). T: 01 44 55 57 50, www.lesartsdecoratifs.fr.

Les Arts Décoratifs, as it is known, is completely autonomous from the Louvre, but housed in the Pavillon de Marsan and part of the Rohan wing of the Louvre Palace. It has three sections: the Museum of Decorative Arts, where the permanent collections are displayed; the Museum of Fashion and Textiles and the Museum of Advertising. The collections of the two last are too fragile for permanent display and are presented in regular temporary exhibitions.

The collections of the Musée des Arts Décoratifs vividly portray the French way of life from medieval times to the present, represented by some 5,000 works permanently on view. They are complemented by regular temporary exhibitions. The museum has depended since the start on donations and bequests, and therefore reflects the tastes of individual collectors down the ages. Among these donations are 600 pieces of 19th-century jewellery from the Vever Collection, and the Chinese cloisonnée works that are the bequest of David Weill. Represented are outstanding examples of decorative and ornamental art and painting ranging through Italian primitives, tapestries, wood panelling, porcelain and furniture. The collections are laid out chronologically, with considerable space devoted to the 19th and 20th centuries. Included are several 'Period Rooms' from the Middle Ages to the 20th century, with reassembled and reconstructed decoration. There are also thematic series of objects exhibited in eye-catching displays. The visit to the permanent collections begins on the Level 3 reception area. The 20th-century rooms are at the far end of the Pavillon de Marsan and extend from the 9th floor down to the 4th.

Middle Ages and Renaissance (Rooms 1–9, 3rd floor)

Glowing colours and gilded frames characterise the sacred works (13th–16th centuries from France and elsewhere) in the Gallery of Retables. Key examples are a rare Spanish piece, the large-scale *Retable of St John the Baptist* by Luis Borrassá and *The Passion of Christ* (1522) from France. Late Gothic figures include the charming *Visitation* (1510–15) on wood. Representative of the International Gothic, the *Virgin and Child* (c. 1275) by the Master of the Magdalene is one of the oldest Italian works in France.

The earliest 'Period Room' is the Bedchamber (late 15th century), with objects predominantly from the Château de Villeneuve Lembron in the Auvergne. It contains a canopied bed, a fireplace, wood panelling and a five-part tapestry entitled the *Romance of the Rose* (c. 1420), representing courtly life.

Late Gothic works include ten unique Spanish monumental reliefs in pine (early 16th century) from Andalucia; 55 painted ceiling panels with portraits, made by Bonifacio Bembo for a monastery in Cremona; and decorated marriage chests or *cassoni* (1466).

Grouped under 'Arts du Feu' are objects made or decorated using firing techniques, including Hispano-Moresque earthenware and Venetian glass and Italian majolicas. Italian Renaissance influences spread to France at the time of François I, including intarsia (marquetry) wall panels; the popularity of personal portraits also increased.

Seventeenth and eighteenth centuries (Rooms 10–18, 3rd floor)

At the turn of the 16th and 17th centuries architectural motifs were adapted in a new ornamental manner, with the development of cabinet-making. From the mid-century, this skill was associated in Paris with sophisticated marquetry techniques and a preference for mainly floral and foliate patterns using a range of materials, exemplified by the casket on legs (c. 1655) by Pierre Gole. Among examples of the most innovative designs in furniture led by Northern European craftsmen is the cupboard with seven columns (1715–20) from Strasbourg. Antique arabesques and grotesques made a comeback in every sector of the decorative arts under the influence of the engravings of Jacques Androuet du Cerceau and of Jean Bérain, designer of sets for Louis XIV's festivities. The same trends are found in ceramics, Moustiers faïences, St-Cloud or Meissen porcelain and Bohemian glass. Two spectacular French pieces, a console table in gilded wood (1710–20) and a handsome two-part dresser of polished oak (c. 1730) demonstrate that by the 18th century decorative sculpture was integral to interior design.

The richly decorated and gilded 'Period Room' of the Hôtel de Rochegude, Avignon (c. 1725) was made by a Parisian artisan, Thomas Lainé, adapting materials and techniques to suit his Provençal commission. Fragile fabrics and wall coverings from the collections are exhibited in a darkened room and will be rotated.

Eighteenth century (Rooms 19–30, 4th floor)

The popularity of *rocaille* (Rococo) spread throughout Europe in the 18th century. Inspired by water, pebbles and shells, its application could be so excessive as to completely transform an object. Among the highlights are the swirling candelabra (1734–5) by Duvivier after Meissonnier, a sauceboat in Vincennes porcelain (1756) by Duplessis, and a Venetian chest.

Also in vogue was *chinoiserie*, decoration based on Chinese influences. A variety of pieces are exhibited in the Lacquered Room from the Hôtel du Châtelet (c. 1770). European objects which imitated those from the East were mainly black or red, but the little desk (1749–50) which belonged to Madame de Pompadour also uses blue lacquer. The finely-carved natural wood panelling *à la capucine* (1730) serves as the background to exhibits of tableware, which are periodically changed. The 'Cabinet des *Fables* de la Fontaine' (1750) comes from a mansion on Place Vendôme, but in the 19th century the panels were gilded, as was the fashion. Two-thirds have now been restored to the original 18th-century colours of pink and green, leaving the rest gilded.

During the later 18th century the frivolities of *rocaille* waned and the formal vocabulary of antiquity gained momentum with a return to Classical sources. The 'Etruscan' fashion is illustrated with furnishings from the end of the *Ancien Régime* (late 18th century), including painted wallpaper, a desk by Jean-Henri Riesener, examples of objects by Josiah Wedgwood, and a remarkable clock which belonged to Marie-Antoinette.

The evolution of the chair is set out in a witty display, a theme which is picked up again later. Early examples of the use of mahogany come from the French provinces, notably Bordeaux, and England. Exotic goods and new ideas filtered through ports such as Marseilles and Toulouse and trading families such as the Gohin, painted in 1787 by Boilly. One room is dedicated to the evolution of gilded bronzework.

Two period rooms conclude the 18th-century section. The Salon Talairac (c. 1790), a rare example of an interior from the end of the century, has panels with *trompe-l'oeil* candelabra motifs framing medallions in the style of Wedgwood. The pink marble fireplace is slightly later and the elaborate clock by Philippe-Jacques Corniquet dates from 1794. The furniture reflects the taste of a connoisseur of the period, following the evidence of paintings and inventories. It also contains valuable scientific instruments and contemporary landscape paintings. The Salon of the Hôtel de Serres (c. 1795) comes from Place Vendôme, with furniture of the 1780s. The room was decorated by Barriol, who bequeathed it to the museum.

Nineteenth century (Rooms 31–42, 4th floor)

At the end of the 18th century, in the search for the '*beau idéal*', artists again sought inspiration from antiquity. The collections reveal the change in direction which stemmed from David's studio in Rome. Brought together are David's painting *Paris and Helen* (1789) and the *Recueil des dessins intérieurs* by Percier and Fontaine, leading architects in Paris under Napoleon who were instrumental in spreading the Empire Style.

The life and times of the Duchesse de Berry (1798–1870), a person of determined views, is recalled in a painting by Alexandre-Jean Dubois Drahonnet. Her husband, Henri d'Artois, Duc de Bordeaux, was assassinated in 1820 and their son, successor to the Bourbon line, was born shortly after. Among objects referring to *l'enfant du miracle*, is the grand ceremonial cradle. The Duchess moved from the Élysée Palace to the first floor of the Marsan wing of the Louvre (this building), where she had to be restrained from endlessly changing the décor. She became involved in a plot to restore the Bourbons to the throne and was arrested and imprisoned in 1832, following a failed rebellion in the Vendée.

The reaction to the sobriety of the Empire Style came around 1820, and the change in direction is dramatically illustrated by the boat-shaped bed by F. Baudry (1827) and a brightly coloured painted panorama by Joseph Dufour.

The Louis-Philippe Bedroom (1830–48), in bright colours with an unusual Renaissance-style décor, is from the mansion in Rue St-Dominique (*map p. 586, B1–B2*) of Baron William Hope, an eminent banker.

The question of 'taste' is addressed by '*Passion de bibelots*' (trinkets), a sumptuous array including a porcelain pitcher by Jacob-Petit, clocks, a crystal paper weight, and the Sèvres porcelain 'Egg and Serpent Teapot' in white and gold. The Mathis-Donnefort collection comprises English and French luxury objects in black lacquer and mother-of-pearl, popular in the second half of the century. The Universal Exhibitions produced showpieces of remarkable technical prowess and originality. Award-winning items include a grand *surtout de table* for Napoléon III by Christofle, a dresser by Pierre Manguin, and one of the first vases created by Émile Gallé (1878). The showy and seductive bed of a famous courtesan, Valtesse de La Bigne (1848–1910), immortalised by Zola in his novel *Nana*, is draped in eau de Nil velvet and enclosed by a gilded balustrade.

The Dining Room of 1880 by Eugène Grasset contains heavy, dark and elaborately carved furniture. In contrast is a collection of brightly-coloured pottery and porcelain influenced by Japan, Turkey and the world of Islam between 1867 and 1880 and works by Bracquemond, Moreau-Nélaton, Eugène Rousseau and others.

The last of the 19th-century rooms is dedicated to Nightmares and Symbolism and ideas which found their roots in myths and mythologies, in pieces by Viardot, a model for a fountain by James Tissot, huge grotesque reliefs by Rodin, and an enamel after Gustave Moreau's *Les Voix*.

Art Nouveau (Rooms 43–49, 4th floor)

The Salon 1900 room, conceived by Georges Hoentschell, commissioned for the UCAD Room at the Universal Exhibition, was modified in 1905 for the opening of the museum. It includes the woodwork, table and chairs, original textiles and a painting by Albert Besnard.

Aspects of Art Nouveau are illustrated in a variety of ways. There are masterly pieces (c. 1904–5) from the workshops of the School of Nancy (the glassmaker Gallé or the cabinet-maker Louis Majorelle). Hector Guimard (who was responsible for the Métro entrances) designed furniture for the industrialist Léon Nozal. Stained glass by Grasset is contrasted with pieces by artists closer to the English Arts and Crafts Movement and to Symbolism. Inspiration from the natural world—fauna, but mainly flora interpreted as an applied motif or to give shape to an object—is evident in vases, which were frequently also given an appropriate name, such as *coloquinte* ('wild gourd'; Daum, 1910) or *chauve souris* ('bat').

Art Deco (Rooms 50–53, 3rd floor)

Furniture of around 1910 demonstrates the transition from Art Nouveau to Art Deco. The latter embraced two extremes: a return to tradition and a preference for colour and rich materials, illustrated by the following three period rooms.

The bathroom, bedroom and boudoir (1921–4) of the apartment of Jeanne Lanvin, the couturier, by Armand-Albert Rateau, incorporate a very personal taste in accessories and luxury. The more restrained and sombre Art Deco dining room by Louis Süe and the Compagnie des Arts Français of 1920–1 looks back to the style of Louis-Philippe. Set apart in a special display is the remarkable clock using jade and diamonds by Louis Cartier and Maurice Couët.

The most innovative artists came together in the design for the Pavilion of the French Embassy for the International Exhibition of Decorative Arts in 1925. Pierre Chareau designed the Ambassador's Office with its domed ceiling, accompanied by drapes by Hélène Henry, a rug by Jean Lurçat and sculpture by Lipchitz. The extraordinary waisted, multi-drawered chiffonier in sharkskin, for the bedroom of the Ambassador's wife, is by André Groult.

Modernity and Tradition highlights different trends across the period. The couturier Jacques Doucet, a major collector of contemporary art, commissioned Pierre Legrain, Marcel Coard and Paul Mergier in the 1920s to design furnishings inspired by Cubism and African art to accompany his collection of contemporary paintings. Also here are pieces made in 1916–33 by Émile-Jacques Ruhlmann, and the contents of Robert Mallet-Stevens' studio. The Union des Artistes Modernes in the 1930s, formed by Mallet-Stevens and other leading designers, was responsible for the first Salon of the UAM at the Musée des Arts Décoratifs in 1930. This period produced rigorous designs typical of Le Corbusier and eclectic pieces by Pierre Legrain, but as time went on, the group as a whole took an increasingly Rationalist approach to interiors, especially in the use of tubular steel, which was pioneered by Marcel Breuer at the Dessau Bauhaus in the 1920s, and revolutionised furniture design.

Modern and Contemporary (9th–5th floors)

This section occupies the five upper floors at the western end of the Pavillon de Marsan, a unique section of the building characterised by the use of metal and glass from its rebuilding in 1873. From here there are magnificent views over the Tuileries. Chronologically the exhibits start on the 9th floor, with the 1940s, and end on the 5th floor with the year 2000. Access is by lift on the 4th floor north, near Room 48.

1937–60: The Vitrine of Objects is a tribute to the wealth of the decorative arts of this period. Experimentation with new forms, materials and techniques took place in ceramics, glass, enamels and metalwork. Works exhibited at the 1937 Exhibition show the diverging trends of Modernist artists such as René Herbst, André Hermant and René Coulon, whereas private and public commissions carried out by André Arbus remained more traditional. The influence of Surrealism and the study of dreams is evident in the spectacular table by Gilbert Poillerat, and in elements from the studio of Diego and Alberto Giacometti. The 1950s are dominated by three architect-designers: Jean Prouvé, illustrated by his work for the Cité Universitaire (*see p. 163*); Jean Royère (banana sofa) and Charlotte Perriand (bamboo chaise longue). Other objects serve new technologies, such as the TV and record player.

1960s–'70s: Here the chair reigns supreme, with a display of around 100 examples including artists' designs such as the Niki de Saint Phalle chair.

À Table is a long trestle with tableware and cutlery of the era along its length. A large vitrine contains around 120 examples of ceramics and glass.

1980s–'90s: Fun, funky, outrageous— the avant garde of these years have become the household names of today: Philippe Starck designs are found all over Paris, for example Ma Cocotte at St-Ouen (*see p. 517*); Olivier Gagnère was responsible for the interior of Café Marly (*see p. 241*); and Roger Tallon designed the seating for the TGV. Marc Newson's curvy three-legged 'Pod of Drawers', laminated in riveted aluminium, contrasts with Alessandro Mendini's elaborate Post-Modernist 'Proust chair'. At other extremes are Gaetano Pesce's 'Samson table' and 'Delilah chairs', and 'Collection Pi', by Martin Szekely, in steel and aluminium.

The 2000s: A group of architectonic pieces, some classic, some extreme, address the new concepts. Examples are the Campana brothers' 'Settimio' cupboard (2012) in the form of a bamboo hut (*for interior design by the Campana* brothers, see *Café Campana in the Musée d'Orsay*), Mathieu Lehanneur's post-Thonet tangled hatstand (2009) and Claude Lalanne's 'Crocodile bench' (2010), its top a mesh of woven bronze fronds, with two crocodiles inhabiting the area between the legs.

Thematic galleries

Toy collections: There are over 12,000 objects, rotated twice a year. The oldest pieces are pre-Revolution but the majority date from the mid-19th century onwards, not exclusively French.

Jean Dubuffet Gallery: The evolution of Jean Dubuffet's work can be followed from the 1940s in his large personal collection, donated to the museum in 1967.

Jewellery Gallery: The oldest pieces in this veritable Aladdin's Cave are Merovingian and Byzantine. Medieval jewellery includes a remarkable pendant of the Paschal Lamb (16th century). In the 18th century production boomed with the increased availability of precious stones, and wealthier customers. In the 19th century, sets of jewellery, or parures, became the fashion. The museum also owns the Nissim de Camondo (*see p. 288*) collection of tie-pins. Delicate and elaborate Art Nouveau pieces include several by Lalique. Art Deco jewellery includes examples by Georges Fouquet, Jean Lambert-Rucki and Boucheron. The Modern collection includes work by Line Vautrin, Jean Schlumberger, Alexander Calder, Georges Braque, Jean Lurçat and Henri Laurens.

Other departments

Fashion and textiles: The collection comprises costumes from the 17th century to the present, along with accessories (umbrellas, hats, fans, shoes, handbags and gloves) and samples of textiles (prints, tapestries, laces, embroideries, braids) since the 14th century, and patterns and pattern-books. The 20th-century fashion houses are well represented.

Publicité et Graphisme: In an exhibition space by Jean Nouvel, this Museum of Advertising mounts temporary exhibitions twice a year from its remarkable collection of posters from the 18th century to the present. The museum also has over 20,000 publicity films (French and foreign) from the 1930s to today.

JARDIN DES TUILERIES

Map p. 586, C1. Métro 1 and 7 to Palais Royal-Musée du Louvre or 1 to Tuileries.

The Tuileries Gardens (Jardin des Tuileries), the best known and oldest of all the gardens of Paris, cover over 28 hectares, between Place de la Concorde and the Place du

Carrousel. Originally an integral part of the royal domain, they still retain the basic framework of Le Nôtre's design of 1664. Re-landscaping and re-planting took place during the 20th century, with the aim of restoring the gardens to something of their original character. In the 19th century the gardens inspired many paintings, including Manet's *Concert dans le Jardin des Tuileries* (1862, London) and *Les Tuileries* by Monet (1876, Marmottan, Paris). The gardens contain around 100 statues, 29 of them 20th-century, beneath 2,800 trees. Since 2005 they have been part of the Musée du Louvre.

THE DEVELOPMENT OF THE GARDENS

This site was a clay pit in Gallo-Roman times. Later there were vineyards and fields and then in the 12th century the area beyond the city walls was occupied by tile kilns (*tuileries*). The area was requisitioned by François I in the 16th century for his mother, Louise de Savoie, but it was not until the mid-16th century that the palace and its gardens took shape. The first designer was a Florentine and the Italian garden was embellished at the time of Catherine de Médicis with grottoes made by the ceramicist Bernard Palissy. Completely independent of the Louvre, surrounded by walls, the garden also contained buildings for its staff. Under Henri IV it was used primarily for hunting and riding, and as a meeting place for high society. During the reign of Louis XIV, André Le Nôtre created a formal layout, enlarging the main avenue and creating two large pools and terraces, and it became the first public garden in Paris. From the 17th century concerts, dances and firework displays were held here and the Tuileries remained fashionable until the Palais Royal came into vogue (*see p. 309*). Louis XV introduced sculptures in the 18th century. The gardens were always intended to be viewed from the palace terrace to the east. After the Revolution many celebrations were held here, and statues were transferred from the former royal estates. Major changes in the 19th century were the construction of the Orangerie (1853), Jeu de Paume (1861), and the creation of the Jardin du Carrousel (1871). More sculptures were added in the 20th century.

VISITING THE GARDENS

The Tuileries Gardens have three distinct parts: the formal gardens and Round Pond of the Grand Carré to the east; the Grand Couvert, a wooded central area; and the Octagon to the west.

In 1993, a terrace designed by I.M. Pei was built over the wide lateral avenue (on the axis of Rue des Pyramides), marked by two huge late 17th-century vases from Versailles and two works by Aristide Maillol, donated in 2001 by Dina Vierny (*see p. 135*). Below (east of) the terrace, the yew hedges of the **Jardin du Carrousel** are the setting for Vierny's major donation of 18 Maillol bronzes, including the allegorical *Île de France* and a cast of the monument to Cézanne, commissioned but then rejected by the town of Aix-en-Provence.

The **Grand Carré** was the original Tuileries palace garden designed by Le Nôtre (parts of his designs were respected during the renovation of 1991–6). From 1831 these were the private gardens of Louis-Philippe; later, under Napoléon III, they were given an informal, English-style layout. The flowerbeds are densely populated by statues, mainly 19th-century, and along the central Allée de Diane are urns and 17th-century statues from the Parc de Sceaux (*see p. 463*). Extending along the south, overlooking the Quai des Tuileries and the river, is the Terrasse du Bord-de-l'Eau, from which a footbridge, Passerelle L. Sédar Senghor, crosses to the Quai Anatole-France near the Musée d'Orsay. On the north side of the gardens, the Terrasse des Feuillants, named after a Benedictine monastery, skirts the Rue de Rivoli. To the east was the site of the palace riding-school, where the National Assembly met from 1789 to 1793 and where Louis XVI was condemned to death.

The wide central avenue of the **Grand Couvert**, the wooded area, is flanked by rows of chestnuts and limes and two marble exedrae, which were the only part of Jacques-Louis David's plan of 1799 to be realised. In the Grand Couvert and to the west are sculptures by 20th-century artists, including Roy Lichtenstein, Henri Laurens, Giacometti, Max Ernst and Germaine Richier, alongside casts of works in the Louvre.

The **Octagon** is an open area determined by a large octagonal pond, originally designed by Le Nôtre and the part of the garden least altered since the 17th century, with replicas of 17th–18th-century statuary (originals in the Louvre) by N. and G. Coustou and Corneille van Cleve. To the north is a copy of Coysevox's bust of Le Nôtre (original in St-Roch, *see p. 299*) and a work called *The Crowd* (1968) by Raymond Mason and Jean Dubuffet's *Bel costumé* (1973). To the south are works by Rodin and Henry Moore. Near the Main Gate is La Librairie du Jardin des Tuileries, a comprehensive garden bookshop (*open 10–7*).

MUSÉE DE L'ORANGERIE

Map p. 586, B1. Open Wed–Mon 9–6; closed Tues. T: 01 44 77 80 07 or 01 44 50 43 00, www.musee-orangerie.fr. Audioguides, free audio-visual. Disabled facilities, bookshop and shop.

The Musée de l'Orangerie, built in 1852 for the orange trees of the Tuileries Gardens, was made over to the Musée des Beaux Arts in 1921 and consequently is now under the auspices of the Musée d'Orsay. This popular small gallery, standing above Place de la Concorde, between the Tuileries and the Seine, contains Monet's *Water Lilies* series and the Jean Walter and Paul Guillaume collection of early 20th-century art, featuring work by many of the most famous French painters of the period.

MONET'S *WATER LILIES*

Claude Monet offered his sensational series *Les Nymphéas* (1914–26) to the state in 1918. The eight compositions (a total of 22 panels) were installed in 1927 in two oval rooms specially designed with the approval of the painter. Impressionism was unfashionable at the time and Monet's paintings did not draw in the crowds. But tastes change, and today's appreciative viewers can feel themselves almost transported to the lily ponds of Monet's gardens at Giverny, drenched in colour and reflected light. The first cycle is orientated with the clear blue of *Morning* to the east and the hazy pinks and golds of *Setting Sun* to the west. *Clouds* and *Green Reflections* are self-descriptive.

The view is directly into the water and the mood is calm. From a distance the tones and staining create a shimmering surface, while up close the energetic commas of paint reveal Monet's expertise—and sheer joy—in putting colour on canvas. The second cycle is based on ever deeper and richer blues and greens. The trunks and branches of weeping willows frame the ponds and give spatial depth. The longest continuous panel on the east wall, *Les Deux Saules* (*The Two Willows*), is acutely curved, and standing close to it creates an effect of almost total immersion.

THE WALTER-GUILLAUME COLLECTION

The collection does not set out to be a representative cross-section of art in Paris during the first decades of the 20th century, but reflects the personal taste of one visionary individual, Paul Guillaume (1892–1934). Guillaume had no artistic background, but he had enough instinctive appreciation of talent—and a natural skill in making the right contacts—to become a successful dealer and collector of modern art. He found African masks in a consignment of rubber and exhibited them, attracting the attention of the high priest of Modernism, Guillaume Apollinaire. The painter and writer Max Jacob introduced him to many rising stars in the art world. In 1914, Guillaume opened a gallery and went on to found the review *Les Arts à Paris*. Such was his reputation that Dr Albert C. Barnes, the American patron of the arts who established the Barnes Foundation in Philadelphia, called on him for advice. He died at the age of 42 and his widow, Juliette Lacaze, known as Domenica, married Jean Walter. She sold some 144 works by ten major artists to the state in 1959 and 1963.

The lower ground floor galleries have been specially created for the collection. During excavation, a section of an old wall, the *Enceinte des Fossés jaunes* (c. 1566) was revealed and can be viewed. The first room provides information on Paul Guillaume and there are portrait tributes to him by Modigliani, Van Dongen and Derain. A reconstruction of an interior from Domenica Walter's home includes paintings by Rousseau and Derain, and photographs show the rooms in which Paul Guillaume originally exhibited his collection in the 1930s.

Renoir: From the 1880s, Renoir began to move away from Impressionism and in the 1890s captured the innocence of youth in his studies of girls at the piano. The 1892 study, a major work of the period, was painted in response to a state commission, and he made four more versions. Renoir's delight in fancy dress is revealed in his portrait of his youngest son Claude (b. 1901, known as 'Coco') as *The Clown* (1909). Renoir was by then in poor health but continued to paint for pleasure, returning constantly to the voluptuous and passive female nude.

Cézanne: The 14 superb works by Paul Cézanne include two versions of *Still Life with Apples*, ten years apart. The earlier is a carefully balanced composition, while the tipped perspective of the later results in a more dynamic work. Typically Cézanne returned time and time again to the same subjects—apples, ginger jar, rustic tabletop—in order to explore structure and the relationships of parts to the whole; the same applies to his studies of bathers, family portraits of the long-suffering *Madame Cézanne* (1885), and landscapes around his home town, Aix-en-Provence.

Rousseau, Modigliani and Laurencin: The museum owns the largest group of works in France by Henri 'le Douanier' Rousseau, including *The Wedding* (c. 1908) and *Père Junier's Cart* (1910), a likeness of his neighbour. The static figures, the flat and detailed painting style, strong colours and outlines, were a refreshing contrast to Impressionism but not so far removed from the monumentality of Seurat or the flat colours of the Symbolists. Picasso admired Rousseau's work and gave a dinner in his honour in 1908.

Paul Guillaume was the first and possibly the only real patron of Amedeo Modigliani. The apparent simplicity of Modigliani's style belies a plethora of influences ranging through the Italian masters, Toulouse-Lautrec and Cézanne, to African primitive art. He was a charming but self-destructive character and his paintings frequently evoke both tenderness and isolation. The portrait of Guillaume stands out vividly.

Marie Laurencin, Apollinaire's lover, friend of the Cubists and designer of ballet sets, produced wistful paintings, mainly elegant and evanescent studies of women, which carry a fleeting reference to Orphic Cubism. She painted a portrait of Madame Paul Guillaume.

Picasso and Matisse: Picasso and Matisse, the two great rivals, stand out from the crowd. Picasso's blue and pink periods are represented in a rare large pastel, *L'Étreinte* (1903), and in *Les Adolescents* (1906), which was painted in Spain. *Nude on a Red Background* (1905–6) just pre-dates *Les Demoiselles d'Avignon* (1907) and shows the influence of African masks in the schematisation of the features. The tonally modelled, monumental *Large Bather* (1921) stands out in contrast to the flat planes and colour of *Woman with a Tambourine* (1925).

All the paintings by Matisse are of women in interiors. In the earliest, *The Three Sisters* (1916–17), Matisse is still organising forms with great clarity. Colours are vivid and contours flattened. The decorative interiors with odalisques, painted during the 1920s in Nice, are more atmospheric, evoking the indolence of warm afternoons and introducing Matisse's deep involvement with fabrics and costumes.

Derain, Utrillo and Soutine: The 28 examples of works by André Derain include the elegant *Portrait of Mme Guillaume* (c. 1929). The solemn realism of these works of 1920–30 reveal explicitly the *'rappel à l'ordre'* in art after the First World War, and the reaction against the pre-1914 Abstract and Cubist experiments. *Le Beau Modèle* (1923) and *Nude with Pitcher* (1924–30) are both monumental nudes, but show a marked change in brushwork. There are also reassuring still lifes such as *Nature Morte au panier* (1927), using a limited palette, as well as landscapes.

Less reassuring is the large collection of works by Maurice Utrillo, the alcoholic son of the painter Suzanne Valadon, who lived on La Butte Montmartre. Like Laurencin and Modigliani, he belonged to no particular group or school. His thickly painted and scraped pictures are of scenes often taken from postcards or photographs, and show a technical affinity with the subjects that he painted, such as the desolate, almost monochromatic, urban landscapes of Paris including *L'Église de Clignancourt* and *Berlioz's House* (both 1914).

The disturbing Expressionist paintings of the Lithuanian Chaïm Soutine, on whom Van Gogh was an early influence, are painted in thick impasto.

Distortions, acrid colours, and a very personal and emotional approach brought him instant fame and concomitant self-doubt. He painted raw flesh in abattoirs, and studies of young people who are stylised almost to the point of caricature as, for example, *The Choirboy* (1928).

THE GALERIE DU JEU-DE-PAUME

Map p. 581, E4. Open Tues–Sun 11–7, closed Mon; T: 01 47 03 12 50.
On the north side of the Tuileries gardens, parallel with Rue de Rivoli, is the Jeu-de-Paume, built in 1851. Its name comes from its original use, as a real (royal) tennis-court. The building once contained the Impressionist collections that were transferred to the Musée d'Orsay in 1986. It now hosts exhibitions of modern and contemporary photography and cinema.

ON & AROUND RUE DE RIVOLI

Map pp. 586, C1–581, E4. Métro 1, 8 and 13 to Concorde.

Rue de Rivoli was named in honour of Napoleon's victory over the Austrians in 1797 and runs from Place de la Concorde to St-Paul in the Marais. It was part of a plan to link the Champs-Élysées and Place de la Bastille, and take the load off the older Rue St-Honoré. An unprecedented 20m wide, the first section, dating from 1800, alongside the Tuileries Gardens and the Louvre, is the grandest, with a uniform range of arcaded buildings. The extension of 1848 between the Louvre and Rue de Sévigné is more ordinary. This part is a strange mixture of Parisian elegance and tourist tat, where smart hotels and boutiques jostle with souvenir shops selling models of the Eiffel Tower and T-shirts emblazoned with Parisian motifs, and an equally heteroclite range of restaurants and cafés.

Opposite the Jeu de Paume gallery is the 18th-century **Hôtel de Talleyrand** (*no. 258, at the corner of Rue St-Florentin*), designed by Chalgrin. It was the inspiration for the later American Embassy building (*see p. 277*). The British bookseller W.H. Smith is at no. 248. Further east is the smartest block, with the **Hôtel Meurice** at no. 228. It was here, on 25th August 1944, that General von Choltitz, commander of the German forces in Paris, was captured after he refused orders to destroy the capital's principal buildings. Next door at no. 226 is **Angelina** (*see p. 261*), a smart place for tea or, even better, hot chocolate. **Galignani's Bookshop** (*T: 01 42 60 76 07, www.galignani.com*), established at no. 224 since 1855, stocks English and French books and magazines. It was established by M. Galignani and his English wife, Anne Parsons, who in 1815 published an English newspaper and guides to Paris. Further east at no. 99 is the entrance to the underground shopping precinct, the Carrousel du Louvre (*see p. 184*).

SAINT-GERMAIN-L'AUXERROIS

Map p. 587, D1. 2 Place du Louvre, Rue de l'Amiral de Coligny. Métro 1 to Louvre-Rivoli or 7 to Pont Neuf. Usually open Tues–Sat 9–7, Sun 9.30–8.15. T: 01 42 60 13 96.

Standing opposite the eastern façade of the Louvre, on the site where reputedly Caesar's legions encamped in 52 BC, is the church of St-Germain-l'Auxerrois, a Gothic structure of the 13th–16th centuries (but much altered) that was once the parish church of the Louvre palace.

Dedicated to the 5th-century St Germanus, Bishop of Auxerre, it stands on the site of a Merovingian sanctuary. The present building was begun in the 13th century at the time of Philippe-Auguste and the only remains of the earlier church are the foundations of the belfry south of the choir.

THE ST BARTHOLOMEW'S DAY MASSACRE

On 24th August 1572, the church bell, *la Marie*, signalled the start of the Massacre of St Bartholomew, the wholesale slaughter of Huguenots on the occasion of the marriage of the Protestant Henri de Navarre (the future Henri IV) to the Catholic Marguerite de Valois, sister of Charles IX, during the Wars of Religion. Prominent Huguenots had gathered in Paris for the nuptials and many lost their lives. Among the victims was Admiral Gaspard de Coligny, after whom the street here is named. De Coligny, a prominent Protestant, correspondent of John Calvin and ancestor of the royal houses of Holland and Germany, had already suffered an attack upon his person two days previously. Suspicion fell on the staunchly Catholic Queen Mother, Catherine de Médicis. On St Bartholomew's Eve, Coligny was attacked and done to death by a band headed by the Duc de Guise, *'le Balafré'*, former lover of Marguerite de Valois and leader of the Catholic League.

Reactions to the St Bartholomew's massacre were mixed in Europe. It enjoyed papal approval (Pope Gregory XIII even sent the King of France a golden rose as a token of favour). When Henri IV became king, although he renounced his Protestant faith in order to quell insurrection, he nevertheless issued the Edict of Nantes, securing freedom of religion for Protestants. This was revoked in 1685 by Louis XIV, leading to widespread emigration of French Huguenots.   A.B.

The most striking exterior feature of St-Germain-l'Auxerrois is its wide porch, by Jean Gaussel (1435–9). Drastic alterations were carried out in the 18th century and, after desecration during the Revolution and ransacking in 1831, the church was badly in

SAINT-GERMAIN-L'AUXERROIS
St Mary of Egypt (15th century).

need of restoration when it reopened in 1837. Fragments of the destroyed rood screen, sculpted by Jean Goujon, are preserved in the Louvre. Between 1838 and 1855, under the direction of Jean-Baptiste Lassus, an attempt was made to recreate the Gothic structure. According to Viollet-le-Duc, the next-door Mairie (Town Hall) of the 1st arrondissement, built in 1859, was intended as a caricature of the adjoining church. The conspicuous neo-Gothic north tower was added to the church in 1860.

Many royal artists and architects of the Valois Court were buried here, including Lemercier, Gabriel and Le Vau (all of whom worked on the Louvre) and De Cotte (who worked at Versailles). Among the painters were Coypel, Boucher and Chardin, and the sculptors Coysevox and N. and G. Coustou, all of whose work is represented in the Louvre. By tradition, court jesters were also buried here.

INTERIOR OF ST-GERMAIN-L'AUXERROIS

The interior (78m by 39m) is double-aisled. The alterations of 1745 mingled 18th-century Classicism with the Gothic by converting piers (in the choir) into fluted columns and heightening their capitals, as well as removing some of the stained glass. The organ case, from the Sainte-Chapelle, was designed by Pierre-Noël Roussel and made by Lavergne in 1756. Opposite the main west entrance are two 17th-century white marble holy water stoups. The brass pendant chandeliers are 18th-century.

Lady Chapel: This large chapel contains a 13th-century **statue of St Germanus (1)**, the 5th-century bishop of Auxerre who exhorted St Geneviève to a life of piety. On the wall opposite is a striking 15th-century polychrome sculpture of **St Mary of Egypt (2)**, clad in her own hair. The **altarpiece (3)**, in the form of a Tree of Jesse, houses a 14th-century painted statue of the *Virgin and Child*, of the Champagne School. Above

it is a 19th-century mural painting of the *Coronation of the Virgin* by Lassus.

South side: Above a doorway at the beginning of the ambulatory is the **Vierge à l'Oiseau (4)**, a late 15th-century wooden sculpture of the *Virgin and Child*. On the Virgin's arm sits perched a small bird, towards which the Christ Child holds out a morsel of food. Diagonally opposite, against the

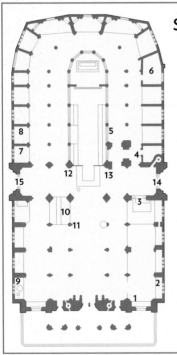

ST-GERMAIN-L'AUXERROIS

1 *St Germanus* (13th century)
2 *St Mary of Egypt*
3 Altarpiece by Lassus
   (with 14th-century *Virgin*)
4 *Vierge à l'Oiseau*
5 16th-century triptych
6 D'Aligre monuments
7 *St Peter Nolasco* by Bourdon
8 *Passion* altarpiece
9 Font
10 Royal pew
11 *Crucified Christ*
12 *St Germanus* (15th century)
13 *St Vincent*
14 *Pentecost* window
15 *God the Father* window

SAINT-GERMAIN-L'AUXERROIS
St Peter Nolasco by Sébastien Bourdon (1665).

wall of the choir, is a remarkable French **triptych** (1530) **(5)**, the central part carved in high relief, the two wings painted, showing scenes from Genesis and the life of the Virgin. In the fourth chapel are marble **monuments to Étienne d'Aligre and his son (6)**, both Chancellors of France (d. 1635 and 1677).

North side: In the first ambulatory chapel, the ante-room to the sacristy, on the right-hand wall, is a fine **painting by Bourdon** (1665) of *St Peter Nolasco taking the Habit* **(7)**. In the next chapel beyond the crossing is an intricately-carved 16th-century Flemish **altarpiece of the Passion (8)**. The scenes in the upper register show the *Way to Calvary*, *Crucifixion* (the Virgin has fainted from grief) and *Descent from the Cross*. The 19th-century **font (9)** was designed by Mme de Lamartine, wife of the poet.

Nave and transepts: The **royal pew** (1682–4) **(10)** is a *tour-de-force* of wood carving designed by Le Brun and executed by François Mercier. The wood is worked to represent a baldachin with draperies above fretworked panels and supported by Ionic columns and pilasters. High up on the pier opposite the pulpit (1635, also by Mercier) is a wooden *Crucified Christ* **(11)** attributed to Bouchardon (18th century). The wrought-iron choir-railings date from 1767. On either side of the choir entrance are a wooden statue of *St Germanus*, seated **(12)**, and a stone figure of *St Vincent* **(13)** (both 15th century).

Only the transepts have their original 15th/16th-century **stained glass**: *Pentecost* **(14)** to the south and *God the Father with Saints, Angels and Doctors of the Church* opposite **(15)**.

NORTH OF ST-GERMAIN-L'AUXERROIS

On Rue St-Honoré is the Mannerist **Temple de l'Oratoire** (1621–30; *map p. 587, D1*), with an 18th-century façade. It was designed by Clément Métezeau the Younger, and Jacques Lemercier and François Mansart also had a hand. Originally the French mother church for the Congregation of the Oratory, it was assigned by Napoleon to the Calvinists in 1811. In front stands a monument of 1889 by Crauk to the Huguenot Admiral Coligny (d. 1572), murdered during the massacre of St Bartholomew's Eve (*see p. 256*), whose residence was nearby.

At the corner of Rue-St-Honoré and Rue de l'Arbre Sec is the **Fontaine du Trahoir**, its stalactites and shells surrounding a nymph sculpted by Boizot. The fountain was rebuilt by Soufflot in 1778, replacing one by Goujon.

Rue-St-Honoré is described on p. 295.

EATING AND DRINKING AROUND THE TUILERIES

€€€€ **Le Meurice**. With its Philippe Starck décor and Alain Ducasse cuisine, this fine-dining establishment in the Hotel Meurice seeks, in its own words, to 'renew the image of haute cuisine'. Menus are short and seasonal. Jackets must be worn. Ties optional (but recommended). *228 Rue de Rivoli. T: 01 44 58 10 55, www.alain-ducasse.com. Map p. 581, E4.*

€€ **Bar Saint-James**. In a smart shopping area, near Pl. de la Concorde/Rue du Fbg St-Honoré. A pleasant and restful oasis with a garden. Brunch Sat and Sun, tea and cocktails. *6 Rue du 29 Juillet (Hotel Saint James Albany, 202 Rue de Rivoli). T: 01 44 58 43 44, www.saint-jamesalbany.com. Map p. 581, F4.*

€–€€ **Le Saut du Loup** ◼. This restaurant has an excellent position. It is accessed from the Carrousel Gardens, which it overlooks, or from the Musée des Arts Décoratifs. The low-key interior is arranged to take full advantage of the garden view, and there is a large terrace for fine weather. It serves brunch and modern, inventive cuisine. Open 10am–2am. *107 Rue de Rivoli. T: 01 42 25 49 55, lesautduloup. fr. Map p. 586, C1.*

€ **Café Diane**. Right in the heart of the the the Tuileries Gardens (same opening hours as the gardens) and offering a range of snacks, a vast seating area and lovely views. *T: 01 42 96 81 12. Map p. 586, C1.*

€ **Le Fumoir**. Opposite the Sully entrance to the Louvre and next to the church of St-Germain-l'Auxerrois, Le Fumoir is a laid-back combination of bar, restaurant and library. The slightly sombre interior helps people take their relaxation seriously. Brunch is served, as well as other meals, and it is ideal for a late-afternoon *café glacé. 6 Rue de l'Amiral Coligny. T: 01 42 92 00 24, www.lefumoir.com. Map p. 587, D1.*

€ **Salon de Thé Angelina**. The charm of the original salon, founded in 1903, remains unchallenged, despite the fact that other Angelinas can be found at smart addresses from the Louvre to Versailles. Angelina's is *de rigueur* for fans of hot chocolate and elegant *pâtisseries. 226 Rue de Rivoli. T: 01 42 60 82 00, www.angelina-paris.fr. Map p. 581, E4.*

Place de La Concorde & the Champs-Élysées

The famous Place de La Concorde is joined to the Étoile and the Arc de Triomphe by the Champs-Élysées, the 'Elysian Fields', the most famous urban avenue in the world.

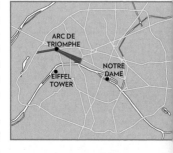

The grandiose Place de La Concorde (*map p. 581, E4; Métro 1, 8 and 12 to Concorde*) is in some respects a discordant urban mêlée—yet even the constantly swirling traffic cannot detract from the superb perspectives it offers, or from the skilful landscaping of this huge open space, which is devoid of buildings on three sides.

In 1757 the empty site to the west of the city limits was chosen to receive a bronze statue of Louis XV, commissioned by the *échevins* (magistrates). The statue, by Bouchardon and Pigalle (model in the Louvre), was unveiled in 1763 and the surrounding square, the creation of Jacques-Ange Gabriel, was named Place Louis XV. In 1770 celebrations with fireworks were held here to mark the marriage of the Dauphin Louis and Marie-Antoinette of Austria, but rejoicing turned to tragedy when 133 onlookers were crushed to death in a ditch. Partly as a reaction to such a disaster, the royal statue was replaced in 1792 by a huge figure of *Liberty*, designed by Lemot. The square was renamed Place de la Révolution. In the same year the perpetrators of the theft of the crown jewels (*see below p. 264*) were executed here by guillotine. On 21st January 1793 the same fate befell Louis XVI, on the site now occupied by the fountain nearest the river. Between May 1793 and May 1795 the blade claimed 1,119 victims.

The square received its present name ('Square of Harmony') in 1795 at the end of the Terror. Though subsequently renamed Place Louis-XV at the Restoration (1815), it reverted to Concorde under Louis-Philippe (1830). Its present appearance dates from 1852, when Jacques-Ignace Hittorff redesigned it. In 1995, the 18 green-bronze and gilded *colonnes rostrales* (rostral columns), made for the July festivities of 1838, were renovated and reinstalled. They resemble the prow of a ship and symbolise, like the city's coat of arms (*see p. 311*), the importance of the river in the history of the Paris.

ARC DE TRIOMPHE
Tricolour vapour trails on Bastille Day.

MONUMENTS AND BUILDINGS ON PLACE DE LA CONCORDE

In the centre, on the site of first Louis XV's statue and then *Liberty*, rises the **Obelisk of Luxor**, a monolith of pink syenite almost 23m high. It originally stood before a temple at Thebes in Upper Egypt and commemorates in its hieroglyphs the deeds of Ramesses II (13th century BC). It was presented to Louis-Philippe in 1831 by Mohammed Ali (the donor of 'Cleopatra's Needle' to London). The pedestal, of Breton granite, bears representations of the apparatus used in its erection in 1836. The two **fountains**, by Hittorff, are copies of those in the piazza of St Peter's in Rome, embellished with figures symbolising inland and marine navigation.

On the north side of the square are two handsome **colonnaded mansions** designed by Gabriel in 1763–72, originally intended as official residences and with pediment sculptures by M.-A. Slodtz and G. Coustou the Younger. The one on the right is the Naval Ministry, previously the Garde-Meuble de la Couronne, or royal furniture store. Public visits were allowed to view the furniture, which the royal family changed according to the season. The crown jewels were stolen from here in 1972. The left-hand building has long been shared between the Automobile Club and the prestigious Hôtel Crillon, being renovated at the time of writing. Between these buildings, Rue Royale leads to the church of the Madeleine (*see p. 281*). The Palais-Bourbon (National Assembly) can be seen to the south across the Seine.

THE CROWN JEWELS OF FRANCE

For a thousand years the monarchs of France were crowned in a symbolic Christian ceremony with a diadem and regalia symbolising divine kingship and the right to rule. The Crown Jewels of the *Ancien Régime* contained some of the most fabled—and valuable—gems in the world: the Regent and Sancy diamonds and the Royal French Blue. During the chaos of the Revolution, in 1792, the jewels were stolen from the Royal Wardrobe in a famous heist. Executions took place in September, but just of hired hands; the ringleaders were never identified or brought to justice. Two thirds of the jewels subsequently resurfaced but the vagaries of repeated revolutions and restorations have played havoc with the integrity of the collection. Most of it was finally sold in 1887. Today the French government buys back items when it can, when they appear at auction. The reassembled jewels, including the Regent and the Sancy diamonds, are in the Louvre. The Ruspoli sapphire and the St Louis emerald are in the treasury of the Minéralogie collection at the Jardin des Plantes. The Royal French Blue, re-cut and now known as the Hope diamond, is in the Smithsonian.   A.B.

Pont de la Concorde, on the south side of the square, with magnificent views up and down river, was built in 1788–90 and widened in 1932. Stone from the Bastille was used in the construction of the upper part, so that Parisians could feel they were treading upon the relics of tyranny.

Eight 18th-century **stone pavilions** around the square, by Gabriel, support statues (restored in 1989) by Caillonette, Cortot and Pradier personifying the eight provincial capitals. Strasbourg (capital of Alsace, ceded to Germany in 1871) was hung with crêpe and wreaths until 1918.

The pillars of the gateway opening from Place de la Concorde to the Tuileries gardens are crowned by replicas of **equestrian statues** of *Fame* and *Mercury*, by Coysevox (brought from Marly in 1719). Balancing these equestrian groups, on the west of Place de la Concorde, the dramatic sweep of the Avenue des Champs-Élysées towards the Arc de Triomphe is framed by replicas of the ***Horses of Marly*** (originals in the Louvre), two groups by G. Coustou which were brought from the Château de Marly in 1794.

THE CHAMPS-ÉLYSÉES

Map p. 581, D4. Métro 1, 8 and 12 to Concorde or 1 and 13 to Concorde-Clemenceau.

The Champs-Élysées, famously sung by Joe Dassin ('Aux Champs-Élysées, aux Champs-Élysées...'), gently ascends northwest of Place de la Concorde for nearly 2km to the striking silhouette of the Arc de Triomphe. Parisians and visitors alike still flock here, although time has taken its toll on the 'Elysian Fields' and their former elegance is a little faded. Three hundred new trees have been planted, however, and when lit up at night, especially at Christmas, the old magic returns.

HISTORY OF THE CHAMPS ÉLYSÉES

At the beginning of the 17th century, this low-lying area was still marshland, but after a decree issued in 1667 to create a promenade on the same axis as the Tuileries gardens, it was drained and in 1670 laid out to designs by Le Nôtre. The name was changed from Grand-Cours to Champs-Élysées early in the 18th century. The Marquis de Marigny, brother of Madame de Pompadour, had the avenue replanted in 1765 and it was extended to the Pont de Neuilly in 1774. It was used from 1814–16 as a military encampment for allied troops and the gardens consequently suffered. When the area became fashionable during the Second Empire, however, they were re-landscaped in the less formal English style (in 1858) and have remained virtually unchanged since then. This processional avenue has seen many parades, celebrations and historic moments. Today it hosts the military parade on Bastille Day, New Year's Eve celebrations, and the grand finale of the Tour de France.

The Champs-Élysées has two distinct parts. The shorter section, from Place de la Concorde to the Rond-Point des Champs-Élysées, has museums (notably the Musée du Petit Palais) and theatres dotted among the gardens, where there are also several restaurants. At no. 25 is the former Hôtel de la Païva (1866), in florid neo-Renaissance style, built for the celebrated courtesan the Marquise de Païva, where artists and writers were entertained. It is now home to the Travellers' Club.

The more commercialised section of the avenue, between the Rond-Point and the Arc de Triomphe, is flanked by offices and showrooms, cinemas and banks, miscellaneous restaurants and fast-food outlets.

MUSÉE DU PETIT PALAIS

Map p. 581, D4. Métro 1 and 13 to Champs Élysées-Clemenceau. Entrance on Av. Winston Churchill. Open Tues–Sun 10–6; during temporary exhibitions 10–8. Closed Mon and holidays. Permanent collections free. Audioguides. Disabled access. Garden café-restaurant and shop. T: 01 53 43 40 00, www.petitpalais.paris.fr.

The Musée du Petit Palais is the fine arts museum of the City of Paris housed in an elegant municipal palace of 1900. Its trapezoid shape encloses a garden courtyard. The permanent collections are of a rare diversity, ranging from antiquity to the 20th century and are rich in 19th-century works.

HISTORY OF THE PETIT PALAIS

The Musée des Beaux-Arts de la Ville de Paris opened its doors in 1902, in a fine building echoing Les Invalides designed for the Universal Exhibition of 1900 by Charles Girault. It is a prime example of a building of the period, whose grandiose Neoclassical public face is a veneer disguising the thoroughly 'modern' aspects of the interior spaces, achieved by the use of materials such as cast iron, concrete and quantities of glass. The entrance hall and main galleries are palatial. Among the stone, stucco, mosaic and paint are two statues in gilded zinc, *Renommées* and *Enfants musiciens*; by the time Albert Besnard was working on the painted decoration of the entrance hall (1903–10), Cubism had arrived. Renovations in 2001–5 returned the museum to its original aspect, re-establishing the interplay between interior and exterior space and re-introducing natural light.

The origins of the collections are responsible for the peculiar diversity of the exhibits. In 1870 the City of Paris began to purchase and commission work in the Salons or directly from artists, and also acquired the contents of workshops. At the same time the museum was enriched by donations of personal collections, some more or less contemporary whereas others introduced new themes and periods. The four major bequests were Dutuit, Tuck, Ocampo and Marie, plus a collection of icons from Roger Cabal in 1998. The result is an interesting cross-section of French fine and decorative arts, from Rococo to Impressionism. Highlights are given below, though the display is rotated, so not all the works mentioned here will be on show at any given time.

Level 1

Paris 1900, Room 1: Superb examples of the **decorative arts** are displayed in the gallery facing Rue F. Roosevelt and the Grand Palais. An emphasis on hand-crafted objects illustrates the reaction against mass-production encouraged by the Universal Exhibitions. Leading artists and craftsmen include Émile Gallé, the Art Nouveau glassmaker from Nancy, who is represented by vases including *Vase Paphiopedilum* (1897), using a complicated procedure of glass

PETIT PALAIS

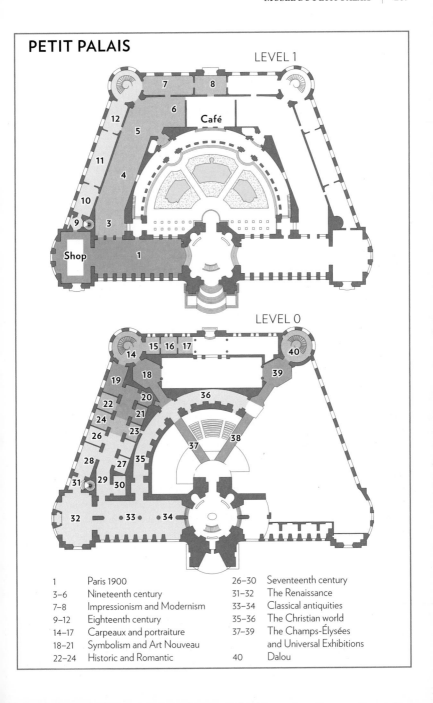

LEVEL 1

LEVEL 0

1	Paris 1900	26–30	Seventeenth century
3–6	Nineteenth century	31–32	The Renaissance
7–8	Impressionism and Modernism	33–34	Classical antiquities
9–12	Eighteenth century	35–36	The Christian world
14–17	Carpeaux and portraiture	37–39	The Champs-Élysées
18–21	Symbolism and Art Nouveau		and Universal Exhibitions
22–24	Historic and Romantic	40	Dalou

marquetry. Armand Point's small coffer borne by peacocks (1899), inspired by medieval enamels, is typical of the eclectic taste of the period. Georges Clairin's studiously nonchalant portrait of Sarah Bernhardt (1876) is echoed by Maillol's study for *La Méditerranée* (*see p. 136*).

The 19th century, Rooms 3–6: The finely executed **Naturalist or Realist works** by Alfred Roll and Fernand Pelez reflect different aspects of Parisian life at the turn of the century, the visual arts' equivalent of Zola's literary portrayals: the Belle Époque for some, but misery for many others. Roll's splendid *Portrait of Alphand* (1888) is the study of a man who contributed to the transformation of Paris in the 19th century, in his 'workplace'; the elegant *Mme Edgar Stern* (1889) by Carolus-Duran contrasts with E-F. Chatrousse's sculpture of a *Jeune Parisienne* (1876), typifying a young working girl.

The Petit Palais owns two glorious Realist works by **Courbet**, donated by his sister Juliette, which demonstrate the painter's skills of observation as well as being influenced possibly by photography and certainly by 18th-century engravings. *Girls on the Banks of the Seine* (1857) presents fully-dressed city girls enjoying a day out and is open to a variety of interpretations. Even more flagrantly sensual is *Sleep* (1866), a celebration of naked female bodies intertwined. It was painted as a commission for the Turkish diplomat and owner of Ingres' *Bain turc* (*see p. 191*). Courbet was greatly admired a generation later by the Impressionists.

Revolutionary themes were popular in their day. Later many artists made their living from commissions from the Third Republic (from 1870), for public works of a celebratory nature confirming the glory of France.

The Vale of Tears by **Gustave Doré** introduces a naturalist approach to the **revival of Christian art**. *The First Funeral* (1883), a sculpture group by Louis-Ernest Barrias, indicates the growing interest in pre-history (the Archaeological Museum in St-Germain-en-Laye opened in 1867).

18th century, Rooms 9–12: Four rooms overlooking the Champs-Élysées contain the Édouard and Julia Tuck donation of 18th-century **decorative arts and paintings**. Remarkable exhibits include a beautiful sedan chair (c. 1700) and French Regency *rocaille* furniture characterised by the use of exotic wood veneers, intricate marquetry and lacquer, decorated with the arabesque or *grotesque* design. Objects in Room 12 typify the period of transition between Louis XV and Louis XVI styles (c. 1760–5), when the curve or volute was modified in favour of a more rectilinear form. Beauvais tapestries include Rococo and *chinoiserie* designs. An elaborate clock with a metal and porcelain case and pipes, *The Orchestra of Monkeys*, comes from Germany. There are also examples of strongly-coloured porcelain pieces from the Sèvres manufactory.

Impressionism and Modernism, Rooms 7–8: The fashion for painting *en plein air* which gave rise to Monet's landscapes could not have happened without practical advances. The technique was pioneered by the Barbizon school of painters, and the **portable painting equipment** on display (folding stool, sunshade, etc.) is a reminder

PETIT PALAIS
Vase (1898) by Émile Gallé.

of how crucial these innovations were. **Impressionist works** here include *Sunset at Lavacourt* (1880), painted by **Monet** at the moment when the river ice was melting. Others who contributed to this revolution include Boudin, Félix Ziem, Jongkind, Sisley and the father of them all, **Pissarro**. Work in the round is represented by **Rodin**, who revolutionised the art of sculpture, freeing it from its Neoclassical, Historicist and Romantic bonds. Works here include a bronze torso (c. 1887) and the marble *Amour et Psyché* (c. 1885).

Three portraits of the influential art dealer Ambroise Vollard include a strong, static pose by Cézanne (1899). Renoir (also c. 1899) depicted him wearing a red scarf around his head; Bonnard painted a busier version in 1924, with a kitten on the dealer's lap.

Cézanne's influence on the future of painting is illustrated by his *Three Bathers* (c. 1880), which Matisse purchased from Vollard in 1899 and kept for 36 years until he and his wife donated it to the Petit Palais, when he wrote: '*it has provided me with moral support in critical moments in my adventure as an artist; I have drawn from it my faith and my perseverance...*' This almost-square composition, one example of many *Bathers* painted by Cézanne, has a concentrated vitality, the paint handling is rapid and dense, and the figures—neither monumental nor especially lyrical—appear self-absorbed, enveloped by the landscape.

Baudelaire was the first to speak of 'modernity', particularly praising the work of Manet and signalling a confidence in the future and a break with 'official art'. Maillol's *La Vague* (c. 1891) shows the influence of Gauguin. There is also a bronze by Bourdelle (*Pénélope*; 1909).

Level 0

Carpeaux and portraiture, Rooms 14–17: From northern France, Jean-Baptiste Carpeaux, leading sculptor of his day, pre-empted Rodin in the use of dramatic light and shade in sculpture and came to prominence with his *Ugolin* (plaster, 1861). Classical and Romantic portraits include Carpeaux's composed portrait bust of Mademoiselle Fiocre (c. 1870) but several of his major public commissions led to controversy and at the end of his career he was racked by increasing persecution mania.

Corot's *Roman Odalisque* (1843) is a beautifully balanced sensual nude study. Manet's full-length 'realist' portrait of the dandified Cognac merchant Théodore Duret is a masterpiece in which the artist typically includes an impeccable still life. Intimate portrait studies include Boilly's charming *Portrait of Mlle. Athénaïs d'Albenas* (1807).

Symbolism, Art Nouveau, decorative murals, Rooms 18–21: The qualities of Symbolism, the antidote to Realism or Naturalism, began to permeate all the arts of this period. Illustrating the range of **Symbolist painting**, of which Gustave Moreau was a precursor, are Bartholomé's *Femme fatale*, landscapes by Ménard and Brokman, experimental works by Henry Cros and Paul Grandhomme, and pastels by Odilon Redon. Cabinet-maker F.-R. Carabin took up the Symbolist gauntlet in his display cabinet of 1895, where the decorative figures represent different materials. Self-taught sculptor, modeller and potter Jean Carriès' bizarre creations included experiments with different materials.

The sinuous lines of Art Nouveau feature in the **dining room designed by Hector Guimard** for his home, and in the superb **jewellery by Georges Fouquet** (whose shop can be seen reconstructed in the Musée Carnavalet). Guimard's designs were initially for private clients but in 1900 he was invited to design the entrances to Métro stations, many of which still (at least partially) exist. Like Lalique, the jeweller Fouquet preferred to use semi-precious stones, on the basis of their colours and shapes.

A young group of artists, **the Nabis** (*see p. 494*), appealing for the combination of beauty and utility, is represented by the four decorative panels commissioned from Édouard Vuillard for a room in a private home c. 1900.

Historic, Romantic and Troubador styles, Rooms 22–24: During the 19th century there was a reawakening of a national historic conscience encouraged by the Third Republic, the historian Michelet, and literary works by Chateaubriand and Dumas. This mood permeates such starkly contrasting works as Cormon's studies for the Natural History Museum and *Departure of the Prodigal Son* (1863), an uncharacteristic work by James Tissot, better known for bourgeois scenes and beautiful women. Romantic nostalgia is evinced in the flourishes and loose paint handling of Delacroix's *Combat du Giaour et du Pacha* (1835), which contrasts vividly with the curiously controlled but richly-coloured 'Troubadour'-style painting by Ingres of an imaginary scene, *François I at the Death of Leonardo da Vinci* (1818): the attendant figures verge on caricature.

17th century, Rooms 26–30: Among work from the Dutuit collection, many major names of the golden age of **Dutch painting** are represented in a variety of characteristic styles: portraits, genre scenes and landscapes. They include works by Jan Steen, Hobbema and Willem van de Velde. Rembrandt's *Self-portrait in Oriental Costume*, with a dog at his feet, is outstanding. French painters include **Poussin** and **Claude Lorrain** (the octagonal *Landscape with the Port of Santa Marinella*) and there is a warm-toned still life by Nicolas de Largillière, *Red Partridge in a Niche*. History painting is represented by **Rubens**' preparatory work for *The Rape of Proserpine*, a remarkable evocation of speed and movement.

The Renaissance, Rooms 31–32: Among the precious objects in this collection is an impressively complex table clock (c. 1550, Marseilles) in the shape of a square tower, with chimes and an astrolabe. The museum owns three of only some 70 pieces known to exist of St-Porchaire or Henri-II ceramics: a heavily decorated candlestick and two elegant ewers. Made from a fine white clay, they were too fragile to be of any practical use. There are also examples of enamelled ceramics with relief decoration by Bernard Palissy.

Artworks include painting, sculpture, furniture, books and precious bindings from the 15th century to the start of the 17th century, divided into two geographic groups: France and Northern Europe; Italy and the Islamic world. There is a tender painting of the *Virgin and Child* by Cima da Conegliano. There are also examples of Limoges enamels and Italian majolica, as well as Venetian glass.

Classical antiquities, Room 33–34 The Dutuit collection has objects from the Greek and Roman worlds. An exceptional Greek white-ground vase with painted and high relief decoration is attributed to Psiax (c. 525 BC). There are some superb Attic rhyta (5th century BC), made in Athens by Sotades and his workshop, in the shape of various animal heads, and one depicting an Ethiopian attacked by a crocodile. The calyx krater with *Heracles in the Garden of the Hesperides* (c. 360 BC) is a rare, technically perfect piece. The beautiful silver *Esquiline Patera* (c. 380) found on the Esquiline Hill in Rome in 1793, depicts Venus at her toilet in the shell-like bowl, with a young hunter on the handle. Among works in bronze are the *Ephèbe des Fins d'Annecy* (c. 30 BC), in the manner of Polyclitus, and three portrait heads.

The Christian World, Rooms 35–36: The collection from the world of Western Christendom includes exquisite ivories, champlevé and Limoges enamels and a lovely *Nativity* (*Adoration of the Child*) by the Netherlandish Maître de St-Barthélemy (c. 1480).

PETIT PALAIS
Attic rhyton in the form of a dog by Sotades (5th century BC).

Petit Palais has the finest collection of **icons** in a French public institution, thanks to a bequest from Roger Cabal (1929–97). The museum owns 76 in total, both Greek and Russian, mainly in tempera on wood. These form the collection entitled The Eastern Christian World.

The selection on display shows a marked contrast of styles. The Greek icons date from the fall of the Byzantine Empire in 1453. The Cretan *Nativity* (c. 1480–1500) combines two styles of painting, Italian and Byzantine, in a diagonally-based composition. Unusual for an icon is the landscape setting and use of perspective; it is perhaps the work of two artists. The icon of *St Martin* (c. 1500) is thought to be from a Creto-Venetian workshop because of the subject and the Latin inscription. Also Cretan is the 17th-century *Lamentation over the Dead Christ*, painted in a more traditional, naïve style.

Russian examples include *St George* (School of Novgorod, 16th century) with a series of scenes from the life of the saint. The *Archangel Michael* and *Archangel Gabriel*, in the style of northern Russia (second half of the 17th century), were probably part of an iconostasis. Also from Russia (late 18th century) is a depiction of events from the book of Genesis, painted in monochrome. In contrast is the colourful and detailed *All of Creation Rejoices in Thee*, signed by Franghia Kavertsas (Crete, first half of the 17th century), an icon type based on a hymn to the Virgin written by St John Damascene.

Rooms 37–39: The display here traces the history of the Champs-Élysées, the Petit Palais and the Paris Universal

Exhibitions which were so important in promoting industrial and artistic innovations in the 19th century.

Room 40: The contents of Jules Dalou's studio were sold to the City of Paris and have been in the Salle Dalou since 1905. The Petit Palais also owns Dalou's plaster model for *Le Triomphe de la République* (1879), the sculpture group commissioned in bronze for Place de la Nation (*see p. 388*). Dalou, a pupil of Carpeaux, was the son of a very humble background who retained staunch working-class sympathies all his life.

The Petit Palais owns some 12,000 works on paper, from the 5th–18th centuries, including drawings, engravings and niellos which, being fragile, are kept in storage. They are available to researchers by appointment.

GRAND PALAIS & ENVIRONS

Map p. 581, D4. Métro 1 and 13 to Champs-Élysées Clemenceau. Open during events (Thur–Mon 10–8, Wed 10–10; closed Tues). Bookshop and two cafeterias open during exhibitions. Visitor entrances for Nave and Southeast Gallery on Av. Winston Churchill; for the National Galleries and the Salon d'Honneur, on Pl. Clemenceau/Sq. Jean Perrin/ Av. du Gen. Eisenhower. T: 01 44 13 17 17, www.grandpalais.fr.

The Grand Palais was built for the Universal Exhibition of 1900, under the supervision of Charles Girault. Like the Petit Palais opposite, iron and glass was used in the construction and the façade is a grand affair surmounted by a lofty portico. It has a long history of hosting major exhibitions in its impressive interior spaces. The Galeries Nationales are used for major exhibitions. In 2012 the Salon d'Honneur reopened for performances by the Comédie Française. In the western section is the Palais de la Découverte (*see p. 522*). The Grand Palais has also become known for its Christmas special events. For the winter of 2014–15, for example, it was transformed into an ice palace, Le Grand Palais des Glaces, with the installation of the largest ice rink in France under the glass nave.

AROUND THE GRAND PALAIS

On Avenue Franklin Roosevelt is the **Théâtre du Rond-Point** (*map p. 580, C4*) by Davioud (1860), which presents about 30 productions a year of works by living writers.

North from Place Clemenceau, Avenue De Marigny runs past the **Théâtre Marigny** (1883) by Garnier. On Avenue Gabriel is an open-air stamp market (*Thur, Sat, Sun and holidays from 10am*). South from Place Clemenceau, Avenue Winston-Churchill leads between the Grand and Petit Palais to the most eye-catching bridge on the Seine, **Pont Alexandre III** (1896–1900), a single elegant steel arch, 107.5m long, abundantly decorated with triple lamps and sculptures. It was named after the Tsar of Russia who laid the first stone at a moment of *entente cordiale* between the two countries. The avenue and bridge create a grand vista over the river to the dome of Les Invalides. In the gardens near Pont Alexandre III is a statue of Simon Bolivar on horseback by Frémiet.

COURS DE LA REINE TO PLACE DE L'ALMA

The Cours de la Reine (*map p. 581, D4*) and its extension, Cours Albert-1er, lead westwards along the river from Place de la Concorde to Place de l'Alma. This was the route laid out in 1616 along the old road to the villages of Chaillot, St-Cloud and Versailles and the Roman canal bringing water from Chaillot. The parallel Port de la Conférence, flanking the river, takes its name from the Conference Gate (demolished in 1730), the entry point of the Spanish ambassadors in 1660 who discussed with Mazarin the proposed marriage between Louis XIV and Maríe-Thérèse. The wedding took place in June of the same year.

Pont des Invalides dates originally from 1827–9 but was rebuilt in 1879–80 and enlarged in 1956. The statue of a zouave (an Algerian soldier belonging to the French light infantry corps) on **Pont de l'Alma** (1974) comes from the original bridge and was once used as a gauge in estimating the height of the Seine in flood. The bridge and the Place de l'Alma at its north end are named after the Battle of the Alma, a victory for France and her allies over Russia at the outset of the Crimean War (1854). On the west side of Place de l'Alma, the **Flame of Liberty**, presented to Paris by the *International Herald Tribune* in 1987, was fly-posted with memorials following Princess Diana's fatal car crash in the nearby underpass in 1997.

The **Théâtre des Champs-Élysées** (*13 Av. Montaigne; map p. 580, C4*) was a pioneering structure (1911–13) by Auguste Perret and decorated by several artists including Bourdelle, who designed the reliefs. In the early days it scintillated with performances by the Ballets Russes as well as the first rendition of Stravinsky's *Rite of Spring*.

On the west side of Avenue George-V, leading northwards, is the **American Cathedral of the Holy Trinity** (1885–8; *map p. 580, B4, www.americancathedral. org*), a neo-Gothic edifice by the English architect G.E. Street.

THE ARC DE TRIOMPHE & ÉTOILE

Map p. 580, B3. Métro 1, 2 and 6 or RER A to Charles de Gaulle-Étoile. Open April–Sept 10am–11pm, Oct–March 10am–10.30pm, and after ceremonies on 8 May, 14 July, 11 Nov. The easiest access is via the tunnel from the Champs-Élysées. T: 01 55 37 73 77, arc-de-triomphe.monuments-nationaux.fr.

Twelve avenues radiate in a star shape from Place Charles-de-Gaulle (formerly Place de l'Étoile and still commonly known as such), around which traffic roars at an alarming rate. In the midst of this broiling chaos stands the serene and grandiose Arc de Triomphe, the largest triumphal arch in the world (almost 50m high and 45m wide), erected to the glory of the French army and a monument to Napoleon's megalomania.

HISTORY OF THE ARC DE TRIOMPHE

Napoleon's desire to raise a triumphal arch to the Imperial armies began to take shape in 1806 after their victory at Austerlitz. Designed by Chalgrin, the arch was completed only in 1836. At the time of the Emperor's marriage to Marie-Louise of Austria (1810), it was necessary to build a mock arch for the wedding procession. Still unfinished by the time of the fall of the Empire in 1814, it was not until 1823, when Louis XVIII dedicated it to his armies returning victorious from Spain, that work began again under Huyot. The project was finally brought to a close at the time of Louis-Philippe when Blouet took over in 1832. He remained faithful to Chalgrin's ideas and supervised the decoration, which was carried out by several of the best sculptors of the day. On an intensely cold day in 1840 the funeral cortège bearing Napoleon's ashes to the Invalides passed under the Arch.

The Place de l'Étoile was designed by Haussmann after the Arch was built. The uniform façades between each avenue are by Hittorff (1854–7). These have no access from the circus but are reached from the encircling rues de Tilsitt (north) and de Presbourg (south).

THE ARCH AND ITS SCULPTURE

The arch contains a museum of the history of the monument, but the greatest attraction is the **observation platform** at the top. From here, until late into the evening, there are spectacular views down to the star pattern of the street below, along the great vista of the Champs-Élysées or towards the huge Grande Arche de La Défense.

The **sculptures** at ground level, especially the colossal groups in high relief on the main façades, are impressive. Facing the Champs-Élysées are (on the right) the *Departure of the Army in 1792* (*La Marseillaise*) by Rude, undoubtedly the most dynamic composition of the four, and (on the left) the *Triumph of Napoleon in 1810*, by Cortot. Facing the Avenue de la Grande-Armée are (right) the *Resistance of the French in 1814*, and (left) the *Peace of 1815*, both by Etex. The four spandrels of the main archway contain figures of *Fame* by Pradier, and those of the smaller archways have sculptures of *Infantry* and *Cavalry* by Achille Valois (south side) and Théophile Bra. Above the groups are relief panels of the campaigns of 1792–1805 including (north) the Battle of Austerlitz. On the row of shields in the attic storey are inscribed the names of battles of the Republic and the Empire, although not all were French victories. Below the side arches are the names of some hundreds of generals who took part in these campaigns, with the names of those killed in action underlined.

Beneath the arch is the **Tomb of the Unknown Soldier**, victim of the 1914–18 War. The flame has burnt constantly since 11th November 1923. At its foot is a **bronze plaque representing the shoulder-flash of SHAEF** (Supreme Headquarters Allied Expeditionary Force), dated 25th August 1944, the day of the Liberation of Paris.

ALONG AVENUE FOCH

From the Étoile two avenues lead directly to the Bois de Boulogne: **Avenue Victor-Hugo** (where in 1885 Victor Hugo died in a house on the site of no. 124) leads to Porte de la Muette. The majestic **Avenue Foch**, the widest avenue in Paris, created by

ARC DE TRIOMPHE
The Departure of the Army in 1792 (*La Marseillaise*), by François Rude.

Napoléon III and Haussmann, ends at Porte Dauphine. Since its inception in 1855 it has had a succession of names, taking the name of Foch following the death of the illustrious general in 1929. At no. 59 is The Musée d'Ennery collection of Far Eastern art (*see p. 519*). No. 80 was the home of Claude Debussy. Southwest of the park entrance is a huge building (1955–9) constructed for NATO but now housing university faculties.

At Porte Dauphine there is a canopied Art Nouveau **Métro station entrance** of 1900 by Hector Guimard, the only complete example to survive *in situ* (the other complete one, at Abbesses in Montmartre, is not original to the site). Nearby (between nos. 17 and 22) is a monument by Dalou to Jean-Charles Alphand, who laid out Avenue Foch, the Bois and many other parks in Paris.

South of Avenue Foch, on Rue Paul Valéry, is the **Musée Dapper**, a collection of the arts of Africa (*see p. 519*).

ON & AROUND RUE DU FAUBOURG ST-HONORE

Map pp. 581, E4–580, B3. Métro 1, 8 and 12 to Concorde.

Rue du Faubourg St-Honoré runs from Rue Royale (*see p. 281*) to Place des Ternes, parallel with the Champs-Élysées. It follows the course of the medieval road from Paris to the village of Roule and became fashionable at the end of Louis XIV's reign. In the 18th century its grand mansions rivalled the prestige of Faubourg St-Germain. Today this is a chic and expensive district, home to the Élysée Palace (residence of President of the Republic) and the British and US embassies. Liberally graced with smart hotels and restaurants, the section up to and around Avenue Montaigne is lined with fashion houses, designer boutiques and jewellers.

The **American Embassy** is at no. 2 Avenue Gabriel, south of Rue du Faubourg St-Honoré, and Rue Boissy d'Anglas runs alongside, past the shopping arcade, the Galerie Royale.

At no. 35 Rue du Faubourg St-Honoré is the **British Embassy**. The building goes back to 1722, when it was built for the Fourth Duc de Charost. During the tenancy of the Comte de la Marck from 1785, much of its interior decoration was completed and the English-style garden laid out. It was bought in 1803 by Pauline Bonaparte (later Princess Borghese), much of whose furniture remains. She sold the house to the Duke of Wellington for £32,000, complete with numerous clocks, chandeliers, candelabras and chimneypieces and it became the Embassy in 1815. In the chapel, the (ultimately unhappy) marriage of Berlioz and Harriet Smithson took place in 1833, with Liszt as best man, and the (also troubled) union of Thackeray and Isabella Shawe in 1836. On either side of the British Embassy are the exclusive **Cercle Interallié** (1714), at no. 33 (the Russian Embassy during the Second Empire) and the **Hôtel Pontalba** (no. 41), designed by Louis Visconti. The Anglican church of **St Michael** (*stmichaelsparis.org*) is in Rue d'Aguessau, opposite the Embassy.

PALAIS DE L'ÉLYSÉE

The **Palais de l'Élysée** (*map p. 581, D4; no admission*), since 1873 the official residence of the President of the French Republic, stands at the corner of Avenue de Marigny. This heavily-guarded mansion was built for the Comte d'Évreux in 1718 and later became the Paris residence of Madame de Pompadour, who commissioned the architect Jean Cailleteau, known as Lassurance the Younger, to make alterations. It was also occupied by Joachim Murat, brother-in-law of Napoleon, who signed his second abdication here in 1815, and by Wellington. Napoléon III lived here as President from 1848 until he moved, as Emperor, to the Tuileries in 1852. It then reverted to its use as a residence for visiting heads of state, including Queen Victoria in 1855 and Elizabeth II in 1957.

Opposite the Élysée Palace, behind a gilded wrought iron gate flanking Place Beauvau, is the **Ministère de l'Intérieur** (Home Office), built in 1769–84. There is a plaque on no. 11 Rue des Saussaies in memory of victims of the Gestapo, which had its headquarters here during 1940–4.

WESTERN RUE DU FAUBOURG ST-HONORÉ

West of the Élysée Palace, beyond Avenue Matignon, stands the church of **St-Philippe-du-Roule** (*map p. 580, C3; opening times vary, see www.stphilippeduroule.org*), built in 1774–84 by Chalgrin on the site of the parish church of Roule and added to in the 19th century. The sculpture *Religion* on the pediment is by Duret and the basilica-style interior contains Chassériau's ceiling painting *Descent from the Cross*.

An old-established concert hall, **Salle Gaveau** (*www.sallegaveau.com*), built in 1906–7 by a piano manufacturer, is at 45 Rue La Boétie.

Honoré de Balzac died in 1850 in a house where 12 Rue Balzac now stands; there is a statue of him at the intersection with Avenue de Friedland (*map p. 580, B3*).

Another concert venue, the Art Deco **Salle Pleyel** (*252 Rue du Fbg. St-Honoré, www.sallepleyel.fr*), was built in 1927 by Camille, son of Ignace Pleyel, friend of Haydn, who manufactured pianos from 1807. The building offers a very high standard of acoustics and comfort.

Round the corner in Rue Daru is the neo-Byzantine **Russian Orthodox Cathedral of St-Alexander-Nevsky** (1859–61; *map p. 580, B2, open for visits Tues, Fri, Sun 3–5pm*). It has five gilded domes and an elaborate interior with frescoes and icons. At no. 19 Rue Daru is a traditional Russian restaurant, Le Daru (*see opposite*).

EATING AND DRINKING AROUND THE CHAMPS ÉLYSÉES

Places to eat in the museums include the **Garden Café of the Petit Palais** for light meals and snacks and € **Le Mini-Palais** in the Grand Palais (*3 Av. Winston Churchill, T: 01 42 56 42 42, www.minipalais.com; map p. 581, D4*). It serves fresh, modern food, something for everyone, in a great setting and at reasonable prices. During exhibitions there are other cafeterias in the Grand Palais. If you are not visiting the museums, a choice of restaurants includes the following:

€€€ **Laurent**. Classic Parisian restaurant in a building which was once a hunting lodge and has a slightly old-fashioned air. The cooking, which is classic with a contemporary twist, is much appreciated in business and government circles. Comfortable in winter, it benefits from a gorgeous garden terrace in summer. *41 Av. Gabriel. T: 01 42 25 00 39, www.le-laurent.com. Map p. 581, D4.*

€€€ **Maison Blanche**. A chic, fasionable, two-level roof restaurant with

Philippe Starck-inspired décor in black and white. The Baie Vitrée level has tables the length of a large window. The Mezzanine level is less angular: both have an excellent view of Paris. The elegant dishes, influenced by the cuisine of the Mediterranean, match the surroundings and are determined by the seasons. *15 Avenue Montaigne. T: 01 47 23 55 99, www.maison-blanche.fr. Map p. 580, C4.*

€€ **Le Pavillon Élysée Lenôtre**. A lovely glazed building of 1900 in the gardens of the Champs-Élysées, opposite the Petit Palais. It is a flagship centre for the upmarket Lenôtre brand. Combined here is a restaurant, cooking school and shop. *10 Av. des Champs-Élysées, T: 01 42 65 85 10, www.lenotre.com. Map p. 581, D4.*

€€ Le Petit Marius. A modern bistrot at a smart address, specialising in seafood, of which there is a large selection in both starters and main courses, which may include mussels from the bay of Mont St-Michel, scallops or *sole meunière*. Menu or *à la carte. 6 Av. George V. T: 01 40 70 11 76, www.lepetitmarius.com.* Next door at no. 4 is its older relation, **Marius & Janette** (*T: 01 48 23 41 88*). Both are open every day. *Map p. 580, B4.*

€–€€ Tante Louise. Tante Louise opened in 1929 under the direction of chef Louise Blanche Lefeuvre and is now part of the portfolio of leading Burgundian chef Bernard Loiseau. Its location makes it convenient both for the business community and for visitors and it still has an Art Deco feel, including some charming stained-glass windows. The dishes, in Burgundian tradition, are cooked with refinement, and include interesting variations on traditional themes while prices range quite widely but remain good value. Unsurprisingly for a restaurant with a Burgundian influence, there is an excellent wine list. Smaller rooms are available for private dining. Good-value lunch *formule*. Closed weekends and all of Aug. *41 Rue de Boissy d'Anglas. T: 01 42 65 06 85, www.bernard-loiseau.com. Map p. 581, E4.*

€ L'Atelier Renault. The Renault car showroom has a vibrantly colourful bar/restaurant and shop on the mezzanine floor overlooking the Champs-Élysées. A fun place to stop by for a drink or a light meal: lunch *formules*, salads and sandwiches. Open Sun–Wed 12–12, Thur–Sat 12–2am. *53 Av. des Champs-Élysées. T: 08 11 88 28 11, atelier.renault.com. Map p. 580, C4.*

€ Le Carré Élysée. In the gardens of the Champs-Élysées, a good address for a not outrageously expensive meal. *49 Av. Roosevelt. T: 01 43 59 91 06. Map p. 580, C4.*

€ Publicis Drugstore Champs-Élysées. A revamp of the '60s–'70s' establishment, using laminated glass, which combines café/brasserie, shop, newsagent and grocer. Open daily until 2am. *133 Av. des Champs-Élysées. T: 01 44 43 77 64, www.publicisdrugstore.com. Map p. 580, B3.*

€ Le Daru. Close to the Russian Orthodox Cathedral. A small Russian restaurant and grocery store. *19 Rue Daru. T: 01 42 27 23 60, www.daru.fr. Map p. 580, C2.*

LA MADELEINE
View down the Corinthian portico.

The Saint-Lazare Quarter

*The part of the 8th arrondissement stretching either side of Boulevard Haussmann
is a district of broad, quiet streets lined by tall, distinguished-looking buildings of
mellow stone. This chapter takes in a chapel built by Louis XVIII, a temple by
Napoleon, and three grand residences of wealthy bankers-cum-connoisseurs,
now public museums that house their precious collections.*

A short way north of Place de la Concorde
is the expansive Place de la Madeleine,
approached along the broad **Rue Royale**
(*map p. 581, E4*), a street that is lined with the
18th-century façades of quality shops and restaurants. At no. 3 (on the left as you approach
Place de la Madeleine) is the famous Maxim's
restaurant-cabaret (*see p. 293*), with awnings in
its trademark red. Orfévrerie Christofle at no. 9
is devoted to the art of the silversmith, and at no.
11 is the main Lalique showroom. René Lalique,

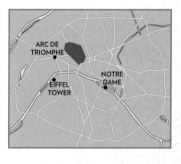

goldsmith and jeweller, caused a sensation when he displayed his designs in glass at the
Universal Exhibition of 1900. Further up Rue Royale on the opposite side is Ladurée,
'*Maison de macarons et fabricant de douceurs*', always with an enticing window display.

LA MADELEINE

*Map p. 581, E4. Métro 8, 12 and 14 to Madeleine or 1, 8 and 12 to Concorde. Open daily
9.30–7.*

La Madeleine, or the church of Ste-Marie-Madeleine, dedicated to St Mary Magdalene,
is built in the style of a Graeco-Roman temple, surrounded by a majestic Corinthian
colonnade which is visually counterbalanced by the Assemblée Nationale building
across the river. Two earlier churches had been demolished unfinished, in 1777 and
1789, before Pierre-Alexandre Vignon started work in 1806 on the orders of Napoleon,
who, prior to building the Arc de Triomphe, had intended it as a Temple of Glory for
the Grande Armée. It was finished by Huvé in 1842. In the pediment is a relief of the
Last Judgement by Henri Lemaire; the bronze doors are adorned with bas-reliefs of the

Ten Commandments by Baron Henri de Triqueti, a commission awarded by the July Monarchy of 1830–48. The works marked a turning point in Triqueti's career. He went on to collaborate in the construction of Napoleon's tomb in the Invalides. Wounded during street-fighting in the revolution of 1848, he left Paris for England, where he was commissioned by Queen Victoria to decorate the interior of the Prince Albert Chapel at Windsor. He is buried in Père-Lachaise, his gravestone decorated with a bas-relief of his own making.

The interior abounds in gold leaf and coloured marble, paintings, mosaics and sculptures, and has a fine Cavaillé-Coll organ. The nave is covered by three coffered domes and the east end by a half-dome, with an enfilade of Ionic columns behind the high altar. In chapels on either side of the entrance are sculpture groups of the *Marriage of the Virgin* by Pradier and the *Baptism of Christ* by Rude. The group of the *Ascension of the Magdalene* (1837) on the high altar is by Carlo Marochetti. Marochetti, like Triqueti, was a native of Piedmont and like Triqueti too was a sculptor much favoured by the July Monarchy. When it fell in 1848, he likewise went to England, where he carried out a number of prestigious commissions. The sculpture group in the Madeleine is an excellent example of his style: high drama suffused with sentiment and—or so his detractors would say—slightly tinged with the absurd.

PLACE DE LA MADELEINE

Standing on the steps of the Madeleine you enjoy a fine prospect to the south, of the obelisk in Place de la Concorde, with the Assemblée Nationale building behind it and behind that again, the vast dome of the Invalides catching the light. It is not a view that evokes the events of Bloody Week in May 1871, when the Commune's barricade on Rue Royale was captured and multiple executions took place here. In retaliation, enraged Communards streamed off to torch the Tuileries Palace. The priest of the Madeleine, Abbé Gaspard Deguerry, whom the Commune had taken hostage, was shot by his captors a day later.

In the former Café Durand (now the Ralph Lauren store at 2 Place de la Madeleine), Zola wrote *J'Accuse*, an open letter denouncing the army and defending Dreyfus (*see p. 23*), which was published in *L'Aurore* on 12th January 1898. On the eastern side of Place de la Madeleine is a small flower market, and at no. 30 (behind the church) is **Fauchon**, the most famous of all Parisian grocery stores, a-delicatessen-cum-tea shop whose window displays are a mouth-watering work of art.

ON & AROUND BOULEVARD HAUSSMANN

Boulevard Haussmann (*map p. 581, E3–F3*), named after the man responsible for transforming Paris in the mid-19th century (*see p. 284*), was begun in 1857 to create an unbroken thoroughfare from Boulevard Montmartre to the Arc de Triomphe. It was only finally completed in 1926. Today it is well known for its famous department stores, Printemps and the Lafayette (*see p. 301*). Where it intersects Boulevard Malesherbes

LA MADELEINE
Detail from 'Thou shalt not commit adultery', one of Triqueti's
Ten Commandments on the basilica's main doors.

(*map p. 581, D3*) is the vast neo-Romanesque church of **St-Augustin** (1871), a work by Victor Baltard, the architect of the famous Les Halles. South of Blvd Haussmann is the Chapelle Expiatoire. To the north is Gare St-Lazare.

CHAPELLE EXPIATOIRE

Map p. 581, E3. Métro 9 to St-Augustin or 3, 12, 13, 14 and RER E to St-Lazare. Open for occasional visits with the CMN (www.chapelle-expiatoire.monuments-nationaux.fr).

The Chapelle Expiatoire stands just off Boulevard Haussmann in Square Louis XVI, formerly the Cimetière de la Madeleine and today a little park surrounded by railings and planted with fragrant evergreen shrubs. Here lie the bodies of the victims of the panic of 1770 in Place de la Concorde (*see p. 262*), together with the members of the Swiss Guard massacred on 10th August 1792 and all those guillotined between 26th August 1792 and 24th March 1794. The chapel was erected in 1815–26 to plans by Fontaine in the style of a Classical funeral temenos. Built by order of Louis XVIII, it was dedicated in expiation of the regicide of Louis XVI and Marie-Antoinette, whose remains, first interred in the graveyard on this site, were removed and formally buried in St-Denis in 1815. Inside the chapel are two marble groups: *Louis XVI and his confessor Abbé Henry Essex Edgeworth* by Bosio, below which is inscribed the king's will, dated 25th December 1792; and *Marie-Antoinette supported by Religion*, by Cortot. Religion bears the features of the queen's sister-in-law Mme Élisabeth. Below is inscribed a letter said to have been written to Élisabeth from the Conciergerie by the queen on 16th October 1793, the day of her execution. Élisabeth herself was guillotined in May 1974. The bas-relief by Gérard above the doorway represents the removal of the royal remains.

BARON HAUSSMANN

Baron Georges-Eugène Haussmann (1809–91), Prefect of the Seine, was responsible for altering the face of Paris in just 16 years during the Second Empire. He demolished slums, drove major routes through the city, created grand vistas, and put in place an efficient infrastructure which largely improved living conditions. It could also be argued that Haussmann's heavy hand was responsible for creating a windy city with tedious boulevards fronted by uniform buildings. Urban regeneration had already been addressed in the Age of Enlightenment. Edmé Verniquet, town planner under Louis XVI, and the philosopher and economist Saint-Simon, had contributed to the impulse. Napoleon's grandiose ideas were partly realised under Louis-Philippe (1830–48) but it was Napoleon's nephew, Louis-Napoléon Bonaparte, who put into action the strong views on the subject that he had developed during his exile in England. As Emperor Napoléon III, he appointed Baron Haussmann to take charge of the overall plan.

A formidable, ambitious, hard-working, artful man of dubious taste, the Baron carried out the emperor's plans with the solid support of Eugène Belgrand, hydraulic engineer, and Jean-Charles Alphand, Director of Public Works with responsibility for landscape architecture. The scheme included a new network of some 135km of major roads across medieval Paris, beginning with the north–south artery of boulevards de Sébastopol, du Palais (crossing and almost obliterating the Île de la Citè) and St-Michel. The area west of the Madeleine was breached by boulevards Malesherbes and Haussmann, and the Left Bank was riven by the creation of Rue des Écoles and the initial section of Boulevard St-Germain. Boulevards Magenta and Strasbourg and Rue de Rennes served the railway stations. Streets were asphalted, pavements laid, trees planted, handsome apartment blocks of prescribed height with uniform stone façades were built on requisitioned land at the cost of many fine *hôtels particuliers* and picturesque older buildings. There was no control over what was built behind the grand frontages. The Louvre Palace was extended by another wing on the north as far as the Tuileries, which became Louis-Napoléon's residence. The rivers Dhuis and Vanne were harnessed for drinking water and the sewers were hugely extended (from 150 to 500km) using the course of the Bièvre river to carry effluent into the Seine. The Bois de Boulogne, Bois de Vincennes and the parks Monceau, Montsouris and Buttes-Chaumont were created on requisitioned land. To realise his plans for modern Paris, Haussmann obtained from the emperor a law authorising the expropriation of land by simple decree of executive power. His daring methods of raising money ultimately came to grief when he was forced to request a loan from the Legislative Body. In 1868 the statesman Jules Ferry issued a violently critical pamphlet *Les Comptes fantastiques d'Haussmann*, which led to the Baron's resignation, while the war of 1870 brutally ended further 'Haussmannising'.

GARE ST-LAZARE

The interior of **Gare St-Lazare** (*map p. 581, E3*), a terminus of the western region of the SNCF, was famously the subject of paintings by Monet in 1877 (examples in Musée d'Orsay). Today it is one of the busiest railway stations in Paris, with a shopping mall in its passenger concourse. To the west of it, Rue de Rome leads north past the **Place de l'Europe**, painted by Caillebotte in 1877. To the south, at no. 8 Rue du Havre, the **Lycée Condorcet**, founded in 1804, occupies the former buildings (with a Doric cloister court) of a Capuchin convent; on the site of its chapel (in the street to the east) is the church of **St-Louis d'Antin** by Brongniart (1782).

MUSÉE JACQUEMART-ANDRÉ

Map p. 580, C3. Métro 9 to St-Philippe-du-Roule or 9 and 13 to Miromesnil. Entrance at 158 Blvd Haussmann. Open daily 10–6; Mon and Sat during temporary exhibitions to 8.30. Audioguides, tea room. T: 01 45 62 11 59, musee-jacquemart-andre.com.

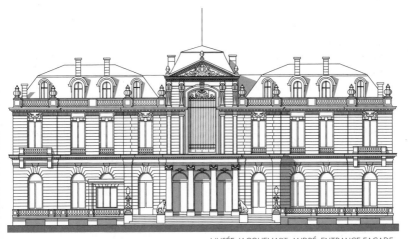

MUSÉE JACQUEMART-ANDRÉ: ENTRANCE FAÇADE

The Jacquemart-André museum's remarkable collection of predominantly Italian Renaissance and French 18th-century art and furnishings is displayed in the 19th-century mansion which has barely changed since the collector Édouard André, who came from a rich Protestant banking family, built it in 1870. In 1881 he married the painter Nélie Jacquemart, and she bequeathed the collection to the Institut de France in 1912. Over two floors are 16 rooms containing *objets d'art* and paintings of great beauty and value. André's portrait, in the uniform of the Imperial Guard, by Winterhalter, hangs in the entrance hall. The former dining room, its ceiling decorated with a Tiepolo fresco, is now a charming *salon de thé*.

Salon des Peintures: The Salon des Peintures, with red damask walls, contains charming 18th-century French works by some of the best artists of the period. They include two oval canvases of typically frivolous subjects by Boucher: *Toilet of Venus* and *Venus Asleep*. These are balanced by two more sober still lifes by Chardin: *The Attributes of the Sciences* and *The Attributes of the Arts*. The furniture and Sèvres porcelain is also 18th-century French, complemented by *St Mark's Square* and *The Rialto, Venice* by Canaletto.

Grand Salon: This spacious room has a curved bay lined with gilded 18th-century wood panelling and mirrors and contains busts by Coysevox, Houdon, Lemoyne and others.

The Private Rooms: The sumptuous **Tapestry Room**, the first of a suite of smaller private rooms, was built to house the three exceptional Beauvais tapestries called *Russian Games*, which had been purchased before the house was built. It also contains a Savonnerie carpet (1663), upholstered furnishings and fine cabinets. The only painting is a gouache by Guardi, *Venetian Portico*.

The couple's **Office** is much as it was in their time, hung with their favourite works, including Fragonard's brilliant *The Model's Début*, where an older woman parades a young girl's charms before a raffishly-dressed artist. Ostensibly he is looking for a nude model, but we know full well what is in store for this girl. On the desk is a portrait of Nélie Jacquemart, who painted Édouard André's portrait in 1872.

The **Boudoir** has a very fine portrait by Vigée-Lebrun of Countess Skravonska, and David's magnificent portrait of Count Antoine Français de Nantes, member of the Conseil d'État.

In the **Library** are Egyptian antiquities as well as works by 17th-century Flemish and Dutch masters much admired by later French painters, among them Van Dyck, Ruysdael and Rembrandt, who is represented by three paintings, including the dramatic *Pilgrims at Emmaus*.

Music Room: The large reception room used as a music room has opulent Second Empire-style red damask walls and ebony furniture. Paintings include a picturesque *Ruined Archway* by Hubert Robert, a bronze bust of André by Nélie Jacquemart (c. 1890), a fine *Portrait of a Man* by N. Largillière and a Beauvais tapestry from a cartoon by Boucher.

Winter Garden and Smoking Room: The most unusual and successful feature of this house, designed by Henri Parent, is the **Winter Garden**, an oval space with a beautiful curved double staircase.

The **Smoking Room** is the repository of souvenirs of travels by Nélie Jacquemart, including a 14th-century mosque lamp (in the cabinet). In this male preserve are English portraits by Sir Joshua Reynolds (of Captain Torryn) and Sir Thomas Lawrence (of the Duke of Buckingham). The staircase is decorated with an illusionistic fresco by Tiepolo, *Henri III's reception at the Villa Contarini*.

First floor: The Italian Museum:
Three rooms on the upper floor contain a prodigious collection of more than 80 Renaissance paintings. The first rooms contain sculptures and reliefs, such as the fine marble bust of Isabella of Aragon by Francesco Laurana; a pair of lamp holders in the form of angels; and a bronze panel of the *Martyrdom of St Sebastian* by Donatello. A number of 15th-century marble door surrounds have been re-erected; terracottas from the Della Robbia workshops include a serene *Virgin and Child*.

The Florentine Room contains four elegant Cinquecento versions of the *Virgin and Child* by different artists including Botticelli, Perugino, Botticini and Baldovinetti. Attributed to Paolo Uccello is a *St George and the Dragon*, purchased in London. Prime examples among the Venetian works, reflecting the taste of Édouard André, are a powerful and poignant *Mocking of Christ* attributed to Mantegna, and *The Virgin and Child between Sts Jerome and Louis of Toulouse*, as well as a strong and dignified *Virgin and Child* by Giovanni Bellini, which contrasts with a small but brilliant *Virgin and Child* by Cima da Conegliano. The visit ends with three small rooms of the private apartments.

PARC MONCEAU & ENVIRONS

Map p. 580, C2. Métro 2 to Courcelles and Monceau or 2 and 3 to Villiers.

Parc Monceau (3.88 hectares) is an appropriately elegant garden for this smart district. It derives its name from a vanished village and is a remnant of a private park laid out as a landscaped garden by Carmontelle in 1778 for Philippe (Egalité) d'Orléans, Duc de Chartres and father of Louis-Philippe. It was then known as the Folie de Chartres. In 1783 the Scotsman Thomas Blaikie took over as gardener and simplified the layout while keeping some of the picturesque details. The four monumental gates are by Gabriel Davioud. Near the northeast corner is the *Naumachie*, an oval lake with a graceful Corinthian colonnade, which may have come from either the Château du Raincy or from the projected Valois chapel at St-Denis. To the east of the lake is a Renaissance arcade from the old Hôtel de Ville. When Paris was enclosed by the wall of the Farmers General in the 18th century (*see p. 405*), Ledoux built a toll-house to the west, which was known as the Rotonde de Chartres, as the Duke had part of it adapted for his use. It later became a keeper's lodge and was disfigured in 1861 when the columns were fluted and a dome added. Scattered among the ornamental trees, shrubs and colourful flowerbeds are several statues, including *Ambroise Thomas* by Falguière (1902) and *Guy de Maupassant* by Verlet (1897).

The park has not changed a great deal since Marcel Proust lived with his mother from 1901–5 at no. 45 **Rue de Courcelles**, in a cork-lined sound-proof room, before moving to 102 Blvd Haussmann, where he remained until 1919. Dickens lodged at no. 38 (then 48) in 1846. The Galerie Pagoda Paris, at no. 48 Rue de Courcelles, is a unique red building in Chinese style, commissioned in 1926 for an Asian art dealer, Ching Tsai Loo.

Close to Parc Monceau are two unique museums housing collections made by the haute bourgeoisie at the turn of the 19th and 20th centuries, when collecting was fashionable. One contains a wide range of Southeast Asian antiquities and art; the other has mainly 18th-century decorative arts.

MUSÉE NISSIM DE CAMONDO

Map p. 581, D2. 63 Rue de Monceau. Open Wed–Sun 10–5.30; closed Mon–Tues. Minimal captions in situ; good audioguides. T: 01 53 89 06 40, www.lesartsdecoratifs.fr.

Belonging to the Musée des Arts Décoratifs, the Musée Nissim de Camondo is a remarkable survival, the former home of an inspired collector of 18th-century artworks, the first collection of its kind. The house reflects the character and ethos of the man and preserves as closely as possible the original layout of the rooms as they are known from photographs taken in 1936. You enter from the courtyard—which was modelled on the Petit Trianon at Versailles, with the addition of curved ends.

The house and its contents were bequeathed to the Arts Décoratifs by the banker Count Moïse de Camondo (1860–1935) as a memorial to his only son Nissim, who was killed in action (as a pilot) in 1917. He is buried in the cemetery of Montmartre. Camondo's only other child, Béatrice, together with her husband and two children, perished in Auschwitz. Moïse de Camondo, descended from the great Sephardic Ottoman banking family, demolished his parents' house to build (in 1911–14) suitable surroundings for his 18th-century collections. René Sergent modelled the façades on the Petit Trianon and reused or reproduced panelling to create an appropriate interior. The result was a comfortable home where the collector could live among the outstanding examples of furniture, carpets, tapestries and tableware that distinguish his taste. Moïse de Camondo stipulated in his bequest that nothing should be altered, and nothing lent. True to his Istanbul background, he always had rugs on the parquet and he loved symmetry in design. Although restoration and reweaving of fabrics cannot be avoided, every object and piece of furniture is, as far as possible, in its original place. The bathroom, kitchen and servants' quarters, testimonies to the functional design of the building, have been refurbished.

Moïse de Camondo was separated from his wife and lived here with his children and his collection. Among the exhibits are numerous bills for the upkeep of the house and garden and other documents revealing the time and care he took over equipping his home with running water, electricity, central heating and other modern conveniences.

Rez-de-chaussée bas: Lower ground floor

Past the plush-seated lift and the servants' entrance is the wide, white-tiled **Kitchen**, with an impressive free-standing range of 1912 and a huge furnace.

There would have been a staff of around twelve to run the house. Their dining room can be seen off the kitchen, as can the scullery and butler's pantry.

MUSÉE NISSIM CAMONDO
Detail of a barometer.

Rez-de-chaussée haut: First floor

Grand Bureau: Unpainted wood panels were unusual in the 18th century but much sought-after later. The two low chairs upholstered in pale blue, made by J.-P.-C. Séné for Madame Élisabeth, sister of Louis XVI, are of the type known as *voyeuses* and were designed for women in voluminous dresses to watch the gaming tables. A writing desk to stand at, such as Victor Hugo used (*see p. 352*), is attributed to David Roentgen (c. 1790–1800) and Aubusson tapestries depict six of the *Fables* of La Fontaine, after Oudry. On a side table are two photographs of Nissim de Camondo. The painting of a *Bacchante*, dressed in a leopard skin, is by Élisabeth Vigée-Lebrun.

Grand Salon: Overlooking the garden, this large drawing room has white and gold panelling from 9 Rue Royale, and above the marquetry cabinet and tables by Riesener is Vigée-Lebrun's *Portrait of Madame Le Couteulx du Molay*, painted just before the Revolution. The Le Couteulx owned the Château de Malmaison before Josephine moved in (*see p. 452*). The six-leaved screen, designed by François Desportes, belonged to the Duvivier family, who directed the Savonnerie carpet works. Also of Savonnerie production is the carpet representing the *Four Winds*, one of many woven for the Grande Galerie of the Louvre (1678). Moïse de Camondo was among the few who appreciated the value of furniture decorated with Sèvres porcelain, such as the dainty lady's desk by Carlin. Also here is a Japanese lacquered bronze perfume flask that once belonged to Madame de Pompadour (its gilt bronze mount is French).

Salon des Huet: This hexagonal room was designed for the seven panels of *Scènes pastorales* painted by Jean-

Baptiste Huet, as were the three *dessus de portes* of 1776. Huet was a designer for the Toile de Jouy fabric company. The little table with porcelain plaques is by Roger Vandercruse (called Lacroix, RVLC), and the superb little marquetry roll-top desk is by Oeben, who taught Riesener and Leleu and worked for Louis XV. The set of carved and gilt chairs were made in such a way that the upholstery could be changed depending on the season. The two Chinese lacquer commodes, originally made as part of a set, were purchased separately by Camondo and reunited here—an aspect of collecting which gave him particular pleasure.

Overlooking Parc Monceau is the **Dining Room**, set as if for a real dinner of 1933, which Moïse de Camondo gave for the Club des Cent, his gourmet dining circle: on this particular occasion the guests tucked in to iced melon, fillets of sole, chicken poached in tarragon, jellied beef, green peas and salad. Here we see part of a silverware set by Roettiers, ordered by Catherine the Great for her favourite, Gregory Orloff. When Orloff fell from grace, she took it back. Much of the set stayed in Russia. The **Porcelain Room** contains a 350-piece Buffon set of Sèvres porcelain, each decorated with a different bird. Behind the Dining Room is the **Servants' Pantry**.

The **Petit Bureau**, or English Drawing Room, its walls in crimson, contains a Riesener *table chiffonnière en auge* (1788) made for Marie-Antoinette, several sketches for Gobelins tapestries of *The Hunts of Louis XV* by Oudry, the *Porte de St-Denis* by Hubert Robert, and four views of Venice by Guardi.

Second floor

On the second floor are the less grand private apartments used by Moïse de Camondo, Nissim and his daughter Béatrice, each with a bathroom. Overlooking Parc Monceau, the **Blue Drawing Room** became Camondo's living room, with watercolours by Jongkind (not to his taste but a present from his cousin Isaac, himself a collector and an admirer of Monet, Degas and Cézanne) and *Views of Paris* by Jean-Baptiste Raguenet.

The **Library** is an oak-panelled rotunda with a circular table, walnut furniture and red-leather bound *Gazettes des beaux-arts* in the shelves. Here too is Count Moïse's **Bedroom** with its alcove bed, and the former Bureau of Nissim de Camondo, with a bronze statuette of Béatrice on horseback.

The **Bathrooms** are equipped with all the comforts of the day, with nickel-plated hot and cold taps, heated towel rails and English porcelain.

MUSÉE CERNUSCHI

Map p. 581, D2. 7 Avenue Vélasquez. Open Tues–Sun 10–6; closed Mon. Free admission. Audioguides. T: 01 53 96 21 50, www.cernuschi.paris.fr.

Enrico Cernuschi (1821–96) bequeathed his collections and this building to the City of Paris, and the museum opened in 1898. Born in Italy, an ardent republican and follower of Garibaldi, Cernuschi fled to Paris in 1850 and then became embroiled with Gambetta and the events leading to the establishment of the Third Republic. Following the uprisings of the Commune, he undertook a world voyage in 1871–3, during which he used his considerable wealth (derived from banking; Cernuschi was a co-founder of the Banque de Paris, later Paribas) to acquire works of art in China. He then commissioned William Bowens de Boijen to design a museum-mansion next to Parc Monceau. The Cernuschi museum owns over 12,000 works and is the second most important museum of Eastern antiquities in France after the Guimet. With views over Parc Monceau, it makes full use of natural light. The permanent collections, from the Neolithic to the 13th century, are displayed chronologically, starting on the first floor, reached via the grand staircase with a portrait of the wildly bearded Cernuschi (1890) by Léon Bonnat, and a Coromandel lacquered screen (17th–18th centuries). Although the collection mainly consists of Chinese works, Cernuschi was one of the first collectors to visit Japan and also acquired Japanese decorative art. Recently-acquired modern Japanese ceramics are also on display. Vietnamese pieces were added in the 20th century.

First floor

The Neolithic collection: Dating from the 8th–1st millennia BC, the Neolithic collection comes mainly from the provinces of Gansu and Qinghai, China, but is not a complete picture. Most objects are of the Majiayao period (c. 3500–c. 2200 BC), whose three phases are represented by terracotta jars with swirling designs, remarkable wafer-thin black ceramics and delicately carved jade (nephrite) pieces.

Representative of Shang-dynasty bronzes (c. 1550–c. 1050 BC) are a number of ritual containers such as the Fanglei vase with a lid. The most outstanding object in the museum is the bronze vase or *you* (1st half of the 11th century BC) from Hunan province, designed for fermented drinks. Known as *The Tigress*, it takes the shape of a small feline (35.2cm tall) propped on its back feet and curling tail to leave its front 'legs' free to clasp a small human figure, whose head is under the fearsome canopy of the animal's upper jaw. The beast is abundantly decorated with abstract and animal motifs, including several *kui*-type dragons.

The Study: Cernuschi's former study now contains objects from the Zhou dynasty, divided between Western Zhou (c. 1050–771 BC), whose capital was Xi'an, and Eastern Zhou (770–256 BC). Characteristic of Western Zhou are imposing bronzes, outstanding among them the two-handled *kui* on a plinth, with a flat ribbon design. Representative of the tumultuous Warring States (Eastern Zhou, 481–221 BC) are swords and lacquered objects such as the wooden drum support, shaped as birds standing on tigers, and small bronze plaques, often in the form of animals.

The Buddha Room: This room, spanning two levels, was adapted to accommodate the large 18th-century bronze Buddha from a temple in Tokyo's Meguro district. Objects from the long-lasting Han dynasty (206 BC–AD 220), founded by Liu Bang who overthrew the Qin dynasty, are exhibited on the lower level.

Rare and very beautiful are the works of the Western Han period, among which is a lacquered wood tabletop in red and black. Also here is a rare sandstone lintel with relief carvings of fantastic birds which fill the intermediary space between heaven and earth that the human soul (*hun*) must cross with the help of Taoist Immortals, one of whom (represented as a wingless figure) is on the right of the composition. The bronze Bear—which represents strength or power—may have served as the base of a screen. Smaller objects include a mythical bird in wood and, the most precious, a pair of gilded bronze handles from a dish incorporating a powerful feline motif.

The Tang Room contains superb Tang period (618–907) ceramics, fired at 800°C, with lead glazes in manganese white, yellow-amber from iron and green from bronze. On occasion, expensive cobalt blue from Persia was used to produce colourful *mingqi* (funerary statuettes) for the well-to-do classes. During the brilliant early Tang dynasty (618–907), Buddhism took a stronger hold but the Taoist Head (early 8th century) is proof that other religions co-existed. New themes were introduced, connected with trade on the Silk Road, or to include servants, concubines and musicians. An example of *mingqi* from Xi'an, Shaanxi province, is the charming orchestra of young female musicians on horseback, delicately tinted, each playing a different instrument. Their hair is tied in bunches and they have plump smiling faces typical of Shaanxi peasants.

Mezzanine level

Statues of different periods indicate the increasing dominance of the Buddhist religion after the fall of the Han in 220. From Yungang, Shaanxi province, at the time of the Northern Wei dynasty (386–534), the seated Bodhisattva reveals Western influence in the draperies, tall headdress and carved decoration of the plinth. Around 534, during the Northern Qi dynasty, borrowings from the Indian Gupta style produced more corpulent and stylised deities. Following reunification under the Sui (581–618), terracotta *mingqi* are varied and elaborate. Protectors of tombs frequently came in pairs, and one of the most celebrated, the *Military Civil Servant*, is the pendant to a *Guardian* in San Francisco's Asian Art Museum.

The marble *Amitâbha*, seated on a lotus flower, was made during the Liao dynasty (907–1125) in the style of the earlier Qi. The deity is surrounded by souls, represented as small figures (as in medieval Christian art) rising from lotus flowers. Among the finest objects from this period are bronze funerary adornments, including funerary masks.

Examples of modern Japanese and Chinese acquisitions (distributed around the museum) include a delightful porcelain watering can by Matsuda (2012), and a bronze vase (c. 1950–60) by Nakajima, and works on paper. The small separate **Smoking Room** contains Cernuschi memorabilia (*visits arranged at the museum entrance*).

BATIGNOLLES

The *quartier* of Les Batignolles gave its name to a school of Impressionist painters under the leadership of Manet, immortalised in a painting by Fantin-Latour in the Musée d'Orsay. In the **Cimetière des Batignolles** (*map p. 578, C1; Métro 13 to Porte de St-Ouen and Porte de Clichy or RER C to Porte de Clichy*) lie Verlaine, André Breton and the Russian Art Deco designer Léon Bakst.

Musée Henner (*43 Av. de Villiers; map p. 580, C2, www.musee-henner.fr*) is devoted to the painting of Jean-Jacques Henner, known for portraits and nudes. The small Art Deco concert hall, **Salle Cortot** (*78 Rue Cardinet, map p. 580, C2*) was designed by Auguste Perret (also responsible for the Théâtre Champs-Élysées) and opened in 1930.

Every Saturday morning an organic produce market is held on Boulevard des Batignolles (*map p. 581, E2; Métro 2 to Rome or 2 and 13 to Place de Clichy*).

EATING AND DRINKING IN THE ST-LAZARE QUARTER

€€€ Maxim's. Restaurant-cabaret. An institution, ever since a waiter by the name of Maxime Gaillard opened a simple bistrot here in 1893. Satisfied customers have included Cocteau and Mistinguett. The Art Nouveau interiors are by the finest artists of the Nancy school. It is now owned by the fashion designer Pierre Cardin. Closed Sun and Mon. *3 Rue Royale. T: 01 42 65 27 94, www.maxims-de-paris. com. Map p. 581, E4.*

€–€€€ Fauchon. Renowned delicatessen founded in 1886, behind the church of the Madeleine. There is also a *pâtisserie*, wine cellar and caviar bar and a café on the first floor which offers a lunch menu. The cuisine is modern French. Closed Sun. *24–26 and 30 Place de la Madeleine. T: 01 70 39 38 39 or 01 73 20 22 97, www.fauchonparislecafe.fr. Map p. 581, E4.*

€–€€ Il Piccolino. A small Italian restaurant. The cooking is genuinely Italian. *10 Rue de Constantinople. T: 01 42 93 73 33. Map p. 581, D2–E2.*

€ Café Jacquemart-André. The former dining room, with a Tiepolo fresco, is now a charming *salon de thé*. Open daily 11.45–5.30, brunch served Sat–Sun 11–3, and during evening openings Mon and Sat open until 7pm. No reservations. *158 Blvd Haussmann. www.musee-jacquemart-andre.com. Map p. 580, C3.*

€ Lazare. Recommended for a good traditional meal in St-Lazare station. Open daily 7.30–midnight. *T: 01 44 90 80 80, lazare-paris.fr. Map p. 581, E3.*

€ Pomze. A play on the French for apple. There is an *épicerie* on the ground floor selling cider etc., and apples are served in a variety of ways in all the dishes in the first-floor restaurant, prepared by Japanese cooks. Good-value lunch *formule*. *109 Blvd Haussmann. T: 01 42 65 65 83, www.pomze.com. Map p. 581, D3.*

OPÉRA GARNIER
La Danse by Carpeaux.

Rue St-Honoré, Opéra & the Grands Boulevards

The ancient Rue St-Honoré runs past Place Vendôme, with the famous column erected by Napoleon in emulation of that of Trajan in Rome. The Opéra Garnier, symbol of Belle-Époque frivolity and decadence, stands beside the enfilade of once-grand boulevards.

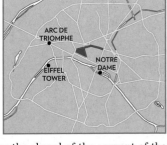

Rue Saint-Honoré (*map pp. 581, E4–587, EI*), one of the oldest streets in Paris, existing since the 13th century, runs parallel to but is very different from Rue de Rivoli, and is much more peaceful and interesting. Many designer boutiques have crossed Rue Royale from Rue du Faubourg St-Honoré to set up shop here.

Heading east along Rue Saint-Honoré, at the point where it meets Rue Cambon, stands the **Church of the Assumption**, built in 1670 as the chapel of the convent of the Haudriettes and now used by the Polish community. At no. 239 (right) is the very chic Hôtel Costes, just before **Rue de Castiglione**, a street of elegant and expensive boutiques, where at no. 7 is Hôtel Lotti, which was described in George Orwell's *Down and Out in Paris and London* (1933). In the other direction from Rue de Castiglione is Place Vendôme (*see below*).

Rue du Marché-St-Honoré (left) has retained some of the neighbourhood atmosphere of small grocer's shops and bars, with a surviving butcher, a fishmonger-cum-oyster bar (L'Écume St-Honoré) and markets on Wed and Sat, although the old market-place itself, **Place du Marché-St-Honoré**, was transformed in 1997 with a building by Ricardo Bofill featuring columns and glass, occupied on the ground floor by furniture and car showrooms. Around the square, though, there is a great variety of places to eat, such as L'Absinthe, Razowski and the Très Honoré brasserie (*see p. 304*). The square was formerly occupied by a Dominican convent, established in 1611. The word 'Jacobin' originally designated a Dominican friar. It came to have its later meaning because of a group of revolutionary thinkers who held meetings in this friary from 1789. With the fall of Robespierre (the leading Jacobin) in 1794, the friary was closed and its premises were made over to a public market.

PLACE VENDÔME
Colonne de la Grande Armée (detail).

PLACE VENDÔME

Map p. 581, E4–F4. Métro 1 to Tuileries or Concorde.

Place Vendôme is one of the most refined and distinguished squares in Paris. It was conceived in 1686 and construction proceeded under the direction of Jules Hardouin-Mansart at the end of the 17th century. It owes its name to a 17th-century *hôtel particulier* built on this site by César, Duc de Vendôme, illegitimate son of Henri IV and Gabrielle d'Estrées. The mansions you see today, with their grand and unified façades, were completed in the 18th century. Homes for bankers gradually became high-class commercial properties and apartments: some of the greatest international jewellers, watchmakers and couturiers now have their emporia on the square. Nos. 11–13 have housed the Ministère de la Justice since 1815; Frédéric Chopin died at no. 12 in 1849. Professor Mesmer, who gave his name to mesmerism, also lived on the square. The Hôtel Ritz, established in 1898, is in the west elevation at no. 15, and has kept much of its 18th-century decoration. The Hôtel Bristol is at no. 3. In the centre stands the tall Colonne de la Grande Armée (or Vendôme Column).

THE COLONNE DE LA GRANDE ARMÉE

The column, 43.5m high, was constructed in 1806–10 by Gondouin and Lepère in the style of Trajan's Column in Rome, to replace an equestrian statue of Louis XIV by Girardon (the left foot of it is now in the Musée Carnavalet). Spiralling up the shaft is a band of bronze bas-reliefs, designed by Bergeret, which was hammered out of the metal of 1,250 Russian and Austrian cannon captured at the Battle of Austerlitz in 1805. The three-month campaign is depicted in chronological sequence. The statue of Napoleon at the summit of the column, replacing the one by Gabriel Seurre that had been commissioned by the July Monarchy in 1833, is a copy by Dumont (1863) of the original by Chaudet that was torn down by royalists in 1814. The present statue narrowly escaped destruction in 1871 when a group of Communards, allegedly encouraged by the artist Gustave Courbet, demolished the column. Courbet fled to Switzerland after being condemned to finance the re-erection of the column in 1875 and died there in 1877.

SAINT-ROCH

Steps ascend from the Rue St-Honoré to the monumental façade of St-Roch (*map p. 581, F4*), one of the largest churches in Paris, rich in paintings and monuments. When it was built, this was already a wealthy and elegant district. The fine Baroque façade was the work of Robert de Cotte in 1736–8, and though its impact improved with cleaning some years ago, the overall effect is hampered by the church's confined position.

INTERIOR OF SAINT-ROCH

The body of the church, which has a classical layout, was begun in 1653 to plans by Jacques Lemercier but only completed in 1719 thanks to a generous donation from the Scottish entrepreneur John Law (*see below*). In the meantime, from 1706–10, Jules Hardouin-Mansart added the circular Chapel of the Virgin at the east end (liturgical east; the church is in fact aligned north–south). The building was consecrated in 1740 and around ten years later was extended by the Chapel of the Calvary to produce a dramatic sequence of Baroque spaces. The total length of the interior is 126m. Between 1750 and 1770, at the instigation of Curé Jean-Baptiste Marduel, St-Roch was endowed with a grandiose ensemble of painted and sculpted decoration. Many of the original works were lost at the Revolution but replacements were commissioned in the 19th century and other works were acquired from defunct churches.

West end: On the west wall is a medallion **memorial to the dramatist Corneille** (d. 1684), who is buried in the church. The organ case dates from 1752, although the instrument has been modified several times.

South side: In the first chapel are a bust of François de Créquy (d. 1687) by Coysevox, the Spanish sculptor to the court of King Louis XIV who also worked at Versailles, and the tomb of the Comte d'Harcourt (d. 1666) by Renard. The second chapel contains a monument

SAINT-ROCH
Guillaume Coustou's tomb statue of Cardinal Dubois (1723), Prime Minister during the regency of Philippe, Duc d'Orléans.

by J-B. Huez to the astronomer and Newtonian mathematician Maupertuis (d. 1759) and the tomb statue of Cardinal Dubois (d. 1723) by G. Coustou. Dubois, Prime Minister during the minority of Louis XV, was a statesman of some skill who found himself attempting to rescue France from the disastrous results of John Law's financial speculations. Law had won the confidence of Philippe, Duc d'Orléans, the young and gullible regent, that he could free France from the debts amassed by Louis XIV. Law was quick to recognise the attractions of credit notes and paper money and founded the national Banque Générale in 1716. He was bankrupted in 1720, after the collapse of his bank and the failure of his 'Mississippi Scheme' to reclaim and settle Louisiana. It was an early example of a financial bubble. Law decamped to Venice, where he died in 1729.

East end: In the dome of the Chapel of the Virgin is a restored painting of *The Assumption* (1756) by Jean-Baptiste Pierre, a forerunner in his style to J.-L. David. The large *Glory* (1756), with rays of light bursting from stucco clouds, is by Mme de Pompadour's favourite Rococo sculptor, Étienne-Maurice Falconet. Part of a now-vanished group, it forms the backdrop to a marble *Nativity* by Michel Anguier, from the church of

Val-de-Grâce. The Communion Chapel behind the Chapel of the Virgin has a curious tabernacle (c. 1840) inspired by the Ark of the Covenant of the Temple in Jerusalem, two many-branched candlesticks (likewise inspired) and some fine stained glass depicting *St Denis the Areopagite* (1849). In the ambulatory hang 18th- and 19th-century paintings by Jean Restout, among others.

North side: On the last pillar on the west side of the ambulatory is a bust of Le Nôtre (d. 1707) by Coysevox and in the transept a plaster of *St Andrew* by Pradier (1823) and a statue of *St Augustine* by Huez (1766); also a canvas of *St Denis Preaching* (1767) by Joseph-Marie Vien and 19th-century murals. The next chapel contains a monument to the Abbé de l'Épée, founder of the first ever school for the deaf (*see p. 68*). His monument incorporates the sign language he invented. Beyond that is the Chapel of Compassion, where ashes and soil from ten concentration camps are enclosed behind an inscribed stone plaque. The next chapel contains the remains (bust and a mourner) of a monument to the Baroque artist Pierre Mignard (d. 1695) by Jean-Baptiste II Lemoyne (1744). And in the last chapel (the baptistery) are two mural paintings by Théodore Chassériau, a gifted disciple of Ingres, showing St Philip and St Francis Xavier baptising.

Choir: In the choir is a sculpture of *Christ on the Mount of Olives*, another work by Falconet (1757). The stalls are 18th-century, as is the dramatic sounding board above the pulpit. This latter is the work of Simon Challe, a triumph of Bernini-esque Italianate Baroque showing the Angel of the Last Judgement brandishing his trumpet.

The **eastern section of Rue St-Honoré**, beyond St-Roch, is where Napoleon suppressed the Royalist rising of 5th October 1795. Look right down Rue des Pyramides towards the river to see a gilt bronze equestrian **statue of Joan of Arc** by Frémiet. A little further down Rue St Honoré, at no. 163, a plaque with a bust overlooking Place Malraux (look up to see it) reminds us that Joan of Arc was wounded near this spot in 1492, close to the old Porte St-Honoré city gate.

OPÉRA GARNIER

Map p. 581, F3. Métro 3, 7 and 8 to Opéra. For the box office, enter at the corner of rues Scribe and Auber, Mon–Sat 11.30–6.30 and 1hr before performances start. Telephone bookings Mon–Fri 9–6, Sat 9–1, T: 0892 89 90 90; from outside France T: +33 1 71 25 24 23; or book online at www.operadeparis.fr.

The public areas may be visited when not in use (enter from Rue Scribe). Open daily 10–5, mid-July–end Aug 10–6; during afternoon performances 10-1. Closed 1 Jan, 1 May, consult website for exceptional closures. Visitors' ticket office is in the second vestibule. Guided visits in English Wed, Sat, Sun at 11.30, 2 and 3.30; audioguides available.

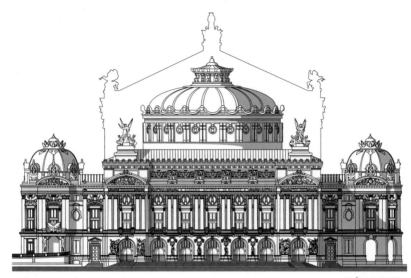

OPÉRA GARNIER

A visit to the interior of the Paris Opera House provides an insight into its drama and opulence even if you are not planning to attend a performance.

The first opera house in Paris was established in 1669, by Perrin, Cambert and the Marquis de Sourdéac, on the Left Bank between the Rue de Seine and Rue Mazarine. The first director was Lully (from 1674), under whom it acquired its secondary title of Académie Royale de Musique. The present Opéra, an appropriately lavish monument to the grandiosity of the Second Empire, was built in 1861–75 to the designs of Charles Garnier. It was inspired by the 18th-century Bordeaux Opera, but aimed to capture a nobler clientèle than the wealthy bourgeois Bordelais. It should have been one of the most splendid symbols of the Second Empire, within easy reach of the Louvre and the Palais Royal, but it was not completed until 1875. The main façade, seen from Avenue de l'Opéra, is elaborately adorned with coloured marbles and sculpture. On either side of the arcade opening into the vestibule are gilded allegorical groups, including (right) a copy of *La Danse* by Carpeaux (original in the Musée d'Orsay). Higher up, between the monolithic columns of the loggia, are medallions and gilt bronze statues of composers and librettists. Behind the low dome of the auditorium is a triangular pediment crowned by a statue of Apollo of the Golden Lyre.

VISITING THE OPÉRA

The visit starts not where the audience would arrive, but via the columned **members' rotunda** leading to the **Pythia Fountain**, an extravagant affair below the Grand Staircase (with a bronze sculpture of the priestess of Apollo at Delphi sitting on her tripod). The white marble stairs are 10m wide and the balustrade of onyx and rosso and verde antico is lit by elaborate chandeliers.

On the first floor where the staircase divides, is the entrance to the stalls and the theatre, flanked by caryatids. The **auditorium**, with five tiers of boxes, is resplendent in red plush and gilt. The dome, resting on eight pillars of scagliola, was painted in disturbing contrast to the rest of the décor in 1964 by Chagall, with murals inspired by nine operas. The huge stage is 60m high, 52m wide and 37m deep. Behind it is the **Foyer de la Danse** (the scene of many paintings of ballet dancers by Degas), with a mirror measuring 7m by 10m. At the end of a long gallery is the **Salon du Glacier**, with Belle-Époque decoration.

From the **avant-foyer** is a fine view of the Grand Staircase, and at its extremities are the Salon du Soleil and the Salon de la Lune. The avant-foyer has glass doors (in the centre of which is Carpeaux's bust of Garnier) leading to the **Grand Foyer**, all pomp and grandeur, lined with mirrors and with a painted ceiling. From here is access to the **loggia** and a splendid view down the Avenue de l'Opéra towards the Louvre.

The **Library-Museum** of the Opéra, now a department of the Bibliothèque Nationale, was created in 1866 to conserve all the documents since the opera's creation. Paintings, photographs and maquettes are exhibited, but the reading room itself is reserved for researchers. The charming museum displays in rotation its collection of the scores of all operas and ballets performed here since the Opéra's foundation, as well as over 100,000 drawings of costumes, photographs, paintings and memorabilia.

CHARLES GARNIER

Garnier (1825–98) began his career as an architect's assistant while studying at the École des Beaux-Arts in Paris. He went on to take top place in the Grand-Prix de Rome in architecture, which qualified him to attend the French Academy in Rome. He remained there from 1849–53 and travelled extensively in Greece and Italy. He presented his fourth-year submission at the Paris Salon in 1853.

After working on a variety of projects he concentrated on the competition for a new opera house, announced by Napoléon III in 1860. He was the winner from among 170 candidates. His neo-Baroque design was fashionable during the Beaux Arts period and its pioneering framework of metal girders assured that it would not only withstand fire, but also support the huge weight of the building.

Garnier's other projects include the Théâtre Marigny (1883; *map p. 581, D4*) and the Grand Concert Hall in the Monte Carlo Casino (1875–9). From 1896 he retired to the house he had built at Bordighera on the Italian Riviera.

The Musée d'Orsay has a display (at the end of the central aisle) which presents all aspects of the construction, decoration and the town planning involved in building the Opéra Garnier, which became the most emblematic building of the Second Empire.

Immediately behind the Opéra, on Boulevard Haussmann, are two famous department stores (*map p. 581, E3–F3*): **Galeries Lafayette** (1898), facing Place Diaghilev (*40 Blvd Haussmann*), with three levels of balconies overlooking the main hall, which is covered with a glass dome; and **Printemps** (1889; remodelled since; *64 Blvd Haussmann*), which has a panoramic view from Level 9.

LES GRANDS BOULEVARDS

Map pp. 581, E4–582, C4. Métro 8, 12 and 14 to Madeleine or 3, 7 and 8 to Opéra.

The once fashionable Grands Boulevards are a succession of wide thoroughfares extending in a curve from Place de la Madeleine (*see p. 282*) to the Bastille. They were laid out in 1670–85 on the site of the inner ramparts built by Charles V in the 14th century and fortifications built by Louis XIII in 1633–7, already demolished some decades earlier (the word 'boulevard' is derived from 'bulwark'). Today they support a combination of banking and commerce with entertainment—opera, theatre, cabaret and cinema—and although not quite the debonair district of the dashing *boulevardiers* who frequented them in the 19th century, there are historic links with developments in art and film in the 19th and early 20th centuries. In terms of nightlife, though, the Grands Boulevards are now a little staid. The more 'happening' clubs and bars are further east, around République and Bastille.

BOULEVARD DES CAPUCINES

Boulevard de la Madeleine, the westernmost of the Grands Boulevards, becomes Blvd des Capucines, off which runs **Square Édouard VII**, built in 1911. It widens out into a circular area with an equestrian statue by Paul Landowski (1913) of Edward VII of England, who was a frequent visitor to Paris and a promoter of the Entente Cordiale which was established between Britain and France in 1904. The theatre here is named after him. On Rue Scribe is the **Musée Fragonard**, a museum of perfume (*see p. 520*).

At no. **35 Blvd des Capucines** (on the other side of the road; right if you are heading east) was the studio of Nadar (Félix Tournachon), the portrait-photographer and aeronaut. The first Impressionist Exhibition was held here in 1874, where Monet's *Impression Sunrise* (1872), depicting the port of Le Havre in the mist, gave the group its name. At **no. 19** the first exhibition of a cinema film was given by the brothers Lumière on 28th December 1895. A few days later the first demonstration of X-rays, a discovery of Dr Roentgen, took place in the same room. Opposite, on the corner of Place de l'Opéra, is Café de la Paix (*see p. 305*). South of the boulevard is **Rue d'Antin**, where Napoleon and Josephine Beauharnais were married in 1796 at no. 3, which was then the Mairie of the 2nd arrondissement. The **Fontaine Gaillon** (1828) in the Rue St-Augustin is by Visconti.

BOULEVARD DES ITALIENS

Boulevard des Italiens, whose once famous cafés have been replaced by cinemas and commercial buildings, derived its name from the Théâtre des Italiens (1783), where Donizetti's *Don Pasquale* was first performed in 1843. Mozart (in 1778) and Chopin (in 1833–6) both stayed at no. 5 **Rue de la Chaussée-d'Antin**. Sir Richard Wallace (*see p. 319*) had a home at no. 2 Rue Taitbout.

Boulevard des Italiens and the eastern extremity of Blvd Haussmann are linked by **Rue Laffitte**, named after the financier and politician Jacques Laffitte (d. 1844), who played a role in the 1830 Revolution. From here there is an almost uninterrupted view of the Sacré Coeur, with the Classical portico of Notre-Dame de Lorette in front. Napoléon III was born on 20th April 1808, at no. 17 Rue Laffitte, where his mother, Hortense de Beauharnais, held brilliant salons. On 14th November 1840, Claude Monet was born at no. 19, and the art dealer and publisher Ambroise Vollard opened his first gallery at no. 39 in 1893 (he later moved to no. 6). It was Vollard who introduced the work of Gauguin and Cézanne to the public and organised the first exhibitions in Paris of works by Picasso and Matisse (1901 and 1904 respectively).

In the parallel **Rue Le Peletier**, Napoléon III narrowly escaped death in 1858, when Orsini attempted to assassinate him, killing or injuring 156 others instead. No. 3 was the Café du Divan, frequented by writers and poets, and Degas painted at the predecessor of the Opéra Comique at no. 6 until 1873. It was in this street that the Second and Third Impressionist exhibitions were held.

South of the Blvd des Italiens in Rue de Marivaux stands the **Opéra Comique-Salle Favart** (*entrance at 2 Rue Boieldieu*), with a diminutive auditorium built 1894–6 and practically no backstage, thus excluding modern opera productions. The Opéra-Comique originated in a company that produced pieces during local fairs, and in 1715 purchased from the Opéra the right of playing vaudevilles interspersed with ariettas. Discord between the two theatres continued until in 1757 Charles Favart finally established the rights of the Opéra-Comique, which moved to this somewhat confined site in 1783, replacing an 18th-century château.

BOULEVARD MONTMARTRE

The short Boulevard Montmartre was very fashionable from its creation in 1676 until 1860 and Haussmann's alterations. Pissarro painted 13 views of it from a window of the Grand Hôtel de Russie, which stood at 1 Rue Drouot. One of the oldest auction-houses in the world, **Drouot**, was established in 1852 at no. 9 Rue Drouot (*open Feb–June Mon–Fri 11–6 and some Sats and Suns; T: 01 48 00 20 20, www.drouot.com. On sale days the public can visit the day before 11–6 and the day of sale 11–12. Sales usually begin at 2pm*). It brings together 74 auction houses and is especially renowned for its art auctions. As well as the main house here, Drouot-Richelieu, which has 16 sales rooms, there is also Drouot-Montmartre at 664 Rue Doudeauville (two rooms; *opens 8.30 or 9; check times in advance*). The monthly *Drouot Gazette* gives details of forthcoming auctions.

At no. 10 Blvd Montmartre is the **Musée Grévin** (*see p. 520*), a waxwork collection, and opposite it at no. 7 is the pretty **Théâtre des Variétés** (*T: 01 42 33 09 92, www.theatre-des-varietes.fr*) built in 1807 for the Comédie-Française (*see p. 306*). It still has its original façade, and in the 1860s it was the scene of several of Offenbach's successes. In the block behind it, between Blvd Montmartre and Rue St-Marc (go through **Passage des Panoramas**, gaslit in 1817), is a labyrinth of 19th-century arcades, offering the double attraction of the arcades themselves and a variety of shops and cafés. This is where the first Académie Julian art school was established in 1868.

Rue du Faubourg-Montmartre, curving northwest towards the former suburb of Montmartre, recalls the time when the boulevard formed the city boundary. This was traditionally a Jewish quarter, with several synagogues. Restaurant Chartier at no. 7 is one of those places that every visitor to Paris knows about. Originally a workmen's canteen or *bouillon*, it has kept its 19th-century décor (*see opposite*).

At no. 32 Rue Richer is the **Folies-Bergère** music hall, founded in 1869 and with an Art Deco interior (*T: 01 44 79 98 60, www.foliesbergere.com*). Manet's *Bar at the Folies-Bergère* (Courtauld Gallery, London) was indeed painted here in 1881.

BOULEVARDS POISSONNIÈRE AND BONNE NOUVELLE

Boulevard Poissonnière is crossed by Rue Poissonnière (south) and its northern extension, the Rue du Faubourg-Poissonnière, which was the route taken by fishmongers on their way to Les Halles.

Beyond this junction is Boulevard de Bonne-Nouvelle, on the northern side of which is the façade (1887) of the **Théâtre du Gymnase** (*www.theatredugymnase.com*), an institution with a formidable reputation on the French comedy circuit. South are steps leading to the church of **Notre-Dame de Bonne-Nouvelle**, rebuilt in 1824 with an earlier belfry. A plaque inside records that the foundation stone was laid by Anne of Austria, Louis XIII's queen. At no. 34 is the popular Delaville Café (*see opposite*).

EATING AND DRINKING AROUND RUE ST-HONORÉ, THE OPÉRA AND GRANDS BOULEVARDS

RUE ST-HONORÉ

€€€ Restaurant at Hôtel Costes. An interior patio, open in summer, is overlooked by a loggia and statues and surrounded by small, intimate dining areas. The service can take a while to warm up and the menu, typically Costes, is quite limited but excellent and resolutely international (club sandwiches, tuna tartare). Book well in advance. *239 Rue St-Honoré. T: 01 42 44 50 00 or 01 42 44 50 25, hotel-costes.com. Map p. 581, E4.*

€–€€ Hotel Regina. The open-air Courtyard Garden in this elegant haven of a hotel offers a good lunch menu. If not fine enough for the courtyard, there is the English bar in the Lounge Club. *2 Pl. des Pyramides. T: 01 42 60 31 10, www.regina-hotel.*

com. *Map p. 581, F4.*

€ L'Absinthe. With a traditional 19th-century bistrot décor, a large terrace and a very good-value lunch *formule*, this makes an excellent choice. Under the auspices of Michelin-starred chef Michel Rostang, the menu offers excellent takes on traditional dishes: grilled duck foie gras with parmesan, rib eye steak pan seared with béarnaise sauce, salmon with sorrel, and iced soufflé with pear and absinthe. *24 Place du Marché-St-Honoré. T: 01 49 26 90 04, www.restaurantabsinthe. com. Map p. 581, F4.*

€ Razowski. American burger bar on Place du Marché-St-Honoré. They have another branch at 169 Blvd St-Germain on the Left Bank. *38 Place du Marché-St-Honoré. T: 01 42 96 53*

20, www.razowski.fr. Map p. 581, F4.
€ **Le Soufflé**. Tucked away in a secluded corner, this place has long specialised in soufflés. There is even a three-course soufflé menu—but there are alternatives. Closed Sun. *36 Rue du Mont-Thabor. T: 01 42 60 27 19, www.lesouffle.fr. Map p. 581, E4.*
€ **Très Honoré**. Bar and restaurant with a neo-'20s décor and reasonable prices. *35 Place du Marché-St-Honoré. T: 01 44 86 97 97, www.treshonore.com. Map p. 581, F4.*

OPÉRA/BOULEVARDS

€€–€€€ **Café de la Paix**. Luxurious café facing Place de l'Opéra, part of the Intercontinental Grand Hotel. The Sunday champagne brunch is superb. There is also the large winter-garden restaurant, €–€€ La Verrière (*2 Rue Scribe, T: 01 40 07 36 35*) which dominates the opera foyer. *12 Blvd des Capucines. T: 01 40 07 36 36. Map p. 581, F4.*
€ **Boco Opéra**. Part of a chain of bistrot/takeaway outlets specialising in prepared dishes presented in '*bocals*' (sealed jars), not new, but a novel concept for fast food. All organic produce and classy recipes, from which a whole meal can be put together (some dishes need heating). Also at St-Lazare, La Défense, Bercy-Village and elsewhere. Closed Sun. *3 Rue Danielle-Casanova. T: 01 42 61 17 67, www.boco.fr. Map p. 581, F4.*
€ **Le Bouillon Chartier**. It still exists, is still budget, and still loved. It has had only four owners since it opened in 1896; reliable, traditional choices,

open 7 days a week 11.30am–10pm. *7 Rue du Faubourg Montmartre. No reservations, www.bouillon-chartier.com. Map p. 582, B3.*
€ **Delaville Café**. A popular and unusual bar/restaurant in the lively area close to République, with several rooms of strangely contrasting décor inherited from previous occupants, including a butterfly collection. The Delaville is stylish yet low-key with a spacious outdoor terrace and a wide choice on the menu: salads, dim sum, hot dogs and fillet of beef. Copious Sunday brunch. *34 Blvd de Bonne-Nouvelle. T: 01 48 24 48 09, delaville-cafe.com. Map p. 582, C4.*
€ **Frenchie**. ■ The creation of Gregory Marchand, who worked with Jamie Oliver and other British and US chefs, where everything is home made and the meat home-cured. *5 Rue du Nil. T: 01 40 39 96 19, www.frenchie-restaurant.com. Map p. 582, C4.* € **Frenchie Wine Bar** is a drop-in place for a drink and a bite to eat (*no reservations*). € **Frenchie to Go** (*9 Rue du Nil*) is a breakfast/coffee shop (*no telephone, very small*) open Tues–Sat, 8.30am-4.30pm, Sat-Sun 9.30–5.30pm for brunch or sandwiches, fish & chips and cheesecake.
€ **Le Richer**. An annexe to L'Office at 3 Rue Richer. Breakfast is served all day and prices are very reasonable. Straightforward and comfortable, it is popular with young people. *2 Rue Richer. No phone, no reservations, www.lericher.com. Map p. 582, C3.*

WALK TWO: AROUND PALAIS ROYAL

The area of the Palais Royal (*map p. 587, D1*), laid out in the 17th century, is central yet discreet. Close to the financial district of Paris, the old palace now encompasses government institutions, shops and restaurants, and elegant old apartment blocks with galleries around a formal Parisian garden. Close by are the Théâtre Français, the Bourse (Stock Exchange) and the Bibliothèque Nationale.

To begin the walk, take Métro 1 or 7 to Palais Royal-Musée du Louvre.

THE THÉÂTRE FRANÇAIS, BETTER known as the **Comédie-Française** (*tickets, T: 0825 10 16 80, www.comediefrancaise.fr; guided visits in French organised by CNM; see p. 540*) and which is part of the Palais Royal, presents a profusion of Tuscan columns to Place André-Malraux and Place Colette. Built from 1786–90 by Victor Louis for the Théâtre des Variétés, it was remodelled in 1900 after a serious fire and much restored. The company originated in the Comédiens-Français created by Louis XIV in 1680, seven years after Molière's death, which brought together two rival troupes: l'Hôtel de Guénégaud, Molière's former company, and the actors of the Hôtel de Bourgogne. The company had many homes before settling here in 1799, led by the great actor François-Joseph Talma. In 1812 Napoleon signed a decree (when he happened to be in Moscow) reorganising the Comédie-Française, which is still a private company with 37 shareholding member actors and 20 contracted actors. The chair in which Molière died in 1673, while playing the part of Argan in *Le Malade Imaginaire*, is in the public foyer protected by a glass case. The theatre also owns several statues of actors and dramatists, including a seated statue of Voltaire by Houdon, *Talma* by David d'Angers, *Dumas fils*

by Carpeaux, *Mirabeau* by Rodin and *George Sand* by Clésinger; also a portrait of Talma by Delacroix and other paintings. The auditorium ceiling was painted by Albert Besnard in 1913.

Follow **Rue de Richelieu** north from Place André-Malraux. The minuscule restaurant L'Incroyable at no. 26 is named after the *incroyables* who, in the 18th century, were the male version of the *merveilleuses*, the post-Terror generation of fops who dressed and behaved outrageously. Further on, on the corner of Rue Molière (left), is the ***Fontaine Molière*** by the architect Visconti (1844), with a bronze statue of the playwright by Gabriel Seurre and supporting marbles by James Pradier.

Slip through the tiny alley of L'Incroyable into Rue de Montpensier, and then turn left and rapidly right into the large rectangle of the **Jardin du Palais Royal**, a calm and decorous oasis giving the lie to the turbulence and notoriety of its past. The buildings on three sides create a harmonious ensemble and under their arcades are specialist shops and varied restaurants. Enfilades of lime trees planted in 1970 flank a formal parterre enlivened by colourful flowers and a fountain. The houses and galleries were the work of the architect Victor Louis and built as a speculative

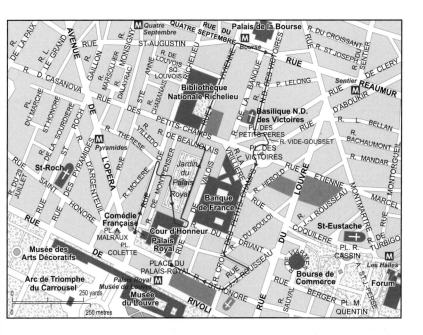

venture in 1781–6 by Philippe-Égalité (so called because of his democratic views), descendant of the Orléans side of the royal family. At the time he was heavily in debt, and shops and cafés were let out. The square became a fashionable place to be seen and smart restaurants opened, including the Grand Véfour (*see p. 312*) under the northwestern arcades. Over the years the cafés became the rendezvous for political activists, literati and—since the police were excluded from entry—for various insalubrious goings-on, especially prostitution. On 13th July 1789 Camille Desmoulins delivered from the garden the fiery harangue which precipitated the fall of the Bastille the following day. Charlotte Corday purchased the knife to kill Marat from one of the shops here. Café du Caveau at nos. 89–92, which had flourished during the *Ancien Régime* and

the Revolution, later became a meeting place of the partisans of the Resistance. Famous residents of Palais Royal have included the multi-talented Jean Cocteau, author of *Les Enfants Terribles* (1929), who spent the latter part of his life at no. 36; and Colette, author of *Le Blé en Herbe* (1923) and *Gigi* (1945), among many other novels, who lived in Palais Royal from 1927–9 and again from 1932 until her death.

The **Cour d'Honneur**, the main courtyard of the old palace, is separated from the gardens by the Galerie d'Orléans, a double Doric colonnade by Fontaine (1829–31), which was restored and cleared of its shops in 1935. In 1985–6 the pools of the Galerie were adorned by Pol Bury's mobile steel spheres (1985) and the Cour d'Honneur received Daniel Buren's 250 black-and-white, candy striped marble columns

PALAIS ROYAL
The Cour d'Honneur with Daniel Buren's striped columns, *Les Deux Plateaux* (1986).

of differing heights, installed above and below ground. Their minimalist brevity is undoubtedly all the more controversial in these surroundings. The north façade of the courtyard was completed by Fontaine, who also restored the east and west wings.

Immediately east of the Palais-Royal is the **Rue de Valois** with, at nos. 6–8, the former Hôtel Mélusine, where the first meetings of the French Academy took place in 1638–43. The ox carved above the door recalls its period as the restaurant *Boeuf à la Mode* from 1792 to 1936. An inscription high up on the corner of Rue de Valois marks the site of the Salle de Spectacle du Palais-Cardinal,

occupied by Molière's company from 1661–73 and by the Académie Royale de Musique from 1673 until the fire in 1763.

Leave Palais Royal to the north, cross Rue de Beaujolais and Rue des Petits-Champs (to the left, at no. 12 Rue Chabanais, was the setting of Toulouse-Lautrec's painting *Au Salon*; 1894) and go up **Rue Vivienne**, past the restaurant Le Grand Colbert (*see p. 313*), to find the **Galerie Colbert**, which opened in 1826 on the site of an *hôtel particulier*, when shopping arcades became all the rage. It is a handsome structure with a rotunda in the middle. It adjoins the L-shaped **Galerie Vivienne**, which opened at the same time. First called Galerie

PALAIS ROYAL

The palace, originally known as the Palais-Cardinal, was designed by Jacques Lemercier in 1634–9 for Richelieu, Louis XIII's chief minister, to be near the Louvre. Richelieu (d. 1642) bequeathed it to the king, who died the following year. Anne of Austria (d. 1666), then queen regent, took up residence with her sons Louis XIV and Philippe d'Orléans, and called it Palais Royal. They had to beat a hasty retreat during the Fronde in 1648 and when Louis XIV returned he preferred to live at Versailles. Queen Henrietta Maria, widow of Charles I of England and sister of Louis XIII, moved in. When her daughter married Monsieur, brother of Louis XIV, the palace passed to him and his male heirs until 1848, and was altered by Mansart. The years up until 1723 were the most brilliant period of the palace, when constant improvements were made. In 1763 the southeast wing, including Richelieu's theatre, burned down and the buildings of the Cour de l'Horloge, facing Place du Palais-Royal, were rebuilt by Constant d'Ivry, with sculptures by Pajou and Franceschi. The so-called Galerie des Proues (prows) on the east is the only relic of Lemercier's 17th-century building. After the Revolution the name changed to Palais-Égalité and it became government offices, only to return, in 1814, to the Orléans family and its earlier name. It was the residence of King Louis-Philippe until 1832, when the seedier establishments were closed down, but in 1848 it was plundered by revolutionaries. The palace was rebuilt by Chabrol in 1872–6 after it was fired during the Commune. Now occupied by the Conseil d'État and the Ministère de la Culture et de la Communication, it is not open to the public.

Marchoux after its owner, who was Président de la Chambre de Notaires, it is abundantly decorated with stuccoes and has an air of faded beauty. It offers a number of small boutiques as well as a popular tea shop, A Priori Thé (*see p. 313*).

Rue Vivienne continues north past the Galeries and **Bibliothèque Nationale Richelieu** (*guided visits by prior arrangement, T: 01 53 79 49 49, visites@bnf.fr*), the buildings of which consist of a group of 17th-century *hôtels particuliers* added to and amended until the end of the 19th century. Formerly known as the Bibliothèque Royale and the Bibliothèque Impériale, the library originated in the private collections of the French kings. It was enriched by the purchase or gift of many famous private libraries and smaller collections (including that of Colbert), and at the Revolution its range was extended with the confiscation of books from numerous convents and châteaux. In 1793 an act was passed that a copy of every publication printed in France should be deposited here by the publishers, making the Bibliothèque Nationale one of the two largest libraries in Europe (the other is the British Library).

The Galerie Mansart, to the right at the foot of the stairs, was formerly Mazarin's sculpture gallery and the Cardinal's coat of arms can be seen above the door. The Musée du Cabinet des Monnaies, Médailles et Antiques (*open daily 1–6*) has precious objects, coins and medals of outstanding quality from antiquity to the present day. The rooms are laid out as a cabinet of curiosities rather than chronologically. Among the treasures are a fabulous emerald which Catherine de Médicis had mounted in gold, and the oldest fan in France, which is purported to have belonged to Diane de Poitiers (1499–1566), favourite of Henri II. There is also the so-called Throne of Dagobert, on which the kings of France were crowned, as well as treasures from the tomb of Childeric I at Tournai, and a Merovingian chalice and oblong paten (6th century) from Gourdon, in the Charollais. A rock crystal bowl, known as the Cup of Chosroes, is studded with garnets and has a central medallion representing the victory of the great Persian warrior-king. The larg-

est antique cameo known, the *Grand Camée*, represents the apotheosis of Germanicus with Tiberius and Livia (Louis XVI ordered it to be moved here from the Sainte-Chapelle. The aquamarine intaglio of Julia, daughter of Titus, is a particularly fine carved portrait. Other objects include a red-figure amphora signed by the Amasis Painter and gold bullae of Charles II of Anjou, King of Naples (1285–1309), Baldwin I, Emperor of Constantinople in 1204–6, and of Edmund, Earl of Lancaster, titular King of Sicily in 1255–63.

HISTORY OF THE BIBLIOTHÈQUE NATIONALE

In 1666 Colbert installed the Bibliothèque du Roi in one of his houses on Rue Vivienne, next to the Hôtel Mazarin. It was first opened to the public for two days a week in 1692. In 1724 the buildings were extended by Robert de Cotte and in 1826 the library spread into Galerie Mazarin, the former Hôtel Chevry and Hôtel Tubeuf, built by Le Muet in 1635, up to Rue des Petits-Champs. Between 1857 and 1873, Henri Labrouste carried out a number of modifications to the building, including the delicate cast- and wrought-iron frame supporting a cluster of faïence cupolas suspended over the Main Reading Room, which seats 259 readers compared to the 2,000 in the new Bibliothèque Nationale-F. Mitterrand (*see p. 83*), to which were transferred printed materials and audio visuals. The emphasis of the Richelieu site is on manuscripts, prints, photographs, maps and plans, coins, medals, antiquities and the performing arts. The Département de la Musique (which has the MS of Mozart's *Don Giovanni*) is at 2 Rue de Louvois.

From the library, continue north to the **Palais de la Bourse** or Stock Exchange (*occasional visits in French with CMN; see p. 540*), also known as the Palais Brongniart after its architect, Alexandre Brongniart. Built in 1808–27, it is a typical Neoclassical building of the period with a grandiose Corinthian peristyle. The north and south wings were added in 1903. In 1864, Rue du Quatre-Septembre was driven through an old district which can has kept some interesting houses around Rue Feydeau,

built on Louis XIII's fortifications, and the Rue des Colonnes.

Turn right now, down Rue Notre-Dame des Victoires, past the church of **Notre-Dame-des-Victoires** (*open 7.30–7.30, Sun and Mon from 8.30*), which stands on the attractive Place des Petits-Pères. The church was dedicated in 1629 by Louis XIII to commemorate the capture of La Rochelle from the Huguenots in the previous year. On the site of a former chapel, it was begun by Pierre Le Muet in 1629–32;

BANQUE DE FRANCE

The 'freighted vessel on a sea argent' has figured in the arms of Paris since the *sceau des marchands de l'eau* (the seal of the water merchants) became the seal of the first municipal administration at the time of St Louis in the 13th century, with its device '*fluctuat nec mergitur*' (tossed but not engulfed). In its stylised form as the logo of the Mairie de Paris, the coat of arms can be found right across the city.

Libéral Bruant designed the transept and last bay of the nave in 1642–6, and it was completed only in 1740 by Sylvain Cartaud. The plan of the interior derives from the Gesù in Rome, with communicating chapels around the nave. Every interior wall is plastered with ex-voto tablets; the organ case and carved stalls date from 1740. The first chapel on the left contains the tomb (above the archway) of the composer Jean-Baptiste Lully (d. 1687) by Pierre Cotton, with a bust by Gaspard Collignon; in the choir are seven paintings of 1746–55 by Carle van Loo, Boucher's great rival as court painter to Louis XV.

From here Rue Vide-Gousset leads southeast into the impressive, circular **Place des Victoires**, laid out by Jules Hardouin-Mansart in 1685; the surrounding houses are harmonious and handsome. The equestrian statue of Louis XIV by Bosio (1822) replaces the original, destroyed in 1792; the bas-reliefs on the pedestal depict the *Passage of the Rhine* and *Louis XIV Distributing Decorations*.

Cross Place des Victoires and take Rue Croix des Petits-Champs, where on the right is the entrance to the **Banque de France** (*occasional visits in French with CMN; see p. 540*), founded in 1800 and relocated here in 1811. The buildings incorporate the former Hôtel de la Vrillière, built by Mansart in 1635–8 and restored by Robert de Cotte in 1713–19, later occupied by the Comte de Toulouse, son of Louis XIV and Mme de Montespan. Within the bank is the profusely-decorated 17th-century Galerie Dorée, one of the first of its kind.

Further on on the left is the entrance to the elegant **Véro-Dodat arcade** (1822), which runs between Rue Croix des Petits-Champs and Rue Jean-Jacques-Rousseau. With its painted ceilings and panelled shopfronts, it was originally lit by gas lamps. It was named after Messieurs Véro and Dodat, two *charcutiers*. Leave the arcade and turn right, then right again down Rue St-Honoré. The building on the right, on the corner of Rue Croix des Petits-Champs, is part of the Ministère de la Culture et de la Communication. It is in fact two buildings, of 1960 and 1989, which were enveloped in a metal fretwork mantle designed by architect Francis Soler in 2002–4 to unify the structure.

Continuing along Rue St-Honoré, on your left is the **Louvre des Antiquaires** (*open Tues–Sun 11–7; closed Mon and also Sun in mid-July–mid-Sept; T: 01 42 97 27 27, www.louvre-antiquaires. com*). This building of 1852, formerly the department store of the Grands Magasins du Louvre, was acquired in 1975 by the British Post Office Staff Superannuation Fund as an investment, then gutted. Since 1978 it has accommodated, on three floors, some 250 professional antique dealers' stalls.

EATING AND DRINKING AROUND PALAIS ROYAL

€€€ **Le Grand Véfour**. This is the city's oldest and one of the greatest restaurants. Situated under the arcades of the Palais Royal, the building is 18th-century and the décor stunningly beautiful with mirrors, painted panels and chandeliers. It has been frequented by diners as diverse as Napoleon Bonaparte and Jean Cocteau—in fact everyone is still drawn to the finest *haute cuisine* from two-star chef Guy Martin, which ranges from classic to very adventurous. One of his most celebrated dishes is *raviolis de foie-gras à l'emulsion de crème truffée*. The kitchens, the cellars and the cigar reserve may be visited. Closed Fri evening, Sat, Sun and holidays. *17 Rue de Beaujolais. T: 01 42 96 56 27, www.grand-vefour.com. Map p. 582, B4.*

€€ **Macéo au Palais Royal**. ■ A fashionable yet traditional address, coolly classy, in the Palais Royal gardens. Light and elegant, a period piece combined with some curious modern fittings, it has four rooms in different styles. The main dining room, Salle Palais Royal, has large windows looking out on the gardens, and the Salon Bar has huge mirrors and crimson walls. The owner, Englishman Mark Williamson (of Willi's Wine Bar; *see below*), takes care of the wine selection and the cuisine is fine and stylish but not over elaborate, and follows the seasons. The Menu Vert is 100 percent vegetarian. *15 Rue des Petits-Champs. T: 01 42 97 53 85, www.maceorestaurant.com. Map p. 582, B4.*

€–€€ **Le Moderne**. Near the Bourse in a busy business quarter, this self-styled 'semi-gastro' bistrot, with clean, sober décor and large windows giving plenty of light, is where professionals come at midday for good-quality, good-value, generous lunch *formules*. In the evenings there is a *menu dégustation*. Closed weekends. *40 Rue Notre-Dame des Victoires. T: 01 73 20 25 60, www.le-moderne.fr. Map p. 582, B4.*

€ **A Priori Thé**. A popular *salon de thé* serving lunch as well as tea Mon–Fri, and brunch Sat–Sun 12–6, in a smart shopping arcade near the Bibliothèque Richelieu. *35 Galerie Vivienne (off Rue Vivienne). T: 01 42 97 48 75, apriorithe.com. Map p. 582, B4.*

€ **Le Grand Colbert**. An attractive brasserie which was a workmen's café in a former draper's shop (the food is up to standard and not too pricey). *2–4 Rue Vivienne. T: 01 42 86 87 88, www.legrandcolbert.fr. Map p. 582, B4.*

€ **Pierre au Palais Royal**. Serves updated traditional French cuisine with an accent on the southwest. *10 Rue de Richelieu/7 Rue de Montpensier. T: 01 42 96 09 17, pierreaupalaisroyal.com. Map p. 582, B4.*

€ **Au Trois Oliviers**. For Provençale specialities. *37bis Rue de Montpensier. T: 01 40 20 03 02. Map p. 582, B4.*

€ **Willi's Wine Bar**. Opened by Englishman Mark Williamson in 1980, this was the first wine bar in Paris and continues to be enormously successful, with a diverse selection of around 250 wines. In a 1930s' building, the bar has a great ambience and a *dégustation* may be accompanied by an attractive 'seasonal and nutritional' meal cooked by the gifted chef, François Yon. The cooking has a Mediterranean slant, with excellent-value daily specials and *à la carte* choices. *13 Rue des Petits-Champs. T: 01 42 61 05 09. Map p. 582, B4.*

PLACE ÉMILE-GOUDEAU
Detail of the Wallace Fountain.

WALK THREE: TO MONTMARTRE
ALONG RUE DES MARTYRS

This walk is a gradual progression uphill towards Montmartre, through a remarkable cross-section of Paris. Rue des Martyrs (*map p. 582, B2*), with many tempting small shops and independent businesses, runs through a mainly residential and lesser-known district, with several interesting twists.

To begin the walk, take Métro 12 to N.-D.-de-Lorette.

NOTRE-DAME-DE-LORETTE (1823–36; *map p. 582, B2*) is a basilican church built by Hippolyte Lebas, characteristic of the July Monarchy, with a Corinthian portico and coffered ceilings inside. It takes its name from the *lorettes*, girls of easy virtue who inhabited this newly-constructed area in the mid-19th century. They were tolerated by property owners seeking a quick return on their investment and were frequently depicted by writers and painters of the time.

In Rue Bourdaloue, which runs up the left flank of the church, at no. 7, is a beautiful *boulangerie*, **Le Pain au Naturel**, which sells organic bread and sandwiches. It is a good place to stock up on refreshments for the walk.

For an interesting detour before embarking on Rue des Martyrs, head left down the casual **Rue St-Lazare**. Among the many places to eat here is the Restaurant Jean at no. 8 (*see p. 327*). Cross Rue St-Georges (where the popular restaurant Georgette is at no. 29; left at the crossroads) and carry on up to **Rue Taitbout** (right), where the atmosphere changes. This area was dubbed 'la Nouvelle Athènes' by Dureau de la Malle in the *Journal des débats* in 1823 for its stately Greek Revival buildings, designed by Auguste Constantin among others. Businessmen and bankers were attracted, but the area also became a haunt of the intelligentsia, favoured by artists, musicians and writers, who met at the Café de la Nouvelle Athènes on Place Pigalle. A typical enclave is **Square d'Orléans** (*at no. 80 Rue Taitbout; entrance through a passageway*), built in 1829 'in the manner of English squares' by the English architect Edward Crecy (the fountain was added in 1856). Always a highly desirable address, this was where George Sand and her lover Chopin had apartments in 1842–7, as well as Alexandre Dumas Père, whose home was decorated by well-known artists.

Leave the square and continue up Rue Taitbout, turning right down **Rue d'Aumale**, where Richard Wagner lived for a while at no. 3, in 1861. At the end of the street is **Rue St-Georges**, with the pretty Le Bon Georges café on the corner. The Goncourt brothers lived on this street in 1849–63 (at no. 43) and Renoir had a studio at no. 35. At the top of Rue St-Georges is a small theatre of the same name, the façade decorated in *trompe l'oeil* (best viewed from the terrace of the friendly café opposite, À La Place St-Georges (*T: 01 42 80 39 32*).

The circular **Place St-Georges** revolves around a fountain-monument to the caricaturist Paul Gavarni (1801–66), who frequently portrayed

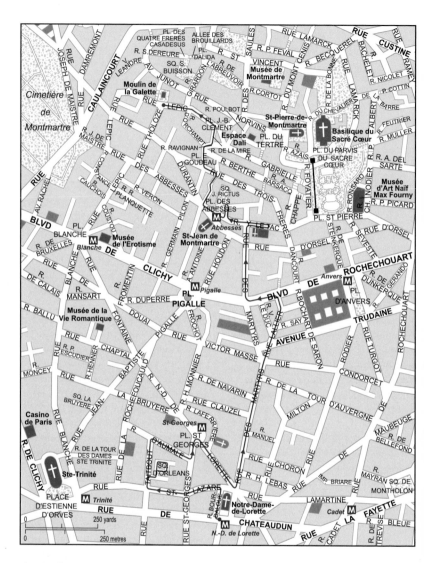

the *demi-mondaines* or *lorettes* of the area, represented here in a sculpture by Denys Puech. The Fondation Dosne-Thiers at no. 27 (to the statue's right) contains the Bibliothèque Thiers, which specialises in Napoleonic and 19th-century French history and is part of the

Institut de France. From 1822–71 this was the residence of President Thiers, who ordered the massacre of thousands of Communards in 1871. The original house (1840) was destroyed by the Communards in 1871 and rebuilt in 1873. Opposite, at no. 28, is an over-ornate

PLACE DES ABBESSES
Detail of Guimard's Métro station entrance, one of only two remaining fully intact.

19th-century Renaissance pastiche, briefly home to the notorious courtesan, the Marquise de Païva, before her *hôtel* on the Champs-Élysées was completed.

With the statue facing you, go down Rue N.-D. de Lorette and at the bottom turn sharp left into **Rue des Martyrs** to admire the shops and, as you ascend, the distant view of Sacré Coeur. The street was well known for its cabarets in the 18th century, but the name refers to the legend of the martyr Denis, and his companions, Rusticus and Eleutherius, who took this route c. 258 to the foot of Montmartre, where they were beheaded. The lower end of Rue des Martyrs is the archetypal Parisian neighbourhood street, nothing fancy and with no pretensions, where locals do their shopping; here you will find grocers, bakers, a fishmonger, cafés and all kinds of shops in succession, and on Sunday there is a morning market. It is a residential district popular with young families and an increasing number of artists. Among the many cafés and restaurants is the Franco-British Rose Bakery and Tea House (no. 46): fragrant, resolutely organic and extremely popular.

At Av. Trudaine, where Rue des Martyrs forks left, turn right up **Rue Lallier**, where at no. 10, on the corner of Boulevard Rochechouart, is the Phonogalerie with an array of old phonographs and records. You are here in the heart of **Pigalle**, the old red-light district. At the meeting point of Blvd Rochechouart and Blvd de Clichy a succession of circuses once stood, the Fernando, which became the Medrano, and latterly the Cirque de Montmartre, which closed in 1972. Today a supermarket occupies the site. After decades of seediness, the foot of the Butte Montmartre, from here to Place des Abbesses, is experiencing a revival.

Rue des Martyrs ends at Rue Yvonne le Tac, traditionally the site of the mar-

SQUARE J.-RICTUS
Detail of the *Mur des je t'aime*.

tyrdom of St Denis, which is marked by the **Chapelle du Martyr** in the convent at no. 9 on the right, originally founded by St Geneviève. It was in the crypt here that Ignatius de Loyola and his six companions, including St Francis Xavier, made a solemn vow, pledging their lives to the service of the Church. Six years later, in 1541, they received papal approval for the foundation of the Society of Jesus.

From here you can choose to continue right up Rue Yvonne Le Tac to visit, at the foot of the Butte Montmartre, in the old Halle St-Pierre (1868) on Rue Ronsard, the **Musée d'Art Naïf Max Fourny** (*open 10–6; T: 01 42 58 72 89, www.hallesaintpierre.org; closed 1 Jan, 1 May, 14 July, 15 Aug, 25 Dec*), a cultural centre which holds the Fourny collection of naïf, brut, outsider and folk art and puts on regular events.

In the other direction, Rue Yvonne Le Tac leads to Place des Abbesses, which has one of only two surviving complete Art Nouveau **Métro entrances by Guimard**, in cast iron and still with its glass roof (it was moved here from Hôtel de Ville in 1974). There is also a Wallace Fountain in the square. Facing it is the

brick-clad **St-Jean de Montmartre** (1894–1904), one of the first churches in reinforced concrete, by Anatole de Baudot. The nave is covered by two cupolas and the interior, which should glitter, is dark with age. Rectangular windows with arched tracery and crazily oblique glazing bars have a variety of glass, dating from 1914 to Max Ingrand windows of 1954.

In front of the church, in Square J. Rictus, is an interesting artwork, **Le Mur des je t'aime** (the 'Wall of I-love-yous'), with declarations of undying affection in over 200 languages including Egyptian hieroglyphs (*www.les-jetaime.com*).

Go up Rue des Abbesses for a short way and then turn right into **Passage des Abbesses**, a cobbled alley which eventually becomes stepped. At the foot of the steps on the right is the gate to the **Jardin des Abbesses**, through which you can see the ruins of the Benedictine convent of Montmartre. At the top of the steps (whose uppermost risers are inscribed '*Aimez-vous*' and '*Prouvez-le*'), on Rue des Trois-Frères, is the grocer's shop Collignon, a famous feature of the 2001 film *Amélie*. Place Émile-Goudeau, a short way further on (and with another Wallace Fountain), is the **site of the Bateau-Lavoir**, the tenement building that was the ramshackle residence at different times of Picasso, Modigliani, Van Dongen, Derain, Gris and Max Jacob, where Picasso painted his ground-breaking *Demoiselles d'Avignon* and where a banquet was held in honour of Henri 'Le Douanier' Rousseau in 1908. Only no. 13A survived a fire in 1970; the rest has been rebuilt.

Until the 1780s, the only access to the summit of Montmartre was **Rue Ravignan** (formerly Chemin Vieux). Steps climb up Rue de la Mire (the name refers to the Paris meridian; *see p. 160*) to arrive in **Place Jean-Baptiste Clément**, named after a hero of the Commune and author of the song *Le Temps des Cerises*. Set to music by Antoine Renard in 1868, it was adopted as the hymn of the Commune of 1871

(today the title is popular as the name of a shop or café). Clément dedicated the song to Louise, a young nurse he met on the barricades.

In Rue Lepic, built in 1852, are the only two remaining (rebuilt) windmills of Montmartre, one behind the other, the old Radet and Blute-fin. The Radet was once known as the **Moulin de la Galette**, a working-class dance hall in the 19th century, where wine and *galettes* (small, round rye cakes) were sold. It was the subject of a painting by Renoir (Musée d'Orsay) in 1876. The Blute-fin now surmounts the Moulin de la Galette Restaurant (*see p. 327*). Van Gogh lived with his brother Theo at no. 54 Rue Lepic in 1886–8. He also painted the windmill.

You are now on the hill of Montmartre and the famous Sacré Coeur is only a few steps away.

WALLACE FOUNTAINS

Known in Paris simply as '*wallaces*', these fountains were donated to the city by Sir Richard Wallace in 1872. Two years previously, upon inheriting his father's estate (*see p. 448*), Sir Richard had been caught up in the Siege of Paris and the painful birth of the Third Republic. Staying on in the city, he paid for an ambulance and a hospital, but the city's violent suppression of the Paris Commune in the following year persuaded Wallace to move his art collection to London for safe-keeping. He offered 50 fountains as a farewell gift. Conceived by Wallace himself in two different models (free-standing and also wall-mounted) and designed by the sculptor Charles-Auguste Lebourg, the fountains provided a free supply of clean drinking water and were enthusiastically received by Parisians. The cast-iron fountains have an ornamental dome supported by four caryatids representing the gowned goddesses of *Simplicity*, *Temperance*, *Charity* and *Kindness*, distinguishable by their knees—whether left or right is covered or bare, held forward or back. The locations of the first batch were chosen by Eugène Belgrand (*see p. 284*). Eighty-two Wallace Fountains can now be found in different parts of Paris, none in the 1st or 2nd arrondissements but an average of five in each of the rest. They still work but are shut down in the winter in case they freeze. They can be found in at least six other French towns. Others exist in more than 20 cities worldwide, with one most recently installed in Macao (the second in Asia after Tokyo).

Montmartre

The hill of Montmartre, the martyrs' mount, has been a sacred place since time immemorial. One of the oldest churches in Paris stands here, St Pierre, dwarfed by the great new church of Sacré Coeur close by, built in the 19th century in a totally different style.

There are several suggestions for the origin of the name Montmartre, but the most likely would be *Mons Martyrum*, referring to the martyrdom of St Denis and his companions. According to tradition, Denis walked from here northwards to the site of his burial, now called St-Denis (*see p. 501*), carrying his severed head (hence the multiple depictions of him with his head literally in his hands). Taking a straight line, he would have gone over the Butte Montmartre, which is 130m at the

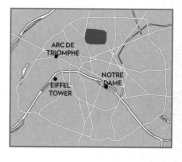

summit with an east–west spine of about 500m. A strategic vantage point, its history is characterised by sieges and battles. Henri of Navarre occupied the hill in 1589 when besieging Paris (*see p. 16*); the final struggle between the French and the Allies took place here in 1814; and on 18th March 1871, to the northeast of the Butte, two generals were murdered by insurgents, precipitating ever more drastic government action against the Communards. In more distant times the hill was covered with vines (a single plot survives) and watered by numerous springs, its rocky cliffs dotted with windmills and gypsum quarries. Until the late 18th century, only one route led south, and one to the north, but as more were built, the Butte attracted poor artists, being both picturesque and cheap, and it remained an artistic centre for about 30 years until the artists gradually retreated towards the Left Bank.

The bohemian past of Montmartre continues to draw the tourist crowds, but despite its popularity the village has retained a distinct atmosphere, best discovered on foot or sitting in a café.

Getting to Montmartre

Métro: Abbesses (line 12) or Anvers (line 2). The Montmartrobus (no. 18) from Pigalle to the Mairie du 18ème runs every 12mins. Otherwise you can follow the example of St-Denis and approach Montmartre on foot (see p. 315).

ST-PIERRE-DE-MONTMARTRE

St-Pierre-de-Montmartre (*map p. 582, B1; open daily 9.30–7*), the successor of an earlier church built to commemorate the martyrdom of St Denis, is a relic of a Benedictine nunnery founded in 1134 by Adélaïde de Savoie. It was consecrated in the presence of her son Louis VII by Pope Eugenius III in 1147 and is one of the oldest churches in Paris. The façade dates from the late 17th century. The **bronze doors** (1980), with scenes from the life of St Peter, were made by T. Gismondi.

Inside, against the west wall, are two ancient columns with 7th-century capitals and two more of the same date at the apse entrance. The Romanesque nave has 15th-century vaulting; the north aisle dates from 1765 and the south c. 1838, was vaulted 1900–5. In the south aisle is a model for the fountain statue of St Denis in Place Buisson (*see p. 324*), by Fernand Guignier. The transept and the choir retain Romanesque elements with, over the choir, one of the earliest examples in Paris of a ribbed vault (1147). There is a modern altar and modern glass by Max Ingrand. In the north aisle, placed upright on the wall, is the tomb slab of the foundress, who died in the abbey here in 1154.

Foundations of a Roman temple were discovered to the north of the church. The **Cimetière du Calvaire**, where the circumnavigator Louis Bougainville (d. 1811) and the sculptor Pigalle (d. 1885) are buried, and its adjoining garden, where there are Stations of the Cross executed for Richelieu, are only open on 1st Nov, All Saints Day.

BASILICA OF THE SACRÉ COEUR

Map p. 582, B1. Open 6am–10.30pm; video and audioguide available for smartphone app. The funicular runs every day at five-minute intervals between 6 and 12.45am from Place Suzanne Valadon (one Métro ticket); journey time 1'30".

This remarkable Romanesque-Byzantine edifice, with its three domes, built in Château-Landon stone which whitens with age, is visible from almost every part of Paris. The façade is composed of two superimposed round-headed bays of three arches and in the niche above is a sculpture of the *Sacred Heart blessing Paris*. The equestrian statues at the front of the basilica, of *Joan of Arc* and *St Louis*, are by Hippolyte Lefèbvre. Bronze doors with a delicate vegetal design welcome visitors.

In 1873 the National Assembly decreed the building of a basilica here as an expiatory offering after the Franco-Prussian War of 1870–1. It was dedicated to the Sacré Coeur, the cult of the Sacred Heart, which became popular after the first pilgrimage in 1873 to Paray-le-Monial in Burgundy, the site of a 17th-century revelation to a young nun. Work on the church began in 1876 after plans by Paul Abadie, who derived his inspiration from St-Front at Périgueux in the Dordogne, itself inspired by Byzantine churches, which he had recently restored. Consecrated in 1891, Sacré Coeur was completed in 1914 and elevated to basilica status in 1919. The square campanile contains the *Savoyarde*, one of the world's heaviest bells at 19 tons.

INTERIOR OF THE SACRÉ COEUR

Despite the monumental scale, the church is always crowded. The nave, in the form of a Greek cross, is surmounted by an 83m high dome on pendentives and the huge choir has eleven tall round arches, seemingly squeezed together. The high altar is a bronze reproduction of the altar at Cluny (Burgundy). The surfaces of the interior are extensively decorated with mosaics by Luc-Olivier Merson, including the largest in the world above the high altar depicting *Christ and the Sacred Heart worshipped by the Virgin, Joan of Arc and St Michael*. The figure of Christ robed in white stands against a blue background, his arms spread wide to reveal the golden heart. He is surrounded by adoring masses, including the Virgin, Joan of Arc and St Michael as well as haloed saints. The 20th-century glass makes an interesting contrast with the rest of the décor. It is possible to climb up into the dome for a remarkable view of the interior and for a close-up of the 80 exterior columns, each with a different capital.

OTHER SIGHTS OF MONTMARTRE

Rue du Mont-Cenis opens into the famously commercialised and crowded **Place du Tertre** (*map p. 582, B1*), where rapid-portrait artists constantly tout for business. In summer or winter it has a holiday atmosphere (and pickpockets).

La Folie Sandrin (1774), at no. 22 Rue Norvins, was a mental clinic whose most famous patient was the schizophrenic poet Gérard de Nerval, in 1841. He eventually committed suicide in 1855. The **Espace Dalí** (*open 10–6; T: 01 42 64 40 10, daliparis. com*), with over 300 works by the Surrealist artist, is close by in Rue Poulbot.

WEST MONTMARTRE

At no. 15 **Avenue Junot** is a Modern Movement house built in 1926 by Adolf Loos, the Viennese purist, for the Dadaist writer Tristan Tzara. No. 13 next door was the home of Francisque Poulbot (d. 1946), famed for her drawings of local children. The painter-engraver Eugène Paul lived on Impasse Girardon.

Square Suzanne Buisson (named after a heroine of the Resistance) is a small public garden with, surmounting a fountain, a statue of St Denis carrying his head in his hands. At the back of the garden to the right, the ground slopes downhill and steps lead into Place des Quatres-Frères Casadesus, at the end of Rue Simon Dereure. The **Paris meridian** is marked in the pavement outside no. 15 Rue Dereure by a small bronze disc engraved 'Arago N S' (*for more on Arago and the meridian, see p. 160*). Steps lead up from the corner of Place Casadesus to the **Allée des Brouillards**, alongside the 18th-century Château des Brouillards (restored 1922–6) built on the site of the Moulin des Brouillards (mists). Renoir's final residence in Monmartre was at no. 6 on the left. The Allée emerges into **Place Dalida**, where there is a bronze bust of the hugely suc-

SQUARE SUZANNE BUISSON
St Denis, by Fernand Guignier (1941).

cessful singer, actress and Miss Egypt, who was born Yolanda Gigliotti in Cairo in 1933 and who lived nearby on Rue d'Orchampt. Despite the success of her career, Dalida's personal life was turbulent and tragic. She took her own life in 1987.

Where Rue de l'Abreuvoir meets Rue des Saules is **La Maison Rose** (now a restaurant), painted by Maurice Utrillo, who was born in Rue du Poteau and buried in the nearby Cimetière St-Vincent. Rue des Saules turns downhill past the **Clos Montmartre**, planted in 1933 with vines which are harvested each October and vinified in the Mairie of the 18th arrondissement. No. 4 in this street is **Au Lapin Agile**, named after sign painted by the caricaturist André Gill of a rabbit jumping out of a cooking pot. Originally made famous by its artistic clientèle (such as Modigliani, Picasso and Utrillo), it has been a cabaret-chansonnier since 1860 (*T: 01 46 06 85 87, www.au-lapin-agile.com*).

Old Montmartre is recaptured in the **Musée de Montmartre** (*open Tues–Sun 10–6, closed Mon; T: 01 49 25 89 39, www.museedemontmartre.fr*) at no. 12 Rue Cortot, a 17th-century house in a garden, which once belonged to one of Molière's troupe. Occupants over the years included Renoir in 1875, Raoul Dufy, Suzanne Valadon and her son Maurice Utrillo. The museum records the history of the district and contains ephemera and material of local interest ranging from Clignancourt porcelain to a reconstruction of a *montmartrois* bistrot. Exhibits evoke local cabarets, notably the Chat Noir, known for its shadow theatre. The composer Erik Satie lived a few doors further down.

CIMETIÈRE DE MONTMARTRE

The Cimetière de Montmartre (*map p. 582, A1*) is one of the three great cemeteries of Paris, along with Père-Lachaise and Montparnasse. The main entrance is on Avenue Rachel (named after the great actress Rachel Félix, sometime lover of Napoléon III, who is buried here). Built on old quarries in 1798 and enlarged in 1825, it now covers over eleven hectares and has around 750 trees. Plans indicating where the illustrious are buried are available at the main entrance. It is fascinating both for its tombstone art (by Bartholdi, David d'Angers, Falguière, Rodin and Rude among others) and the names of those who lie here. Zola was entombed in a red marble monstrosity before his remains were translated to the Panthéon. Among others buried in Montmartre are the comedy *artiste* La Goulue, immortalised by Toulouse-Lautrec; writers as varied as Stendhal and Feydeau; composers including Berlioz, Delibes and Offenbach; painters such as Fragonard and Degas; the dancer Nijinsky; Mme Récamier, Marie Duplessis (*La Dame aux Camélias*) and Nissim de Camondo (*see p. 288*).

CLICHY

Map p. 581, E2. Métro 2 and 13 to Place de Clichy.

Place de Clichy was the site of the Barrière de Clichy, which on 30th March 1814 was defended against the approaching Prussian troops by pupils from the École Polytechnique and the Garde Nationale under Marshal Moncey. The action is commemorated by a bronze group by Doublemard (1869). The French failed to secure a victory and an armistice was signed. A week later, Napoleon abdicated and departed for Elba. The Place and Boulevard de Clichy were frequently painted by Renoir, Van Gogh (in 1887), Signac and other artists working and living in the vicinity during the 19th century and into the 20th. Rue de Douai (*map p. 581, F2*) was particularly popular with painters and writers, including Charles Dickens. Henri de Toulouse-Lautrec, who kept studios at no. 21 Rue Caulaincourt (*map p. 581, F1*) and 5 Av. Frochot (*map p. 582, B2*), also vividly brought this bohemian *quartier* to life. Renoir had studios at 73 Rue Caulaincourt c. 1910, and Degas died at no. 6 Blvd de Clichy, where Mary Cassatt had painted. Seurat and Signac also worked for a while on Blvd de Clichy (at no. 39 Rue André Antoine, off the boulevard to the left, Seurat died of diphtheria in 1891, aged 31). In 1909 Picasso lived on the boulevard, at no. 130. Reminders of the era are the museums dedicated to Gustave Moreau and also to La Vie Romantique, as well as vestiges of its seamier side. Although today the area is experiencing a revival, the **Moulin Rouge** (founded 1889) grinds on undaunted (*82 Blvd de Clichy, www.moulinrouge.fr*) and at no. 72 is the Musée de l'Érotisme (*see p. 519*).

MUSÉE DE LA VIE ROMANTIQUE

Map p. 582, A2. 16 Rue Chaptal. Open Tues–Sun 10–6; closed Mon and public holidays. T: 01 55 31 95 67. Teashop open March–Oct.

Tucked away at the end of a cobbled courtyard with a small garden is the delightful Musée de la Vie Romantique, in the Maison Renan-Scheffer (built 1830), with collections devoted to George Sand and Ary Scheffer including paintings by Scheffer as well as memorabilia, portraits and furniture; it is also used for temporary exhibitions. Scheffer brought together here the artistic luminaries of the era and the area. His great-niece, daughter of the philosopher Ernest Renan, carried on the tradition. The house remained in the family for about 150 years. As well as the house, there are the studios built by Scheffer for teaching and receiving guests. George Sand, the prolific and unorthodox novelist and writer famous for wearing men's clothes and for taking radical political stances as well as many lovers (de Musset, Liszt and Chopin among them), was an occasional guest of Scheffer's, who here introduced her to Delacroix and Géricault. The celebrity designer Jacques Garcia had a hand in the look of the museum, which was founded in the 1980s as an outpost of the Musée Carnavalet.

MUSÉE GUSTAVE MOREAU

Map p. 582, A2. 14 Rue de la Rochefoucauld. Open Mon, Wed, Thur 10–12.45 & 2–5.15, Fri–Sun 10–5.15; closed Tues. T: 01 48 74 38 50, www.musee-moreau.fr.
The Musée Gustave Moreau contains a collection of some 18,000 paintings and drawings left by Moreau to the state. Moreau himself laid out the museum, which cannot be altered—though it did receive some enhancements in 2013–14, including the private apartment. The walls of the creaking, evocative studio on two floors are covered with paintings by the leading Symbolist, whose use of colour and surprisingly liberal teaching methods profoundly influenced the next generation of artists. A former pupil, Georges Rouault, was the first curator of the museum. Among the works on display are *The Apparition* and *Salomé* (1874–6), *Mystic Flower* (1890), *Hesiod and the Muse, Jupiter and Semele* (1895). A picturesque spiral staircase leads to the upper floor where watercolours are exhibited in rotation and drawings are presented in hinged panels. Degas' *Portrait of the Artist*, dated 1867, also hangs here. On the first floor it is possible to see the tiny apartment in which Moreau and his parents lived, full of family memorabilia.

CASINO DE PARIS AND LA TRINITÉ

At no. 16 Rue de Clichy is the **Casino de Paris** (*map p. 582, A2; T: 01 49 95 22 22, www. casinodeparis.fr*), where Josephine Baker once starred. It originated in 1880, the successor of a disreputable cabaret, which was demolished in 1851 to be replaced by **La Trinité**, identifiable by its 63m-high tower. The church was built 1863–7 by Théodore Ballu in a hybrid 'historic' style characteristic of the Second Empire with a heavy interior. Olivier Messiaën was organist here for some years in the 1930s. In front of the church is a welcome patch of greenery, with fountains and sculptures.

EATING AND DRINKING IN MONTMARTRE

MONTMARTRE

€ Au Clocher de Montmartre. Below Sacré Coeur, a popular bistrot with food combinations that take you by surprise, such as red onions with oxtail stuffing and *religieuse au cassis* (a choux pastry cake). There are also lighter choices on the menu. Good value. *10 Rue Lamarck. T: 01 42 64 90 23, www.auclocherdemontmartre.fr. Map p. 582, B1.*

€ Au Grain de Folie. A vegetarian/vegan restaurant with fairly simple fare. *24 Rue La Vieuville. T: 01 42 58 25 57. Map p. 582, B1.*

€ Le Moulin de la Galette. On the site of the last remaining windmill of the Butte de Montmartre. Nostalgic and touristy, but fun to visit. There are good-value *formules* and menus. *1 Rue Norvins. T: 01 46 06 84 77, www. lemoulindelagalette.fr. Map p. 582, B1.*

€ Bistro Poulbot. Below Sacré-Coeur, offering good Franco-Italian cooking in a modern setting. *Formule*, menu or *à la carte*. *39 Rue Lamarck. T: 01 46 06 86 00, www.bistropoulbot.fr. Map p. 582, B1.*

AROUND RUE DES MARTYRS

€€€ Jean. ■ In a lively area near Rue des Martyrs, the modest exterior belies the fact that it has a Michelin rosette. The cooking is mainly based on traditional French food (though always with a twist) and there are some pasta dishes. Chef Attilio Marazzo trained under Joël Robuchon. Cosy décor with *toile de Jouy* on the walls. *8 Rue St-Lazare. T: 01 48 78 62 73, www.restaurantjean.fr. Map p. 582, B3.*

€€ Les Coulisses Vintage. Modest and unassuming from the exterior, and more about the food than the décor. The choice includes veritable French dishes such as *os à moelle*, *blanquette de veau* and *mousse au chocolat*, and generous servings. *19 Rue Notre-Dame-de-Lorette. T: 01 45 26 46 46. Map p. 582, B3.*

€ La Cantine de la Sigale. Near the corner of Boulevard Rochechouart and Rue des Martyrs, this is a brasserie under the direction of Christian Etchebest and serves dishes with a Basque flavour, such as Ossau-Iraty cheese with black cherry jam. Helpings are generous. Closed Sun. *124 Blvd Rochechouart. T: 01 55 79 10 10, www.cantinelacigale.fr. Map p. 582, B2.*

€ Georgette. Between Rue Lafayette and Pl. St-Georges, this is an unpretentious place where the décor combines exposed beams with '50s' formica. Very local, very seasonal, and the *patronne* (who is not called Georgette) is very much in charge. Traditional *cuisine de grandmère* includes, for example, *velouté de topinambours* (Jerusalem artichokes) or *oreilles de cochon* (pig's ears). *29 Rue St-Georges. T: 01 42 80 39 13. Map p. 582, B3.*

€ Le Pain au Naturel. A *boulangerie* selling organic bread and sandwiches. *7 Rue Bourdaloue. Map p. 582, B3.*

PLACE STRAVINSKY
Blind wall covered with public street art by Jef Aérosol.

Les Halles & Beaubourg

*Les Halles Centrales, the central markets memorably described by Zola as
'Le Ventre de Paris' (the belly of Paris), are long gone, and 'Le Trou' ('the Hole')
of the 1970s is now 'La Canopée'. The area is being regenerated and there is
plenty to see and do. Most famous of all is the Centre Pompidou.*

The fame—and the name—of Les Halles (*map p. 587, E1*) goes back to the markets which were held here from the early 12th century, although in 1969 the commercial activity was moved from central Paris to Rungis, near Orly. The ten huge pavilions constructed by Victor Baltard in the 1850s, plus two of 1936, were all demolished by 1974 (only one was preserved, at Nogent-sur-Marne.)

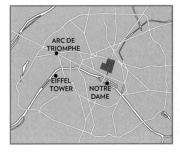

Now a vast translucent canopy hovers above the enhanced urban space at ground level. The scheme, designed by architects Patrick Berger and Jacques Anziutti, also provides much-improved access to underground transport and a modernised RER station, one of the busiest in the network. Cultural spaces are diverse, including a library and an area dedicated to hip-hop, and there is a shopping mall and swimming pool. The last stage is the re-landscaping of the gardens, including the Nelson Mandela Garden. The final result will allow uninterrupted views of the surroundings, notably the church of Saint-Eustache, the Bourse de Commerce and the artworks, which include the large sandstone sculpture of a head, *l'Écoute* (1986) by Henri de Miller, its ear to the ground.

BOURSE DE COMMERCE

The Bourse de Commerce at Place des Deux-Écus, to the west of the Canopée, is the only remaining evidence in Paris of the old markets. A circular mid-18th-century building, formerly the Corn Exchange, it received a metal-framed dome in 1811 and was remodelled in 1888. Inside is a fresco representing international commerce around the upper part of the hall covered by a glass dome. Adjoining its southeast side is a fragment of the Hôtel de la Reine, built by Bullant for Catherine de Médicis in 1572. It was later known as the Hôtel de Soissons and from 1720 stock-jobbing or brokering took place in the garden. Rue Coquillière, which runs into Rue Rambuteau, is lined with shops and restaurants, including Au Pied de Cochon, the brasserie where all-night revellers used to eat oysters for breakfast when the old market was in full swing.

SAINT-EUSTACHE

Map p. 587, E1. Open Mon–Fri 9.30–7, Sat 10–7, Sun 9–7.15. Organ recitals on Sundays and frequent concerts. T: 01 42 36 31 05, www.saint-eustache.org.

Keeping watch over the Jardins des Halles is the church of St-Eustache. Begun in 1532, perhaps by Pierre Lemercier, it was consecrated in 1637. At first sight it appears to be a thoroughly Gothic structure with supporting flying buttresses but, typically of this transitional period, it has Renaissance details and decorations. The Neoclassical colonnade of the west front, completed only in 1754–88, is strangely out of keeping with the rest of the church. The openwork bell-tower, known as the *Plomb de St-Eustache*, above the crossing, has lost its spire, and above the Lady Chapel in the east is a small tower built in 1640 and rebuilt in 1875. Molière was baptised in the church and lived in the district. During the Revolution the church was the scene of the riotous Festival of Reason in 1793, when revellers drank themselves senseless in the square outside around bonfires stoked with the choir stalls. In 1795 it became the Temple of Agriculture. Here Berlioz conducted the first performance of his *Te Deum* (1855) and Liszt his *Messe Solenelle* (1866). St-Eustache has always been noted for its music and holds an organ festival in June and July.

INTERIOR OF SAINT-EUSTACHE

The interior is a striking combination of Gothic plan and Renaissance decoration. The nave is short and the double aisles and chapels continue round the choir, while the wide transepts do not extend beyond the chapel walls. The square piers are decorated with squared shafts in three storeys of superimposed orders, while the vaulting is Flamboyant with heavy pendant bosses. Above the high arcades there is a small gallery. The chapels contain restored paintings from the time of Louis XIII, and the eleven lofty windows of the apse were executed by Soulignac (1631), possibly from cartoons by Philippe de Champaigne. The churchwardens' pew is the work of Pierre Lepautre and Jean-Sylvain Cartaud (c. 1720) and the unadorned stalls were acquired from the convent of Picpus (*see p. 388*). The organ, with an ornate case by Victor Baltard (1854), was rebuilt by the Dutch firm Van den Heuvel in 1986–9 and is one of the most important in Paris.

The **Musicians' Chapel**, second on the south, commemorates Rameau, Franz Liszt and Mozart's mother. The trumeau of the transept doorway supports is a 16th-century statue of *St John* and the second choir chapel has a *Pietà* attributed to Luca Giordano. In the fifth chapel, the glass featuring *St Anthony* was given by the Société de la Charcuterie de France—one of St Anthony's attributes being a pig.

On the altar of the **Lady Chapel** is a *Virgin* by Pigalle (1748) accompanied by murals by the great historicist Thomas Couture (1856).

The very fine but incomplete **tomb of Colbert** (d. 1683), in the first choir chapel of the north aisle, was designed by Le Brun with statues of Colbert and *Fidelity* by Coysevox, and *Abundance* by Tuby. In the next chapel is a painting of the *Supper at*

Emmaus by the school of Rubens and a 17th-century French painting of the *Burial of a Martyr*. *The Ecstasy of the Virgin* (c. 1627) is by Rutilio Manetti and in the west chapel is an *Adoration of the Magi* after Rubens. Over the northwest door is the *Martyrdom of St Eustace* by the early 17th-century French master of the Italian Baroque, Simon Vouet.

RUE SAINT-DENIS

Rue de Turbigo leads northeast from St-Eustache towards Place de la République (*see p. 401*), soon reaching Rue Étienne-Marcel, in which, to the left (at no. 20), rises the **Tour de Jean-sans-Peur**, a graceful defensive tower (c. 1400), the tallest medieval civil tower in Paris, last relic of the palace of the Dukes of Bourgogne. Part of this mansion (see no. 29) was used from 1548 until the turn of the 18th century as a theatre, where plays by Corneille and Racine were performed.

Rue St-Denis (*map p. 587, E1*), which crosses Rue de Turbigo north–south, is one of the oldest routes in Paris. Parallel to the old Roman road of Rue St-Martin, it runs north from Place du Châtelet and leads eventually to the Royal necropolis of St-Denis (*see p. 501*). Pedestrianised near Les Halles, this narrow, bustling street is lined with sandwich bars and seedy shops (and in its northern reaches is a favoured haunt of prostitutes).

At no. 92 Rue St-Denis, the church of **St-Leu-St-Gilles** was built in 1235, the nave reconstructed after 1319. The aisles were added in the 16th century and the choir, still partly Gothic, in 1611 (but reconstructed in 1858–61 to make way for the adjacent boulevard). The façade and windows were remodelled in 1727 and a crypt was excavated in 1780. The church contains three alabaster reliefs (in the sacristy) moved from the Holy Innocents Cemetery (*see below*) and a sculpted group, *St Anne and the Virgin* by Jean Bullant (second chapel south). The organ case is by Nicolas Rimbert (1659). The church also has a painting by Jean Restout: *Disciples à Emmaus* (1735).

Further south, the small **Place Joachim du Bellay** stands on part of the site of the medieval Cimetière des Innocents, the main burial ground of Paris until 1785, when the remains, probably including those of La Fontaine, were transferred to the catacombs (*see p. 162*). Traces of the arches of the cemetery galleries are still to be seen on nos. 11 and 13 in Rue des Innocents off Rue St-Denis. The restored Renaissance *Fontaine des Innocents* in the middle of the square was originally erected in 1548 in the neighbouring Rue St-Denis by Pierre Lescot, with bas-reliefs by Jean Goujon (now in the Louvre). It was remodelled and set up here by Poyet c. 1788; the south side was decorated by Pajou.

At no. 135, in the northern section of Rue St-Denis, an inscription indicates the position of the former Porte St-Denis or Porte aux Peintres, a gateway in the walls of Philippe-Auguste. No. 142 is the *Fontaine de la Reine* (1730). On no. 133 are statues from the medieval Hôpital de St-Jacques, once on this site. The road ends at **Porte St-Denis** (*map p. 582, C4*), a triumphal arch 23m high, designed by Blondel and erected in 1674 to commemorate the victories of Louis XIV in Germany and Holland. The bas-reliefs were designed by Girardon. Rue St-Denis was once known as the Voie Royale, the processional route of entry into Paris, and was used as such on the occasion of Queen Victoria's visit in 1855.

The short Blvd St-Denis leads east to the **Porte St-Martin** (*map p. 583, D4*), another triumphal arch built in 1674 in honour of Louis XIV. It is c. 18m high, vermiculated and decorated with bas-reliefs of contemporary campaigns. Just east of it on Blvd St-Martin are two famous theatres, the **Théâtre de la Renaissance** (*theatrede-larenaissance.com*), managed by Sarah Bernhardt from 1893–9, and the **Théâtre de la Porte-St-Martin** (*www.portestmartin.com*). Both were burnt down during the Commune and rebuilt. They are a reminder of the many playhouses that opened in this area after 1791, with the emancipation of French theatre. In fact so frequent were performances of passionate and bloody melodramas that this street became known as the Boulevard du Crime. Close by is the **Musée de l'Éventail** (Fan Museum; *see p. 520*).

MUSÉE NATIONAL DES ARTS & MÉTIERS

Map p. 583, D4. 60 Rue Réaumur. Métro 3 and 11 to Arts et Métiers. Open Tues–Wed 10–6, Thur 10–9.30, Fri–Sun 10–6; closed Mon, 1 May, 25 Dec. Audioguides. Included in the entrance ticket are guided visits and demonstrations, including of Foucault's pendulum. T: 01 53 01 82 00, www.arts-et-metiers.net.

The Musée National des Arts et Métiers has outstanding historic collections relating to technical innovation and applied sciences in industry. Incorporated in the museum is the Abbey Church of St-Martin-des-Champs. At the northwest corner of the building is the *Fontaine du Vertbois* (1712) and a tower going back to the 12th century.

SAINT-MARTIN-DES-CHAMPS

The priory of St-Martin-des-Champs, founded in 1060 by Henri I and presented to the Abbey of Cluny by Philippe I in 1079, stood outside the city walls until the early 14th century. After the Revolution it became an educational institution and its dependencies were later used as a small-arms factory. In 1798 the buildings were assigned to the Conservatoire des Arts et Métiers, founded in 1794. The collections of Vaucanson and other scientists were assembled here and in 1802 it opened as the Musée des Techniques. The library (42.8m by 11.7m) is now installed in the former refectory, a 13th-century masterpiece, possibly built by Pierre de Montreuil (*see p. 503*), its vaulting supported by a central row of columns and with a reader's pulpit at the east end. The external side of the southern doorway is a good example of decorated Gothic and the sole relic of the original cloister. Further south is the restored 13th-century doorway of the church (enter from the museum). The turret is a comparatively recent addition, restored in 1854–80. The choir has perhaps the earliest Gothic vault in Paris (1130–40), while the aisleless nave dates from the 13th century.

THE MUSEUM COLLECTIONS

The museum is arranged over three floors and divided into seven themes (Scientific Instruments, Materials, Construction, Communication, Energy, Mechanics and Transport, each sub-divided chronologically into pre-1750, 1750–1850, 1850–1950, and 1950 onwards. Exhibits demonstrate the evolution of inventions since the 16th century, not only the technically and scientifically brilliant ones but also the beautiful, skilful or curious. The suggested sequence is to begin the visit on the second floor (lifts).

Second floor

Scientific instruments: In this extensive collection are astronomical and surveying instruments for calculating time, distance, weight, temperature and so forth, including Arsenius's great astrolabe of 1569; Pascal's calculating machine of 1642; and timepieces and clocks by Berthoud, Lepaute, Bréguet, Janvier and other famous 18th-century horologists. There are also Abbé Nollet's instruments of natural philosophy (early electrostats), the laboratory of Jacques-César and Alexandre Charles, Buffon's circular mirror with variable focus, an anemometer (1734) for measuring the speed of wind—the oldest known instrument integrating a system of recording data—and Lavoisier's laboratory (1743–94). Exhibits range from Foucault's experiments with the measurement of the speed of light (1862) to the cyclotron of the Collège de France (1937) and a Cray-2 super computer (1985).

Materials: Includes natural products—paper, ceramics, iron, linen, wool and glass. It addresses the organisation of production techniques, such as the use of fire, various stages of production, especially during the Industrial Revolution, and the evolution of taste leading to objects such as those produced by Émile Gallé at the turn of the 20th century. It also covers the manufacture of aluminium and the development of plastics.

First floor

Construction: This section follows the development of architecture, building and civil engineering in all its aspects, from traditional methods to the greatest revolutions in construction. Ancient methods using wood and stone are described with models and series of relevant tools which underline the individual skills of the craftsman-builder. The great revolution in construction occurred in the 19th century with the introduction of metal frames and concrete; and finally in the 20th century the combination of these developments resulted in reinforced concrete such as used in the Théâtre du Champs-Élysées (1911–13) by Perret.

Communication: Many techniques are covered: writing, and printing, from

Gutenberg (1438) to the mechanised printing press (1750–1850); the development of photographic equipment and the apparatus used by Daguerre, Niépce, Lumière and others in the pioneering days of photography and cinematography; historical equipment such as the optical telegraph invented by Chappe and Edison's phonograph (1877); objects illustrating the development of recording, radio and television; discoveries by Bell; global satellites in the 20th century; and current means of communication, including the internet.

Energy: The display begins with water and windmills, including the Machine de Marly (*see p. 496*). Next is the discovery of steam power, which includes a model of Watt's steam engine, followed by the development of electricity over 200 years. There is also an example of energy economy, with a model of a modern bioclimatic house (1999).

Mechanics: Automation, machine tools, levers and mills are among the subjects of this section. Innovatory objects include everything from the potter's wheel to clocks, and an example of the 18th-century sliding lathe by Vaucanson, agricultural machinery and industrial machine tools. There are also enchanting examples of automata.

Ground floor and chapel

Transport: This area contains examples of early modes of mechanised transport, following the development from wind and animal power to steam, then motorised vehicles. Among the museum's excellent collection are two prototypes of the motor car, Cugnot's steam-carriage of 1770 and one by Serpollet (1888). Early petrol-driven vehicles include a Panhard (1896), Peugeots of 1893 and 1909, a Berliet phaeton (1898), a De Dion-Bouton (1899) and a Renault of 1900. Pioneering aeroplanes include those of Ader (1897), Esnault-Pelterie (1906), the plane in which Blériot made the first flight across the Channel (1909), and a Bréguet of 1911. Foucault's pendulum is in the chancel of the chapel. There is also Scott's steam engine; the first steam-powered bus, called *L'Obéissante*, made by Amédée Boillée; a model for the *Statue of Liberty* by Bartholdi; and a model of the Vulcan engine from the *Ariane* rocket.

QUARTIER DU TEMPLE

Map p. 583, D4. Métro 3 to Temple or 3 and 11 to Arts et Métiers.

Square du Temple is one of the 24 squares created during the Second Empire. The landscaped garden boasts many different trees, a lake and a cascade made with rocks from the Forest of Fontainebleau.

Until the late 12th century it was the site of the stronghold of the Knights Templar, who owned land between this point and Place de la République to the northeast,

SAINTE-ÉLISABETH
Adam and Eve (17th-century wood carving).

the headquarters of their Order in Europe, but it was seized by the spendthrift King Philippe IV (1284–1314) with the connivance of the French pope Clement V, who subjected the knights to the Inquisition. The Grand Master was burned at the stake roughly where the statue of Henri IV stands on the Île de la Cité (*see p. 44*). From 1313 the building was occupied by the Order of St John and a new palace for the prior was built in 1667. Before the Revolution the area was occupied by wealthy families, by artisans who did not belong to the corporations, and therefore were free from many restrictions, and by debtors who were protected here from legal action. With the Revolution, the Tour du Temple (1265) and palace were transformed into a prison where, in August 1792, Louis XVI and the royal family were incarcerated after being taken from the Tuileries (objects from the prison are now in the Musée Carnavalet). Louis XVII is thought to have died here, of tuberculosis, aged ten.

ENVIRONS OF THE SQUARE DU TEMPLE

At 195 Rue du Temple (north of the square) is the **church of St Elisabeth of Hungary**, founded in 1628 by Marie de Médicis and now the church of the Knights of the Order of Malta. The main feature is the woodwork, including, in the ambulatory, 17th-century carvings of biblical scenes from the abbey of St-Vaast at Arras. The *Temptation of Adam and Eve*, as in the carving on the façade of Notre-Dame, features a human-headed serpent rearing up between the forked branches of an apple tree. There is a much-venerated 16th-century *Pietà* in the north aisle.

There are interesting houses in the quarter, including **no. 3 Rue Volta** (corner of Rue Au Maire) which, dating from c. 1300, is possibly the oldest surviving house in Paris (although another house claims that distinction). It is now a Chinese restaurant, and in fact this district is a predominantly Chinese part of town, with numerous Chinese shops and businesses.

SAINT-MERRY
Detail of the west façade.

On **Rue de Montmorency**, the Hôtel de Montmorency (no. 5; *map p. 587, F1*) was the residence of Fouquet, Louis XIV's *Surintendant de Finances*, in 1652. The Maison au Grand-Pignon at no. 51 was built in 1407 by Nicolas Flamel, a wealthy merchant with a reputation as an alchemist in search of the philosopher's stone. The house was restored in 1900 and is now a restaurant (*see p. 348*). It is decorated with scratched designs of angel musicians. A number of early 17th-century houses have survived in Rue Michel-le-Comte.

BEAUBOURG

Map p. 587, F1. Métro 1, 4, 7, 11 and 14 to Châtelet. RER A, B and D to Châtelet-Les Halles.

Bounded by the functional Boulevard de Sébastopol to the west and by the Rue du Renard to the east, the Beaubourg is an old quarter probably best known for the Pompidou Centre, although there are plenty of other attractions as well. Literally translated as 'beautiful market town', the Beaubourg was once a small rural community outside Paris, surrounded by vineyards. It came within the boundaries of the city when Philippe-Auguste's walls were built in the 13th century, the main artery being Rue Beaubourg, focused on St-Merry. This ancient quarter was carved up in the 19th century when Rue Rambuteau and Boulevard Sébastopol were driven through it. By the 1930s it had fallen into neglect and was partially demolished. Its character was radically altered when the Centre Georges Pompidou opened in 1977, but relics of the old Beaubourg still can be found in narrow streets such as Rue Quincampoix (between Rue des Lombards and Rue aux Ours), with houses from the 17th–18th centuries.

SAINT-MERRY

Map p. 487, E1–F1. Open Mon–Sat 12–12.45 & 3–7, Sun 9.30–9. T: 01 42 71 93 93.

The church of St-Merry stands at the intersection of two major Roman roads, the present Rue St-Martin and Rue de la Verrerie. It replaced at least two older churches that covered the grave of St Medericus of Autun (d. c. 700), and was built in Flamboyant Gothic style at a time when Renaissance ideas were taking over in the late 16th century. The porch, although damaged, is carved with pinnacles and friezes and the Gothic tower was completed in 1612 in the style of the period. The west front is notable for its rich decoration, but the statues are mostly poor replacements of 1842. The northwest turret claims the oldest bell in Paris (1331); the southwest tower lost its top storey in a fire. Houses are still built up alongside part of the exterior.

INTERIOR OF SAINT-MERRY

In the 18th century the interior received a Baroque décor, and from 1796–1801 it became the Temple of Commerce. The nave and choir are of equal length and have simple quadripartite vaults except over the crossing, which has lierne vaults and a pendant boss. There is a double aisle on the right (south)—one for the canons and one for the public—and a single on the left. The church has retained many original furnishings but lost its 16th-century wooden *jubé* early in the 18th century. A frieze of animals, leaves and human figures runs around the nave above the arcades and the window tracery has flame-like (Flamboyant) curves. The Slodtz brothers were responsible for the sculptured embellishments in the 18th century: Michel-Ange Slodtz designed the pulpit (1753) and the gilded Glory above the main altar, and added marble veneer and stucco to the choir chapels. The dark oak organ case dates from 1647, modified in the 18th century and in 1857. Saint-Saëns was organist here.

Immediately to the left of the west door (as you face it) is a Renaissance screen enclosing a chapel retaining remains of the 13th-century church. The first south chapel is by Boffrand (1743–4), with three oval cupolas, beautiful bas-reliefs by Paul-Ambroise Slodtz (1758) and Charles-Antoine Coypel's *Supper at Emmaus* (central painting).

On the south pier of the entrance to the choir is the 17th-century *Vierge Bleue*, originally one of a pair by Carle van Loo but its opposite number was stolen.

The third north chapel contains a *Pietà* (c. 1670) attributed to Nicolas Legendre from Étampes. From the fifth chapel a staircase descends to the crypt (1515; *no access*), which has grotesque corbels and the tombstone of Guillaume le Sueur (d. 1530). The painting of *Sts Peter, Merry and two other Saints Adoring the Holy Name* in the north transept is by Simon Vouet (c. 1647). The church was decorated with murals in the 19th century, some by Théodore Chassériau in the third chapel north of the choir.

There is some good stained glass contemporary with the church in the upper windows, although much was taken out in the 18th century, and the lower windows are mainly 19th century. The nave windows belong to the early 16th century; outstanding are the two south windows, depicting the lives of St Nicholas of Myra and of St Agnes. The stained glass of the choir and transept is attributed to Pinaigrier and dated c. 1540.

ENVIRONS OF SAINT-MERRY

The quarter around St-Merry, with its narrow and picturesque alleys, retains several characteristic old houses that survived the rage for demolition during the Halles-Beaubourg redevelopment. The cobbled **Rue des Lombards**, named after the Italian bankers and moneychangers active in the Middle Ages, is the continuation to the east of Rue de la Verrerie. It is said that the writer Boccaccio (1313–75), whose mother was French, was born near the junction of Rue des Lombards and Rue St-Martin.

In the plaza between the north flank of the church and the Pompidou Centre (Place Stravinsky) is the **Stravinsky fountain**, created in 1983, with colourful mobile sculptures by Niki de St Phalle and Jean Tinguely.

THE POMPIDOU CENTRE

Map p. 587, F1. Métro 11 to Rambuteau. Open Wed–Mon 11–9 (last admission at 8), Thurs until 11pm for certain exhibitions; closed Tues. Atelier Brancusi open 2–6, closed Tues. There is a 'View of Paris' ticket for the escalator. Audioguides, guided visits Sat and Sun. Level 0 has a large bookshop and a shop selling artist-designed objects. Café and restaurant (see p. 349). T: 01 44 78 12 33, www.centrepompidou.fr.

The Centre National d'Art et de Culture Georges-Pompidou, or Centre Pompidou, which opened in 1977, initially caused an uproar but is now Beaubourg's main attraction and much patronised. Its fame rests partly on its architecture but more importantly on its collection: as the home of the Musée National d'Art Moderne (MNAM), it is one of the most important collections of modern and contemporary art in the world and its photographic reserve is considered a vital document in the history of photography from the 1960s onwards. Equally important are the architecture and design collections, with drawings, models, furniture and other aids to design from Russian villages to Bernard Tschumi. In a separate building is the Atelier Brancusi. The Paris City Museum of Modern Art (in Palais de Tokyo) complements the Pompidou.

The Pompidou Centre is renowned for the animation of the sloping piazza in front of it and for its exterior escalators to the upper floors, from where there are stunning views of Paris (though sadly it is no longer a free ride up the escalators to see them). There is a smart restaurant on the 6th floor, and the Centre offers a vast programme of exhibitions, cinema, concerts and live shows, debates and activities for children and young people.

HISTORY OF THE POMPIDOU CENTRE

The centre is named after President Georges Pompidou, who proposed in 1969 the establishment of a centre focused on modern creation. The winning design for the building, which had to answer the inter-disciplinary needs of the centre, came from the Anglo-Italian team of architects Richard Rogers and Renzo Piano, in association with G. Franchini and the Ove Arup group. It was the first great project of its kind and was inaugurated on 31st January 1977. It introduced innovative ideas to provide maximum free-flowing space which could be adapted to a variety of uses. It is, in fact, a 15,000 ton metal box, 166m long, 60m wide and 42m high with a glazed surface of 11,000 square metres with its functional elements—air conditioning, elevators and so on—mainly on the exterior, picked out in primary colours. The interior space over seven floors (five above ground) totals 70,000 square metres. One of the most daring— and successful—features of the building is the external escalator encased in a glazed tube which writhes up the façade. The Centre became one of the most controversial buildings constructed in Paris since the Eiffel Tower and the publicity generated by this tended to overshadow the importance of the collections that it houses. Of the two hectares available only part was built on, leaving space for Piazza Beaubourg, which slopes from Rue St-Martin down to the main entrance. It has become a popular meeting place and the setting for a variety of street entertainment. Despite the controversies, the building was hugely successful, especially the escalators, to the extent that by 1997 it was suffering from excessive wear and tear. A complete overhaul was carried out 1997–2000 under the direction of Renzo Piano. The galleries underwent further improvements in 2005–6, reopening on 31st January 2007, to coincide with the 30th anniversary of the centre's inauguration.

The National Museum of Modern Art encompasses all the creative arts, from painting to architecture, and including photography, cinema, installations, sculpture and design. It has around 100,000 works by architects and designers representative of artistic creation in the 20th and 21st centuries. The permanent collections, divided into Modern (1905–70) and Contemporary (1980–present), are presented in rotating themed displays (changed every 12–18 months) on Levels 4, 5 and 6.

MODERN COLLECTIONS 1905–70

The Modern Collections include works by major artists of the first half of the 20th century, from Matisse to Germaine Richier, representing the major movements from Fauvism to Art Brut.

Fauvism: Exponents of the first great 20th-century art movement, which was crucial in liberating the palette of many artists, include Georges Braque (*L'Estaque*, c. 1906), Raoul Dufy (*Posters at Trouville*, 1906), Vlaminck (*Red Trees*, 1906) and André Derain (*Two Barges*, 1905–6). Matisse emphatically adopted the Fauve effect, illustrated in *Algerian Woman* (1909) and *Window at Collioure* (1914), windows and odalisques becoming constant motifs in his work c. 1925–6, as in *Decorative Figure against an Ornamental Background. Large Red*

Interior (1948) pursues the expressive qualities of colour. The cut-outs of the 1930s were a technique for working directly with colour.

Cubism: The development of Cubism (1907–14) can be followed through its creators, Braque and Picasso. The broadly monochromatic Analytic phase (until c. 1911) divided objects up into their constituent planes; the Synthetic phase brought objects together, often in collages. Masks and carvings from Gabon and the Ivory Coast influenced the Cubist vision. Among seminal Cubist works of c. 1907–13 are Picasso's study for one of the *Demoiselles d'Avignon*, and Braque's *Still Life with a Violin* (*Le Guéridon*). A later, subtle still life is his Venice Biennale prizewinner *Le Billard* (1944). The third major Cubist is Juan Gris, *Breakfast* (1915). Cubist sculpture includes Henri Laurens' *Bottle of Beaune* (1918), Duchamp-Villon's *The Horse* (1914–61) and Lipchitz's *Head of Gertrude Stein* (1920). Robert Delaunay (*Joie de Vivre*, 1930) and Sonia Delaunay (*Electrical Prisms*, 1914) were characterised by Apollinaire as 'Orphic' Cubists, for their lyrical use of colour. Fernand Léger shifted from Orphic forms (*The Wedding*, c. 1911) to Purism (*Contraste de formes*, 1913), a geometric form of Cubism introduced by Amédée Ozenfant and Charles Jeanneret (Le Corbusier). Léger's *Composition with Two Parrots* (1935–9) was intended to appeal to the proletariat.

School of Paris: The School of Paris were a disparate group of international artists who gravitated to Paris between the wars, among them the Italian Amedeo Modigliani, Chaïm Soutine from Russia and Foujita from Japan. Later arrivals included abstract painters such as Maria Elena Vieira da Silva from Portugal (*The Library*, 1949) and the Catalan Antoni Tàpies. Marc Chagall's personal poetic imagery blended memories of his native Russia with Orphic Cubism in *To Russia, Donkeys and Others* (1911) and *Death* (1908). The Pompidou Centre is particularly well endowed with works by Picasso, from the post-Cubist *Portrait of a Young Girl* (1917) and 'Neoclassical' *Girl Reading* (1920) to mature works including *Women with Pigeons* (1930) and the colourful *Muse* (1935).

Dada and Surrealism: Dada emerged in 1916 in Zurich in reaction to the First World War: anti-art, provocative, funny and obscene, among its leaders were Marcel Duchamp, George Grosz (*Remember Uncle August, the Unhappy Inventor*) and Kurt Schwitters, who created his own movement which he called Merz. Marcel Duchamp broke through the accepted boundaries of art with notorious ready-mades, especially *Fountain*, the famous urinal signed 'R. Mutt'. Surrealism, a 'new reality' synthesising conscious and unconscious experience, developed in the 1920s, its roots in Dada, literature, Freud's theories, and the hallucinatory paintings of Giorgio di Chirico, such as *Melancholy of an Afternoon* (1914). Its poet-painters, led by André Breton, had a far-reaching effect on all aspects of the visual arts. Seminal Surrealist works include Max Ernst's *Ubu Imperator* (1923), an assemblage of unrelated elements which create a new reality in the shape of a spinning top-man based on Alfred Jarry's character *Ubu*. *Loplop*, an imaginary bird, inhabits

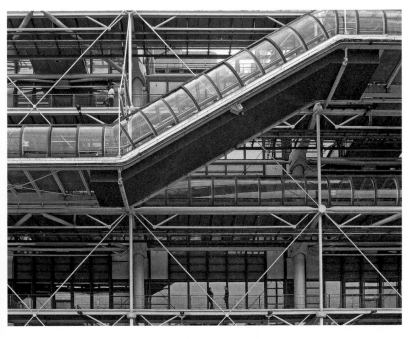

POMPIDOU CENTRE
Detail of the exterior.

many of Ernst's works, and *La Femme cent têtes* (1929) is a page from a collage 'novel'. Salvador Dalí's *Putrefied Donkey* (1928) is a slick, hallucinatory version of Surrealism. Other notable Surrealists in the collections include René Magritte and André Masson. The American artist Man Ray settled in France in 1921 and joined the Surrealists. Others who remained with Surrealism, or passed through it, include Hans Bellmer, Hans Arp, Wifredo Lam, Victor Brauner, Yves Tanguy and the sculptor Julio González. Francis Picabia embraced Cubism for a while but moved on to more aggressive anti-Salon-art tendencies in *L'Oeil*

cacodylate (1921). In Luis Buñuel's *L'Âge d'or* (1930), Surrealism spread to the cinema. The poetic Catalan artist Joan Miró's earlier style is typified by *Interior, The Farmer's Wife* (1922–3). Profoundly influenced by Surrealism, he shaped from it his own particular brand of imagery of detached floating shapes on flat colour planes and assembled derelict objects to create sculpture, either playful or threatening. The chilling earlier works of Alberto Giacometti (*Sharp Point in the Eye*, 1931) were replaced by the pared down, skeletal figures of *Venetian Woman V* (1956). Germaine Richier, a major 20th-century French 'existentialist' sculptor, was influenced by Giacometti and Marino Marini: among her works is *The Storm* (1947–8).

Abstraction: In the second decade of the 20th century Abstraction was born was born from the fertile breeding ground of the Bauhaus, and cross-pollinated with movements throughout Europe, notably Orphism, De Stijl in Holland, Futurism in Italy and Constructivism in Russia, all of which are represented in the collections. Russian-born Wassily Kandinsky progresses from early Fauve-type landscapes to abstract shapes in *Yellow Red Blue* (1925). His colleague at the Bauhaus (1922–3), Paul Klee, produced small, subtle works including *Arrow in the Garden* (1929). Constructivism hovered between utopia and utilitarianism, and Antoine Pevsner produced finely-balanced geometric works such as *Construction in Space* (1923–5). The Ukrainian Kasimir Malevich's *Black Cross* (1915) influenced the Minimalists. The Dutch abstract artists of De Stijl artists include Piet Mondrian (*New York City I*, 1942), Van Doesburg and Georges Vantongerloo (*S x R3*, 1933–4). Alexander Calder bent wire into witty sculptures but is better known for delicate abstract mobiles such as *White Disk, Black Disk* (1940–1).

French art movements: Art movements in France in the mid-20th century included *Art Informel*, non-geometric abstraction practised by Jean Fautrier with his *Hostages* (1945) series, fired by the brutality and agony he observed during World War II. Jean Dubuffet was Art Brut's main exponent, exemplified by primitive, graffiti-like works such as *Dhôtel Tinted in Apricot* (1947). The 'CoBrA' artists, northern painters such as Pierre Alechinsky, Karel Appel and Bram Van Velde, focused on unconscious spontaneous creation. 'Individualists' include the pure abstract painter described as 'poet of space and musician of line', Hans Hartung, and Nicolas de Staël (*Les Musiciens, Souvenir de Sidney Bechet*, 1953).

Expressionism: The exaggerated forms and colour of Expressionism developed as a movement out of the symbolic use of colour by the Fauves, and the de Brücke and Blaue Reiter groups in northern Europe. Pioneers were František Kupka (*Autour d'un Point*, 1911) and Ernst-Ludwig Kirchner (*The Toilette–Woman in Front of a Mirror*, 1912–13). Francis Bacon is well represented. Abstract Expressionists from the USA (1940–50) include Jackson Pollock, whose drip technique produced lyrical and subtle works such as *Silver over Black, White Yellow and Red* (1948) and *The Deep* (1953).

Nouveau Réalisme: Yves Klein was the driving force behind Nouveau Réalisme, founded in Paris in 1960. Among its adherents was Arman, whose *Home Sweet Home*, an 'accumulation' of rubbish, is a criticism of 20th-century consumerism. Others were Daniel Spoerri and Gérard Deschamps. Klein himself is best known for monochromatic works in deep ultramarine that he patented as IKB (International Klein Blue) in the belief that blue has no tangible reality and that by painting in monochrome, colour is deprived of subjective associations. Martial Raysse moved on from Nouveau Réalisme to become a brilliant interpreter of European Pop, illustrated by *America, America*, a huge neon-lighted metal hand.

The 1960s: César is famous for 'compressions' of discarded objects, prompted initially by lack of money: *Compression Ricard* (1962) is a car reduced to a rectangle; then came 'expansions'. Raymond Hains and Jacques de la Villeglé worked together making inventive *décollages* from peeled and shredded posters, such as *Ach Alma Manetro* (1949).

A major artist of the 20th century, Joseph Beuys, was associated with the group Fluxus. The mysterious *Infiltration for Grand Piano* (1964–6) is reminiscent of a rhinoceros; *Skin* (1984) is the felt that was discarded when the artist changed the piano's wrapping. Other Fluxus members were Ben, Robert Filliou and Erik Dietman. There is also a representative selection of British and American Pop Art, including Andy Warhol's *Ten Lizes* (1963), Claes Oldenburg's *Ghost Drum Set* (1972), Robert Rauschenberg's *Oracle* (1962), Christo's *Package and Wrapped Floor* (1968) and James Rosenquist's *President Elect* (1960–1).

Abstract Expressionists in France are headed by Pierre Soulages, the grand old man of French abstract painting, who has remained constant to the possibilities of black, or black on white, and sometimes sombre browns, on huge canvases, with designs which trace a form in space and are often reminiscent of hugely magnified Chinese characters. The works depend on paint textures and the absorption or reflection of light, as for example *All-black Painting* (1979). Objective titles such as *Painting 1985,*

324 x 362cm or *Polyptych C*, deliberately avoid figurative reference.

Arte Povera, 'Impoverished Art', is a mainly Italian movement which appeared in 1967. It confronts the materialism of the established art world by employing simple, worthless materials. The main movers were Giuseppe Penone, Jannis Kounellis and Mario Merz (*Che fare*, c. 1968–9). Antiforme is a sub-group of Arte Povera in which temporary forms and 'soft, non-fixed sculptures' were developed in the work of Eva Hesse (*Seven Poles*, 1970) and the eloquent felt *Wall Hanging* (1969–70) by Robert Morris.

Conceptual Art, the art of ideas, which began with Marcel Duchamp, gave its name to a wide-ranging movement in the 1960s. Joseph Kosuth opined that art should only be conceptual and therefore must break with aesthetics, epitomised in *The First Investigation (Art as Idea as Idea)* of 1968.

Installations and special works: Large, playful fantasies of mechanised sculpture focus on 'representation'. Some of the best-loved are Jean Tinguely's mobiles, such as *Requiem for a Dead Leaf* (1970). Claes Oldenburg's *Giant Ice Bag* (1969–70) is marginally threatening. *Le Magasin* (1958–73) by Ben is a monumental montage of disparate objects making an anti-art statement. Niki de Saint Phalle was influenced by Art Brut, Tinguely and Klein. Her assemblages, such as *The Bride* (1963), are an extraordinary comment on life, both disturbing and humorous. Annette Messager specialises in series such as *Les Pensionnaires* (1971–2), a sequence of 14 vitrines. Christian Boltanski's *The Archives of Christian*

Boltanski (1965–88) is an installation of 644 biscuit boxes containing around 1,200 photographs and 800 documents. Other installations include *While Visions of Sugarplums Danced in their Heads* (1964) by Edward Kienholz and *Container Zéro* (1988) by Jean-Pierre Raynaud (b. 1939).

CONTEMPORARY COLLECTIONS 1980–PRESENT

The range of disciplines in the contemporary collection has expanded to include casting, mechanical installations, photomontage, photography, video, drawing, recycling, performance art and kinetics. At the same time, there is a geographic expansion to acknowledge the variety and innovation in artistic expression coming from the Americas, Asia, the Middle East and Africa, as well as Europe. Increasing globalisation from 1989, triggered by major global events such as the fall of the Berlin Wall and the uprising in Tiananmen Square, are reflected in a concomitant breakdown of barriers in artistic creation. A new focus of creativity and greater cross-fertilisation of production is part of an art scene which is constantly in flux as the role of the artist evolves in reaction to contemporary socio-political upheavals, as narrators or autobiographers, fictionalising their lives, pushing boundaries and finding inspiration in everyday objects.

1970–90: This was a time of crisis, questioning and reaffirmation, represented in France by the Support/Surfaces group. Typical are the striped installations *Jamais Deux Fois la même* (1967–2000) by Daniel Buren, who is best known for his site-specific installations, exterior and interior, to enhance, or set up a contrast with their setting (*to see one in situ, visit Palais Royal; p. 308*). Also representative are the neo-Expressionist violence of Markus Lüpertz (*Untitled MLZ 2546/00*, 1992), of a firing squad, as well as Malcolm Morley, who shifted from photorealism to a painterly style combining two scenes, a beachscape and the Trojan Horse in *Cradle of Civilisation with American Woman* (1982). *Ralf III* (1965) and also *Die Mädchen von Olmo* (1981), designed to be hung upside-down, are typical of Georg Baselitz. Martin Szekely and Dominique Perrault, and more recently Bernard Tschumi, Rem Koolhaas, Toyo Ito and designers Marc Newson and Jonathan Ive are also represented. Works from 1990 to the present involve cross-disciplinary observations of the human figure by artists such as Claude Closky, Thomas Schütte, Valérie Jouve and Marie-Ange Guilleminot.

1990–present: The themed exhibit brings the presentation up to date with examples of work by photographers, body artists, film-makers, sculptors, sound artists, installation artists, architects, interdisciplinary and multi-media artists, designers and performance artists from across the globe.

ATELIER BRANCUSI

It is all too easy to miss this relatively small building on the north of the Piazza Beaubourg—but don't. Designed by Renzo Piano, it is a dignified haven of Constantin Brancusi's monumental sculptures. Brancusi reacted against the dynamism of Rodin to create taut, coherent shapes. The four studios of the Atelier, from his workshop at 11 Impasse Ronsin (*map p. 586, A4*), have been precisely reconstructed, complete with works such as *Le Coq* (1935), along with models, plinths and other memorabilia, and are designed so that visitors can move around the exterior of the studios viewing them through glass from different angles.

PLACE DU CHÂTELET

The hectic Place du Châtelet (*map p. 587, E2*), undermined below by a maze of Métro and RER tunnels, is named after a small fortified gatehouse to the Cité, built by Abbot Suger under the authority of Louis VI (d. 1137). It was transformed into the Grand Châtelet by Louis IX, more château than gatehouse, once the headquarters of the Provost of Paris and the Guild of Notaries, demolished in 1802–10. A plan of the fort can be seen on the **Chambre des Notaires** building to the north. On the east side of the square is the **Théâtre de la Ville** and opposite the **Théâtre du Châtelet** (1862), a vast Renaissance-style hall where Communards were court-martialled in 1871. In the centre, once the site of the Parloir aux Bourgeois, seat of the municipality from the 13th century until 1357, is the **Fontaine du Châtelet** (1808–59).

Just north is Square St-Jacques, a public garden since 1856 and the first green space created by Haussmann. It frames the Flamboyant Gothic **Tour St-Jacques** (1508–22) which, since 1797, is the only relic of a succession of churches that stood on this site from the 9th century. Dedicated to St James the Greater, it was always known as St Jacques-de-la-Boucherie, after the butchers who were established on this marshy spot. It was a rallying point for pilgrims on the road to Santiago de Compostela in Spain. In the 17th century, Blaise Pascal carried out experiments here and there is a statue of him. From 1836 it was used as a shot tower, where shot was made by pouring molten lead through a sieve at the top into water at the bottom. In 1858 it was creatively restored by Ballu. From the end of the 19th century to 2000 it was a meteorological station. A magnificent restoration was completed in 2009.

Avenue Victoria, named in honour of Queen Victoria's visit to Paris in 1855, runs between Place du Châtelet and Place de l'Hôtel-de-Ville.

PLACE DE L'HÔTEL DE VILLE

Map p. 587, F2. Métro 1 and 11 to Hôtel de Ville.

Place de l'Hôtel-de-Ville is a large pedestrianised square which is frequently used for public gatherings. Until 1830 it was known as Place de Grève, as ships had moored on the strand or *grève* in this area since the 11th century. It was the location for public executions, many incredibly barbarous, of Protestants, assassins, sorceresses, highwaymen, murderers, revolutionaries and criminals. It was often a rendezvous for unemployed or dissatisfied workers, who were said to *faire grève*, which came to mean to go on strike. The square was also the centre of the great midsummer bonfire, the *Feu de la St-Jean*, lit on the eve of the feast of St John the Baptist, the summer solstice. Crowds gather now for a variety of activities, such the ice rink in winter, big screens during major sporting events, and exhibitions. Since 2005 it has hosted the beach games extension to Paris Plage, a 3km stretch of river bank between Quai des Tuileries and Quai Henri IV.

THE HÔTEL DE VILLE BUILDING

Free guided visits by appointment, T: 01 42 76 54 04/01 42 76 50 49, www.paris.fr.
The Hôtel de Ville or City Hall is the seat of the Mairie de Paris and the administrative centre of the municipal authorities.

In 1264 Louis IX created the first municipal authority in Paris by allowing the merchants to elect magistrates (*échevins*), led by the Prévôt des Marchands, who was also head of the *Hanse des marchands de l'eau*. This merchant guild, which had the monopoly of the traffic on the Seine, Marne, Oise and Yonne, took as their emblem a ship, a device which still graces the arms of the city (*see p. 311*). They had two temporary meeting places, The Parloir aux Bourgeois and then the Grand-Châtelet (*see above*), until in 1357 the provost, Étienne Marcel (*see p. 14*), purchased a mansion in Place de Grève for their assemblies. In 1532, plans for an imposing new building had been drawn up but nothing was completed until 1628. In 1789 the 300 electors nominated by the districts of Paris met here and, on 17th July, Louis XVI received the newly-devised tricolore cockade from the hands of Jean-Sylvain Bailly, the Mayor. However, on 10th August, 1792, the 172 commissaries elected by Paris gave the signal for a general insurrection. Robespierre took refuge here in 1794 but was arrested on 27th July and dragged, injured, to the Conciergerie. In 1805 it became the seat of the Préfet de la Seine and his council, and was the scene of numerous official celebrations. The Swiss Guard put up a stout defence of the building during the 1830 July Revolution. In 1848 it became the seat of Louis Blanc's provisional government and witnessed the arrest of the revolutionary agitators Armand Barbès and Louis-Auguste Blanqui. The Third Republic was proclaimed here on 4th September 1870 and, in the following March, the Commune. On 24th May 1871, the building was evacuated before being set ablaze by its defenders. It was rebuilt from 1874–84 with elaborate façades, on a larger scale than before, in the style of the French Renaissance, to the plans of Ballu and Deperthes. The façades are embellished with statues of eminent Frenchmen and its interior is lavishly adorned in accordance with the official taste in architecture of the period, including sculpture, elaborate carvings and murals by Puvis de Chavannes. In 1944 the Hôtel de Ville was a focus of opposition to the occupying forces by the Resistance movement who, by 19th August, had established themselves in the building, repelling German counter-attacks until relieved by the arrival of Général Leclerc's division five days later.

The visit takes you to the great reception rooms inspired by the Hall of Mirrors at Versailles, with paintings recalling the history of Paris.

HÔTEL DE VILLE
Science by Jules Blanchard (1882).

EATING AND DRINKING AROUND LES HALLES AND BEAUBOURG

€€€ **Benoit**. A very traditional, refined bistrot, where the service is impeccable and the setting small and intimate with an old-world charm. Part of Alain Ducasse's portfolio, it has a Michelin star. The choices are mainly traditional Burgundian: *pâté en croûte* (a meat pie) and *tête de veau* (calf's head). It offers a set menu at lunchtime. *20 Rue St-Martin. T: 01 58 00 22 05, www.benoit-paris.com. Map p. 587, E1.*

€€ **Au Bascou**. ■ Close to the Musée des Arts et Métiers, the cuisine is based on typical recipes from Brittany to the Basque country. The décor reflects the warm colours of the south, as do the dishes, frequently flavoured with the red-hot *piments d'Espelettes*, or sweet red peppers. Basque seafood is a must, including squid in its ink (*chipirons à l'encre*) and cod (*morue*). A set menu is offered at lunchtime. Best to book. Closed Sat evening and all day Sun. *38 Rue Réaumur. T: 01 42 72 69 25, www.au-bascou.fr. Map p. 583, D4.*

€€ **Le Pharamond**. Happily Le Pharamond's Belle-Époque décor of 1832, with its mirrors and *pâte de verre* panels, is protected, and the establishment has been revived by Jean-Michel and Josette Cornut. The dishes here were traditionally inspired by the cuisine and ingredients of Normandy and the reference continues. The brasserie fare is copious, good quality and affordable and waiters in white aprons are efficient.

All-time classics include *escargots*, *foie gras*, *tripes maison*, *onglet* (beef) and *coupe glacée normande* with Calvados and apples. There is also a terrace. *Formule* at lunchtime. Closed Mon and Tues. *4 Rue de la Grande-Truanderie (just south of the church of St-Leu). T: 01 40 28 45 18, www.pharamondparis.com. Map p. 587, E1.*

€–€€ **Auberge Nicolas Flamel**. In a block of houses that avoided destruction when the Beaubourg quarter was being modernised, this is perhaps more an historic and architectural experience than a gastronomic one, but you can eat fairly well in this ancient and historic building close to the Pompidou Centre. It claims to be the oldest house in Paris and was home to the wealthy scrivener Nicolas Flamel and his wife Pernelle. On the top floor Flamel provided free lodging for poor tenants, on condition that they recite a daily *Pater Noster* for the souls of their benefactor and his wife. Flamel died in 1418 and gained a posthumous reputation (based on fairly flimsy evidence) as an alchemist. He appears as such in one of the Harry Potter novels. His tombstone is preserved in the Musée du Moyen Âge. *51 Rue de Montmorency. T: 01 42 71 77 78, www.auberge-nicolas-flamel.fr. Map p. 587, F1.*

€ **L'Acanthe**. ■ This small, neat cocktail bar/restaurant just off Rue de Rivoli was reputedly an opium den at the time of Baudelaire and Delacroix. Now it serves fresh-cooked, fairly light dishes with an emphasis on fish, and pasta as well as decent sandwiches, and good ice cream and desserts. *22 Rue Saint-Martin. T: 01 40 27 85 28. Map p. 587, E1.*

€ **Au Pied de Cochon**. The 'Pig's Trotter' is an historic Les Halles restaurant, which traditionally served early breakfasts to market traders. Today it is still going, though its *raison d'être* is less authentic. But you can still get a platter of *fruits de mer*—and of course pig's trotter, with chips and béarnaise sauce. *6 Rue Coquillière. T: 01 40 13 77 00, www.pieddecochon. com. Map p. 587, E1.*

€ **Pompidou Centre**. On Level 6 is **Restaurant Georges** (closed Tues; *T: 01 44 78 47 99*), with a separate lift and marvellous views over Paris. The space is glassed over and has curious 'pods' and seating in a variety of colours, and there is also an open terrace with seating: an excellent spot for a sundowner on a fine evening (though the food is variable in quality).

On Level 1 is **Le Café Mezzanine**, a self-service cafeteria open 11–9. *Map p. 587, F1.*

€ **Le Zimmer**. This brasserie has lots of red plush and mirrors, a revamp by Jacques Garcia of the 19th century décor. Fairly traditional, on the menu are lamb tagine and veal liver. Open until 1am every day, though best of all is breakfast or brunch on the terrace on a sunny spring morning. *1 Place du Châtelet. T: 01 42 36 74 03, www.lezimmer.com. Map p. 587, E2.*

For restaurants in the nearby Marais district, see p. 380.

HÔTEL DE SULLY
The element Earth, on the courtyard façade.

The Marais

The Marais, one of the most interesting districts of old Paris, remains substantially as it developed in the 17th century. It contains buildings of outstanding architectural interest and a number of important and inviting museums. Part of the Marais is traditionally a Jewish area. The Place des Vosges has royal and aristocratic associations. There is a great variety of places to eat and a number of charming small green spaces.

A marshland (*marais*) on the northern banks of the Seine (*map p. 588, A2–B2*), this district only became habitable with the arrival of the Knights Templar and other religious houses that settled here in the 13th century and drained the marshes for arable land. Royal patronage began with Charles V who, anxious to forget the associations of the Palais de la Cité with the rebellion of Étienne Marcel in 1358, built the Hôtel St-Paul. The Hôtel de

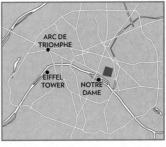

Lamoignon and Hôtel Carnavalet were built in the 16th century, but the seal of royal approval came with the construction of the Place Royale (1605), later known as Place des Vosges. Courtiers built themselves houses in the district and the Marais remained the most fashionable residential area of Paris until the Faubourg St-Germain took over in the early 18th century. At the Revolution, the state confiscated the property of the nobles for sale to craftsmen, mechanics and merchants and the grand buildings were neglected. Now re-animated, the Marais is again a very fashionable place to live.

PLACE DES VOSGES & HÔTEL DE SULLY

Map p. 588, B2. Métro 1 to St-Paul or 8 to Chemin Vert.

Place des Vosges, built in 1606–11 at the heart of the Marais, has a specific charm unlike any other square in Paris. This large quadrangle is surrounded by 39 houses built on a uniform plan with brick, stone and stucco façades, arcaded ground floors and simple dormers. Trees were not planted in the central gardens until 1783, upsetting the over-all symmetry: ideally visit in winter when the leaves have fallen. The main approach, from Rue St-Antoine, is by Rue de Birague, through the Pavillon du Roi. The square in its present form was laid out for Henri IV, possibly by Louis Métezeau or Jean-Baptiste du Cerceau, and was inaugurated by Louis XIII in 1612. The slightly taller king's pavilion was built above the gateway in the centre of the south side, and the queen's was the corresponding building on the north (no. 28). In the centre of the square is a park with benches and an equestrian statue of Louis XIII (1829), replacing a bronze original of 1639. The horse is curiously supported in the centre of its belly by a stout stone column. In the angles of the square are fountains of 1816.

JOUSTERS, REVOLUTIONARIES & *PRÉCIEUSES RIDICULES*

Place des Vosges occupies the site of the royal Palais des Tournelles, the residence of the Duke of Bedford, English regent of France in 1422 after the death of Henry V. In 1559, during the double marriage celebrations of Henri II's daughter Elisabeth to Philip II of Spain and of his sister Marguerite to Emmanuel-Philippe of Savoy, a tournament was held on the exceptionally large Cours St-Antoine near the square. During the last joust, Henri II was wounded by Montgomery, Captain of the Scottish Guard, dying after ten days of agony. His widow, Catherine de Médicis, consequently abandoned the palace.

In the earlier part of the reign of Louis XIV this was one of the most fashionable addresses in Paris, haunt of the kind of *Précieuses Ridicules* satirised by Molière. It acquired its present name in 1799, after the Département of the Vosges was the first to discharge its liabilities for the Revolutionary Wars.

Under the cloister-style arcade that runs around the square are numerous cafés, galleries and a comfortable hotel, Pavillon de la Reine. No. 21, on the same side (north), was the **mansion of Cardinal Richelieu**. On the east side is the **Temple des Vosges** synagogue (recognisable from the large menorah on its façade). Théophile Gautier lived at no. 8, the **Hôtel de Fourcy**, in 1831–4, writing *Mademoiselle de Maupin*. A later resident was the journalist and novelist Alphonse Daudet (*Lettres de mon Moulin*; 1866). At no. 6, on the corner, is Maison Victor Hugo.

MAISON VICTOR HUGO

Open Tues–Sun 10–6, closed Mon and holidays, T: 01 42 72 10 16; free entry
In the southeast corner of Place des Vosges is the former Hôtel de Rohan-Guéménée, which Victor Hugo rented from 1832–48. Already successful (the *Hunchback of Notre-Dame* was published 1831), Hugo lived here with his family; he received artists and literati of the day including Dumas, Lamartine, Mérimée and David d'Angers, and began *Les Misérables*. Seven rooms reflect his life before, during and after his self-imposed exile to the Channel Islands (1851–70), precipitated by Napoléon's III's coup.

The visit starts on the first floor in the **Antichambre**, with references to the period from childhood to his first literary successes, illustrated by family portraits painted by friends or members of the family. The literary and political life of Hugo among the Romantic idealists of the day such as Lamartine, Dumas and Mérimée, is conjured up by The **Salon Rouge**, swathed in red damask. Hugo's talent for interior design is revealed by the ornate **Salon Chinois**, which he conceived in 1863–4 for his lover

SAINT-PAUL-SAINT-LOUIS
Germain Pilon's *La Vierge de la Douleur* (1586).

Juliette Drouet's house in Guernsey; their monograms, JD and VH, are concealed in the décor. Hugo's leanings towards Gothic design are evident in the **Dining Room** décor, also designed for Juliette Drouet. The '**Return from Exile**' room, once the writer's study, contains his portrait by Léon Bonnat and that of Juliette Drouet in 1883 by Bastien-Lepage. In the **Bedroom**, recreated from his last years, is the desk where Hugo wrote standing up and, in a style favoured by Hugo, an 18th-century Aubusson tapestry is on the ceiling.

HÔTEL DE SULLY

Main entrance at 62 Rue St-Antoine but also accessible from the southwest corner of Place des Vosges (no. 7), through the garden.

The Hôtel de Sully (1624–30), the most elegant *hôtel particulier* in the Marais, is thought to be the work of Jean du Cerceau. It was acquired in 1634 by Maximilien de Béthune, Duc de Sully, Henri IV's chief minister. The courtyard, a fine example of Louis XIII style, abounds in carved decorations, notably around the dormers and the six bas-reliefs in niches, the females representing the *Elements* and the males *Autumn* and *Winter* (*Spring* and *Summer* are on the garden façade, a subdued echo of the courtyard). The entrance pavilions and the interior, extensively restored, still have 17th-century ceilings and panelling.

The buildings are occupied by the Centre des Monuments Nationaux (CMN), where there is an extensive bookshop. The CMN organises guided tours, mainly in French (*see p. 540*). The *Visites Conférences* booklet is available at the CMN, 62 Rue St-Antoine. There is no formal registration for individuals participating in a guided tour: simply go to the rendezvous shortly before the start.

SAINT-PAUL-SAINT-LOUIS

Map p. 588, B2. Métro 1 to St-Paul. Entrance on Rue St-Antoine. Open Mon–Fri 8–8, Sat 8–7.30, Sun 8–8; T: 01 42 72 30 32.

The church of St-Paul-St-Louis, or the Grands-Jésuites, was built for that Society by Louis XIII in 1627–41, replacing a chapel of 1582. The Jesuits were suppressed in 1762, and St-Paul was added to the original dedication in 1796 to commemorate the demolished St-Paul-des-Champs, traces of whose belfry remain on Rue St-Paul (*see p. 379*).

Building work, including the handsome Baroque portal, was supervised by Martellange until 1629, and François Derrand saw it through to its completion in 1641, while the Jesuit Charles Turmel supervised the interior decorations. Its florid style, inspired by 16th-century Italian churches, is a good example of French Jesuit architecture. The clock on the façade came from the old church of St-Paul. The church was restored by Baltard in the 19th century and the statues on the façade are 19th-century (by Lequesne, Etex and Préault). Madame de Sévigné was baptised here in 1629. Cardinal Richelieu said the first Mass in 1641. Robespierre preached his cult of Reason here in 1793 (though the following year he was to desert Reason for his own Cult of the Supreme Being).

INTERIOR OF SAINT-PAUL-SAINT-LOUIS

The ornate interior, imposing but light, has retained the original clear glass with floral friezes. The 55m high dome over the crossing was the third to be built in Paris (after the Petits-Augustins (now the École des Beaux-Arts) and the Carmelite Chapel on Rue de Vaugirard. In the pendentives are medallions of the four Evangelists and, in the drum, 19th-century *trompe l'oeil* paintings of saintly kings: Clovis, Charlemagne, Robert le Pieux and St Louis. Most furnishings have been dispersed, some to the Louvre and the tomb of Henri II (whose death followed a jousting wound sustained in the nearby Place des Vosges) to Chantilly. The suspended silver angels carrying the embalmed hearts of Louis XIII and XIV have, of course, long gone, but the church still contains some fine works.

In the north transept is the dramatic *Christ on the Mount of Olives* by Delacroix, and opposite is *St Louis Receiving the Crown of Thorns* by the school of Vouet (1639). In the chapel off the north transept is *La Vierge de la Douleur* (1586) by Germain Pilon, commissioned by Catherine de Médicis for the Valois dynasty chapel at St-Denis (never completed) and placed here by Anne of Austria, consort of the church's founder Louis XIII. In the south transept (right-hand side) is *Louis XIII offering a Model of*

RUE PAVÉE
Synagogue by Hector Guimard, built for an orthodox Russian congregation in 1913.

the Church to St Louis by Vouet. There is good-quality wood carving and 17th-century ironwork. Buried here are Bishop Huet of Avranches (d. 1721; plaque in south transept) and Louis Bourdaloue, confessor to Louis XIV (plaque in north transept).

ENVIRONS OF SAINT-PAUL-SAINT-LOUIS

East along Rue St-Antoine, on the corner with Rue Castex, is the circular **Temple de Ste-Marie** (*map p. 588, B2*), originally the chapel of the Convent of the Visitation, and now a Protestant church. It was built by François Mansart in 1632–4. The unscrupulous *Surintendant des Finances*, Nicolas Fouquet (d. 1680), and Henri de Sévigné (Mme de Sévigné's husband, killed in a duel in 1651) were buried here. Vincent de Paul was almoner of the convent for 28 years. A few paces to the west, at no. 21, is the **Hôtel de Mayenne** (or d'Ormesson), with a turret and charming staircase. Now the École des Francs-Bourgeois, it was built by Jean or Jacques II du Cerceau in 1613–17 and modified by Boffrand in 1709. To the east, a tablet on 5 Rue St-Antoine marks the position of the court of the Bastille, by which the Revolutionary mob gained access to the fortress. Near the junction of this street and the Place de la Bastille was the site of the great barricade of 1848, and also the last stronghold of the Communards in 1871.

The **Hôtel Lamoignon** on the corner of Rue Pavée (no. 24; *map p. 588, A2–B2*), with its colossal Corinthian pilasters and curved pediments, was built in 1584 for Diane de France, legitimised daughter of Henri II, and is possibly the work of Jean-Baptiste Androuet du Cerceau. Named after a 17th-century occupant, it now houses the Bibliothèque Historique de la Ville de Paris, containing over 400,000 volumes and 100,000 manuscripts relating to the history of the city and to the Revolution.

Rue Pavée itself has an Art Nouveau synagogue designed by Hector Guimard (better known for his Métro stations). Opening off it is **Rue des Rosiers**, in the old Jewish quarter (parallel with Rue des Francs-Bourgeois), with interesting restaurants.

On the south side of Rue des Francs-Bourgeois, no. 31 is the **Hôtel d'Albret**, built c. 1640 by François Mansart, with an 18th-century street façade. At the end of the courtyard of no. 33 is a **fragment of Philippe-Auguste's walls**.

MUSÉE CARNAVALET

Map p. 588, B2. 16 Rue des Francs-Bourgeois (corner of Rue Sévigné). Métro 1 to St-Paul or 8 to Chemin Vert. Open Tues–Sun 10–6, closed Mon and holidays. Free entry. T: 01 44 59 58 58, www.carnavalet.paris.fr.

Anyone wishing fully to get to grips with Paris should head for the Musée Carnavalet, the museum of the city's history, which has a varied collection of objects and works of art ranging from pre-Roman dugout canoes to 20th-century paintings. It is housed in two of the most outstanding historic buildings in the Marais, the Hôtel Carnavalet and the Hôtel le Peletier de St-Fargeau.

The museum has a vast collection of artworks, by lesser-known as well as well-known artists but valuable chiefly as historic documents recording cityscapes and monuments, events and people. There are views of medieval Paris on the Île de la Cité and the Left Bank and many painters captured the Seine and the Quais on canvas. Gradually the emblematic buildings and monuments which still define Paris appear, such as the Louvre and Tuileries, Pont Neuf (c. 1633 when it was still new), Place des Vosges, the Hôpital St-Louis, Les Invalides and the Eiffel Tower. Nicolas Raguenet, the 'Parisian Canaletto', left a rich source of information on Paris during the Enlightenment and *La Tour Eiffel et le Champ de Mars en janvier 1889* by Paul-Louis Delance is a rare record in paint of the of the Eiffel Tower under construction.

Tips for visiting
This is a complicated museum to get around, over two buildings, three floors and some 155 rooms. As it is free, however, there is less pressure to see all in one visit.

The collection is displayed according to periods or themes. The 17th- and 18th-century rooms, the Revolutionary period and the 20th-century section are all particularly popular. The description below describes the collections in chronological order, not in the order that the rooms are visited. Room numbers refer to the plans.

The visit starts beyond the cloakroom, in the L-shaped Salle des Enseignes, which evokes old Parisian streets with shop and tavern signs (15th–19th centuries) and maquettes of Paris during the 19th century. Beyond this is the Escalier de Luynes, which leads up to the first floor of the Hôtel Carnavalet. The connecting gallery between the two buildings is hung with paintings on one side, while the other is devoted to temporary exhibitions.

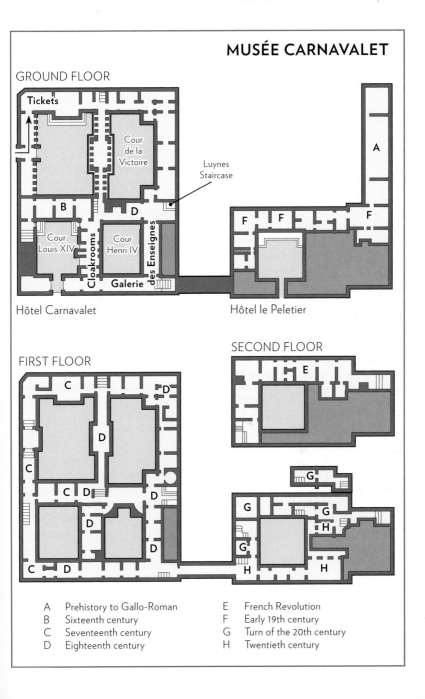

MUSÉE CARNAVALET

GROUND FLOOR

Tickets

Cour de la Victoire

Luynes Staircase

A

B

D

F   F   F

Cour Louis XIV

Cloakrooms

Cour Henri IV

des Enseignes

Galerie

Hôtel Carnavalet

Hôtel le Peletier

FIRST FLOOR

SECOND FLOOR

E

C

D

D

C

C   D

D

D

D

C   D

G

G   G

H

G

H   H

A	Prehistory to Gallo-Roman	E	French Revolution
B	Sixteenth century	F	Early 19th century
C	Seventeenth century	G	Turn of the 20th century
D	Eighteenth century	H	Twentieth century

THE BUILDINGS

HÔTEL CARNAVALET

The imposing, Renaissance-style Hôtel Carnavalet was begun in 1548 for Jacques de Ligneris, president of the *Parlement*. It originally consisted of the main building overlooking the courtyard with two wings at right angles. From this period come the four magnificent reliefs on the main façade, *The Seasons*, from the workshop of Jean Goujon, and four signs of the Zodiac: Aries, Libra, Cancer and Capricorn. In 1578 the building was acquired by the widow of François de Kernevenoy, called Carnavalet by the Parisians. Around 1660, François Mansart designed new wings and altered the street façade, while Gérard van Obstal added allegorical reliefs to the Rue des Francs-Bourgeois façade and those of *Juno, Hebe, Diana* and *Flora* in the courtyard. The sculptor of the allegories of the *Four Elements* on the left is unidentified. Some years later Mme de Sévigné rented the building and lived here until her death in 1696 (*see p. 360*).

Hôtel Carnavalet was acquired in 1866 by the City of Paris and, renovated and adapted, opened as a museum in 1880. The front courtyard became known as Cour Louis XIV after the bronze by Coysevox was moved from the courtyard of the Hôtel de Ville in 1890, having miraculously survived the Revolution. As the collection grew, more space was created to the west using elements from three demolished Parisian buildings: on Rue des Franc-Bourgeois is the Arc de Nazareth (1552–6) from the Île de la Cité; to the west, the façade of the Bureau des Marchands Drapiers (1660) from Rue des Déchargeurs; and north, the central part of the Hôtel de Marêts (c. 1710) from Rue St-Augustin, named the Cour des Drapiers. Further extensions were carried out early in the 20th century around the two courtyards: Cour de la Victoire was named after the original lead statue *Winged Victory* (1807) by Simon Boizot for the Châtelet fountain (replaced by a copy in 1898); and Cour Henri IV after the bronze relief (1834) by Henri Lemaire for the Hôtel de Ville, placed here in 1907.

HÔTEL LE PELETIER DE ST-FARGEAU

In 1895 the museum acquired an *hôtel* that had been built by Pierre Bullet for Michel de Peletier in 1687–90 on Rue de Sévigné. A sober building, the Rue Payenne façade (around the gardens of Square Georges-Cain) is less austere than those facing the courtyard. The Orangerie is decorated with an allegory of *Truth*, and on the main façade is a figure of *Time*. The building has retained only the main stairwell and one room with gilded panelling and mirrors on the first floor.

THE COLLECTIONS IN CHRONOLOGICAL SEQUENCE

A: Prehistory to Gallo-Roman (Orangerie, Le Peletier)

These collections occupy the 17th-century orangery, which is a rare survival of this type of structure in Paris. Interesting objects here include mammoth molars, gold coins of the *Parisii* era, Gallo-Roman divinities and 7th-century damascened buckles. Especially exciting was the discovery in the Bercy quarter in 1991 of ten ancient

MUSÉE CARNAVALET

Fragment of 2nd–3rd-century Roman wall painting showing an idealised male head.
Found at Rue de l'Abbé de l'Épée (*map p. 587, D4*).

oak pirogues (dug-out canoes). The oldest (c. 4500 BC) and the best preserved is here, measuring nearly 6m long. These and other finds introduced new insights into the origins of Paris.

B: Sixteenth century (Rooms 7–10, Carnavalet ground floor)

Sixteenth-century Paris was a time of cultural expansion and religious and political conflict. Portraits from the School of Clouet picture two royal widows: Mary Stuart (1561), widow of François II and later the Queen of Scots, wearing a white mourning veil; and Catherine de Médicis (1519–89), widow of Henri II, who failed to find a solution to the religious problems that resulted in the St Bartholomew's Day Massacre (*see p. 256*). There is also a portrait of Diane de France, Duchesse d'Angoulême, the natural daughter of Henri II by Diane de Poitiers, Catherine's triumphant rival. She built the nearby Hôtel de Lamoignon (*see p. 355*). The Duc de Guise, known as *le Balafré* because of a facial scar, was from a hard-line Catholic dynasty opposed to the Huguenot supporters of Henri of Navarre. St Geneviève, patron of Paris (*see p. 12*), is portrayed in front of the 17th-century Hôtel de Ville. Two huge 17th-century mascarons removed from the Pont Neuf during renovations in the 19th century can also be seen here.

C: Seventeenth century (Carnavalet first floor)

The history of Paris in the 17th and 18th centuries is illustrated by series of reconstructed period interiors, including Madame de Sévigné's apartments, together with impressive collections of topographical art and fine furniture. The transformation of the city during the reigns of Louis XIII and Louis XIV is represented through paintings, sketches for decorative schemes inspired by Italy, and the interiors of grand town houses, including the Sévigné Rooms of the Hôtel Carnavalet itself.

Rooms 13–15: Painted views of Paris, including three of the Place Royale (now Place des Vosges).

Room 17: Contains the sumptuous drawing-room of the nearby Hôtel Colbert de Villacerf (*23 Rue de Turenne*; c. 1655), with cream and gilt wood panelling decorated with polychrome grotesques.

Rooms 19 and 20: Notable are the richly painted and gilded *boiseries* of c. 1656 of the *Grande chambre* and the *Cabinet doré* of the Hôtel de la Rivière (*14 Pl. des Vosges*). Abbot La Rivière, Bishop of Langres, purchased the property in 1652 and called on the architect François Le Vau (*see p. 46*) and the painter Charles Le Brun to refurbish it. These rooms represent the most remarkable decorative ensembles of the Carnavalet and were the first to be reassembled here, from 1872. The project was one of Le Brun's first major decorative commissions and prompted Fouquet to engage him to work at Vaux-le-Vicomte (which ultimately led him on to work at the Château de Versailles).

Rooms 21–23: Apartments containing memorabilia which belonged to Marie de Rabutin-Chantal, Marquise de Sévigné (d. 1696), who occupied two wings of the *étage noble* of Carnavalet from 1677 until her death. Her daughter, Mme de Grignon, lived on the ground floor in an apartment adapted by Libéral Bruant (c. 1636–97). Mme de Sévigné's *Lettres de la Marquise*, written mainly to her daughter and which span 30 years, are a brilliant and lively testament of the society of the day, written in an unusually informal style for the time. Her portrait by Claude Lefèbvre was reproduced in an engraving used as the frontispiece for the second edition, published in 1754, and her japanned desk from the Château des Rochers, near Vitré, is below it. There are also likenesses of contemporary literary figures, including Jean de la Fontaine by Rigaud and the playwright Molière, depicted in Corneille's *La Mort de Pompée* (c. 1657).

Rooms 24 and 25: An evocation of Paris during the *Ancien Régime* with municipal paintings. The original grand fireplaces still grace the main rooms.

D: Eighteenth-century (Carnavalet ground and first floors)

This section is divided into four different periods or styles: Louis XIV, Regency of Philippe d'Orléans, Louis XV and Louis XVI.

Rooms 27–29: Views of Paris in the 18th century and Rococo panels colourfully painted with garlands of flowers, cameos and mirrors from a mansion that once stood in Rue de Varenne.

Rooms 30–31: On the ground floor is a room from the Café Militaire on Rue St-Honoré (1762), which was reserved for officers. It is a rare survival of the decorative work of Claude-Nicolas Ledoux (*see p. 405*) and was his first commission in Paris. Cafés came into fashion at the end of the 17th century, the first being Le Procope, founded in 1675 (*see p. 98*). Also by Ledoux is the magnificent gold and white panelling from the Salon de Compagnie of the Hôtel d'Uzès (1767), with golden trees garlanded with musical instruments. The reconstructed stairwell from the Hôtel de Luynes is decorated with *trompe-l'oeil* paintings of peopled balconies by P-A. Brunetti (1748).

Rooms 37–41: The early 18th century, during the Regency of Philippe d'Orléans, demonstrates the wealth of invention of Rococo decoration. After Louis XIV's death in 1715, during the eight years that the young Louis XV spent at the Tuileries, high society evolved to include financiers and intellectuals. Women also had a greater influence in defining tastes. Paris eclipsed Versailles and architects, cabinet-makers, sculptors and haberdashers were hugely in demand. Representative paintings include Boucher's *Le Pied de Mlle O'Murphy* (Room 39), a tiny study for the odalisque *Mlle O'Murphy*, and Chardin's *Game of Billiards* (Room 41).

Rooms 46–58: The varied themes of these rooms are religious, theatrical (with statuettes from the Comédie Italienne) and literary (with a portrait of Voltaire aged 24 and the chair in which he wrote). The Blue Room has a variety of chairs, a harp of c. 1780 and a table by Adam Weisweiller, who was patronised by Marie-Antoinette. The superb painted decoration of Room 58, the work of Boucher and Fragonard c. 1765, is from the house of the engraver Gilles Demarteau in Rue de la Pelleterie.

DECORATIVE ARTS IN THE MUSÉE CARNAVALET

The Decorative Arts are a key part of the collections. Painted and sculpted wood panels and ceilings saved from *hôtels particuliers* originally situated in smart *quartiers* such as the Faubourg St-Germain and Faubourg St-Honoré, many of them demolished during Haussmann's urban reconstruction in the mid-19th century (*see p. 284*), have been reassembled in the museum. Following scrupulous research, some of these décors have been meticulously restored using the original technique of *peinture à la colle* or distemper, using water-based pigments combined with animal glue or milk protein. The colour schemes, all of which are different, vary according to the period, as does the relief decoration of the panelling, which may be either wood or stucco. Rooms were also smaller then. Fabrics were specially woven to match the original decoration, carefully differentiating between what is authentic and what has been remade. The museum has around 800 examples of furnishings, and the rooms are brought to life with relevant *objets d'art*, tapestries and pieces from the workshops of leading cabinet-makers such as Migeon, Riesener, Weisweiller and Roger Vandercruse (called Lacroix, RVLC).

E: The French Revolution (Le Peletier second floor)

These rooms hold a central place in the museum and vividly evoke this turbulent period in Parisian history.

Rooms 101–106: Paintings and engravings which record key moments include *The Tennis Court Oath* (1789), in the Jeu de Paume at Versailles, by Jacques-Louis David; *The Declaration of the Rights of Man* (c. 1789) by J.-J.-F. Le Barbier (Room 103); *The Storming of the Bastille* (1793) by Charles Thévenin and *Demolition of the Bastille* (1789) by Hubert Robert; and the huge *Fête de la Fédération,* on the Champs de Mars on 14th July 1790, when the oath to the republic was sworn. *Capital Punishment* (1793–4) by Pierre-Antoine Demachy shows an execution during the Terror declared on the 5th September 1793, by Robespierre on Place de la Révolution (now Pl. de la Concorde). A major element of the display is the multitude of surviving curiosities: the chest that carried letters from the Bastille; the keys of the Bastille; a model of the Bastille cut from one of its stones; and Danton's toiletries case. Royal memorabilia include Louis XVI's shaving dish, a portrait of the young Louis XVII and a reconstruction (in Room 106) of the room in the Temple where the royal family were imprisoned from 10th August 1792.

Rooms 107–109: These are dedicated to the Convention, the Terror and the Thermidor. Immortalised on canvas or in sculpture are the key players of the time, such as Count Mirabeau (d. 1791) and the great orator and beau Barnave (d. 1793), whose likeness was sculpted by Houdon. Both men were constitutional monarchists. There is also a bust of the Jacobin demagogue Marat, stabbed to death in his bath by Charlotte Corday in 1793. Le Peletier de St-Fargeau, owner of this *hôtel*, was himself a revolutionary aristocrat who voted for the death of Louis XVI and was assassinated in 1793 by one of the king's guard while dining in a restaurant of the Palais Royal. There are also portraits (anon) of Robespierre, dominant member of the Jacobins and chief architect of the Reign of Terror, who had Danton and Camille Desmoulins, also pictured here, 'eliminated' in 1794, though he too went to the guillotine the same year. Dr Guillotin is commemorated in a portrait and in a model of the guillotine (Room 108), which was adopted in 1789.

Rooms 110–113: The focus here is on the European wars, patriotic fervour, and the Generals, including Bonaparte at the start of his rise to power. *The Desecration of the Royal Vaults* (1793) by Hubert Robert is a reminder of the vandalism of the time. These acts did, however, engender an interest in the safeguarding of national heritage, in which Alexandre Lenoir played a major role (*see p. 93*). Popular imagery of the period is recorded in some 50 gouaches by Pierre-Étienne Le Sueur, and a gruesomely direct image shows a man whose arm has just been amputated (it lies on the table) declaring his devotion to *la patrie* (with his other arm).

F: Early nineteenth-century (Le Peletier ground floor)

The period from Napoleon to 1848 is covered in rooms next to the Orangerie that contain paintings and furnishings from the Consulate and First Empire.

Rooms 115–116: The portrait of Napoleon in the uniform of *Colonel des Chasseurs de la Garde* (1809) was commissioned from Robert Lefèvre by the city for the Hôtel de Ville. Also here are Napoleon's preferred *nécessaire de campagne*, with 110 pieces, and his death-mask. The fine portrait, *Mme Récamier Seated* (1805), by Gérard, depicts the famous beauty of post-Revolutionary Paris, Juliette Récamier, who was credited with the introduction of the 'Empire' style, sparked by a general interest in antiquity following new archaeological discoveries in Italy.

The Restoration Period under Charles V is evoked in Room 116 by furnishings from the Duchesse de la Gaëte's home in Rue du Faubourg St-Honoré, and a painting by Corot, *The Pont St-Michel and Quai des Orfèvres*.

Rooms 117–118: Painted views of Paris in the first half of the 19th century.

Rooms 119–120: These two rooms are dedicated to events surrounding the revolution of July 1830 and the July Monarchy. The three days when the barricades went up following Charles X's suppression of the freedom of the press on 27th July, *Les Trois Glorieuses*, lost him the throne. A maquette depicts the arrival of the Duc d'Orléans at the Hôtel de Ville on 31st July 1830 to accept the lieutenant-generalcy of France. On 8th August Charles X abdicated and Louis-Philippe was acclaimed *Roi des Français*, the only member of the House of Orléans to reign. His overthrow came in February 1848, with more barricades, depicted in the *Burning of Louis-Philippe's Throne on Place de la Bastille*.

Rooms 122–127: The years between 1830 and 1848 were the height of the Romantic period in France, embracing figures such as the historian Michelet and the novelist Victor Hugo. The last two rooms (on the first floor) display paintings of the city during the Romantic era, several by visiting Englishmen.

G: Turn of the twentieth century (Le Peletier first floor)

The display traces the story of the city during the Second Empire (1852–70), through the Belle Époque up to the years preceding the First World War.

Rooms 128 and 129: In pride of place is the Prince Imperial's grand ceremonial cradle (1856), a gift from the City of Paris to Emperor Napoléon III and Empress Eugénie on the birth of prince Eugène-Louis-Joseph. The large painting *Napoléon III hands over to Haussmann the Decree of Annexation of the Suburban Communes* (16th June 1859) refers to the expansion of Paris under Baron Haussmann's direction to embrace eleven suburbs, doubling the size of the city and creating the 20 arrondissements of today. Part of the scheme is shown in *The Building of Av. de l'Opéra* by Giuseppe de Nittis. The portrait of Prosper Mérimée by Simon Rochard depicts the author of the novella *Carmen* (1845), on which Bizet's opera was based. Mérimée was also first

MUSÉE CARNAVALET

Waterlilies by Alphonse Mucha, part of the decoration for the Fouquet jewellery shop (1900).

Inspector of Historic Monuments, a post created in 1830 to protect and preserve national heritage. Giraud's painting *Le Bal de l'Opéra* is of the same period. This was also the time of Universal Exhibitions in 1855 and 1857, for which many foreign dignitaries, including Queen Victoria, visited Paris.

Rooms 130 and 131: *Gambetta Leaving Paris by Balloon* and small sketches made by Puvis de Chavannes, *The Pigeon* and *The Balloon* (finished works at the Musée d'Orsay), refer to episodes during the Siege of Paris at the time of the Franco-Prussian war (1870–1). The tiny work *Paris Burning* by Corot records the collapse of the Second Empire and the extremely violent repercussions are summed up in the *Execution of a Trumpeter* by Alfred Roll, when

Versaillais troops indiscriminately executed all suspects, officially numbered at 17,000. The 19th century ends with paintings of events and personalities of the Third Republic.

Rooms 133–137: In a different mood, Paris at the turn of the 19th and 20th centuries as seen by the painters of the period includes two versions of the *Moulin de la Galette* in Montmartre, one by Paul Signac in 1884, at a time that witnessed the gradual urbanisation of the villages around Paris. The mill was demolished in 1925 but its neighbour still stands. Other glimpses of Paris include *Views of the Seine* by Guillaumin, Jongkind's *Rue St-Séverin at Night* (1877) and the *Cité et Port St-Michel* by Maximillien Luce. Among portraits of literary figures are *Edmond de Goncourt* by Carrière and *Daudet Writing*. The great music-hall performer Yvette Guilbert is captured in a sculpture by Leonetto Cappiello. Famous for her expressive gestures and mimicry, and identified by her long black gloves and butterfly bows, she was happy to be portrayed by Cappiello but had a love-hate relationship with Toulouse-Lautrec, who made studies of her which she considered 'caricatures'. Jean Béraud's *Les Coulisses de l'Opéra* shows the backstage of the opera house invaded by portly gentlemen in top hats, every one of them preying upon a lissom young dancing girl.

H: Into the twentieth century (Rooms 141–148, Le Peletier first floor)

This section illustrates radical changes in taste. Art Nouveau, or the new style, which did not imitate the past, took off in the 1890s, mainly in architecture and the decorative arts. In the collections are two remarkable Art Nouveau interiors: one, of 1899 by Henri Sauvage, is a private room from the Café de Paris, a famous restaurant at 39 Av. de l'Opéra (demolished in 1954); the other example of this short-lived fashion is Georges Fouquet's jewellery shop (1900) from Rue Royale, a unique and complex piece entirely created by Alphonse Mucha, best known for poster design. By 1923 Fouquet had decided to remodel his boutique: the old one was dismantled and stored until 1941, when it was donated to the Carnavalet. It was restored and finally reassembled here in 1989. Slightly later is the Art Deco decoration of the Hôtel de Wendel ballroom (1925) by the Catalan artist José Maria Sert. This is an extraordinary example of the decorative arts during the Roaring Twenties, its theme the *Procession of the Queen of Sheba*.

Three alcoves (Room 147) contain furniture and mementoes from the homes of three writers: Marcel Proust, Anna de Noailles and Paul Léautaud. They had little in common except for the fact that they each worked in their bedrooms, and in the case of the first two, in bed (the iron bedstead in which Proust wrote much of *À la Recherche du Temps Perdu* is preserved). Paul Léautaud (d. 1956), life-long author of the *Journal Littéraire*, was something of a marginal, indifferent to fame, who lived in run-down conditions at Fontenay-aux-Roses in the company of around 300 cats and 100 dogs. Very different is the room of Anna de Noailles (d. 1933), from 40 Rue Scheffer, where she moved in 1909. This is a pleasant, feminine retreat where she reclined on cushions on her bed to receive visitors and to compose poetry. The bedroom of Marcel Proust (d. 1922) is recreated from the three places he occupied as a recluse. The cork tiles are a reminder of their use to line the walls and ceiling at 102 Blvd Haussmann, where he lived from 1906. The room also contains his childhood bed, a Chinese screen and a portrait of his father.

The great variety of paintings in this section range from elegant Belle-Époque works to late 20th-century Parisian subjects. They include *Young Woman holding a Book* by Alfred Stevens; *The Young Jean Cocteau in the Garden at Offranville* (1913) by J.-É. Blanche; a portrait of the couturier who liberated women from the corset, Paul Poiret (1927); and another of Princesse Jean de Broglie (1914), depicted in a dress by Poiret. There are also works by Paul Signac, Marquet, Foujita and Marcel Gromaire.

MUSÉE COGNACQ-JAY

Map p. 588, B2. 8 Rue Elzévir. Métro 1 to St-Paul. Open 10–6; closed Mon and holidays. Free. T: 01 40 27 07 21, www.museecognacqjay.paris.fr.

Musée Cognacq-Jay occupies the intimate Hôtel de Donon, built c. 1575 and altered about a century later. The remarkable collection of 18th-century objects was put together from 1900–25 by Ernest Cognacq, founder of the Magasins de la Samaritaine, and his wife Marie-Louise Jay, and bequeathed to the Ville de Paris on his death in 1928. A profusion of objects is displayed in 20 small rooms on four floors and in the beamed attic. The result is a charming evocation of a luxurious 18th-century inte-rior. Several rooms have *rocaille* panelling, some removed from the Château d'Eu (Normandy) and some of it original to the house.

THE COLLECTION
Some of the best-known artists of the time are represented, including Chardin, whose *Still Life with a Copper Cauldron*, a small painting on wood, is deliciously satisfying. Light-hearted Rococo works include Watteau's *Gilles à l'Orée du Bois*; and, illustrating one of Fontaine's *Fables*, Fragonard's *Perrette et le Pot au Lait*. Examples of François Boucher's painterly virtuosity include *Mme Baudouin*, his daughter, and *Diana's Return from the Hunt* (1745). The portraitist Jean-Baptiste Lemoyne, a protégé of Louis XV, produced a remarkably lifelike yet unflattering terracotta portrait bust of the Count de Lowendal, who became *Maréchal de France* in 1749. Among portraits by Maurice-Quentin Delatour are a pastel of Mme la Présidente de Rieux (1742), dressed in a grey silk ballgown with blue taffeta frills. It is a masterpiece of light and textures.

Rare for a Parisian collection is the large number of English works, including Thomas Lawrence's *Princess Clémentine de Metternich* and Wright of Derby's *Young Bird-Catchers*. There is also an early work by Rembrandt.

Among delicate pieces of furniture are a bureau in ebony by Boulle inlaid with a variety of materials, and a charming oval oak writing table on two levels (c. 1770) by Lacroix, which contains a sliding writing desk with compartments for ink and pens. Jean-François Oeben was probably responsible for the mechanical table (c. 1760) with a secret drawer. A pair of commodes by Martin Carlin illustrates the transition between Louis XV and Louis XVI styles: the curved legs and marquetry floral medal-lions are still Louis XV but the overall shape and decorative elements, such as the urn and acanthus leaves with marquetry floral medallions, are typical of the latter.

The collection of ceramics and porcelain includes a pair of Kien-Lung cranes in white porcelain, symbols of longevity and favourite images in Chinese art.

BETWEEN MUSÉE COGNACQ-JAY AND MUSÉE PICASSO

At no. 11 Rue Payenne, the Hôtel de Marle houses the **Swedish Cultural Centre**, the Institut Tessin, the only one of its kind in the world, administered by the Swedish

MUSÉE COGNACQ-JAY
Detail of Boucher's *Diana's Return from the Hunt* (1745).

Institute in Stockholm (*open Tues–Fri 10–1 & 2–5; closed Sun–Mon except during temporary exhibitions; T: 01 44 78 80 20*).

The **Hôtel Libéral-Bruant**, at no. 1 Pl. de Thorigny (off Rue de la Perle), is named after one of the architects of Les Invalides and was built in 1685 for his personal use. It has a perfectly harmonious pedimented elevation, decorated with four busts in niches.

MUSÉE PICASSO

Map p. 588, B1. Métro 8 to St-Sébastien Froissart. Open Tues–Fri 11.30–6, Sat–Sun 9.30–6; open to 9pm on third Fri of the month; closed Tues. Free entry for disabled visitors. Booking your visit in advance (online or by phone) is strongly recommended, and book online for guided visits. Visioguide available in French, English, Spanish and sign language, and can be uploaded as an app. T: 01 85 56 00 36, www.museepicassoparis.fr.

Reopened after costly refurbishment in 2014, the museum takes as a leitmotif Picasso's witty *Tête de Taureau*, created in 1942 from a bicycle saddle and handlebars.

The Hôtel Salé, an elegant 17th-century mansion on Rue de Thorigny, acquired its name on account of the huge profits that its owner made from the salt tax. The largest house in the Marais, it is a prime example of a *hôtel particulier* between court and garden. It received the collection of works by Pablo Picasso from the French state in lieu of death duties in 1985 and has been remodelled to show off the exceptional collection to the very best advantage. The large entrance hall is formed from part of the courtyard and a major feature is the elegant central staircase of the original building. The exhibits are shown over five floors in light, white rooms of varying proportions which incorporate the vaulted basement and original beams in the attic area. There are views over the garden from the upper floors.

The collection covers Picasso's *oeuvre* and evolution from 1894–1973 as painter, sculptor, ceramic designer and photographer. It includes 5,000 works by Picasso himself and 200,000 objects from his personal archives, including 150 works by other artists. The display is chronological and falls into three major sequences: *Picasso Magistral* on the three main floors (Levels 0–2); *Dialogues* under the eaves (Level 3); and *Ateliers* in the cellars (Level -1).

Picasso Magistral (Levels 0–2)

This section follows the entire evolution of Picasso's work from the earliest beginnings to his death in 1973.

Early years (1895–1906): Picasso was taught drawing by his father at his art school in Málaga and by the age of 14 was influenced by the Golden Age of Spanish art. Hints of Velázquez and Murillo appear in *La Fillette aux pieds nus* and *L'Homme à la casquette*. A stay in Barcelona resulted in an echo of Art Nouveau in the poster *Els Quatre Gats*; and in Madrid (1897–8) he copied portraits by Goya. He represented Spain at the Universal Exhibition of 1900 in Paris with *Derniers Moments* and joined the Spanish painters in Montmartre. Captivated by Parisian life, he was influenced by Toulouse-Lautrec, Degas and Steinlen, and his palette lightened. Around 1901 the influence of Van Gogh, Gauguin and Cézanne is perceptible in *Death of Casagemas*. Picasso's 'Blue Period' resulted in a haunting *Self-portrait* (1901) and *La Celestina* (1904), a woman with a blind eye. Other monochromatic works followed.

During 1905–6 Picasso met Apollinaire, Gertrude Stein, Gauguin and Matisse; he discovered Iberian sculpture at the Louvre and when visiting Catalonia, and the *Self-portrait* of 1906 shows a simplification of form and space. He began to experiment with the relationship between sculpture and painting.

Primitivism and Cubism (1906–15): Picasso abandoned perspective and freed his work from local colour, while introducing Deconstruction and Abstraction. Between *The Two Brothers* (summer 1906) and *Self-portrait* (autumn 1906) he undertook a major project of preparatory drawings, the culmination of which was *Les Demoiselles d'Avignon* (1906–7), now in New York. He also studied African and Oceanic art, which produced *Nu assis, Femme aux mains jointes* and *Buste*. In his large wooden sculpture *Figure* (1907), he adopted Cézanne's rule for treating volumes in nature as the cylinder, the sphere and the cone. He simplified, flattened and fragmented surfaces into successive or transparent planes, opened structures and broke volumes down into facets, resulting in *Guitares* (1912). The monochromatic washes *Homme à la guitare* and *Homme à la mandoline* (1911–13) were important in affirming the new principles of what became known as Cubism. *Nature morte à la chaise cannée* (1912), arguably the first collage in modern art, of rope and oil-cloth printed with a design of chair caning, is a three-dimensional interpretation of Cubism. The synthesis of collage and sculpture produced the construction *Violon* (1913).

Polymorphism/Metamorphoses (1915–36): Colour, moulding and tactile qualities came into Picasso's Cubist work, leading to 'cubo-collages' such as *Bottle of Bass* (1913) and his controversial sets for Diaghilev's ballet, *Parade* (1917). Graeco-Roman classicism, Ingres and photography all merge in *Olga dans un fauteuil* (1918), and *Paul en arlequin* (1924) recalls children painted by Velázquez, Goya or Manet. Monumental figures appear in *Femmes à la fontaine* (1921) and *La Course* (1922).

Although never part of the Surrealist group, its influence and the impact of personal problems emerge in the aggression of *Le Baiser* (1925) and *Grand Nu au fauteuil rouge*, as well as *Figures au bord de la mer* (1931). The three-dimensional wire 'drawings in space' were maquettes for a *Monument à Apollinaire* (d. 1918), in acknowledgement of the poet's support. Large, curvaceous sculptures made at Boisgeloup (1930–1) are based on his model Marie-Thérèse, pared down to the barest essentials.

War Paintings (1936–46): Picasso expressed the horrors of the Spanish Civil War and World War II in brutally explicit figures skinned alive, *La Femme qui pleure, La Suppliante* (with the traits of Dora Maar and Marie-Thérèse), and *Chat égorgant un oiseau*. Following the bombing of Guernica (April 1937), Picasso began a cycle of propagandist works culminating in the famous *Guernica*. He painted a series of portraits (1937–9) in homage to Van Gogh, whose canvases were confiscated by the Nazis.

Picasso managed to remain in Paris during the war years. Works such as *L'Enfant aux colombes* (1943) express the depth of feeling against all forms of domination and indoctrination, and sculptures such as *Homme au mouton* or *Tête de taureau* (1943) acknowledge the tragedy of war. *Massacre en Corée* (1951) concludes the cycle of war paintings.

Les Années 'Pop' (1947–51): Living in Vallauris, close to the Mediterranean, Picasso put a new slant on works made from the *objet trouvé*, such as *Le Guenon* (1951), *Petite Fille sautant la corde* (1950) and *La Chèvre* (1950), and he took to decorating ceramics from the Madoura pottery. *La Femme-fleur* (1946), painted in a flat, colourful technique, symbolises a new world rising from the rubble. As homage to Matisse (d. 1954), from whom he had taken inspiration but with whom he always had a competitive relationship, Picasso painted *L'Atelier de la Californie*. Tributes to other painters who inspired him include versions of Velázquez's *Las Meniñas*, Manet's *Déjeuner sur l'herbe* and Delacroix's *Femmes d'Alger*.

Picasso's Private Collection (Level 3)

A photograph of 1908 taken at the Bateau-Lavoir (*see p. 319*) shows that Picasso had already acquired a number of African figures and masks. There are canvases by Rousseau, Matisse, Braque, Derain and Van Dongen, with whom Picasso was in regular contact before 1914. Among other works from his collection by artists who inspired him are *Landscape* by Gauguin (1885–90), Cézanne's *La Mer à l'Estaque, Le Château noir, Cinq Baigneuses*, and *Still Life with Oranges*; Van Dongen's *La Vigne*; still lifes by

Matisse; Miró's *Self-portrait*; Degas' *La Fête de la patronne* and Henri Rousseau's *Self-portrait with Lamp*; also paintings by Le Nain, Renoir, Modigliani and Victor Brauner.

The Ateliers (Level -1)

This vaulted space completes the Picasso Magistral section with a photographic record of Picasso's creativity over five different periods and covering painting, sculpture, photography, ceramics and the graphic arts. The Bateau-Lavoir studio was photographed by Picasso between 1900 and 1912. The Boisgeloup workshop, in images by Brassaï, shows the extent of the sculpture carried out in 1929–35. During the war Picasso worked at the Grands-Augustins studio and during the Pop Period at the Fournas studios. Between 1959 and 1960, he worked on monumental canvases in the studios at La Californie and Vauvenargues. The Mougins workshop, gathered around his press, show the sequence of engravings on copper for *La Celestina* (1968–70).

THE ARCHIVES NATIONALES

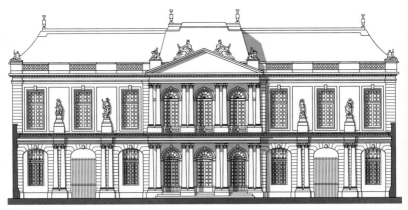

HÔTEL DE SOUBISE

Map p. 588, A1. 60 Rue des Francs-Bourgeois. Métro 11 to Rambuteau. Open Mon, Wed–Fri 10–5.30, Sat–Sun 2–5.30; closed Tues and holidays. Guided visit first Sat of month 2.30–4, by reservation only, T: 01 75 47 23 07, service-educatif.an@cultures.gouv.fr. For general information, T: 01 40 27 60 96, www.archives-nationales.culture.gouv.fr.

The Archives Nationales de France occupy the Hôtel de Soubise, Hôtel de Rohan and other buildings. It is well worth visiting for the rare examples of Rococo decoration which have remained *in situ*. Frequent temporary exhibitions are held here.

HISTORY OF THE HÔTEL DE SOUBISE

The first mansion here was the Hôtel de Clisson, built in the 14th century by Constable Olivier de Clisson, supporter of Charles V against the English. The turreted Gothic gateway of 1380 (*58 Rue des Archives*) is a remnant of this building and a rare example of 14th-century architecture in Paris. Bolingbroke (later Henry IV) gave a farewell banquet here in 1399 before setting out for England. Purchased in 1553 by François de Lorraine, Duc de Guise and his wife Anna d'Este, as the Hôtel de Guise, it is possible that this was where the St Bartholomew's Day Massacre of 1572 (*see p. 256*) was planned. In 1700 the mansion was sold to François de Rohan-Soubise and Anne de Rohan-Chabot and became known as the Hôtel de Soubise. Between 1705 and 1712 the architect Delamair transformed the building and re-orientated it, making the main entrance on Rue des Francs-Bourgeois. The Hôtel de Rohan was begun in 1705 by Delamair and successively inhabited by four cardinals of the Rohan family, all bishops of Strasbourg. The National Archives, covering the 7th century to 1958, have used these buildings since 1808 and have five specialised centres on this site.

VISITING THE ARCHIVES

The semicircular monumental gateway opens into a colonnaded **Cour d'Honneur**, with copies of *The Four Seasons* by Robert le Lorrain on the main façade.

The interior of the building has been drastically altered; nevertheless there are examples of the campaign of renovation led by Boffrand at the time of Prince Hercule Mériadec de Rohan, between 1735 and 1740, which represent the pinnacle of Rococo art by Adam and Lemoyne, and a remarkable number of paintings created for the *hôtel* by Boucher, Carle van Loo and others. The **Prince's Apartments** (Bedchamber, Oval Salon and Grand Cabinet) have remnants of the original décor as well as furniture of the period from the national collections. There are also some examples of objects from the National Archives, such as a terrestrial and celestial globes.

The 19th-century staircase from the vestibule leads to the **Princess's Apartments**, where the Antechamber, large and empty, was the guard room at the time of the Guise. The Ceremonial Bedroom is a glorious and busy apartment decorated by Boffrand in 1735–6, with gilded stuccos and Boucher paintings, and a reproduction of the princess's bed. The Princess's Oval Salon is one of the best Parisian Rococo interiors, by Boffrand and Natoire, in white and gold with large windows and mirrors. The chapel bears traces of the Chapelle de Clisson of 1375, transformed in 1533. There follow the small rooms of the Princess's Private Suite, decorated with paintings and a portrait of Anne de Rohan-Chabot, Princesse de Soubise, who was the favourite, for a time, of Louis XIV.

ON AND AROUND RUE DES ARCHIVES

The magnificent Hôtel de Guénégaud, designed by François Mansart (c. 1650), at 62 Rue des Archives, houses the **Fondation François Sommer pour la Chasse et de la Nature** (*map p. 588, A1; open Tues–Sun 11–6; Thur to 9.30; closed Mon and holidays, T: 01 53 01 92 40, www.fondationfrancoissommer.org*). This is a unique venue conceived as the private house of a rich collector, and was completely renovated in 2007. Regular exhibitions explore all aspects of nature and man's interaction with the natural world. There is a large collection animal paintings of all periods by a wide range of artists. The Foundation is particularly concerned with the conservation and protection of buildings and decoration connected with hunting and fishing.

Notre-Dame des Blancs-Manteaux, on the street of the same name (*map p. 588, A1–A2*), refers to the white habits of an order of mendicant monks established here in 1285 by Louis IX. Rebuilt in the late 17th century, the church's 18th-century door came from St-Barthélemy on the Île de la Cité, demolished in 1863. Inside the church is a Flemish-style Rococo pulpit (1749).

The **Temple des Billettes** (*22 Rue des Archives; map p. 588, A2*) was built in 1756 for the Carmelites, with a galleried interior, and since 1809 has been used by a Lutheran congregation. On the north side is the only surviving medieval cloister in Paris (1427), a Flamboyant relic of an older convent constructed on the site of the so-called 'Miracle des Billettes' of 1290, when the Communion bread is supposed to have dripped blood when a Jew, not deeming it the body of the Messiah, attempted to put it to ordinary use in his kitchen. The miracle was later used in support of the Catholics' argument with the Protestants over transubstantiation. Occasional temporary exhibitions, guided visits and concerts are held here (*www.egliselutherianne-paris.com*).

MUSÉE D'ART & D'HISTOIRE DU JUDAÏSME

Map p. 588, A1. Métro 11 to Rambuteau. Open Mon–Fri 11–6, Sun 10–6; closed Sat. Audioguides, guided tours. T: 01 53 01 86 60, www.mahj.org.

On the west side of Rue du Temple is a charming ensemble of 17th-century houses, one of the best of which is Hôtel de St-Aignan, home to the Museum of Jewish Art and History. A main theme of the museum is Jewish communities that have congregated on French soil over the centuries, such as European Jews who migrated to France in the 19th century, or those from North Africa in the 20th. Three sections are reserved for specifically French-Jewish history and art: the Middle Ages; the process of emancipation from the French Revolution to the Dreyfus Affair; and the 20th century.

THE BUILDING
The Hôtel de St-Aignan, designed by Pierre Le Muet, was completed in 1650 for Cardinal Mazarin's superintendent of finance. An unprecedented example of civil architecture in Paris, the giant Corinthian order is deployed in the magnificent courtyard. On the south side, masking a section of Philippe-Auguste's boundary wall, is a *trompe l'oeil* façade creating an illusion of space and symmetry. The mansion was acquired by the Duc de St-Aignan in 1688, at which time the main staircase was installed and the garden façade enlarged. Le Nôtre was involved in the design of the original garden. The Hôtel St-Aignan was later at the heart of the Jewish quarter known in Yiddish as the *Pletzl*. It was made available for a museum at the initiative of

Jacques Chirac in 1986, then Mayor of Paris, and opened in 1998. The museum brings together collections from the former Musée d'Art Juif in Montmartre and collections previously in the reserves of the Hôtel de Cluny.

THE MUSEUM

The entrance is beneath the St-Aignan family coat of arms. The main staircase leads to the permanent collections, which begin on the first floor with the **Introductory Room**. Here the antiquity of the Jewish people is evoked through the relationship to a text, a language and a homeland, and its particular destiny of exile, using handwritten Hebrew texts and translations. Discovered in 1868 in Dhiban (Jordan), the *Mesha stele* (in the Louvre; Near Eastern Antiquities, ground floor, The Levant, Room D) provides the most important direct archaeological history of the Kingdom of Israel.

The Middle Ages: The display includes gravestones, manuscripts and four rare objects: a Hanukkah lamp, a wedding ring, an alms box and a seal. Jews in Italy from the Renaissance to the 18th century are represented by synagogue furniture, a marriage ring and illuminated marriage contracts. The meeting of two diaspora in Amsterdam in the 16th and 17th centuries is narrated through engravings. A *sukkah* (tabernacle hut) decorated with a view of the Holy City is the focal point for a display concerning the central role of Jerusalem.

Rooms divided between the first and second floors are devoted to the traditional Ashkenazi and Sephardi worlds, with models of synagogues and silverware including a highly ornate 17th-century Torah case from Vienna.

The Era of Emancipation: Jewish emancipation in France began with the Revolution. Vital events in 19th-century French Judaism are illustrated by documents, paintings and other objects. They include more than 3,000 items from archives donated by the grandchildren of Dreyfus.

Also explored is the intellectual contribution of Jews in Europe at the turn of the 20th century, the emergence and spread of Zionism and Yiddish culture, as well as the Jewish cultural renaissance in Germany and Russia at the beginning of the 20th century.

The Jewish presence in 20th-century art: Featured here are School of Paris artists such as Lipchitz, Soutine, Marcoussis, Modigliani, El Lissitsky, Zadkine and Chagall, all of whom absorbed contemporary artistic developments in a very personal manner, often breaking away from the exclusively religious iconography which had once dominated Jewish art.

A documentary picture of European Judaism is built up around the theme of the Jewish community which inhabited the Hôtel de St-Aignan in 1939. The only reference in the museum to the Holocaust is very personal to this community: in a tiny courtyard is a moving installation by Christian Boltanski which consists of plaques naming former residents. During the round-up of Parisian Jews in 1942, seven were arrested and in all 13 were deported and died. (*For Paris' main Holocaust memorial, Mémorial de la Shoah, see p. 376.*)

SAINT-GERVAIS-SAINT-PROTAIS

Map p. 588, A2. Métro 1 and 11 to Hôtel de Ville. Open for worship Mon–Sun 5.30–9. Guided visits some Sundays. If the front door is closed, entrance from Rue des Barres (back left).

Dominating the eastern side of Place St-Gervais, which is closed at the other end by the Hôtel de Ville (*see p. 346*), is the church of St-Gervais-St-Protais, dedicated to SS Gervase and Protase, martyrs from Milan whose cult was popular in the early Middle Ages. This was one of the oldest parishes on the Right Bank, going back to the 6th century. It is supposed that the sanctuary was rebuilt in the 13th century, and despite the Classical façade, the body of the present church is a late Gothic structure begun in the late 15th century.

The original plans are attributed to Martin Chambiges, whose work was continued by his son Pierre. The lower stages of the tower are an early 15th-century survival. The façade (1616–21), by Clément II Métezeau, is posited as an early example in Paris of the received sequence of the three Classical orders: Doric, Ionic and Corinthian. The painter Philippe de Champaigne (d. 1674), the writer Paul Scarron (d. 1660) and the dramatist Crébillon the Elder (d. 1762) are buried here. Since 1975 the church has been the headquarters of the Fraternities of Jerusalem.

INTERIOR OF SAINT-GERVAIS-SAINT-PROTAIS

The interior, impressively lofty and stylistically unified, is extremely atmospheric, particularly on dark winter mornings when the gloom is pierced only by a few candles. The high windows of both nave and choir contain painted glass of c. 1610–20 by Nicolas Chaumet among others. François Couperin (d. 1733) and seven members of his family served as organists here from 1653 to 1830. The organ (16th–17th century), known as the Couperin organ, survives, the case rebuilt in the 18th century. The choir and transepts date from rebuildings of 1494–1578 and the nave was continued in Flamboyant Gothic style c. 1600–20, with lierne and tierceron vaults, despite the strength of Italian Renaissance influence at this time.

South aisle: The third chapel **(A)** has an altar commemorating some 50 victims of the bombardment on Good Friday, 1918, when a German 'Big Bertha' shell struck the church. In the fourth **(B)** are seven 17th-century painted panels of the life of Christ. Painted glass of 1531 in the fifth chapel **(C)**, restored in the 19th century, represents the *Martyrdom of St Gervais and St Protais*, and in the sixth the *Judgement of Solomon* **(D)** by Jean de Chastellain (1533). The chapel at the end of the aisle **(E)** contains the tomb of Chancellor Michel le Tellier (d. 1685), supported by bearded heads from the tomb of Jacques de Souvré (d. 1670), by François Anguier, the rest of which are in the Louvre.

East end: The Lady Chapel **(F)** is a heady example of Flamboyant Gothic (1517) with complicated vaults and a

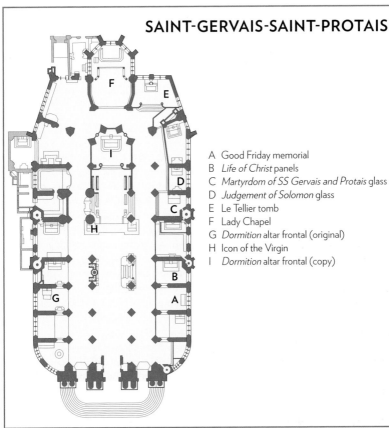

SAINT-GERVAIS-SAINT-PROTAIS

A Good Friday memorial
B *Life of Christ* panels
C *Martyrdom of SS Gervais and Protais* glass
D *Judgement of Solomon* glass
E Le Tellier tomb
F Lady Chapel
G *Dormition* altar frontal (original)
H Icon of the Virgin
I *Dormition* altar frontal (copy)

bravura pendant boss. It retains fine original glass by Jean de Chastellain (restored in the 19th century) of the life of the Virgin.

North aisle: The Chapelle Dorée (1628) conserves its original decoration (*sadly no admission*); in the adjacent chapel **(G)**, the altar frontal is a 13th-century high relief of the *Dormition of the Virgin* and there is a portrait by Pajou (1782) of Mme Palerme de Savy.

Choir: Against the north entry-pillar is a 14th-century icon of the Virgin, known as *Notre-Dame de Bonne-Délivrance* **(H)**. The first seven stalls in the upper row were remade in the 17th century; the rest are mid-16th century with interesting misericords. The 18th-century bronze-gilt candelabra and cross on the altar were designed by Soufflot and on either side of the altar are wooden statues of the patron saints, by Michel Bourdin (1625). The altar frontal **(I)** is a copy of the *Dormition of the Virgin* from the north aisle chapel.

WALK FOUR: THE SOUTHERN MARAIS

The southern section of the Marais, a wedge-shaped zone cut off from the rest of the quarter when Rue de Rivoli was built in the mid-19th century, is bounded by the Seine and the Bastille. It has developed a rarefied character and discreet charm in its quiet streets, with a number of fine old buildings, restaurants and specialist boutiques.

To begin the walk, take Métro 1 or 11 to Hôtel de Ville (map p. 588, A2).

PLACE ST-GERVAIS, IN FRONT OF THE church of St Gervais and St Protais (*see above*), is planted with a single elm in its central part, a reminder of the elm of St Gervais, beneath which justice used to be administered, and from which comes the proverbial expression for waiting for Doomsday: *attendre sous l'orme*.

Rue François-Miron, to the left of the church façade, is part of the Roman road leading east from Lutetia to Melun, which was paved above the marshes. Much later it was named after François Miron, *Prévôt des Marchands* from 1604–6, who carried out many improvements in the area, including the enhancement of the quays. The stepped terrace on the right-hand side of the street was built c. 1735; the wrought-iron first-floor balconies of the building above it carry an elm tree motif. The Couperin family, organists and composers for the church, lived in this terrace; François Couperin, prodigiously talented, was born on the site of no. 2 in 1668.

Go up the steps to the right and into **Rue des Barres**. Behind the gate at no. 15 are the remains of the church's charnel house. Rue des Barres descends gently towards the Seine. At the bottom is a house with a small garden with a Baroque pediment and sundial. From here there is an impressive view of the south flank of the church.

Turn left at the end of the street, past the restaurant Chez Julien (*see p. 380*), with Belle-Époque décor, and left into **Rue du Pont Louis-Philippe**, where you will find specialist shops for paper and calligraphy, artefacts, framing and musical instruments. At the corner of Allée des Justes is the Shoah Memorial bookshop. Turn right into the alley (which has a Wallace Fountain; *see p. 319*) to see the **Mur des Justes**, with its plaques recording the names of righteous Gentiles who, at great personal risk, helped Jews to find safety. The modern building here on the right is the **Shoah Memorial** (*open Sun–Fri 10–6, Thur until 10; closed 1 Jan, 1 May, 14 July, 15 Aug, 25 Dec and some Jewish holidays; free; T: 01 42 77 44 72, www.memorialdelashoah.org*), inaugurated in 1956. It combines the memorial to an unknown Jewish martyr, archives, a photo library and library of the Centre de Documentation Juive Contemporaine (CDJC), the Memorial Crypt and a museum. The names of 76,000 Jews deported from France are engraved on the Wall of Names in the forecourt.

From outside the Shoah Memorial, turn left up Rue Geoffroy-l'Asnier, past the **Hôtel de Chalon-Luxembourg** (1608) at no. 26, which has a magnificent doorway (1659). Back on Rue

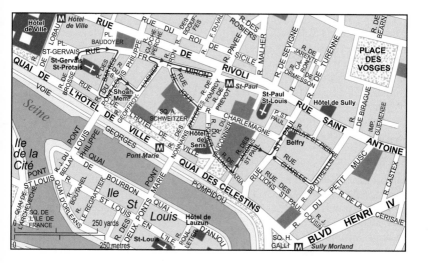

François-Miron, look left to see **two medieval houses** (at nos. 11 and 13), both of which were known to exist in the early 1500s; the façade of no. 13 is leaning perilously into the ancient Rue Cloche Perché. Overhanging jetties were forbidden from 1508, and in 1607 wooden beams had to be rendered with plaster to reduce fire risk, but during restoration of these houses in 1967 the old plaster was removed and the wooden beams replaced. All along this street are interesting details such as mascarons, wrought-iron balconies and shop signs. **La Maison d'Ourscamp** at nos. 44–46 (1585) is an outstanding structure built around a timbered and jettied courtyard and over a vaulted 13th-century cellar (*open daily 11–6.30; T: 01 48 87 74 31*). It was formerly the town house of the Cistercian Abbey of Ourscamp (near Noyon) and is now occupied by the l'Association de Paris Historique, who mount exhibitions here and organise guided walks.

If you feel in need of refreshment, the **Au Petit Versailles du Marais bakery**, at the corner of Rue Tiron, is a good place to stop before continuing down the street to admire its star building, the Baroque **Hôtel de Beauvais** (no. 68). Now occupied by the Cour Administrative d'Appel de Paris, the courtyard can usually be visited. The building (1654–7) is a *tour de force* by Antoine Lepautre, built on land purchased from the Cistercian Abbey of Châlis by Pierre de Beauvais and his wife, Catherine Bellier, first lady of the bedchamber to Anne of Austria. Le Pautre's design was an ingenious solution for dealing with what were in fact two adjacent plots with no parallel lines, between Rue François-Miron and Rue de Jouy. The François-Miron wing is two rooms deep, with shops over the medieval cellars, pierced by a long *porte cochère* leading to a circular peristyle. The lobby on the left contains a grand stone staircase supported by four Corinthian columns and the main courtyard façades are a subtle play of curves and counter-curves ending in an apse-like form. Cleverly disguised, the left is simply a curtain wall while on the right is a structure with depth, incorporating a corridor, stables and the Rue de Jouy entrance. Around the courtyard the *étage noble*, outlined by a beautiful balcony, was the level of the main living quarters, including a hanging garden, terrace and chapel. It was from this building in August 1660 that Cardinal Mazarin, Marshal Turenne, the Queen Mother Anne of Austria and Queen Henrietta Maria of England, watched the arrival in Paris of Louis XIV and Marie-Thérèse of Spain on the occasion of their marriage. By 1686 Catherine Bellier had tired of her mansion and moved to the increasingly fashionable St-Germain. Mozart, with his father and sister, stayed here for five months in 1763 when Maximilien d'Eyck, Ambassador of Bavaria, was renting the *hôtel*. It was sold at the Revolution.

The early 18th-century Hôtel Hénault de Cantobre at 82 Rue François-Miron, with a handsome wrought-iron balcony supported by carved corbels, is home to the **Maison Européenne de la Photographie** (*entrance on Rue de Fourcy; open Wed–Sun 11–8; free Weds 5–8; www.mep-fr.org*), a centre for contemporary photography which holds regular exhibitions. The zen courtyard is designed to illustrate the significance of light to the medium.

Retrace your steps now and turn left up **Rue de Jouy**. The refined decoration and heavy door surround adorned with a grinning head at no. 7 announce the Hôtel d'Aumont (1648), a grand affair designed by Le Vau (*see p. 46*). It was altered by François Mansart in 1656, with the addition of the garden façade

visible from Rue de Fourcy, and is home to the Administrative Tribunal.

At the end of Rue de Jouy you come to a crossroads. To the left is Rue de Fourcy, and to the right Rue Nonnains d'Hyères. Look up to see, on the building on the corner of Rue de Fourcy, the relief carving of a knife grinder, '*Le Rémouleur*', a copy of an 18th-century *enseigne* now in the Musée Carnavalet. Turn into Rue Nonnains d'Hyères. On the left a sunken garden with parterres creates a romantic foreground to the turrets, ogees, dormer windows and steep roofs of the **Hôtel de Sens** (1475–1519; *entrance on Rue du Figuier*). This was designed as the Paris base for the archbishops of Sens when the bishopric of Paris was suffragan to the metropolitan see of Sens (before 1623), and is older than the Hôtel de Cluny (*see p. 54*), the only other important extant example of 15th-century domestic architecture in the city. Once Paris became an archdiocese, the building was rented out by the archbishops of Sens. Among the occupants were the Catholic League, which opposed the succession of the Protestant Henri of Navarre (the future Henri IV) and briefly, in 1605, Queen Margot, Henri IV's extravagant first wife. Later it became a stagecoach depot, and among other commercial uses in the 18th century it was used for a time as a jam factory. The much-needed restoration in the 19th century unfortunately transformed it into a medieval pastiche. Since 1911 it has housed the Bibliothèque Forney, a fine-arts reference library. When the library is open, and during exhibitions, the courtyard can be visited; a cannon-ball has been embedded in the courtyard wall since 1830.

Walk through the short dog-run (past the left flank of the building) into Rue du Figuier and from there straight on into **Rue de l'Ave Maria**. At the end of this street are views of the Île St-Louis. At the level of no. 32 Quai des Célestins once stood the Tour Barbeau, which completed the northern perimeter of Philippe-Auguste's defences linked by chains to the island. Retrace your steps and turn right into Rue des Jardins-St-Paul, where one of the best sections of **Philippe-Auguste's wall**, including the bases of two towers, can be seen across the school playground. The church at the far end is St-Paul St-Louis (*see p. 354*). Between Rue des Jardins-St-Paul and Rue St-Paul (go right under the arch marked '10–12–14'), the former gardens of King Charles V were restored and rearranged in 1970–81 to provide a labyrinth of small courtyards. Now known as the **Village St-Paul**, there are around 200 antique dealers and boutiques here.

Emerge from the 'Village' and turn left into **Rue St-Paul**, which acquired its name before 1350 from the church of St-Paul-des-Champs, of which only a fragment of the belfry survives at no. 32. Rabelais died in this street in 1533.

Turn right past the old belfry up Rue Neuve St-Pierre, which brings you to **Rue Beautreillis**. From 1858–9,

Baudelaire lived at no. 22, the Grand Hôtel de Charny (1676), which has woodcarvings in purest Louis XIII style beneath the carriage-entrance. Jim Morrison (1943–71), lead singer and lyricist of The Doors, died at no. 17 when he was staying here with his girlfriend Pamela Courson; he was buried in Père-Lachaise Cemetery (*see p. 393*). No. 10 was the Hôtel des Princes de Monaco, built c. 1650, but altered in the 18th–19th centuries. Opposite, at nos. 7 and 9, are two much restored late 16th-century bourgeois houses.

Rue Charles V is a dignified street with handsome 17th-century houses. No. 10, the Hôtel de Maillé, retains its Louis XIII façade. The imposing Hôtel d'Aubray (1620) at no. 12 belonged to Balthazar Gobelin, Marquis de Brinvilliers, whose daughter-in-law Marie-Madeleine would later be sensationally accused of murdering her father and two brothers, having been taught to manufacture poisons by her lover. She was tortured and beheaded.

Also elegant, **Rue des Lions-St-Paul** is where Madame de Sévigné, famous for her *Lettres*, lived from 1644 to 1650, at no. 11. Until it fell out of favour, the Hôtel St-Pol was a royal residence occupying much of this district.

EATING AND DRINKING IN THE MARAIS

The Marais is well-endowed with all kinds of restaurants, cafés and takeaway outlets and has evolved from a slightly dilapidated to an extremely chic *quartier*, with gay bars and pet stores (such as Moustaches on Rue des Archives, selling every accessory that your pet could desire). Rue de Rosiers (*map p. 588, A2*), once the Jewish quarter, still has some takeaways and bakeries.

€€ **Chez Julien**. Modern bistrot with a Belle-Époque décor, where the cooking of traditional dishes is inventive and attractive. *1 Rue du Pont Louis-Philippe. T: 01 42 78 31 64. Map p. 588, A2.*

€ **L'As du Fallafel**. This place in the old Jewish neighbourhood has become a must-stop on a lot of tourist itineraries and queues can be very long. But the falafel is excellent. *34 Rue des Rosiers. T: 01 48 87 63 60. Map p. 588, A2.*

€ **La Boutique Jaune**. In the tradition of this former Jewish quarter is Sacha Finkelsztajn's high-quality bakery producing Jewish specialities, to eat on the spot or take away. The choice is vast and delicious: generously filled Yiddish sandwiches in soft rolls, phyllo-pastry pies, pastrami, gelfite fish, and outstanding pastries. No need to go hungry. *27 Rue des Rosiers. T: 01 42 72 78 91, www.laboutique-jaune.com. Map p. 588, A2.*

€ **Café des Musées**. Close to the Carnavalet and the Picasso museums, very traditional, very reliable, in a 19th-century setting, just the job for sustenance during a heavy day at the museums. Daily menu, specials on the board or *à la carte. 49 Rue de Turenne. T: 01 42 72 96 17, www.cafedesmuses. fr. Map p. 588, B1.*

€ **Le Comptoir du Saumon**. For all things salmony, as well as caviar, champagne and vodka. Closed Sun evening. *60 Rue François-Miron. T: 01 42 77 23 08, www.autourdusaumon.eu. Map p. 588, A2.*

€ **Cuisine de Bar**. This was the first café/shop on the Right Bank to sell Poilâne bread (*see p. 135*). It is a handy for baked goods, salads and sandwiches (open and toasted). Closed Sun. *38 Rue Debelleyme. T: 01 44 61 83 40, www.cuisinedebar.com. Map p. 588, B1.*

€ **Enoteca**. Italian food including delicious *antipasti*. *25 Rue Charles V. T: 01 42 78 91 44, www.enoteca.fr. Map p. 588, B2.*

€ **Mère et Filles**. Run by sisters, Flavie and Mélodie (the mother/daughter concept is in the photos on the wall, and the desserts on the slate are suggested each month by a mother and daughter team). A small, friendly place with a select choice of dishes which change regularly and are based on traditional French cooking but enhanced with Asian spices, e.g. chicken teriyaki. Closed Sun. *8 Rue St-Paul. T: 01 48 04 75 89, meresetfilles.fr. Map p. 588, B2.*

€ **Le Petit Célestin**. ■ This modest and friendly establishment on the riverbank takes you back to the days when francs were still in use. A cheery welcome, a board with daily specials, slightly scruffy, and the chef will recommend the dish of the day. Good stalwarts include *terrine de campagne maison*, *ris d'agneau et salsifis* (sweetbreads) and *tarte tatin*. Splash out on the wine. *12 Quai des Célestins. T: 01 42 72 20 81, www.lepetitcelestin.fr. Map p. 588, A2.*

€ **Le Petit Marché**. In a quiet street close to Place de Vosges, this is a very popular place with 'new-bistrot' food and a bistrot ambience: small and a bit squashed, but speedy service. Dishes have an Asian influence and include duck breast with ginger or ceviche of tuna with sesame and a Thai sauce. Good-value two-course lunch menu. *9 Rue de Béarn. T: 01 42 72 06 67. Map p. 588, B2.*

€ **Au Petit Versailles du Marais**. Bakery with delicious baguettes. *1 Rue Tiron (corner of Rue François-Miron). T: 01 42 77 70 97. Map p. 588, A2 (larger scale on p. 377).*

€ **Picasso Museum**. There is a café-tea room on the first floor, Café sur le Toit (On the Roof), with a communal table or bar stools. It serves salads, sharing plates and sandwiches at midday and pastries in the afternoon. *T: 01 44 61 79 19. Map p. 588, B1.*

€ **Le Potager du Marais**. This vegan restaurant is a welcome discovery for vegetarians in Paris, with a varied choice and good standard of cooking. Close to the Musée du Judaïsme. Closed Mon and Tues. *22 Rue Rambuteau. T: 01 57 40 98 57, www. lepotagerdumarais.fr. Map p. 588, A1.*

€ **Rose Bakery**. A stopping point for excellent cakes and pastries. Closed Mon. *30 Rue Debelleyme. T: 01 49 96 54 01. Map p. 588, B1.*

€ **Le Wood**. The bright interior of this modern venue is veneered with a variety of types of wood and combines wine bar snacks, tapas and good fresh salads. Close to the Picasso Museum. *1 Pl. de Thorigny. T: 09 67 27 39 08. Map p. 588, B1.*

€ **Breizh Café**. Serves delicious Breton pancakes and galettes, both savoury and sweet, made with organic flour and butter. They come with many fillings, from delicate sour cream and chives to far more hearty ones. Very popular: you need to book. Closed Mon. *109 Rue Vieille du Temple. T: 01 42 71 39 44, breizhcafe. com. Map p. 588, A1.*

Bastille, Bercy, Père-Lachaise & Belleville

Place de la Bastille is one of the most famous road junctions in Paris. In the Gare de Lyon is the opulent Train Bleu restaurant. Bercy is an interesting area to explore. Père-Lachaise is the eternal resting place of saints and sinners.

Place de la Bastille (*map p. 588, B2; Métro 1, 5 and 8 to Bastille*), laid out in 1803, has no remaining visible remnant of its Revolutionary history except for the ground plan of the famous fortress-prison marked by a line of paving stones in Blvd Henri-IV. Beneath the Place, some of its cellars are said to survive. The keep stood on the west side, across the end of Rue St-Antoine, and the main drawbridge was slightly north of the junction with Blvd Henri-IV. The July Column stands approximately in the centre of what was the east bastion. This is a young, lively *quartier*, especially around rues de la Roquette, de Lappe, de Charonne and Keller.

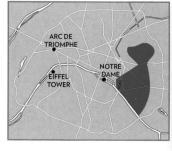

THE BASTILLE

The Bastille (or Bastille St-Antoine), originally a bastion-turret defending the eastern entrance to Paris, developed during Charles V's reign into a fortress with eight massive towers, immensely thick walls and a wide moat. Prisoners still managed to escape, however. By the reign of Louis XIII, the Bastille had become almost exclusively a state prison for political offenders, among whom were the mysterious Man in the Iron Mask (1698–1703) and Voltaire (twice). Arbitrary arrests by *lettre de cachet* and imprisonment without trial made the Bastille a popular synonym for oppression. Many illustrious persons were held here, often for obscure reasons, but confined in relative comfort. Among them were John Vanbrugh, the English architect and playwright (for most of 1692), and from 1784–9 the notorious Marquis de Sade, who wrote *Justine* and other salacious novels here. On 14th July 1789, the Revolutionary mob, aided by a few troops, attacked and overwhelmed the Bastille's defenders, murdered the governor, the Marquis de Launay, and freed a handful of prisoners. Work on the demolition of the fortress was immediately put in hand.

BELLEVILLE
Street detail.

THE JULY COLUMN

The July Column is not connected with the storming of the Bastille but was erected by Louis-Philippe in 1840–1 to commemorate the 504 victims of the *Trois Glorieuses* (three days of street-fighting) of July 1830, who are buried in vaults beneath the column's circular base. Their names are picked out in gold all down the length of the column shaft. The victims of the Revolution of February 1848 were subsequently also interred here, and their names added to the inscription. The bronze-faced column, 51.5m high, is surmounted by a gilt-bronze figure of Liberty.

OPÉRA BASTILLE

Map p. 588, C2–C3. Box office at 130 Rue de Lyon, Mon–Sat 2.30–6.30 and 1hr before performance (open from 11.30 on opening day). T: 0892 89 90 90 (from outside France, T: 00 33 1 71 25 24 23), www.operadeparis.fr. For guided visits check times (T: 01 40 01 19 70). Tickets are sold 10mins prior to start of tour.

On the southeast corner of the Place de la Bastille, on the site of the former Gare de la Bastille, is the Opéra National de Paris Bastille, a costly structure with a convex façade and clinical appearance, built to celebrate the bicentenary of the Revolution. The design, by the Uruguayan-born Canadian architect Carlos Ott, is in deliberate contrast to Garnier's opera house (*see p. 299*). Incorporating sophisticated technical equipment, Opéra Bastille is noted for its excellent acoustics. The building covers a vast area and comprises a main auditorium with seating for 2,700, a multi-purpose space for 600–1,000, and a studio seating 280. Granite, wood and glass are used in the uncluttered décor of the main auditorium. Both ballet and opera are performed here.

THE ARSENAL AREA

With the July Column behind you and the Opéra Bastille on your left, an esplanade shaded by plane trees opens out ahead, closed at the end by railings. Beyond these, across the Métro tracks, is **Port de Plaisance de l'Arsenal**, which flows into the Seine. This is the last reach of the Canal St-Martin (*see p. 401*). Boat trips start from here (*see p. 529*) and the area between it and Blvd de la Bastille is maintained as a park. The area as a whole takes its name from the armoury (arsenal) established here by Henri IV, and the Bibliothèque de l'Arsenal, on Rue de Sully, occupies the former residence of the Grand Master of Artillery, built in the 18th century.

BIBLIOTHÈQUE DE L'ARSENAL

Map p. 588, B3. Open for guided visits Wed 3pm and Sat 11am; book in advance, T: 01 53 79 49 49, visites@bnf.fr, www.bnf.fr. The visit can be arranged in English.

The library, founded in 1757 by the Marquis de Paulmy, was purchased by the Comte d'Artois (Louis XVI's brother) in 1785. Supplemented by other collections, it became state property in 1792, opened to the public in 1797 and has been part of the Bibliothèque Nationale since 1934. Among its more famous librarians were Prosper Mérimée and Anatole France. It has an encyclopaedic collection of early specialised printed volumes and music, and is known particularly for its incomparable series of

PLACE DE LA BASTILLE
Detail of the July Column and its gilt-bronze *Liberty*.

illuminated manuscripts, including the *Psalter of St Louis*. The tour is of the Rococo rooms, which have retained most of their original décor from the 18th century.

The **Pavillon de l'Arsenal** (*T: 01 42 76 33 97, www.pavillon-arsenal.com*), at 21 Blvd de Morland, is a large metal-framed space built 1878–9. It is home to an information centre for architecture and urban planning in Paris, and mounts permanent and temporary exhibitions. The Mayor of Paris, Anne Hidalgo, launched an international competition here in 2014 for projects to redevelop 23 prime sites in the city.

THE VIADUC DES ARTS, COULÉE VERTE AND GARE DE LYON

Avenue Daumesnil (*map pp. 588, C3–589, E4*) is animated by two imaginative installations making use of the old elevated railway line, unused since 1969, which once terminated where the Opéra Bastille now stands. The **Viaduc des Arts** (*T: 01 44 75 80 66, www.leviaducdesarts.com*) is a series of shops which occupy the 71 attractive brick arches of the old railway. Here some 50 craftsmen and artists create and sell items as varied as musical instruments, textiles, paper, pigment, glass, furniture and sculpture, made to traditional and contemporary designs.

The tracks themselves, above the viaduct, have been turned into a green walkway crossing the whole of the 12th arrondissement. The **Coulée Verte René-Dumont** (or *Promenade Plantée*) consists of some 4.5km of planted walkways and gardens created in 1988, leading from Bastille to Vincennes. A footbridge, the Passerelle Diderot, was recently opened, and the elevated garden descends at Rue Montgallet (*map p. 589, D4–E4*) to street level. It then follows Allée Vivaldi, a shopping area, and continues through tunnels and trenches to end at Porte-Dorée and Vincennes. Along the way are a number of access points as well as four gardens, Hector-Malot, de Reuilly, de la Gare de Reuilly and Charles-Péguy.

GARE DE LYON,

The Gare de Lyon (*map p. 588, C4*) serves the southeast and south of France, as well as Italy, and has a distinctive tall belfry. It preserves a grand and beautiful *fin-de-siècle* bar-restaurant, Le Train Bleu, on the upper floor behind the Beaux-Arts façade. Opposite the station once stood the Mazas Prison, where 400 Communards were rounded up and massacred by Thiers' troops in 1871. In this redeveloped business area, the two banks of the Seine are linked by Pont Charles-de-Gaulle (1995) and Pont d'Austerlitz (originally 1802–7, rebuilt in stone in 1855 and widened in 1886). For the Jardin des Plantes and Docks on the opposite side of the river, see pp. 78–82.

BERCY

Map pp. 588, C4 and 579, E3–E4. Métro 6 and 14 to Bercy.

Bercy was extensively redeveloped in the 1980s and is now a place where Parisians come to relax. In fact, history suggests that it was always so, as here the first wine warehouse was established in the 16th century and by the 19th it was a very lively area. The 20th-century transformation began with the hexagonal Palais Omnisports in 1984, which holds 17,000 spectators. The Ministère des Finances followed in 1989, when it vacated the Louvre, to occupy a specially-designed building next to the Seine on Blvd de Bercy, necessitating the widening of the Pont de Bercy. The Parc de Bercy, completed in 1997, which covers 14 hectares parallel to the Seine opposite the Bibliothèque Nationale Mitterrand, is where the bonded wine warehouses once stood.

CINÉMATHÈQUE FRANÇAISE–MUSÉE DU CINÉMA

Map p. 579, E3. 51 Rue de Bercy. Cinématèque open daily except Tues, 1 Jan, 25 Dec. Ticket sales Mon, Wed–Sat from 12pm, Sun from 10am. Musée du Cinema open Mon and Wed–Sat 12–7, Sun 10–8; closed Tues and 1 Jan, 1 May, 25 Dec. Bookshop open Wed–Sat 12–8. For daily screenings T: 01 71 19 33 33, www.cinematheque.fr.

The former American Centre building (1994, Frank Gehry) is now home to the Cinémathèque Française and Musée du Cinéma and holds around 40,000 films, 4,000 pieces of equipment, 1,500 objects and 1,000 costumes. The first collector of film was an Englishman, Will Day, after whose death in 1936 Henri Langlois, with Lotte H. Eisner, continued the project. Langlois founded the Cinémathèque Française, which acquired Day's collection in 1959, and it has become the best of its kind in the world. Film archives were created in 1969 by the engineer-technician and historian Jean Vivié, and the collecting and preservation of films continues.

The Musée du Cinéma's permanent exhibition is a treasure trove covering the evolution of the cinema in the USA, England and France, from magic lanterns, phonographs, Muybridge's photos and Edison's kinetoscope in 1894, through to the birth of the 35mm film, Lumière's cinematograph and beyond. It has memorabilia including all types of pioneering cinematographic equipment, posters and documents. There are also early sets and props, including the head of the dead Mrs Bates from Hitchcock's *Psycho*, the robot from Fritz Lang's *Metropolis* (1927) and costumes which include one worn by Vivien Leigh in *Gone with the Wind*. There are tributes to film-makers such as Jacques Demy, Man Ray and Luis Buñuel and excerpts of films through the ages. There are also regular temporary exhibitions.

PARC DE BERCY

Parc de Bercy (*map p. 579, E4*) occupies the site of the old bonded wine warehouses which in the 19th century were the largest of their kind anywhere. They closed in the 1950s, though some of the old buildings have been preserved along with stretches of old rail track. During excavations, ancient dug-out canoes were discovered here (*see p 358*). Next to the Palais Omnisports is a novel fountain, **Canyoneaustrate** (canyon, water and stratum), by Gérard Singer. Opposite the Musée du Cinéma is the **Grande Prairie**, an open grassy area.

The central **Parterres** around the Maison du Jardinage (*temporary exhibitions*) are intimate themed spaces including the spring, rose and scented gardens and a small maze, as well as a kitchen garden, the columned Pavillon du Vent protecting measuring instruments, an orchard with an orangery, a vineyard signalled by a brick chimney and 400 vines. Beyond is a sunken garden and wisteria-covered pergolas lining a canal. Protecting the garden from the embankment is a high terrace and steps leading up to a view of the Seine. The light, transparent, single-span **Simone de Beauvoir footbridge** (304m) is by Dietmar Feichtinger. It opened in 2006, at the same time as a swimming pool with a retractable roof, named after the singer Josephine Baker.

The hump-backed bridge over Rue Joseph-Kessel leads to the **Romantic Garden**, with a variety of trees, lawns and ponds and a sculpture, *La Demeure 10*, surrounded by waterlilies. The **Maison du Lac** holds exhibitions. The **Chai de Bercy**, the old bottling workshops, is another exhibition centre.

The **Musée des Arts Forains** (*see p. 518*) at no. 53 Av. des Terroirs de France, is a fairground museum.

Beyond Rue François-Truffaut is the very popular **Bercy Village** (*open daily, shops 11–9, restaurants until 2 am, Métro 14 to Cour St-Émilion*), an attractive pedestrian centre which has transformed the 19th-century wine cellars and cobbled streets into an area of shops and restaurants.

FAUBOURG SAINT-ANTOINE

Map p. 598, D3. Métro 1, 5 and 8 to Bastille or 8 to Ledru-Rollin.

Rue du Faubourg-St-Antoine leads from Bastille to Place de la Nation through an area memorable in the violent history of the Revolutions of 1789 and 1848. It was also the scene of skirmishes during the Fronde (1652; *see p. 17*), when Turenne defeated Condé. From the late 13th century cabinet-makers were active here, and there are still a few signs of this activity in the courtyards behind the 18th-century façades. At **no. 1 Rue du Faubourg-St-Antoine**, Joseph Fieschi hatched a plot in 1835 to assassinate King Louis-Philippe—it failed, but 18 others were killed. At the corner with Rue de Charonne is the old ***Fontaine Trogneux*** (1710) and to the north via Rue de la Forge Royale, in the much-altered church of **Ste-Marguerite** (1634) on Rue St-Bernard, is a *Pietà* by Girardon behind the high altar. It is believed that the ten-year-old Louis XVII, who in all probability died at the Temple (*see p. 335*), was buried in the graveyard here in 1795, together with other victims of the Revolution.

PLACE DE LA NATION

Several thoroughfares converge on the spacious circus known as Place de la Nation (*map p. 589, E3–F3*). Formerly its name was Place du Trône, after the throne erected for Louis XIV's triumphal entry in 1660 with Marie-Thérèse, along the Cours de Vincennes. In 1794 no fewer than 1,306 victims of the Terror were guillotined here. Between 1793 and 1880 it was known as the Place du Trône-Renversé. Today's Place de la Nation is dominated in its centre by a colossal bronze group, the *Triumph of the Republic* (1899), by Dalou. The female personification of the Republic is shown victoriously riding the Chariot of the Nation, drawn by lions guided by Liberty. Beside the chariot are *Work* and *Justice*, while *Peace* spreads abundant fruitfulness in her wake. To the east of the circus there were originally two toll-houses designed by Ledoux (*see p. 405*) in 1788. Two columns 30.5m high are still standing, one with a statue of Philippe-Auguste by J.-E. Dumont; the other, of Louis IX, by Antoine Etex.

CIMETIÈRE DE PICPUS

Map p. 589, F4. 35 Rue de Picpus. Métro 6 to Picpus or 1, 2, 6 and 9 to Nation. Opening times are erratic. Normally mid-April–Aug Tues–Sun 2–6, Oct–mid-April Tues–Sat 2–4; closed Mon and holidays. Guided tours in French at 2.30 and 4.30. T: 01 43 44 18 54.

At the end of the garden of a convent of Augustinian nuns, is a tiny private burial ground for émigrés and descendants of victims of the Revolution, including the Marquis de Lafayette and the families of Chateaubriand, Montmorency, Noailles, Salignac-Fénelon, the Romantic poet André Chénier and many others. The 17th-century convent on this site was confiscated in 1792 and on 13th June 1794, the Commune of Paris requisitioned the garden and dug two ditches to receive the bodies of those executed on Place du Trône-Renversé (La Nation; *see above*). Closed in 1795, the cemetery was secretly sold in 1797 to Princess Amélie de Salm de Hohenzollern-Sigmaringen, whose brother was buried there. In 1803 the families of the deceased were able to purchase the old convent land with the right to be buried in an adjoining cemetery. A very simple chapel was built by the Congrégation des Sacrés-Coeurs et de l'Adoration. In it is a painting of the 16 Carmelites of Compiègne, who were beheaded on 17th July 1794 and beatified in 1906. The names of those buried here are engraved on marble plaques on the chapel walls.

PÈRE-LACHAISE CEMETERY

Map p. 589, E1. Métro 2 and 3 to Père-Lachaise or 2 to Philippe-Auguste. Open mid-March–Oct Mon–Fri 8–6, Sat 8.30–6, Sun and holidays 9–6; Nov–mid-March Mon–Fri 8–5.30, Sat 8.30–5.30, Sun and holidays 9–5.30. Main entrance on Blvd de Ménilmontant.

Père-Lachaise, or Cimetière de l'Est, on a hill overlooking the city, is the largest (47 hectares) and most celebrated necropolis in Paris. It is, however, much more than a burial ground. It is a park and meeting place, designed for quiet contemplation with green spaces and flowerbeds, trees and benches. It is not laid out entirely in rigid chequerboard order but has an extensive free-flowing central area *à l'anglaise*. The rows of sombre graves and mausolea are visited by over a million people a year. Among the monuments are some fine works of art by leading 19th- and 20th-century French sculptors, but also some outrageous kitsch. It receives the greatest number of visitors on All Saints Day (1st November), the Day of the Dead, when it will be ablaze with chrysanthemums.

HISTORY OF PÈRE-LACHAISE CEMETERY

Père François de La Chaise (1624–1709) was confessor to Louis XIV and lived in the Jesuit house rebuilt in 1682 on the site of a chapel on the side of the hill. At the time of the Fronde (uprisings against Mazarin during the minority of Louis XIV, 1649–53), the king watched the skirmishes between Condé and Turenne from here. The land was bought by the city in 1804 and laid out by Brongniart, but has been extended several times.

The burial ground is not reserved for Roman Catholics, nor even exclusively for Christians; buried here side-by-side are also Jews, Buddhists, Muslims and non-believers. The first to be interred were La Fontaine and Molière, whose remains were translated here in 1804. Today it is also possible to reserve your plot, as the photographer and designer André Chabot has done, renovating an abandoned 19th-century mausoleum as his own future resting place. A self-described 'cemetery ethnographer', he is, with Anne Fuard, the founder of Mémoire Nécropolitaine, a society dedicated to recording and creating an archive of funerary monuments around the world. The mausoleum, still preserving the original carved pelican in its piety, is at present occupied by a giant sculpted camera. It is also equipped with a QR code so that inquisitive passers-by with smartphones can read about the society and its aims.

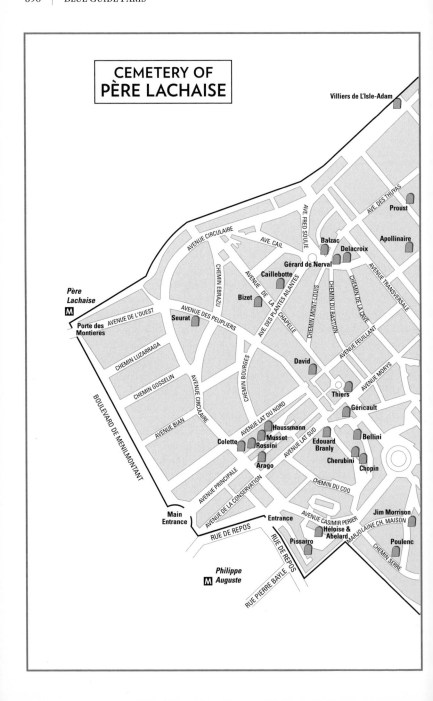

CEMETERY OF
PÈRE LACHAISE

Villiers de L'Isle-Adam

Proust

Balzac
Delacroix
Apollinaire

AVE. DES THUYAS

AVENUE CIRCULAIRE
AVE. CAIL
AVE. FRED SOULIE

Gérard de Nerval
Caillebotte
AVENUE DE LA

CHEMIN EBRAZU

AVENUE TRANSVERSALE

Bizet

Père
Lachaise
Ⓜ

AVENUE DES PEUPLIERS
AVE. DES PLANTES AILANTES
CHAPELLE
CHEMIN MONTRUIS
CHEMIN DU BASTION
CHEMIN DE LA CAVE

Porte des
Montieres

AVENUE DE L'OUEST

Seurat

AVENUE FEUILLANT

CHEMIN LUZARRAGA

David

AVENUE MORYS

CHEMIN GOSSELIN

CHEMIN BOURGES

Thiers

Géricault

BOULEVARD DE MENILMONTANT

AVENUE CIRCULAIRE

AVENUE LAT DU NORD

Haussmann

Bellini

AVENUE BIAN

Colette

Musset
Rossini

AVENUE LAT SUD

Edouard
Branly

Cherubini

Chopin

AVENUE PRINCIPALE

Arago

CHEMIN DU COQ

AVENUE DE LA CONSERVATION

Jim Morrison

Main
Entrance

Entrance

AVENUE CASIMIR PERIER

MARJOLAINE CH. MAISON

RUE DE REPOS

Héloise &
Abelard

Poulenc

Pissarro

CHEMIN SERRE

RUE DE REPOS

Philippe
Ⓜ Auguste

RUE PIERRE BAYLE

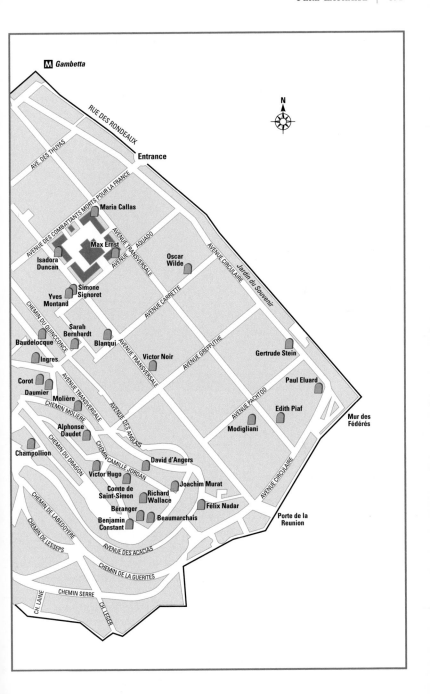

PÈRE-LACHAISE CEMETERY
Detail of Jacob Epstein's tomb of Oscar Wilde. To protect it from the lipstick,
it is now surrounded by a perspex barricade.

The main alley, **Avenue Principale**, runs through the central sector (24 hectares), which is classed as an historic site. Among those buried here are Colette, Rossini, Alfred de Musset and Baron Haussmann, and opposite them the astronomer and politician Arago (*see p. 160*). At the end of the avenue is the large and deeply moving **Monument to the Dead** (1895) by Albert Bartholomé, who turned to sculpture on the advice of Degas after his wife's death and then specialised in funerary masks and tomb statuary.

The eastern part of the central sector, designated **Secteur Romantique**, contains the graves of La Fontaine and Molière and in the southern corner is the monument to Abélard and Héloïse (*see p. 54*), first erected in 1779 at the Abbey of the Paraclete (near Nogent-sur-Seine) and moved here in 1817. Its canopy is composed of fragments collected by Lenoir (*see p. 93*) from the abbey of Nogent-sur-Seine.

One of the most visited burial sites is the simple **grave of Jim Morrison**, lead singer of The Doors, who died in Paris in 1971 (*see p. 379*). It vies in popularity with the **tomb of Oscar Wilde** in the eastern sector (his body was moved here nine years after his death in 1900), designed by Jacob Epstein. In the 1990s a cult of kissing and leaving lipstick traces on it necessitated regular cleaning which began to damage the stonework. The Paris authorities were reluctant to subsidise frequent renovations, but in 2011 the Irish stepped in to pay for cleaning, de-greasing and a protective glass barrier.

Huge mausolea such as that of the Princess Elisabeth Demidoff contrast with the realistic bronze by Dalou of the young journalist **Victor Noir**, shot in 1870 by Pierre Bonaparte, Napoleon's nephew, during a squabble with an anti-imperialist newspaper whom Bonaparte felt had defamed his famous uncle. Bonaparte had struck an innocent man: Noir was not the author of the article. He instantly became a republican hero. The life-size recumbent effigy of Noir, who was no dashing lothario, has become too popular with Parisiennes as a fertility symbol for its own safety.

West of the cemetery, off Rue de la Roquette, stood the Prison de la Grande-Roquette, where in the latter half of the 19th century condemned prisoners were held while awaiting execution. In 1871 many Commune hostages were taken here, and although around 130 were released, some 50 were shot. Thiers' victorious government forces of 'law and order' then proceeded to round up thousands of Communards—both repentant and defiant—and in two days executed 1,900 of them in retaliation or 'in expiation'. In the eastern corner of Père-Lachaise is the **Mur des Fédérés**. The cemetery was the scene of the Paris Commune's final and bloody stand on 28th May, 1871. At dawn, 147 surviving Communards were shot against this wall and buried where they fell. Adolphe Thiers is also buried in Père-Lachaise.

Here too is a monument to the many thousand Frenchmen who died either in German concentration camps or during the Resistance of 1941–4, and other deeply moving tributes to victims of Nazism. A service for the victims of the *Charlie Hebdo* shooting was held here in 2015.

Writers, composers, singers, artists and sculptors are numerous in Père-Lachaise but there is also a representative selection of Napoleon's marshals, including Masséna, Ney, Murat and Suchet, and generals Foy and Baron Larrey (*see p. 161*). Other famous names include René Lalique and Édouard Branly. Among the British are Sir William Keppel (d. 1754), second Earl of Albemarle; Admiral Sir Sidney Smith (d. 1840); General Sir Charles Doyle (d. 1842); and Sir Richard Wallace (d. 1890), art connoisseur and benefactor of Paris (*see p. 319*).

ENVIRONS OF THE CEMETERY

The **church of St-Jean-Bosco** (1937), made of concrete and with a lofty tower, stands a short distance southeast of the cemetery on Rue Alexandre-Dumas. Further east off Rue de Bagnolet is **St-Germain-de-Charonne** (*map p. 589, F1*), a rustic church of the 13th–14th centuries, restored in the 19th. It still has its village graveyard, the only other in Paris being St-Pierre-de-Montmartre (*see p. 322*). France had decreed in 1804, for reasons of hygiene, that burials should take place in cemeteries on the city outskirts. The stonemason Pierre de Montreuil (*see p. 503*) had a vineyard in Charonne.

WALK FIVE: BELLEVILLE & MÉNILMONTANT

This is a fairly long walk and may be done in stages, but it gives a fascinating glimpse of an increasingly popular area of Paris. Belleville-Ménilmontant was once a village on a steep hill, higher than Montmartre, with a rural community gathered around the church of St-Jean-Baptiste. Surrounded by vines, there were abundant springs which were a source of water for Paris from Gallo-Roman times, and again from the 12th century, when monks, Templars, and King Philippe-Auguste constructed aqueducts or channels to carry the water to Paris, a system that lasted for some five centuries. Today the only reminders are a few street names and four inspection chambers. Gypsum quarries were also known here; the gypsum began to be seriously exploited in the late 18th century but the community remained outside the Farmers General walls (1784–7; *see p. 405*) and therefore exempt from tolls. Consequently, it became a free and easy extra-mural location for *bals* and *guinguettes*. Until 1830, there was much merrymaking during Mardi Gras, when the *courtille* descended Rue de Bellemont. During the Second Empire's grand project for Paris under Haussmann (*see p. 284*), when insalubrious industries were banished from the centre and many homes were forcibly requisitioned, the suburbs became centres of political ferment. Belleville-Ménilmontant today has a lively, multicultural immigrant community, where Berbers and Jews have been joined by Poles, Japanese and Pakistanis. Improvements in housing were begun in the 1970s, and today there is a desire to protect the surviving 19th- and early 20th-century buildings and to promote urban regeneration. Over the last few decades the quarter has been evolving into a fashionable 'village', considered more authentic than its beautiful but touristy neighbour Montmartre and attracting younger newcomers, artists and intellectuals. Look out for the late-September open days at the artists' studios: the Ateliers de Belleville and Ménilmontant claim around 250 artists and about 23 groups that offer studio visits (*Ateliers d'Artistes de Belleville, 1 Rue Francis Picabia, Métro Couronnes, ateliers-artistes-belleville.fr*) and Ateliers de Ménilmontant (*43 Rue des Panoyaux, Métro Père-Lachaise/Ménilmontant; www.ateliersdemenilmontant.org*).

To begin the walk, take Métro 11 to Pyrénées.

BOULEVARD DE BELLEVILLE RUNS downhill from the Pyrénées Métro station. A lively produce market (reputedly one of the cheapest) is held on Tues and Fri 7–2.30, and alongside the vegetables are fabrics and some bric-à-brac. The street is also something of a pilgrimage site for fans of Edith Piaf (1915–63), since legend (and a plaque) say that she was born on the steps of **no.72**, and perhaps she sang on the doorstep of no.

115. (*The **Musée Edith Piaf** is at 5 Rue Crespin du Gast; map p. 396, A2*). Piaf, known as *La Môme Piaf* (the 'Piaf Kid', the 'Little Sparrow'), was considered the archetypal Parisian singer after making her career début in 1935. She became instantly recognisable for her distinctive, strident voice and emotive songs such as *Je ne regrette rien* and *Milord*.

Further downhill, the street widens out into **Place Fréhel**, a small, dilapi-

PLACE FRÉHEL
Don't trust words (public art by Ben).

dated square created in 1972 on the corner of Rue Julien-Lacroix, but with important pieces of public art: *Le Passé* by Jean Le Gac and a mural by Ben, *Il faut se méfier des mots* (1993). Turn left into **Rue Julien-Lacroix**, where at no. 85 is the small café/bar Le Petit Navire, which has a collection of model boats. Lacroix Synagogue is further along the street, on the corner of Rue Pali Kao. Walk back up Rue Lacroix for a short distance and turn right up Rue Jouy Rouve (opposite the Navire, next to Les Ateliers du Tayrac). At the end of it, go through the gates, which have a triangular relief and mosaic and a plaque commemorating the last stand of the Commune. Go up the steps and bear

right up a rising path. This is the **Parc de Belleville**, an interesting modern garden (1988) designed by François Debulois on a site eight metres higher than the Butte Montmartre and with superb views over Paris. It is extremely popular on a sunny day.

Climb the rising path, keeping right, to emerge at a concrete theatre outside the **Maison de l'Air**, which is dedicated to the Parisian environment and air quality. From here paths descend into the gardens, with rocky grottoes and a stepped water-feature as well as steep, tree-lined paths and a flight of steps under wisteria arches.

At the very top of the gardens, behind the Maison de l'Air, you come out into

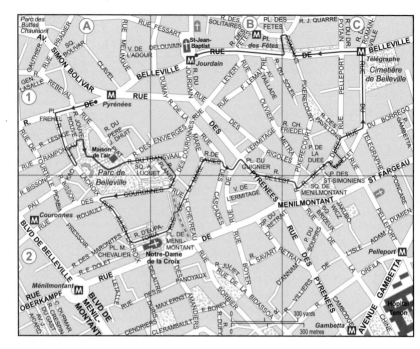

Rue Piat. Here, on the corner of Rue des Envierges, is a *boulangerie-pâtisserie* and the highly popular café-bar O'Paris, with a terrace (*see p. 399*). In front is an open cobbled area with a Wallace Fountain (*see p. 319*) and a **belvedere** with a panoramic view over Paris. Just inside the railings is the **Jardin Luquet**, planted with vines, a reminder of how the area was once used.

Go downhill now along **Rue du Transvaal**, passing on the right at no. 16 (beyond the modern houses with the same number) the gated, 19th-century Villa Castel, where a scene from the film *Jules et Jim* (1962) was shot. Turn right into the tiny **Passage Plantin**, lined with pretty houses and streetlamps. After the steps, turn right (Rue des Couronnes). At the junction you have a choice. To see the huge church of Notre-

Dame-de-la-Croix, turn right (**1**). To cut short the walk, turn left and then left again into Rue de la Mare (**2**).

(**1**) Rue des Couronnes leads into the continuation of Rue Julien-Lacroix. Turn left into it to arrive at the garden at the east end of the neo-Romanesque **Notre-Dame-de-la-Croix** (1860–9), by Héret, the third longest church in Paris after Notre-Dame and St-Sulpice, with a belfry of 78m. There have been churches on this site since the 15th century. Monumental steps lead up to the west door from Pl. Maurice-Chevalier, which lies at the heart of Ménilmontant. Here is a Wallace fountain (*see p. 319*) and across Rue de Ménilmontant is La Boulangerie restaurant-bistrot (*see p. 399*). From the east of the church, cross the railway bridge and take Rue de la Mare, an old river bed which ran into a pool (*mare*) on the spot where the church now stands. Continue along it and cross Rue H. Chevreau.

(**2**) At the top of **Rue de la Mare**, turn right into Rue des Savies, at the top of which is the **Regard St-Martin** or de Savies, a small stone building with a pointed roof and an inscription giving its date as c. 1722. This was an inspection chamber over the collecting point of spring water which was carried to Paris via an aqueduct built by monks from St-Martin-des-Champs. In **Rue des Cascades**, the area of numerous springs and where much of the land was owned by Parisian abbeys, are two more *regards* (look beyond the housefronts into the yards below street level to see them): de la Roquette (no. 37) and des Messiers (no. 17). These structures were part of Philippe-Auguste's Belleville aqueduct. The street was the backdrop in 1952 for Jacques Becker's classic film *Casque d'Or*, starring Simone Signoret.

A street market is held on Sun and Thur on **Place du Guignier**, and at the corner of Rue des Pyrénées with Rue Ménilmontant is an elegant Neoclassical *folie* (1770), a former country retreat, but now the main cultural centre of the area, known as the **Pavillon Carré de Baudoin** (*www.carredebaudouin.fr*). In the 19th century it was owned by an uncle of Edmond de Goncourt.

Turn left up Rue de l'Est to reach **Square de Ménilmontant et St-Simoniens** (115m). This garden was the site of the house of the followers of the early Socialist, industrial entrepreneur, economic theorist and mystic aristocrat Claude Henri de Rouvroy, Comte de Saint-Simon (1760–1825). The St-Simoniens gathered at no. 145. Off Rue de la Duée (small spring) is **Passage de la Duée**, reputedly the narrowest street in Paris.

Continue up Rue de la Duée, making a detour around Rue Tarclet to enjoy the gardens of **Villa Georgina**, and turn right along Rue du Borrégo then left into Rue du Télégraphe, to arrive at the highest part of Ménilmontant, the **Cimetière de Belleville**, at 128m. It was created in 1880 in part of the Château de Ménilmontant belonging to the St-Fargeau family. An inscription on the gatepost records that here in 1792 Claude Chappe experimented with the *tachygraphe*. His first attempts were regarded by the mob as a plot to communicate with Louis XVI, imprisoned in the Temple below: the installation was burned and Chappe was imprisoned. The following year he was successful in using the aerial telegraph to announce the Republican victory. By 1794 a communication link was established between Paris and Lille, taking three hours rather than three days. The tomb of Léon Gaumont, promoter of the cinema industry (d. 1946), can be found about 20m to the right on the central alley. South of the cemetery are the Reservoirs de Belleville.

Turn left down Rue de Belleville to see the **Regard de la Lanterne**, the most monumental of the inspection chambers, in a little children's play area on Rue des Compans. King Philippe-Auguste channelled water from the hills above and this domed chamber was semi-submerged to allow access by underground steps to the Aqueduct de Belleville. **Place des Fêtes**, just beyond, was once the focal point of festivities in the area but was engulfed in concrete in 1970. Further down the main road is the church of **St-Jean-Baptiste** (1854–9) by J.-P. Lassus. The artist Georges Rouault was born at 51 Rue Fessart, west of the church.

EATING AND DRINKING AROUND BASTILLE, BERCY, PÈRE-LACHAISE, BELLEVILLE AND MÉNILMONTANT

BASTILLE / BERCY

€€–€€€ **Au Trou Gascon**. This restaurant deserves its accolades, offering both excellent service and fine food and wine. A long-established family affair, chef Alain Dutournier (also Carré des Feuillants near Place Vendôme) has handed over the reins of Au Trou Gascon to his wife, Nicole. The menu is based on the high-quality, fresh and varied produce typical of Gascony (southwest France): beef from the Chalosse, *charcuterie* and cured ham, plump duck and foie gras, a wide range of cheeses, and delightful desserts such as warm and crisp *tourtière*. Closed weekends. *40 Rue Taine. T: 01 43 44 34 26, www.alaindutournier.com. Map p. 589, E4.*

€€ **Bofinger**. Established in the mid-19th century, this Alsatian brasserie was the first in Paris to serve draught beer. During the 1920s it received its Belle-Époque décor, including the coloured glass cupola over the main dining area. Always popular and very busy, it is renowned for its seafood in season, including seafood *choucroute*. *5 Rue Bastille. T: 01 42 72 87 82, www.bofingerparis.com. Map p. 588, B2.*

€€ **Le Train Bleu**. When the Gare de Lyon was revamped for the 1900 Universal Exhibition, it not only received a new façade and a 64m-high clock tower, but also a splendid brasserie, all designed by Marius Toudoire. The brasserie was named Le Train Bleu in 1963, after the Paris–Ventimiglia train which transported Parisians to the Côte d'Azur. Many famous people have patronised Le Train Bleu, including Brigitte Bardot and Jean Cocteau (and more recently scenes from *Les Vacances de Mr Bean* were shot here). Renovated in 2014, it is now absolutely splendid in its Belle-Époque glory, lavishly endowed with gilt, chandeliers and paintings of the destinations served by the trains. Meals, snacks and drinks are served daily from 7.30am (9am Sun) until 10pm, as well as meal trays for your journey (order in advance). *Gare de Lyon. T: 01 43 43 09 06, www.le-train-bleu.com. Map p. 588, C4.*

€–€€ **Au Vieux Chêne**. The reference to the 'old oak' is a tribute to the Saint-Antoine *quartier*, formerly of cabinet-makers, now of artists and craftspeople. The bistrot has a long history and retains a friendly neighbourhood atmosphere. The cooking is straightforward and good. *7 Rue du Dahomey. T: 01 43 71 67 69, www.vieuxchene.fr. Map p. 589, D3.*

€ **L'Auberge Aveyronnaise**. From the beautiful and remote Aveyron come some of the best-quality products in meat and cheese (as well as the famous Laguiole knives). The dining area is intimate, with a terrace for summer days. Traditional hearty dishes include *aligot* (potato mashed with cheese and garlic), *tripoux* and cassoulet, a rich dish of duck and white beans. However, there are lighter alternatives, using seasonal seafood or wild mushrooms and traditional desserts. *40 Rue Gabriel-Lamé. T: 01 43 40 12 24. Map p. 579, E4.*

€ À La Biche au Bois. A small affair, with set-price classic French menus. As its name would suggest (*biche* means doe), it specialises in game. Good wine. Closed Mon lunch and Sat–Sun. *45 Av. Ledru-Rollin/Rue de Lyon. T: 01 43 43 34 38. Map p. 588, C3.*

€ Le Bistrot du Peintre. Art Nouveau brasserie (founded 1902) with an attractive bar and large heated terrace. The cooking is traditional and the helpings generous: main courses change daily, although staples such as *confit de canard* and *entrecôte de salers* (beef from the Auvergne) are usually available. *116 Av. Ledru-Rollin (north of Rue du Fbg St-Antoine). T: 01 47 00 34 39, bistrotdupeintre.com. Map p. 588, C2.*

€ Chai 33. Wine shop offering tastings and a restaurant, in an old wine warehouse. *33 Cour St-Émilion, Bercy Village. T: 01 53 44 01 01, www.chai33.com. Map p. 579, E4.*

€ Viaduc Café. Under the arches of the Viaduc des Arts near Bastille, with musical events. *43 Av. Daumesnil. T: 01 44 74 70 71. Map p. 588, C3.*

BELLEVILLE / MÉNILMONTANT AND PÈRE-LACHAISE

€ La Boulangerie. ■ Formerly a baker's shop, it is now a pleasant restaurant, with a calm and unfussy décor. Excellent bread, a vast wine selection, organic produce and good, simple cooking. Closed Mon, Sat lunch and Sun. *15 Rue des Panoyaux. T: 01 09 53 60 97 35, www.laboulangerie.fr. Map p. 396, B2.*

€ Les Cascades. Café-bar and haunt of the local arty/music community, serving excellent, reasonably-priced sandwiches and salads. Closed Mon. *82 Rue des Cascades. T: 01 46 36 56 92, bar.cascades.free.fr. Map p. 396, B1–2.*

€ Mama Shelter. Bar/restaurant close to Père-Lachaise with eclectic décor by Philippe Starck. A bit of everything happens here: beauty, fashion, shopping and celebrated brunch menus. *109 Rue de Bagnolet. T: 01 43 48 45 45, www.mamashelter.com. Map p. 589, F1.*

€ Le O'Paris. On the heights of Belleville, a friendly place with a large terrace and a great view, ideal for an evening rendezvous. On fine Sundays it is packed out with young locals for brunch. Occasional Jazz evenings. *Rue des Envierges. T: 01 43 66 39 54, www.le-o-paris.com. Map p. 396, A1.*

€ Le Perchoir. A popular rooftop from where to admire Paris while sipping a cocktail and nibbling on tapas. On the level below is the minimalist restaurant (essential to book). Dinner only Tues–Sat. *14 Rue Crespin du Gast (near the Piaf museum). T: 01 48 0618 48, leperchoir.fr. Map p. 396, A2.*

€ Le Petit Navire. A long-standing neighbourhood café/bar (lunch only), decorated with a collection of model boats. *85 Rue Julien-Lacroix. T: 01 77 19 58 73. Map p. 396, A1.*

€ Le Petit Vingtième. Pleasing bistrot in a former textile workshop serving simple, tasty dishes. The ingredients are mainly organic and seasonal. Evenings only. Closed Sun. *381 Rue des Pyrénées. T: 01 43 49 34 50, petit20.com. Map p. 396, B1.*

CANAL SAINT-MARTIN

République

Place de la République is the largest pedestrian area in Paris and a popular centre for nightlife. Canal Saint-Martin is an animated stretch of water (particularly in its higher reaches) leading all the way to Parc de la Villette, with its Science and Music parks.

Place de la République *(map p. 583, D4–E4)* covers two hectares at the junction of seven important thoroughfares and straddles three arrondissements (3rd, 10th and 11th). Watched over by the large **Monument de la République** (1883) with its allegorical female figure, *Marianne*, it is now a sleek piazza, shaded by 150 trees and with two water features. The square, glass-sided Café Monde et Médias serves '*bio et équitables*' (organic and fair trade).

The Place was originally laid out in 1856–62 by Haussmann on the site of the Porte du Temple, as an anti-revolutionary planning scheme, but it continues to be the rallying point for demonstrations. Bronze reliefs by Dalou around the monument recount the history of the Republic from its inception to 1880. In January 2015, following the killings at the office of the satirical magazine *Charlie Hebdo*, more than three million people, including world leaders, gathered in Place de la République to express their solidarity, grief and horror. It was the largest rally of its kind.

At the corner of Rue Léon-Jouhaux, leading northeast from the Place, was the workshop from 1822–35 of Jacques Daguerre, pioneer of photography, who produced his first *daguerréotypes* in 1838. The Cirque d'Hiver (Winter Circus), offering a variety of events, at 110 Rue Amelot (off Blvd Voltaire southeast of the Place), has existed since 1852.

CANAL SAINT-MARTIN

Map p. 583, E4–E2. Métro 3, 5, 8, 9 and 11 to République or 11 to Goncourt.

The Canal St-Martin has evolved into an animated and fun place to visit, by day or night, or on summer evenings, whether by boat, by bike or on foot; and as the result of a determined effort at regeneration, it is also a fashionable and popular area to live.

Inaugurated in 1825, the canal was built to extend the De l'Ourcq and St-Denis canals, which run into the holding basin of La Villette, thus linking two sections of the Seine and reducing the journey by 12km. The canal covers the extent of the 10th arrondissement over some 4.5km, between the Bassin de l'Arsenal and La Villette. Along this stretch are nine locks, two swing bridges, and several arched iron footbridges but commercial shipping and its related industries have disappeared. Old buildings have been transformed, shops, restaurants and a large cinema complex have sprung up, and new apartment complexes line the banks. The area just beyond Place de la Bataille de Stalingrad, at the start of the Bassin de la Villette, was landscaped and planted some years ago, and the proximity of water and trees is pleasant on a hot day.

To the east of Place de la République, the busy, commercial Rue du Faubourg du Temple runs over the point where Canal St-Martin emerges from beneath Blvd Jules Ferry. In **Square Jules Ferry** (the park to the right) is a statue called *La Grisette* (1880), a coy interpretation of the young working-class girls who once frequented the quarter. In **Square F. Lemaître** (left) is the bust (1899) by Pierre Granet of Frédérick Lemaître (d. 1876), the famous 19th-century entertainer who played the boulevards. Behind it, the canal appears between the green banks of the square and heads north, flanked by the Quai de Valmy on the west and Quai de Jemmapes on the east, which are linked by a succession of bridges, some moveable, some pretty arched footbridges. The Passerelle de la Douane, level with Rue Léon-Jouhaux, is followed by the Pont Tournant de la Rue Dieu (1884–5), a lifting road bridge. The arched *passerelle* beside it makes an ideal vantage point to watch the procedure.

A short detour from Quai de Jemmapes down Avenue Richerand arrives at the **Hôpital St-Louis** (*map p. 583, E3*). A working hospital, it was built by Claude Vellefaux in 1607–12 and is a superb rare example of early Louis XIII-style in brick and stone. It is announced by an entrance lodge with central archway, emblazoned *Liberté, Égalité, Fraternité*, leading to a courtyard and a second, taller pavilion with a clock in the high roof. It leads to a large square garden court planted with a variety of trees and enclosed by identical façades,each with a central pavilion, reminiscent of Place des Vosges. The elevations are mainly in brick, with stone quoins and central pavilions with high slate roofs; the lower roofs have red tiles. The hospital was built at the orders of Henri IV and all the old buildings are still in use. Beyond are the newer wings.

Rue de la Grange aux Belles leads back to the canal. Since the 13th century and until 1790, the Gibet de Montfaucon, the Tyburn of Paris, stood near. The gallows proved fatal to three *Surintendants des Finances*: Enguerrand de Marigny, who erected it; Jean de Montaigu, who repaired it; and Semblançay, who tried to avoid it.

Beyond the swing bridge, where the canal veers northeast around the site of the old hospital, is **Square des Récollets**, a tree-lined double lock. The square and the **Hôtel du Nord** (*www.hoteldunord.org*), at 102 Quai de Jemmapes, were the setting for the novel *L'Hôtel du Nord* by Eugène Dabit, made famous in Marcel Carné's film of the same name in 1938, starring Louis Jouvet and Arletty. The bar-brasserie building has been revamped in retro-1930s' style. The floor is original and there is a zinc bar; it still has character.

Cross to Quai de Valmy, where there are a number of interesting stores, pop-up shops and eating places. The most important public garden in the 10th arrondissement, **Jardin Villemin** (*map p. 583, D3*), has a wide variety of well-established trees and shrubs, a bandstand, playground, and an elaborate drinking fountain of 1848. It is built on the gardens of a military hospital dating from 1870, named after Dr Jean-Antoine Villemin (1827–92), who demonstrated how easily tuberculosis can be transmitted. The hospital was an extension to the existing buildings of the **Convent of the Récollets** (*entrance at 148 Rue du Faubourg St-Martin; top end, outside Gare de l'Est*), since 2003 home to the Centre International d'Accueil et d'Échanges providing accommodation for researchers from all over the world, and the Ordre des Architectes en Île-de-France. Inside, on the right are the café, old chapel and exhibition space. In 1604, the Récollets, an offshoot of the Franciscan Order vowed to poverty, were authorised by Henri IV to establish their house on land given them by Jacques Cottard, a weaver, close to the church of St-Laurent. It amassed an important library and many leading preachers were educated here. The convent, rebuilt in the 18th century, closed in 1790 and became a hospital for incurables. During World War II and the Algerian War (1954–62), it was used as a military hospital because of its proximity to Gares du Nord and Gare de l'Est.

GARE DE L'EST & GARE DU NORD

Map p. 583, D3–D2. Métro 4, 5 and 7 and RER E to Gare de l'Est; Métro 4 and 5 and RER B and D to Gare du Nord.

Across from the Récollets convent, **Gare de l'Est**, one of the oldest stations in Paris, built in 1849 and extended and altered in 1930, is in good shape following the makeover for the TGV line to Strasbourg. The forecourt occupies the site of the medieval St Lawrence's fair. Rue d'Alsace, west of the station, recalls its role serving eastern France.

Between Blvd Faubourg St-Martin and Blvd de Magenta is the **church of St-Laurent** (*open Mon 8.30–7.15, Tues and Thur 7.15–8, Wed 7.15–10, Fri 7.15–7.15, Sat 9.30–7, Sun 8.30–8*). There has been a church on this site since the Merovingian era (6th century). The present building dates from before 1429, with an older north tower. The nave was vaulted (with some splendid pendant bosses) and the choir remodelled in 1655–9, with a high altar by Antoine Lepautre. The Lady Chapel dates from 1712. The 17th-century façade was demolished in 1862–5 in favour of a neo-Flamboyant one.

AROUND GARE DU NORD

Boulevard de Magenta runs northwest from Place de la République past Gare de l'Est and then **Gare du Nord**, designed by Jacques Hittorff in 1863, with an iron and glass interior and Neoclassical façade.

The Hôpital St-Lazare was built on the site of the headquarters of the Lazarists or Priests of the Mission, founded in 1625 by Vincent de Paul. Part of the site is now occupied by the **Hôpital Lariboisère**, built in 1854 in response to the outbreak of cholera that had swept Paris in 1832. Also by Hittorff is the church of **St-Vincent-de-Paul** (1824–4; *map p. 582, C2*). Two square towers dominate a pedimented portico of twelve Ionic columns approached by a cascade of steps. The interior frieze was painted by Hippolyte Flandrin and the dome by François-Édouard Picot. On the altar is a *Crucifixion* by Rude and there is a Cavaillé-Coll organ.

The **Petit Hôtel Bourrienne** (1789–98) at 58 Rue d'Hauteville (*map p. 582, C3; guided visits first two weeks of July and all Sept daily 12–6; rest of year by appointment, T: 01 47 70 51 14*) is a rare example of *hôtel particulier* built at the time of Napoleon Bonaparte's Consulate immediately after the Revolution. It was occupied in 1795–8 by Fortunée Hamelin (1776–1851). A *merveilleuse*, she was born in Santo Domingo, a creole like her friend (and rival) the Empress Josephine, and was notorious for her dress: she once paraded down the Champs-Élysées in a flesh-coloured gown so diaphanous that she appeared half naked. A room painted with tropical birds was decorated for her, and the mansion contains an Egyptian-style bathroom.

BASSIN DE LA VILLETTE

Map p. 583, E2–F1. Métro 2 and 5 to Jaurès or 2, 5 and 7 to Stalingrad.

The busy Place de Stalingrad, with its flyover railway, can be a daunting place but the effort of crossing it is rewarded by Bassin de la Villette, older and wider than Canal St-Martin (*see p. 401*), inaugurated in 1808 by Napoleon. It boasts a fine example of 18th-century architecture in the **Rotonde de la Villette** toll gate by Ledoux, the most complete of the four that remain out of all those that he designed for the barrier which surrounded Paris at the time when La Villette was still a village. It has lost the four sentry-boxes which controlled the Grande Rue de la Villette (now Av. de Flandre) and Route de Meaux (now Av. Jean-Jaurès) and has had many uses since the Revolution. Following a major programme of restoration, it began a new life as a restaurant (*see p. 409*), which provides a marvellous opportunity to explore the interior of the building. From the upper terrace there is a view down the Bassin de la Villette, which flows between the **Quai de la Seine** on the northern side and **Quai de la Loire** opposite. Both have wide terraces, café/restaurants, and bars on boats. This area is full of activity: in June the Fête du Bassin offers a variety of events; and an extension of Paris Plage. Old warehouses lining the pool have been converted and repurposed.

At the northeast end the pool narrows to become the **Canal de l'Ourcq** with a lifting bridge (1884) carrying Rue de Crimée across, and a footbridge. In the little garden which is Place de Bitche (*for the story of the square's name, see p. 430*) is a bandstand in front of the Neoclassical basilica-style church of **St-Jacques et St-Christophe** (1901). Inside, at the head of the south aisle, is a statue of St Peter with one very highly-polished foot, like its prototype in Rome. Beyond here is The Parc de la Villette.

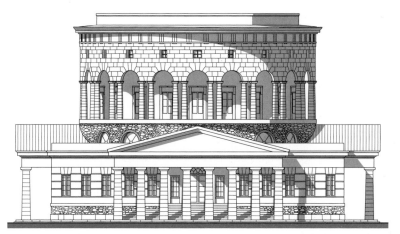

ROTONDE DE LA VILLETTE

CLAUDE-NICOLAS LEDOUX

Ledoux (1725–1806) was a visionary and far-sighted architect of the Age of Enlightenment. Born in Champagne, he studied in J.-F. Blondel's atelier in Paris and became architect attached to the Département des Eaux et des Fôrets. His knowledge of antiquity was indirect, through engravings and Palladio, reinforced by a visit to England. In Paris he built mansions (1765–79) in the Chaussée-d'Antin and Poissonnière districts, but most were demolished by the creation of Rue Meyerbeer. Examples of Ledoux's decorative work survive in the Musée Carnavalet.

In the 1780s the Farmers General (in the sense of tax farmers, not agriculturalists) built a wall to surround Paris to prevent smuggling and they chose Ledoux to design the toll gates (*postes d'octroi*), collection points for duties. The barrier, 24km long and nearly 4m high, fed public discontent: Paris wailed about being walled in: *le mur murant Paris rend Paris murmurant*. Ledoux's toll gates, of which there were over 50, were all different. Many were damaged at the Revolution; most were destroyed in the 19th-century reorganisation of the city. There are four surviving examples (1785–8), of which La Villette is the finest. The most serious and imposing, appropriately monumental for this important entrance to Paris, it takes the pure classical form of a Greek cross with porticoes, surmounted by a circular drum ending in a rotunda, using the Doric Order, square columns and heavy rustication.

Ledoux's career ended with the Revolution and he spent his last years preparing a summary of his theories, published in 1804 as *L'architecture considérée sous le rapport de l'art des moeurs et de la législation*. The book contains a repertory of his designs, which involve ideas on the symbolism of geometric forms and thinking that anticipates the Romantic era. His interpretations of Neoclassical architecture were the most advanced in France and his simple and functional shapes are the historic antecedents of the Modern Movement.

PARC DE LA VILLETTE

Map p. 579, E1–E2. Métro 5 or Tram 3 to Porte de Pantin for the south entrance; Métro 7 or Tram 3 to Porte de la Villette for the north entrance. Park open 6am–1am. Some gardens have specific opening times. For thematic guided tours, T: 01 40 03 74 82. Seasonal gardens open April–Sept Wed, Sat, Sun 2–6. T: 01 40 03 75 75, www.villette.com. Canal boat trips, T: 01 42 39 15 00, www.canauxrama.com.

What is now a popular modern quarter, La Villette, to the northeast of Place de la République, was once the site of the abattoirs and meat markets. The area was completely transformed in the 1980s into the Parc de la Villette, a large green urban area crossed by the Canal de l'Ourcq. It is a place for relaxing, for learning and for entertainment. It encompasses La Cité des Sciences et de l'Industrie and La Cité de la Musique and is home to the Philharmonie de Paris. To the west of La Villette is a contemporary arts centre, Le Centquatre.

The park which lies between the two Cités was designed by Bernard Tschumi, whose 26 bright red enamelled metal 'follies', each with a unique form and function, punctuate the space; Philippe Starck designed the park furniture. Three kilometres of walkways link the Porte de Pantin and Porte de la Villette across seven hectares of meadows. Numerous themed gardens, designed to be informative and fun, especially for children, divide the space into areas such as a bamboo forest, a 'scary garden', 'the dragon's garden', and one that evokes the seaside. The wide variety of entertainment on offer embraces music, theatre, film, popular arts, circus, modern forms of musical expression and current affairs. La Grande Halle is a survival from the old market.

CITÉ DE LA MUSIQUE & PHILHARMONIE DE PARIS

Métro: Porte de Pantin. Open Tues–Sat 12–6, Sun 10–6; closed Mon. T: 01 44 84 44 84, www.citedelamusique.fr, www.philharmoniedeparis.com.

On the southern side of the Parc de la Villette, the spectacular new building for the **Philharmonie de Paris** was inaugurated in 2015. Designed by Jean Nouvel, it is the new home of the Orchestre de Paris and of the Baroque Ensemble. Despite its size (seating for 2,400 people), it is designed to create an impression of intimacy, with seating arranged in long, organically-shaped modular balconies. To create an all-enveloping acoustic the design has synthesised many ideas and includes cloud-like panels suspended above the audience. The concert hall has also been sound-proofed against external noise.

It is linked to the **Cité de la Musique** (opened 1995), which was conceived by Christian de Portzamparc. The Médiathèque (Music Resource Centre) is open to all, offering a huge collection of documents that can be consulted on site or online, covering all types of artistic trends. A mix of concerts and other activities is offered at weekends.

MUSÉE DE LA MUSIQUE

Open Tues–Fri 12–6, Sat–Sun 10–6; closed Mon. Free audioguides (in French, English and Spanish) include samples of recorded music relevant to the instruments in the collection and a musician is present every day to give live demonstrations.

This is one of the finest collections of musical instruments in the world, covering the broad sweep of Western music as well as music from other parts of the globe. The display is imaginatively presented to illustrate the evolution of instruments and music as well as the role of composers, musicians and patrons. Some items in the collection are unique. In the string collection are 17th-century Venetian archlutes and guitars by Voboam, an outstanding collection of French stringed instruments from the 18th and 19th centuries, and Cremona violins by Amati, Stradivarius and Guarnerius del Gesù. There are Flemish harpsichords by the celebrated Rucker dynasty and 18th-century French harpsichords, as well as pianofortes by Érard, including one that was played by Franz Liszt. The exceptional brass collection includes instruments invented by Adolphe Sax (1814–94). Representing the 20th century are an electronic violin by Max Mathews, a MIDI saxophone and Frank Zappa's E-Mu synthesizer. Recent acquisitions include guitars which belonged to Django Reinhardt and a Hel violin owned by Stéphane Grappelli. Instruments from around the world include a 17th-century Sarangi from northern India and a 19th-century chest drum from Zaire. An enlarged section dedicated to 20th-century popular music is planned.

At the entrance to the Cité de la Musique is the Café des Concerts (*see p. 409*).

CITÉ DES SCIENCES ET DE L'INDUSTRIE

Métro: Porte de la Villette. Open Tues–Sat 10–6, Sun 10–7; closed Mon and 1 Jan, 1 May, 25 Dec. Géode open Tues–Sun 10.30–8.30; check opening times for individual attractions. Audioguides (ID required). T: 01 40 05 79 99, www.cite-sciences.fr.

A massive rectangular steel and glass structure contains the Cité des Sciences et de l'Industrie, covering over three hectares, which opened in 1986. It was a project of President Giscard d'Estaing. Adrien Fainsilber's design cleverly incorporates the auction-hall of a slaughter-house, begun on this site but abandoned incomplete in 1973. The structure is surrounded by a moat and the main hall or nave is 100m long and 40m high. There are five levels to explore.

The Cité is a giant communications centre whose aim is to demystify and popularise science. There are both temporary and permanent exhibitions to explain how scientific experiments and discoveries, innovative technology and revolutionary changes evolve hand-in-hand with industry and business. There are many and varied activities using models, videos, multimedia displays and hands-on experiences and touch screens to encourage discovery and exploration. On the central concourse are spherical domes through which sunlight is transmitted via a system of movable mirrors. The interior is in the form of a full-sized replica of an American space station. In front of the south entrance is the **Argonaute** submarine, flagship of the French navy from 1957, and pensioned off in 1989. At the core of the Cité, covering 30,000 square metres is **Explora**, a series of exhibitions in four sections: Language and Communication; From the Earth to the Universe; The Adventure of Life; and Matter and the Work of Man. In addition there are large areas for special exhibitions and conferences. There is an **Aquarium** in the basement, the **Inventorium** for children from 3 to 12 years, to encourage teamwork and logical thinking, as well as a **Planetarium**, a cinema and a multi-media library.

The huge **Géode**, completed in 1985, is a polished steel mirror ball 36m in diameter. Designed by Adrien Fainsilber and the engineer Félix Chamayou, it took two years to build. Inside are some 395 tiered seats facing a huge hemispheric cinema screen of 1000 square metres, 26m in diameter. Specially-adapted films are projected at a vertiginous optical angle of 180° to produce an impression of total immersion. **Cinaxe** is a 'total film experience' simulator with seating for 56 people.

LE CENTQUATRE

Map p. 583, E1. Rue Curial and Rue d'Aubervilliers. Métro 7 to Riquet. Open Tues–Fri 12–7, Sat–Sun 11–7; closed Mon. T: 01 53 35 50 00, www.104.fr.

Le Centquatre in Rue Curial, founded in 2008, occupies the magnificent space of a former *pompes funèbres* (municipal undertakers' building) of 1874, built under the supervision of Victor Baltard. It has become a creative centre supporting young artists where the public is encouraged to experience work-in-progress of all forms, including theatre, dance, music, cinema, video, culinary, landscape-gardening, digital and urban art. An ambitious project, it has struggled but there are encouraging moves being made under the directorship of José Manuel Gonçalves. It has a community garden, a café and restaurant, Les Grandes Tables du 104.

EATING AND DRINKING AROUND RÉPUBLIQUE AND CANAL SAINT-MARTIN

CANAL SAINT-MARTIN AND RÉPUBLIQUE

€ **L'Atmosphère**. Local bar-restaurant just off Quai Valmy. *49 Rue Lucien Sampaix, T: 01 40 38 09 21. Map p. 583, D3.*

€ **Les Enfants Perdus**. Good-value lunch menus, Sunday brunch until 4pm, this is a fine place tucked away behind Canal Saint-Martin. *9 Rue des Récollets. T: 01 81 29 48 26, les-enfants-perdus.com. Map p. 583, D3.*

€ **Hôtel du Nord**. Cocktails, music, wifi, excellent wine list, next to Canal Saint-Martin in an old-established venue. *102 Quai de Jemmapes. T: 01 40 40 78 78, www.hoteldunord.org. Map p. 583, E3.*

€ **L'Îlot**. An unpretentious, small, busy oyster bar near Place de la République, a place for shellfish and seafood aficionados. The produce is fresh, and reasonably priced. Closed Sun. *4 Rue de la Corderie. T: 06 95 12 86 61. Map p. 583, D4–E4.*

€ **Chez Jenny**. Close to Place de la République and Canal Saint-Martin, this claims to be the most Alsatian of all Alsatian brasseries in Paris and is a must for lovers of shellfish. On a fine autumn's day, the restaurant terrace is the perfect place to eat oysters and sip a glass of white wine. Come here with a good appetite: after the oysters you might be tempted by a *choucroute royale au crémant d'Alsace* prepared in front of you, followed, by a *kouglof au rhum. 39 Blvd. du Temple. T: 01 44 54 39 00, www.chez-jenny.com. Map p. 583, E4.*

€ **Chez Prune**. This is a good place, next to the Canal Saint-Martin, for a drink or light lunch. *36 Rue Beaurepaire. T: 01 42 41 30 47. Map p. 583, E3–E4.*

LE CENTQUATRE

There are several choices in this public arts centre (*104 Rue d'Aubervilliers/5 Rue Curial; map p. 583, E1*). € **Café Caché** is a friendly place and a meeting point for artists. It serves snacks and tapas.

€ **Le Camion à pizzas** is literally a piazza van (a sophisticated black version), standing alongside the Centrequatre. It serves excellent pizzas with toppings that might include roasted aubergine or smoked salmon.

€ **Le Grand Central** is described as a 'neo-brasserie'. Designed by Sébastien Wierinck, it is a long, sleek ultra modern functional space where the choice ranges from roast free-range chicken

to Welsh rarebit. They also offer meals for children.

GARE DU NORD

€ **La Pointe du Grouin**. Convenient for travellers to and from Gare du Nord, a convivial wine bar and bistrot which serves meals and snacks, home-baked bread and delicious desserts. Open weekdays until 2am, closed Sat–Sun. No phone or website. *8 Rue de Belzunce. Map p. 582, C2.*

LA VILLETTE

There are a number of bars, cafés and restaurants beside the Bassin de la Villette in warm weather. In the Parc de la Villette, at the entrance to the Cité de la Musique, is € **Café des Concerts**. next to the Philharmonie and with a large west-facing terrace looking out over the esplanade of the Grande Halle. The restaurant has an open kitchen and the service is continuous. It serves cocktails, sharing plates and standard salads, burgers, sandwiches and pasta-based dishes. *211 Av. Jean-Jaurès. T: 01 42 49 74 74. Map p. 579, E1–F1.*

€ **La Rotonde**. Ledoux's great toll gate (*see p. 405*) has come to life as a restaurant. Open Tues–Sat and until 8pm Sun, happy hour Tues–Thur 6pm–8pm. With an English chef who trained in Paris and worked in London, it serves Sunday brunch, a Tues–Fri lunch *formule* and there is also an art gallery showing contemporary work. Pleasant upper terrace with good views. *6–8 Place de Stalingrad T: 01 80 48 33 40, www.larotonde.com. Map p. 583, E2.*

Trocadéro & Passy

Place du Trocadéro, named after a fort near Cadiz in Spain that was occupied by the French in 1823, is known for its splendid views of the Eiffel Tower and its many nearby museums, including the Guimet collection of Asian art and the Musée d'Art Moderne. Further west across the Ranelagh gardens is the Musée Marmottan, with its collection of works by Monet.

Six avenues fan out from the Place du Trocadéro, in the centre of which is an equestrian statue of Maréchal Foch, Allied commander in the final year of the First World War. West of the square, in Rue du Commandant-Schloesing, is the entrance to the **Cimetière de Passy**, created in 1820. It contains the graves of Debussy, Gabriel Fauré, Manet and Berthe Morisot.

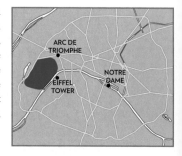

PLACE DU TROCADÉRO & PALAIS DE CHAILLOT

Map p. 584, C1. Métro 6 and 9 to Trocadéro.

Tour buses often park in Place du Trocadéro because from the raised piazza between the two wings of Palais de Chaillot is one of the finest prospects of the Eiffel Tower to be had in all Paris. Indeed, the view from here has been prized for centuries, before the Eiffel Tower was ever thought of. This prestigious site overlooking the Seine, the Colline de Chaillot, was chosen in the 16th century by Catherine de Médicis as the site of a royal palace, later embellished by Anne of Austria. In 1651 Henrietta Maria established the Convent of the Visitation here, destroyed at the Revolution. Here too Napoleon planned to build a palace for his son that would eclipse the Kremlin, but the disasters of 1812 intervened and this dream was never realised.

The Palais de Chaillot that occupies the hill today was erected for the Paris Exhibition of 1937, replacing the earlier Palais du Trocadéro built by Davioud for the 1878 Exhibition. The plan of the present building, by Carlu, Boileau and Azéma, was determined by the old one, though the stripped Classicism of the architecture belongs unmistakably to the 1930s. The former central pavilion of the old palace was

PLACE DU TROCADÉRO
View of the Eiffel Tower from Palais de Chaillot.

removed to create a terrace and the wings were encased within the two curved extensions. In 1948 the palace became the HQ of the United Nations, where the Universal Declaration of Human Rights was signed. Today the two curved wings house the Musée de la Marine and Musée de l'Homme (west) and the Cité de l'Architecture et du Patrimoine and Théâtre National de Chaillot (east).

From the terrace, flanked by gilded bronze statues, the Trocadéro Gardens descend to the Seine, and provide the setting for fountains which include a battery of 20 jets shooting almost horizontally. On the opposite bank, beyond Pont d'Iéna (1806–13; named in commemoration of Napoleon's victory over the Prussians at Jena in 1806), the Eiffel Tower pierces the horizon and orchestrates a dramatic vista across the Champ de Mars to the École Militaire, the UNESCO buildings and Musée du Quai Branly. In the Trocadéro Gardens is the Paris Aquarium (*see p. 518*).

MUSÉE NATIONAL DE LA MARINE

Map p. 584, C1. Open Mon and Wed–Fri 11–6, Sat–Sun 11–7; closed Tues. T: 01 53 65 69 53, www.musee-marine.fr.

The Musée National de la Marine is one of the oldest maritime museums in the world. Arranged in large rooms and with a great variety of objects, it combines art, history, science and technology with adventure and seafaring customs. As the national repository and showcase for all nautical activity in France, with a collection begun in the 15th century, it illustrates French naval history up to the 21st century. The collections are derived from the historic naval shipyards of France and from Versailles. There are beautiful models of vessels throughout the ages, as well as navigational instruments and fine maritime paintings. It also offers the unique opportunity to observe a team of restorers working in the model repair shop. Exhibits are displayed mainly in chronological order.

SHIPS AND SHIP MODELS

Among the older exhibits are souvenirs of galleys, including the magnificent carved **stern of the *Réale*** (c. 1694), lead ship of the Regiment of Galleys made in the Marseilles dockyard for Louis XIV. Over 300 rowers were needed to propel this vessel. Surviving from **Marie-Antoinette's barge** (1777), used on the Grand Canal at Versailles, are the prow and poop decorations including a voluptuous female figure holding a crayfish (a painting in the museum confirms the original aspect of the barge). Impressively complete is the 18m-long **Emperor's Barge** (1810). Richly ornamented, it was originally built in just 21 days for Napoleon's visit to the Antwerp shipyard to inspect the fleet. In 1858 the décor was altered for Napoléon III and Empress Eugénie to include the imperial arms and a large crown supported by angels. Abandoned until 1943, it arrived at Chaillot with a German escort but it was not placed inside the building until 1945, after the decision was finally taken to breach a wall.

There are numerous finely-sculpted French **figureheads and reliefs** from the period 1650 to 1850 and many smaller objects in wood and brass. Particularly fine is the

MUSÉE DE LA MARINE
Prow decoration from the barge of Marie-Antoinette (1777).

museum's remarkable collection of meticulously crafted **model ships** representing all types of vessel from every period. Among the most impressive are the three-decked fighting ships with detailed decoration and complicated rigging. The *Sans-Pareil*, a 1/30 model of 1757, has one side left open to reveal the interior arrangement including barrels, stone ballast and chicken coops. The *Louis XV* is the scale model of a great late-18th-century vessel, with 110 cannons and three decks that could house the command of a squadron. An earlier model is the *Royal-Louis*, built during the reign of Louis XIV in 1692. Its poop decoration is consistent with late 17th-century ships of this rank but it presents the king in the guise of a Roman general, suggesting that it was probably not a model of an existing vessel, which would have carried the Sun King's emblem, but rather a teaching aid for the initiation of the young king into naval affairs. Fighting ships were standardised by Colbert at the time of Louis XVI and inspired the ships which were used successfully in the American War of Independence. A remarkable piece, *La Ville de Dieppe*, is the ivory model of a warship under sail made by the town of Dieppe for Napoleon on the birth of the King of Rome (1811).

In 1783, Claude Jouffroy d'Abbans sailed up the Saône to Lyon in a paddle boat, or *pyroscaphe*, driven by steam. The beautifully-made model of 1784 is not a replica but is based on the mechanics used and was submitted to the Académie des Sciences.

Unfortunately for d'Abbans, the head of the selection committee was a rival, Perier, whose own experiments on the Seine had lamentably failed. He made sure that d'Abbans never succeeded in exploiting his designs.

The last and largest French warship under sail, the three-decker *Valmy*, went to the Crimea in 1854, just ten years before *La Gloire*, the first steam-powered armoured frigate of the French navy. *La Gloire* was about 20 years ahead of her time, but because of her steel hull, conditions below deck were very poor. Although her glory lasted only for one year, further frigates were built to this design.

The *Paraguay* is a shipyard model of a mixed sail and propeller vessel, a type which carried thousands of European *émigrés* to America from 1820, in search of political and religious freedom. Freighter companies competed in a price war for this human cargo (which required neither loading nor unloading) until controls were introduced in 1892.

MARINE PAINTINGS

There are many interesting and fine paintings in the collection, including 13 views of the ports of France (only 15 of the 24 originally commissioned were completed), painted in 1754–65 by Claude-Joseph Vernet, considered a major artist in his day. The most important ports—Toulon, Bordeaux and Bayonne—get two views each. *Interior Port of Marseilles* (1754) presents a busy, cosmopolitan Mediterranean city that has not changed much to this day. Among the crowds are the painter, his wife and his son. Louis-Philippe Crépin's painting of the *Redoutable at Trafalgar* (1807), a masterpiece of naval drama, shows the *Redoutable* trapped between HMS *Victory* on the right, and HMS *Téméraire*.

Crew in the Battery (c. 1890) by Julien le Blant won a gold medal in the 1889 Universal Exhibition. It pictures the crew aboard a battleship taking their meal among the cannons and the anchor chain. It documents the way sailors dressed and the furnishings below deck at the time.

MODERN PERIOD

The parallel galleries record the development of modern shipping and naval warfare, from an air balloon to the latest in aircraft carriers, through ocean liners, cargo ships, training ships, the development of the submarine, and 100 years of aeronautical evolution (1910–2010).

The ocean-liner style was born at the 1925 Exposition des Arts Décoratifs: a glass panel, enhanced in silver and gold, designed by Jean Dupas and made by the artist and glassmaker Charles Champigneulle, was part of the décor for the salon of the huge liner *La Normandie* (1935). Built at St-Nazaire in 1931, she won the Blue Ribbon during her inaugural voyage but was so large that a special dock had to be built for her in New York. A showcase of French art and lifestyle, she came to a sad end in 1941, with the entry of the USA into the war, when she was commandeered. Fire broke out in 1942 and she sank ignominiously in the Hudson River. More modest is the reconstruction of the cabin of the Chief Mate of the *Mogador* (1937–42), with authentic furnishings.

The museum also has naval accessories, compasses, diving suits, a lighthouse display, yachts and an exhibition about daily life on board the nuclear aircraft carrier *Charles de Gaulle.* Displayed in the last room is the Trophée Jules Verne, a prize awarded to the yacht which completes the fastest round-the-world sail (in under 80 days).

The **model repair workshop**, which is on the Seine side of these galleries, can be viewed from outside but not entered by visitors.

MUSÉE DE L'HOMME

The Musée de l'Homme (Museum of Mankind), a major scientific and cultural centre since 1938, was closed at the time of writing for major refurbishment. Its holdings of prehistory, anatomy and the environment lend themselves to explorations of the themes of the natural and cultural history of mankind.

CITÉ DE L'ARCHITECTURE ET DU PATRIMOINE

Map p. 585, D1. Open Wed–Mon 11–7, Thur 11–8.45; closed Tues, 1 Jan, 1 May, 25 Dec. T: 01 58 51 52 00, www.citechaillot.fr.

The east wing of the Palais de Chaillot contains the Cité de l'Architecture et du Patrimoine, a museum of French architecture bringing together the former Musée des Monuments Français and the Institut Français d'Architecture (IFA). The latter, created in 1981, has combined with the Centre des Hautes Études de Chaillot (CEDHEC), which has trained architects for over a century. The Cité is made up of the Mouldings and Wall Paintings Galleries of medieval architecture, and the Modern and Contemporary Gallery illustrating the evolution of architecture since the mid-19th century. From several of these rooms are stunning views.

Mouldings and wall paintings (levels 0–3): The collection of casts of medieval monuments of France goes back to the 19th century. The architect and passionate conservator of national heritage, Eugène Viollet-le-Duc, proposed the creation of a Museum of Comparative Architecture, which opened in 1882 in the Palais du Trocadéro. In 1937 Paul Deschamps added the Fresco Gallery, with full-size copies (not reproductions) of medieval and Renaissance mural paintings on reconstructions of their original architectural supports. The display of 350 casts (both 19th-century and modern) and 60 scale models is arranged chronologically and geographically.

Entering the museum is a disorientating yet breathtaking leap into the Middle Ages. Gathered here are replicas of the most celebrated decorated church portals, tympana and medieval sculptures from all over France. They include examples from the southwest (Moissac, Conques and Toulouse); from Charente Maritime, the Saintonge and Clermont Ferrand. Examples of Burgundian masterpieces include the portal of Autun, a section of Cluny III and a scale model of Notre-Dame at Paray-le-Monial. The Gothic period is represented by casts of Chartres' etiolated column figures, the smiling angel in Rouen Cathedral doorway and Dijon's magnificent well-head from the Chartreuse de Champmol, sculpted by Claus Sluter. Replicas of Renaissance secular architecture include the Hôtel Jacques Coeur, Bourges and the Hôtel de Bernuy, Toulouse. In the galleries facing the Seine are casts of 17th–19th-century monuments, including *La Marseillaise* (1833–6) from the Arc de Triomphe in Paris.

The process of making casts is demonstrated by models and films. Casts were used in the royal academies in France in the 17th century. The technique has not changed whereas the materials have. Originally the impression was made with clay but, since its discovery in the 20th century, silicon is now used, allowing greater flexibility.

On the upper floors are recreations of painted interior walls and vaults, and three stained-glass windows (Level 3). Interest in, and the conservation of, medieval wall-paintings was galvanised by Prosper Mérimée when he published an album dedicated to the Romanesque murals at Saint-Savin-sur-Gartemps, which became known as the 'French Romanesque Sistine Chapel'. Copies of murals include Saint-Savin's vaults.

Modern and Contemporary Architecture Gallery (level 2): This sets out the evolution of architecture in France from 1851 to the present, demonstrating the many innovations since the Industrial Revolution. Among the examples of 19th-century buildings or projects which profoundly altered the course of architecture are Paxton's Crystal Palace in London; and the transformations Baron Haussmann made to Paris. The responses to changes in the use, purpose or evolution of materials, varying climates, styles and fashions are recorded. The evolution of the Palais de Chaillot itself is one theme. The vision of individual architects and their projects are set out as a chronological progression: among them Auguste and Gustave Perret's Théâtre des Champs-Élysées; Bernard Tschumi's visions for the Parc de la Villette; the 1980s' industrial steel-roofed building for Renault at Boulogne-Billancourt by Claude Vasconi (transformed into a communications centre for Renault in 2005) and La Grande Arche de la Défense, the controversial design of Johan Otto von Spreckelsen.

The last section is the re-creation of one unit of Le Corbusier's Unité d'Habitation or Cité Radieuse, built in 1947–52 in Marseilles. It can be entered, allowing visitors to experience the efficient use of space at first hand, as well as the view from the back balcony of the Bay of Marseilles.

MUSÉE NATIONAL DES ARTS ASIATIQUES-GUIMET

Map p. 580, A4–B4. Métro 9 to Iéna. Open Wed–Mon 10–6; closed Tues, 1 May, 25 Dec, 1 Jan. Free audioguides with photo ID; detailed handbills in the galleries. Salon des Porcelains restaurant open as the museum. Shop. T: 01 56 52 53 00, www.guimet.fr.

Occupying a triangular site between Avenue d'Iéna and Rue Boissière, the Musée

National des Arts Asiatiques, usually known as the Guimet, is the most important museum of Asian art in Europe. It contains an outstanding collection illustrating the diversity of cultures and civilisations throughout Asia.

The **Buddhist Pantheon** in the adjacent building (Panthéon Bouddhique; *19 Avenue d'Iéna*) consists of some 150 Japanese and 30 Chinese Buddhist works. In 2001 a Japanese tea house was created in the Japanese garden, where tea ceremonies can be attended (*by reservation only; garden open 10–5 except during tea ceremonies; telephone before visiting*).

Close by is another collection of Asian art, the **Musée d'Ennery** (*see p. 519*).

ÉMILE GUIMET AND HIS COLLECTION

Émile Guimet (1836–1918) was the son of a Lyonnais industrialist who inherited and managed, out of a sense of duty, the family pigment factory but whose true passion was for philosophy and ancient religions, which led him to collect Egyptian and Classical antiquities and Asian art. His collections were transferred from Lyon to this specially-designed building in Paris in 1889, where they have remained ever since. In 1905, Guimet launched the career of Mata Hari when he arranged for her to perform three 'Javanese temple dances' at his museum. Her performance left the audience spellbound.

The Guimet collection passed to the nation in 1927 and merged with the Musée Indochinois du Trocadéro. The Egyptian section was gradually phased out in favour of Asian art. During the reorganisation of national museums in 1945, the Louvre's Asian art collection, which had been formed in the late 19th century, also passed to the Guimet. The Buddhist Pantheon annexe was inaugurated in 1991. The calm, open display area is arranged over four main levels around the naturally-lit central atrium. The displays are arranged geographically.   A.B. & D.G.-D.

Ground floor

India: The Indian section contains sculptures from the 3rd millennium BC to the 18th and 19th centuries, and paintings from the 15th–19th centuries. The art of ancient and medieval India (1st–2nd centuries to the 17th century) is related mainly to the Buddhist and Hindu religions in the form of sculptures in bronze, sandstone, wood or terracotta. Some of the prime pieces in this section are from the earlier period, namely the Amaravati School marble *Head of Buddha* (2nd century). Amaravati, in Andhra Pradesh in the southern Deccan, witnessed the devel-opment of highly original art which flourished in the 1st–3rd centuries, an enduring style which was to influence the art of Sri Lanka and the Indianised kingdoms of Southeast Asia. The *Nagaraja* or *Serpent King* of the 2nd century, from the Mathura region in Northern India, is distinctive for its red sandstone. The Mathura School flourished from the 3rd century until the Gupta period (4th–6th centuries), which was considered the Golden Age of Indian Art. The style is demonstrated by the Buddha torso (early 6th century) from the Mathura region, dressed in fine monastic robes that seem to cling to the body. The female bust from Madhya Pradesh (10th–11th centuries), also known as a female tree spirit or *shalabhanjika*, is representative of sculptures which embellished the walls of many Indian shrines. Seventeenth-century Indian miniatures from the Mughal Court are also on display.

Southeast Asia: This section comprises part of the Asian mainland and the islands of Indonesia, Malaysia and the Philippines. Three groups on the mainland dominated in the 1st millennium: the Cham along the east coast of Vietnam; the Khmer in the central Mekong valley; and the Mon to the west (Thailand and Burma).

The **Cambodian department** contains some of the most beautiful Khmer sculptures outside Cambodia. It is divided into three periods: Pre-Angkorian (1st–8th centuries); from the foundation of Angkor to Angkor Wat (9th–11th centuries); and the apotheosis and the end of Angkor (12th–15th centuries). The first temple at Angkor, capital of the kingdom, built c. 900, was dedicated to Shiva and called the Bakheng. It had five terraces and 109 sanctuary towers. The Banteah Srei pediment (c. 967), in pink sandstone, was part of a *gopura* or tower. It features a high-relief carving of Krishna in an animated struggle during an episode from the Sanskrit epic the *Mahabharata* and reflects the emergence of the style of Banteah Srei. The *Head of Jayavarman VII* (r. 1181–1219) is typical of the Bayon style, with downcast eyes and an enigmatic smile. The *Buddha Protected by the Naga Mucilinda* is very typical of the Angkor Wat style (1st half of the 12th century), with the hieratic figure of the Enlightened One seated on the serpent's coiled body and protected by its many heads. A section of the huge Giants' Causeway, Preah Kahn, Angkor Wat (12th or early 13th centuries) is part of a serpent balustrade on the bridge that crossed the temple moat, alluding to the passage from one world to another.

The **Kingdom of Champa**, east Vietnam, was Indianised from the 7th century. A rare group of Cham sculptures includes the iconic figure of *Shiva of the Silver Tower* (11th–12th centuries), which displays classic iconography of Shiva, with a central eye, a crescent moon in his matted hair, and a snake across the torso.

The influence of India was felt in **Burma** from the 1st century AD, as represented by a huge number of temples and stupas. Delicate Buddhas finely carved in teak with traces of polychrome and lacquer include the *Crowned Buddha* (14th century). Indian culture also shaped **Javanese development** via the trade routes through the region, and inspired the astounding Temple of Borobudur, erected in the 8th century, with over 500 lifesize Buddhist images and nearly 3km of relief carvings.

Objects from **Thailand and Laos** from the period of Mon kingdom of Dvaravati, which emerged by the 5th century, include the *Wheel of the Law* (8th or 9th centuries), emblem of the Buddha's first sermon. The bronze *Head of Buddha* (14th century), of the Ayutthaya period, displays classic features such as the tight hair curls surmounted by a pointed flame. Most works from Laos here are 18th–19th-century.

First floor

Ancient China: Archaeological evidence has identified three outstanding separate but concurrent Neolithic cultures: the painted pottery culture of **Yangshao**, northwest China, represented by the slender *Jandipin amphora* (4800–4000 BC) from Shaanxi, for carrying liquids; the **Hong Shan culture**, in the east, which produced pottery and carved hard green nephrite or jade to represent a magic creature, the *zhulong* or dragon-pig; the **Liangzhu** in the lower Yangtze, who used jade or bone to produce the *cong* or tube, which carried a mystical and authoritative significance. Cult objects in jade include pierced *bi* discs, representing heaven and earth, which were placed on corpses. Terracotta pottery of this era shows sophisticated form and decoration.

The **Shang dynasty** in the 16th century BC learned to cast bronze earlier than Western civilisations. Typical of bronze production are the *liding*, a sacrificial vessel used in ancestor worship, and libation vessels such as the *Camondo tsun*, from Southern China, in the shape of an elephant. The lacquered doe (481–221 BC, Warring States period) supported a drum.

The Empire under the **Qin dynasty** was founded in 221 BC by Emperor Huangdi, who began the Great Wall and amassed a terracotta army of 6,000 figures. The **Han dynasties** which followed (206 BC–220 AD), produced a wide repertoire of *mingqi* (funerary statuettes) including musicians, servants and spirited horses. The **Northern Wei dynasty** (386–589) continued the production of graceful terracottas, but the most outstanding figures are

from the **Tang dynasty** (618–907). The Tang ruled over a vast empire crossed by trade routes, with their capital at Ch'ang, and fostered a period of artistic exuberance. The production of superbly modelled *sancai* figurines for tombs includes graceful dancers and courtiers. The *Bactrian camel with Rider and Load* (2nd half of the 7th century) is a superb example of a popular motif during the Wei and Tang periods.

The introduction of **Buddhism along the Silk Road** is explicit in a 9th-century painting on silk of a monk carrying books, surrounded by all his attributes. The painting came from the cave at Dunhuang where some 500 manuscripts were discovered. **Mediterranean influence** contributed to the increasing naturalism found in the *Bodhisattva sitting in Royal Relaxation* (6th century), from the Longmen caves, Henan province, and *Head crowned with Feathered Tiara* (6th–7th centuries) from Xingjiang province.

Pakistan and Afghanistan: From the 1st–3rd centuries AD, the Kushans ruled over a vast area of Northern India and Afghanistan and Pakistan. Their culture blended Graeco-Roman, Iranian and Indian influences into the Gandhara style. Typical is the expressive standing Bodhisattva carved in green-grey schist. White and blue blown glass and other luxury objects come from Begram, north of Kabul. The art of Hadda, southeast Afghanistan, combines Hellenistic and Indian characteristics in 3rd–4th-century stuccoes such as the *Spirit with Flowers*. Giant Buddhas were sculpted in the cliffs during the occupation by

Persian Sassanids (c. 5th century). Typical of the last Buddhist art is the heavily adorned Bodhisattva from the Monastery of Fondukistan (7th century).

Nepal and Tibet: The art of the Himalayas shows both Tibetan Buddhist and Nepalese Hindu influences. Nepalese art is colourfully represented by several painted book covers in wood (12th–14th centuries), and the gilded, inlaid copper *Manjusri* is a prime example of finely-wrought 13th–18th-century metal sculpture. Paintings on fabric—linen, cotton or silk—are called *thangka*, literally 'rolled-up' and therefore portable. A colourful *thangka, Vajrasattva and his Consort* (1st half of the 13th century), shows many characteristics of Indian miniatures, such as geometric faces and a gentle modelling of forms. The *Mandala of Vajramrita* (1st half of the 16th century) is a prime example of a *thangka* which borrows themes and colours from Nepal.

Riboud Gallery: The decorative arts of India (16th–19th centuries) include jewels, fabrics including saris, and jade dagger handles, as well as pieces from the Mughal dynasty. In the small circular space at the apex of the building is Guimet's original library.

Second floor

Classical China: Brush painting is represented by 1,000 works ranging from the Tang to the Qing dynasties, including a large group from the 13th–18th centuries. There are similarities in style across the centuries although some, such as the 10th-century Northern Song, are more spiritual, and the 12th-century Southern Song show a lyrical quality.

Chinese **calligraphy** and painting are closely linked through their spiritual and meditative qualities, and also technically, as both are executed with brush and ink. The depiction of bamboo holds an elevated position in the established canons of Chinese painting, falling somewhere between calligraphy and tree painting. This is epitomised in the perfectly controlled use of numerous tones of black in the vertical, Yuan-period scroll *Bamboo* (1279–1368). In traditional Chinese painting, the effect of perspective and depth is created by graduated colour and diminishing size.

The collection of **ceramics** under the Tang and the Song is a comprehensive panorama of around 10,000 pieces going back some 8,000 years to handcrafted earthenware. During the Neolithic period, stoneware was produced and the potter's wheel invented. The major contribution of Tang dynasty (AD 618–907) potters was their bold introduction of three-coloured ware, using yellow, green and white glazes, and the influence of Sassanid Persia. Tang pottery peaked in the 10th century with the development of pure porcelain from kaolin fired at very high temperatures to create vessels with a creamy white glaze. The success of ceramic production in the Song dynasty (960–1279) was based on monochromatic wares, the most spectacular of which was celadon, a type of transparent glaze. A beautiful example of early Song production is the globe-shaped celadon ewer (11th century) in porcelain-like stoneware, from Shaanxi, northern China, with a phoenix-head spout and extensive carved floral decoration under a blue-green glaze. The Liao dynasty (916–1125) from Mongolia, established in northeast China, adopted many Chinese customs including ceramic techniques which they adapted to produce a unique repertoire of forms modelled on everyday objects. A very rare Yuan dynasty (1280–1368) ceramic is the porcelain Meiping vase (mid-14th century), which uses a strong cobalt blue glaze with a white slip dragon motif. The Yuan capital, Tatu, on the site of Beijing, was rebuilt by the Ming dynasty (1468–1644) and raised to the rank of Imperial City. Porcelain was produced in great quantity, the most important centre being Jingdezhen. A flourishing export business developed, and blue and white ware was adjusted to the taste of European customers.

Korea: This department has some 1,000 objects covering the main periods of Korean art. Buddhism and writing were introduced from Han China early in this era, and a particular style of **Buddhist art** emerged from the 4th century. The three kingdoms are represented here. From the Paekche Kingdom in the southwest is a small, cross-legged Bodhisattva meditating (6th century); from the Silla Kingdom, the last to convert to Buddhism, comes a remarkable gilded bronze crown (5th–6th centuries), influenced by Siberian shamanist art. The Koryo dynasty which unified the Kingdom of Korea in 918 produced large, serene Buddha sculptures such as the meditative *Teaching Buddha* (11th–12th centuries) in gilded wood.

Very high-quality celadon, or *mae-byong*, developed characteristics specific to Korea and brought renown to its ceramicists. With the **Choson dynasty** (1392–1592), the capital was established in Seoul and Confucianism became the official religion. The near-caricatures of *Three Sitting Monks* (14th–15th centuries), carved in stone, were not unusual. The production of ceramics was revived; green Punch'ong replaced celadon, and white porcelain was developed.

Japan: The Japanese department is extremely rich, with around 11,000 works from the 3rd–2nd millennia BC to the beginning of the Meiji era (1868). The production of ceramics, from c. 10,500 BC to c. 300 BC, the **Jomon period**, is identified by the rope-cord pattern on terracotta pots and figurines. The succeeding culture, **Yayoi**, when rice was introduced, made undecorated ceramics, and bronze and iron objects. The **Kofun period** (AD 300–538) was named after the large tombs (*kofun*) built for the political leaders of that era, during which time (c. AD 400) the country was united as Yamato Japan. Remarkable clay figures or *haniwa* (meaning clay cylinders) developed in conjunction with funerary rituals. During the **Nara period** (710–49) Japanese Buddhist art followed in the wake of Chinese paradigms. From the mid-8th century, works of the **Heian period** showed greater independence and the country was indeed liberated from China in 894.

Under the **Fujiwara** (until 1185) and the shogun warriors of **Kamakura** (until 1333), Zen Buddhism appeared. The art of Zen emphasised portraits, austere ink paintings, calligraphy and direct aids to meditation, including gardens, tea rituals, and Noh theatre. The *Kannon Bodhisattva* which portrays the Great Being of Compassion, placed on a lotus-flower pedestal, symbol of purity, is typical of the Fujiwara period.

Ceramics were the ultimate manifestation of the art of the **Momoyana period** (1558–1637), epitomised in the *Raku tea bowl. Raku*, meaning enjoyment or ease, is a form of pottery fired at low temperatures using lead glazes and removed from the kiln while glowing hot. It is the traditional hand-made manufacturing technique for bowls for the Japanese tea ceremony, ensuring that each bowl is unique.

Western influences arrived with the Portuguese in 1543 and a direct result is the **Edo period** painting *The Portuguese* (17th century) on the fold-ing screen of Namban Byobu. In 1603, Edo (modern Tokyo) was established as the military and administrative centre, while Kyoto remained the artistic centre. Subsequently Edo overtook Kyoto artistically and became famous for wood-block prints in colour, known as *ukiyo-e* (pictures of the fleeting or floating world). Leading artists were Kitagawa Utamaro, Katsushika Hokusai and Utagawa Hiroshige. The iconography includes genre pleasure scenes, portraits and landscapes. Their fame spread worldwide, to influence many Western painters such as Degas and Whistler. In 19th-century France, the portrait prints of elegant and beautiful women by Kitagawa Utamaro were popular and widespread, but very few were authentic originals.

Third and fourth floors

Qing China: China was ruled by foreigners for a second time under the Manchu, who founded the Qing dynasty (1644–1911). The arts flourished again under Emperor Kangxi (1662–1722) when skills in porcelain, enamel, inlay and lacquer techniques were perfected. The colour-palette of enamels expanded: to green (*famille verte*) was added pink (*famille rose*); later in the 18th century, still more colours and the *cloisonné* technique became sought after. The *Vase of a Thousand Flowers* (1736–95, Qianlong period) is a spectacular example.

PALAIS DE TOKYO

Map p. 585, E1. Métro 9 to Iéna or Alma-Marceau. Entrance on 11–13 Av. du Président-Wilson.

The Palais de Tokyo was constructed for the International Art and Technical Exhibition in 1937, fronting the Seine on what was then Avenue de Tokyo (it was re-named Avenue de New York after the Second World War). The building is in two parts, divided by a terrace with views towards the Seine. On the façade and terrace walls are reliefs of the Muses by Alfred-Auguste Janniot and statues by Bourdelle including the bronze *La France*, installed in 1948. The eastern half is occupied by the City Museum of Modern Art. In the western part is the Site de Création Contemporaine.

MUSÉE D'ART MODERNE (MAM)

Open Tues–Sun 10–6, Thur during temporary exhibitions 10–10; closed Mon and holidays. Audioguides. As a museum of the Ville de Paris, there is free entry to the permanent collection. There is a well-stocked bookshop, self-service café and two restaurants (see p. 436). T: 01 53 67 40 00, www.mam.paris.fr.

The museum was inaugurated in 1961 to house the municipal collection of 20th-century art consisting of donations and acquisitions since the 1930s, to which have been added 21st-century works. The bequest of Dr Maurice Girardin in 1953 of over 500 works formed the basis of the collection. A recent donation of 127 paintings and sculptures was made by Michael Werner, and bequests have come from the De Chirico foundation. Acquisitions or bequests have created an original collection of some 10,000 works, a rotating selection of which is on permanent display. Full benefit is derived from the generous original architectural spaces and natural light, especially in the galleries facing the Seine. Because of the rotating nature of the displays, the description below focuses on major highlights, artists particularly well represented, and themes.

The Modern Collections

Salle Dufy: In 1964 a room on the upper floor was created to receive the unique celebratory decoration (10m by 60m) of 250 panels, *Fée Eléctricité* (1937), painted by Dufy for the Pavilion of Light designed by Mallet-Stevens at the 1937 International Exhibition. This ode to electricity, based on Lucretius' poem, *De Rerum Natura*, reads from right to left on two registers, mixing myth and historical fact. The upper level begins with the natural landscape and gradually transforms into an industrial urban setting with neon lights and floodlit buildings. In the apse is the temple to electricity, a power station linked by thunder to Zeus, while Hermes acts as go-between. On the lower register is a frieze of 110 savants and inventors, philosophers and electrical engineers who contributed to the development of electricity, beginning with Archimedes and including Ampère, Faraday, Bell and Morse, all named, set against a background of bright, translucent colours depending on zones. The climax is the Electricity Fairy or Iris, Messenger of the Gods, associated with the rainbow, soaring above an orchestra in the last movement of a symphonic poem.

Salle Matisse: This room (downstairs) contains two large **triptychs by Henri Matisse**. These began as a commission in 1930 for the Barnes Foundation in the USA, for which Matisse returned to a dance theme. *La Danse Inachevée* (1931) was sketched on scaled-up paper using charcoal fixed to a bamboo stick, and painted in grey oils on a blue ground. It contains eight figures, two largely obscured, intended to create a continu-

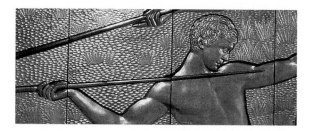

MUSÉE D'ART MODERNE
Detail from *Les Sports*, part of the decoration of the transatlantic liner *Normandie* (1935).

ous chain as in *La Danse* of 1909–10 for Shchukin. In 1931 Matisse, exhausted, abandoned it. He began a new version using cut-outs of coloured paper, which was discarded in 1932 because of an error in the dimensions. The Merion mural was finally completed in 1933. Matisse then returned to the 1932 version, which became known as *La Danse de Paris*. Against orthogonal pink, black and blue bands are energetic, muscular dancers, setting up a vibrant surface pattern. This work revolutionised architectural decoration and Matisse's work from then on. It was bought by the Ville de Paris in 1937 to decorate a specially designed room in the museum; *Danse Inachevée* was acquired in 1993. In the same room is a Matisse bronze, *The Back*.

Mur de Peintures is hung with 20 panels of different coloured vertical stripes—black, red, blue, grey and orange—in varying sizes, painted between 1966 and 1977 by Daniel Buren. When first presented here it was arranged on two walls. Since 2006, when it entered the collection, it has, according to the artist's wishes, become a coherent whole. Buren's installations follow a precise practice. Different formats and colours and the inherent rhythm and ornamental dimensions of the group are underpinned by a rigorous positioning which nevertheless avoids leaving any structural evidence. His works are totally dependent on the places for which they are conceived, to a certain extent reversing the traditional accepted autonomy of an artwork. For an example of Buren's work *in situ*, see Palais Royal (*p. 308*).

Robert Delaunay (1885–1941) plays an important part in the collections. Delaunay became interested around 1908 in the Bergsonian concepts of simultaneity and dynamism, duration and time. He celebrated modernism and the technical age, including the Eiffel Tower, as well as movement, although his main concern was the primacy of colour over form. He was closely associated with Orphic Cubism, so named by Apollinaire, which led to the first abstract works by a French painter. *The Cardiff Team* (1912–13) is a colourful variation of a Cubist collage, influenced by Chevreul's law of simultaneous contrasts. There are also works by his wife Sonia Delaunay, including the mural *Rhythm* (1938).

Art Deco Room: in keeping with the period of the building, the splendid gallery overlooking the Seine contains examples of the Art Deco style of the 1930s, including furniture and objects by Émile-Jacques Ruhlmann, Eugène Printz and Jean Dunand, among others. Dunand's *Les Sports* (1935), glazed stucco panels of javelin-throwing athletes, was made for the first-class smoking cabin of the transatlantic steamer *Normandie* (more decorations from which are in the nearby Musée de la Marine). There are also large-format decorative works by Albert Gleizes and André Lhote, both of whom painted in a colourful pseudo-Cubist style with overlapping planes.

James Lee Byars, on a quest for perfection, found himself turning to Minimalism plus Conceptualism and Performance Art and, inspired by Eastern cultures, bringing in Noh theatre and Buddhist and Western philosophy. Simple but satisfying contemplative forms, such as *Moon Books* and *The Triangle Book*, are made from precious materials, gold or marble. The *Star Book* was donated by Michael Werner in 2012.

Jean Fautrier's desire to create a living reality was first received with incomprehension, and he remained a solitary figure. The 14 works he donated to the museum include an ironic early work, *Sunday Walk* (1921–2), of doll-like figures painted during the inter-year wars in the Tyrol. From his black period is *The Great Black Boar* (1926) and *The Jewess* (1943), in thick impasto layers, painted during executions which took place near his home and linked to his important *Hostage Series* (1945; *see p.*

342). From *Objects* comes 'The Ink Well' (1948), which uses plaster impasto with a sprinkling of pigment or diluted oil paint. His work is seen as the forerunner of Art Informel, spontaneous abstract painting which dominated the 1950s.

The Italian artist **Giorgio de Chirico** first visited Paris in 1911 and met, among others, Apollinaire, Picasso and Max Jacob. He returned in 1920 and became an important influence on early Surrealism. MAM, which already owned seven works by him, including *Mélancolie hermétique* (1919), received a legacy of 61 works, including drawings and sculptures, from the Fondation Giorgio et Isa de Chirico in 2011, making the collection of de Chirico's later works the second largest after Rome.

Pierre Bonnard (*see below*) is famous for emotionally charged canvases luminous with colour. **Édouard Vuillard**, like Bonnard, started by painting small-format, intimate interiors. The 'Anabaptists' is the title given to a group of portraits of former Nabis painters: Aristide Maillol, Ker Xavier Roussel, Pierre Bonnard and Maurice Denis. Vuillard's studies reveal his colleagues at work in their studios in 1936–7.

Matisse was fascinated by fabrics, having grown up in a textile manufacturing area in the northwest of France. The sensation of interior light, colour and pattern was always important to him. He visited north Africa in 1906 and brought fabrics back. The odalisque was a recurrent motif in Matisse's work, presenting the opportunity to combine the sensuality of a female with that of fabrics, as exemplified in *Odalisque au fauteuil turc* (1928).

PIERRE BONNARD

Bonnard (1867–1947) initially used decorative pattern in contrast to areas of flat colour, but in later paintings, texture and colour become as important as the subject. The painter would take a daily walk, jotting down small compositions on tiny scraps of paper or in his pocket diary, with a blunt pencil. These drawings, which he called his 'sensations', were his emotional response to the walk. For Bonnard, colour was 'reasoning', and many of his works took him years to complete as he agonised over colour balances, trying to find equivalents in paint for his pencil notations. There are stories of him revisiting his works, even in museums, secretly touching up areas that did not satisfy him. One of his main sources of inspiration was his life-long partner Marthe, who is frequently depicted in the bathroom. She was a reclusive figure, apparently suffering from a nervous condition (hydrotherapy was then a popular medical treatment) but the bathroom itself gave Bonnard the chance to wrestle with the problem of painting white. In many of his paintings the walls and floor of the bathroom blaze with colour while Marthe's ageless figure glows in the tub. Bonnard's pictures have a slightly disorientating shifting viewpoint. He said of them that they should give you the sensation of walking into a room where you see 'everything and nothing at the same time'. They are very carefully composed but loosely painted. 'To tell you the truth, I have trouble with painting,' he said. But it is through his struggle with colour that he gives us back the emotion that he first felt on his morning walk.

Raoul Dufy: 104 works by Dufy were among the Girardin bequest, covering his career from his brief brush with Fauvism to a more graphic and distinctive pre-war style, in works such as the *Abandoned Garden* (1913). In the 1930s his style softened into a technique reminiscent of watercolour, such as *Nu couché* (1930) and *Races at Epsom* (1934), where line and colour are separated. Throughout much of his career he was well known as a fabric designer.

Dada and Surrealism: Covering a multitude of styles, the Surrealist collection includes collages by Dada artist Kurt Schwitters, for example *Miroir Collage* (1920–2), made of rubbish and framed by Tristan Tzara, who donated it to the museum; others are *Vase de fleurs* (1924–6) by Francis Picabia, elegantly 'drawn' in wire and straw; Max Ernst's *Fleurs* (c. 1928–9), using the technique of *frottage*; and Jean Crotti's *Le Clown* (1916), on glass. Among the host of Surrealist memorabilia is the 1938 International Surrealist Exhibition catalogue, works by André Masson, and examples of the *Cadavre exquis* (1927–31), a group game where each participant in succession draws on folded paper. The large collection of works by Victor Brauner includes a portrait of the Surrealist leader André Breton. Marcel Duchamp's input includes *La Mariée mise à nu par ses célibataires, même* (1934), *La Bôite en valise*, *Le Surréalisme en 1947* and works of the 1960s, *Rotoreliefs* and *À L'infinitif* (*La Bôite blanche*).

Abstraction in the 1920s and '30s: Abstraction was evolving in Europe from c. 1910 and came to permeate the French artistic consciousness around 1925. In 1931 the Abstraction-Création group was formed, by a disparate band of Cubists, Dadaists and Constructivists including Auguste Herbin, Jean Hélion, Jean Arp, Kurt Schwitters and Étienne Bééthy. Among the works are the rigorous *Plans diagonaux* (1925) by František Kupka, the hard-edged, painted wood *Polychrome Relief* (1920) by Auguste Herbin, and the biomorphic shapes of *Constellation aux cinq formes blanches et deux formes noires* (1932) by Jean Arp.

School of Paris: A disparate group of foreign artists living in Paris in the 1920s were grouped under this title. Their diverse interpretations of the human figure include a typically stylised and flat painting by Modigliani, *Femme aux yeux bleus* (c. 1918), and the enigmatic beauty *The Sphinx* (c. 1925) by Kees Van Dongen. *The Dream* (1927) by Chagall is inspired by the circus but open to deeper interpretation. Ossip Zadkine was an inspired woodcarver who combined Cubism and Classicism in *Orpheus* (1928–30). There are also Expressionist portraits by Chaïm Soutine, deformed and almost caricatural; and sculptures by the Bulgarian dandy Jules Pascin. Marcel Gromaire evokes the conditions of toil and resignation in his monumental compositions such as *Le Faucheur flamand* (1924). Among the works by Foujita is the seductive nude *Femme couchée à la toile de Jouy* (1922), which borrows from Manet's *Olympia*. 'Toile de Jouy' refers to the curtains used as a framing device in the painting, made of a type of fabric which goes back to the 18th century, traditionally printed with flirtatious scenes.

Fauvism and Cubism: The Fauve movement was born in 1905, when the art critic Louis Vauxcelles ironi-

cally described the brightly-coloured canvases of a number of artists, such as Maurice de Vlaminck, Derain and Braque, as 'wild'. The cross-fertilisation of colour and energy leaps out in Vlaminck's *Berges de la Seine à Chatou* (1906). Other works include *L'Olivier près de l'Estaque* (1906) by Georges Braque. The collection of works by Derain covers most periods of his creative activity, from Fauvism (*La Rivière* and *Le Phare de Collioure*; 1905); experiments with Cubism (*Baigneuses*; c. 1908); ceramics, bronze heads (1930s–50s); and prints and drawings. Derain described Fauvism as colours which should explode with light. In *Trois Personages assis dans l'herbe* (1906), the three figures, seated in a field, contain the components of a traditional theme: the nude in nature. But here nature is simplified to a cool green swathe and a band of blue against which the three figures, painted in warm blocks of colour, stand out. The faces are reduced to a mask-like expression (Derain had recently seen African masks in London).

In 1908 Braque and Picasso worked together for a time, deconstructing and researching a new way of expressing volume, in part inspired by African masks. They came up with a solution which made a radical break with established traditions, for which once again Louis Vauxcelles coined a term: 'Cubist'. *Le Verre* (1911), *Pigeon aux petits pois* (1911) and *Tête d'homme* (1912) became known as Analytical Cubism. Among the long list of artists influenced by Cubism, most of whom adapted it to a more colourful, decorative version (Synthetic Cubism), are Delaunay, de la Fresnaye, André Lhote (*Nature Morte à la tasse de café*) Albert Gleizes (*Les Baigneuses*, 1912)

Metzinger (*L'Oiseau bleu*) and Juan Gris (*Le Livre*, 1913).

Georges Rouault: The museum is rich in mainly pre-1918 works by Rouault, who was born in Belleville and trained in stained glass before studying under Gustave Moreau. The collection includes his entire production of copper engravings. He painted recurring themes in a singular graphic, Expressionistic style including *À Tabarin—Le Chahut* (1905) depicting the popular dance hall; later he became a well-known religious painter, producing biblical landscapes such as *Crépuscule* (1938–9). He remained mainly independent of groups and later in life designed stained-glass windows.

Art Brut or 'Raw Art' was a term coined by Jean Dubuffet to describe art that stood beyond the pales of conventional styles and isms. Often described as 'outsider art', it includes graffiti, art by prisoners, children and the mentally disturbed. Among those who espoused the style were Jean Bazaine (*Objets du soir*; 1943), inspired by Cubism and medieval stained glass; Alfred Manessier and Joseph Sima. Dubuffet himself is represented by *Chaussée boiseuse* (1959), made from plant material, part of a series entitled *Eléments botaniques*.

Lyrical Abstraction: This post-1960s movement owes a debt to Japanese calligraphic painting and experimented with single colours. Pierre Soulages' *16 December, 1959* was one of his earliest predominantly black works. Jean Degottex's *Écriture* (1962) is a product of his introduction to Zen. Simon Hantaï introduced folded and crumpled painted surfaces. Bram van Velde was influenced by Picasso's Expressionism of the 1930s.

Raymond Mason was a realist sculptor who spent much of his life in Paris. He worked in clay, casting in epoxy resin and sometimes using colour to animate his condensed, and on occasions controversial, figurative works for public places. He was inspired by medieval statuary and in his work aimed to minimise the distance between art and the viewer.

African and Oceanic art: As a result of the Girardin bequest the museum owns a collection of African works, including a variety of seated, standing or crouching figures and two remarkable animal sculptures from the Congo.

Brassaï, a Hungarian sculptor and draughtsman, arrived in Paris in 1924 and took French nationality in 1948. He turned to photography and became internationally famous. His first collection of photographs, *Paris de nuit*, published 1933, is a haunting portrait of the city at night that established his reputation.

The Contemporary Collections

The contemporary section is arranged around French movements such as Nouveau Réalisme and Fluxus through to Abstraction and the renewed interest in painting and sculpture since 1980. Considerable space is dedicated to the exploration of experiments in new materials and techniques, including installations, photography and video.

Nouveau Réalisme: Influenced by Marcel Duchamp and the urge to desacralise the work of art, Nouveau Réalistes are represented by Jacques Villeglé, Niki de Saint Phalle and Raymond Hains. There is also an 'Accumulation' by Arman, a 'Compression' by César, and a 'Néon' by Martial Raysse. There are a number of works by Yves Klein, leader of the movement, including *2 Blue, Portrait-relief de Martial Raysse (PR2)* and *Red Monochrome, M26* (1949). Other artists associated with Nouveau Réalisme are Daniel Spoerri, Gérard Deschamps and Robert Filliou.

Fluxus: An international movement which appeared in the 1960s, Fluxus drew its inspiration from music, science and the theatre, to create improvised works of art or 'events'. The objective of Fluxus artists Ben, Marcel Broodthaers and Jean Dupuy has been to abolish the frontier between art and life, with works frequently composed of a multitude of objects, often treated with humour. A work by Ben *in situ*, for example, is his *Il faut se méfier des mots*, where two life-size (and lifelike) mannequins are hoisting a huge advertising hoarding into place (*see p. 395*). Works in the museum include Ben's cupboard entitled *In the Spirit of Fluxus* and Annette Messager's *vitrines* with collections of photos and text. Broodthaers' installations such as *Le Corbeau et le renard* (1967) combine film, sound and the written word. One of a group of five robots created for the bicentenary of the French Revolution, *Olympe de Gouges* (1989) by the Korean-born Nam June Paik was assembled from a number of video screens. Alain Jacquet's witty, neo-Impressionist *Le Déjeuner sur l'herbe* (1964) looks sharp from a distance and 'pixellates' the closer you get to it.

Audiovisual: Glasgow-born Douglas Gordon (Turner Prize 1996) is a film and video creator. MAM Paris has the world's largest collection of his video works. His installations frequently refer to film, particularly Hitchcock classics, which introduce a new interpretation and engage the memory of the viewer. Among his works are *24 Hours Psycho* (1993) and *Feature Film* (1999).

The Salle Noire is set aside for video projections and there are further screenings throughout the museum by artists such as Francis Alÿs, Gillian Waring, Rosemarie Trockel and Clarisse Hahn. Camille Henrot's *Grosse Fatigue*, which received the Silver Lion at the 55th Venice Biennale, attempts to trace the history of creation and the universe in six parts totalling 13 minutes.

Christian Boltanski: The museum exhibits a selection of iconic works by Boltanski, who turned from painting to varied media, including installations. To evoke human presence he uses multiples of discarded items or photographs, in *Rêves du Musée des enfants I* (1989) and *Rêves du Musée des enfants II*. A collection of international telephone directories, *Les Abonnés du téléphone* (2001), is evidence of the existence of millions.

1980–present: New acquisitions include work by emerging young French painters and international artists such as Damien Cabanes, Marc Desgrandchamps, Peter Doig, Mathieu Mercier, Philippe Parreno, Xavier Veilhan, Françoise Vergier, Charline von Heyl and Christopher Wood.

SITE DE CRÉATION CONTEMPORAINE

Open Wed–Sun 12–12, closed Mon. T: 01 81 97 35 88, www.palaisdetokyo.com.

In the vast expanses of the west wing of the Palais de Tokyo, this contemporary arts centre holds regular exhibitions and events. The informal restaurant Tokyo Eat is also here, with inventive cuisine (*see p. 437*), as well as a self-service snack bar, Smack.

PALAIS GALLIÉRA & MUSÉE BACCARAT

Map p. 580, B4. Métro 9 to Iéna.

PALAIS GALLIÉRA

10 Av. Pierre 1er de Serbie. Open 10–6 during exhibitions; closed Mon and public holidays. T: 01 56 52 86 00, www.palaisgalliera.paris.fr.

The exhibition space here presents intermittent temporary exhibitions; there are no permanent galleries. Set in gardens, the Hôtel Galliéra (1888–92) was built in Italian Renaissance style to house the collection of 17th-century Italian art belonging to the Duchesse de Galliéra (d. 1889). Since 1977 the building has housed the Musée Galliéra de la Mode et du Costume (fashion and costume). Selections of the vast collection, enriched by donations, are shown in rotation in a series of temporary exhibitions covering specific themes or periods. The holdings include dresses, designs, costume and fashion-plates, photographs and an astonishing variety of accessories, lingerie and other forms of clothing, from costume jewellery to shoes, as well as dolls and wigs, dating from the 18th century to the modern era.

MUSÉE BACCARAT

11 Place des États-Unis. Open 10-6.30; closed Tues, Sun and public holidays. T: 01 40 22 11 00, www.baccarat.fr.

The prestigious manufacturer of crystalware, Baccarat, which celebrated its 250th anniversary in 2014, has a glittering showroom and private museum housed in the elegant former private mansion of Marie-Laure de Noailles. The manufacture was founded in Lorraine with the authorisation of Louis XV, and there are displays of historic works and spectacular examples of its production. Tableware and jewellery are on sale. There is also a very elegant restaurant, Cristal Room Baccarat on the first floor (*see p. 436*).

Place des États-Unis, where the museum is situated, was originally called Place de Bitche, after a town in Lorraine which held out valiantly during the Franco-Prussian war. At the end of the 19th century, when the United States legation took up residence here, the name was deemed unsuitable and it was deported to the 19th arrondissement, to the former Place de l'Église in front of the church at the end of the Bassin de la Villette, where it remains (*see p. 404*).

PASSY & THE JARDINS DU RANELAGH

Map p. 584, C2. Métro 6 to Passy.

Rue de Passy is the high street of the former village of that name. Off Rue Raynouard are steps to Sq. Charles Dickens and the **Musée du Vin** (*open Tues–Sat 10–6, closed Sun–Mon; T: 01 45 25 63 26, www.museeduvinparis.com; also a restaurant, lunch only until 3.30*), in the vaulted 14th-century cellars of Passy Abbey, which were originally quarries. Tucked away at no. 47 Rue Raynouard is the **Maison de Balzac** (*open Tues–Sat 10–6, closed Sun, Mon and holidays; T: 01 55 74 41 80*), which is not only a memorial to the writer but also to rural Passy. Balzac lived in the late 18th-century house from 1840, enjoying the garden and the proximity to Paris. He organised his day around a strict routine of writing. His study is barely altered and contains the small table where he proofread *La Comédie humaine*, wrote to Mme Hanska and wrote *La Cousine Bette*, among other novels. Memorabilia include his coffee pot (he was heavily dependent on caffeine). The house has become a literary museum and the library is a centre for research.

Further west are the **Jardins du Ranelagh** (*map p. 584, A1–A2*), part of the ancient royal park of La Muette. 'Le Petit Ranelagh' was named in 1774, after its fashionable namesake in London, a favourite place to go dancing for over a century. Nearby in 1783, the first balloon ascent in France was made by François d'Arlandes and Pilâtre de Rozier in a balloon created by the Montgolfier brothers. The royal Château de la Muette, originally a hunting-lodge, restored by Louis XV for Mme de Pompadour, was demolished in 1920. The modern mansion just north of the Jardins du Ranelagh and east of the Porte de la Muette, on Rue André-Pascal, was built by Baron Henri de Rothschild. It is now the property of the OECD (Organisation for Economic Cooperation and Development).

MUSÉE MARMOTTAN MONET

Map p. 584, A1. 2 Rue Louis-Boilly. Métro 9 or RER C to La Muette. Open Tues–Sun 10–6, Thur until 8pm. Closed Mon. T: 01 44 96 50 33, www.marmottan.com.

On the west side of Ranelagh gardens is the Musée Marmottan Monet, a very popular small museum best known for the outstanding collection of paintings by Claude Monet and other Impressionists. The building was bequeathed in 1932 to the Académie des Beaux Arts by Paul Marmottan, who inherited it from his father and enlarged and redecorated it in First Empire style as a foil to his collections of art and furniture. The core of the museum is in fact its collection of First Empire paintings, furniture and bronzes. The Impressionist collections came later, as a result of several bequests. The museum received the Donop de Monchy bequest of a number of Impressionist paintings in 1957 and in 1966, Michel Monet bequeathed a hugely important group of works by his father, the artist Claude. The museum now holds 94 of his canvases, the largest collection in the world. A room inspired by the Orangerie in the Tuileries has been built to house them.

An exceptional collection of illuminated manuscripts was donated by Daniel Wildenstein in 1980 and this eclectic but already brilliant collection was further enhanced with works from the Duhem bequest in 1987. The Marmottan also owns the largest single collection in any public holding of works by Berthe Morisot, resulting from bequests by the Rouaut family (Denis and Julien Rouaut were Morisot's grandsons). The Marmottan is also rich in other Impressionist paintings, including works by Renoir, Pissarro and Sisley.

FIRST EMPIRE COLLECTIONS: GROUND FLOOR

The First Empire artworks and furnishings have been returned, as far as possible, to their original settings, including the clocks, which are in working order. An example is the geographical clock (1813) in the hallway. Altered after the fall of the Empire, it is inlaid with Sèvres porcelain medallions.

The tour begins here, with works from the Napoleonic Empire (Paul Marmottan's passion) and continues on the first floor. Impressionist paintings are displayed in some of these rooms. In the **Dining Room**, overlooking Ranelagh gardens, is an oval dining table and a *surtout de table* in gilded bronze by P-P. Thomire as well as a sideboard by Georges Jacob-Desmalter (c. 1810). On the walls are several Impressionist works, including *Au Bal* by Berthe Morisot, Caillebotte's *Rue de Paris, temps de pluie* (1877), Renoir's *Paul Monet reading a Newspaper* and Gauguin's wonderful *Bouquet de fleurs* (1867).

In the **Hallway** are landscapes by Carmontelle and a portrait of Hortense de Beauharnais (c. 1806) by F.-P.-S. Gérard and a pair of marble sculptures of *Antinous as Osris* (Beauvallet, c. 1807). The **Rotunda** contains paintings of ateliers of the period: by Massé is *The Interior of Gros' Studio* (all men with a female model) and by Adrienne-M-L. Granpierre-Deverzy *Abél de Pujol's Studio for Women* (lady artists being taught by a man). There is also a *Portrait of Paul Marmottan in his Study* by Count von Rosen and a series of busts including Napoleon's mother and sister. The **Small Salon** contains a painting of the Duchesse de Feltre and her children by Fabre and *Little Girl Eating Cherries* (1817) by Jeanne-Élisabeth Chaudet.

FIRST EMPIRE AND MEDIEVAL COLLECTIONS: UPPER FLOOR

Here are more objects by Thomire and portraits, including *Napoleon Bonaparte as First Consul* by Franque and a charming painting of a female painter, pupil of David wearing a hat. The **upper Rotunda**, Paul Marmottan's former office, contains a portrait of landscape painter Jean-Victor Bertin (1805) by Robert Lefèvre, and one of Bertin's own landscapes. In the **Bedroom** is Napoleon's bed by Jacob-Desmalter (c. 1807–8), in mahogany, bronze and gilded bronze.

From the original collection of Jules Marmottan, father of Paul, are **medieval Flemish, German and Italian works**, including an elegant *Virgin and Child* (c. 1500) set in a charming landscape. The Wildenstein Collection of **illuminated manuscripts and miniatures** has over 300 works. Initially produced in monastery scriptoria for devotional and liturgical purposes, their uses and techniques changed over time. They gained in popularity and were commissioned by individuals for Books of

Hours, bestiaries, herbals and scientific tracts. Styles became less prescribed and the individuality which developed is evident in these brilliant little paintings. Among the French works are a page from the *Hours of Étienne Chevalier* by Jean Fouquet, and an episode from the life of St Vrain, showing an exorcism in Notre-Dame, an important early record of the interior of the cathedral. In contrast is the animated and vigorous 'Admiral de Graville Hunting Wild Boar' (after 1493), from a manuscript called *Le Terrier de Marcoussis*, recording events in the life of a medieval nobleman. *The Kiss of Judas* (late 15th century) by Jean Bourdichon, who was court painter and Fouquet's successor, evokes the intensity of the episode with a crowded scene.

BERTHE MORISOT ROOMS

The varied collections of works by Berthe Morisot include 25 canvases and around 50 watercolours as well as pastels and drawings. Morisot, sister-in-law of Édouard Manet, was an accomplished artist who exhibited in all but one of the Impressionist Exhibitions. Her daughter Julie was her most frequent model. Among beautiful examples of Morisot's work, revealing her delicate and subtle palette, are *Eugène Manet on the Isle of Wight* (1875), *Small Girl with a Basket* and *Little Girls on the Banks of a Lake* (1883), as well as a strong *Self-portrait* (1885). The collection also holds a magnificent portrait of Morisot by Édouard Manet (1873). Morisot lived in Passy, not far from the Jardins du Ranelagh. In a second room are watercolours, sketchbooks, photos and letters. Everyone in Morisot's circle painted and sketched, including Ernest Rouaut, her son-in-law, who was Degas's only student. There are also examples of Morisot's works on paper and family memorabilia.

THE CLAUDE MONET COLLECTION: LOWER FLOOR

The collection of works by Claude Monet is displayed in the lower gallery. The impact of this room is both breathtaking and intimate. The paintings collected here include the most celebrated of all Impressionist works, *Impression Sunrise*. First exhibited in 1874, it gave its name to the most important artistic movement of the 19th century. It shows a hazy blue dawn with indistinct outlines of boats, suggesting the chill of the early day, with a hint of colour from the rising sun reflected in the sky and in the water. The paint handling is loose and the sun's reflection is accomplished in vibrant impasto strokes. This priceless canvas—among others—was stolen from the Marmottan in 1985, but all were recovered five years later in Corsica.

Many of the pictures here are drawings and sketches of Monet's family. *The Beach at Trouville* was painted after his marriage in 1870, when he went with his wife and their son Jean to this mid-19th century fashionable resort. Shortly after war was declared on Prussia, Monet left for London, but returned to live in Argenteuil, which became the subject of several works here: *Walking near Argenteuil*, the *Railway Bridge* and *Argenteuil in the Snow*. Trains, stations and bridges are characteristic of Monet's repertoire. *A Train in the Snow* (1875) is a symphony of grey with the bright lamps of the train shining through the mist. Monet travelled by train from St-Lazare to Argenteuil, making many studies and paintings en route, including of the great 19th-century bridge, the *Pont de l'Europe*, outside the Gare St-Lazare.

IMPRESSIONISM

The style that became known in 1874 as Impressionism changed the art world for ever. It revolutionised painting techniques, altered the way colour was used, and threw open the choice of subject. It represented a new approach to capturing nature on canvas, using the fleeting effect of light on different objects through the analysis of tone and colour with a heightened palette. It represented a rupture with the accepted norm of a laboriously outlined image. To a confused and unprepared public, it appeared unfinished and blurred; yet this revolution had been underway since the 1860s. When Monet's *Impression Sunrise* (1872), of the dawn over the port of Le Havre, was exhibited in 1874, the journalist Louis Leroy wrote a derisory article, calling it *L'Exposition des Impressionistes*. The name stuck and the event became known as the First Impressionist Exhibition. As well as Monet, another 38 artists contributed over 165 works, including Degas, Renoir, Sisley, Pissarro, Cézanne, Guillaumin, Boudin and Berthe Morisot. The exhibition ran for a month from 15th April in studios formerly used by the photographer Nadar, on Boulevard des Capucines (*see p. 302*). Despite the ridicule, this was a major turning point for the *plein-air* painters, several of whom had been turned down by the Salon. The group had established its solidarity and identity. Eight more Impressionist exhibitions were held, the last in 1886.

The threads that were drawn together can be found in philosophy, in the work of earlier painters, in social and demographic changes and scientific developments. In the early part of the 19th century, the philosopher Jean-Jacques Rousseau and the novelist George Sand drew attention to the healing properties of country life and solitude. Life was changing for the general public during the Second Republic, with the creation of public parks and gardens, the vogue for sea bathing and boating, and the *guinguettes* or *bals*, open-air dances. In the first half of the 19th century colour theory was also topical, based on research by the chemist Michel-Eugène Chevreul, whose colour wheel for the Gobelins tapestry house illustrated how colours influence each other. In 1839 he published his law on simultaneous contrasts (demonstrating that the eye demands that opposite colours or contrasts be generated) and on optical mixing (the way that the eye fuses colours). He codified something that painters probably already knew instinctively, such as the complementary colour of a shadow.

Impressionist artists are described as painters of modern life. Their aim was to record life as it was experienced, in opposition to the studied and overworked academic classics of history, religion, mythology or artificially picturesque landscapes. The young painters came from all walks of life and were generally apolitical, making little comment on social hardships even though some suffered deprivation themselves. They captured the spontaneity of regattas, celebrations, boating parties and picnics, in beautiful settings; also city streets, railway stations, factory chimneys and frozen landscapes, to record an effect. Their subject matter also proved to be more accessible to the public. The use of bright prismatic colours applied in small patches produced a flickering effect and vivacity never previously encountered in finished paintings.

In the 18th century painters made oil studies out of doors, and landscape as a genre had begun to be appreciated seriously in the wake of English and Dutch landscape painters and in France through Corot, Boudin and Jongkind. Changes in technique were encouraged by the freer brush-strokes and more innovative use of colour that had been pioneered by Delacroix and Courbet. The most direct influence on the future Impressionists was the Barbizon group, who experimented with painting in the Forest of Fontainebleau.

The capture of the moment out of doors, however, and the application of new colour theories, could never have been fully explored without the more affordable synthetic pigments developed in the 19th century. They offered a greater choice of hues and provided the saturated colours necessary for the new movement. Ready-mixed with a support such as oil or gum Arabic, and after 1841 available in collapsible metal tubes, they greatly facilitated painting en *plein air*. Alongside came improvements in the type of brushes available and outdoor painting kits with lightweight easels.

Photography was also challenging the reasons for painting, and providing a new way of seeing. In 1826 Nicéphore Niépce took the first steps on the road to photography, and by 1850–60 the medium had made great strides. Early photographs on glass plates were either blurred or else showed the effect of strong sunlight eating into solid objects, destroying the clarity of contour. The work of photographers in the Forest of Fontainebleau was secretly admired by the Barbizon painters. The influence of Japanese art also opened up new possibilities—unconventional viewpoints, seemingly arbitrary cut-off points, a rejection of traditional perspective, patches of flat colour and the omission of detail.

By the 1880s Impressionism was going through a crisis, triggered by disunity, attacks by critics and new trends such as Symbolism. Many who were connected with Impressionism for a time, such as Cézanne, Manet, Renoir, Van Gogh, Gauguin and Seurat, moved off in different directions. Speed and spontaneity began to be shunned in favour of the monumental and the timeless. Yet by the end of the century Impressionism had provided the impetus and inspiration for many movements and artists, notably Post-Impressionism and Fauvism, Matisse and Léger. Pissarro and Sisley continued to embrace the Impressionist ethos, but it was Monet above all who pushed to the limit the quest for effects of light and colour that would produce canvases as ephemeral as music. In the 20th century, Impressionism came to be seen as decisive in preparing the way for Modernism.

A fascination with light reflected in water runs throughout Monet's work. He captured different effects in *Vertheuil in the Mist* (1879), *The Beach at Pourville, Sunset* (1882), The *Cliff at Étretat* (c. 1885), and *London, Houses of Parliament* (1899), with a glinting Thames. *Rouen Cathedral, effects of Sunlight–Sunset* (1892) is one of some 20 canvases over which he toiled to achieve the variations created by light in different atmospheric conditions, making the cathedral an insubstantial shimmering object.

Most haunting perhaps are Monet's views of the gardens at Giverny, where he went to live in 1883. He later bought the house and created the gardens, planting waterlilies, willows and wisteria which, with the Japanese bridge, became his constant inspiration. From 1912 he suffered eye problems, and following a cataract operation in 1916 his perception of colour remained irreversibly distorted. The beautiful soft blues and mauves of the earlier lily ponds, the soft oranges and yellows of the *Hemerocallis* and *Iris*, intensify into exciting stronger tones in the *Japanese Bridge* (1918), while the views across the garden painted in the 1920s, of barely decipherable form, remain extraordinary crescendos and celebrations of colour.

FONDATION LE CORBUSIER

Map p. 584, A3. Métro 9 to Jasmin. Open Mon 1.30–6, Tues–Sat 10–6; closed Sun, Mon morning and public holidays. T: 01 42 88 75 72, www.fondationlecorbusier.fr.

Maison La Roche and Maison Jeanneret are adjacent villas designed in 1923 by Le Corbusier (Charles-Édouard Jeanneret). The latter contains the offices of the Corbusier Foundation. Maison La Roche can be visited. Situated at 8–10 Square Dr-Blanche, it is a prime example of the spirit of Le Corbusier and an essential visit for anyone interested in the Modern Movement. Built for a Swiss banker, Raoul La Roche, the house is designed around a main hall leading to two different sections—private and public—and contains paintings, sculpture and furniture. The overall impression is of light and carefully articulated space.

EATING AND DRINKING AROUND TROCADÉRO AND PASSY

€€€ **Astrance**. Smart cooking for a very smart district is offered at this small and select restaurant. Chef Pascal Barbot's remarkable culinary talent creates superb dishes according to the availability of the freshest products each day. Lunch menus with or without wine, from under €100; dinner menu with wine quite a bit more. Absolutely essential to reserve. Closed Mon and weekends and public holidays. *4 Rue Beethoven. T: 01 40 50 84 40, www.astrancerestaurant.com. Map p. 584, C2.*

€€€ **Cristal Room**. Among the great and glorious restaurants of the 16th arrondissement, at the Maison Baccarat. This is an exclusive and truly glitzy affair which combines gallery, boutique and museum. Designed by Philippe Starck, the eclectic décor is a setting for beautiful and luxurious food. There is a five-course tasting menu. Closed Sun. *11 Place des États-Unis. T: 01 40 22 11 10, www.cristal-room.com. Map p. 580, B4.*

€€ **Monsieur Bleu**. ■ In the west wing of Palais de Tokyo (below the museum, looking towards the river), this 'neo-brasserie' occupies a high space and terrace looking out towards the Eiffel Tower and is decked out in inspired greys and olive green and gold, with simple lines. The gourmet dishes, which follow the seasons, include traditional ingredients (you will even find *cuisses de grenouilles* here) but cooked with flair and originality. Open every day. *T: 01 47 20 90 47, monsieurbleu.com. Map p. 585, E1.*

€ **Bon**. The cooking here is a delicate blend of Asian and European with a wide range of fish meat dishes, served in spaces of different character: La Vinothèque, La Salle Cheminée, La Terrace, among others. Open every day. *25 Rue de la Pompe. T: 01 40 72 70 00, www.restaurantbon.fr. Map p. 584, B1.*

€ **La Gare**. As its name suggests, this really is an old station. It serves affordable food from a fairly wide-ranging menu and is not too far from the Marmottan museum. Open every day. Brunch on Sunday. *19 Chaussée de la Muette. T: 01 42 15 15 31, www.restaurantlagare.com. Map p. 584, B2.*

€ **Le Grenier à Pommes**. Small and friendly crêperie, serving all kinds of freshly-made pancakes, sweet and savoury. *19 Rue de Longchamp. T: 01 47 04 48 36. Map p. 585, D1.*

€ **Palais de Chaillot** has a self-service café-restaurant overlooking the Trocadéro gardens, with a marvellous panorama across the Seine. For those attending a performance at the Théâtre National de Chaillot, the Foyer de Chaillot is open before performances (*T: 01 60 04 24 75*) and there is a bar for light refreshments.

€ **Le St-Didier**. An unassuming place serving freshly-cooked fare. *23 Rue Saint-Didier (between Av. Poincaré and Av. Kléber). T: 01 47 04 73 81. Map p. 580, A4.*

€ **Salon des Porcelains**. Small restaurant-cum-tea shop in the Musée Guimet, on the lower ground floor, serving Asian-style food (open same hours as museum). Tea ceremonies are occasionally performed in the garden (*see p. 417*). *T: 08 99 96 92 87. Map p. 580, A4–B4.*

€ **Le Tokyo Eat**. Relaxed restaurant in the west wing of Palais de Tokyo, with interesting décor and traditional French cuisine. Open daily 12–12. *T: 01 47 20 00 29. Map p. 585, E1.*

OUTSKIRTS OF PARIS

*Paris is in the middle of the Île de France region, which includes six
further départements: Hauts-de-Seine, Yvelines, Seine-Saint-Denis,
Val-de-Marne, Essonne, Seine-et-Marne and Val-d'Oise.*

*The visits described in this section fall outside the main ring road, the Boulevard
Périphérique, but can easily be reached by Métro or RER (and sometimes by bus).
Those to the west are defined by the Seine which, after crossing Paris, makes a series
of tight meanders before turning towards Le Havre and the English Channel.*

*Hauts-de-Seine, which is in the first tight loop of the river,
includes La Défense, Nanterre, Rueil-Malmaison, St-Cloud,
Boulogne-Billancourt, Sèvres, Meudon and Sceaux.*

*The former royal palaces of Versailles and St-Germain-en-Laye are further west,
in the Département d'Yvelines, also on the banks of the Seine, as are
Maisons-Laffitte and Poissy.*

*St-Denis is in the Département de Seine-Saint-Denis
and beyond (in Val d'Oise) is the Château d'Écouen.*

*Vincennes, with a once-important royal château and large park,
is also just beyond the eastern confines of Paris in the Val-de-Marne.*

LA DÉFENSE
On one of the passerelles.

La Défense, Bois de Boulogne & Neuilly

*This western fringe of Paris is home to Europe's largest business 'city',
an ancient hunting reserve now landscaped as a public park,
and the fashionable residential suburb of Neuilly.*

LA DÉFENSE

*Map p. 578, A1. Métro 1 or RER A to La Défense Grande Arche. Also tram T2 between La
Défense and Versailles.*

The distinctive silhouette of La Défense, rising beyond the Arc de Triomphe in the
département of Hauts-de-Seine, announces Europe's largest purpose-built business centre, which celebrated its 50th anniversary in 2008 with a Jean-Michel Jarre
extravaganza. It is a two-tier city: the upper level is pedestrianised, while the rail and
road traffic networks, including the RER and Métro, bus stations and car parks, are
below ground. Now home to 2,000 companies and 2,500 corporate headquarters, it is
the workplace for some 150,000 people and an increasing number, presently around
20,000, live here. It is a compelling experience with its modern architecture and soaring glass towers, the perfect foil for large-scale modern and contemporary artworks,
some of which are integral to the development and include installations and water
features, on the concourses and in the many green spaces. La Défense also serves as
an open-air theatre for a wide range of entertainment and activities, from fun runs to
concerts, and also has a Christmas market. Around eight million people a year come to
visit. During the working week it is at its liveliest during lunch hour, when office workers break out of their confines. La Défense, like a small city, is organised into twelve
numbered *quartiers* or sectors (*see map overleaf*).

HISTORY OF LA DÉFENSE

La Défense is divided in two by the 1.5km-long Axe de la Défense, which is the modern
prolongation of the greatest of all Parisian thoroughfares, planned in the 17th century
as a royal highway between Paris and St-Germain-en-Laye. The project was never
completed, but by 1863 Napoléon III had extended the Avenue de la Grande Armée as

far as Chantecoq hill and placed a statue of Napoleon there. This statue was replaced by Barrias' *La Défense de Paris* (1883), commemorating the defence of the city against the Prussians in 1871, from which the area takes its name. In 1958 a government project to set up a business centre took shape and 750 hectares belonging to the three adjacent communes of Courbevoie, Nanterre and Puteaux were selected. The CNIT (Centre for Industry and Technology), a private initiative, was inaugurated in 1955–8. Its triangular-shaped flat-domed exhibition hall, designed by a group of five architects (Jean Prouvé, Robert Camelot, Jean de Mailly, B.-L. Zehrfuss and Nicolas Esquillan) has the largest concrete vaulted roof in the world. In 1958 a government body was set up to manage La Défense: EPAD (Établissement public pour l'aménagement de la région de la Défense), whose role was defined by government decree. In 1964 the first layout plan was adopted, requiring all the office towers to observe the same rules.

THE BUILDING PHASES OF LA DÉFENSE

Examples of 'first-generation' towers include **Europe** (Place des Corolles; sector 2), **Atlantique** and **Opus 12** or **PB12** (south of Place de La Défense; sector 9); all first-generation towers are due to be replaced or updated.

Between 1965 and 1969 the first skyscraper was erected, designed by Jean de Mailly, who co-drafted the EPAD layout plan of 1964. The completion of the RER rail link assured La Défense's success and the expansion of Nanterre. In 1972 a new layout plan was adopted and 'second-generation' towers were built (**CB21** at the eastern end of sector 2 and **Areva** in sector 6) along with landscaping and the installation of art-works. After a hiatus when the height of the buildings drew criticism, another recovery in 1978–82 allowed EPAD to fund more construction and the 'third-generation' phase began. **Les Quatre-Temps** (sectors 7–8), the largest shopping centre in Europe at the time, opened in 1981, and narrower towers of varying height, such the angular **Pascal Towers** (1983; sector 7) went up. Hotels were built, the Imax Dome (now Ciné Cité) was created, architecture diversified, and La Défense's image changed spectacularly. The CNIT was refurbished, the Métro arrived and most importantly, in 1989, the **Grande Arche** was inaugurated (*see below*).

From 2000 the oldest buildings were becoming obsolete and began to be replaced or remodelled. All new buildings must now conform to environmental standards and there is an increasing commitment to sustainable development. Services have been improved and Société Générale moved in, as did more high-tech companies, improving the district's image. Residential building is increasing and new outdoor events add to the animation of the area. The administration of the site was divided in 2007 between two separate bodies: EPAD retains responsibility for development and Defacto has taken over promotion and public programmes. It aims to make La Défense a gastronomic centre combining great architecture with top-of-the-league chefs and cuisine.

Useful information on the buildings, gardens, artworks and events is available at the Defacto information kiosk in front of the CNIT on the Parvis. They also offer guided walks (book online, numbers limited). T: 01 47 74 84 24, www.ladefense.fr.

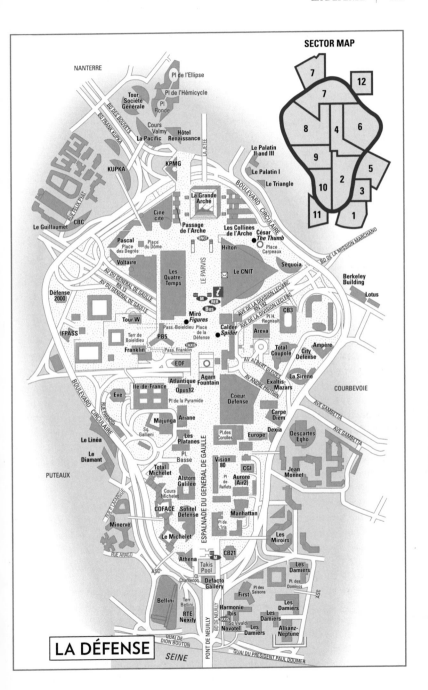

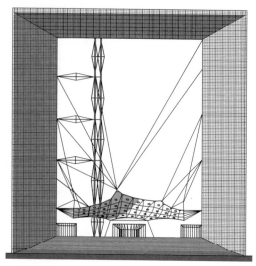

GRANDE ARCHE DE LA DÉFENSE

ARC DE TRIOMPHE

LA GRANDE ARCHE

The focal point of this forest of high-rise structures is La Grande Arche de la Défense (sector 7), inaugurated 1989, which easily dwarfs the historic Arc du Carrousel and the Arc de Triomphe (*NB: because of structural problems, the roof and visitor viewing gallery were closed at the time of writing*). Rather than an arch, it might be better described as a colossal hollow cube. Its design, by the Danish architect Johan Otto von Spreckelsen, was selected by President Mitterrand from 424 submissions. It sits on twelve huge piles which sustain a weight of 300,000 tons and the whole is pivoted very slightly from the main axis of La Défense. The wide flight of steps beneath it is a popular gathering place, over which is suspended a 'cloud' awning.

In front of the Arche is the Parvis de La Défense, a forecourt flanked by the enormous CNIT building to the north and a vast shopping centre, Les Quatre-Temps (1981), to the south. Ahead is the Axe de La Défense, the main historic thoroughfare running east towards Paris; in the opposite direction, behind the Arche, is Nanterre.

TOWERS OF LA DÉFENSE

At the eastern edge of La Défense, north of the Esplanade, stands the **CB21 Tower** (1972–4, 179m; sector 2) by Max Abramovich, which provoked a protest campaign from Parisians because it was visible from the historic centre. In the far north, in sector 12, are the lower-rise **Le Palatin I** (2001), **Le Palatin II and III** (2005) and **Le Triangle de l'Arche** (2001). Between the Arche and the CNIT, on Place Carpeaux (sector 6), building began in 2013 on the ambitious 71-floor **Tour Phare**, with two entwined towers (297m high), designed by the American architect Thom Mayne. Innovative in terms of sustainable development, it will be topped with a forest of wind turbines. As well as office space, it promises a panoramic restaurant and exterior elevators and is due for completion in 2017. It will be just 20m shorter than the Eiffel Tower.

East of the CNIT, in Quartier Coupole-Regnault (sector 6), is **Total Coupole**, Total's HQ, consisting of five superimposed parts up to 187m high, the highest with 49 floors. Just east of it again, the **Exaltis-Mazars Tower** (2006; sector 4) is a 16-storey glass monolith 70m high and 23m wide, with one curved side. The **EDF Tower** (2001) in Quartier Boieldieu on the south side of the Place de la Défense fountain (sector 8), is an elegant elliptical shape. Opposite, in Quartier Corolles (sector 4), is the huge and distinctive multiple complex of **Cœur Défense** (2001), behind which is the 'structural expressionist' **Tour Carpe Diem** (162m, 2013). East of it, close to the ring road, stands **Tour Dexia** (2002–6, altered in 2007, 142m; sector 2), reminiscent of the hull of an ocean liner and one of the few towers with an inclined roof. Its asymmetrical blade-like form changes according to direction of viewing; the monumental entrance is 18m high. The third-generation **Tour Descartes** (1988, also known as Tour Eqho) rising to 130m (40 levels) on the far side of the ring road (sector 5), has aluminium cladding flanking a hollowed-out semi-cylindrical shape.

On the south side of the Axe de la Défense, in Quartier Michelet (sector 10), is **Tour Michelet** (PB17, 117m). Quartier Saisons (sector 1) is the site of **Allianz-Neptune** and the prismatic 231m **Tour First** (formerly AXA, renovated 2007–11). The proposed Hermitage Plaza, a Foster and Partners design, consists of a podium and six buildings of which two towers, of 85 and 86 floors, would reach 323m, the tallest in the European Union. It is scheduled to be finished by 2019.

ARTWORKS IN LA DÉFENSE

Public art in La Défense responds to the space available, to the huge scale and modernity of the architecture, and is at times integral to the buildings and service constructions. For example, Dewasne's colourful geometric *Monumental Fresco* in and around La Grande Arche was created at the behest of the architect and installed gradually, as building work progressed, in fragments over a large area. Covering another large area behind the Arche, is Takis' installation *Light Signals* and beyond that is Richard Serra's *Slat*, five metal sheets 11m high.

West of the CNIT is one of the most iconic pieces, César's steel version of his own *Thumb*, and behind the CNIT is Anthony Caro's monumental sculpture *After Olympia*. Among a wealth of sculpture on the Parvis in front of the Arche is the sparkling *Monumental Light Sculpture* in Swarovski crystal by Lopez and on the façade of Les Quatre-Temps is the botanist Patrick Blanc's *Vegetal Wall*. Behind Les Quatre-Temps is *Place des Degrés*, the work of Piotr Kowalski, on three terraces.

Place de la Défense has Miró's unmistakable *Characters*, Rieti's *Face* and Calder's *Great Red Stabile*, known as the *Spider*. From here is a view down onto the 19th-century monument *Defence of Paris* by Barrias. In the large grassy space is Christine O'Loughlin's *Displaced Arc*, an 'artistic circle' cut out of the lawn, and beyond is the beautiful *Agam Fountain*, with a mosaic of Venetian enamel and 66 jets of water. *La*

Défonce (meaning 'break up') by Morellet is a challenging and brutal metal structure which ironically is placed above the reserve of the National Contemporary Art
Collection, seemingly piercing it.

Esplanade Général de Gaulle, the continuation of the Axe, is lined with disciplined
plane trees. On the south side, Place Basse is a small square with clipped evergreen
oaks and Mediterranean and Chinese shrubs in tubs in the shape of female heads.
Around this area are Guy-Rachel Grataloup's huge mosaic column ***Three Trees*** and
Édouard François' ***Vegetable Chimney***, both of which ingeniously mask utility constructions. In sector 10 is Bernar Venet's ***Two Indeterminate Lines***, an elegant 3D
steel doodle inscribed on the sky, and in Quartier Reflets (sector 2) to the north of the
Axe is Moretti's ***Le Moretti***, a 32m-high ventilation shaft stunningly transformed by
672 fibreglass tubes in different colours; Jakober's ***BC1*** is an assembly of solid tubes
of iron bent into the shape of an American footballer's helmet and at the eastern end
of the Axe, the 49 multi-coloured lights at different heights reflect in the ***Takis Pool***.
Close by is the **Defacto Gallery**. Vines are cultivated in the **Clos de Chantecoq**.

NANTERRE

West of the Grande Arche is Nanterre (*map p. 577, B2*), an extensive development
which incorporates the 25-hectare Parc André-Malraux, the largest park created in
Paris since the beginning of the 21st century, using soil extracted from La Défense
when its towers were constructed. The Paris West University Nanterre La Défense,
established in 1960 as one of the 13 successors to the University of Paris, was where
student unrest famously began in 1968. St Geneviève was born in Nanterre in 423.

THE BOIS DE BOULOGNE

Map pp. 578, A2 and 584, A1. Métro 1 and RER C to Porte Maillot; Métro 2 to Porte
Dauphine; RER C to Avenue Foch; Métro 10 to Porte d'Auteuil.

The Bois de Boulogne, at 846 hectares, is slightly smaller but much better known than
its counterpart at the opposite side of the city, the Bois de Vincennes (*see p. 516*). It
encompasses gardens, lakes and the Longchamp and the Auteuil racecourses. The suburb of Boulogne-Billancourt lies to the south. To the west is the Seine, on the far side of
which rise the hills of Mont Valérien, St-Cloud, Bellevue and Meudon. There are four
main entrances to the Bois from central Paris: Porte Maillot (northeast corner); Porte
Dauphine (western end of Av. Foch); Porte de la Muette (southern end of Av. Victor-
Hugo); and Porte d'Auteuil (southeast corner). Between the last two is the subsidiary
Porte de Passy. The Bois is divided diagonally by the long Allée de Longchamp, leading
southwest from Porte Maillot towards Carrefour de Longchamp, a popular equestrian
rendezvous. There are 28km of tracks for horse riders, 15km for cyclists, and a circuit
of 2.5km for joggers. It has two lakes, ponds and streams.

BOIS DE BOULOGNE
Enjoying the paper on a tranquil bench.

HISTORY OF THE BOIS DE BOULOGNE

The Bois de Boulogne is a tiny remnant of the Forest of Rouvray, part of the band of woodland once surrounding ancient *Lutetia* which became a hunting ground for the kings of France. Although the châteaux of La Muette, Madrid and Bagatelle, and the Abbey of Longchamp were erected on its periphery, the Bois was neglected until the mid-19th century. Quantities of timber went for firewood during the Revolution and a large part of the Allied army of occupation bivouacked here after Waterloo. It was the haunt of footpads and often the scene of suicides and duels. Parts of the Bois today are well known as a cruising ground. In 1852 the Bois was handed over by the state to the City, tamed, landscaped and subdivided into an extensive park, becoming a favourite promenade for Parisians. The model was Hyde Park in London, which had so impressed Napoléon III. More trees were felled in 1870 to reduce protective cover for the Prussians. Now the Boulevard Périphérique tunnels below the eastern and southern edges of the Bois, which is bounded on the north by Neuilly.

PARC AND CHÂTEAU DE BAGATELLE

Map p. 577, B2. Garden open May–Sept daily 9.30–8, Oct daily 9.30–6.30; admission charge. Château open during temporary exhibitions in summer 11–6, winter 11–4.30. Guided tour of the château 3pm Sun and public holidays; T: 01 45 01 20 10. Métro 1 to Porte Maillot then bus 244 to Bagatelle; buses 43 from Gare du Nord (direction Neuilly) or 93 from Pont des Invalides (direction Suresnes) to Place de Bagatelle.

Skirted by the Route de Sèvres at Neuilly are the walls of the **Parc de Bagatelle** (24 hectares), a delightful and well-tended oasis made up of several gardens in different styles but most famous for its rose garden, at its best in mid-June, when the annual International New Rose competition takes place in the Orangerie. Earlier in the year it is carpeted with spring flowers and later it has a display of asters. Concerts are held here. Landscaped, with a wide selection of trees, as well as follies, streams, waterfalls and lakes, the planting shows the influence of the Impressionists' preference for massed blooms (J.-C.-N. Forestier, the garden conservator in 1905, was a friend of Monet).

The small and elegant **Château de Bagatelle**, a *folie* or country residence, was built for a wager within 64 days in 1779 by Bélanger for the Comte d'Artois, later Charles X. Napoleon afterwards occupied it and in 1815 it returned to the Comte d'Artois, before passing to the Duc de Berry. Purchased in 1835 by the English eccentric Richard Seymour-Conway, 4th Marquess of Hertford (who added the dome in 1852), it passed on his death in 1870 to his natural son Sir Richard Wallace, together with its fine art collection and the apartments at no. 1 Rue Laffitte and no. 2 Rue Taitbout, where Seymour-Conway also collected art treasures. Created baronet in 1871, Richard Wallace became a Member of Parliament in 1873 and took up residence in London, taking with him much of his art collection. A great benefactor of Paris, he provided 50 drinking-water fountains (*see p. 319*) and also built the Anglican church of St George (1887–8) in Rue Auguste-Vacquerie (*map p. 580, B4*). He was buried in Père-Lachaise. In 1890 Lady Wallace inherited Sir Richard's property, and bequeathed the English collection to

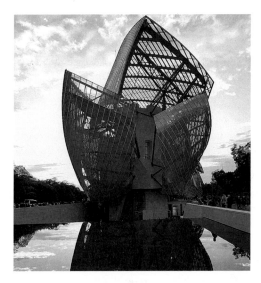

BOIS DE BOULOGNE
Frank Gehry's Fondation Louis Vuitton.

the Wallace Collection in London and the French property, including the contents of Bagatelle and Rue Laffitte, to her adviser, John Murray Scott. Bagatelle was acquired by the City of Paris in 1904. The contents of Rue Laffitte went via Lady Sackville of Knole to a Parisian dealer, thus ultimately dispersing the art collections throughout the world.

LOUIS VUITTON FOUNDATION FOR CREATION

Map p. 578, A2. Métro 1 to Les Sablons-Jardins d'Acclimatation. Open Mon, Wed, Thur 12–7, Fri 12–11, Sat–Sun 11–8; closed Tues. Ticket also gives access to the Jardin d'Acclimatation. Shuttle bus (navette) every 15mins from Place Charles de Gaulle/Av. Friedland (near Métro exit) daily 12–7 (except Tues when Fondation is closed).

This unique structure by Frank Gehry, with billowing roofs of glass, wood and steel, floats above the treetops of the Bois de Boulogne which are reflected in a specially-created water feature. Opened in 2014, it is home to the Louis Vuitton permanent collection of contemporary art and hosts temporary exhibitions, concerts and debates, particularly aimed at young people. The twelve glass sails (some clear, some cloudy) are firmly anchored to eleven white concrete galleries although the impression produced is that everything is floating. The modular auditorium has glass walls bringing interior and exterior together, and from the rooftop terrace Paris is seen from a new angle. The building achieves Gehry's aim to create a 'magnificent vessel for Paris' and is also designed to display the wealth and taste of the corporation and its chairman, Bernard Arnault. The permanent collection includes works by Christian Boltanski, Giacometti, Mona Hatoum, Nam June Paik and many others. This is the first major privately-funded cultural institution in France and will pass to the City of Paris in 2061; above the entrance is the logo of LVMH (also designed by Gehry).

OTHER SIGHTS IN THE BOIS DE BOULOGNE

The **Hippodrome de Longchamp** (*beyond map p. 578, A2*) opened in 1857. To the north of it, a windmill (restored) is almost the only relic of the Abbey of Longchamp, founded in 1256 by St Isabelle of France, sister of Louis IX.

From the Carrefour de Longchamp (just east of the windmill), a road leads due east past the **Grande Cascade** (an artificial waterfall) to skirt the enclosure of the **Pré-Catelan** (according to legend, named after the troubadour Arnaud Catelan, murdered here c. 1300 by bandits who believed that he was carrying gold. When they opened his pack, all they found were *herbes de Provence*). The **Jardin Shakespeare** has specimens of plants and trees mentioned in Shakespeare's plays and an open-air theatre which stages performances for adults and children. Further east are buildings of the Racing Club de France, flanking the west bank of the **Lac Inférieur** (*map p. 578, A2*), the larger lake, with two linked islands. Boats may be hired on the east bank. To the south is the **Lac Supérieur**, beyond the Carrefour des Cascades; in the southeast corner of the Bois is the **Hippodrome d'Auteuil** (steeplechasing).

NEUILLY-SUR-SEINE

Map p. 578, A1. Métro 1 to Porte Maillot.

From the Arc de Triomphe, Avenue de la Grande Armée descends northwest to Porte Maillot, a great meeting of principal routes and the site of extensive blocks of buildings. Beyond it, the wide Avenue Charles-de-Gaulle bisects Neuilly-sur-Seine, once the most fashionable suburb of Paris. Part of the district covers the park of Louis-Philippe's former château (burned down in 1848), which was developed as a colony of elegant villas, although later apartment blocks temper the distinctive character of the neighbourhood. In the old **cemetery** lie Anatole France and André Maurois and in the **Cimetière de Levallois-Perret** (*map p. 578, B1*), the suburb north of Neuilly, are the tombs of the revolutionary anarchist and Communard Louise Michel (d. 1905) and the composer Maurice Ravel (d. 1937).

ÎLE DE LA GRANDE JATTE
Map p. 578, A1. Métro 3 to Pont de Levallois-Bécon. Follow Rue Anatole France towards the Seine, bear left and walk along the embankment to the footbridge from where steps lead down to island.

Spanning the *quartiers* of Neuilly and Levallois-Perret, on the edge of Paris, the Île de la Grande Jatte is the setting for Seurat's famous painting of 1884, *Sunday Afternoon on La Grande Jatte* (in Chicago) and Sondheim's musical *Sunday in the Park with George.* Much of the island is now occupied by expensive homes, and large houseboats are moored here, but there is still a green area shaded by large trees and it is a pleasant place for a stroll. At the Levallois end are beehives, the bee being the symbol of Levallois.

EATING AND DRINKING IN LA DÉFENSE, THE BOIS DE BOULOGNE AND NEUILLY

BOIS DE BOULOGNE

€€ **Le Frank**. At the Fondation Louis Vuitton, under the auspices of award-winning chef Jean-Louis Nomicos. Open Wed–Mon noon–7pm, Wed and Thur dinner by reservation only, Fri–Sat late-night opening; closed Tues. *T: 01 58 44 25 70, contact@restaurant-frank.fr, www.restaurantlefrank.fr. Map p. 578, A2.*

€€€ **Le Pré Catelan**. This famous three-Michelin-rosette restaurant inhabits a Napoléon-III pavilion and orangery set in beautiful gardens in the Bois de Boulogne. Top chef Frédéric Anton is renowned for top-class modern French cooking and minute attention to combinations of flavours. A very special place. *Route de Surenes. T: 01 44 14 41 1, www.restaurant-precatelan.com. Map p. 578, A2.*

LA DÉFENSE

There are numerous fast-food and takeaway outlets open during the day, but at night everything closes. The major hotels (Mercure, Sofitel, Hilton and Renaissance) have good restaurants, often busy with business lunches. On the Parvis de La Défense there are many food outlets such as Café Moutarde, Les Quatre-Temps, Lavinia, Daily Monop, and others. In Courbevoie is €€ **Le Tournesol** *(65bis Av. Gambetta. T: 01 47 89 07 40, www.restaurant-letournesol.com; map p. 578, A1)* run by Thierry Chauvel who did his apprenticeship with several starred chefs. The cuisine is traditional with seasonal variations. Also in Courbevoie, in La Défense, is €€ **Le Mond**, which does a *formule express* and set lunch menu (*1 Place des Corolles, T: 01 47 75 97 11, www.le-mond.com; map p. 443*).

NEUILLY/GRANDE JATTE

There are places to eat on the island (*map p. 578, A1*), including the bistrot **La Guinguette de Neuilly** (*Blvd Georges Seurat, T: 01 46 24 25 04, www.la-guinguette-de-neuilly.com*) and Café de la Jatte, with a terrace (*60 Blvd Vital Bouhot, T: 01 47 45 19 32, cafejatte.com*).

€ **L'Entredgeu**. A small, authentic bistro just inside the Périphérique, with choices on the slate and good-value lunches. *83 Rue Laugier (close to Porte de Champerret métro). T: 01 40 54 97 24. Map p. 580, A1.*

Hauts-de-Seine

Southwest of central Paris, beyond the Périphérique, excursions can be made to
a former home of Napoleon and Josephine at Rueil-Malmaison, three buildings by
Le Corbusier, the royal park at St-Cloud, Sèvres, the home of fine porcelain,
Rodin's studio at Meudon and the Château de Sceaux.

RUEIL-MALMAISON

Map p. 577, B2. RER A to Rueil-Malmaison (Zone 3; make sure you get on a St-Germain-en-Laye train) and then bus 27 to Église de Rueil (for the town centre) or direct to Le Château. Or bus 258 from La Défense to Le Château. Information office at 33 Rue Jean le Coz. Open Mon–Tues 10–12.30 & 1.30–6, Wed–Fri 10–12 & 1.30–5. T: 01 47 32 35 75, www.rueil-tourisme.com.

Rueil-Malmaison, on the banks of the Seine west of Paris, has close associations with the early Empire period through the châteaux of Malmaison and Bois-Préau. This is an attractive town offering pleasant outdoor visits, including a Japanese garden, walks along the Seine and to the Second World War memorial on Mont-Valérien, as well as 850 hectares of wildlife parkland.

MUSÉE NATIONAL DU CHÂTEAU DE MALMAISON

Open April–Sept Mon 10–12.30 & 1.30–5.45, Sat–Sun 10–12.30 & 1.30–6.15; Oct–March Mon and Wed–Fri 10–12.30 & 1.30–5.15, Sat–Sun 10–12.30 & 1.30–5.45. Closed Tues. Audioguides. Park open 10–6. T: 01 41 29 05 55, www.chateau-malmaison.fr.

The château was built c. 1620 and became, from 1799, the country residence of Napoleon and Josephine, who chose it for the park which then covered 800 hectares, with the intention of rebuilding the house. Napoleon considered that the best days of his life were spent here, when all was going well, in the large country house which became an official residence. The work of transforming the interior was entrusted to Fontaine and Percier.

Joséphine (Marie-Josèphe Rose) Tascher de la Pagerie was born in Martinique in 1763, the daughter of a nobleman. She had married Alexandre, Vicomte de Beauharnais, in December 1779; he was guillotined in 1794. In 1796 she married Bonaparte, who crowned her Empress in 1804. Josephine retired here with her children, after her

CHÂTEAU DE MALMAISON
Portrait of the Empress Josephine, by Gérard.

divorce in December 1809, and continued to develop her passion for botany and gardening. She died at Malmaison five years later of a chill caught while entertaining visiting allied sovereigns. Malmaison was later purchased by María Cristina of Spain, but in 1861 Josephine's grandson, Napoléon III, bought back the despoiled château with the intention of restoring it. It was sold again in 1896 to the philanthropist Daniel Iffla, known as Osiris, who presented it refurbished to the state as a Napoleonic museum.

THE MUSEUM

Malmaison's collections concentrate on the earlier Napoleonic period, the Consulate and on Josephine and her two children by her first husband: Eugène and Hortense, mother of Napoléon III. On display are paintings, furniture and fittings, carpets, porcelain, silver and clocks (all in working order) of the early Napoleonic period. There are several pieces of furniture made specifically for the Consul and his wife by Jacob Frères and other *ébenistes*, and such personal pieces as Josephine's bed (designed by Jacob-Desmalter), dressing-table, dressing case and embroidery frame. Showcases display a large number of smaller mementoes. All the rooms on the ground floor were returned to their former character according to Fontaine and Percier's original drawings for the interior. Restoration work in the 1980s recreated the original Neoclassical décor by the painstaking removal of up to eight layers of paint, followed by retouching where necessary. The antechamber of the Salon was restored in 2003.

Ground floor: The entrance is through an enclosed porch or vestibule in the form of a tent, which was added in 1800. The Main Hall, on the ground floor, in antique style, contains marble busts of the Bonaparte family; further busts are displayed throughout the building.

The paint on the moulded panels of the **Billiard Room**, installed in 1812, was stripped back to the original dark green picked out in purple-red, which contrasts with the earth colours of the shutters. It is furnished with stools by Jacob-Desmalter, card tables and an Empire-style billiard table from Burgundy. In the **Drawing Room** (*Salon Doré*), combining decorative schemes of 1800 and 1810–11, are armchairs by Jacob Frères in blue and gold (c. 1800) decorated with Egyptian heads. Other chairs come from the Palais de St-Cloud. Romantic-style paintings by Gérard and Girodet were inspired by the poems of Ossian.

Published in 1761–5, these poems purported to be written by a mythical Gaelic bard and inspired many a 19th-century northern European painter and writer; in fact they were the work of the Scots poet James Macpherson.

The delightful **Music Room** contains Josephine's harp and the pianoforte that belonged to Hortense. In Josephine's day the room was used as a gallery, especially for troubadour-style pictures as depicted in the painting by Garneray. From the window can be seen the famous cedar planted by Josephine to celebrate the victory of Marengo in 1800. On the left of the Main Hall, the **Dining Room** has a splendid floor of black and white marble, frescoes of dancers by Louis Lafitte inspired by Pompeii, and two Thomire candlelabra.

The **Council Chamber**, the setting for the creation of the Legion of Honour, has been returned to its original design by Percier of a military tent. It contains a portrait of the Emperor's mother and a copy of *Joséphine Seated* (1801) by Gérard (the original is in the Hermitage). The rotating chair is from the Emperor's study at the Tuileries.

The elegant **Library** has around 500 books retrieved from Napoleon's personal collection of some 4,500, a travelling chest for books used during his campaigns, and a desk by Jacob Frères. At the foot of the stairs is a *Head of Napoleon* by Canova.

First floor: The **Emperor's Apartments**, in part reconstructed, display various memorabilia and the draped bedroom replicates the original as far as possible and contains an Empire-style timepiece, *'Oblivion of Time'*, by Claude Galle. In the Marengo Room is *Napoleon Bonaparte Reviewing his Troops after the Battle of Marengo* by Gros. Gros' painting of Josephine (c. 1809) shows the park of Malmaison. Also here is David's original painting of *Bonaparte Crossing the St-Bernard Pass* (there are five other versions elsewhere), signed on the harness *'L. David, l'an IX'* (1800). This great propagandist work shows the First Consul on a rearing white charger (Bonaparte in fact crossed the Alps on a mule). Beneath the horse's feet, etched into the rock, is the name of a famous predecessor across the Alps: Hannibal. The Vienna version of the painting bears the name Charlemagne in this location. Here too is one of Napoleon's grey coats, as worn at St Helena, and his *nécessaire de toilette*.

The **Empress's Bedroom** was redesigned after her divorce in 1812 while she was absent in Milan. The result is an unusual but elegant red and gold tent-like 16-sided room with many mirrors to brighten it. The only original piece is the bed by Jacob-Desmalter. This was shared by the couple until 1803 and is where Josephine died on 24th May 1814, when she was 51. The fireside chairs, known as *paumiers*, have one armrest lower than the other to benefit from the warmth of the fire. There is also a mahogany paper tidy. The display of luxury items in a room created from the apartments of Prince Eugène and Queen Hortense (Napoleon had married her to his brother Louis, whom he created King of Holland) include many mementoes such as a table service with a design of exotic plants (1807) and a double service of some 50 pieces commissioned by the Empress and her son from the porcelain manufacturer of Dihl et Guerhard. The two firedogs (late 18th century) are from Napoleon and Josephine's first residence in Paris, the Hôtel de la Victoire.

The **Empress's Private Bedroom**, which she preferred, is an altogether brighter and lighter room. The *nécessaire* for keeping small articles, such as her jewels, and looked after by her senior lady-in-waiting, was made by Martin-Guillaume Biennais, whose shop, the Violet Monkey, was well known in Paris. The box is decorated with polished steel rosettes and linked by a pearl latticework set in facetted steel, fashionable at the time. The octagonal **Boudoir**, easy to keep warm, was a favourite of Josephine's and was used as a small dining room when only one or two people were present.

Second floor: The **Frieze Room** has a bed and a night table in mahogany which belonged to Hortense and the frieze is from the salon of the *hôtel* on Rue de la Victoire in Paris. There are also two tables and several pieces of furniture from the Tuileries.

The **Wardrobe Room** still has the cupboards which were made for the Empress. She had a passion for clothes and luxury goods and owned huge numbers of garments which were regularly sorted. Those no longer to her taste were discarded.

THE PARK

Only six hectares remain of the original 200 hectares of gardens. Josephine was an enthusiastic horticulturalist and passionate about roses, which she had gathered from all over the world for Malmaison. Until 1805 she was helped by an English gardener, Mr Howatson. The gardens were celebrated in their time and the blooms were later reproduced in coloured drawings by Pierre-Joseph Redouté. For the bicentenary of her death the beds were replanted with 750 bushes of the varieties that she had selected.

The **Pavillon Osiris** (*included in the visit; open as the Château*) houses an eclectic collection of fine arts and decorative arts typical of late 19th-century collections in Paris.

Beyond the other side of the entrance drive is a **summer house**, used as a study by Napoleon when First Consul. To the left of the entrance lodge, on the way out, is the old coach house (*closed*).

CHÂTEAU DE BOIS-PRÉAU AND PETITE MALMAISON

The Château de Bois-Préau (*closed for restoration at the time of writing; T: 01 41 29 05 55; park open Wed–Mon 9.30–8 in summer, 9.30–6 in winter*) dates from 1700 and was acquired by Josephine in 1810 as an annexe in which to accommodate her entourage and visitors and to house part of her collections. It was later sold and in 1926 bequeathed to the state by its American owner, the millionaire Edward Tuck. The **Petite Malmaison** (*visits by appointment at 229bis Av. Napoléon-Bonaparte, T: 01 47 49 48 15, petitemalmaison.fr*), now privately owned, was constructed in 1805 for Josephine as a place to receive and entertain visitors when they visited the greenhouses, which were originally attached but no longer exist.

RUEIL-MALMAISON TOWN

In the **church of St-Pierre-Saint-Paul** (1584, west façade of 1635 by Lemercier) is the Carrara marble tomb of the Empress Josephine (1825); that of Hortense de Beauharnais is in the chapel erected in 1858 by her son, Napoléon III. He also donated the 15th-century Florentine organ case by Baccio d'Agnolo.

Atelier Grognard, very close to the château (*6 Av. du Château de Malmaison, T: 01 47 14 11 63*), holds temporary art exhibitions. In the former Mairie, a handsome building in brick and stone, is a **Museum of Local History** (*Rue Paul Vaillant-Couturier, open Mon–Sat 2.30–6; closed Sun and Aug, T: 01 47 32 66 50*) with items ranging from the Neolithic era to the time when the Impressionists patronised the *guinguettes* on the banks and the islands of the Seine nearby. A footpath follows the Seine from Gennevilliers to Bougival passing the scenes that they painted. There is also a museum of the Swiss Guard (*visits by appointment*).

ÎLE DE CHATOU

Rueil 2000 is an attractive modern area on the banks of the Seine looking out towards the **Île de Chatou** (*map p. 577, B2*), also known as the Île des Impressionnistes. The island became popular with young Parisians from the 1860s for boating and bathing. Among the visitors were some of the Impressionist painters who captured scenes of the island and its rowing enthusiasts. Among them were Caillebotte and Renoir: the island was the setting for Renoir's *Le Déjeuner des canotiers* (1881, Washington), the famous scene of a boating party sitting around a lunch table. A main attraction of the island was the Maison Fournaise, a *guinguette*, but once this closed Châtou was gradually abandoned. However, in 1980 it was reanimated when the Parc des Impressionistes was created and the Restaurant Fournaise opened (*see p. 465*).

Just beyond Rueil, at **Bougival** on the Seine, is the house where Georges Bizet died in 1875 as well as the dacha built by the Russian novelist Ivan Turgenev (*open Sat 2–6, Sun 10–6; T: 01 39 18 22 30/06 08 58 18 94, www.tourgueniev.fr*). He died of cancer here in 1883, urging his arch rival Tolstoy to 'return to literature'.

BOULOGNE-BILLANCOURT

Map p. 577, B2. Metro 9 to Marcel-Sembat, or 10 to Boulogne-Jean-Jaurès. Information office at 25 Av. André-Morizet, open Mon 2–6.30, Tues–Fri 9.30–6.30, Sat 9.30–1, closed Sun; T: 01 41 41 54 54, www.otbb.org.

Boulogne-Billancourt, known as such since 1925, is celebrated as the town of the Modern Movement because of the remarkable concentration of buildings of the 1920s and '30s. The automobile (Renault, in 1898) and aeronautical industries took root in the area, but in the 1920s it was still empty and inexpensive, and as the Métro had just extended this far, it was an attractive prospect for artists and architects making their name: Juan Gris and Chagall, Landowski and Lipchitz, Le Corbusier, Auguste Perret, Robert Mallet-Stevens and Tony Garnier. The film industry was represented by Abel Gance and Jean Renoir. André Malraux lived here for 17 years.

The **Parcours des Années 30** is an architectural walk—or cycle ride—past the best of the Modernist buildings (*booklet available from the Tourist Office, the Musée des Années 30, or download online*). Around Rue Denfert-Rochereau are buildings by L.-R. Fischer, Le Corbusier and Robert Mallet-Stevens; at the corner of Rue des Arts and Allée des Pins are two *résidences-ateliers* of 1924 by Le Corbusier; and there are more examples of experimental architecture of the 1920s by Auguste Perret and André Lurçat in Rue du Belvédère. In Rue Nungesser-et-Coli (near Parc des Princes) is an apartment block (1932) by Le Corbusier. The Musée-Jardin Paul-Landowski at 14 Rue Max-Blondat (*T: 01 46 05 82 69*) is included in the route.

MUSÉE DES ANNÉES 30-ÉSPACE LANDOWSKI

28 Av. André-Morizet. Open Tues–Sun 11–6, closed Mon, holidays and last two weeks of Aug. T: 01 55 18 53 00 and 01 55 18 46 42, www.annees30.com.

This museum of the Art Deco era is in the old Hôtel des Postes (1938) by Charles Giroud. It has a rare collection of Neoclassical and avant-garde works of the inter-war period covering most disciplines and reflects the artistic and industrial heritage of Boulogne-Billancourt which developed at the time. The Central European artists of the School of Paris are also well represented; the art dealer who supported them, Henry Kahnweiler, lived in the town at 12 Rue de l'Ancienne-Mairie. There are some 800 paintings by artists such as Boutet de Monvel, who painted in a naïve style, and Tamara de Lempicka, who is best known for her portraits of women. There are also many landscapes by Henry de Waroquier, the result of his travels in Spain and Italy in the early 1920s, and sculpture is well represented with about 1,500 pieces by artists such as Belmondo and the monumental sculptor Paul Landowski, as well as the Art Deco sculptor Alfred Janniot. The decorative arts include a glass screen by L. Barillet in the white glass that he pioneered, a chaise longue by Jean Prouvé and chairs designed by Kahnweiler and Juan Gris. There is also a collection of decorative objects, furniture, ceramics and maquettes of buildings, and interior designs by Émile-Jacques Ruhlmann.

MUSÉE ALBERT KAHN

14 Rue du Port. Métro 10 to Boulogne-Pont de St-Cloud, then bus 52, 72, 126, 160, 175, 460 or 467 to Rond-Point Rhin et Danube. Open May–Sept Tues–Sun 11–7, Oct–April Tues–Sun 11–6; closed Mon and holidays. T: 01 55 19 28 00.

The Musée Albert Kahn has a collection of early photographs, *Archives of the Planet*, and a garden which presents a variety of international landscapes.

Albert Kahn (1860–1940), banker and humanist, lived here between the two wars. His vision was to create a utopia where all nations might coexist and communicate in perfect harmony through deeper knowledge and understanding. Such was his wealth that he was able to finance photographic and film records of the customs and environments of about 50 countries between 1900 and 1931. The result amounts to 72,000 autochrome images—the earliest colour photography—on glass plates, 4,000 black and white images, and around 183,000m of black and white filmed sequences, all of which form a remarkable and precious record (as well as frequently being beautiful images in themselves) and include China in 1905, Ireland in 1913 and Patagonia in the early 20th century. Annual exhibitions draw on the collections, which can also be viewed on interactive terminals. Kahn was ruined by the stock market crash in 1929.

His garden, the **Jardin du Monde**, covers 3.9 hectares, landscaped between 1895 and 1920, and continues the theme of bringing nations together. The informal English garden is juxtaposed with the formal French one, a palmarium and a rose and fruit garden. Beyond are wooded landscapes representing the Vosges and the North American Blue Forest divided by prairie and swamp. Close to the gallery are Kahn's original Japanese Village and a modern Japanese Garden (1990) which evokes Mount Fuji and symbolically represents the life of Albert Kahn himself.

DOMAINE NATIONAL DE SAINT-CLOUD

Map p. 577, B2. Métro 9 to Pont de Sèvres or 10 to Boulogne-Pont de St-Cloud. Open daily May–Aug 7.30–10, March–April and Sept–Oct 7.30–9, Nov–Feb 7.30–8. Museum open Wed, Sat and Sun 2–6. T: 01 41 12 02 90.

The great park of St-Cloud (460 hectares) is on a ridge overlooking Paris, with grand prospects and sophisticated cascades and fountains. Philippe d'Orléans (Monsieur), younger brother of Louis XIV, employed Lepautre and Hardouin-Mansart to design a palace and fountains and Le Nôtre to create the gardens. In 1785 it was sold it to Marie-Antoinette, who transformed it. The château was fired by the Commune in 1870 and razed in 1891, by which time the estate was enclosed in walls and wrought-iron railings.

The site of the vanished château is marked out on the terrace with flowerbeds and yews. To the north is the English-style **Jardin de Trocadéro** with a small lake, created at the time of Louis XVIII, and in the opposite direction is the **Bassin du Fer à Cheval**, extended by an alley to a green amphitheatre created in the 18th century. Below the château terrace is a large pond that serves as reservoir for the **Grande Cascade**. This magnificent example of hydraulic magic, using only gravity, is brought to life on Sundays in June. The upper part of the cascade, all of which is decorated with sculptures of figures, sea monsters, masks and *rocailles*, was the work of Le Pautre in 1660–5 and the lower part was by Hardouin-Mansart in 1698–9. Not far from here is the **Grand Jet**, which dates back to the 16th century, and a fountain with six nymphs. To the west, beyond the terrace, is a fountain with 24 water jets, long perspectives, alleys, more basins, fountains and woodland. There is a small **museum** of the history of the Château. St-Cloud's porcelain factory, which produced the first soft-paste porcelain at the end of the 17th century, burned down during Prussian occupation of 1870–1.

SÈVRES

Map p. 577, B2. Information office: Hotel de Ville, 54 Grande Rue; open Mon–Fri 8.30–12.30 & 1.30–5.40, Sat 8.30–12. T: 01 41 14 10 10, www.ville-sevres.fr.

Sèvres is a pleasant town on the banks of the Seine which has retained something of a village atmosphere. Illustrious residents have included Sisley, Balzac, Eiffel and Gambetta. Once an important port on the Seine, it is now most closely associated with the Manufacture de Sèvres, which is both factory and museum of glass and porcelain.

SÈVRES, CITÉ DE LA CÉRAMIQUE

2 Pl. de la Manufacture. Métro 9 to Pont de Sèvres and a short walk (or bus) across the bridge; Tramway T2 from La Défense. Open Wed–Mon 10–5; closed Tues, 1 Jan, 1 May,

25 Dec. Guided visits to the permanent collection and temporary exhibitions, as well as to the workshops (book in advance, T: 01 46 29 22 05, visite@sevresciteceramique.fr). Also themed visits on Mon (no reservation necessary). A free app in French and English introduces 26 works; and a selection of works have a QR code for smartphone or tablet. Shop selling replicas and modern pieces. T: 01 46 29 22 05, www.sevrescitedeceramique.fr.

The porcelain factory founded in 1740 at Vincennes was transferred to Sèvres in 1756 and has been state-controlled since 1760. It continues to produce high-quality objects manually, and contemporary designs count for over 50 percent of the production. The museum was established in 1824 by Alexandre Brongniart, director of the factory in 1800–47, who followed his father Théodore and combined the national museum and the national manufactory. The idea behind the museum was to collect wide-ranging samples as an inspiration for production, and these later developed into a collection. The collection gathered pace in the 19th century, stimulated by an increasing number of excavations of sites where ancient pottery was uncovered, as well as universal exhibitions bringing in new ideas. In 2010 it became the Cité de la Céramique and in 2012 the Musée National de Porcelaine Dubouché in Limoges came under its wing. Among the multitude of artists and designers associated with Sèvres production are Boucher, Rodin, Calder, Poliakoff and Louise Bourgeois.

This vast collection conserves and exhibits the '*arts du feu*' (fired arts', i.e. anything made of fired clay, including glass). Porous ceramics include faïence, pottery and terracotta, which can be rendered watertight by the use of a glaze. Stoneware and porcelain, using a vitreous paste with a high content of silica, are watertight. Examples come from many parts of the world, from the earliest times to the present day, covering Europe, the Islamic world, Asia and the Americas.

EUROPEAN EARTHENWARE, FAÏENCE AND MAJOLICA

The technique for making faïence was originally developed in Baghdad in the 9th century and was introduced into Spain by Arab potters. It was used to imitate Chinese porcelain before kaolin was found in Europe. Faïence combined with a metallic glaze in 15th-century Spain spread through Europe, and became known as majolica through the 16th century. Italy had been an important centre of faïence since the mid-14th century (the name in fact derives from Faenza, a town in the Po valley). Faïence was adopted by the Della Robbia dynasty of ceramicists and in Delft by producers of tiles and tulip-vases patterned in blue. Production at Nevers in France can be traced from the end of the 17th century. Louis Poterat at Rouen produced the first soft-paste porcelain (*porcelain tendre*) in France, followed by St-Cloud (late 17th century/ early 18th century). The process spread to Chantilly (between 1730 and 1745) and to Mennecy. The presentation here highlights the evolution of designs and colours at Vincennes (later Sèvres), the foremost centre of French production. English soft-paste porcelain, pioneered in England at Bow, is known as bone china as it contained animal bone; and statuettes made at the Chelsea factory became very popular.

The first European manufacturer to discover true porcelain was Meissen (Germany), launching hard-paste porcelain in 1710, made from a mixture of feldspar and kaolin ('china clay'). The recipe remained a secret and when Maria Amalia, grand-daughter of Augustus the Strong, founder of the Meissen manufactory, set up the Capodimonte works in Naples in 1739, the ware that they produced was soft-paste porcelain. In France the history of hard-paste porcelain started in 1768 with the discovery of kaolin at St-Yrieix, near Limoges. Among notable commissions from Sèvres was the service of 65 pieces for Marie-Antoinette's dairy at Rambouillet (1787–8; only 17 pieces have survived). By 1804 Alexandre Brongniart had abandoned the production of soft-paste porcelain. Representative at the turn of the century was the production by Parisian factories, notably Dagoty, of porcelain in a refined Neoclassical style, much favoured by Empress Josephine, such as the Pompeian Service (c. 1810), with a frieze of gold birds on a dark ground.

Changes in taste from the end of the 19th century led to the traditional manufactories of Sèvres, Limoges and Meissen being replaced by a large number of individual workshops such as Pusaye, Berry, Savoie and Mâconnais. In the 20th century individual practice was encouraged by Bernard Leach's *A Potter's Book* and communities of potters gathered in villages such as Vallauris, where Picasso worked in 1947, which opened the way to artists such as Alechinsky, Jean Arp, Calder, Arman and Pierre Soulages, who were welcomed to Sèvres in the 1960s. The contemporary collection continues to grow.

MAISON JARDIES (MUSÉE LÉON GAMBETTA) & VILLE D'AVRAY

Train from Gare St-Lazare or Métro 9 to Ville d'Avray (map p. 577, B2). Villa Jardies, Gambetta's house, is a 5-min walk from the station at 14 Av. Gambetta. Open Thur and Fri 2.30–6.30 and alternate weekends. T: 01 45 34 61 22, www.maisonjardies.monuments-nationaux.fr.

In Sèvres (off the N10 towards Ville d'Avray) is the Maison des Jardies, now the **Léon Gambetta Museum**. The small 17th-century house was originally built by a wine-grower. Some 40 years after Balzac stayed there, Léon Gambetta became the owner. He made very few alterations and it is now preserved as it was when inhabited by the man who proclaimed the Republic in 1870. Gambetta died here in 1882. A monument to him by Bartholdi was erected in 1891 in the garden.

The 18th-century church of **St-Marc-St-Nicolas** in Ville d'Avray contains frescoes by Corot, who often painted the lakes in the Bois de Fausses Reposes, further to the southwest.

MEUDON-SUR-SEINE

Map p. 577, B3. RER C to Meudon Val Fleury (Zone 3), then bus 169 for one stop and walk along Av. Rodin. You can also simply walk from the RER station (about 20mins).

Meudon, whose benefice Rabelais enjoyed in 1551–2 and where Wagner wrote *The Flying Dutchman* in 1841, is visited chiefly for the **Musée-Atelier de Rodin** (*open Fri–Sun 1–5; T: 01 41 14 35 00*). Rodin lived at the modest Villa des Brillants with Rose Beuret, from 1895 until his death in 1917. The Rodin Museum in Paris (*see p. 130*) was never the sculptor's home. The house is set in a garden above the Seine, and behind it is a large, glazed atelier. A few rooms can be visited, including the dining room, which contains Rodin's academic gown from Oxford. In the atelier are numerous plasters, large and small, which demonstrate the inventive re-use and reassemblage he made of parts of existing works. In the garden is part of his collection of antiquities.

MUSÉE ET CHÂTEAU DE SCEAUX

Map p. 577, B3. RER B to Bourg-la-Reine/Sceaux/Parc de Sceaux (Zone 3). Open April–Oct Mon–Fri 10–1 & 2–6, Sat 10–6, Sun 10–6.30; Nov–March 10–1 & 2–5, Sat–Sun 10–5. Closed Tues, some holidays and during winter holidays. Guided visit including Pavillon de l'Aurore: in summer, Sun 3pm; winter, 1st Sun of month 3pm. Park open every day from dawn to dusk. T: 01 41 87 29 50.

The Château de Sceaux, which is set in a magnificent park, has since 1937 been home to the Musée du Domaine Départemental de Sceaux. Its collections are divided between the château and other buildings (the Orangerie, Pavillon de l'Aurore, Petit Château and Écuries), which were part of the estate.

The château itself, a somewhat disappointing 19th-century pastiche of a Louis XIII mansion, replaced the sumptuous 17th-century château built here for Jean-Baptiste Colbert (1619–83), Secretary of State to Louis XIV. Colbert and his son, the Marquis de Seignelay, created the magnificent park and gardens. In 1699 the estate passed to the Duc du Maine, son of Louis XIV and Madame de Montespan. The duke spent his time translating Latin works, while the ambitious duchess created a literary and artistic court. Voltaire wrote *Zadig* here; and works by Racine, Molière and Lully were performed in the Orangerie. Sold during the Directoire, the house was razed and the gardens levelled, but in 1856–62 the Duc de Trévise had the present house built by Joseph-Michel le Soujaché. The interior is decorated in the Louis XIV and Louis XV styles, fashionable during the Second Empire.

MUSÉE DU DOMAINE DEPARTEMENTAL DE SCEAUX

A long, broad Allée d'Honneur leads across a stone bridge over a dry moat to the château entrance, grandly announced by gates with crowns and the monogram 'NT' (Napoléon-Trévise), between two sentry posts (1670–3) with sculptures of a unicorn overcoming a dragon and a dog overpowering a wolf, symbolising probity and fidelity respectively. Just inside is the 18th-century steward's house.

The **Écuries** (stables) house temporary exhibitions, the shop and restaurant. The domed **Pavillon de l'Aurore** (*guided visits only, see above*), designed by Claude

CHÂTEAU DE SCEAUX
View of the 19th-century building and its flanking topiary.

Perrault in 1670–2, is east-facing to catch the morning sun. The interior of the cupola is decorated with an allegory of Aurora, Roman goddess of the dawn, by Charles Le Brun. This is a rare surviving example in France of a garden pavilion, an Italian fashion. The **Orangerie**, (1686), the work of Jules Hardouin-Mansart, was built at the time of the Marquis de Seignelay. Originally about 88m long, it was damaged in 1870s and reduced by about a third and is now a gallery exhibiting sculptures from the time of Colbert. There are also a tea room and bookshop. The **Petit Château** (1661) is one of the oldest buildings in the park, and was the guest house at the time of Colbert. Its formal garden has been reinstated.

The **Château** itself contains artworks and furnishings. Among the portraits of the owners of the château is one of Colbert, attributed to Lefèbvre, and of the Duchesse de Maine by François de Troy, who also painted the large *Banquet of Dido and Aeneas* (1704). The varied reserve of works on paper from the 17th century onwards includes original plans and drawings from the time of Colbert and the Marquis de Seignelay. A late 18th-century work by Carmontelle, measuring 42m, records great houses (many lost) of the Île de France. Among donations from artists are watercolours by Dunoyer de Segonzac and versions of Jean Fautrier's *Hostages* series (*see p. 342*). Furniture and furnishings from Sceaux and other châteaux in the Île de France include a collection of predominantly 18th-century ceramics and porcelain from the Paris area.

THE PARK OF THE CHÂTEAU DE SCEAUX

The majestic Parc de Sceaux, with open spaces and grand perspectives, covers 151 hectares and straddles three municipalities. Originally laid out by Le Nôtre but gradually abandoned and ruined from the Revolution onwards, it was bought by the Département in 1923 and renovation and replanting began. There are now around 50 varieties of trees and the formal vistas have been preserved.

South of the château is a series of **cascades** leading to the Octagon; parallel to the west is the **Grand Canal**. There is a view towards the **Pavillon de Hanovre**, moved here in 1934 from the Blvd des Capucines.

Many of the **statues** which originally embellished the park were taken to the Louvre and the Jardins de Luxembourg, but in recent years they have again become an important feature, following a campaign to restore or replace them with replicas plus the addition of modern works. Near the cascades, for example, are bronze mascarons by Rodin, and around the Octagon are 17th-century copies from the antique. At the end of the Tapis Vert, west of the château, are four statues, two 17th- and two 19th-century.

ENVIRONS OF SCEAUX

A short distance northwest of the château, across the park, is the old **churchyard of Sceaux**, where the fabulist Florian (d. 1794) is buried. The simple tombs of Pierre and Marie Curie (née Sklodowska), who discovered radium, are in the local cemetery (though their remains have been translated to the Panthéon).

In the **Parc de la Vallée aux Loups**, at Châtenay, about 2.5km west of Sceaux (*map p. 577, B3*), is the beautifully-restored Maison de Chateaubriand (*open March–Oct Tues–Sat 10–12 & 2–6, Sun 11–6; Nov–Feb Tues–Sun 2–5; closed 1 Jan, 25 Dec; guided visits, T: 01 55 52 13 00*). The great Romantic writer, politician and historian François-René de Chateaubriand (1768–1848) purchased the property in 1807, transforming the residence from a simple dwelling into an elegant 19th-century residence set in a ten-hectare park. The visit consists of eight rooms on the ground floor and four on the first, a library dedicated to Chateaubriand and Romanticism, and the Tour Velléda, where Chateaubriand could retire to write. There is a *salon de thé* in the orangery.

North of Sceaux, the double **Aqueduct d'Arcueil** crosses the valley of the Bièvre, 2km south of the Boulevard Périphérique. The lower part was built in 1613–23 by Marie de Médicis to supply the fountains of the Jardin du Luxembourg. It was preceded by a Roman aqueduct, built in the 4th century to bring water to the baths of Lutetia. Both the composer Erik Satie and the artist Victor Vasarely lived in the suburb of Arcueil.

EATING AND DRINKING IN HAUTS-DE-SEINE

BOULOGNE-BILLANCOURT/ PONT DE ST-CLOUD

€–€€ **L'Auberge**. An excellent bistrot with a modern bar, and tables for seated dining in a more traditional setting. The quality of the food is excellent, the meticulous cooking incorporating skill with fine ingredients. Lunch menu and *à la carte*. *86 Av. J.-B. Clément. T: 01 46 05 67 19 (Métro: Boulogne-Pont de St-Cloud).*

€ **Chez Michel**. A simple setting with a warm welcome, offering good choices which really do adapt to the seasons, at very affordable prices. Menus and *formules*. A popular place. Closed Aug, 12 Dec–1 Jan, Sat midday and Sun. *4 Rue Henri-Martin. T: 01 46 09 08 10 (Métro: Porte de St-Cloud).*

ÎLE DE CHATOU

€ **Restaurant Fournaise**. Pleasant place on the island with a terrace on the river, open all year every day (orders taken midday–2pm and 7pm–11pm). *Menu du jour* for lunch and dinner. Its main attractions are the setting and the history. *3 Rue du Bac. T: 01 30 71 41 91, www.restaurant-fournaise.fr.*

RUEIL-MALMAISON

€ **Le Patte Noire**. An attractive, very popular place in the town centre, with a *menu dégustation*. Closed Sun eve and Mon. *50 Rue du Gué. T: 09 81 20 81 69, www.lepattenoire.com.*

SCEAUX

At the Château de Sceaux there are two good choices:

€€ **Le Trévise**. Gourmet restaurant near the old stables. Closed Sun and Mon. *8 Av. Claude Perrault. T: 01 40 96 95 50, www.letrevise.fr.*

€ **Le Kiosque**. Just outside the château itself, offers drinks, light meals (salads, sandwiches, crêpes, quiches) and good views of Le Nôtre's gardens. Closed Sun and Mon.

In the orangery of the Maison de Chateaubriand, € **Les Thés Brillants** serves tea, snacks and also light lunches, with set menus Wed–Sat and brunch on Sun. Closed Mon and Tues. *T: 01 46 15 21 49.*

VERSAILLES
View of the château across the Bassin d'Apollon.

Versailles

The town of Versailles (*map p. 577, A3*) is dignified and affluent, as befits its regal history, with regularly laid-out streets and imposing avenues that converge on the château and park, meeting at Place d'Armes. With a population of some 90,000, it lies on a low sandy plain between two lines of wooded hills and is the Préfecture of the Département of Yvelines. The town is well worth exploring and makes a very pleasant alternative base to Paris, especially in the summer. It has many elegant 17th- and 18th-century buildings, a lively market area, and hotels and restaurants of all categories. Avenue de Paris divides the centre into two distinct *quartiers* around its two main churches, the Cathedral of St-Louis and the church of Notre-Dame.

Getting there
Versailles can easily be reached from Paris on RER line C5 to Versailles Rive Gauche (Zone 4; the nearest station to the château) and on SNCF mainline trains from Gare St-Lazare to Versailles-Rive Droit or Montparnasse to Versailles-Chantiers.

CHÂTEAU DE VERSAILLES

Versailles is possibly the most famous palace in the world. Begun by Louis XIV in the 17th century, it was, right from the outset, the model that royalty all over Europe sought to emulate. Adapted and amended by succeeding monarchs, Louis XV and Louis XVI, the combination of palace, museum and gardens is almost overwhelming, both in splendour and size; to appreciate it thoroughly ideally requires two days. There are several routes that can be taken inside the palace, and the 815 hectares of grounds encompass two smaller palaces, the Grand Trianon and the Petit Trianon on Queen Marie-Antoinette's estate, as well as the Hameau de la Reine. There is also the Baroque garden designed by Le Nôtre, with pools and *bosquets* (groves) and the wooded park along the Grand Canal. It is advisable to plan your visit in advance. The château is much visited and can be extremely crowded.

Visitor information
Château open *1 April–31 Oct Tues–Sun 9–6.30; 1 Nov–31 March 9–5.30; last admission 30mins before closing. Closed Mon, 1 Jan, 1 May, 25 Dec and during official ceremonies. Trianon and Marie-Antoinette's estate open April–Oct 12–6.30; Nov–March 12–5.30. Closed Mon, 1 Jan, 1 May, 25 Dec and during official ceremo-*

nies. **Gardens open** *April–Oct daily 8–8.30; Nov–March 8–6. Park open April–Oct daily 7–8.30; Nov–March 8–6 (except during special events and bad weather). Tickets can be bought online or on the day but it is advisable to buy in advance online. Prices vary depending on what is included. T: 01 30 83 78 00, www.chateau-versailles.fr. Free entry on first Sun of month in Nov–March. Gardens free on Tues, Sat, Sun in April–Oct.*

Guided tours *in French and selected tours in English include parts of the château not normally open to the public. Book in advance, T: 01 30 83 78 00 or at the North Ministers Wing from 9am; dome tours can be booked online. There are also guided visits to temporary exhibitions.*

Refreshments: *There is a choice of places to eat and drink both inside the château and in the grounds. For details, see p. 487.*

A mini **train shuttle** *runs between the Parterre du Nord and Marie Antoinette's Estate (www.train-versailles.com). Individual guided rides can be taken around the Grand Canal on Segways (T: 01 78 52 54 00, www.viator.com/versailles.segway).*

The **Prince's Bookshop** *is in the south wing. Throughout the year there are concerts and operas. During the summer there is a variety of outdoor performances, including the* **Grandes Eaux** *(Musical Fountains). Each summer an artist is invited to exhibit his/her works in the grounds: www.chateauversailles.spectacles.fr.*

HISTORY OF THE CHÂTEAU

Versailles emerged from obscurity in 1624, when Louis XIII built a hunting lodge on this site, which was extended into a small château with a garden laid out in 1639. The royal estate once covered an area of 8,000 hectares, surrounded by a 43km-long wall and entered by 22 gates. It was reduced to 815 hectares after the Revolution. The château was the birthplace of Louis XV in 1710, Louis XVI in 1754, Louis XVIII in 1755 and Charles X in 1757. The real creator of Versailles, however, was the Sun King, Louis XIV, who conceived the building as a lasting monument to his reign. Louis le Vau (*see p. 46*) was entrusted with the embellishment of the old building around the Cour de Marbre, while Le Nôtre laid out the park. After Le Vau's death in 1670 the work was continued by his pupil François d'Orbay, and the interior decoration was supervised by Charles Le Brun. Jules Hardouin-Mansart, appointed chief architect in 1678, radically remodelled the main body of the château, replacing Le Vau's terrace with the Hall of Mirrors. The South Wing and then the North Wing followed, resulting in the immense façade (over half a kilometre long) with 375 windows. In 1682, Louis XIV announced his intention to make Versailles the seat of government. The workforce employed on the building and in draining and laying out the grounds numbered 22,000 men and 6,000 horses, which emptied the coffers of France. Nevertheless, building continued and the Trianon was built in 1687–8. Louis XIV lived on a construction site for the whole of his reign.

After Louis XIV's death in 1715, the château was abandoned until Louis XV attained his majority in 1722, when the court returned, remaining until the Revolution. Under Louis XV the building was transformed to the current style. The Salon d'Hercule, the interior of the opera and the Petit Trianon were all built around this time by Jacques-

Ange Gabriel. Louis XVI redecorated a suite of apartments for Marie-Antoinette and completed the rustic village or Hameau in 1783.

LIFE AT THE COURT OF LOUIS XIV

Life at Court was a superficially brilliant existence that disguised monotonous routine, rigid protocol and ceremonious etiquette. Members of the Court fluttered in the orbit of the king during the daily drama of Versailles, which was rife with intrigue and hypocrisy, all superbly described by the Duc de Saint-Simon in his *Mémoires*. The king, absolute monarch by divine right, kept the nobility close to him to avoid plotting, reinforced by a network of spies. The main wings of the château were divided up into numerous diminutive suites to house individual courtiers and their families. Here is Saint-Simon on the king's reaction, after he had attempted to leave his service:

After supper that evening, and when about to undress, [the King] paid me a compliment, a mere trifle I admit, and one which I should be ashamed to mention if it were not so characteristic of him. Although the disrobing chamber was very well illuminated, the chaplain officiating at vespers there always held a lighted candle, which he afterwards gave to the valet-de-chambre, who bore it before the King until he reached his chair, and then handed it to whomever the King ordered him to deliver it to. On this occasion the King, glancing about him, let his eye fall upon me, and commanded the valet to give me the candle. It was a distinction which he bestowed sometimes upon one man, sometimes upon another, as the fancy took him, but which, by his manner of bestowing it, was always looked for as a great honour. My surprise may be imagined when I heard myself named aloud for this favour—and the performance was on many occasions repeated. This was not for any want of persons of due standing; but the King was sufficiently nettled by my desire for retirement to wish that no one might perceive it. For three years he laboured without fail to make me feel to what extent he was displeased with me. He no longer spoke to me; he scarcely threw me a glance. And to show that his vexation did not extend to my wife, but that it was entirely aimed against me, he bestowed several marks of favour upon Madame de Saint-Simon. She was repeatedly invited to suppers at the Trianon, an honour which had never been granted her hitherto.

From the Mémoires de Saint-Simon, *chapter XXIV.*

The independence of the United States was formally recognised by Britain, France and Spain at Versailles in 1783. The Assembly of the Estates-General met in Versailles in 1789, where on 20th June the deputies of the Third Estate formed the National Assembly. On 6th October an angry mob, some 7,000 strong, led by the women of Les Halles, marched to Versailles and forced the royal family to return with them to Paris, where they were confined to the Tuileries. The incomparable collection of works of art was then split up. The furniture was publicly auctioned; paintings, antiques and gems went to the Louvre, and books and medals to the Bibilothèque Nationale.

The château was preserved by the Republic (it hosted a museum, school and library), but the Grand Canal had run dry. With the proclamation of the Empire, Versailles became Napoleon's residence and he commenced refurbishment. During the Restoration, more work was done but it was not occupied by royalty. Louis-Philippe

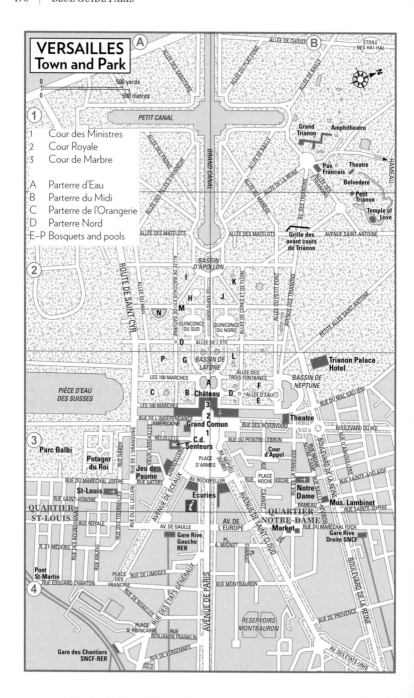

VERSAILLES
Town and Park

0 — 500 yards
0 — 500 metres

1 Cour des Ministres
2 Cour Royale
3 Cour de Marbre

A Parterre d'Eau
B Parterre du Midi
C Parterre de l'Orangerie
D Parterre Nord
E–P Bosquets and pools

PETIT CANAL

GRAND CANAL

ALLÉE DE CHOISY
ÉTOILE DES HAI-HAI

ALLÉE DU PLAFOND
ALLÉE DES SABOTIERS
ALLÉE DE BAILLY

Grand Trianon
Amphitheatre

ALLÉE DES PAONS
ALLÉE DE LA REINE
ACCÈS TRIANONS
ALLÉE DES 2 TRIANONS

Pav. Français
Theatre
HAMEAU
Belvedere
Petit Trianon
Temple of Love

ALLÉE DES VILLES D'HONNEUR
ALLÉE DU MANÈGE
ALLÉE DES MATELOTS
ALLÉE DES MATELOTS

Grille des avant cours de Trianon
AVENUE SAINT-ANTOINE

BASSIN D'APOLLON

ALLÉE DE BACCHUS ET DE SATURNE
LE TAPIS VERT
ALLÉE DE CÉRÈS ET DE FLORE
ALLÉE DU PETIT PONT
AVENUE DES TRIANONS
AVENUE SAINT-ANTOINE
PETITE ALLÉE SAINT-ANTOINE

I
H
K
M
J
F
N
O
QUINCONCE DU SUD
QUINCONCE DU NORD
ALLÉE DE L'ÉTÉ
BASSIN DE LATONE
ALLÉE DES TROIS FONTAINES
BASSIN DE NEPTUNE

ROUTE DE SAINT-CYR
ALLÉE DU MAIL

P
G
L
Trianon Palace Hotel

PIÈCE D'EAU DES SUISSES

LES 100 MARCHES
C
B
A
Château
D
E
ALLÉE D'EAU
LES 100 MARCHES
3
2
1
Grand Comun
Theatre
RUE DES RÉSERVOIRS
BOULEVARD DU ROI
RUE DU MAL GALLIEN

RUE DE L'INDÉPENDANCE AMÉRICAINE
C.d. Senteurs
RÉCOLLETS
RUE DU PEINTRE LEBRUN
Cour d'Appel
BOULEVARD DE LA REINE

Parc Balbi
Potager du Roi
RUE HARDY
RUE DE L'ORANGERIE
VIEUX-VERSAILLES
CHANCELLERIE
PLACE D'ARMES
RUE NEUVE NOTRE-DAME
RUE SAINTE-ADÉLAIDE

Jeu de Paume
RUE DE MARÉCHAL JOFFRE
RUE SATORY
AV. ROCKEFELLER
AVENUE DE SCEAUX
AVENUE DE SAINT-CLOUD
RUE CARNOT
PLACE HOCHE
RUE HOCHE
RAMEAU
Notre Dame
Mus. Lambinet
RUE SAINTE-SOPHIE

St-Louis
RUE ROYALE
RUE SAINT-HONORÉ
RUE DES TOURNELLES
RUE DU GL LECLERC
Ecuries
i
QUARTIER NOTRE-DAME
Market
RUE DU MARÉCHAL FOCH

QUARTIER ST-LOUIS
R. ST-MÉDÉRIC
RUE DE BOURGOGNE
RUE ANJOU
AV. DE GAULLE
Gare Rive Gauche RER
AV. DE L'EUROPE
PL. A. MIGNOT
RUE DU MARÉCHAL FOCH
Gare Rive Droite SNCF

Pont St-Martin
RUE ÉDOUARD CHARTON
PLACE DES FRANCINE
RUE DE LIMOGES
RUE DE NOAILLES
AVENUE DE PARIS
RUE MONTBAURON
BOULEVARD DE LA REINE

PLACE R. POINCARRÉ
RUE BENJAMIN FRANKLIN
RUE DES ÉTATS GÉNÉRAUX
RUE DE VERGENNES
RESERVOIRS MONTBAURON
RUE DE PROVENCE
AV. DES ÉTATS-UNIS

Gare des Chantiers SNCF-RER

(1830–48) rescued the palace from destruction, yet did irreparable damage to the apartments in order to house his Glories of France museum, inaugurated in 1837. During the Franco-Prussian War (1870–1), Versailles was used as a hospital and became the headquarters of the German armies. On 18th January 1871, King Wilhelm I of Prussia was crowned German Emperor in the Hall of Mirrors and on 26th January the peace preliminaries were signed at Bismarck's quarters at 20 Rue de Provence (*map p. 470, B4*). The French Government took refuge here from 1871–5 and the National Assembly proclaimed the Third Republic from the opera house, on 25th February 1875. A general restoration began after the appointment of Pierre de Nolhac as curator in 1887.

During the First World War, Versailles was the seat of the Allied War Council. The Peace Treaty with Germany was signed in the Hall of Mirrors on 28th June 1919. Further extensive restorations were made in 1928–32, thanks largely to the Rockefeller Foundation, and continued after the Second World War under the curatorship of Gerald van der Kemp. During that war, the Allied GHQ was at Versailles from September 1944 until the following May, and many buildings were requisitioned for military use.

VISITING THE CHÂTEAU

Everything at the Château de Versailles is designed to impress, in dimensions and opulence. There are scarcely superlatives sufficient to describe the whole ensemble of palace, gardens, park, water features and Trianon palaces. The first view of it is designed to resemble a great Baroque theatrical set.

Three wide Avenues (St-Cloud, de Paris and de Sceaux; *see plan opposite*) converge on **Place d'Armes** east of the château, which is separated from the courtyards by a monumental curtain of railings designed by Hardouin-Mansart. Opposite the château entrance, between the avenues, are the **Écuries**, the royal stables, in grand buildings of equal size. The main gate leads to the wide forecourt of the château, **Cour des Ministres (1)**, which is flanked by detached buildings, once assigned to Ministers of State. Adding to the splendour of the forecourt are two groups of allegorical sculptures: *Victories over the Empire* by Gaspard Marsy and *Victories over Spain* by Girardon. In contrast are *Peace* by Tuby and *Abundance* by Coysevox, themes repeated in the Hall of Mirrors and in the gardens. Beyond between two colonnaded pavilions dating from 1772 (right) and 1829, is the **Cour Royale (2)**. An equestrian statue of Louis XIV (erected in 1836) stands here. At the time of Louis XIV, only those who possessed the 'honours of the Louvres'—called cousin by the king—had the right to enter by this route and to bring their carriage and liveried servants into the great courtyard. The small Marble Courtyard or **Cour de Marbre (3)**, at the end of the Cour Royale, indicates the position of Louis XIII's château, which was enveloped in later extensions by Le Vau and Hardouin-Mansart.

THE STATE APARTMENTS OF THE KING

The State Apartments (*Grands Appartements du Roi*) on the first floor are the most frequented part of the palace, usually less crowded in the early morning or late afternoon. They have preserved their original decoration, inspired by Italian palaces, including marble inlay, sculptured and gilded bronzes, carved doors and painted ceilings, carried out for Louis XIV under the supervision of Charles Le Brun. They were intended as His Majesty's living quarters but from 1684 he had apartments prepared in the older part of the palace, and this suite of rooms was used instead for entertainment. Designed for the glorification of the Sun King, it derived its planetary theme (*Abundance, Venus, Diana, Mars, Mercury* and *Apollo*) from the Pitti Palace in Florence, and made allegorical reference to the king's actions. In 1710 the theme was interrupted with a new room dedicated to the mythological hero Hercules. The original furniture was sold after the Revolution.

Stairs lead up to the **Vestibule de la Chapelle (1)** on the first floor, from where there is a striking view of the **Chapel (2)**, dedicated to St Louis (Louis IX). On this first-floor level is the Royal Gallery, from which the king heard Mass daily at 10am for about 30mins, descending to the nave only for major ceremonies. Mass was accompanied by music. The ensuing enfilade of rooms served as a grand entry to visitors seeking audience with the king.

Salon d'Hercule (3), one of the most impressive in the château, was decorated by Louis XV in the Louis XIV style and inaugurated in 1739. It replaced a chapel demolished in 1710. The marbles and bronzes are of exceptional quality and announce the decoration of the Hall of Mirrors. The room is dominated by a great work by Paolo Veronese, *Supper in the House of Simon* (1570), given to Louis XIV in 1664 by the Republic of Venice, in a grand frame moulded by Jacques Verberckt. The painting was installed only in 1730, at the time of Louis XV, and inspired the décor and colours of the room, including the vast *Apotheosis of Hercules* on the ceiling, painted by François Lemoyne in 1733–6.

Salon de l'Abondance (4) (1680, recently renovated) was a small reception room that Louis XV used for showing off rare paintings and *objets d'art*, as well as for refreshments during major receptions. It has royal portraits by Rigaud and by J.-B. van Loo.

The **Salon de Vénus (5)**, the main entrance to the State Apartments until 1752 and named after its painted ceiling, has marble decorations in early Louis XIV style and original *trompe l'oeil* perspectives by Jacques Rousseau. In the central alcove is a statue of Louis XIV in antique costume.

The former billiard room, the **Salon de Diane (6)**, features the goddess of the hunt on the ceiling and a bust of Louis XIV aged 27 (1665) by Bernini. Louis XIV was a skilled billiards player.

The **Salon de Mars (7)**, dedicated to the God of War, was originally the guard room but went on to have various uses, as gaming-room, concert hall and ballroom. Paintings include Louis XV and Queen Marie Leszczynska by Carle van Loo. *Mercury on his Chariot* on the ceiling of the **Salon de Mercure (8)** is by J.-B. Champaigne. Originally this was Louis's ceremonial bedchamber (a public room not intended for sleeping in), where the king received visitors. It has been refurbished and returned, as far as possible, to its original décor. Louis XIV lay in state here for eight days. Some of the furnishing has been replaced or remade. The present bed was ordered

CHÂTEAU DE VERSAILLES

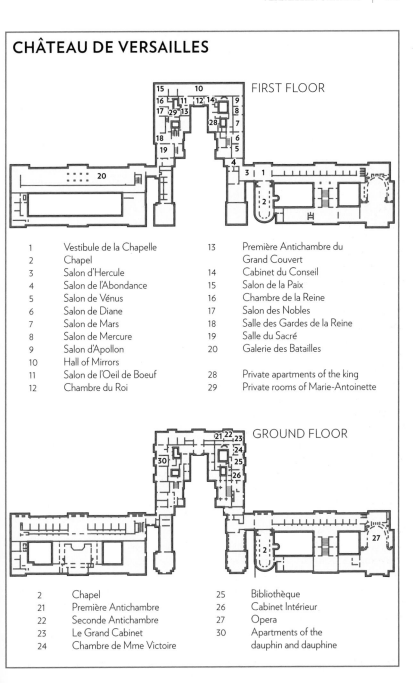

FIRST FLOOR

1	Vestibule de la Chapelle	13	Première Antichambre du Grand Couvert
2	Chapel	14	Cabinet du Conseil
3	Salon d'Hercule	15	Salon de la Paix
4	Salon de l'Abondance	16	Chambre de la Reine
5	Salon de Vénus	17	Salon des Nobles
6	Salon de Diane	18	Salle des Gardes de la Reine
7	Salon de Mars	19	Salle du Sacré
8	Salon de Mercure	20	Galerie des Batailles
9	Salon d'Apollon		
10	Hall of Mirrors	28	Private apartments of the king
11	Salon de l'Oeil de Boeuf	29	Private rooms of Marie-Antoinette
12	Chambre du Roi		

GROUND FLOOR

2	Chapel	25	Bibliothèque
21	Première Antichambre	26	Cabinet Intérieur
22	Seconde Antichambre	27	Opera
23	Le Grand Cabinet	30	Apartments of the
24	Chambre de Mme Victoire		dauphin and dauphine

from Jacob-Desmalter in 1833, when the château became a museum at the time of Louis-Philippe and at that time old embroidered covers were acquired. These are now protected by a crimson *gros de Tours* bedspread.

The **Salon d'Apollon (9)**, dedicated to the god of the Sun, the Arts and Peace, with whom Louis XIV identified, was, from 1673, the grandest of the sequence of rooms. It became the throne room in 1682 and housed a nearly three-metre-high silver throne (melted down in 1689). In the centre of the ceiling is Charles de la Fosse's masterpiece: *Louis XIV (Le Roi Soleil) as Apollo in a Chariot Escorted by the Seasons*. The fine stucco work was sculpted by the Marsy brothers.

The **Hall of Mirrors (10)**, together with its antechambers at either end, the Salon de la Guerre and the Salon de la Paix (the War and Peace Rooms), form a brilliant ensemble occupying the west front of the building. The **Salon de la Guerre**, completed in 1686, still has three of the six busts of Roman emperors bequeathed by Mazarin and a stucco medallion of Louis XIV on horseback by Antoine Coysevox. The ceiling painting, the first of a series designed by Le Brun, represents *France Victorious*, bearing on her shield the portrait of Louis XIV.

The 73m-long Hall of Mirrors (*Galerie des Glaces*, the '*Grande Galerie*' in the 17th century, is the best known of all the rooms at Versailles and represents the apogee of the Sun King's palace: a scintillating masterpiece which other European monarchs desired to reproduce. It was used daily by courtiers and the public as an access route or meeting place. Begun by Jules Hardouin-Mansart in 1678, it was completed in 1684

(and most recently restored in 2007). Seventeen windows overlook the park, and opposite each is a bevelled mirror of equal size, made by the Manufacture Royale de St-Gobain. Arches, surmounted by Apollo and the Nemean lion, are separated by red marble pilasters with bronze capitals featuring *fleurs-de-lys* and Gallic cocks. The gilded stucco cornice is adorned with crowns and the orders of chivalry. There are marble copies from the antique of Venus, Paris, Mercury and Minerva. At the time of Louis XIV it was lit with candlelight from 20 silvered bronze Bohemian glass chandeliers reflecting in the mirrors and falling on lavish furnishings and fabrics. Le Brun used his creative genius to the full in the decorations, which include the central ceiling painting, *Louis XIV Omnipotent*, and images which illustrate the civil and military achievements of Louis XIV over the course of some 20 years. Heads of state are still entertained here during official visits.

Halfway down the Hall of Mirrors, detour left to the King's Bedchamber (*Chambre du Roi*). The *Antichambre*, known since 1701 as the **Salon de l'Oeil-de-Boeuf (11)**, after the oval bull's-eye window, was the room where courtiers waited for admission to the king's levée (rising). Decorations include the stucco frieze showing children frolicking on a gold background and busts of Louis XIV by Coysevox, Louis XV by Gois, and Louis XVI by Houdon.

The lavishly restored **Chambre du Roi (12)**, facing the sunrise and overlooking the Cour de Marbre, became Louis XIV's bedchamber in 1701. Here the ceremonial *levée* (arising) and *couchée* (retiring) of the king took place. Up to 100 members of the Court might attend the king as he prepared for the day. He would lunch daily at a little table placed before the middle window. It was here that he died on 1st September 1715. The decorations of carved wood, including the balustrade separating the (reconstructed) bed from the rest of the room have been regilded but are in part original. Most of the rich brocades and other fabrics are modern remakes, scrupulously copied at Lyon from original samples. The sculpture of gilded stucco above the bed is by Nicolas Coustou and the chimneypieces (1761) have bronzes by Caffieri. There is a bust of Louis XIV by Coysevox and two portraits by Van Dyck. On 6th October 1789, it was from the balcony of this room that Marie-Antoinette and Louis XVI, at Lafayette's suggestion, showed themselves to the mob.

In the **Première Antichambre du Grand Couvert (13)** the royal family took their meals in public. Known as the *grand couvert*, the ritual was part of daily protocol and Louis XIV was accompanied by his family; at the *petit couvert* the king dined alone. The custom was less frequently observed during Louis XV's reign; on 1st January 1764, Mozart (barely 8 years old) was invited with his father to attend the *grand couvert*. By the time of Louis XVI, the *grand couvert* occurred only on Sundays and holidays, an exercise that Marie-Antoinette found particularly tedious.

The large **Cabinet du Conseil (14)**, a more sober room where meetings were held, dates in its present form from 1755, with *boiseries* by Antoine Rousseau. It contains the table on which the Treaty of Versailles recognising American Independence was signed in 1783.

THE STATE APARTMENTS OF THE QUEEN

The *Grand Appartement de la Reine* overlooks the southern garden.

The **Salon de la Paix (15)** was the queen's card room. The ceiling, with *France Bringing the Benefits of Peace to Europe*, completes Le Brun's scheme.

The **Chambre de la Reine (16)**

(Queen's Bedchamber), the main room of the apartment, was where the queen spent most of her time. It was where formal public rituals were held such as the *toilette*; and where queens gave birth in public (19 children were born here). The room retains the memory of three queens: Marie-Thérèse, Marie Leszczynska and Marie-Antoinette (the first two died in this room, in 1683 and 1768 respectively). The décor has been lavishly returned to its appearance at the time when Marie-Antoinette fled on 6th October 1789. The chimneypiece is from the Trianon and the ceiling painting, by François Boucher, was commissioned by Louis XV c. 1730. The silk hangings were copied in 1976 from original pieces that Marie-Antoinette had made in Lyon in 1787. Her jewellery cabinet is by Schwerdfeger (1787) and the bust is by Félix Lecomte.

The **Salon des Nobles (17)** was Marie-Thérèse's *antichambre* and is where Marie Leszczynska later held audience. It was sumptuously made over by Marie-Antoinette. To alleviate the tedium of her days, she insisted on having accompanying music.

The **Salle des Gardes de la Reine (18)**, at the head of the stairs, still has the marble decoration of Louis XIV's time and the original ceiling by Noël Coypel. It was here that the revolutionary mob, having mounted the staircase to demand bread from Louis XVI and Marie-Antoinette, burst in. Three of the Swiss Guard died in the queen's defence.

GALERIES DES BATAILLES

This **(20)** is the largest of the historic galleries at Versailles and the most important remaining part of Louis-Philippe, Duc d'Orléans's history galleries dedicated to 'All the Glories of France'. It has remained intact since its inauguration. Created between 1833 and 1837, it was prompted by a desire to reunite the French people, divided into four factions at the time: Legitimists (supporters of Charles X and the Bourbon line); Orléanists (partisans of the July Monarchy); Republicans; and Bonapartists. The 33 large battle scenes cover a period from 496 (Battle of Tolbiac; victory of Clovis over the Alamanni) to 1809 (Battle of Wagram; victory of Napoleon over Austria). The four largest works in the gallery were commissioned by preceding régimes: the Empire (*Austerlitz*) and the Restoration (*Henri IV's Entry into Paris*), both by Gérard; and the *Battle of Bouvines*, and *Battle of Fontenoy* by Vernet. Two paintings were commissioned from Delacroix, the *Battle of Taillebourg*, fought during the Revolutionary period, and the *Entry of the Crusaders into Constantinople*. These, like the rest, were painted between 1834 and 1845. The gallery also contains the busts of 80 officers, and bronze plaques.

The **Salle du Sacré (19)** (Coronation Room) occupies the former large Salle des Gardes, restored following alterations by Louis-Philippe in the 19th century. Here hang the two largest paintings in the History of France collection, *Le Serment fait à l'Empéreur par l'Armée après la distribution des Aigles, le 5 Dec 1804*, finished by Napoleon's official painter David in 1810; and *Le Sacré de l'Empéreur Napoléon et le Couronnement de l'Impératrice Joséphine*, commissioned by the emperor from David in 1806–7. The original hangs in the Louvre. The Versailles version is a copy by David, begun in 1808 and completed during the painter's exile in Brussels in 1816–25. A third painting, *La Bataille d'Aboukir* by Gros, was commissioned by Bonaparte's brother-in-law, Murat. The paintings above the door are by Gérard.

APARTMENTS OF MESDAMES, THE DAUGHTERS OF LOUIS XV

This succession of charming 18th-century rooms was used by the Mesdames, the six daughters of Louis XV. Victoire and Adélaïde remained unmarried and stayed in these apartments for 20 years, until the Revolution. The rooms reopened in 2013 following extensive renovations to return them to their original form. Six of the nine rooms are entirely refurnished, which entailed reweaving silk wall hangings and curtains in Lyon using the 18th-century designs. The painting *La Tasse du Chocolat* by Jean-Baptiste Charpentier affords a glimpse of court life and dress in the 18th century.

Première Antichambre (21): Over the doors are paintings of ministers of Louis XV by Michel van Loo and Alexandre Roslin. Madame Adélaïde occupied this room in 1752–3; Mme Sophie in 1755–67; and from 1769, Mme Victoire.

Seconde Antichambre (22): The shutters and windows are remnants of the former bathhouse, while the panelling was probably from the time of Mme Victoire. This room was occupied by Mme Adélaïde and later Madame Victoire, with her sisters Sophie and Louise (before the latter took the veil; *see p. 508*). Above the doors are *The Fables of La Fontaine* painted by Oudry for the Dauphin; there are also a chest of drawers by Riesener, a Savonnerie screen and a Chinese-style *cartel* in imitation lacquer.

Le Grand Cabinet (23): Originally the octagonal room of the bath house of Louis XIV, this was transformed in 1763 by Madame Victoire when the cornice, angle woodwork and fireplace were installed. The princesses were great lovers of the arts. The Blanchet harpsichord is a reminder that Madame Victoire was an accomplished musician, to whom Mozart dedicated his first six harpsichord sonatas in 1784. In the apartments are also a small organ and a Gagliano violin which belonged to Mme Adélaïde.

Mme Victoire's Chambre (24) has fine *boiseries* by Antoine Rousseau. The Chinese design on the taffeta in the alcoves reproduces the 'summer décor'. The two corner cupboards by Péridiez were sold in 1769, to be repurchased in 1982, having in the meantime been in Russia and then England. Returned to their original place are three superb vases made at the Royal Manufactory at Sèvres, painted by Nicolas Dodin. Originally they were part of a set of five (the others are in New York's Metropolitan Museum).

The **Bibliothèque (25)** of Madame Victoire has bookcases still in place with some books carrying the arms of the Mesdames. The woodwork and fireplace of the **Cabinet Intérieur (26)** are again by Rousseau and on the chest by Foullet (1768) is an alabaster cup, and the writing desk which was made by Levasseur for the Mesdames.

THE CHAPEL

The sumptuous chapel **(2)**, on two levels, with a colonnade of Corinthian columns, was designed and begun by Jules Hardouin-Mansart in 1699 and completed in 1710 by Robert de Cotte. Four chapels had preceded it. The high altar is of marble and bronze with sculptures by Van Cleve, and the organ was created by Robert Clicquot, the king's organ builder. François Couperin played here on Easter Sunday, 1711. The Chapel Choir was of great renown. The central ceiling painting is by Antoine Coypel and above the royal pew is a *Descent of the Holy Spirit* by Jouvenet. The court would attend Mass every morning, the king seated in the Royal Gallery surrounded by his family, while the court ladies sat in the side galleries and others, including the public, were in the nave. The king only descended to the nave to take Communion on important religious festivals.

THE OPERA

At the far end of the North Wing, the Opera **(27)** perfectly exemplifies a court theatre and is remarkable for its architecture and decoration as well as theatrical and technical details (*operas are performed here during the Summer Music Festival; see www.cha-*

teauversailles.spectacles.fr). Designed in the 1680s by Hardouin-Mansart, it was built for Louis XV by Gabriel in 1770. It was first used on the occasion of the marriage of the Dauphin (Louis XVI) and Marie-Antoinette, when Lully's *Perseus* was performed. The Foyer retains its 18th-century decoration by Pajou. It was greatly transformed under Louis-Philippe and in 1855 was the scene of a banquet given in honour of Queen Victoria. Modelled on the King of Sardinia's theatre in Turin, it was returned to its original aspect in 1955–7, even the upholstery being copied from the original specifications. It underwent more renovations in 2007–9.

PRIVATE APARTMENTS

The sets of rooms described below are normally not open to the public but can be seen on guided tours; see p. 468.

Private apartments of the king (28): Known as the *Cabinets du Roi* in Louis XIV's day, it is here that the king kept precious art treasures. The suite of rooms was transformed by Louis XV in 1735 to provide a retreat from the tedious etiquette of the court. He died of smallpox here on 10th May 1774. The **Cabinet de la Pendule** houses a clock, by Dauthiau and Caffieri, placed here in 1754, surmounted by a crystal globe marking the phases of the sun, moon and planets. The **Cabinet Intérieur du Roi** is the grandest, with panelling and mirror frames considered the finest made by Verberckt. The original furniture of the time of Louis XV is still in place, including a famous rolltop desk by Oeben and Riesener (1760–8).

The private rooms of Marie-Antoinette (29): This small and very secluded suite between the state rooms and courtyards offers a fascinating insight into the private life of Marie-Antoinette. The rooms retain their superb original decoration, although fabrics have been remade. In the **Salon de la Reine** the Queen received her intimate friends and her musicians, Gluck and Grétry, and sat for portraits to Mme Vigée-Lebrun. The **Méridienne** is an octagonal room redesigned by Mique in 1781, with original furniture. Other small rooms were used for informal entertaining. There was a discreet route between the king's and queen's bedroom along back corridors.

Apartments of Mme de Pompadour and Mme du Barry: On the attic floor of the North Wing, a diminutive suite was occupied by Mme de Pompadour from 1745–50 after which, no longer the king's mistress but still his confidante, she moved to the ground floor. Mme du Barry lived in the same apartments from 1769–74.

Apartments of the dauphin and dauphine (30): On the ground floor overlooking the gardens, these apartments, were successively occupied by eight *dauphins* and their wives. They were repeatedly remodelled but their present arrangement corresponds to the period when Louis XV's son Louis Dauphin and his second wife, Marie-Josèphe de Saxe, lived here, between 1747 and 1765. At the start of the Revolution, the future Louis XVII and his sister Madame Royale occupied the rooms.

The apartments are sumptuous. There are portraits of Queen Marie Leszczynska and flower paintings by Monnoyer. Louis XV is depicted in his coronation robes by Hyacinth Rigaud (1715). Marie-Josèphe, daughter of King Augustus III of Poland, gave birth in the bedchamber to three future kings of France: Louis XVI, Louis XVIII and Charles X. Paintings by Nattier include the daughters of Louis XV, *Madame Henriette as Flora* and *Madame Adélaïde as Diana*. Among superb pieces of furniture by Bernard Van Rysenburgh are a red lacquer Chinese style cabinet or library, and a flat-topped desk (1745). The terrestrial and celestial globe enclosing a second one, on which are reliefs of the sea floor, was made by Mancelle in 1781 for Louis XVI, who intended it for his son's education. A console table classified as National Treasure was made by Claude-Charles Saunier in 1787 for the same Dauphin.

THE PARK & GARDENS

The gardens and groves are open daily, except during official ceremonies (see p. 468 for opening times). Picnics are not allowed. Cycle hire is available. The Grandes Eaux Musicales take place between 11 and 5.30 at weekends in April–Oct; Grandes Eaux Nocturnes take place at 9pm in July; Fêtes de Nuit take place at 9.30pm on certain evenings in Aug–Sept (for information, T: 01 30 83 78 88).

The gardens of Versailles are a *tour de force* of geometry creating a link between the architecture of the château and its surroundings. They divide into three main sections: the formal ornamental gardens or parterres immediately surrounding the château; the forest in the distance, crossed by broad radiating alleys; and the area of the *bosquets* or groves, which provide the transition between the two. Louis XIV was as much involved in the gardens as in the palace and the whole project combines many devices to enhance the vistas and sense of drama, such as artificial lakes and ponds, rigorous alleys of trees, formal parterres designed to be viewed from above, statues and vases of marble and bronze, and—the ultimate embellishment—the spectacular fountains.

HISTORY OF THE GARDENS

Louis XIV commissioned the celebrated landscape gardener André le Nôtre to design the gardens, which were first laid out in 1661–8. The land was unpromising, with a sharp escarpment and marshes, entailing prodigious preliminary work in levelling and draining, and the importation of thousands of trees. Inspired by Italian originals but on an unprecedented scale, Versailles represents the pinnacle of formal 17th-century French garden design. In their general lines and their Classical sculptural decoration, the gardens remain as planned, but it was not until the 18th century, at the time of Louis XV, that trees were planted to the present extent. Le Nôtre was aided by Jean-Baptiste Colbert, who managed the overall project, and by Le Brun for sculptural decoration and fountain designs. The supply of water to the fountains, was, and still is, a subject of concern. Louis XIV's engineers devised a remarkable hydraulic system to bring water from the Seine via Marly. There are around 400 sculptures, the majority of them in place for some 300 years (the more fragile have been replaced by plaster copies). Each of the kings incorporated their own ideas, for example areas inspired by the paintings of Hubert Robert at the time of Louis XVI. During the 19th century much was lost or altered. A long-term programme of replanting to recreate the contrasting styles of Le Nôtre and Hubert Robert began in 1990 but was violently interrupted by a devastating storm in 1999, when some 10,000 trees were blown down. Among the rare species and historic trees lost were two junipers planted by Marie-Antoinette, the Virginian tulip tree, and the cedar planted in 1772 near the Hameau. The huge task of replanting began in March 2000.

THE PARTERRES

West of the château is a large terrace from which the eye is led the full length of the central axis past ponds and formal flowerbeds, along a straight lawn and the canal lined with serried ranks of trees, to the woodland beyond. The terrace was designed to be viewed from the first floor and is adorned with bronze statues and marble vases including *War* by Antoine Coysevox, and *Peace* by Tuby. Corresponding to the centre of the château façade, below the Hall of Mirrors, is the **Parterre d'Eau (A)** or Water Garden, laid out in 1683 with two large ornamental basins which mirror the building, decorated with bronzes (1690) of water nymphs and the *Kingdom of France*, represented by allegorical figures of the four great rivers and their main tributaries. From the top of the steps of the Bassin de Latone (Latona fountain) there are the magnificent views of the gardens. In the opposite direction, the whole façade of the château comes into focus with the centrally placed statues of *Apollo* and *Diana*, central to the theme and symbolic layout of the gardens. The sculpted group at the foot of the steps, *Latona with her Children Apollo and Diana*, depicts Latona insulted by Lycian peasants who are turned into frogs by Zeus at her request.

To the south steps lead to the **Parterre du Midi (B)**, with elaborately trimmed box designed to combine with flowers and 17th-century sculptures of children mounted on sphinxes. The Cent Marches (Hundred Steps) descend from here to the formal **Parterre de l'Orangerie (C)**, which was been returned to Le Nôtre's original design. The Orangery (1681–8), one of the largest in the world, designed by Le Vau, has 5m-thick walls and double glazing to withstand the cold. Over 1,000 trees in containers, including ancient orange and lemon trees, are over-wintered here and returned to the Parterre de l'Orangerie in spring. The Communards were herded into the Orangery in 1871 prior to their imprisonment. Beyond the Orangery is the **Pièce d'Eau des Suisses** (Swiss Lake), 682m long by 134m wide (13ha), excavated in 1678–82 by the Swiss Guard, many of whom are said to have died of malaria during the operation. It provided the Château with a lateral perspective behind the Orangerie.

The **Parterre Nord (D)** (*from where the shuttle bus leaves for the Trianon*) leads to the elegant Pyramid Fountain and the Bath of Diana's Nymphs (both by François Girardon, 1679) and on either side are the **Bosquet de l'Arc de Triomphe (E)**, with *France Triumphant* (Coysevox and Tuby), and the **Bosquet des Trois Fontaines (F)**.

Restored in 2005, an ancient plan records that the king desired it thus. Between them, the Allée d'Eau (Water Avenue), designed by Perrault and Le Brun (1676–88), leads directly to the theatrical **Bassin de Neptune** (1740), the largest fountain-basin in the gardens (*from here is the most direct route on foot to the Trianons*).

Beyond the oval Bassin de Latone extends the Allée Royale or **Tapis Vert** (Green Carpet), a lawn 330m long and 36m wide, lined with marble vases and statues, many of them copies from the antique. It leads to the **Bassin d'Apollon**: the sun god, setting out on his daily journey, is represented by *Apollo's Chariot Rising from the Waves to start its Course Across the Firmament* (Tuby, 1671). To the right is Petite Venise ('Little Venice'), where Louis XIV's Venetian gondoliers were housed.

Beyond the Bassin d'Apollon, and separated from the gardens by railings, is the Petit Parc, divided by the **Grand Canal**, 1650m long and 62m wide, the scene of Louis XIV's boating parties. It is crossed by a transverse arm (c. 1070m), extending from the Grand Trianon to the north to the few remaining buildings of the former royal menagerie.

THE BOSQUETS

The bosquets or groves, carefully planned and furnished al fresco 'rooms' within walls of greenery, were used for amusement and entertainment at the time of Louis XIV. Of the original 14, just six survived although some of the sculptures have been lost. They include the **Salle de Bal** or Ballroom **(G)**, south of the Bassin de Latone and further west the **Bosquet de la Colonnade (H)**, with a circle of marble arches (Hardouin-Mansart, 1885–8), whose central sculpture of the *Rape of Prosperine* by Girardon has disappeared. The **Salle des Marronniers (I)** is a chestnut grove behind the Colonnade. North of the Tapis Vert is the **Bosquet des Dômes (J)**, with several statues including *Acis and Galatea* (Tuby), and the **Bosquet de l'Encelade (K)**, heavily restored. In a work by Marsy, the giant Enceladus is about to throw a last rock and utter a final curse, symbolised by a jet of water, to save Jupiter from earth-born giants. In a Romantic spirit, very different from Le Nôtre's formal symmetry, is **Bosquet des Bains d'Apollon (L)**, within a grove laid out by Hubert Robert for Louis XVI. *Apollo served by Thetis's Nymphs* (Girardon and Renaudin, 1672) is the survival from the Grotto of Thetis. Always a delightful discovery, the bosquets are at their most enchanting during the Grandes Eaux Musicales. Also to explore are the **Bassin de Saturne** or Winter Pool **(M)**, the **Bassin du Miroir (N)** and the **Bassin de Bacchus** or Autumn Pool **(O)**, with sculptures by Girardon and Marsy and the glade known as the **Bosquet de la Reine (P)**.

THE TRIANON PALACES & MARIE-ANTOINETTE'S ESTATE

Map p. 470, B1. Open April–Oct Tues–Sun 12–6.30; Nov–March Tues–Sun 12–5.30. Includes the Grand Trianon, Petit Trianon, gardens, Chapel, French Pavilion, Queen's Theatre, Temple of Love, Grotto, English Garden, Dairy, Queen's Hamlet. Ticket office closes 5.50. Closed Mon, 1 Jan, 1 May, 25 Dec and during official ceremonies. Gardens open daily April–Oct 8–8.30, Nov–March 8–6.

THE GRAND TRIANON

The Grand Trianon is a miniature palace designed by Hardouin-Mansart and Robert de Cotte for Louis XIV in 1687. It replaced a modest summer house tiled inside with blue and white Delftware known as the Porcelain Trianon, erected on the site of the village of Trianon, which was razed in 1663. The Grand Trianon was Louis XIV's retreat from court life, where he could commune with nature. The low, U-shaped building with an Italian-style roof, also known as the Palais Rose because of its pro-fusion of French pink marble and porphyry, has extensive wings to the north which are not immediately obvious. Baroque rhythms and a play of light are set up by the flat pilasters and round-headed windows of the wings, accelerated by the colonnade or loggia. The loggia's huge French windows and mirrors brought the outside inside, creating a 'palace of flora' for Louis XIV. Botanical motifs also permeate the interior decoration,with woodwork and paintings based on nature and featuring mythological subjects such as Europa and Narcissus, in contrast to the Apollo myth of the château. During Louis XIV's reign, apartments here were occupied by members of the royal family, including the king's sister-in-law, the Princess Palatine, and the Duchesse de Bourgogne, mother of Louis XV of whom the king was very fond. Peter the Great also stayed here in 1717, as did Stanislas Leszczynski in 1741. Marie Leszczynska came during the summer months. Louis XV himself rarely used it and Louis XVI gave the estate to Marie-Antoinette as a place where she could be less formal, inviting only personal friends. Napoleon, after his divorce from Josephine in 1809, was a frequent visitor with Marie-Louise, his second wife; some Napoleonic and Empire furnishings have remained. Louis-Philippe's younger son lived here and introduced 19th-century Romantic furnishings. At the time of President de Gaulle, one entire wing was restored to receive heads of state on official visits and this custom continues, with visits from President Hollande at certain times.

INTERIOR OF THE GRAND TRIANON

During the time of Louis XIV there were apartments here for him and the queen, as well as for his favourite, Madame de Maintenon, and also a Salle de Théâtre. The visit includes rooms on both sides of the courtyard, and while the décor is largely Louis XIV, the furnishings are mainly 19th-century pieces from Napoleon and Marie-Louise's time. The Salon des Colonnes, originally Louis XIV's bedroom, is one of the finest rooms in the Trianon. The furniture was installed by Empress Marie-Louise. The beautiful mirrored Salon des Glaces has a view of the canal. The Chapel became an antechamber in 1691, but continued to be used for its original purpose and the cor-nice is decorated with heads of wheat and bunches of grapes, symbols of the Eucharist. The Salon de Musique and Grand Salon precede the Malachite Room, named after the malachite bowl given by Alexander I of Russia after the Treaty of Tilsit in 1807. The Salon Frais was built to protect fragile blooms from the upper garden, and has four

Views of Versailles by J.-B. Martin. *The Gardens of Versailles and the Trianon at the time of Louis XIV* in the adjoining gallery, mostly by Jean Cotelle and his brother, were valuable documents in the restoration of the *bosquets*. The Salon des Jardins faces the Grand Canal and the Salon des Sources has *Views of Versailles* by P.-D. Martin and Charles Chastelain.

GARDENS OF THE GRAND TRIANON

The gardens, laid out by Mansart, echo the traditional garden design of Le Nôtre with pools, vistas and borders of colour. The parterres are on two levels, the Upper Garden with two basins and statues by Girardon, and the Lower Garden, with one basin. The central axis leads to the Plat Fond (flat-bottomed basin), decorated with dragons. To the west is the secondary branch of the Grand Canal. The large Water Buffet (the main fountain) of 1703, designed by Mansart, has the only mythological theme, Neptune and Amphitrite. Louis XIV collected scented plants, which were kept in pots and could be rearranged and replaced. It took around a million to fill the garden. A bridge leads from the Jardin du Roi, behind the palace, to the gardens of the Petit Trianon.

THE PETIT TRIANON

The Petit Trianon is closely associated with Marie-Antoinette, although it was conceived for Louis XV as a country retreat for himself and Madame de Pompadour. Built in 1762–8 by Jacques-Ange Gabriel, it is a small Grecian-style masterpiece with two floors and an attic storey. It was later occupied by Madame du Barry and it was here in 1774 that Louis XV was taken fatally ill and then moved to the château to die. It became a favourite residence of Marie-Antoinette, who at first came only during the day, but as time passed, she also slept here. It was subsequently occupied by Pauline Borghese, Napoleon's sister. Each of the four façades is different; the most elegant columned façade faces the French garden. To the left of the courtyard is the chapel.

INTERIOR OF THE PETIT TRIANON

The sober, elegant interior (*guided visits only to the attic storey*) is an antidote to the florid Rococo style which preceded it. Many of the rooms in the Petit Trianon retain their original woodwork, including chimneypieces by Guibert in the dining room and grand salon, and sliding panels to obscure the windows to provide screens from prying eyes. In the dining room, traces of a trap-door, through which tables would appear ready-laid, are still visible in the floor, but Marie-Antoinette did away with the device. The entrance is in the former billiard room and the first floor is open to the public for a non-guided visit of ten rooms, all containing paintings and furnishings of high quality. It was entirely restored in 2008.

GARDENS OF THE PETIT TRIANON

The gardens of the Petit Trianon were originally a *ménagerie* and botanical garden laid out by Bernard de Jussieu for Louis XV, a passionate botanist who cultivated rare plants in large hothouses (now gone). During Louis XV's time there was a French

Garden Pavilion in Rococo style, but Marie-Antoinette had the gardens altered in the English style (1774–86) and Louis XVI liked to gather his own herbs here. The queen loved music—Gluck was a regular guest—to dance and to play cards, and to act. To satisfy her enthusiasms, in 1776–83, Richard Mique, the last of the royal architects at Versailles, built a circular Temple of Love, a Grotto and the Belvedere, on rocky outcrops, with a stream running between small artificial islands. Mique also built a mechanised Chinese tilt ring and a theatre (which can be viewed), where the queen made her acting début (not meeting with universal approval). Among the varied entertainments arranged by Marie-Antoinette were country balls to which ordinary people were invited. Rather than endearing her to them, however, her behaviour was considered un-queenly and unnerving.

HAMEAU DE LA REINE

Some few minutes' walk to the northeast of the Trianons is Marie-Antoinette's hamlet, also built by Mique in 1783. A charming ensemble, it consists of rustic buildings picturesquely arranged around a lake in a contrivedly rural setting. Here the queen could indulge her taste for nature, as popularised by Jean-Jacques Rousseau and Diderot, but this flight of fancy was more authentic than most *hameaux* built for the aristocracy at the time. It was a working concern with a farmer and his wife, where the queen could introduce her children to milking and other aspects of rural life. Five buildings were reserved for the queen and four for the farmers. The produce was used in the château—although in the nearby village of St-Antoine farmers were dying of hunger. The main building is the Queen's House (restoration began in 2014), with several rooms, decorated with blue earthenware pots carrying Marie-Antoinette's initials. Other buildings include the Boudoir (for resting), dairies, the Tour de Marlborough, the remains of a barn, and a dovecote.

THE TOWN OF VERSAILLES

Tourist office at 2bis Avenue de Paris (map p. 470, A3); T: 01 39 24 88 88, tourisme@ ot-versailles.fr, www.versailles-tourisme.com. A variety of themed and cultural visits are organised.

THE QUARTIER ST-LOUIS

The Quartier St-Louis, south of Place d'Armes, was begun at the time of Louis XIV and replaced a medieval village centred on Rue du Vieux-Versailles. The Petite Écurie du Roi (south stable), which echoes the Grande Écurie (north stable), was built for the queen's horses and carriages. The former **Hôtel de la Chancellerie** (1674; *24 Rue de la Chancellerie*) is typical of the houses which once surrounded the Place d'Armes. Accessed from alongside the Chancellerie, **La Cour des Senteurs** is the route to a charming 'scented' walk, through an urban garden (also an outlet for major perfume manufacturers) with a small café (*www.parfumsetsenteurs.fr*). It exits on Rue du Vieux Versailles.

Immediately south of the château is the **Grand-Commun**, built by J. Hardouin-Mansart in 1684, used by for the '*Services de la Bouche*', the centre of catering for the courtiers. The former **Hôtel de la Guerre** (1759; *13 Rue de l'Indépendance Américaine*) is now the Centre of Works for France's armed forces and the former Hôtel des Affaires Etrangères et de la Marine (1761; *5 Rue de l'Indépendance Américaine*), with Louis XV decoration, is now the **municipal library** (*open Tues and Thur 2–7, Wed and Sat 10–6, Fri 2–6*). On the corner with Rue du Vieux Versailles is the old Surintendance des Bâtiments du Roi (c. 1702), the base of the king's ministers for Fine Arts, and diagonally across is the Hotel du Grand Côntrole, built in 1681 for the Duc de Beauvilliers, Colbert's son-in-law. Bought back by Louis XV, he installed his finance ministry here. Across from here is the Pièce d'Eau des Suisses (*see p. 480*).

The **Potager du Roi** (King's Vegetable Garden; *10 Rue du Maréchal Joffre; open Jan–March Tues and Thur 10–6; April–Oct Tues–Sun 10–6, Nov–Dec Tues and Thur 10–1; guided visits at 11, 2.30 and 4 (in French), www.potager-du-roi.fr*) was created by Jean-Baptiste La Quintinie in 1678–83 to provide for the court. It covers nine hectares and has retained its original 16 divisions, in which serried ranks of fruit and vegetables are still cultivated, especially pears, the king's favourite fruit. It is next to a small lake and incorporates Parc Balbi, a small 18th-century Anglo-Chinese-style landscaped garden. The Potager is host to the École Nationale Supérieure de Paysage.

The **Jeu de Paume** (*Rue du Jeu de Paume; open Tues–Sun 2–5; guided tours on Sat*), built in 1686, became the most famous of all the real tennis courts on 20th June 1789. L'Hôtel des Menus Plaisirs, where the États Généraux generally met, being closed, the Third Estate gathered at the largest alternative space: the tennis court. It was here, with the astronomer Jean-Sylvain Bailly acting as president, that they swore not to separate until they had given France a proper constitution. This act became known as the 'Tennis Court Oath'. Real Tennis was a royal indoor sport with varied rules, which went in and out of fashion.

At the end of Rue de Satory, a pedestrian street lined with cafés and restaurants, is the **Cathédrale St-Louis** (1743–54) by Jacques Hardouin-Mansart de Sagonne (grandson of Louis XIV's architect), a rare example of a church of the period of Louis XV. A restrained version of the Baroque, it was designated a cathedral in 1802.

QUARTIER NOTRE-DAME

The Quartier Notre-Dame is northeast of Place d'Armes. Where Avenue de Paris meets Place d'Armes is the **Grande Écurie**, built by Jules Hardouin-Mansart for the royal cavalry. It is now occupied by the Academy of Equestrian Arts, which offers a programme of equestrian performances most of the year (*T: 01 39 02 07 14, www.acad-equestre.fr*).

Place Hoche (1671) is an octagonal square, unique for its time. Just to the west, on **Rue Carnot**, is the Pavilion of the Springs, a two-storey building of 1683 which covered a reservoir fed by natural springs to provide water for the town. Beyond is the Court of Appeal in the former Queen's Stables (1682), once used for the horses of

Marie-Antoinette and Marie Leszczynska. Further west, at 7 Rue des Réservoirs, is the *hôtel* built by Lassurance for Mme de Pompadour, still bearing the marquise's arms. Proust isolated himself here for almost five months in the latter half of 1906. At no. 13 is the elegant **Théâtre Montansier** (*box office open Tues, Fri, Sat 4–6; T: 01 39 20 16 00*), founded by the actress Mlle Montansier and built by Heurtier. It was inaugurated in 1777 in the presence of Louis XVI and Marie-Antoinette.

At the heart of this busy district, on Rue de la Paroisse, is the classical-style **Church of Notre-Dame** (1684–6, Hardouin-Mansart), bearing the royal coat of arms on its façade. Northeast, at 54 Blvd de la Reine, is the **Musée Lambinet**, housed in a mid-18th-century mansion. Its collection includes objects relating to the history of Versailles and to the Revolution.

On **Rue Rameau**, the Quartier de la Geôle (the old jail and courthouse of 1724) has become an antiques area with numerous picturesque passageways, some leading to the covered market. There is a wide choice of places to eat around here. Rue Saladin brings you back to Avenue St-Cloud and on the other side is **Place Charost**, with pavement cafés and the Palais de Justice (1888; *3 Pl. André-Mignot*).

Back on **Avenue de Paris** are various municipal buildings, including the Hôtel du Département (no. 11, 1866, in 18th-century style). The Hôtel de Ville (no. 4) is in two parts; one dating from the time of Louis XIV and the other neo-Louis XIII. No. 21 is the house which belonged to Madame du Barry, Louis XV's mistress (1751; *private*), with a monumental portal by Claude-Nicolas Ledoux (*see p. 405*). The Hôtel des Menus Plaisirs (1741–8; no. 22), was the warehouse used for storing theatrical scenery, props and other equipment. Comte Robert de Montesquiou (d. 1921), on whom Proust based Baron Charlus and Huysmans Jean des Esseintes in *À Rebours*, lived at no. 53.

TRIANON PALACE HOTEL

At the extreme west of Bouelvard de la Reine, next to the park of the château, is the Trianon Palace (*map p. 470, B3*), a luxury hotel built by René Sergent, the architect of the Plaza Athénée, in 1910. During the First World War it served a hospital for British troops and in April 1917 the Allied Military Committee installed its permanent War Council here. It was chosen by Allied politicians for meetings preceding the signing of the Treaty of Versailles in the château. In the conference room is a plaque recording the handing of the conditions for peace by Georges Clemenceau to the German High Command on 7th May 1919. The building was requisitioned by the Royal Air Force in 1939, by the Luftwaffe in 1940 and by the Americans in 1944, when it was again the meeting place for decisions that settled the peace. Since then the Trianon Palace Hotel's original architectural splendour has been lavishly restored and is a Waldorf-Astoria hotel with several bars and restaurants.

EATING AND DRINKING IN VERSAILLES

IN THE CHÂTEAU
Salon de Thé Angelina. On the first floor near the Galeries des Batailles. Part of the same small chain as the grand tea room opposite the Tuileries (*T: 01 39 20 08 32*).

Grand Café d'Orléans. On the garden level (*access also via Cour des Princes*), serving light refreshments or more substantial meals, either self-service with modern seating, or waiter service (*T: 01 39 50 29 79*).

IN THE PARK
€ **La Flotille**. Restaurant, brasserie and tea shop in 1900s style with waiter service, and with a terrace overlooking the Grand Canal. Open every day. *T: 01 39 51 41 58, www.laflottille.fr*.

€ **La Petite Venise**. Between the Bassin d'Apollon and the Grand Canal. It occupies the former gondola workshop, built at the time of Louis XIV, where the vessels were constructed by Venetian experts. The menu is essentially modern Italian, and good quality (also takeaway). Open daily 12–6 (5.30pm in low season). *T: 01 39 53 25 69*.

For takeaway snacks in the gardens are **La Parmentier de Versailles**, serving baked potatoes with various fillings (in high season at Place du Grand Trianon and the south bank of the Canal; in low season at Place du Grand Trianon and Allée du Bosquet); and **Brasserie La Girandole** (fast food and takeaway),

open April–Oct, with outdoor seating, south of the Grand Canal. There is also an Angelina tea shop/takeaway on Marie-Antoinette's estate (close to the Petit Trianon) and various other places for ice creams and drinks.

IN TOWN
There are several restaurants of varying quality along Rue de Satory (*map p. 470, A3*) and around the market (*map p. 470, B4*), including one on Rue au Pain on the market's south side: € **Le Boeuf à la Mode** (*no. 4; T: 01 39 50 31 99, leboeufalamode-versailles.com, open daily 9am to midnight*), a good traditional French '*selon le marché*'. Not far from the château is € **La Tour** (*6 Rue Carnot, T: 01 39 50 58 46; map p. 470, B3*), an impeccable yet congenial restaurant which specialises in all cuts and kinds of meat.

The **Trianon Palace Hotel** (*1 Blvd. de la Reine, T: 01 30 84 50 18, www.trianonpalace.com; map p. 470, B3*), has two restaurants: the exclusive €€€ **Gordon Ramsay au Trianon**, which has only ten tables, specialises in traditional French cuisine and has earned two Michelin stars; and €€ **La Veranda**, with black and white décor and a modern take on classic cooking. For those who enjoy cooking per se, the **Chef's Table** at Gordon Ramsay au Trianon allows for a small group not only to sample but also to watch the preparation of a menu. The **Gallery Bar** serves light meals and tea and there is a **Garden Bar Lounge** for fine weather.

Saint-Germain-en-Laye & Yvelines

St-Germain-en-Laye, within easy reach of Paris,
makes a pleasant expedition from the city. Also in the département
are Poissy, Marly-le-Roi and Maisons-Laffitte

On the edge of the Forest of St-Germain (the suffix 'Laye' is thought to derive from a Celtic word connected with forest), Saint-Germain is an interesting and attractive town with royal connections, well-kept mansions and elegant shops. The impressive former royal château, now home to the Musée d'Archéologie Nationale, stands on the edge of a park with panoramic views of Paris. This and the museum dedicated to the painter Maurice Denis make a visit to Saint-Germain well worthwhile. Claude Debussy was born here in 1862.

Getting there and information
Map p. 577, A2. RER A1 to St-Germain-en-Laye (Zone 4). Debussy's birthplace is now the Information Centre (38 Rue au Pain, T: 01 34 51 05 12, www.tourisme.saintgermainenlaye.fr).

CHÂTEAU DE SAINT-GERMAIN-EN-LAYE

The Château de St-Germain-en-Laye is strategically positioned on an escarpment dominating a bend in the Seine on the edge of the former royal forest. Louis IX built the first of three Gothic royal chapels here and it remained one of the principal seats of the French Court until abandoned by Louis XIV. The Renaissance château was restored and adapted in the 19th century to house the collections of French archaeology: an interesting visit on both counts.

THE CHÂTEAU
A château was first built here c. 1122 by Louis VI, of which only the square tower to the left of the entrance remains. In the late 12th or early 13th century St Louis (Louis IX) completed the feudal castle, described as the '*Petit Châtelet*', and had a free-standing chapel built (*see below*), to house relics from the Holy Land. The chapel is attributed to

the unconfirmed architect of the Sainte-Chapelle, Pierre de Montreuil. Château and chapel were enclosed within the same enceinte. In 1346, during the Hundred Years War, the English fired the château and the village, but the chapel was spared. Charles V, in the 14th century, rebuilt the château and linked the chapel and keep.

The marriage of François I and Claude de France took place here in 1514 and in 1539 began rebuilding in brick, under the direction of Pierre Chambiges, following the uneven pentagon outline of the earlier building. By 1559 the château covered some 8000m square and included a ballroom and a prison. The ballroom, with a grand fireplace, now part of the museum, was considered the greatest in the land and went on to be a theatre, where works by Molière and Lully were performed. The terraced roofs of the château are reminiscent of the Loire Valley. Henri II completed the building and began the Château-Neuf below the original castle, a vast structure which was completed by Henri IV. Louis XIV was born there and lived in St-Germain from 1660, when major improvements were carried out and Le Nôtre designed the terrace. In 1682 he moved his court to Versailles.

This was home to the infant Mary Stuart from October 1548 until her marriage to François II in April 1558; it also afforded refuge in 1644–8 to Henrietta Maria of England, sister of Louis XIII; and after 1688 it became the residence and court-in-exile of James II of England, cousin of Louis XIV. King James and his wife, Mary of Modena, helped the impoverished English who filled St-Germain. King James died here in 1701 but loyal Jacobites remained in St-Germain until 1793.

In 1776 the Château-Neuf was demolished except for the Pavillon Henri-IV. Dilapidated after the Revolution, the main château was also due for demolition but Queen Victoria, visiting James II's place of exile in 1855, persuaded Napoléon III to save it. A decree for the establishment of a museum was signed in 1862 and restoration of the château was directed by Eugène Millet (pupil of Viollet-le-Duc). Napoléon III, who took a major interest in the archaeological past of France, decided to bring together here the finds from archaeological digs, particularly those from Alésia, where Caesar had defeated Vercingetorix. The emperor opened the first rooms of the museum in 1867.

THE CHAPEL OF ST LOUIS

The graceful Rayonnant Gothic chapel of St Louis, built in 1280–8, ten years before La Sainte-Chapelle in Paris, is a single-nave structure which, having lost its furnishings over the years, contains only copies of tombs from the Alyscamps at Arles. It is nevertheless elegant in its emptiness. Unique in a Gothic building, it has square-headed windows, which had appeared in no great church of the period. In the vaults are keystones with images of Louis IX and his mother, Blanche of Castile. In Henri II's time the château was built up against the west rose window with elegant tracery, which once had coloured glass. In this chapel in 1238, Baldwin II of Constantinople relinquished the relics of Christ, including the Crown of Thorns (*see p. 35*), for which La Sainte-Chapelle in Paris was constructed. Royal marriages as well as royal baptisms, legitimate and illegitimate, were performed here. Louis XIV and his son, the Grand Dauphin, were both baptised here.

MUSÉE D'ARCHÉOLOGIE NATIONALE

Open Wed–Mon 10–5; closed Tues. Free first Sun of month and for under-18s and to chapel and courtyard. T: 01 39 10 13 00, www.musee-archeologienationale.fr.

The Museum of National Archaeology is presented in 18 rooms over two floors of the old château. It is one of the most important archaeological collections in Europe, holding some two million objects of which around 30,000 are on display. It traces man's existence in France from his origins to the Middle Ages: c. 500,000 BC to the 8th century AD.

Mezzanine floor

Palaeolithic to Mesolithic: Early evolution can be followed through the production of flint tools used by hunter-gatherers of the Lower Palaeolithic era. The first humans to emerge in France some 800,000 years ago, Tautavel man, made rudimentary tools from pebbles. Neanderthal man produced more diversified stone implements and was the first to bury his dead accompanied by offerings. Cro-Magnon man, who emerged some 35,000 ago, was present-day man's direct ancestor, and developed a greater variety of tools for precise applications such as scraping, cutting and piercing, reaching perfection with the 'laurel leaf' shape. From c. 25,000 BC we encounter the prehistoric art, for which France is so well known. Images tended to be restricted to animals, including mammoths, reindeer, horses and bovines: examples in the museum include a limestone relief of antelopes facing each other (c. 18,000 BC) from the Charente; a reindeer horn engraving from La Madeleine, in Dordogne, of a bison licking itself (c. 13,000 BC), and of the same period, a horse from Lourdes (Hautes-Pyrenees), carved in the round from mammoth ivory. One of the oldest and most remarkable examples, however, is the *Lady with the Hood* (c. 21,000 BC), from Brassempouy (Landes), also of mammoth ivory. Human figures, usually associated with female fertility, are described as Venuses.

Neolithic: During the New Stone Age (c. 12500–7000 BC) more organised societies and farming demanded new types of polished stone tools for cultivation and working with wood. At this time the first long-distance networks were established, mainly via rivers. Neolithic-period objects which bear witness to the skills acquired, such as weaving and pottery, were found mainly in cairns or tumuli. A find of polished axe heads from Brittany demonstrates the high-quality finish given to these tools. A unique production was the statue-menhir or standing stone, found outside tombs and exclusive to a part of southwest France where around 50 have been identified; an example from the Aveyron of a female figure is engraved on all four faces.

Bronze Age (c. 2000–750 BC): The last period of prehistory is characterised by technical innovation and the technique of casting bronze, which produced increasingly elaborate decorative objects, arms and tools. Hierarchies emerged: there was competition for metal deposits, skills developed and pottery acquired a variety of shapes, while gold objects became more frequent. Most pieces in the collection are associated with votive cults or sacrifice. An unusual juxtaposition of gold goblets and adornments (1600–1300 BC) was found in the Marne and a group of seven bronze breastplates (9th–8th centuries BC) from Haute-Marne is thought to be a votive offering. A deposit of 65 pieces from the Franco-German border highlights the importance of a military hierarchy, with examples of jewellery, a harness and chariot attachments for parades, culminating in a sword on top. A superb gold belt is from Guines (Pas-de-Calais).

First Iron Age (c. 850–c. 450 BC): This was a time of demographic change and economic upheaval. Iron was still rare and communities gathered in areas where it was available. Fortifications protected commercial routes with the Etruscans and Greeks. Individual burials were granted only to high-ranking members of society, who were buried with their possessions in wooden funeral chambers inside burial mounds. In the so-called chariot tombs found at Sainte-Colombe-sur-Seine and Apremont (Haute-Saône), the deceased was placed on the chassis of a chariot, with its wheels and other valuable objects placed alongside, including bronze swords, harnesses, ceramics, gold jewellery, and on one tomb a remarkable helmet in bronze (c. 375 BC).

The Gauls: From 490 BC to start of the present era, the Gauls (Celts) occupied the centre of France. Theirs was a warring society which grew in strength when power was centralised in fortified *oppida*. Skilled in the 'arts of fire', they produced fine pottery, glass and metal objects, such as the gold torque and earrings. The gradual Romanisation of the Gallic world came with the conquest of Gaul by Caesar at the beginning of the 2nd century BC. A large find of Celtic and Roman weapons comes from the battlefield of Alésia (Côte-d'Or, Burgundy), where the Gauls, led by Vercingetorix, were defeated by the Romans in 52 BC. A coin or weight in gold carrying an effigy of the Gallic leader was found at Puy-de-Dôme.

First floor

Roman Gaul (52 BC–AD 486): The collection is arranged thematically to evoke life in the Gallo-Roman period and show the cross-fertilisation of cultures, both social and religious. The curious statue with glass eyes and a neck torque (Essonne, late 1st/early 2nd century) shows little Roman influence except in the hair, whereas the statuette of *Mercury* from the Lyon area (1st–3rd centuries AD) has Classical attributes.

Small objects include the charming *Amants de Bordeaux*, of a couple in bed, embracing, with a dog at their feet. A collection of military equipment and coins was found in a Roman soldier's sepulchre and a large 3rd-century mosaic pavement from St-Romain-en-Gal (on the Rhône) depicts a rustic calendar of the seasons. A variety of domestic objects includes sigillated pottery and silver; new skills include blown or moulded glass.

Early Middle Ages, Merovingian era (mid-5th–mid-8th century): This is an exceptional collection, presenting fine objects as well as those associated with everyday life. Germanic tribes, from whom Clovis, founder of the French monarchy descended, brought new influences from the north. These merged with the influence of Rome, which held to the pagan custom of burying possessions with the deceased. Christianity gradually took root and Dagobert I was the first to be buried at St-Denis (*see p. 507*), whose rich tombs yielded two fibulae and a gold cross buried in the late 5th century and a late 6th-century bronze belt buckle engraved with a relief of Daniel in the Lions' Den. A 5th-century marble altar table found in the Ardèche has a frieze of the Apostles in the form of sheep and doves. Metalworkers employed cloisonné and damascene techniques, and semi-precious stones were imported from India and Ceylon.

Comparative Archaeology: This section occupies François I's ballroom. The aim is to compare and contrast evolution in France from prehistory to the early Middle Ages against objects of the same periods from other parts of the world: Africa, from the Mediterranean Basin, the Middle East, the Caucasus and Europe.

The Salle Piette (*accessible to pre-booked groups or special visits, T: 0134 51 65 36*): The collections here come from searches made by Édouard Piette of six caves in the Pyrenees and include prehistoric tools, arms and art donated to the museum in 1904.

THE PARK

Open daily day 8–8; July–Aug 8–9.30.

Standing in the dry moat of the château are a menhir, engraved blocks and a replica of Trajan's Column, installed in 1867. To the north of the château are the gardens and terraces initially laid out by Le Nôtre in 1662–74, which cover a large area on the edge of the forest. Le Nôtre's masterpiece is the seemingly infinite Grande Terrasse (1.95km), extending northeast. Paris is to the east and the towers of La Défense are visible. In the park are French and English gardens and a vineyard and in its southeast corner is the Pavillon Henri-IV, all that remains of the Château-Neuf (it has been a hotel since 1836; *see p. 536*). It was here that Alexandre Dumas wrote *The Three Musketeers* and *The Count of Monte Cristo*.

THE TOWN OF SAINT-GERMAIN-EN-LAYE

The **church of St-Louis** (opposite the château), the third church on this site, is a Neoclassical building designed c. 1765 by N.-M. Potain but not completed until the early 19th century. It was re-orientated to face the château (*enter on the north*). It contains a monument to James II of England (d. 1701), who lived in the château during his exile. He requested that he should be buried in St-Louis, and in 1824 his partial remains were discovered. Louis-Philippe, with the participation of George IV of England, financed the erection of a monument in 1827. The decoration of the chapel in which it stands was paid for by Queen Victoria. James II's skull was translated to the Collège des Écossais in the Latin Quarter (*see p. 77*). The town centre is worth a stroll.

MUSÉE CLAUDE DEBUSSY/TOURIST OFFICE

38 Rue au Pain. Open March–Oct Tues–Fri 2–5.45, Sat 10–12.45 & 2–5.45; Nov–Feb 10.30–12.15 & 2.30–5.45. Closed Sun, Mon. T: 01 30 87 20 63, www.ot-saintgermainen-laye.fr.

This building, also the Tourist Office, was the birthplace of the composer Claude Debussy in 1862. Debussy spent his childhood in this fine 17th–18th-century house, built around a courtyard, where his parents owned a small shop. The museum, on the first floor, contains a collection of memorabilia, arranged to follow the development of Debussy's career, presented by Madame de Tinan, the composer's daughter-in-law. On the second floor is a Salon de Musique with a Bechstein of c. 1915 for faithful recitals of Debussy's oeuvre.

The **Pâtisserie Grandain**, at 13 Rue au Pain, makes St-Germain specialities.

MUSÉE MAURICE DENIS

2bis Rue Maurice-Denis. Open Tues–Fri 10–5.30, Sat, Sun and holidays 10–12.30 & 2–6.30. Closed Mon, 1 Jan, 1 May, 25 Dec. T: 01 39 73 77 87.

A short walk along the continuation of rues au Pain, A. Bonnefant and de Mareil, the museum occupies a former royal hospital founded by Madame de Montespan in 1678. Maurice Denis rented a studio here in 1905 and bought the property in 1914. With the help of Auguste Perret, he built a workshop and restored the ruined chapel before moving in with his large family. He called the house the Priory and lived here until his death. The late 17th-century building, which was never completed, is in a garden setting and has a vaulted entrance and a double-helix staircase. The museum, inaugurated in 1980, throws an interesting light on the development of Modern Art. The bequest by the artist's family and collection of works by Denis' contemporaries have been added to by acquisition to include paintings, sculptures, decorative arts, engravings, pastels and manuscripts. There are eight rooms and a chapel, over two floors.

There are works from the whole career of Maurice Denis, whose famous dictum was that a painting is first and foremost a flat surface with colour assembled on it in a certain order. Among Denis' early experimental Symbolist works is the small *Le Chemin dans les arbres* (c. 1891), a spectral scene with figures dwarfed by tall straight trees. The road disappearing into the distance was to become a recurrent theme in his work. *Madame Ranson and her Cat* (1892) explores the Nabis principles of flat pattern and colour, with no attempt at depth, and is heavily influenced by Japanese prints. Similarly, *Ladder in Foliage* (1892), intended as a ceiling decoration for music publisher Henri Lerolle, shows variations on a theme of the same woman. *Échelle* (ladder) also means a musical scale in French. Works inspired by Brittany include the colourful *Regatta at Perros Guirec* (1897), with a disturbing use of perspective. Breton subjects by other painters include Sérusier's sombre *The Old Breton Woman* (c. 1898) and Émile Bernard's *Landscape with Wrack* (seaweed), painted in 1888. From 1906, under the influence of Cézanne, whom Denis met in Provence that year, Nabis paintings became more colourful and luminous: *The Beach and a Red Bonnet* (1909) is an example. Denis was married twice: in *Self-portrait* he is shown at his easel in the garden of the Priory with both his wives and his children in the background. The museum also has paintings by Édouard Vuillard and Paul Gauguin.

Maurice Denis was commissioned to decorate a narrow room for Baron Denys Cochin's property in Melun, taking the themes of the legend of St Hubert and of Beau Pécopin as told by Victor Hugo in *Le Rhin*. The seven panels, painted in 1896–7, bring together all the Nabis precepts of harmony, decoration, symbolism and colour and introduce members of the Cochin family as well as Victor Hugo. Gabrielle Thomas's dining room in Meudon is reconstructed here with the ten panels of *Eternal Spring* (1908), painted by Denis.

In 1919 Denis (with Auguste Perret) restored the badly neglected chapel, which was re-consecrated in 1922. Perret designed the woodwork while Denis planned the decorative scheme. Colleagues helped with the murals and Denis's family and friends modelled for the *Life of Christ* and the *Last Supper*; *St Louis* introduces an element of patriotism and the geometric *Crucifixion* refers to the horrors of the First World War. There are objects designed by Denis, together with glass by Daum.

The gardens contain bronzes by Bourdelle and the workshop built by Auguste Perret in 1912 when Denis (with Perret and Bourdelle) began the large decorations for the Théâtre des Champs-Élysées. The gardens have been adapted for public use.

> ## THE NABIS
>
> Maurice Denis was co-founder and principal theorist of the Nabis, a group named by the poet Cazalis. *Nabi* is the Hebrew word for prophet and the members of the group were all were searching for a new way forward in painting. Maurice Denis (*le Nabi aux belles icônes*), Pierre Bonnard (*le Nabi très japonard*) and Paul Ranson studied at the Académie Julian and were inspired by a painting on a cigar-box by fellow student Paul Sérusier, which became known as *Le Talisman* (it is now in the Musée d'Orsay) and was crucial in disseminating new ideas learned from Gauguin. Édouard Vuillard and Ker-Xavier Roussel, Felix Vallotton and Aristide Maillol also joined the group and adapted the Nabis principles to their personal approach. They are represented in the museum.

CHAMBOURCY & POISSY

MAISON ANDRÉ DERAIN

64 Grande Rue, Chambourcy. RER A to St-Germain-en-Laye and bus R4 (direction Chambourcy Collège) to the Mairie, then a 3-min walk. Closed for renovations at the time

POISSY
Villa Savoye by Le Corbusier.

of writing, www.maisonderain.free.fr or inquire at the Tourist Office (T: 01 39 22 31 31).
This 18th-century house, La Roseraie, was from 1935 the home of André Derain. It is now privately owned. The studio, which can be visited, is preserved intact.

VILLA SAVOYE

82 Rue Villiers, Poissy. Map p. 577, A1. RER A to Poissy (Zone 5) and then bus 50 to Les Œillets. Open Wed–Sun May–Aug 10–6; March–April and Sept–Oct 10–5; Nov–Feb 10–1 & 2–5. Closed Tues and 1 May, 1 Nov, 11 Nov, 25 Dec–1 Jan. Guided tour in English Wed and Fri, 11.00 T: 01 39 65 01 06, www.villa-savoye.monuments-nationaux.fr.
At Poissy, 33km northwest of Paris, is Le Corbusier's Villa Savoye, built in 1919–31 for Pierre and Eugenie Savoye, who lived here until 1940. The villa was damaged when expropriated during the Second World War but has since been returned as near as possible to its original state. Known as *Les Heures Claires*, the house was designed to take advantage of the site which then commanded views towards Paris (now obscured). A seemingly simple design, it incorporates the architect's basic tenets. From the exterior it presents a white box on *pilotis* or stilts, with a flat roof and a horizontal rhythm. The interior reveals a more complex articulation of space and light, combining large windows and a roof terrace with practical living spaces.

MAISON D'ÉMILE ZOLA

Closed at the time of writing; T: 01 39 75 35 65. SNCF train from Gare St-Lazare (direction Mantes) to Villennes-sur-Seine and then on foot for c 1.5km.

In Médan, near Poissy, is the house where Émile Zola lived from 1878–1902, and where he wrote *Nana, Germinal* and *La Bête Humaine*. Zola lived a rural idyll here, in a neo-Gothic mansion surrounded by a garden, both of which he designed himself. He and his wife received many illustrious guests here, including Cézanne. Something of a time capsule (many of the writer's belongings are still in place), it preserves a collection of original manuscripts and photographs taken by Zola.

MARLY-LE-ROI

Map p. 577, A2. SNCF train from Gare St-Lazare (direction St-Nom-La-Bretèche) to Marly-le-Roi, and then bus 10 to Les Lampes (or 15mins walk along Av. Général Leclerc). Tourist information office at 2 Av. des Combattants. T: 01 30 61 61 35, www.marlyleroi.fr.

The now-vanished royal Château de Marly, built in 1679–86 by Jules Hardouin-Mansart for Louis XIV, 25km west of Paris, was a favourite retreat from the formality of Versailles. Unlike other royal residences, Marly was a completely new creation, and was planned as a group of twelve guest houses around the central royal pavilion, a design based on the signs of the Zodiac and dedicated to carefree conviviality. The buildings were fully integrated into the parkland setting and much use was made of *trompe l'oeil* and water. The famous Marly horses, by Coysevox and Coustou, which adorned the pools, were gradually transferred to the Tuileries between 1719 and 1794. Sold at the Revolution, the château was used as a factory until 1809, plundered for its stone, and demolished in 1816.

Vestiges remain of the park where the famous *Machine de Marly* stood, a hydraulic device designed in 1681 to raise water from the Seine to the Marly aqueduct, which in turn carried it to Versailles. New machinery was installed in 1855–9, taking water from an underground source, but it was dismantled in 1967. Since 1985 there have been efforts to recapture some of the magic of Marly and copies of the statuary have been installed.

MUSÉE-PROMENADE DE MARLY-LE-ROI/LOUVECIENNES

Open Wed–Sun April–Sept 2–6.30, Oct–March 2–5.30; closed Mon, Tues and holidays; frequent temporary exhibitions; T: 01 39 69 06 26.

In Marly Park, the **Musée-Promenade** illustrates the splendours of the former residence of the Sun King with the help of an interactive model. There is a room devoted to Madame du Barry, Louis XV's favourite, and to Élisabeth Vigée-Lebrun, the portrait artist, both of whom lived in Marly-le-Roi.

The **church** of Marly-le-Roi was also built by Hardouin-Mansart (1689) and contains some works originally in Versailles.

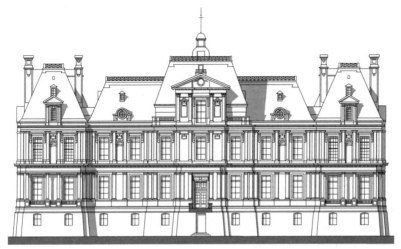

CHÂTEAU DE MAISONS-LAFFITTE

CHÂTEAU DE MONTE-CRISTO

Square des Ormes, Port-Marly (map p. 577, A2). RER A1 to St-Germain-en-Laye (Zone 4), then bus 10 (stop Av. Kennedy), or SNCF from Gare-St-Lazare to Marly-le-Roi and then bus 10. Open April–Nov Tues–Fri 10–12.30 & 2–6, Sat and holidays 10–5; T: 01 39 16 49 49, www.chateau-monte-cristo.com.

This Renaissance-style château was built by Alexandre Dumas as a haven in which to live and work, but it bankrupted him a year after its completion in 1847. It is surrounded by English-style gardens and inside is a Moorish living room.

CHÂTEAU DE MAISONS-LAFFITTE

Map p. 577, B1. RER A3 or A5 (a Cergy or a Poissy train) to Maisons-Laffitte (Zone 4). Open Wed–Mon 10–12.30 & 2–5 (summer to 6). Closed Tues, 1 Jan, 1 May, 1 Nov, 11 Nov, 25 Dec. Audioguides. Guided visits on Sun at 2.30 and 4 (places limited). Free on first Sun of month. T: 01 39 62 63 64, www.maisonslaffitte.net.

The Château de Maisons-Laffitte, in the pleasant residential town of Maisons-Laffitte on the Seine northwest of Paris, is the most complete surviving work by François Mansart, representing his genius better than any other building. It is also the only building by Mansart in which his interior decoration survives.

The château was built c. 1642–50 for René de Longueil, first Marquis de Maisons, president of the *Parlement* and governor of the châteaux of Versailles and St-Germain.

The property was bought in 1777 by the Comte d'Artois (brother of Louis XVI, later Charles X), who built the stables and created a racecourse. At the Revolution, the house passed to the state and the contents were dispersed. Maréchal Lannes owned the house from 1804, when Napoleon was a regular visitor. It was sold in 1818 to Jacques Laffitte, head of the Banque de France, who demolished the stables and sold off the estate, which was divided up for development. Further fragmented by a subsequent owner, the shell of the château was saved from demolition in 1905 when acquired by the state. Recently it has received additional furnishings, some of which originate from here, including an exceptionally fine billiard table which was purchased by Louis-Philippe for the Tuileries in 1834. Despite the vagaries of time, the interior has retained its fine Baroque proportions and some of its original decoration. Voltaire wrote *Marianne* when a guest here in 1720.

VISITING THE CHÂTEAU

On the ground floor is the apartment of René de Longueil, where the **Salon des Captifs** takes its name from the fireplace carved by Gilles Guérin with the *Triumph of Louis XIII*, shown in Roman guise representing victories during the Thirty Years War. The magnificent **Entrance Vestibule** is richly restrained, without gilt or colour. It has Doric columns with allegorical reliefs and the eagles of the Longueil on the entablature, and spans the width of the château. The two sets of wrought-iron doors leading to the exterior (1650) were transferred to the Louvre in 1797. The **Ceremonial Staircase** around an open square, embellished with putti by Philippe de Buyster, has a particularly fine balustrade.

The Neoclassical decoration of the **Dining Room of the Comte d'Artois**, on the first floor, was directed by F.-J. Bélanger. It uses the Corinthian Order and includes a grand chimneypiece with a scene of Bacchus. In niches around the room are sculptures representing the fruits of the earth.

L'appartement à l'Italienne comprises the Grande Galerie in grey and gilt paint with a musicians' gallery and paintings of the Italian countryside. The **King's Bedroom**, designed by Mansart, is like a theatre set, with the original ceiling and floor and a replica 17th-century bed. The domed **Cabinet aux Miroirs**, with a marquetry floor, was also designed for the king.

Maréchal Lannes' Apartment, formerly the Queen's suite, was transformed by Lannes, including the bedroom furnished in Empire style, with a painting of the *Remains of Napoleon I Returning to Paris*. A small bedroom in 19th-century style contains souvenirs collected by Jacques Laffitte.

THE TOWN OF MAISONS-LAFFITTE

Tourist information at 43 Av. de Longueil. T: 01 39 62 63 64,
www.tourisme-maisonslaffitte.fr.

The land adjacent to the château, after its sale by Laffitte, was developed in the 19th century with attractive villas for Parisians and is well known as a horse-racing centre. The railway station was built in 1843 and in 1882 the town was officially renamed Maisons-Laffitte. Jean Cocteau was born here in 1889.

EATING AND DRINKING IN AND AROUND SAINT-GERMAIN-EN-LAYE

MAISONS-LAFFITTE

A couple of recommended restaurants at Maisons-Laffitte are € **La Plancha de Kiko** (*5 Av. de St-Germain, T: 01 39 12 03 75*), close to the RER station, a bar and restaurant which combines French cooking with a hint of Spanish and Japanese; and €–€€ **Tastevin** (*9 Av. Eglé, T: 01 39 62 11 67, www. letastevin-restaurant.fr*), in an attractive old building in the park, which serves classic cuisine with interesting combinations.

SAINT-GERMAIN-EN-LAYE

€–€€ **Cazaudehore La Forestière**. A family affair since 1928, this is also hotel, in a beautiful woodland garden setting. The cooking is modern and light, beautiful to look at, with hints of southwest France. Tasting Menu, Menu Forestière and *à la carte*. Closed Sun evening, Nov–March and Aug. *1 Av. du Président Kennedy. T: 01 30 61 64 64, www.cazaudehore.fr.*

€–€€ **La Feuillantine**. Run by a husband-and-wife team, in an 18th-century building in the centre of St-Germain. The restaurant presents a calm and very personalised setting for contemporary creative cuisine and delicate flavours. Lunch and weekday dinner menus, or *à la carte*. There are also guest studios to rent. *10 Rue de Louviers. T: 01 34 51 04 24, www. lafeuillantine.com.*

€–€€ **Pavillon Henri-IV**. Built on the site of the first royal castle, the Pavillon acquired its name in the 19th century and has been a luxury hotel since 1836, established by a Welshman. It is famous for *pommes de terre souflées*, invented by the chef in 1837. During the 1870–1 invasion of Paris it was the headquarters of Commander von Kleist; and there is a long list of celebrated guests, including many musicians and writers. The elegant restaurant is in a superb position with views over the Grande Terrasse and park, with La Défense in the distance. The cuisine is equally *soignée* under the direction of Patrick Käppler, one of his creations being *terrine de chevreuil à la pistache*. Closed Sat lunch and Sun dinner. *19 Rue Thiers. T: 01 39 10 15 15, www. pavillonhenri4.fr.*

€ **L'Amnésia**. Café/bar-brasserie just across from the château, a regular local place for a drink and a light meal before setting off for more sightseeing. *2 Pl. André Malraux. T: 01 39 73 07 07.*

€ **Restaurant Le Manège**. Open every day for lunch and dinner, Sunday by reservation. A combination of a pub/bar/bistrot, this is a friendly local place with home-cooked traditional food. *5 Rue Saint-Louis. T: 01 39 73 22 12, www.restaurant-le-manege. com.*

CHÂTEAU DE VINCENNES
Apocalyptic angel in the east window of the Sainte-Chapelle.

Saint-Denis, Écouen & Vincennes

To the north of Paris is historic Saint-Denis, burial place of French kings.
The château at Écouen is home to the important Musée de la Renaissance.
Just outside the Périphérique to the east is the forest and château of
Vincennes, with its lovely Sainte-Chapelle.

SAINT-DENIS

Map p. 577, C1. Métro 13 to St-Denis-Basilique or RER D2 to St-Denis. Information office at 1 Rue de la République. T: 01 55 870 870, www.saint-denis-tourisme.com.

The historic cosmopolitan suburb of St-Denis has drawn visitors for many centuries. Its two main attractions are the magnificent Gothic Basilica Cathedral of St-Denis, and the much more recent Stade de France, an arena used for sports, concerts and other events. Today, the local population embraces some 130 different ethnicities and this is reflected in the colourful market (*Tues, Fri and Sun mornings*), the largest in the Île-de-France with an exotic array of produce from all over the world. The town also has a museum of art and history and holds an annual summer music festival. Pilgrims came—and still come—to venerate the shrine of St Denis and the basilica and stadium are linked by the 'Historic Trail', starting from the garden north of the basilica and marked out by 20 steel markers engraved with information on past and present events and monuments. Along the banks of the Canal St-Denis are footpaths which lead to the Parc de la Villette, and canal boat rides can be taken (*www.canauxrama.com*).

HISTORY OF SAINT-DENIS

According to a legend which developed in the 6th century, Dionysius, or Denis, was a missionary apostle sent to Lutetia in 250. By the 9th century he was confused with two others, also called Dionysius, and the tradition developed that after his martyrdom at Montmartre c. 150 he had carried his own head to the Gallo-Roman settlement known as *Catolacus*, close to a bend in the Seine 11km north of Paris on the Paris–Beauvais route. At some point he was acclaimed as first bishop of Paris and by the 12th century he was ousting St Martin of Tours as national saint. Very early on this area became an important pilgrimage site. The suburb was already an important commercial centre in the Middle Ages: the Foire de St-Denis fair began in the 8th century and the celebrated Foire du Lendit, established in 1050, was the most important fair in the Île-de-France until the 16th century. The town was rebuilt after the Hundred Years War and the walls were reconstructed in the 15th century. The 19th-century Grande Halle of the market and the 18th-century Maison des Arbalétriers (drying house) have been restored.

When Paris was purged of heavy industry in the mid-19th century, much of it relocated to St-Denis, serviced by new canals. Subsequently those industries gradually disappeared and much of the town was transformed in the 1970s by imaginative redevelopment of commercial, domestic and civic buildings, involving architects such as Roland Simounet and Oscar Niemeyer. Again in the 21st century the landscape is changing with new, exciting buildings including the main centre for the National Archives by Massimiliano Fuksas at Pierrefitte-sur-Seine. Such is the history of this ancient settlement, close to a bend in the river, that it is one of the most researched towns in France. There is ongoing archaeological exploration of the medieval town, 'La Fabrique de la ville' (for guided visits, T: 01 49 33 80 28, ville-saint-denis.fr). Saint-Denis is one of eight neighbouring communities of La Plaine Commune.

THE ROYAL BASILICA-CATHEDRAL OF ST-DENIS

Open April–Sept 10–6.15, Sun 12–6.15; Oct–March 10–5, Sun 12–5.15. Closed 1 Jan, 1 May, 25 Dec. T: 01 48 09 83 54, www.saint-denis.monuments-nationaux.fr. Audioguides; guided tours in French on weekdays at 11 and 3, Sun at 12.30 and 3. CMN tour Fri 2.30, T: 01 44 54 19 33.

The Gothic basilica church of St-Denis stands over what is believed to be the Gallo-Roman cemetery where c. 250 Denis, the first bishop of Paris, and his companions Rusticus and Eleutherius (*see p. 317*), were laid to rest. The abbey of St-Denis was founded c. 475, traditionally at the instance of St Geneviève (*see p. 12*), and it became a site of pilgrimage, enlarged in 630–8 by King Dagobert, who also founded a Benedictine monastery. The first substantial church on the site was built by Abbot Fulrad in 750–75 and here, in 754, Pope Stephen II anointed Pepin the Short, his wife and sons (one of them the future Charlemagne), thus establishing them securely on the throne that Pepin had recently usurped. Fulrad's church was replaced by another built by the powerful Abbot Suger, a momentous occasion in the history of architecture: the new style adopted was the prototype of what would eventually become known as Gothic. The narthex (c. 1135–40), crypt and apse (1140–4) survive from this period. The rebuilding of the nave had barely begun before Abbot Suger's death and the rest of the building, notably the nave and transepts, dates from 1231–81, following the designs of Pierre de Montreuil (*see opposite*). The chapels on the north side of the nave were added c. 1375. The strong links between the Crown and the Abbey were reinforced at the time of Abbot Suger who, from 1127, was adviser to Louis VI and Louis VII, and regent during the Second Crusade (1147–9). Dagobert had chosen to be buried close to the saintly relics of Denis and, during the reign of St Louis (Louis IX), the abbey church became the royal mausoleum. With the exception of Philippe I, Louis XI, Louis-Philippe and Charles X, all the French kings since Hugh Capet were buried here. As well as being the last resting place of royalty, the abbey was entrusted by Louis VI in 1120 with the royal insignia, including the *oriflamme* (the military standard) and the coronation regalia. The association with royalty, and the fact that 13 bishops attended the dedication of the choir in 1144, assured the spread of its style of architecture throughout northern France. In 1422 the body of Henry V of England lay in state at St-Denis on its way from Vincennes to Westminster, and here Joan of Arc came seven years later to dedicate her armour. Henriette d'Angleterre, daughter of Charles I, was buried here in 1670 where her mother, Henrietta Maria, widow of Charles I, had been buried the previous year.

At the Revolution the abbey was suppressed and its roof stripped of lead. During the Terror in 1793, the tombs were rifled, their contents dispersed and the corpses of the kings tossed into a common pit. The best of the monuments were saved from destruction by Alexandre Lenoir (*see p. 93*) and preserved in the Musée des Petits-Augustins, later to be returned and drastically restored. Renovation of the basilica was taken in hand in 1805, but in 1837 the north tower was struck by lightning. François Debret undertook its rebuilding but it was again destabilised by storms and, as a precaution, was dismantled in 1847 by Viollet-le-Duc, who accused Debret of technical errors. Since then St-Denis has remained bereft of a north tower. There is, however, a long-term project underway to rebuild it, based on the detailed descriptions and drawings left by Debret.

PIERRE DE MONTREUIL

When Pierre de Montreuil died in 1267, he was buried in a chapel of his own design, dedicated to the Virgin, at the church of St-Germain-des-Prés. That chapel no longer exists; it was torn down after the Revolution. But it is known that Pierre's tombstone named him as '*doctor latomorum*', 'teacher of masons', and that in his lifetime he enjoyed a considerable reputation—and a rare one, in that age of anonymous stonecarvers. The Chapel of the Virgin at St-Germain would have been splendid indeed, its rose window a grand example of the Rayonnant Gothic style of which Pierre was such a brilliant and early exponent. Its doorway survives (preserved in the Musée du Moyen Âge), and it is carved with luxuriant foliage, with recognisable maple leaves. Pierre seems to have been fond of this motif. He uses it again in his Porte Rouge at Notre-Dame, where maple leaves form a garland with wild roses. But most extraordinary of all Pierre de Montreuil's works—or at least, of those few works of probable attribution—is his *Adam*, carved for the transept façade of Notre-Dame and now also in the Musée du Moyen Âge. In approaching this work, we must dispense with any preconceptions about medieval sculpture. This is an Adam almost of the Renaissance in his naked lineaments, grasping the fig tree against his nudity like a Classical Venus surprised while bathing, but poised at the same time in proud, S-shaped contrapposto like an athlete of Polyclitus. We know next to nothing of Pierre de Montreuil's life, but he must surely have been acquainted with Roman copies of Greek sculpture. A.B.

EXTERIOR OF SAINT-DENIS

The west front, a development from the great Norman churches, notably St-Étienne in Caen, inspired generations of Gothic façades. Mighty buttresses divide the elevation vertically into three sections, corresponding to the internal structure of the church. An original element is the crenellated caesura between the façade and the set-back tower (originally twin towers; *see above*). Three west portals, deep and finely profiled, animate the lower part of the façade, the central one larger than the others. The sculptures in all three were badly damaged, and reworked in the 19th century. The *Last Judgement* in the central tympanum has a few original elements—the images of God and Christ, and the Dove and the Lamb. The signs of the Zodiac on the jambs are 12th-century. The south door tympanum is decorated with scenes from the life of St Denis, mainly 12th-century but with 19th-century heads. The *Labours of the Month* on the jambs are 12th-century. The high-relief statues of Old Testament kings in the jambs (destroyed in 1771) marked a turning point in the integration of sculpture with architecture, coming before those at Chartres. Another innovation is the large oculus high in the central bay of the west façade (its original subdivision is unknown), the precursor of the Gothic rose window.

Abbot Suger undertook the enlargement of the east end to allow for the increasing number of pilgrims. The exterior of Suger's apse appears less innovative than the west end, with Romanesque round-headed windows and relieving arches around the crypt, although the windows of the chapels are Gothic and the upper storeys with their flying buttresses date from the 1230s. By Suger's death in 1151, the two ends of the church were still linked by the 8th-century construction. When the rebuilding of the nave and transepts was undertaken during the mid-13th century, the upper level of Suger's choir was destroyed. The transept portals, each with a pioneering Rayonnant rose window, are mid-13th-century work. A small garden was created in 1998 on north side of the basilica, setting off the north door with its 12th–13th-century sculptures and indicating on the ground the extent of the unfinished Valois rotunda with the monogram of Henri II and Catherine de Médicis in the centre. The west façade has undergone restoration to return it to the aspect which it acquired during the work carried out by François Debret in 1838–40.

INTERIOR OF SAINT-DENIS

Suger added large narthex supporting three chapels to the west of the existing 8th-century church. Consecrated in 1140, this is recognised as the first example of a Gothic façade flanked by towers. The reconstruction of the east end began immediately afterwards. Work consisted of enlarging the crypt, the choir and the double ambulatory. The use of slender columnar supports in the ambulatory, rather than compound piers, looks back to Romanesque east ends—perhaps stemming from a desire to harmonise the ambulatory with the existing 8th-century structure. The shallow chapels are linked by ribbed vaulting (an ingenious combination of round and pointed ribs). In 1144, 20 new altars were consecrated. The rib vaults and the vast ratio of glazed to solid wall are what secures St-Denis' reputation as the birthplace of Gothic. Also characteristic of early Gothic are the ribs springing from strong piers enlivened by

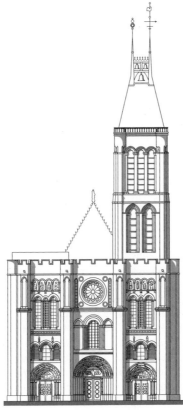

SAINT-DENIS: WEST FRONT

clusters of elongated shafts, and the tall openings between them. From Suger's records it is known that the central nave was rib-vaulted. This elegant arrangement allows an uninterrupted view through to the large windows of the radiating chapels, two in each, thus fulfilling Suger's aim of flooding the church with 'wonderful and uninterrupted light'. The axial chapels of the crypt and ambulatory were both dedicated to the Virgin.

Nave, transepts and choir: Work to rebuild the 8th-century nave began in earnest in 1231 and for part of the time (c. 1247) was under the direction of Pierre de Montreuil. The elegant effect created by expanses of glass in the clerestory lives up to its comparison with a lantern of light. Generous transepts allowing for the royal tombs are pierced north and south with magnificent rose windows squared up to fill the bay and continuing behind the open triforium below, the first of their kind, emulated at Notre-Dame in 1258. The glass is

19th-century. The carved high stalls of the choir (1501–7) come from Georges d'Amboise's chapel at the Château de Gaillon; the low stalls are 15th-century (from St-Lucien, near Beauvais), and the charming 12th-century *Virgin* is from the abbey of Longchamp. On the south side of the ambulatory are a copy of the *Oriflamme* and statues of Louis XVI and Marie-Antoinette at prayer, commissioned by Louis XVIII.

Crypt: This was constructed by Suger around the original Carolingian martyrium built by Abbot Fulrad, the site of the grave of St Denis and his companions. There are 12th-century capitals and traces of wall paintings. Excavations revealed Gallo-Roman Christian tombs and the tomb of Queen Arégonde, Clovis's daughter-in-law, as well as fragments of preceding churches. The central chapel was the Bourbon burial vault until the Revolution, and contains the sarcophagi of Louis XVI and Marie-Antoinette (their remains are no longer here; *see p. 283*) and those of Louis XVIII, among other 18th- and 19th-century sovereigns. The ossuary on the north side contains, since 1917, the remains of the kings, queens, princes and abbots of St-Denis that were thrown into a pit when the tombs were rifled during the Terror in 1793. On the south side is a 19th-century cenotaph in memory of the Bourbon kings, including Henri IV and Louis XIV.

Stained glass: The glass in the **Lady Chapel** dates from the 12th century, placing it among the oldest in France, albeit restored in the 19th century. Among the 15 panels that have survived, mounted in modern glass in the east end, is a *Tree of Jesse*, in which Abbot Suger himself is depicted.

The **baptistery** window, designed by J.-J. Gruber in 1932, is vividly different.

The Tombs: south side: The collection of over 70 tombs and funerary sculptures at St-Denis dates from the mid-12th to the mid-16th centuries.

In the **south aisle** are the tombs of Louis d'Orléans (d. 1407) and of Valentine de Milan (d. 1408), the latter an Italian work of 1502–15 combining a figure in repose, in the French tradition, on an Italian-style sarcophagus with the Twelve Apostles. Opposite, against the southwest pillar of the crossing, is the heart-tomb of François II (d. 1560) by Germain Pilon and Ponce Jacquiau and in the south aisle, an urn (1549–55) by Pierre Bontemps containing the heart of François I.

In the **south transept**, the tomb of François I (d. 1547) and his consort Claude de France (d. 1524), a masterpiece begun in 1547 by Philibert de l'Orme, is a classicised version of the tomb of Louis XII in the north aisle, in the form of a triumphal arch with coloured marbles by Bontemps. The royal pair and their children kneel on the upper level (recumbent, below). On the east side of the transept is the tomb of Charles V (d. 1380), with a remarkable likeness sculpted by André Beauneveu, commissioned before the king's death. The statue of his queen, Jeanne de Bourbon, was brought from the Célestins church in Paris. Bertrand du Guesclin (c. d. 1380), High Constable of France and hero of the Hundred Years War, is one of the few commoners buried here.

The tombs: choir: At the west end of the choir is the tomb of Philippe III, le Hardi (d. 1285) by Jean d'Arras, using black and white marble, one of the first portrait statues, and a masterly effigy of his queen, Isabella of Aragon (d. 1271); also the tomb of Philippe IV, le Bel (d. 1314). At the right of the steps to the sanctuary is the 13th-century tomb of Dagobert (d. 638), with relief sculptures showing the torment and redemption of the king's soul, and a beautiful statue of Queen Nanthilde (13th century). The figures of Dagobert and his son are 19th-century restorations. Also in the choir are the tombs of Louis X (d. 1316) and his son Jean I (d. 1316).

The tombs: north side: In the **north ambulatory** are the tombs of Blanche and Jean (both d. 1243), children of Louis IX, a rare example in metalwork and enamel. Transferred from St-Germain-des-Prés is an 11th-century cloisonné mosaic of Frédégonde (d. 597), queen of Chilperic I. Childebert I's (d. 558) is the oldest funerary effigy in France (mid-12th century). In the sanctuary is the Altar of the Relics (by Viollet-le-Duc), with the reliquaries, given by Louis XVIII, of St Denis and fellow martyrs.

Recumbent marble effigies by Germain Pilon of Henri II and his queen, Catherine de Médicis, are on the **north side** at the top of the sanctuary steps. The **north transept** contains the temple-like tomb of the royal couple, part of a grandiose scheme on the part of Catherine de Médicis, which was to have been housed in a huge rotunda in the Italian style built onto the north transept (never completed, it was demolished in the 18th century). Artists linked with its construction were Primaticcio, Lescot, Bullant and Jean-Baptiste du Cerceau. The tomb itself, designed by Primaticcio in 1560–73, was placed in its present position by Henri IV. The bronze kneeling figures of the king and queen on top of it are by Germain Pilon. Below, in the mortuary chamber, are recumbent effigies of the royal pair in death. Here also are the tombs of Philippe V (d. 1322), Charles IV (d. 1328), Philippe VI (d. 1350) and Jean II (d. 1364), the last two by André Beauneveu.

The **north aisle** contains the tomb of Louis XII (d. 1515) and Anne de Bretagne (d. 1514), commissioned by François I and made by the Florentine Giovanni di Giusto c. 1515–31: above, the royal couple is represented in life; below, after death, in a remarkably sensitive manner. The chapel-like tomb enclosing the effigies introduces a new element in funerary monuments.

Among other 13th–14th-century tombs are that of Louis de France (d. 1260), the eldest son of Louis IX, with Henry III of England as one of the *pleurants* around the base—an early example of this imagery.

On the north side of the basilica is a small garden, **Place Pierre de Montreuil**, where you can rest and regain your strength. The **Bigoudène café** opposite serves delicious crêpes. To the south of the basilica are restored monastic dependencies. Rebuilt in the 18th century by Robert de Cotte and Jacques V Gabriel, they were occupied after 1809 as a Maison d'Éducation de la Légion d'Honneur, for the daughters of members of the Legion (*guided visits during school holidays; information from the Tourist Office on Rue de la République, T: 01 55 870 870*).

MUSÉE D'ART ET D'HISTOIRE

22bis Rue Gabriel-Péri. Open Mon, Wed, Fri 10–5.30, Thur 10–8, Sat–Sun 2–6.30. Closed Tues and holidays. T: 01 42 43 05 10, musee-saint-denis.com.

The town's history museum occupies a former Carmelite convent, founded in 1625. Three wings of the cloister are original and the fourth was rebuilt. The pious 18th-century mottoes on the convent walls have been restored.

In the former chapter house is the reconstituted **Pharmacy of the Hôtel-Dieu** (demolished 1907), with other mementoes of the former hospital. The archaeological and history section, in the former refectory and kitchen, presents the **history of Saint-Denis** over the centuries: *Catolacus*, on the ancient tin route across northern Europe; medieval pilgrimages and town fairs; the supplanting of monarchist by Communist associations; modern industries, as varied as Pleyel pianos (until 1962), chemicals, Christofle glass and gas—evoked in André Lhote's painting *Usine à Gaz, St-Denis et Gennevilliers* (1937).

The **history of the Carmelites** themselves is recorded in the restored cells on the upper floor, one with memorabilia specific to Madame Louise, youngest daughter of Louis XV, who became a nun here in 1770, taking the name Thérèse de Saint-Augustin. She died in 1787 and was later declared Venerable by Pope Pius IX. In adjacent rooms are works from the Besson Donation, notably by Albert André, friend of Renoir. On the second floor is a huge and fascinating collection devoted to the **Paris Commune** (1870–1). The museum owns some 4,000 engravings and lithographs by Daumier (not necessarily on view). The modern wing of the cloister leads to the section devoted to the poet **Paul Éluard**, who was born in St-Denis in 1895. The collections include some of Éluard's manuscripts and works by Zadkine, Picasso, Max Ernst, Cocteau, Giacometti and Françoise Gilot, a portrait of Paul Éluard (1952) by André Fougeron, as well as rare editions illustrated by his painter friends. The **chapel**, by Mique, with an Ionic portico and fine compartmented cupola (1780), was commissioned by Madame Louise. It is used for exhibitions of contemporary art. The **Garden of the Five Senses** was planted in 2009.

STADE DE FRANCE

Map p. 577, C1–C2. Métro 13 to St-Denis-Port de Paris or RER B and D to Stade de France. Open for guided visits lasting around 1hr, check times and reserve online: accueil. stadefrance.com. Closed Mon outside school holidays. Restaurant (see p. 517).

The Stade de France was opened in 1998 at Plaine St-Denis. Designed mainly for football, rugby and athletics as well as major concerts and other events, it was built in two years. A spectacularly well-organised complex, it seats over 80,000 and the elliptical roof over the seating, suspended from steel beams, appears to hover like a flying saucer. Included in the guided visit is a permanent exhibition covering all aspects of sport and entertainment.

ST-OUEN AND LE BOURGET

Close to St-Denis is the **Marché aux Puces de St-Ouen** (flea market), with over 1,500 dealers in around 16 markets and small streets (*Rue des Rosiers; map p. 579, D1; open Sat 9–6, Sun 10–6, Mon 11–5; Métro 13 to Porte de St-Ouen or 4 to Porte de Clignancourt; www.parispuces.com*).

At the old airport at Le Bourget is an air and space museum, **Musée de l'Air et de l'Espace** (*map p. 577, C1; closed Mon, check opening times: T: 01 49 92 70 00, www. museedelair.org*).

CHÂTEAU D'ÉCOUEN

Map p. 577, C1. Trains from Paris Gare du Nord to Écouen-Ézanville (suburban lines direction Luzarches/Persan-Beaumont via Montsoult); then bus 269 (direction Garges-Sarcelles) to the Mairie/Église. Alternatively, it is a 20-min walk from the station through the woods: a footpath leads to the château. Château open Wed–Sun 9.30–12.45 & 2–5.15 (5.45 in summer); closed Tues, 1 Jan, 1 May, 25 Dec. Park open daily summer 8–7, winter 8–6; free. T: 01 34 38 38 52, www.musee-renaissance.fr. Restaurant and tea shop (see p. 517).

Écouen is a small town in a rural setting, dominated by the magnificent Renaissance Château d'Écouen which houses the Musée National de la Renaissance, inaugurated in 1977. It is the furthest museum from the centre of Paris in this book, but it is important because the collection follows on chronologically from the Musée du Moyen Âge. There is little to see in the town except for the church of St-Acceul, which has some notable stained glass (1544) in the choir.

MUSÉE NATIONAL DE LA RENAISSANCE

This elegant, well-organised, and lesser-known museum provides an overview of the decorative arts of the Renaissance in a château which itself is a prime example of Renaissance architecture. Construction of the château began c. 1538 for the High Constable Anne de Montmorency. Among major artists employed were the sculptor Jean Goujon and the architect Jean Bullant. The building was put to a variety of uses during the Revolutionary period and in 1805 became a school for girls. Many of its embellishments, including an altar by Goujon from the chapel, were removed during the Revolution and reverted to the Duc d'Aumale, who chose to include them in his château at Chantilly. The second stage of construction began in 1547.

The château is arranged around a courtyard, with square pavilions at the corners and moats on three sides. The elevations are simply articulated with pilasters and string courses, and ornamentation confined to the dormer windows, which show a progression in styles from the west to the north wings. After 1547, work began on the interior to provide luxurious apartments for the owners and King Henri II, and porticoes were added. Those on both sides of the north wing have Henri II's insignia. The south portico, which uses the Colossal Order for the first time in France, is ascribed to Jean Bullant. It was intended as the setting for Michelangelo's *Slaves* (*see p. 240*) given to Montmorency by Henri II.

The entrance, through the east wing, is a replacement (1807) of the superimposed galleries. Above was an equestrian statue of the High Constable, designed by Goujon or Bullant, destroyed in 1787 (a fragment of its decorative sculpture is in the museum).

Ground floor

The visit begins with the **Chapel**, whose decoration is totally in keeping with the spirit of the French Renaissance, combining traditional Gothic vaulting with a return to antiquity. The preponderance of heraldry, especially on the vaults, makes reference to the owner of the château.

The **Armoury** has a profusely decorated chimneypiece in the School of Fontainebleau style, the first of twelve depicting biblical themes which are a feature of Écouen. The arms and armour include stirrups with the emblem of François I and armour from the workshops of Maximilian I of Germany (c. 1510–20).

The **Kitchens** contain a collection of fragments of stonework from Écouen, carved wooden screens and other pieces from the Château of Gaillon (Normandy).

The **Room of Roman Heroes** contains rare painted leather hangings from Normandy depicting Roman heroes and the chimneypiece shows *The Tribute to Caesar*. There are also collections of alabasters, carved wooden plaques and panels and small sculptures; also pearwood and box-wood statuettes, mainly German or Flemish. Outstanding bronze figurines include *Jupiter* by Alessandro Vittoria, a *Virgin and Child* by Niccolò

Roccatagliata and *Fornicating Satyrs* by Il Riccio. There are also superb examples of damascened metalwork, cutlery and a collection of Renaissance doorfurniture.

The **Clock Room** contains mathematical instruments and watches, including a celestial sphere in gilded copper and an exquisite automated timepiece masquerading as a miniature ship, by Hans Schlotheim of Augsburg. An unusual object is the inlaid silversmith's workbench from Germany (1565), a full-scale working model made for a nobleman's pleasure rather than as a craftsman's tool.

Catherine de Médicis' Bedchamber and Great Hall: This corner room has three tapestries showing the *Battle of St-Denis* (10th November, 1567, a victory for Anne de Montmorency's Catholics over an army of Huguenots) and a portable triptych with painted enamels. The monumental fireplace is from Rouen. In the next room are sculpted and enamelled ceramics by Luca della Robbia as well as French sculptures including *The Three Fates*, in marble, by Germain Pilon, and *The Compassion of the Father* in terracotta. The museum owns a precious collection of portraits in wax in the form of medallions.

First floor

The first floor has been arranged to evoke the owners' and the king's residence as it was after 1547. In the South Wing were the apartments of Anne de Montmorency and his wife, Madeleine. The royal apartments were in the West Wing.

South Wing: The décor incorporates reminders of Montmorency's role as commander of the army—an unsheathed sword accompanying his coat of arms. The decorated chimneypiece in the **High Constable's Apartments** has a scene of *Esau Hunting* and there are two School of Fontainebleau paintings.

The **Apartments of Madeleine de Savoie**, are mainly a reconstruction. The antechamber contains an Italian spinet (1570) and the main rooms contain a 16th-century Venetian bureau inlaid with painted mother-of-pearl and notable carved doors (from elsewhere). **Abigail's Pavilion** takes its name from the painted decoration of the fireplace, which shows and episode from the story of Abigail and David.

The long **Psyche Gallery** originally had sumptuous stained glass and paving (remnants of which are exhibited elsewhere), as well as murals. The finely carved stone fireplaces are from Châlons-en-Champagne (1562), with reliefs of *Christ and the Samarian Woman* and *Actaeon Surprising Diana at her Bath*. This room houses the *raison d'être* of the museum, the celebrated *David and Bathsheba* series of tapestries (Brussels c. 1510). It is possible that Jan van Roome was involved in their creation. An individualistic, typically Renaissance portrayal of the figures and architectural settings is combined with a foreground reminiscent of medieval *millefleurs*. Stylised flowers form the border and the colours are still strong.

The story, reading from left to right, begins with a scribe before an open book recording the episodes. Each of the ten tapestries contains several scenes. David, despised by his wife, brings the ark to Jerusalem, then departs for battle against the Ammonites at Rabbah, with Uriah, husband of Bathsheba. After seducing Bathsheba, David sends Uriah to his death and Bathsheba is received at David's court. The prophet Nathan predicts the death of their child, while allegorical figures put Lust to flight. David and Bathsheba's child dies and David appeases God's anger by fasting and praying. He then resumes the battle and takes Rabbah. As the story ends the scribe closes the book.

West Wing: Here were the royal apartments. **Henri II's Chamber** has a painted ceiling with the king's monogram and crescent and a chimneypiece featuring *Saul in Anger Slaughtering Two of his Cattle*. Beyond a carved wooden staircase, from the Chambre des Comptes of the Palais de la Cité, is the **Salle d'honneur**, which has the only sculpted marble chimneypiece at Écouen. Attributed to Jean Bullant (c. 1558), the coloured marble was a gift of Cardinal Farnese. The paved floor, originally in the Psyche Gallery, was made by Masséot Abaquesne (mid-16th century), who made his name at Écouen. Displayed in this room are two tapestries of the *Fructus Belli* series woven in Brussels (1546–8) by Jean

Baudouyn from cartoons by Giulio Romano, which show the soldiers' payday and the general's dinner. There are also painted leather panels with scenes from Scipio and a chimneypiece with the *Judgement of Solomon*, as well as secular stained glass. The last room on this floor has embroideries made for Sully when he was Grand Master of the Artillery and occupied the Arsenal in Paris.

Second floor

The first room on the second floor is devoted to a fine group of Iznik ceramics dating largely from 1555–1700. French ceramics are represented by 16th-century tile panels and ceramics by Masséot Abaquesne, including a magnificent tiled floor of 1550 and pharmacy pots; also two rare pieces from the Saint-Porchaire workshops (c. 1560) and faïence attributed to Bernard Palissy. There is a room dedicated to painted panels from 15th-century Florentine *cassoni* (marriage-chests) and Limoges enamel plaques; also collections of majolica and glass, and among the jewellery, a swan pendant from Germany. Among fine examples of the gold and silversmith's craft are a statuette of *Daphne* by Wenzel Jamnitzer, a goblet in the shape of a snail (Netherlands, c. 1700) and several magnificent examples from Nuremberg and Augsburg. Here also is the High Constable's Library.

VINCENNES

Map p. 577, C2. Métro 1 to Château de Vincennes.

The Cours de Vincennes, which runs east from Place de la Nation to the Porte de Vincennes, is a royal processional route laid out by Le Vau for Louis XIV. The Château de Vincennes, with its chapel, was one of the glories of the French monarchy in the 14th and 15th centuries. Although badly damaged, the presentation of the keep and remaining fortifications give an interesting insight into medieval building, and renovation work is in progress. In the Bois de Vincennes, formerly a royal chase, are a Parc Floral and a Zoological Garden.

CHÂTEAU DE VINCENNES

Open mid-Sept–mid-May 10–5; mid-May–mid-Sept 10–6. Closed holidays. Main entrance through the Tour du Village. Audioguides. Guided visits available in French. Shop. T: 01 41 74 19 12, www.chateau-vincennes.fr.

The impressive bulk of the former royal residence of the Château de Vincennes played a very important role in French history. A royal property since 1178 under Louis VII, it

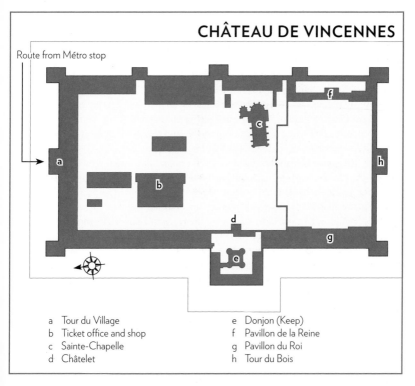

CHÂTEAU DE VINCENNES

Route from Métro stop

a Tour du Village
b Ticket office and shop
c Sainte-Chapelle
d Châtelet
e Donjon (Keep)
f Pavillon de la Reine
g Pavillon du Roi
h Tour du Bois

became the second residence after Paris of Louis IX (St Louis, d. 1270) and remained a royal stronghold until the 14th century. The keep or *donjon*, begun by Philippe VI, the first of the Valois, in 1337 at the beginning of the Hundred Years War, was completed c. 1370 by his grandson Charles V, who built the ramparts in about seven years and started work on the chapel in 1379, replacing the one built by Louis IX. This great fortress was at this time the political capital of the kingdom. The illustration for December in the *Très Riches Heures du Duc de Berry*, as well as Fouquet's panel for the *Hours of Étienne Chevalier* (both in the Musée Condé, Château de Chantilly, north of Paris), give an idea of its splendour and importance in the 15th century. By the 16th century this huge rectangular construction comprised nine square towers linked by fortified walls surrounded by a moat. Enclosed within were a keep, chapel and buildings of different periods.

The foundations of the Pavillon du Roi and the Pavillon de la Reine (named after the Queen Mother, Anne of Austria) to the southeast, were laid in the 16th century and completed nearly a century later when the château, then in Cardinal Mazarin's possession, was altered and decorated by Le Vau. It was used as a refuge for the court during the Wars of Religion, and by Mazarin to protect his collection during the Fronde (*see p. 17*). Louis XIV preferred Saint-Germain, and when his court finally moved to Versailles, Vincennes was gradually stripped of its furnishings to become first a porcelain manufactory (until that transferred to Sèvres in 1756), then a cadet school, and finally a small-arms factory. By 1788 it had been put up for sale but found no purchaser. It was rescued by Lafayette from the Revolutionary mob in 1791. When in 1808 Napoleon converted it into an arsenal, the surviving 13th-century buildings were demolished. Later in the 19th century all the towers were reduced to the level of the walls. By 1840 it was being used as a fortress again, to the detriment of much of Le Vau's decoration. Degradation continued during the Second World War, when German occupying forces installed a supply depot here, and the Pavillon de la Reine was partially destroyed by an explosion in 1944 when they evacuated.

There are many historical associations, some sombre, with Vincennes: Louis X died in the castle in 1316; Charles IV in 1328; and Charles V was born here in 1337. Both Charles IX (in 1574) and Cardinal Mazarin (in 1661) died here, as well as Henry V of England in 1422, seven weeks before the death of Charles VI, whom he should have succeeded as King of France. During the reign of Louis XIII, the keep was used as a state prison. The Duc d'Enghien (1772–1804), related to the Bourbon monarchs of France, was arrested on trumped-up charges on Napoleon's orders, was tried by court-martial and shot the same night in the château. Général Daumesnil, governor at different periods between 1809 and his death in 1832, famously retorted, when summoned to surrender to the Allies in 1814: 'First give me back my leg' (lost at the Battle of Wagram). Mata Hari, the exotic dancer whose career had been launched by Émile Guimet (*see p. 417*) was shot here in 1917, on charges of spying for the Germans. Part of the fortress is today occupied by the armed forces.

Visiting the château
The 48m-high Tour du Village stands over the entrance. Access is across a draw-bridge over the high moat and through the gatehouse. The visitor's route then passes between buildings in military occupation to the ticket office on the right-hand side of the vast inner ward.

THE KEEP GATEHOUSE
In the *châtelet*, or gatehouse to the vast keep, you can climb spiral stairs to visit the machicolated ramparts and bell-tower. The tower was rebuilt in 2000 and reproduces a clock installed by Charles V in 1369, an innovatory and costly undertaking at that time. The bell, which is struck from outside, is also a reproduction (original in the Sainte-Chapelle; *see below*), and would originally have been used for liturgical purposes, although being semi-public (the reason it survived), its tolling also came to mark the hours of the working day. From the terrace here you get an excellent view of the château, its huge courtyard, the Sainte Chapelle and Le Vau's monumental screen dividing the medieval ward from the 17th-century ward. On the right is the Pavillon du Roi (now containing military archives) and opposite, the Pavillon de la Reine, where Mazarin died in 1661. Both were completed by Le Vau in 1654–60. The gateway, the Tour du Bois, was remodelled for Mazarin as a triumphal arch. He would have used it as his principal entrance.

CHÂTEAU DE VINCENNES
Prisoner graffiti: 'My Lord and My God, behold me here because you called me.
May you be blessed for ever. 1724.'

THE KEEP

The huge *donjon* or keep, a 52m tall square tower buttressed by round turrets, rises above its free-standing turreted enceinte with ditches that were always dry. The finest of its type still standing in France, the *donjon* is a sophisticated construction consisting of a series of superimposed vaulted chambers using iron girders to stabilise the upper floors. To ensure its impenetrability were two drawbridges and portcullises and access was exclusively from an external staircase in the gatehouse. Today you cross a narrow drawbridge to enter the first floor. Here a large central chamber is preserved and opening off it are a chapel, latrines and remains of rooms converted into prisons during the *Ancien Régime*. A stout door with two massive iron bolts leads into the room where Napoleon condemned his erstwhile confessor, Monseigneur Boulognes, to solitary confinement. The walls are adorned with mural paintings and graffiti made by former inmates.

Charles V's quarters were on the second floor, where renovations have revealed evidence of the comfort and luxury of the period. Henry V of England died here in 1422. His body was then taken to Westminster for burial. King Charles' former garderobe, study, treasury and oratory can be visited. The walls are scratched with the graffiti of later prisoners.

On the ground floor is an exhibition on Vincennes as a royal prison. Famous men incarcerated here include the future Henri IV, Fouquet, Diderot and Blanqui.

SAINTE-CHAPELLE

The elegant chapel stands alone opposite the entrance to the *donjon* enclosure. Like the Sainte-Chapelle on the Île de la Cité, it takes the shape of a reliquary casket and was originally intended to receive part of the relics of the Passion. Slightly wider and longer, it is the same height as the Cité church, but has no lower level and it was once graced with a spire above the second bay of the nave. Begun in 1379 by Charles V, there are signs that further work was carried out towards the end of the 14th century, but it was not completed until 1552, at the time of François I and Henri II. The west end, including a magnificent Flamboyant rose window and gable tracery, was completely rebuilt during restoration work begun in 1987.

The interior, although empty, is lofty with graceful vaulting and sculptures and seven stained-glass windows (1555–6) by Beaurain, illustrating the Apocalypse. On either side of the nave are the king and queen's private oratories. The one on the left as you face the high altar, Oratoire de la Reine, is filled by a monument to the executed Duc d'Enghien by Deseine (1816).

The monograms of François I and of Henri II and Catherine de Médicis, the salamander, crescent moon and the initial 'C', as well as the *fleur de lys*, are visible in the vaults. Behind the high altar is a lapidary fragment with another salamander. Beside the altar is the original 14th-century bell from the gatehouse tower (*see above*), the earliest public 'clock' in Paris.

BOIS DE VINCENNES

The Bois de Vincennes, which at 995 hectares is slightly larger than the Bois de Boulogne, has many attractions, both botanical and sporting. The forest was first enclosed in the 12th century. Joinville, author of the *Life of King Louis* (1309), tells how after Mass, the saintly Louis IX would go to the Bois de Vincennes and seat himself under an oak tree, where he would hear disputes and dispense popular justice. The forest was replanted in 1731 by Louis XV, who opened it to the citizens of Paris. In 1855 the first embellishments, including three lakes, were carried out by Haussmann and the engineer J.-C. Alphand. After further land was ceded to the Bois in 1860, more lakes and avenues were created. The **Parc Floral** (*open summer 9.30–8, winter 9.30–6.30*), a botanic garden covering 28 acres, was created in 1969 to the southeast of the château. The naturally flat terrain was given a contoured relief. Lac Daumesnil to the southwest, with a grotto, a waterfall and two bridges, is a boating lake with a small island. To the south of the park, near the most popular trotting racecourse in Paris, is the organic **Ferme de Paris** (*open April–Sept daily except holidays 1.30–7; Oct–March weekends 1.30–7*), created from a genuine old farm and still a working concern.

The **Parc Zoologique de Paris**, or Zoo de Vincennes (*Métro 8 to Porte Dorée; open mid-March–Oct weekdays 10–6, weekends 9.30–7.30; mid-Oct–mid-March 10–5; T: 01 44 75 20 10, www.parczoologiqueparis.fr*), the main zoo of Paris, presents animals in as appropriate an environment as possible. A 3km trail runs through five biozones: Patagonia, the Sudano-Sahelian plains, Europe, Amazon-Guyana and Madagascar. The sometimes dramatic landscapes are laid out around the Great Boulder; the tropics are simulated by a large greenhouse. Among the 180 species are giraffe, zebra, a puma, an African lion, giant tortoises, birds, reptiles, amphibians and fish. The zoo also claims 870 different plant species. It is designed to be an animal-friendly environment aimed at preserving and protecting species.

EATING AND DRINKING IN SAINT-DENIS AND ÉCOUEN

ÉCOUEN

€ **Delyan**. Restaurant/tea shop at the château. Open daily except Tues midday–4.30pm (until 5pm on Thur). *T: 09 54 53 86 23*. There is also a good Japanese restaurant, € **Yagura** (*47 Rue de la Gare, T: 08 99 37 66 67*).

SAINT-DENIS

€ **La Bigoudène Café**. ■ No need to go to Brittany for fresh and delicious authentic Breton crêpes: the Bretons are making them here, in a garden café on the north side of the basilica. *11 Allée des 6 Chapelles, Pl. Pierre de Montreuil. T: 06 09 68 91 56.*

€ **Les Mets du Roy**. A traditional, pleasant place using seasonal produce and in an excellent position opposite the basilica; it has terrace for outdoor eating. *4 Rue de la Boulangerie. T: 01 48 20 89 74.*

€ **La Table Gourmande**. Not far from the basilica, a 1900s-style brasserie offering French cooking (and halal). *32 Rue de la Boulangerie, T: 01 48 13 06 95.*

€ **Au Petit Breton**. Central, with a good-value menu and *formule. 18 Rue de la Légion d'Honneur. T: 01 48 20 11 58.*

There are a number of restaurants in or close to the **Stade de France**: €€ **La Panoramique** (*T: 01 55 93 04 04; lunch only; no service during events*) has an unusual setting on the 8th floor above the stands, with a remarkable view of the stadium. The quality of the food is good, especially the desserts, and it boasts a high-class wine cellar. Other places to eat, in Rue Jules Rimet (*see www.restaurant-sta-dedefrance.com*), include € **La 3ème Mi-Temps**, at no. 29 (*T: 01 55 93 16 81; open 6am–midnight; no service during events*), which has a terrace and serves light meals and snacks; €€ **Balyann** (*T: 01 49 98 49 10; open during events*) is a lounge bar and restaurant with traditional French cooking; € **Le Chalet Crêpes** (*T: 01 49 51 14; open during events*) is an informal eatery which, as the name suggests, specialises in pancakes.

There is also the wonderful **produce market** at St-Denis on Tues, Fri, and Sun mornings, for buying ingredients for a picnic.

SAINT-OUEN

€€ **Ma Cocotte**. Philippe Starck-designed restaurant with an open kitchen and a *rôtisserie*, offering dishes that range from classic French (*côte de boeuf*) to wannabe Anglo Saxon (fish and chips de Portobello). Open for lunch and dinner on weekdays and all day from 9am at weekends. Best to book. *106 Rue des Rosiers. T: 01 49 51 70 00, www.macocotte-lespuces.com.*

Appendix

The selected sites listed alphabetically below are not treated in the main body of the text. They are given here with brief details in order to assist in wider exploration of the enormous wealth and variety of Paris.

Aquarium du Trocadéro–Cinéaqua
Map p. 585, D1.
Av. Albert-de-Mun, 16th.
Open daily 10–10, closed 14 July.
T: 01 40 69 23 23; www.cineaqua.com.
Over 3600m², the aquarium has 43 pools, over 10,000 fish and invertebrates. Access is by tunnel resembling an underwater walk. Cinéaqua has two cinemas for underwater films; also a Japanese restaurant.

Bibliothèque Polonaise de Paris
Map p. 587, F2.
6 Quai d'Orléans, 4th.
Open 2.15–6, closed public holidays.
T: 01 55 42 83 83, www.bibliotheque-polonaise-paris-shlp.fr.
This Polish library has mementoes of émigrés; also the Adam Mickiewicz collection, the Salon Chopin with memorabilia of the composer, and the Musée Boleslas Biegas, of the Symbolist sculptor.

Mundolinga
Map p. 587, D3.
10 Rue Servandoni, 6th.
Open daily 10–7. T: 01 56 81 65 79,
www.mundolingua.org.
Museum of language, languages and linguistics worldwide, past and present.

Among various themes are the 'bricks of language' syntactic and semantic: a verb roll, how different species communicate; how we produce sound; how we link words in sentences in different languages and so on. Facsimiles of the Rosetta Stone, the Enigma encryption machine and the Dead Sea Scrolls plus an example of a text translated into the six languages of the UN: English, Arabic, Spanish, French, Mandarin and Russian. However, most of the display is in French.

Musée des Arts Forains
Map p. 579, E4.
53 Avenue des Terroirs de France, 12th.
Open Sat–Sun only by prior reservation online, www.pavillons-de-bercy.com.
Museum of the Fairground in old wine warehouses. An enchanting collection of attractions of the 1900s, including fairground organs, carousels and sideshows and five special areas: Theatre of Marvels, Venetian Rooms, the Theatre of Verdure and the Magic Mirror.

Musée de l'Assistance Publique–Hôpitaux de Paris
Map p. 587, F2.
47 Quai de la Tournelle, 5th.
Closed at the time of writing,

musee-aphp.fr.
Overview of the history of Paris hospitals from the foundation of the Hôtel-Dieu (12th century) to the beginning of the 20th century through 9,000 objects, documents and art works, including 260 paintings.

Musée Curie

Map p. 587, E4.
11 Rue Pierre et Marie Curie. 5th.
Open Wed–Sat 1–5; closed Sun, Mon, public holidays, Aug and Christmas holidays. T: 01 56 24 55 33, musee.curie.fr.
In the oldest part of the Institut Curie, the museum conserves the office and laboratory (decontaminated in 1981) where Marie Curie worked. It pays tribute to her life and work and that of Pierre Curie, as well as Irène and Frédéric Joliot-Curie, and describes the important stages in the history of the discovery of radioactivity and its applications.

Musée Dapper

Map p. 580, A3.
35 Rue Paul-Valéry, 16th.
Open Wed–Mon 11–7, closed Tues and Thur. T: 01 45 00 91 75,
www.dapper.com.fr.
An excellent small museum dedicated to the art and culture of Africa and its diaspora. The Dapper Foundation was established in 1983 in Amsterdam and is named after a 17th-century Dutch humanist. It moved to Paris in 1986, and into its present location, designed by Alain Moatti, in 2000. Its original objective was to promote the arts of Sub-Saharan Africa, but it has since broadened to promote the arts of Africa and the Caribbean, African-American and mixed-race communities of Europe, Latin America and the Indian Ocean. It mounts regular thematic exhibitions. There is an attractive modern café (*T: 01 45 00 31 73*).

Musée Dupuytren/Fondation Déjerine

Map p. 587, D3.
15 Rue de l'École de Médecine, 6th.
Open Mon–Fri 2–5, closed Sat, Sun and holidays. T: 01 42 34 68 60.
This museum of anatomical pieces was first created in 1835 thanks to the bequest of Guillaume Dupuytren (1777–1835), Professor of Surgery. The collection dates from 1820 to 1935 and illustrates diseases and malformations. Among the 600 objects are skeletons, and preserved organs; some of the most spectacular pieces, the wax models, are some of the oldest.

Musee d'Ennery

Map p. 578, B2.
59 Av. Foch, 16th.
Open Sat, by reservation via resa@guimet.fr (no tickets issued); closed end-June–mid-Sept; check changes on T: 01 56 52 54 23, www.guimet.fr. Free.
A unique and personal Asian art collection formed from 1890 by Clémence d'Ennery, wife of dramatist Adolphe d'Ennery, who was an enthusiast of Oriental objects when this fashion was at its peak. The collection includes Ming vases, superb Japanese porcelain, netsuke and furniture. The house was specially adapted to display the collection, which was bequeathed to the state at Madame d'Ennery's death on the condition that it remained unchanged.

Musée de l'Érotisme

Map p. 582, A2.

72 Blvd de Clichy, 18th.
Open daily 10–2am. T: 01 42 58 28 73,
www.musee-erotisme.com.
A unique collection of international
erotic art through the ages.

Musée de l'Éventail (Fan Museum)
Map p. 483, D4.
2 Blvd de Strasbourg, 10th.
Open Mon–Wed 2–6; T: 01 42 08 90 20,
www.annehoguet.fr
Created in 1893, four generations of the
same family have been making fans and
the large collection is rotated annually
in the original room. The stages of the
fan-making process are also part of the
display.

Musée de la Fédération Française de Tennis
Map p. 578, A3.
2 Av. Gordon Bennett, 16th.
(Métro 10 to Porte d'Auteuil).
Open during school time Wed, Fri, Sat,
Sun 10–6; during school holidays daily
except Mon. T: 01 47 43 48 48, www.fft.fr.
The first multimedia tennis museum,
covering 2,200 square metres in the
Roland Garros Stadium. Guided visits
on request.

Musée Fragonard du Parfum
Map p. 581, F3.
9 Rue Scribe, 9th.
Open Mon–Sat 9–5.30, Sun and holidays
9.30–4. T: 01 47 42 04 56,
www.fragonard.com.
Five thousand years of the history of
perfume in an elegant Napoléon III-
style mansion

Musée de la Franc-Maçonnerie
Map p. 582, B3.
16 Rue Cadet. 9th.

Open Tues–Sat 2–6. T: 01 45 23 74 09,
www.museefm.org.
Material relating to the story of
European freemasonry, with medals,
seals, portraits, etc.

Musée Grévin
Map p. 582, B3.
10 Blvd Montmartre, 9th.
Open Mon–Fri 10–6.30; Sat, Sun and
holidays 9.30–7. T: 01 47 70 85 05,
www.grevin-paris.com.
Waxworks museum with over 300 figures including 80 contemporary ones,
on the same lines as Madame Tussaud's
in London. Café.

Musée Hébert
Map p. 586, B3.
85 Rue du Cherche-Midi. 6th.
Closed at the time of writing. Check for
updates on www.musee-orsay.fr.
Works by Ernest Hébert (1817–1908),
painter of Italian landscapes and society
portraits, cousin of Stendhal, in an 18th-
century mansion.

Musée de l'Histoire de la Médecine, Université de Paris Descartes
Map p. 587, D3.
12 Rue de l'École de Médecine, 6th.
Open mid-July–Aug 2–5.30, closed Sat,
Sun and 15 Aug; 1 Sept–15 July 2–5.30,
closed Thur, Sun and holidays; closed two
weeks at Christmas. T: 01 76 53 16 93,
www.univ-paris5.fr.
On the 2nd floor of the Faculty of
Medicine, a museum of medicine from
antiquity to the present illustrated
by collections among the oldest in
Europe. Some 1,500 historic medical
instruments include rare medical and
surgical kits and operating equipment.
Remarkable model of a human body in

poplar wood, made in Italy at Napoleon's request

Musée des Lettres et Manuscrits

Map p. 586, C2.
222 Boulevard Saint-Germain, 7th.
Open Tues–Sun 10–7, Thur to 9.30, closed Mon, 1 Jan, 1 May, 25 Dec. Visioguide. T: 01 42 22 48 48.

An unusual museum dedicated to old letters and rare manuscripts and also including musical scores and scientific manuscripts. The display is regularly rotated. Among the precious documents are a score by Mozart, an original manuscript by George Sand and numerous letters written by Voltaire, Napoleon, and the artists Géricault and Manet. In the collection is also a manuscript relating to Einstein's calculations for the Theory of Relativity. Regular visits and workshops are offered.

Musée de la Magie

Map p. 588, B2.
11 Rue St-Paul, 4th.
Open Wed, Sat, Sun 2–7, and daily during school holidays except July–Aug. T: 01 42 72 13 26, www.museedelamagie.com.

History of magic through a unique collection: posters, automata, courses in magic, special effects, optical illusions, robots, interactive games and a permanent conjuring show.

Musée Maxim's

Map p. 581, E4.
3 Rue Royale, 8th.
Open Wed–Sun, guided tours at 2, 3.15, 4.30; closed holidays. T: 01 42 65 30 47, www.maxims-musee-artnouveau.com.

Above the restaurant, a grand courtesan's luxurious three-floor apartment is laid out with over 550 superb international Art Nouveau objects including furniture and tableware. Tea room and recitals late afternoon.

Musée Mendjisky–Écoles de Paris

Map p. 585, E4.
15 Square de Vergennes, 15th.
Open Tues–Sat 12–7. T: 01 56 23 00 22 or 01 45 32 37 70, www.fmep.fr.

The first museum dedicated to the two Schools of Paris, the first School (1905–39) refers to the numerous foreign artists who settled in Montparnasse. The Second brings together abstract and figurative artists who made Paris the world capital of art in 1945–60. It occupies a 1930s' building designed by Robert Mallet-Stevens as a workshop and home for master glazier and engraver Louis Barillet, and is the only Mallet-Stevens house that can be visited in Paris. A window the height of the building incorporates the white or opalescent 'stained' glass that Barillet invented, combined with a geometric pattern. On the third floor there is another example of Barillet's work. The building, which had been radically altered, was restored by industrialist Yvon Poullain to display the ingenious modern design work of Yonel Lebovici. There is also a materials library, and regular temporary exhibitions are mounted.

Collection de Minéraux–Université Pierre et Marie Curie

Closed at the time of writing: collection being relocated. Check for updates on www.upmc.fr.

Mineralogy and crystallography laboratory of the Curie University, a fascinating collection of 2,000 minerals from all over the world.

Musée de Minéralogie

Map p. 587, D4.
Mines ParisTech, 60 Blvd St-Michel, 6th.
Open Tues–Fri 1.30–6, Sat 10–12.30 &
2–5; closed Mon, Sun and holidays.
T: 01 40 51 91 39,
www.musee.mines-paristech.fr.
Major museum of minerals founded in
1783 with 100,000 samples exhibited
in a gallery overlooking the Jardin du
Luxembourg. Among exhibits are hundreds of meteorites, the most important
of which is the Canyon Diablo Meteorite
found in 1890 at the bottom of a ravine
in Arizona.

Musée Pasteur

Map p. 585, F4.
Institut Pasteur, 25 Rue du Docteur-
Roux, 15th.
Open Mon–Fri 2–5.30; closed Sat, Sun
and Aug. T: 01 45 68 82 83,
www.pasteur.fr.
Founded by Louis Pasteur in 1887 and
built by private subscription. Pasteur's
apartment has become a museum containing family memorabilia and the
mausoleum with the chemist's tomb.

Musée Pierre Cardin

Map p. 587, F1.
5 Rue St-Merri. 4th.
Open Wed–Fri 11–6, Sat–Sun 1–6.
T: 01 42 76 00 57.
A representative and fascinating display
of the diverse creations of Pierre Cardin,
revolutionary and highly influential couturier from the 1960s, 'modelled' on 130
mannequins.

Musée de la Poupée

Map p. 588, A1.
22 Rue Beaubourg, Impasse Berthaud,
3rd. Open Tues–Sat 1–6; closed Sun, Mon
and holidays. T: 01 42 72 73 11,
www.museedelapoupeeparis.com.
Collection of dolls, from France and
from around the world.

Musée de la Préfecture de Police

Map p. 587, E3.
5 Rue de la Montagne-Ste-Geneviève, 5th.
Open Mon–Fri 9.30–5; closed Sat, Sun
and holidays. T: 01 44 45 52 50,
www.prefecturedepolice.interieur.gouv.fr.
Exhibits associated with police history, including a section devoted to the
Resistance and the Liberation of Paris,
records of important conspiracies,
arrests, famous characters, archives,
unique weapons and uniforms, and evidence from famous criminal cases.

Musée du Service de Santé des Armées

Map p. 587, D4.
1 Place A.-Laveran, 5th.
Open Tues–Wed, Sat–Sun 12–6. T: 01 40
51 51 92, www.ecole-valdegrace.sante.
defense.gouv.fr.
The collections of the Army Health
Department displayed in the historic
building of the Val-de-Grâce illustrate
the history of French military medical
service. The Salle Debat has a complete
pharmacy, and a travelling pharmacy.

Palais de la Découverte

Map p. 581, D4.
Av. Franklin-D.-Roosevelt, 8th.
Open Tues–Sat 9.30–6, Sun and holidays
10–7; closed Mon. T: 01 56 43 20 20,
www.palais-decouverte.fr.
In the western extension of the Grand
Palais, this centre developed in 1937
with the aim of bringing science to life
in central Paris. Demonstrations, films
and interactive displays explore the

basic laws of mathematics, astronomy, computing, physics, chemistry, earth sciences; there is also a planetarium.

Parc André-Citroën

Map p. 584, B4.
2 Rue Cauchy, 15th.
Open Mon–Fri 8am–dusk, Sat, Sun and public holidays 9am until dusk.

On the riverside beyond Pont Mirabeau, the site of the former automobile factory was transformed in 1992–9 into the Parc André-Citroën. Rigorous, architectonic and Modernist, it was created by Alain Provost and Gilles Clément working in association with three architects, Patrick Berger, Jean-Paul Viguier and François Jodry. Four themes prevail: artifice, architecture, movement and nature. There are three principal sections: the White Garden to the east, the Black Garden to the south, and the main park dominated by two huge rectangular greenhouses. The principal vista descending towards the Seine is flanked by banks of evergreen magnolias and beech hedges, with box and yew, trimmed into disciplined shapes. Water is a determining element of the park—a large fountain, canals, lily-ponds, water courses and *jets d'eau* account for about a hectare of the total. On the northeast side is a series of parallel rectangular gardens each planted to a different colour scheme. Opposite each is a tall greenhouse. The plants in the Jardin des Métamorphoses, on the other side, are inspired by alchemical transmutations. In contrast to the formal gardens closer to the river there are stretches of wild gardens described as the Jardin des Roches and Jardin en Mouvement.

Parc des Buttes Chaumont

Map p. 583, F2.
Rue Botzaris/Rue Manin, 19th.
Open May–Sept 7–10, Oct–April 7–8.

The Parc des Buttes Chaumont (southwest of La Villette) is one of the most picturesque but least known of Parisian parks. The 25 hectares were laid out during Haussmann's régime in 1866–7 by Alphand and Barillet from decidedly unpromising terrain. The bare hills (*monts chauves*) of extensive gypsum (plaster of Paris) quarries, where rubbish was dumped, were transformed into craggy scenery and there are fine views of the city. Lawns slope down to a lake spanned by a suspension bridge leading to a rocky promontory topped off with a tiny Classical temple. The landscaping was of Anglo-Chinese inspiration, and therefore less formal than typical French gardens. Among the well-tended flowerbeds are three restaurants and various entertainments for children. Outside the park, off Rue de Mouzaïa, is a delightful series of little cobbled streets with terraced houses.

Parc Georges-Brassens

Map p. 578, B4. 15th.

Laid out 1977–85, the park is named after the famous poet-singer who lived nearby. In the former hamlet of Vaugirard, the site was an important vineyard until the end of the 18th century. There are still vines and vestiges of old buildings. The Monfort Theatre offers a varied programme and there is a puppet theatre and a stream and pond, a small bridge and a belvedere. Honey is on sale one Saturday a month from the local beehive.

PRACTICAL INFORMATION

Planning your Trip

WHEN TO GO

Parisian weather is temperate and variable, and while spring in Paris is most people's ideal, the autumn can also be glorious with long periods of fine weather. Average temperatures from March to May range from 4° to 20°C, June to August 13° to 25°C, September to December 12° to 21°C, and January and February 1° to 7°C. The heaviest rainfall can be in August.

PARIS WEBSITES

www.paris.fr	City of Paris
www.parisinfo.com	Paris Tourist Office
www.visitparisregion.com	Tourist information for Paris and Île de France
www.rendezvousenfrance.com	French Government Tourist Board
www.francetourism.com	French Tourist Office
www.parismuseumpass.com	Paris Museum Pass official website
www.monuments-nationaux.fr	Centre des Monuments Nationaux
www.voyages-sncf.com	European rail services: Information and bookings
www.disneylandparis.co.uk	Disneyland Paris

TOURIST INFORMATION OFFICES

Bureau des Pyramides: 25 Rue des Pyramides, 1st (*map p. 586, C1*)
Gare du Nord: 18 Rue de Dunkerque, 10th (*map p. 583, D2*)
Anvers: 72 Blvd Rochechouart, 18th (*map p. 582, B2*)
Gare de Lyon: 20 Blvd Diderot, 12th (*map p. 588, C4*)
Gare de l'Est: Pl. du 11 Novembre (Rue du 8 Mai), 18th (*map p. 583, D3*)
Espace Accueil de Tourisme: 1 Pl. de la Porte de Versailles, 15th (*map p. 578, B4*)
Syndicat d'Initiative Montmartre: 21 Pl. du Tertre, 18th (*map p. 582, B1*).

DISABLED TRAVELLERS

Considerable progress has been made in providing access for the disabled to historic buildings, monuments, entertainment venues as well as hotels and restaurants. A list of Paris hotels and restaurants with the 'Toursime & Handicap' label, meaning they are able to offer facilities for the disabled, is available on the Paris Tourist Office website (*see above*) and at information offices in Paris. General information can be found on the City of Paris and Paris Tourist Office websites.

Getting Around

TO PARIS BY EUROSTAR

Eurostar trains link the UK Eurostar Terminal at St Pancras station in London directly with Paris, Gare du Nord in about 2hrs 30mins. There are also departures from Ashford International Terminal, Kent (journey time c. 2hrs) and from Ebbsfleet International (journey time c. 2hrs 10mins. For information and reservations, see www.eurostar.com. For help with existing bookings, call T: 03432 186 186 (from outside UK +44 1233 617 575).

GETTING TO AND FROM THE AIRPORTS

CDG (ROISSY)

Charles de Gaulle airport is 23km northeast of the capital (*map p. 577, D1*). For flight schedules, see www.aeroportsdeparis.fr.

Air France coaches: (Cars Airfrance, *www.cars-airfrance.com*).
Line 2: every 30mins between CDG and Porte Maillot (*map p. 578, B2*) and Étoile (*map p. 578, B2*), 5.30am–11pm.
Line 3: every 30mins between CDG and Paris Orly airport, 5.30am–11pm.
Line 4: every 30mins between CDG and Gare de Lyon (*map p. 579, E3*) and Gare Montparnasse (*map p. 578, C3*), 6am–10pm.
Roissybus (*www.ratp.fr*) every 15 to 20mins between CDG and Opéra-Rue Scribe (*map p. 578, C2*), 5.15am–1.30am (journey time 60mins). Tickets are sold in advance at all Métro stations and automatic ticket machines.
RER B links CDG (Terminals 2 and 3) and Paris (inc. Gare du Nord, Châtelet-Les Halles, Denfert-Rochereau); for Orly, transfer to OrlyVal Métro at Antony. NB: When travelling from Paris to CDG, some non-rush hour trains are non-stop between Gare du Nord and the airport, which can save a good deal of time. To check timetables, see the RATP website (*www.ratp.fr*). When alighting, make sure you leave the train at the right terminal.

ORLY

Orly airport is 14km south of Paris (*map p. 577, C3*). For flight schedules, see www.aeroportsdeparis.fr.

Orlybus (every 15–20mins) between Orly South and West and Denfert-Rochereau (*map p. 578, C4*) from 6am–11.30pm Thur, Sun and holidays, 6am–1.30am Fri, Sat and day before public holidays (journey time 30mins).

OrlyVal to Antony, and transfer to RER B for central Paris.

Shuttle bus to Pont de Rungis (every 20mins 6am–11pm, journey time 25mins), then RER C.

Noctilien night buses to Orly run from Châtelet (line 22), Gare de Lyon (lines 31 and 131) and Gare de l'Est (line 144).

NATIONAL RAIL (SNCF)

For information and reservations, see www.voyages-sncf. The main stations in Paris are Gare d'Austerlitz (*map p. 579, E3*), Gare de l'Est (*map p. 579, D2*), Gare de Lyon (*map p. 579, E3*), Gare Montparnasse (*map p. 578, C3*), Gare du Nord (*map p. 579, D1–D2*) and Gare St-Lazare (*map p. 578, C2*).

Most stations have left-luggage offices (*consignes*) or lockers (automatic or manual), trolleys and information bureaux. NB: French Railways do not have ticket control at platform barriers. Passengers travelling in France must validate (*composter*) their ticket in an orange-red machine (which punches and date-stamps it) at the platform entrance before boarding the train.

PUBLIC TRANSPORT

The Paris public transport authority, RATP (*54 Quai de la Râpée; map p. 579, E3*) operates the Métro, RER trains and buses. It is an efficient system except for the lack of late-evening buses. The same tickets are valid for Métro, RER, buses and trams. For information for all services, see www.rafp.fr (or call T: 0 892 68 77 14, information in French only). Combined maps are available at Métro ticket offices.

Paris Métro lines and trains are being replaced over ten years by safer, streamlined automatic models. Métro Line 1, the oldest and busiest, is now fully automated. Line 14 is the only other fully automated line. A €20.5 billion plan to invest in 200 km of rapid transit lines and 57 stations, has been agreed.

Travel passes and tickets

The same tickets are used on Métro, RER, tram and bus lines. They can be purchased at all RATP stations individually or in tens (*carnet*), over the counter or by automatic machine. Various passes exist for combined travel and sightseeing: **Paris Museum Pass, Paris Attraction Pass**, and **Paris Visite Pass**. They can be purchased at all major tourist and transport hubs. The Paris Visite Pass is valid for 1, 2, 3 or 5 consecutive days in Zones 1–3 or 1–5 and includes other offers. If you plan to stay longer, the **Navigo Découverte** is a weekly or monthly pass giving unlimited travel.

On the maps in this guide, a letter M on a blue square denotes a Métro stop, while a plain blue square denotes an RER stop.

Métro and RER tickets activate the turnstile. Sometimes there is a heavy gate which you push your way through. The ticket will automatically be date stamped; keep it for the duration of the journey in case it is checked and for the exit. The ticket includes interchanges. On the bus, after validating it, the ticket pops out again and you need to retrieve it.

THE PARIS MÉTRO

The Métro (underground; *Métropolitain*) runs between 5.30am and 0.30am and is frequent and efficient. There are 14 lines identifiable by their number and colour. The direction of the train is indicated by the final station: arm yourself with that information before plunging underground, as maps of the network are sometimes not posted up. Interchanges are marked '*Corréspondance*'. One ticket is valid for one Métro journey including changes. Note that some older trains do not have automatic doors: either press the button or twist the lever. For passes and season tickets, see above.

RER TRAINS

The RER (suburban express railway) is a fast under- and overground service on lines identifed by letters of the alphabet: A, B, C, D and E. Métro tickets are valid on these lines within central Paris but beyond Zone 2, RER fares are different (Métro tickets are valid for all zones at no extra charge).

BUSES AND TRAMS

Bus routes are numbered and most operate 6.30am–8.30pm. One ticket is required per person per journey (excluding changes) and must be date stamped (*composté*) in the machine near the driver. Routes and timetables are clearly displayed at individual bus stops, which are all request stops (*arrêt facultatif*), and each is indicated by name on the stop and, on most lines, announced in advance on the bus. A few late-night buses run until 0.30am. The Noctambus (night service) operates 18 bus routes seven days a week, between 1am and 5.35am.

The **Balabus** (included in the Paris Visite ticket, *see above*) stops at the main tourist sites between Bastille and La Défense between 12.30pm and 8pm, from April to Sept; stops are marked Balabus (Bb). The **Monmartrobus** is a round trip of Montmartre between the 18th arrondissement Mairie (Town Hall) and Pigalle. Both services are operated by RATP.

Paris l'Open Tour (*T: 01 42 66 56 56, www.paris-opentour.com*) is a sightseeing hop-on-hop-off service.

Paris/Île de France has seven **tram lines**. Only the T3 runs inside the city of Paris, following the exterior boulevards (trams run 5am to 12.30am). The T2 serves the Cité de la Céramique at Sèvres).

BICYCLES AND SCOOTERS

There are bikes on hire from most train stations and principal tourist routes. Parisians take to the streets on rollerblades on Friday evenings and Sunday afternoons; for more information see parisinfo.com.

Parisvélib' is a self-service bike system available is 24rs a day: 1-day or 7-day tickets available online or at Vélib stations. Pick up and return when you choose (*www. en.velib.paris.fr*).

Paris Bike Tour (*13 Rue Brantôme, south off Rue du Grenier St-Lazare, map p. 587, F1; T: 01 42 74 22 14, www.parisbiketour.net*).

Maison Roue Libre (*37 Blvd. Bourdon, map p. 588, B3; T: 08 99 96 58 19, www.cityvox.fr*).

Motorail (*190 Rue de Bercy, map p. 588, C4; and also at Orly Airport; T: 08 92 35 00 25, www.motorail.fr*) offers bikes, motorbikes and scooters.

BOAT TRIPS

ON THE SEINE

A variety of cruises is offered. **Batobus** (*T: 01 44 11 33 99, www.batobus.com*) specialises in a hop-on-hop-off service of eight stops between the Eiffel Tower and the Jardin des Plantes (1- or 2-day tickets). The **Vedettes du Pont Neuf** are sightseeing barges (*Square du Vert-Galant, T: 01 46 33 98 38, vedettesdupontneuf.com; map p. 587, D2*). **Bateaux Parisiens** are another company offering boat trips (*Port de la Bourdonnais, T: 01 44 11 33 44, www.bateauxparisiens.com; map p. 585, D1*).

ON CANAL ST-MARTIN

Canauxrama (*Bassin de la Villette, 13 Quai de la Loire, www.canauxrama.com; map p. 583, F1*) and **Paris Canal** (*Bassin de la Villette, 19–21 Quai de la Loire, www.pariscanal. com; map p. 583, F1*) both offer canal trips.

TAXIS AND AUTOLIB'

Taxis have no particular distinctive form or colour, except for the white 'Taxi' sign on the roof (lit up when available). They can be found at train stations, airports, near major road junctions, at 470 taxi ranks, and can be hailed. At taxi ranks there are telephones to call taxis. A minimum fare is charged and thereafter the price is metered by the kilometre. Night-time fares are slightly more expensive. A small supplement is charged for luggage from the second piece placed in boot. No supplement can be requested from disabled passengers using a wheelchair and/or animals accompanying them. It is advisable to request a receipt for each journey, in case of dispute or lost property. In case of complaint, contact the Préfecture de Police Service des Taxis (*36 Rue des Morillons, T: 01 55 76 20 05, map p. 578, B4*). At the time of writing the average taxi fare from airports (CDG and Orly) to Paris was between €55 and €65, depending on the number of passengers. Tipping is not strictly necessary.

Autolib' is an electric car-sharing scheme (the four-wheel equivalent of Vélib') set up by Bolloré Bluecars for public use on a subscription basis. There are over 4,000 charging points in the city.

Accommodation

Paris has around 2,700 hotels in a huge range of styles, value and prices. Some of them are famous and historic names, known for their elegance and luxury: the Plaza Athénée (now part of the Dorchester group), Le Bristol, the George V (now a Four Seasons) and Costes being prime examples. The list below aims to give a good cross-section. Booking in advance assures a better rate than the walk-in price: the more expensive the hotel, the more worthwhile is the search for special offers. The tourist tax (€0.20 to €1.50 per person per night) is usually included in the quoted price. Breakfast is rarely included, unless on special offer. The price per room per night ranges approximately from €60 for a one-star hotel to well over €600 for the grandest.

Three famous five-star hotels were undergoing a total refurbishment at the time of writing: the Hôtel Crillon on Place de la Concorde, the Ritz on Place Vendôme and the Lutetia on Bouevard Raspail.

Price categories (double room per night) are a guideline only:

€€€ = €400+
€€ = €200–350
€ below €200

HOTELS IN CENTRAL PARIS

€€€ **Hôtel Bel Ami**. *7–11 Rue St-Benoit, 75006. T: 01 42 61 53 53, www.hotelbela-mi-paris.com. Map p. 587, D2.* Cool and contemporary combined with warm and welcoming, the Bel Ami is at the heart of St-Germain. Comfortable bedrooms include four suites, each with a different character. The bar is light and restful and the restaurant, Les Mots Passants, has a novel and colourful book theme in its decoration. A copious organic brunch is served Saturday noon to 3pm, and Sunday noon to 4pm. There is also a spa.
€€€ **L'Hôtel**. *13 Rue des Beaux-Arts, 75006. T: 01 44 41 99 00, www.l-hotel.*

com. Map p. 587, D2. A gorgeous boutique hotel in St-Germain-des-Prés in a *fin-de-siècle* building. Architecturally, its unique characteristic is a central six-storey circular balconied atrium supported by ancient vaulted cellars which have been cunningly adapted to contain a hammam/*contre-courant* swimming pool. Currently owned by Peter Frankopan and Jessica Sainsbury (who also own Cowley Manor Hotel in England), this has been a hotel of distinction since the time of Oscar Wilde, who famously took his last breath here in 1900. Fashionable designer Jacques

Garcia carried out the transformation, giving a different theme to each of the 30 bedrooms. Apart from the famous Wilde bedroom, which has English furniture, a peacock mural and tiny balcony, others include the elegant '30s-style Mistinguett room, with objects from her home, the Cardinal room with a view of the belfry of St-Germain and the Restoration-style Roi de Naples room. The lounge, bar and restaurant are intimate and comfortable, decked out in Garcia-Directoire style. Le Restaurant (*T: 01 44 41 99 01*) has a Michelin rosette.

€€€€ **Le Meurice**. *228 Rue de Rivoli, 75001. T: 01 44 58 10 10, www.dorchester-collection.com. Map p. 581, E4.* The long history of this sumptuous hotel goes back to a coaching inn established at Calais in 1771 by Charles-Augustin Meurice to receive weary British travellers after a Channel crossing. In 1817, Meurice built another refuge in Paris (which was then 36 hours away) and in 1835 the Hotel Meurice moved to its present site close to Place Vendôme and the Tuileries. Crowned heads and celebrities from all over the world have stayed here, including Queen Victoria in 1855; and in 1931 Picasso and Olga Koklova chose the Meurice for their wedding. In 2007 Philippe Starck brought an air of Louis XIV revisited to the public spaces, and including the three-star Michelin restaurant, inspired by the Salle des Glaces at Versailles and taken over by Alain Ducasse in 2013. The Dali Restaurant, where tea may be taken, is named after one of their more eccentric guests, and the Bar 228 prides itself on record choice of drinks and aperitifs. Its 160 rooms are super elegant, and there is every facility one could wish for. The restaurants and bar are open to non-residents.

€€€ **Hôtel Pavillon de la Reine**. *28 Pl. des Vosges, 75004. T: 01 40 29 19 19, www.pavillon-de-la-reine.com. Map p. 588, B2.* Opening off Place des Vosges, this historic building has been known as Pavillon de la Reine since the 17th century. The hotel and spa entrance is across a pretty courtyard. Old and modern are happily combined here. The 54 discreetly luxurious rooms and suites maintain authentic features of the building. There are characterful duplexes under the roof, and some suites have four-poster beds and beamed ceilings.

€€€ **The Peninsula Paris**. *19 Av. Kléber, 75016. T: 01 58 12 28 88, www.peninsula.com. Map p. 580, A4.* This is the first of the Peninsula Group enterprises in Europe (Peninsula is part of SEHK, founded in 1928 and based in Hong Kong). It occupies a 19th-century *hôtel particulier* and has 200 ultra-luxurious rooms and suites in a flawless style using tones of grey and cream combined with clean lines, which do not detract from the mouldings and other 19th-century details. There is a spectacular rooftop terrace and among the choices of places to eat and drink are the LiLi Cantonese testaurant, the Kléber Terrace, and l'Oiseau Blanc rooftop restaurant.

€€–€€€ **Hôtel Le Sénat**. *10 Rue de Vaugirard, 75006. T: 01 43 54 54 54, www.hotelsenat.com. Map p. 587, D3.* With 41 rooms, including 6 suites, this is a well turned-out and comfortable hotel with fresh modern décor and air-conditioned rooms, some with terrace and views over Paris. Opposite the Senate and a stone's throw from the Jardin du Luxembourg, it is in a prime position for the Quartier Latin and Montparnasse. Look out for special offers.

€€ **Hôtel Bourg Tibourg**. *19 Rue du Bourg Tibourg, 75004, T: 01 42 78 47 39, www.hotelbourgtibourg.com. Map p. 587, F2*. The fashionable designer Jacques Garcia is responsible for the Viollet-le-Duc look—combining neo-Gothic-Victorian with Oriental—in this luxurious hotel owned by the Frères Costes, and designed as a voyage in itself. No surface is ignored and no detail spared. Thirty or so smallish, warmly-coloured rooms are luxuriously appointed with superb touches such as fringed lampshades and Gothic-style gilded fretwork. Black granite and mosaic tiles feature in the bathrooms. There is also a tiny garden with just about room for two for breakfast. The whole effect is opulent, even somewhat over-egged: romantic or bordering on a 19th-century upmarket bordello.

€€ **Hôtel Buci**. *22 Rue Buci, 75006, T: 01 55 42 74 74, www.bucihotel.com. Map p. 587, D2*. A charming hotel in a 16th-century building which gets the balance just right, and is beautifully situated on a little street deep in St-Germain, close to galleries, antiques shops and boutiques. The attractive entrance lobby sets the tone for the subtle and thoughtful décor. There is a very comfortable under-stated lounge and the breakfast room, which doubles up as a bar, is a small haven of tranquillity. The decoration of the bedrooms, some with exposed beams, is luxurious but not overwhelming. They are also a surprisingly good size and all have elegant marble bathrooms.

€€ **Hôtel Design La Sorbonne**. *6 Rue Victor-Cousin, 75005, T 01 43 54 58 08, www.hotelsorbonne.com. Map p. 587, E3*. Very good boutique hotel. The redecorated rooms are beautifully turned out, with interesting colours and features. In the ancient student quarter, it is close to the Panthéon and the Palais du Luxembourg. The shower-rooms are narrow, but there are some with bath. The Panthéon can be glimpsed from some rooms.

€€ **Hôtel Édouard VII**. *39 Avenue de l'Opéra, Paris 75002, T: 01 42 61 56 90, www.edouard7hotel.com. Map p. 581, F4*. Built as a hotel in 1877 during the time of Entente Cordiale at the end of the 19th century, it was patronised by King Edward VII, who enjoyed the view of the Opera House from the balconies on the corner between Avenue de l'Opéra and Rue Louis-le-Grand. The lobby is an open space with an eclectic choice of décor combining traditional marble, mahogany, Italian chandeliers and modern carvings by Nicolas Cesbron. Off the lobby is a very comfortable bar with the original stained-glass windows and modern furnishings. Meals, including the copious buffet breakfast, are served in the dining-room/restaurant, l'Angl'Opéra. The refurbished bedrooms have parquet floors and deep luxurious colour schemes and all the rest of the rooms are being renovated; bathrooms have granite floors, double basins and good lighting.

€€ **Les Fontaines du Luxembourg**, *4 Rue de Vaugirard, 75006, T: 01 43 25 35 90, www.luxembourghhotel.com. Map p. 587, D3*. A luxurious affair around a patio, where Louis XIV's grooms once resided, it picks up on the atmosphere of the *quartier* in its (slightly over-the-top) 'neo-Baroque'-style decor. Prices can fluctuate wildly according to season and length of stay.

€€ **Hôtel du Jeu de Paume**. ■ *54 Rue St-Louis-en-l'Île, 75004, T: 01 43 26 14 18, www.jeudepaumehotel.com. Map p. 587, F2*. This is a very smartly converted

17th-century building, the core of which is a raftered court where real tennis was once played. It is very quiet, off a secluded small yard on the main street of Île St-Louis, which is an idyllic setting in itself. The old tennis court is now the breakfast room, with a painting of a game in progress; modern combines harmoniously with old beams and stone walls. There is also a small, cosy bar and lounge with a fire. The thirty bedrooms are modern and comfortable. There are also two well appointed apartments on the first and second floors and a spa. Staff are extremely helpful and friendly.

€€ **Hôtel Lenox**. *9 Rue de l'Université, 75007, T: 01 42 96 10 95, www.lenox-saintgermain.com. Map p. 586, C2.* This is a great corner of St-Germain, an area of narrow streets with lots of interesting places to visit. This boutique hotel offers simple, elegant rooms and there is an attractive bar which makes reference to the jazz age. Breakfast is served in the vaulted cellars.

€–€€€ **BLC Design Hotel**. *4 Rue Richard-Lenoir, 75011, www.blcdesign-hotel-paris.com. Map p. 589, D2.* White and minimalist, the carefully uncluttered surroundings are chic but a bit unnerving. It describes itself as 'the hotel of blissful harmony and balance'. Each of the 29 all-white bedrooms is an artistic creation, and each has a diffused light and sound system to help you drift into sleep. Rates vary; check for special offers.

€ **Hotel Arvor St Georges**. ■ *8 Rue Laferrière, 75009, T: 01 48 78 60 92, www.hotelarvor.com. Map p. 582, B2.* The hotel is situated in an interesting residential quarter, full of history and atmosphere. Place St-Georges is located between Pigalle/Montmartre and the Grands Magazins. The 24 rooms and 6

suites are simple and bright, some under the eaves, with one suite opening onto the courtyard and some with superb views. The old staircase has an attractive wrought-iron balustrade (there is also a lift). There is a bar-lounge with a library corner for guests and the continental breakfast is good quality. Tariffs are very modest and vary according to season and time of booking: the earlier you book, the more favourable the rate.

€ **Hotel Aviatic**. *105 Rue de Vaugirard, 75006, T: 01 53 63 25 50, www.aviatic. fr. Map p. 586, B3.* This is a comfortable period piece in the Montparnasse district just off Rue de Vaugirard; Tour Montparnasse is nearby for a high cocktail (*see p. 172*). A three-star establishment, it occupies a historic site. In the 17th century this was the site of a house owned by the Marquise de Maintenon, who brought up the illegitimate children of Louis XIV and Madame de Montespan. A hotel since 1856, the building became the principle residence of aviators based at the Issy-les-Moulineaux airfield during the First World War, and it was also a centre for artists and writers. Bedrooms are not large but are individually decorated in a mix of styles and with harmonious fabrics. The executive rooms can accommodate up to three people. The entrance hall is typical of an old Parisian house, with old, small, attractively decorated Empire-style lounge. The staff are very helpful, and the breakfast room has a café atmosphere.

€ **Hôtel de la Bretonnerie**. *Rue Ste-Croix-de-la-Bretonnerie, 75004. T: 01 48 87 77 63, www.bretonnerie.com. Map p. 587, F2.* This is an intimate hotel deep in the Marais with a pretty entrance hall and a fine 17th-century staircase.

Although the old building does not allow for very spacious rooms, each of the 28 bedrooms (some are small suites), is individually decorated in lush warm colours or chintzes appropriate to the building and the bathrooms are nicely appointed. The breakfast room is in a stone-vaulted undercroft.

€ **Hôtel Brighton**. *218 Rue de Rivoli, 75001. T: 01 47 03 61 61, www.esprit-de-france.com. Map p. 586, C1.* The Brighton, like many other hotels with English names, was named during the period of cordial relations between England and France at the time of Queen Victoria. The interior has kept much of its original 1850s charm, including faux-marble and mosaics and it is in an excellent location overlooking the Tuileries gardens—an ideal base for visits to the Louvre or the Musée des Arts Décoratifs. The rooms are good quality and quite traditional, remarkably spacious and with decent-sized bathrooms. Those at the back are quieter, but on the Rue de Rivoli side there is the advantage of the view, even better from the corner rooms and the higher rooms with balconies. The hotel belongs to the Esprit de France group, whose portfolio of reasonably-priced hotels aim to put charm, character and authenticity first, offering hotels with a true sense of place. They have a number of other hotels in Paris, including in St-Germain (**Hôtel des Saints Pères**), near the Orsay (**Hôtel d'Orsay**), Montparnasse (**Hôtel Aiglon**) and Place Vendôme (**Hôtel Mansart**).

€ **Hotel du Champ de Mars**. *7 Rue du Champ de Mars, 75007. T: 01 45 51 52 30, www.hotelduchampdemars. Map p. 585, E2.* This slightly old-fashioned hotel has a certain charm and 25 pretty rooms. Situated very close to the Champ

de Mars gardens and a stone's throw from the Eiffel Tower and Les Invalides. The Orly shuttle bus terminal at Les Invalides is also nearby.

€ **Hôtel Claret**. *44 Blvd. de Bercy, 75012. T: 01 46 28 41 31, www.hotel-claret.com Map p. 589, D4.* This is a former *relais-de-poste* in the old wine-trading area of Paris, now the Jardins de Bercy. Close to the Seine and the Bastille, this has become a popular district. On the Bercy site are the Cinemathèque and Museum of Cinema, as well as Bercy Village with a multitude of shops, restaurants and wine bars. The hotel has 52 sound-proofed, modern, colourful rooms in three grades: standard, superior (overlooking the gardens), and mansart (the largest), under the sloping roof. There is a restaurant, Le Bouchon Bistrot; outside dining in good weather. Room prices are reasonable.

€ **Hôtel Le Clément**. *6 Rue Clément, 75006. T: 01 43 26 53 60, www.hotel-clement.fr. Map p. 587, D2.* This is a gem of a two-star hotel in a brilliant situation opposite the renovated Marché St-Germain, now a shopping mall. The hotel is discreet, quiet, and charming: everything is small (if you have a large suitcase it will probably have to travel alone in the lift) but perfectly presented. Bijou bedrooms have pretty prints on the walls and curtains. They are all comfortable and well equipped. The brightest rooms overlook the street and two-bed rooms are especially good; there are some family rooms. From the fourth floor is a rooftop view including the belfry of St-Sulpice. There is a pretty breakfast room. Close to excellent shops, it is also within a stone's throw of St-Germain des Prés and the Luxembourg Gardens.

€ **Hôtel Ferrandi**. *92 Rue du Cherche-Midi, 75006. T: 01 42 22 97 40; hotel.ferrandi@wanadoo.fr. Map p. 586, B3.* This pleasant hotel in a 19th-century building is in great position between the Luxembourg Gardens, St-Sulpice and St-Germain. The rooms have recently been renovated and although the décor may be a bit overloaded, the rooms are nevertheless a good size and with well-maintained bathrooms.

€ **Hôtel Floride Étoile**. *14 Rue St-Didier, 75016. T: 01 47 27 23 36, www.floride-paris-hotel.com. Map p. 580, A4.* Discreetly tucked away in the smart 16th arrondissement, close to the Champs-Élysées and Trocadéro, this small hotel has recently been renovated. The rooms are mainly in whites and creams with touches of colour and measure around 12–16m². The lounge, breakfast room and bar are all restful and pleasing.

€ **Grand Hôtel des Gobelins**. *57 Blvd St-Marcel, 75013. T: 01 43 31 79 89, www.hotel-des-gobelins.com. Map p. 591, D1.* The 13th arrondissement has a lot to offer. On the Left Bank, it is close to Rue Mouffetard, the Jardin des Plantes, and the interesting Butte aux Cailles district. The hotel takes its name from the Gobelins tapestry workshops (*see p. 163*). It has plenty of character, and is comfortable without trying too hard. The bedrooms are modern and there are public spaces on different levels. All rooms have flat-screen TV. The bathrooms vary in size—some are fairly large—but all have with good showers, although storage space may be lacking.

€ **Hôtel Louvre-Opéra**. *4 Rue des Moulins, 75001. T: 01 40 20 01 10, www.hotel-paris-louvre-opera.com. Map p. 581, F4.* This Best Western hotel occupies an old building in a quiet street, a central and prestigious location on the Right Bank between the Opéra and the Louvre. The rooms are modern, uncluttered and fairly small, although the bathrooms are a reasonable size.

€ **Grand Hôtel Malher**. *5 Rue Malher, 75004. T: 01 42 72 60 92. www.grandhotelmalher.com. Map p. 588, B2.* A family affair—and has been so for several generations—the 30 rooms in this old building have recently been refurbished. It is in a great position in the Marais, close to Place des Vosges, the Musée Picasso and Musée Carnavalet. The rooms are have a 'zen' feel, with good bathrooms, and certain architectural features have been highlighted. It is worth booking early to get the best prices, which fluctuate depending on the season.

€ **Hôtel de la Tulipe**. *33 Rue Malar, 75007. T: 01 45 51 67 21, www.hoteldelatulipe.com. Map p. 585, E1.* This small, cheerful hotel, in the shadow of the Eiffel Tower and close to lively shopping streets, has a Provençal feel. Once a convent, the building is arranged around a small interior courtyard where the breakfast tables are set out in the summer. Sunny yellow fabrics contrast with old beams and stone walls. The rooms are simple, but well equipped and reasonably priced.

€ **La Villa des Artistes**. *9 Rue de la Grande-Chaumière, 75006. T 01 43 26 60 86, www.villa-artistes.com. Map p. 586, C4.* Close to the Luxembourg gardens and near Montparnasse, this unassuming hotel is in a quiet street. It has a patio-garden, and a pretty breakfast room—outside in summer—and agreeable salon-bar. The functional rooms make reference to artistic styles; good bathrooms.

HOTELS OUTSIDE PARIS

€€€ **Trianon Palace Hotel**. *1 Blvd. de la Reine, Versailles 78000. T: 01 30 84 50 18, www.trianonpalace.com. Map p. 470, B3*. On the edge of the Parc de Versailles and set in extensive gardens, the Trianon Palace has innumerable historic associations (*see p. 486*). Built in 1910, it is a lavishly modernised Waldorf Astoria hotel presented with elegant and luxurious simplicity. There are two restaurants. The exclusive Gordon Ramsay au Trianon, which has earned two Michelin stars, is confined to ten tables and specialises in traditional French cooking. La Veranda offers a modern take on classic cooking, and a black and white décor. For those who enjoy the process of cooking as well as the results, the Chef's Table at Gordon Ramsay au Trianon allows for a small group to not only taste but watch the preparation of a tailor-made menu. The Gallery Bar also serves light meals and tea, and there is a Garden Bar Lounge for drinks outside.

€€ **Pavillon Henri-IV**. *21 Rue Thiers, 78100 Saint-Germain-en-Laye. T: 01 39 10 15 15, www.pavillonhenri4.fr*. To the west of Paris, St-Germain-en-Laye is an elegant town (*see p. 488*). The hotel was built in the 19th century on the site of the Château-Neuf, where Louis XIV was born. It has a handsome entrance and lounge the length of the building with calm colours, and the restaurant opens onto a large terrace, all of which command superb views. The bedrooms are huge and comfortable, and with good bathrooms. This hotel is good value compared to the centre of Paris.

€€ **Hôtel la Résidence du Berry**. *14 Rue d'Anjou, 75000 Versailles. T: 01 39 49 07 07, www.hotel-berry.com. Map p. 470, A4*. This is a small but nicely turned out hotel with 39 rooms, situated in the centre of Versailles. Its most unusual feature is the 18th-century cellar where vintage wines are stored. To get the most out of Versailles, staying in this lovely little town is a pleasure in itself, and it provides an opportunity to enjoy all the special visits or performances at the château and park, especially in the summer. An added bonus is that Paris is easily accessible from Versailles by public transport.

> ## BLUE GUIDES RECOMMENDED
> Hotels and restaurants that are particularly good choices in their category—in terms of location, charm, value for money or the quality of the experience they provide—carry the Blue Guides Recommended sign: ■. These have been selected by our authors, editors or contributors as places they have particularly enjoyed and would be happy to recommend to others. We only recommend establishments that we have visited. To keep our entries up to date, reader feedback is essential: please do not hesitate to contact us (*www.blueguides.com*) with any views, corrections or suggestions.

Paris Food & Drink

G reat cooking and fine dining have a long association with Paris (which now has around 40,000 restaurants) and the French language is the source of many expressions connected with *haute cuisine* in the western world.

The ubiquitous café has always been associated with coffee drinking. The word coffee or café comes from the Arabic for strength or vigour, *qhawa* or *kaweh*, which became caffé via French explorers to the Ottoman Empire. The oldest café in Paris is Le Procope (*see p. 98*), established in 1686 by Francesco Procopio dei Coltelli, a Sicilian. Cafés abound in Paris, from very simple corner cafés to the very grand, such as Café de la Paix opposite the Opéra. Like cafes everywhere, they serve more than just coffee and in Paris it is still possible to find an occasional establishment which has kept its old zinc bar.

The word restaurant goes back to the 15th century when it referred to a highly-concentrated restorative consommé or broth, produced by the prolonged cooking of a variety of meats without the addition of any liquid. (In the earliest recipes the addition of gold pieces or precious stones was recommended.) The 'restaurateur's room, where the restorative was served, was originally promoted as a health centre. As time went on the room and the broth merged to become the restaurant. The oldest restaurant in Paris is the beautiful Le Grand Véfour (*p. 312*), founded 1784–5. A *bouillon*, from the verb *bouillir*, to boil, is similar to a broth but less concentrated, made using liquid and possibly vegetables as well as meat. A *bouillon* once also denoted a type of restaurant: a rare survival is Chartier (*p. 305*). The bouillon, or stock, cube was produced by *traiteurs* or caterers who provided transportable food for *table d'hôte* guests (communal eating). The expression *table d'hôte* is still occasionally used at rural B&Bs.

During the mid 18th century, the time of the Enlightenment, there was an increasing interest in the healthy properties of food. Places to eat and drink such as inns, taverns and cabarets already existed and eating had already became more convivial prior to the Revolution. After the Revolution, as court etiquette and the spectacle of the *grand couvert* (where members of the public watched royalty dine), disappeared, dining out became fashionable. The restaurant was an attractive place to be and be seen and, unlike England or the USA, a place where women were accepted. By the first decades of the 19th century British and American connoisseurs were delighted with the culinary standards in Paris

The name bistrot, first recorded in the 1800s, is possibly derived from *bistouill* or *bistrouille*, a type of aperitif, although popular legend dates it from the Russian occupation of France when impatient clients would call out '*bystro!*' (quickly). The typical bistrot is unpretentious, with red checked tablecloths and traditional, inexpensive fare.

Brasserie comes from *brasser*, to malt or brew, and although brasseries rarely now brew beer, they do usually have beer on tap. Many were established by refugees from Alsace-Lorraine during the occupation of the region by Germany in 1871–1939 (and again in 1940–4). They have a specific character and as many were opened in Paris during the Belle Époque, a number have kept their Art Nouveau or Art Deco look. Waiters wear long white aprons and meals are served all day, often including Alsatian specialities such as *choucroute* (sauerkraut) and charcuterie. Traditional brasseries include Chez Jenny, Bofinger, Brasserie Lipp and La Coupole. In the winter months, one of the most typical and evocative sights in Paris is the colourful displays of shell fish (*coquillages, crustacés et fruits de mer*) resting on beds of ice and seaweed outside the brasserie, while waiters open the oysters at amazing speed and pile up platters of *fruits de mer*.

The word menu, which is used worldwide (literally meaning small), originally referred to a summary account of the bill of fare, which then developed into a list of choices on offer with their cost. In the 19th century, with the development of printing, the menu printed on card was introduced and became *La Carte*. The difference today between the *Le Menu* and *La Carte* is that the former is usually fixed-price and limited choice (the *Menu du Jour* or *Plat du Jour* change according to the day of the week), and dining *à la Carte* tends to be a more expensive option but offers a wider choice, better quality and probably larger portions.

There are numerous Michelin-starred French chefs in Paris: Guy Savoy, Philippe Labbé, Alain Passard, Joël Robuchon (who introduced the 'open kitchen'), Pierre Gagnaire, Yannick Aliéno to name but a few. Their food is exquisite, as are the settings in which it is served. Several of them manage an entire portfolio of restaurants. They are constantly innovative and the *Menu dégustation* or tasting menus are well worth trying.

There are also great chefs from the regions of France bringing the best of Basque or Périgord flavours to the capital. The influence of Anglo-Saxon cooking is pronounced too, with the introduction of Le Brunch, good sandwiches and excellent fish and chips. Frenchie to Go is based on a New York deli.

It is interesting to note, however, that the French are the second largest consumers of McDonalds, which they call McDo. And while on the subject of abbreviations: restaurant is *resto*, *apéro* is apéritif, *les fasts* is fast-food outlets and *les softs* are soft drinks. *Bon appétit!*

A small selection of **recommended restaurants and cafés**, mainly traditional or modern French, is given at the end of every chapter. **Paris by Mouth** is a reliable online listing (*www.parisbymouth.com*). The least expensive way to eat a good meal are the *prix fixe* or *formule* menus at lunch, which most restaurants offer, including some of the top ones. It is always advisable to book in advance to book and to check opening times. The price ranges given in the text are a guideline only.

€€€	€100+
€€	€50–€100
€	€30–€50.

General Information

CHEMISTS

Most chemists are open during normal working hours. Late-opening pharmacies are as follows:

British and American Pharmacy, 1 Rue Auber (9th), until 8.30pm.
Pharmacie Européenne, 6 Place de Clichy (9th), 24hrs.
Pharmacie Malherbes, 84 Av. des Champs-Élysées (8th), 24hrs.
Pharmacie des Arts, 106 Blvd du Montparnasse (14th), until midnight Mon–Sat.
Grand Pharmacie Daumesnil, 6 Pl. Félix-Eboué (12th), until 9pm.

VISITING CHURCHES

Visits to all churches in Paris are free of charge, including Notre-Dame and Sacré Coeur. However there is an entrance fee at the Basilica of St-Denis and also for La Sainte-Chapelle and the Sainte-Chapelle in the Château de Vincennes.

Note that church descriptions in this guide use the concept of liturgical east, being the end at which the high altar is placed, regardless of whether this faces compass east on the street grid.

CRIME AND PERSONAL SECURITY

General emergency services (ambulance, fire, police): T: 112.
Alongside 112, the following emergency numbers are also available:

15: medical emergency,
17: police,
18: fire brigade,
115: social emergency,
119: abused children,
116000: missing children,
114: emergency calls for deaf and people with hearing problems.

Look out for pickpockets, especially on the Métro and in crowded tourist areas. Lost items should be reported immediately to the nearest police station in order to process insurance claims. Visitors to Paris should carry identification. For the nearest police station, contact: Préfecture de Police, 9 Blvd du Palais (4th), T: 01 53 71 53 71, www.prefecturedepoliceinterieur.gouv.fr.

ENTERTAINMENT

For all information on theatres, cinemas, cabarets, night clubs, cultural events, sporting events, fairs, exhibitions and shows, consult the Paris Convention and Visitors Bureaux (*www.parisinfo.com; list on p. 525*). Weekly information can also be found in *Pariscope, l'Officiel des Spectacles*, or *Zurban*, on sale at newsagents.

MUSEUM ADMISSIONS AND OPENING TIMES

National museums and monuments are closed on Tuesdays and municipal museums are closed on Mondays. The exception is the Musée d'Orsay, which closes on Mondays. Several museums have late openings once or occasionally twice a week. Some museums will not allow entry after 45mins before closing time. Details of admission times are given in the text, but these are subject to change and it is always useful to check. Tourist offices (*list on p. 525*) have up-to-date admission times and charges.

The **Paris Museum Pass** (*La Carte Musées et Monuments*) gives reduced-price and unlimited access to over 60 museums and monuments in Paris and the surrounding region. It can be bought at participating museums and monuments, tourist offices and the Espace de Tourisme d'Île-de-France (Carrousel du Louvre), major Métro stations and FNAC shops. It is available for two, four or six consecutive days and avoids the need to queue in the busier museums. It does not include temporary exhibitions or guided tours.

Admission to national museums is free on the first Sunday of each month. There is free access every day to the permanent collections of most museums belonging to the Paris City Council (Ville de Paris) including the Musée d'Art Moderne, Petit Palais, the Carnavalet, Cernuschi, Cognacq-Jay, Bourdelle and Zadkine, Musée de la Vie Romantique, Maison de Balzac, Maison de Victor Hugo, Mémorial de la Libération de Paris. The Musée Galliéra, Catacombes and Crypte Archéologique are fee-paying.

Guided tours to a variety of monuments (including some which are difficult to access), and areas of Paris (in French unless arranged in advance), are organised by the **Centre des Monuments Nationaux (CMN)**. The Visites-Conférences booklet is available from their office at 62 Rue St-Antoine (Place des Vosges; *map p. 588, B2*) as well as at most museums; or see www.monuments-nationaux.fr. There is no formal registration for individuals participating in a guided tour: simply go to the meeting point shortly before the start. Maximum 40 people. Visits last about 90mins.

PUBLIC HOLIDAYS

Almost everything closes on 1st January, 1st May and 25th December. Post offices, banks, and some museums and shops are also likely to be closed on the following:

Easter Monday
8th May (VE Day)
Ascension Thursday
14th July (Bastille Day)
15th August (Feast of the Assumption)
1st November (All Souls)
11th November (Armistice Day)

SHOPPING

There are a great many different parts of Paris which are known for smart shopping. The two most famous department stores are Printemps and Galeries Lafayette (*map p. 581, E1–F1*). Designer boutiques are found in the 1st and 8th arrondissements, Rue St-Honoré. Place Vendôme has a number of famous jewellers. Rue du Faubourg St-Honoré, Av. Montaigne and Passy, in the 16th, are alternative districts. St-Germain, on the edge of the 6th/7th arrondissements, around Rue du Four and Place St-Sulpice, has many designer shops, and the Marais district is cutting-edge in design. The Marais remains the most interesting place for Sunday shopping, but there other places that open, such as the Carrousel du Louvre, some stores on the Champs-Élysées including Drugstore, Virgin Megastore and FNAC. The Quatre-Temps at La Défense is a vast shopping centre with 230 shops and 30 restaurants. Other varied places for shopping are Bercy Village-Cours St-Emilion, and Rue d'Orsel in Montmartre. Most supermarkets remain closed on Sundays. There are several Sunday street markets..

Shops are usually open from between 9 and 10, until around 6 or 7. Fashion shops are generally closed Sunday and some also on Monday morning. Food shops often open earlier and stay open until 7, and some open on Sunday morning.

Markets

There are markets all over Paris, selling flowers, birds and small animals, artisanal cheese, vegetables and fresh produce. Many are mentioned in the text of this guide. They are also listed by arrondissement on the Paris City website (*www.paris.fr*). The Viaduc des Arts (*see p. 385*) near Bastille is an arts and crafts market. An open-air stamp market is held Thur–Sun at Av. Matignon, Rond-Point des Champs-Élysées. There are *brocanteurs* (second-hand dealers) in the 6th arrondissement. The Marché aux Puces at St-Ouen (Sat–Mon; *www.parispuces.com*), a few minutes' walk from Porte de Clignancourt Métro, is the most extensive and best-known flea market and might still produce a bargain among the bric-à-brac. In the last few years the number of Christmas markets in Paris has grown (*www.christmasmarkets.com*). Along the Seine, many of the traditional *bouquinistes* still operate, selling antiquarian books and prints.

TELEPHONES AND THE INTERNET

There is free wifi in most hotels in Paris (ask at reception for the code). The Mairie de Paris gives information on how to access wifi free in Paris (*www.paris.fr/wifi*).

The international country code for France is +33. The area code for Paris is 01. Telephone numbers in this guide assume that you are calling from within France. If you are dialling a Paris number from outside the country, dial the country code first and drop the initial zero of the area code.

TIPPING

A 15% cover charge is always added by law to the price of a meal and is shown on the bill. There is no obligation to tip extra, but obviously, as everywhere else, the recognition of good service is appreciated.

Glossary

Ambulatory, the section of a church, with side chapels, that curves around and behind the high altar

Annunciation, the delivering of the news to the Virgin that she is to bear the Son of God

Antependium, altar frontal

Aquamanile (pl. aquamanilia), a jug or other vessel for pouring water shaped like an animal or human

Architrave, the horizontal beam placed above supporting columns, the lowest part of an entablature (*qv*); the horizontal lintel above a door or window

Art Deco Stylised, often geometric art and architecture of the 1920s and '30s

Art Nouveau design style originating in the late 19th century, curving and feminine, asymmetrical, making use of floral motifs, leaves and vine tendrils

Atlantes, sculpted figures of the god Atlas, used as supporting columns

Baldachin, canopy supported by columns or other uprights

Basilica, originally a Roman building used for public administration; in Christian architecture, an aisled church with a clerestory and apse

Bas-relief, sculpture in low relief

Bauhaus, design school founded by Walter Gropius which came to be associated with clear, clean, austere Rationalism

Black-figure ware, ancient Greek pottery style of the 7th–5th centuries BC where the figures appear black against a clay-coloured ground

Boiserie, decorative interior woodwork

Boss, carved or otherwise decorated block at the join of two vault ribs

Cartel, decorative surround, often of ormolu (*qv*), for a wall or bracket clock

Capital, the top or head of a column

Caryatid, supporting column in the form of a sculpted female figure

Cenotaph, literally 'empty tomb', a monument to someone whose body is lost or buried elsewhere

Champlevé, metalwork technique whereby elements of a design are scraped hollow, then filled with enamel before firing

Chancel, part of a church to the liturgical east of the crossing (*qv*), where the clergy officiate

Charnier, a charnel house, typically a vaulted precinct where bones exhumed from a graveyard to make way for new burials were placed and allowed to dry out. Many Paris churches had charniers; the one at St-Sévérin is the only survivor

Choir, part of a church or cathedral reserved for the singers, usually with stalls. It is situated in the centre of the building, to the east of the crossing (*qv*), with the ambulatory (*qv*) encircling it

Clerestory, uppermost part of the nave wall of a church, above the side aisles, pierced by windows

Cloisonné, type of enamel decoration, where areas of colour are partitioned by narrow strips of metal

Colossal, order of architecture where the columns or pilasters have a vertical span of two or more storeys

Convention, France's revolutionary governing assembly in 1792–5

Corbel, projecting block, usually of stone, to support an arch or beam

Corinthian, ancient Greek and Roman order of architecture, a characteristic of which is the column capital decorated with sculpted acanthus leaves

Couchant, heraldic term to describe a beast as lying down

Cour d'Honneur, a monumental forecourt, often characterised by architectural symmetry

Crenellated, of a wall or parapet, indented with alternate crenels (the indented sections) and merlons (the sticking-up sections), so as to form a battlement

Crossing, the part of a church where the nave (central aisle) and transepts (side arms) meet

Damascened, of metalwork, denoting an object typically of iron or steel inlaid with a pattern in other metals such as gold and silver

Doric, ancient Greek order of architecture characterised by fluted columns with no base, and a plain capital

Dormition, the death of the Virgin, represented in art as a 'falling-asleep'

Ébeniste, a cabinet-maker, especially one making fine, highly decorated luxury pieces. The profession came into its own in the Rococo age

Entablature, the continuous horizontal element above the capital (consisting of architrave, frieze and cornice) of a Classical or Neoclassical building

Étage noble, the *piano nobile*, the first floor of a town house where the grandest apartments are located

Evangelists, the writers of the gospels, Matthew, Mark, Luke and John, often represented in art by their symbols: a man's head, a lion, a bull and an eagle

Exedra, recessed area projecting from a room, a large alcove

Faïence, glazed decorative earthenware or terracotta, named after the town of Faenza, Italy, where it originated

Flamboyant, from the French for 'flaming', a florid style of Gothic architecture originating in the mid-14th century and characterised by rich tracery with S-shaped curves, reminiscent of leaping flames

Giant Order (*see Colossal*)

Greek cross, cross with vertical and transverse arms of equal length

Grisaille, painting in tones of grey

Grotesque, grotesques (*grottesche*), painted or stucco decoration in the style of that found during the Renaissance in Nero's Golden House in Rome, then underground, hence the name, from 'grotto'. The delicate ornamental decoration usually includes patterns of flowers, sphinxes, birds, human figures etc, against a light ground

Guinguette, an out-of-town café offering music and dancing

Hôtel particulier, the private town residence of a nobleman or other wealthy person

Impasto, technique where the paint is applied very thickly, so that brushstrokes and marks of the palette knife can often be seen

Incunabulum (pl. incunabula), any book printed in the same century as the invention of movable type (i.e. between 1450 and 1500)

Ionic, an order of Classical architecture identified by its capitals decorated with volutes (scrolls)

Jaune d'argent, clear and beautiful yellow colour in stained glass made of silver and ochre compounds

Jubé, in French churches, the rood screen, a screen (often highly elaborate) dividing the nave from the chancel in a church, originally bearing a Rood (Crucifix) or with a Rood hanging above it

Krater, large ancient Greek vessel for mixing wine and water

Lady Chapel, often the most important lateral chapel in a church, dedicated to the Virgin. In Paris churches, the Lady Chapel is usually at the centre of the east end, behind the high altar.

Latin cross, cross where the vertical arm is longer than the transverse arm

Lierne, kind of ribbing in a vault producing an intense veined pattern, with shorter, linking ribs running between the main structurally necessary ribs

Lost wax, method of metal casting whereby a mould is made around a wax model, which is then melted away so that molten metal to be poured in

Lunette, semicircular space in a vault or ceiling, often decorated with a painting or relief

Machicolated, of a parapet, having holes in the floor through which stones, boiling oil etc. could be dropped on attackers

Mascaron, decorative element in the form of a carved head or face

Metope, square ornamental relief on a Doric frieze

Millefleurs, literally 'a thousand flowers', a tapestry style where figures appear against a grassy background spangled with multiple small blooms

Misericord, decorated wooden block attached to the underside of the seat in a choir stall, against which choristers can lean for support during long periods of standing. From the Latin word for mercy

Naos, the enclosed inner part of a temple; the main body of a church

Narthex, the enclosed west porch or entrance vestibule of a basilica

Niello, a black substance composed of silver and lead inlaid into stone to make an incised design stand out

Oculus, round window or other aperture

Ogee, of an arch, shaped in a double curve, convex above and concave below

Oriel, a window projecting from an upper storey

Ormolu, originally a film of gold applied to the surface of furniture mounts, it later came to be made of a zinc and copper alloy

Passant, heraldic term to describe a beast walking or striding towards the left, with its front foreleg raised

Pediment, gable above the portico of a classical building; also above a window, either triangular in form or curved (segmental)

Pendentive, concave spandrel (*qv*) beneath the four 'corners' of a dome

Pier, a square or compound pillar used as a support in architecture

Pilaster, shallow pier or rectangular column projecting slightly from the wall

Pietà, painting or sculpture group showing the mourning of the dead Christ, usually by the Virgin

Porphyry, an extremely hard, dark blue or purplish igneous rock

Porte-cochère, canopied entranceway that allows a conveyance to drive up to a doorway and discharge its passengers under cover from the elements

Putto (pl. putti), sculpted or painted

figure, usually nude, of a male child, without wings

Quatrefoil, four-lobed design

Quoin, from the French *coin* (corner), stones placed in courses at the outer corners of buildings

Rayonnant, a style of 13th-century Gothic architecture typified by radiating tracery in rose windows and slender-shafted columns

Red-figure ware, Greek pottery style of the 6th–4th centuries BC where the figures appear in red against a black ground

Retable, screen behind an altar, often a frame or setting for the altarpiece

Rhyton, ancient, horn-shaped libation vessel often shaped at the tip in the form of an animal

Rocaille, a type of design of the 18th century using pebbles and shells; another term for Rococo, denoting a decorative style of sinuous foliate forms

Rococo, frothy, highly ornamented design style of the 18th-century

Romanesque, architecture of the Western (not Byzantine) Empire of the 7th–12th centuries, preceding the Gothic, and typified by sturdy columns supported round arches

Rosso antico, red marble from the Peloponnese; Tenaros red

Scagliola, a material made from selenite, used to imitate marble or other fine stone

Sgraffito, decorative technique whereby a surface is coated in two layers of contrasting colours and a design is scratched into the surface, revealing the colour of the layer underneath

Soffit, the underside of an arch

Spandrel, surface between two arches in an arcade or the triangular space on either side of an arch

Stele (pl. stelae), upright stone slab with a commemorative function

Stoup, vessel for Holy Water, usually near the entrance of a church

String course, horizontal band of masonry, either plain or moulded, stretching across an elevation of a building

Storiated, decorated with figures from history, mythology or legend

Temenos, a sacred enclosure

Tierceron, a type of vaulting even more crowded than lierne (*qv*), where an additional, third group of ribs radiates outward from the wall shafts

Tracery, system of carved and moulded ribs within a window aperture dividing it into patterned sections

Transept, the side arm of a church leading to right (liturgical south) or left (liturgical north) of the nave

Trefoil, decorated or moulded with three leaf or lobe shapes

Triforium, arcaded gallery above the nave of a church, below the clerestory (*qv*)

Triton, a sea god

Trompe l'oeil, literally, a deception of the eye: illusionist decoration, painted architectural perspectives, etc.

Trumeau, in medieval architecture, the central supporting partition or mullion between two sections of an aperture, typically a doorway

Tympanum, the area between the top of a doorway and the arch above it or the triangular space enclosed by the pediment

Vermiculated, carved with a worm-like pattern

Verde antico, a green marble from Thessaly in Greece

Volute, tightly curled spiral scroll

Rulers of France

MEROVINGIANS

Clovis I	481–511
Childebert I	511–58
Clothair I	558–61
Charibert	561–7
Chilperic I	567–84
Clothair II	584–629
Dagobert I	629–39
Clovis II	639–57
Clothair III	657–73
Childeric II	673–5
Clovis III (usurper)	675–6
Thierry (Theuderic)	675–91
Clovis IV	691–95
Childebert II	695–711
Dagobert II	711–15
Chilperic II	715–21
Theuderic	721–37
Charles Martel (as Maire)	737–41
Childeric III	743–51

CAROLINGIANS

Pepin the Short	751–68
Carloman I	768–71
Charlemagne	768–814
Louis I	814–40
Charles the Bald	840–77
Louis II	877–9
Louis III	879–82
Carloman II	882–7
Charles the Fat	884–7
Eudes (Odo)	887–98
Charles the Simple	898–922
Robert I	922–3
Rudolph	923–36
Louis IV	936–54
Lothair	954–86
Louis V	986–7

CAPETIANS

Hugues Capet	987–96
Robert II, le Pieux	996–1031
Henri I	1031–60
Philippe I	1060–1108
Louis VI	1108–37
Louis VII	1137–80
Philippe-Auguste	1180–1223
Louis VIII	1223–6
Louis IX, St Louis	1226–70
Philippe III	1270–85
Philippe IV, le Bel	1285–1314
Louis X	1314–16
Jean I	1316
Philippe V	1316–22
Charles IV	1322–8

HOUSE OF VALOIS

Philippe VI	1328–50
Jean II, le Bon	1350–64
Charles V	1364–80
Charles VI	1380–1422

[Henry VI of England claims French throne, 1422–53]

Charles VII	1422–61
Louis XI	1461–83
Charles VIII	1483–98

Louis XII	1498–1515
François I	1515–47
Henri II	1547–59
François II	1559–60
Charles IX	1560–74
Henri III	1574–89

HOUSE OF BOURBON

Henri IV, le Vert Galant	1589–1610
Louis XIII	1610–43
Louis XIV, le Roi Soleil	1643–1715
Louis XV	1715–74
Louis XVI	1774–92
Louis XVII (never crowned)	

FIRST REPUBLIC 1792–1804

FIRST EMPIRE

Napoleon I	1804–14

HOUSE OF BOURBON (RESTORED)

Louis XVIII	1814–15

FIRST EMPIRE (RE-PROCLAIMED, THE 'HUNDRED DAYS')

Napoleon I March–June	1815
Napoleon II June–July	1815

HOUSE OF BOURBON (RESTORED)

Louis XVIII	1815–24
Charles X	1824–30

HOUSE OF ORLÉANS

Louis-Philippe, le Roi Citoyen	1830–48

SECOND REPUBLIC 1848–52

SECOND EMPIRE

Napoleon III	1852–70

THIRD REPUBLIC

Adolphe Thiers	1871–3
Patrice de MacMahon	1873–9
Jules Grévy	1879–87
Sadi Carnot	1887–94
Jean-Casimir Périer	1894–5
Félix Faure	1895–9
Émile Loubet	1899–1906
Armand Fallières	1906–13
Raymond Poincaré	1913–20
Paul Deschanel	1920
Alexandre Millerand	1920–4
Gaston Doumergue	1924–31
Paul Doumer	1931–2
Albert Lebrun	1932–40

FRENCH STATE 1940–4

Head of State: Marshal Pétain

PROVISIONAL GOVERNMENT OF THE FRENCH REPUBLIC

Governors: Charles de Gaulle	1944–6
Félix Gouin	1946
Georges Bidault	1946
François Auriol	1946
Léon Blum	1946–7

FOURTH REPUBLIC

Vincent Auriol	1947–54
René Coty	1954–8

FIFTH REPUBLIC

Charles de Gaulle	1958–69
Alain Poher	1969
Georges Pompidou	1969–74
Valéry Giscard d'Estaing	1974–81
François Mitterand	1981–95
Jacques Chirac	1995–2007
Nicolas Sarkozy	2007–2012
François Hollande	2012–

THE REPUBLICAN CALENDAR

With the aim of breaking with the Christian tradition, a republican calendar was introduced in the autumn of 1793. It remained in force until January 1806, when France reverted to the Gregorian Calendar. The first year of the republican calendar was considered to have begun on the autumn equinox (22nd September) of 1792, when the republic had been proclaimed. The year was divided into twelve months, each of exactly 30 days, which in turn were subdivided into three ten-day *décades*. Five extra days known as *sansculottides* were added at the end of each year (six days in leap years) to be observed as national holidays.

The days were named numerically: primidi, duodi, tridi, quartidi, quintidi, sextidi, septidi, octidi, nonidi and décadi, the day of rest. The months had more poetic names: Germinal, Floréal and Prairial were the spring months of seed-time, flowers and meadows; Messidor, Thermidor and Fructidor were the summer months of harvest, heat and fruit; Vendémaire, Brumaire and Frimaire the autumn months of vintage, fog and frost; and Nivôse, Pluviôse and Ventôse the winter months of snow, rain and wind.

THE REVOLUTIONARY GOVERNMENTS

The turbulent decade of 1789–99 saw a bewildering succession of different ruling bodies each stepping forward into the chaos. They were as follows:

1789–91: National Constituent Assembly (*Assemblée Nationale Constituante*): In June 1789, members of the Third Estate (the 'common people', that is to say, neither nobles nor clergy; most of them were lawyers), formed themselves into a body aimed at radical government reform. Their aim at this stage was not to remove—and certainly not to execute—the king. Indeed, their vision of governance still incorporated him, but as a constitutional monarch. They swore the Tennis Court Oath at Versailles, vowing to establish a constitution. They also abolished feudal privileges. The National Assembly's most famous act was the Declaration of the Rights of Man, in August 1789.

1791–2: Legislative Assembly (*Assemblée Législative*): The National Assembly provided France with a constitution and then dissolved itself, making way for a unicameral parliament known as the Legislative Assembly. The king was the head of this body, but his character was weak, and rumblings of republicanism from the left-wing, Jacobin flank of the Assembly began to prevail over the conservative, constitutional monarchist Feuillant wing (led by Lafayette). In April 1792 France embroiled itself in a war with Austria and Prussia. In August, a republican mob marched on the Tuileries and forced the king to flee to the safety of the Legislative Assembly. Jacobin members of the Assembly called for the king to be deposed and for a new constitution to be drawn up. The royal family was imprisoned in the Temple.

1792–5: The Convention: These were the years when the French Revolution, as it is commonly understood, reached its height. It was the time of the First Republic and of the guillotining of Louis XVI and Marie-Antoinette. Republican fervour descended into the Terror, a system established to purge the new republic of all its enemies. The two most famous instruments of this were Danton and Robespierre (the latter had famously declared that 'The king must die that the nation may live.'). The aim of the Convention was to provide France with a republican constitution, but once again, internal political strife ruled the day. The two main factions were the Girondins (republican moderates) and Montagnards (radical Jacobins). The latter went into alliance with the Sans-culottes, the revolutionary army of peasants and urban labourers, known as '*sans-culottes*' because they did not wear the knee-breeches of the gentility. Revolution turned on itself, however, as factions, sub-factions and counter-revolutionaries began to destroy each other. The Jacobin hero Marat was stabbed by the Girondin Charlotte Corday. Anyone seen as an opponent of the measures of the so-called 'Committee of Public Safety' was executed. Danton fell victim, and so, eventually, did Robespierre, with what is known as the Thermidorian Reaction. Opposition to his measures, widely seen as a Jacobin dictatorship, resulted in his summary execution on 28th July 1974 (10 Thermidor according to the Republican calendar). Yet another constitution was drawn up and power was vested in a committee known as the Directory.

1795–9: The Directory (*Directoire*): A five-member executive council supervised two legislative chambers, the Council of Ancients and the Council of Five Hundred, taxed with bringing stability to France. The Directory was unpopular, weak and tottering and could do little in the face of repeated attempts to bring it down. Eventually a coup on 18 Brumaire (9th November) 1799, led by a military leader called Napoleon Bonaparte, who had won fame for himself with his campaigns in Egypt. He overthrew the Directory and instituted the Consulate in its place, with himself as one of three consuls. Not very much later he ousted the other consuls and created the post of First Consul, to be filled by himself.   A.B.

Index

Numbers in bold are major references. Numbers in italics refer to illustrations.

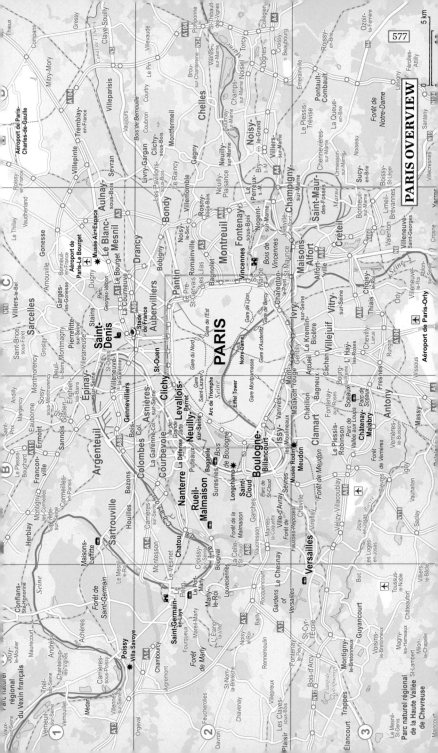

PARIS OVERVIEW

577

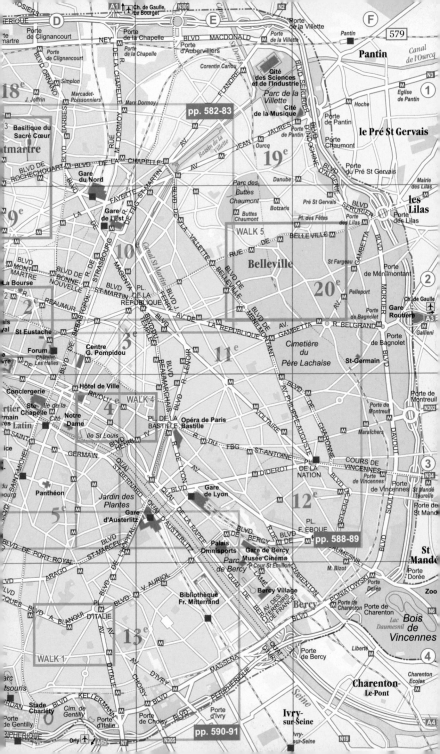

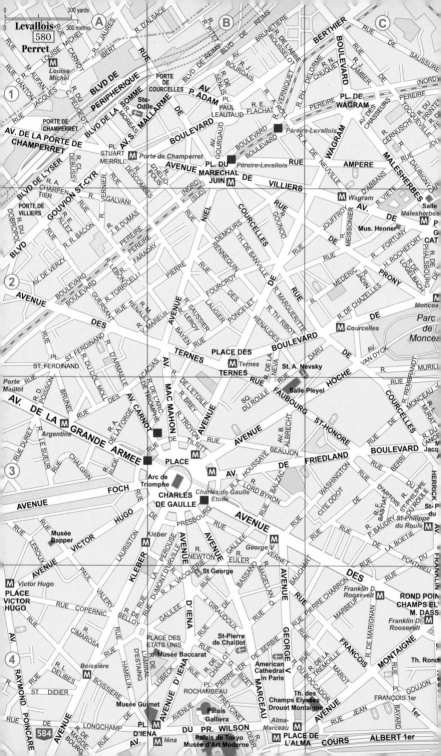

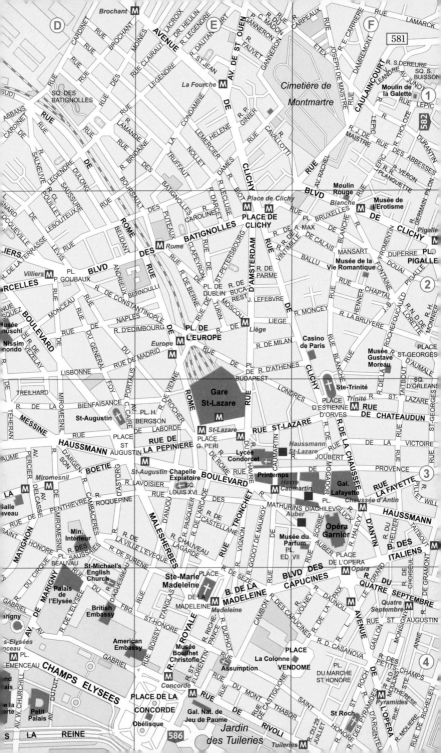

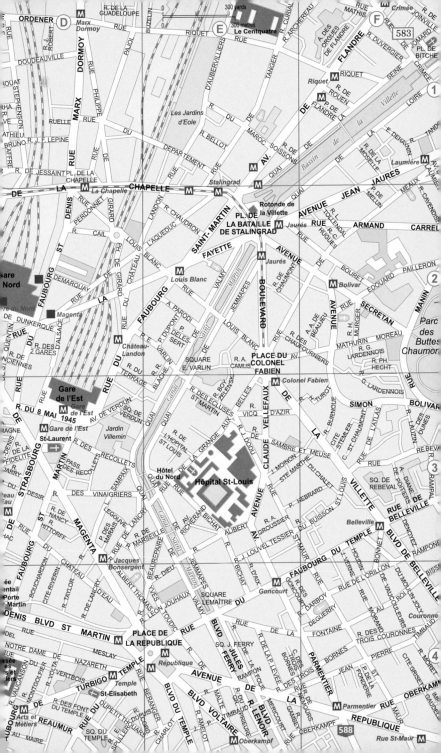

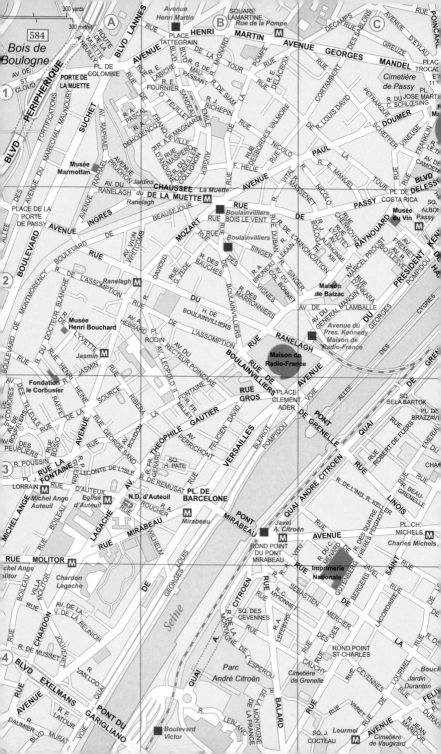

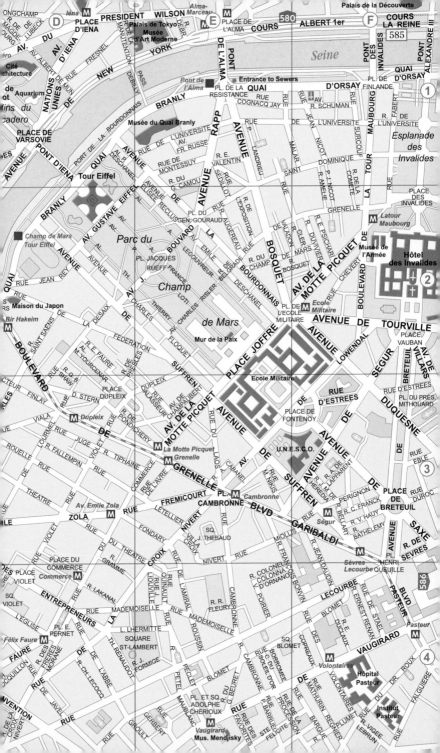

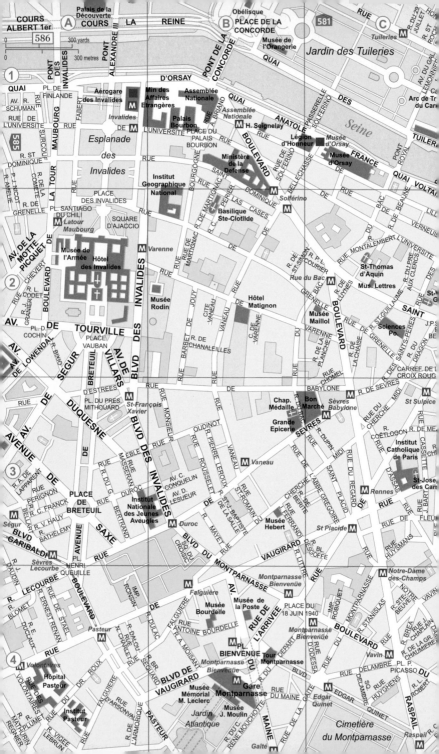

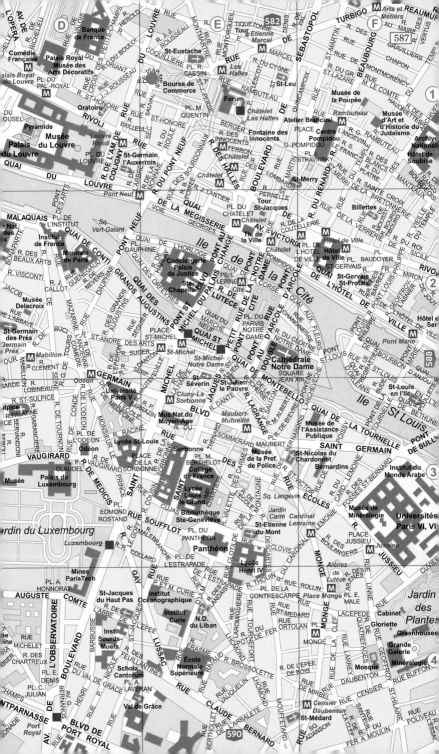

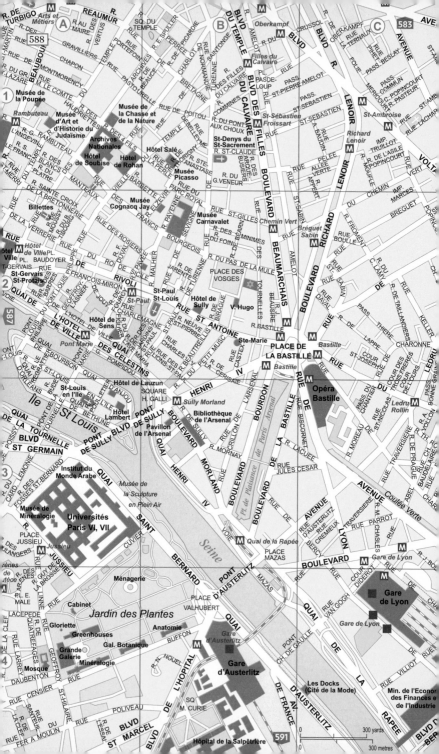

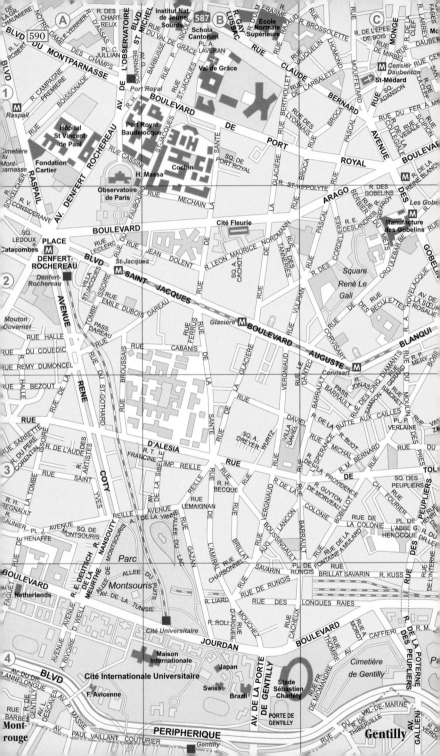

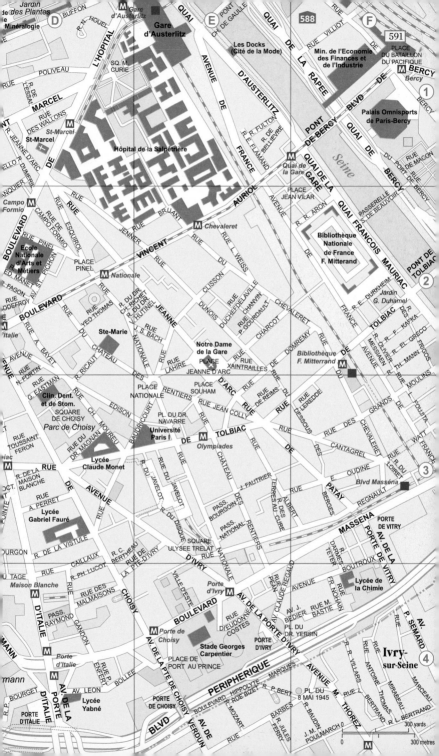

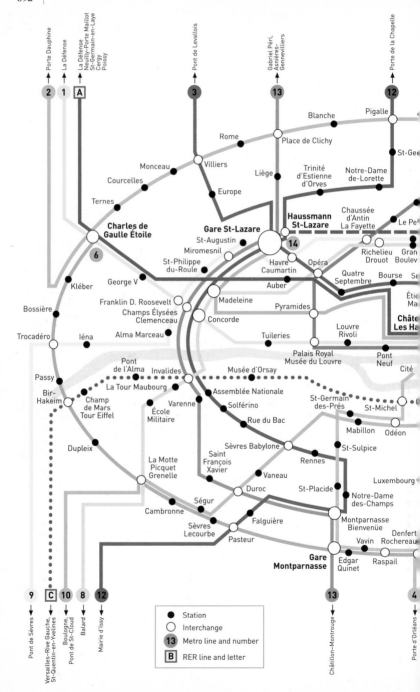

2 Porte Dauphine

1 La Défense

A La Défense Neuilly-Porte Maillot St-Germain-en-Laye Cergy Poissy

3 Pont de Levallois

13 Gabriel Péri, Asnières-Gennevilliers

12 Porte de la Chapelle

Blanche

Pigalle

Rome

Place de Clichy

St-Ge

Monceau

Villiers

Liège

Trinité d'Estienne d'Orves

Notre-Dame de-Lorette

Courcelles

Europe

Ternes

Haussmann St-Lazare

Chaussée d'Antin La Fayette

Le Pe

Charles de Gaulle Étoile

6

Gare St-Lazare

14

Richelieu Drouot

Gran Boulev

St-Augustin

Miromesnil

Havre Caumartin

Opéra

Kléber

St-Philippe du-Roule

Quatre Septembre

Bourse

Se

George V

Auber

Bossière

Franklin D. Roosevelt

Madeleine

Pyramides

Éti Ma

Champs Élysées Clemenceau

Concorde

Louvre Rivoli

Chât Les Ha

Trocadéro

Iéna

Alma Marceau

Tuileries

Passy

Pont de l'Alma

Invalides

Musée d'Orsay

Palais Royal Musée du Louvre

Pont Neuf

Cité

Bir-Hakeim

La Tour Maubourg

Assemblée Nationale

St-Germain des-Prés

St-Michel

Champ de Mars Tour Eiffel

Varenne

Solférino

Mabillon

Odéon

École Militaire

Rue du Bac

Dupleix

Sèvres Babylone

St-Sulpice

La Motte Picquet Grenelle

Saint François Xavier

Rennes

Luxembourg

Vaneau

St-Placide

Notre-Dame des-Champs

Ségur

Duroc

Cambronne

Montparnasse Bienvenüe

Sèvres Lecourbe

Falguière

Denfert Rochereau

Pasteur

Vavin

Gare Montparnasse

Edgar Quinet

Raspail

9 Pont de Sèvres

C Versailles–Rive Gauche, St-Quentin-en-Yvelines

10 Boulogne, Pont de St-Cloud

8 Balard

12 Mairie d'Issy

13 Châtillon-Montrouge

4 Porte d'Orléans

	Station
○	Interchange
13	Metro line and number
B	RER line and letter